Aviation Maintenance Technician Series

General
Second Edition

Dale Crane

Terry Michmerhuizen
Technical Editor

School of Aviation Sciences
Western Michigan University

Aviation Supplies & Academics, Inc.
Newcastle, Washington

Aviation Maintenance Technician Series: General
Second Edition
by Dale Crane

Aviation Supplies & Academics, Inc.
7005 132nd Place SE
Newcastle, Washington 98059-3153
Email asa@asa2fly.com
Internet http://www.asa2fly.com

Cover photo © Gary Gladstone/The Image Bank
Photos pp. 3, 5 and 7 courtesy Museum of Flight Foundation
Photos pp. 4 and 6 courtesy The Boeing Company
Photo p. 480 courtesy Dowty-Rotal, Inc.

ASA-AMT-G2
ISBN 1-56027-422-0

Library of Congress Cataloging-in-Publication Data:

Crane, Dale.
    Aviation maintenance technician—general / Dale Crane
        p.   cm.   — (Aviation maintenance technician series)
    Includes index.
    ISBN 1-56027-152-3
    1. Airplane—Maintenance and repair. I. Title. II. Series.
TL671.9.D66467 1993
629.134'6—dc20   92-1292
                            CIP

CONTENTS

iv

L

PREFACE

Aviation maintenance technology has undergone tremendous changes in the past decades. Modern aircraft, with their advanced engines, complex flight controls, and environmental control systems, are some of the most sophisticated devices in use today, and these marvels of engineering must be maintained by knowledgeable technicians. The Federal Aviation Administration, recognizing this new generation of aircraft, has updated the requirements for maintenance technicians and for the schools that provide their training. The FAA has instituted an Aviation Maintenance Technician Awards Program for technicians and their employers to encourage technicians to update their training.

New technologies used in modern aircraft increase the importance of maintenance technicians having a solid foundation in such basic subjects as mathematics, physics, and electricity. The *Aviation Maintenance Technician Series* has been produced by ASA to provide the needed background information for this foundation and to introduce the reader to aircraft structures, powerplants, and systems.

These texts have been carefully designed to assist a person in preparing for FAA technician certification, while at the same time serving as a valuable reference for individuals working in the field. The subject matter is organized into the categories used by the FAA for the core curriculum in 14 CFR Part 147, "Aviation Maintenance Technician Schools" and for the Subject Matter Knowledge Codes used in the written tests for technician certification. These categories have been rearranged in the ASA series to provide a more logical progression of learning. For example, in the General textbook the basic subjects are covered first, then the technical subjects common to both airframe and powerplant certification, and finally the maintenance publications, forms, and records that are so important.

The author and publisher of the *Aviation Maintenance Technician Series* wish to express our appreciation to the various manufacturers, aviation maintenance technician schools, and FAA personnel who have assisted us in producing this coordinated training series. Special appreciation goes to Terry Michmerhuizen of Western Michigan University School of Aviation Sciences for his valuable assistance in editing these texts.

Dale Crane

AN INTRODUCTION TO AVIATION

1

An Introduction to Aviation

Aviation History

In only 100 years, aviation has progressed from just the dream of flight to the reality of thousands of people traveling by air each day. All first-class mail now travels by air, and air express is becoming one of the most popular ways of shipping. Aviation has evolved through a number of key eras, each with their own advancements in the way airplanes connect people and places of the world. Let's look at some of the most outstanding happenings in each of these eras.

1903–1918

The airplane evolved from a machine that could barely support itself in the air, into the pursuit planes, bombers, and observation airplanes of World War I. These aircraft were, for the most part, dangerous, undependable, and inefficient, but they did fly.

With their Flyer, the Wright brothers solved the basic problem of control which finally allowed man to fly.

1919–1926

The government sold surplus WWI airplanes to ex-military aviators who became barnstormers and who carried thousands of passengers on their first airplane ride. This was the age of the flying circus when aviators flew without government regulation.

1927–1939

During this period the federal government began to control aviation by licensing airplanes and airmen, and by helping to develop airports and airways. This period includes the "Golden Age of Aviation" in which surplus WW I airplanes were disappearing and the aviation manufacturing industry began to come into its own. The Wright Whirlwind engine proved reliable enough for trans-Atlantic flights, and the world became aware of the airplane as a means of serious transportation.

Hundreds of aircraft manufacturers operated during this era, and the National Air Races attracted thousands of onlookers each year. Heroes and heroines in the persons of Charles Lindbergh, Wiley Post, Jimmy Doolittle, and Amelia Earhart, and names such as Lockheed, Travelair, Waco, and Stinson were as familiar to the average person as Chevrolet, Ford, Chrysler, and Honda are to us today.

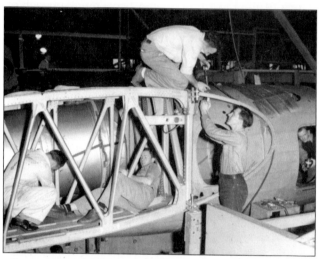

All-metal construction replaced wood & fabric, as the state-of-the-art technology in the early 1930s.

The fast all-metal, low-wing, cantilever monoplane replaced the slower and more clumsy trimotor airplane for regular airline service.

1940–1949

World War II dominated this era. High-performance fighters and high-altitude, long-range bombers were designed and built by the thousands. During this period, the jet engine and the helicopter were developed, but the war ended before either was perfected. Flight by instruments was common in the military, but was not generally used by civilian pilots.

After the war, the GI Bill provided flight training for thousands who had wanted to fly during the war but who served on the land or the sea. These new pilots, along with the thousands of returning military pilots, caused the industry to anticipate "an airplane for everyone." Airplane manufacturers, flight schools, fixed-base operators, and nonscheduled airlines flourished, but many soon fell by the wayside.

1950–1959

This era ushered in the first commercial jet transport aircraft, and the war in Korea brought about the acceptance of the helicopter as a practical aircraft. Aerospace activity began with the launching of the first satellite.

The long-range jet transport airplane made it possible for people and things to cross oceans in hours rather than weeks.

1960–1969

This was a time of accelerated development of aerospace and high-speed aircraft. During this time, both the Concorde supersonic transport and the widebodied Boeing 747 made their first flights.

1970–1979

The "Cold War" caused most aviation development to center around high-speed, high-performance military aircraft, and it was during this time that computerized systems became of extreme importance in aviation technology.

1980–1989

During these years the skyrocketing costs of ownership and maintenance of private planes caused most general aviation manufacturers to stop producing them. Deregulation of commercial airlines and the increase in carriage of mail and express-by-air multiplied the demand for transport aircraft. The increased number of flight hours for these aircraft has expanded the importance of aviation maintenance.

The widebodied Boeing 747, with its large seating capacity and long range, has made air travel the most efficient way for the public to travel.

1990 –

The small airport has lost its economic importance, but the large airports serviced by both major and commuter airlines are vital to our economy. The major airlines all have their own extensive maintenance facilities, and there are now large, well-equipped facilities that service independent operators and operators in foreign countries. Airplanes are flying so many hours and lasting for so many years that the "aging fleet" has become a special challenge in aviation maintenance.

Many private pilots and aviation buffs are involved with amateur-built aircraft that are in many instances more state-of-the-art than some of the commercially built aircraft. Each year, the Experimental Aircraft Association fly-in at Oshkosh, Wisconsin, gives general aviation another boost and keeps the interest in private flying alive.

The Importance of Aviation to Our World History

The railroad opened up travel in the United States shortly after the Civil War ended in 1865, and during the 1930s, highway development increased the utility of buses and private automobiles. But the development of practical, long-range, high-speed, pressurized jet airplanes has broken down greater barriers. Airplanes can take us to any point on the earth in a matter of hours. Air freight and air express move all but the largest bulk cargoes much faster and more economically than ships, trucks, and trains. Today, airplanes have almost completely replaced trains, busses, and ships for moving people over long distances.

Research and development in the aerospace industry and military aviation, both sustained by the federal government, impact all aspects of our lives. Computer technology, new composite materials, high-strength and lightweight metals, and new breakthroughs in turbine engine technology are examples of the way our entire economy profits from aviation.

Your Future in Aviation Maintenance

Aviation maintenance has undergone many changes over the years. In the early days, airplanes were often designed, built, flown, and maintained by the same person, but today's high-tech aircraft are so complex that specialized training and experience are needed to maintain them. Expertise with the welding torch and dope brush, so important to the A&E (aircraft and engine) mechanic of the 1930s and 1940s, have given way to the skills of troubleshooting electrical systems and turbine engines that are the stock in trade of today's aviation maintenance technician (AMT). To these skills are being added flight control systems analysis and composite repair that have become of increasing importance to the AMT.

The space shuttle is today's state-of-the-art flying machine. Spin-offs from its complex and sophisticated systems provide challenges for the technician today and in the future.

Civilian aviation maintenance is different from all other types of transportation maintenance because it is so carefully controlled by the Federal Aviation Administration. For a person to be allowed to work on an aircraft certificated by the FAA, he or she too must also be certificated by the FAA. The basic maintenance license is the mechanic certificate with an airframe and/or powerplant rating.

The requirements for the mechanic certificate, along with its privileges and limitations, are discussed in Chapter 12, beginning on Page 698.

The highly complex systems in our modern aircraft are impossible to troubleshoot using the methods that were used in the past. These systems use BITE (Built-In Test Equipment), and such systems as ECAM (Electronic Centralized Aircraft Monitor), EICAS (Engine Indicating and Crew Alerting System), FADEC (Full Authority Digital Engine Control, and FMCS (Flight Management Computer System) are all computer controlled and do much of their own troubleshooting. It is the responsibility of the AMT to interpret the output from these systems and make intelligent decisions regarding which components to replace when a system malfunctions.

The ASA Aviation Maintenance Technician Series (AMTS)

This series is part of a collection of training materials produced by ASA for aviation maintenance technicians. These include the *General* textbook, *Airframe* textbook (in two volumes), *Powerplant* textbook, the *Dictionary of Aeronautical Terms*, *Aviation Mechanic Handbook*, the *General, Airframe and Powerplant Technician Knowledge Test Guides*, *Inspection Authorization Test Prep*, and the *Prepware for Aviation Maintenance Technician Knowledge Exams*.

ASA also reprints certain FAA publications that are of vital concern to the AMT. These include copies of pertinent Federal Aviation Regulations, Advisory Circulars AC 43.13-1B and -2A *Acceptable Methods, Techniques and Practices: Aircraft Inspection, Repair, and Alterations*, and the questions that are used on the General, Airframe, and Powerplant knowledge tests. To conserve space and increase their utilization, ASA has put the *Dictionary of Aeronautical Terms* and the FAA reprints on a single compact disk (*Pro-Flight Library* CD).

MATHEMATICS 2

Continued

MATHEMATICS

2

Why Study Mathematics?

Mathematics is an exact science that gives us the basic language for all technology, and without it, aviation as we know it could not exist. We use mathematics daily for a variety of tasks, from figuring our paycheck to determining the strength of a riveted joint.

Today, a knowledge of mathematics is more important than ever before. All aircraft, engines, and the systems they contain must obey the laws of physics, and only by using the tools of mathematics are engineers able to design equipment that follows these laws. And only by understanding and using mathematics are we as technicians able to maintain this equipment so it will continue to function properly.

The miracle of modern engineering and production is possible only because of computers that quickly and accurately make the vast number of mathematical computations that are needed. Pocket-size calculators help to take the boredom out of mathematics and free the technician to concentrate on the practical use of this science.

In this section, we begin with a review of the number systems commonly used and progress through the four basic procedures in arithmetic, through a discussion of common and decimal fractions, percentage, ratio and proportion, powers and roots, signed numbers, and trigonometry, and conclude with mathematical sequences and practical problems.

To gain the most from this chapter, work all of the study problems by hand and check your answers with a pocket calculator; then check with the answers in the back of this chapter. By practicing the old-fashioned way of working problems, you will sharpen your skills and better understand the mathematical process.

Numerals

Numerals are the symbols used in mathematics to represent values. We are most familiar with the Arabic numerals, but Roman numerals have some special functions.

Arabic Numerals

Practically all modern mathematics are performed with Arabic numerals. This series of ten symbols is thought to have been developed by the Hindus in India and introduced in Europe by the Arabs.

Arabic numerals. The symbols 0, 1, 2, 3, 4, 5, 6, 7, 8, and 9 used to represent values in the decimal number system.

The ten symbols may be arranged in such a way that they represent any quantity we want, and we use Arabic numerals, also called digits, in both the decimal and binary number systems.

The ten Arabic numerals are: 0, 1, 2, 3, 4, 5, 6, 7, 8, and 9.

Roman Numerals

Roman numerals were used in an ancient number system, and are occasionally used as the chapter numbers in some books and on some of the more decorative clock faces. Seven capital letters represent numbers, and combinations of these letters may be used to make up any value we want. Mathematical manipulation of these numerals is too awkward for us even to consider here.

The seven Roman numerals and their Arabic equivalent are seen in Figure 2-1.

Roman	Arabic
I	1
V	5
X	10
L	50
C	100
D	500
M	1,000

Figure 2-1. *Comparison of Roman and Arabic numerals*

Number Systems

Decimal System

The number system used every day in aviation maintenance is the decimal system. It is based on the ten Arabic numerals, and we can arrange these ten digits so they represent any value we want. We do this by observing the position the digits occupy in the string of digits. The value of the digits in a decimal number is determined by their placement relative to the decimal point.

The easiest way to understand the decimal system is to use a number line, Figure 2-2. The center of the number line is marked with a small dot similar to a period used in writing. This is called the decimal point or, more generally, just "the decimal."

1,000,000	100,000	10,000	1,000	100	10	1	(.)	.1	.01	.001	.0001	.000 01	.000 001

Figure 2-2. *On the number line, all numbers to the left of the decimal point are whole numbers, and all numbers to the right of the decimal point are fractional parts of a whole number.*

The digit in the first place to the left of the decimal point has a value between 1 and 9. The digit in the second place has a value between 10 and 90, and the digit in the third place has a value between 100 and 900. This continues on, with each place to the left increasing the value by ten times.

To find the exact value of any number, just add all of the place values to the left of the decimal point. For example, we can break the number 52,496 down as shown in Figure 2-3.

In the United Kingdom, the decimal is placed above the line (·), but in the United States the decimal is placed on the line (.), and the raised dot (·) is used to indicate multiplication. All numbers to the left of the decimal point are numbers greater than 1, and those to the right of the decimal are fractions, or numbers less than 1.

The digit in the first place to the right of the decimal point has a value between $\frac{1}{10}$ and $\frac{9}{10}$, and the digit in the second place has a value between $\frac{1}{100}$ and $\frac{9}{100}$. The value of the digits becomes smaller by a factor of ten for each place the digit is to the right of the decimal point (*see* Figure 2-4). The number 347.69 can be broken down as we see in Figure 2-5.

For whole numbers greater than 1, the decimal point is normally omitted, and for numbers less than 1, a zero is normally placed before the decimal point.

Binary System

All data used by digital computers is represented with only two electrical conditions, OFF or ON. This can also be LOW or HIGH, or NEGATIVE or POSITIVE. Computers can do many different things when they are commanded by combinations of these two conditions.

To get the most value from digital computers, we must be able to reduce all of the data we use to a series of numbers, and since the computer recognizes only two conditions, we use the binary number system. This system uses only two symbols, 0 and 1. These are called bits (**BI**nary digi**TS**).

$$
\begin{array}{rcl}
50{,}000 & = & 5 \cdot 10{,}000 \\
2{,}000 & = & 2 \cdot 1{,}000 \\
400 & = & 4 \cdot 100 \\
90 & = & 9 \cdot 10 \\
6 & = & 6 \cdot 1 \\
\hline
52{,}496 & &
\end{array}
$$

Figure 2-3. *Place values for numbers greater than 1 in the decimal system*

$$
\begin{array}{lcl}
0.1 & = & 1/10 \\
0.01 & = & 1/100 \\
0.001 & = & 1/1{,}000 \\
0.000\ 1 & = & 1/10{,}000 \\
0.000\ 01 & = & 1/100{,}000
\end{array}
$$

Figure 2-4. *Place values for numbers smaller than 1 in the decimal system*

$$
\begin{array}{rcl}
300. & = & 3 \cdot 100 \\
40. & = & 4 \cdot 10 \\
7. & = & 7 \cdot 1 \\
0.6 & = & 6 \cdot 0.1 \\
0.09 & = & 9 \cdot 0.01 \\
\hline
347.69 & &
\end{array}
$$

Figure 2-5. *Place values for mixed numbers in the decimal system*

In the binary system the value of the bits doubles as they progress from right to left. The values of the first ten bits, reading from right to left, are: 1, 2, 4, 8, 16, 32, 64, 128, 256, and 512, as shown in Figure 2-6.

To find the binary equivalent of a decimal number, start with the left side of the chart and subtract the binary place values from the decimal number. Proceeding to the right, every time a place value goes into the decimal number, put a 1 for the place value. When a place value does not go into the decimal number, put a zero for that place value. For example, the binary equivalent of 152 is 10011000:

- 152 – 128 = 24, so 1 goes in the 128 column
- 64 is greater than 24, so 0 goes in the 64 column
- 32 is greater than 24, so 0 goes in the 32 column
- 24 – 16 = 8, so 1 goes in the 16 column
- 8 – 8 = 0, so 1 goes in the 8 column
- There is nothing left, so 0 goes in the 4, 2, and 1 columns

Any zeros to the left of the first 1 may be omitted without changing the value of the binary number.

To find the decimal equivalent of a binary number, add all of the place values in which there is a 1. The decimal equivalent of 0100111000 is 312.

- Start at the right and add the place values in which there is a 1
- 0 + 0 + 0 + 8 + 16 + 32 + 0 + 0 + 256 = 312

Decimal	Binary place values										Binary
	512	256	128	64	32	16	8	4	2	1	
1	0	0	0	0	0	0	0	0	0	1	0000000001
10	0	0	0	0	0	0	1	0	1	0	0000001010
97	0	0	0	1	1	0	0	0	0	1	0001100001
152	0	0	1	0	0	1	1	0	0	0	0010011000
312	0	1	0	0	1	1	1	0	0	0	0100111000
1,000	1	1	1	1	1	0	1	0	0	0	1111101000

Figure 2-6. *Conversion between the binary and decimal system*

Arithmetic

Arithmetic is essentially the branch of mathematics in which we use addition, subtraction, multiplication, and division to solve problems that may contain positive and negative numbers and zero.

The pocket calculator has just about spoiled us for working arithmetic problems the old-fashioned way, but it is a good idea to review a few principles. Practicing may prevent some common mistakes.

Addition

Addition is the process of finding the combined values of two or more numbers, their sum. The symbol for addition is the plus sign (+).

To find the sum, arrange the numbers in a vertical column with the decimal points all in a line, and combine the values of the numbers in each column. Since most whole numbers are written without a decimal point, just align the numbers with the least significant digits, the digits on the right, all in a straight vertical line. *See* Figure 2-7.

1. Arrange the numbers for addition, and combine the values of all of the digits in the ones column, the column on the right. When all of these digits are added together, they total 21. Twenty-one is 2 tens plus 1 one. Place the 1 below the ones column, and carry the 2 above the tens column. *See* Figure 2-8.

2. Combine the value of all of the digits in the tens column, including the 2 you just carried. The sum of these four digits is 14. This is 1 hundred, plus 4 tens. Put the 4 below the tens column and carry the 1 at the top of the hundreds column.

3. Now, combine the values of the digits in the hundreds column. This is 7 plus 1, or 8. Place the 8 below the hundreds column, and this gives the sum of the four numbers, which is 841.

The best way to check the accuracy of an addition problem is to add the numbers in a different sequence. If you added them the first time from the top number down, check by adding them from the bottom to the top.

Before leaving addition problems, there is one fact that will help in practical problems: It makes no difference in which order we add numbers.

```
   6        4        4
   4       19        5
  19        5        6
+  5      + 6     + 19
 ----     ----    ----
  34       34       34
```

addition. The process of finding the combined value of two or more numbers.

```
    64
    32
   736
+    9
```

Figure 2-7. *Arrangement of numbers for addtion*

```
    12
    64
    32
   736
+    9
  -----
   841
```

Figure 2-8. *The process of addtion*

sum. The answer in an addition problem.

least significant digit. The digit on the extreme right in a decimal number.

```
   486
 −  32
  454
```

Figure 2-9. *This subtraction process does not involve borrowing.*

A

```
   12
  234
 − 76
```

B

```
      2
  2 3(14)
 −  7 6
      8
```

C

```
  1 (12)
  2 3 4
 −  7 6
    5 8
```

D

```
    1
  2 3 4
 −  7 6
  1 5 8
```

Figure 2-10. *This subtraction process does involve borrowing.*

Subtraction

Subtraction is the process of finding the difference between two numbers. The symbol for subtraction is the minus sign (−).

The number you begin with is called the minuend, and the number you subtract, or take away, from this is called the subtrahend. The answer is called the difference.

In Figure 2-9 we find the difference between 486 and 32. Place the subtrahend, 32, under the minuend, 486, with the least significant digits, the right-hand digits, lined up. Find the difference between the values of the digits in the ones column. 6 − 2 = 4. Place the 4 below the 2 in the ones column.

Find the difference between the values of the digits in the tens column. This is 8 − 3 = 5. Place the 5 below the tens column.

Since there is no number in the hundreds column of the minuend, just place the 4 in the answer in the hundreds column.

The difference between 486 and 32 is 454.

Some subtraction problems have digits in the subtrahend that are larger than those in the minuend, and we have to do some borrowing.

In Figure 2-10, we see this situation:

A. We want to find the difference between 234 and 76.

B. Six ones is larger than 4 ones, so we must borrow 10 ones from the 3 in the tens column. This gives us 14 ones, and 6 from 14 leaves 8. Place the 8 in the ones column of the answer.

C. Seven is larger than 2, so we must borrow 10 tens from the hundreds column to get 12 tens. Seven from 12 gives us 5 tens in the answer.

D. We had to borrow 10 tens, or 1 hundred from the 2 hundreds, so we have 1 left in the hundreds column. Place a 1 in the hundreds column of the answer.

To check a subtraction problem, add the subtrahend to the difference, and if the problem has been worked correctly, the sum will be the same as the minuend.

Multiplication

Multiplication is a process in which one number is added to itself a given number of times.

Various symbols are used to indicate the multiplication process. These are the letter "x," or a small dot placed in the center of the space "·," or parentheses. Parenthesis are used in problems in which other functions must be applied to terms before they are multiplied.

$$5 \times 8 \times 10 = 400$$
$$5 \cdot 8 \cdot 10 = 400$$
$$(3 + 2)(12 − 4)(6 + 4) = 400$$

The number to be multiplied is called the multiplicand, and the number used to multiply is called the multiplier. The answer is called the product.

The multiplication problem 4 · 3 = 12 is the same as four added to itself three times: 4 + 4 + 4 = 12.

When multiplying numbers having more than one digit, the way we arrange them is important. This is shown in Figure 2-11.

A. To multiply 365 by 124, begin by multiplying 365 by 4.

   1. First, multiply 5 by 4. 5 · 4 = 20

      Place the 0 in the ones column of the answer and carry the 2 above the tens column.

   2. Now, multiply 6 tens by 4 and add the 2 tens we carried.

      4 · 6 = 24 + 2 = 26 (This is actually (4 · 60) + 20 = 260.)

      Place the 6 in the tens column of the answer, and carry the 2 (200) above the hundreds column.

   3. Multiply 3 hundreds by 4, and add the 2 hundreds we carried.

      4 · 3 = 12 + 2 = 14 (This is actually (4 · 300) + 200 = 1400.)

      Place the 4 in the hundreds column of the answer and the 1 in the thousands column. The answer for our first step is 1,460.

B. The second stage is to multiply 365 by 2 in the tens column (20).

   1. Multiply 5 by the 2 in the tens column. 5 · 2 = 10
      (This is actually 5 · 20 = 100.)

      Place the zero in the tens column and carry the 1 (10) above the tens column.

   2. Multiply 6 tens by 2 tens, and add the 10 tens we carried.

      6 · 2 = 12 + 1 = 13 (This is actually (60 · 20) + 100 = 1300.)

      Place the 3 in the hundreds column and carry the 1 (100) above the hundreds column.

   3. Multiply 3 hundreds by 2 tens, and add the 10 hundreds we carried.

      3 · 2 = 6 + 1 = 7 (This is actually (300 · 20) + 1000 = 7000.)

      Place the 7 in the thousands column.

C. The final stage is to multiply 365 by 1 in the hundreds column (100).

   1. Multiply 5 by 1 hundreds. 5 · 1 = 5 (This is actually 5 · 100 = 500.)

      Place the 5 in the hundreds column.

   2. Multiply 6 tens by 1 hundreds. 6 · 1 = 6
      (This is actually 60 · 100 = 6000.)

      Place the 6 in the thousands column.

Continued

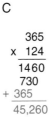

A

```
  2 2
   365
x  124
  1460
```

B

```
   11
   365
x  124
  1460
   730
```

C

```
   365
x  124
  1460
   730
+  365
 45,260
```

Figure 2-11. *The process of multiplication*

multiplicand. The number in a multiplication problem that is multiplied.

multiplier. The number in a multiplication problem by which the other number, the multiplicand, is multiplied.

product. The answer in a multiplication problem.

3. Multiply 3 hundreds by 1 hundred. $3 \cdot 1 = 3$ (This is actually $300 \cdot 100 = 30{,}000$)

   Place the 3 in the ten thousands column.

4. Add all the numbers we have just created to get the product of $365 \cdot 124 = 45{,}260$.

To check a multiplication problem, divide the product by the multiplier, and you should get the multiplicand.

$$45{,}260 \div 124 = 365$$

In a multiplication problem involving several steps of multiplication, the order in which the numbers are multiplied has no effect in obtaining the correct answer.

$$6 \cdot 5 \cdot 9 \cdot 20 = 5{,}400$$
$$20 \cdot 5 \cdot 6 \cdot 9 = 5{,}400$$
$$9 \cdot 6 \cdot 20 \cdot 5 = 5{,}400$$
$$5 \cdot 20 \cdot 9 \cdot 6 = 5{,}400$$

Division

Division is the process of determining the number of times one number will go into another. The number to be divided is called the dividend, the number that is to go into the dividend is called the divisor, and the answer is the quotient. The symbols for division are $\div$, and $/$.

Division can actually be thought of as a series of subtractions. We can find the number of times 7 will go into 56 by subtracting 7 from 56 until we get zero. Seven will go into 56 eight times. *See* Figure 2-12.

If the divisor does not go into the dividend an even number of times, the number left over is called the remainder.

$$42 \div 5 = 8, \text{ remainder } 2$$

Long division is the term we generally use when the divisor has two or more digits. To solve a long division problem, we arrange it as we see in Figure 2-13.

1. Place the dividend under the division sign, and the divisor to the left of it.

   The 24 of the divisor will go into 136 of the dividend 5 times, with some remainder. Place the 5 above the 6. Multiply the 24 by 5, to get 120. Place the 120 below the 136.

   Subtract 120 from 136 to get 16 as the remainder for our first step.

---

dividend. The quantity in a division problem that is divided.

divisor. The quantity in a division problem by which the dividend is divided.

quotient. The answer in a division problem.

remainder. The number left in a division problem when the divisor does not go into the dividend an even number of times.

$56 - 7$	$=$	49	(1)
$49 - 7$	$=$	42	(2)
$42 - 7$	$=$	35	(3)
$35 - 7$	$=$	28	(4)
$28 - 7$	$=$	21	(5)
$21 - 7$	$=$	14	(6)
$14 - 7$	$=$	7	(7)
$7 - 7$	$=$	0	(8)

Figure 2-12. *Division is actually a series of subtractions.* $56 \div 7 = 8$

$$\begin{array}{r} 57 \\ 24\overline{)1368} \\ \underline{120} \\ 168 \\ \underline{168} \\ 000 \end{array}$$

Figure 2-13. *The process of long division*

2. Bring the 8 from the dividend down and place it after the remainder to give us a new dividend of 168.

The 24 of the divisor will go into the new dividend 7 times. Place the 7 above the 8 and multiply the 24 by 7. Place the product of 168 below the new dividend and subtract. Since there is no difference, there is no remainder in this problem.

Twenty-four will go into 1,368 fifty-seven times.

$$24\overline{)1368} \text{ or } 1368 \div 24$$

$$\text{or } \frac{1368}{24}$$

Figure 2-14. *Ways of writing division problems*

Division problems may be written in any of the ways we see in Figure 2-14.

STUDY QUESTIONS: ARITHMETIC

Work all of these problems by hand, and then you may check your accuracy with a calculator.
Answers begin on Page 58. **Page numbers refer to chapter text.**

1. Find the sum of each of these columns of numbers:
   Page 19

a.	b.	c.	d.
321	65	7	936
66	681	47	72
59	6385	371	7931
6	83	849	365

2. Find the difference between each of these numbers:
   Page 20

a.	b.	c.	d.
458	756	5296	39
196	47	4805	18

Continued

3. Find the product in each of these multiplication problems:
   Page 20

a.	b.	c.	d.
248	1969	306	9841
62	142	212	77

4. Find the quotient and remainder of each of these division problems:

   a. $3685 \div 92 =$ _____ remainder _____

   b. $5694 \div 23 =$ _____ remainder _____

   c. $148 \div 53 =$ _____ remainder _____

   d. $98 \div 7 =$ _____ remainder _____

   Page 22

---

fraction. The mathematical term that denotes a whole is divided into several parts, and the number of the parts is identified.

common fraction. A fraction written in the form of one number above another. The number on the bottom is the denominator, indicating the number of parts into which the whole is divided, and the top number is the numerator indicating the number of parts being considered.

denominator. The quantity below the line in a common fraction, indicating the number of parts into which the numerator is divided.

numerator. The number in a common fraction written above the line.

Fractions

Up to this point, we have been working with whole numbers, but now we want to see how to work with only parts of a number. These parts are called fractions. There are two kinds of fractions: common fractions, in which the whole number can be divided into any number of parts, and decimal fractions, in which the whole number may be divided only by numbers that are multiples of 10.

Common Fractions

A common fraction is written as two numbers, one above the other, or if the numbers are all on the same line, they are divided by a slash mark. Examples of common fractions are ¼, ⅜ and ¹⁵⁄₆₄.

The number below the line or following the slash is called the denominator, and it represents the number of parts the whole object is divided into. The number above the line is called the numerator, and it represents the number of parts of the object we are considering.

If we speak of ⅜ of a load, the denominator tells us that the load is divided into 8 equal parts. The numerator tells us that we are talking about 3 of these parts.

Addition of Common Fractions

In order to add common fractions, we must first make all of the denominators the same, then add the numerators and place the sum above the common denominator. In Figure 2-15, the sum of $\frac{1}{8} + \frac{1}{3} + \frac{2}{5}$ is found.

1. Find a common denominator by multiplying all of the denominators together. $8 \cdot 3 \cdot 5 = 120$

2. Make three new fractions, using 120 as the denominator.

    For the first fraction, 8 will go into 120 fifteen times. Multiply the numerator 1 by 15 to get the new numerator.

    $1 \cdot 15 = 15$

    For the second fraction, 3 will go into 120 forty times. Multiply the numerator 1 by 40 to get the new numerator.

    $1 \cdot 40 = 40$

    For the third fraction, 5 will go into 120 twenty-four times. Multiply the numerator 2 by 24 to get the new numerator.

    $2 \cdot 24 = 48$

3. Add the numerators, and place their sum above the common denominator:

$$\frac{15}{120} + \frac{40}{120} + \frac{48}{120} = \frac{103}{120}$$

4. Therefore:

$$\frac{1}{8} + \frac{1}{3} + \frac{2}{5} = \frac{103}{120}$$

$$\frac{1 \, (\cdot \, 15)}{8 \, (\cdot \, 15)} = \frac{15}{120}$$

$$\frac{1 \, (\cdot \, 40)}{3 \, (\cdot \, 40)} = \frac{40}{120}$$

$$+ \frac{2 \, (\cdot \, 24)}{5 \, (\cdot \, 24)} = \frac{48}{120}$$

$$\frac{103}{120}$$

Figure 2-15. *To add common fractions, first change them into fractions with a common denominator, and then add.*

Subtraction of Common Fractions

In subtraction, like addition, we must first find a common denominator and then find the difference between the numerators. Finally, that difference is placed above the common denominator.

In Figure 2-16, we find the difference between $\frac{3}{5}$ and $\frac{1}{8}$.

1. Find a common denominator by multiplying the two denominators together.

    $5 \cdot 8 = 40$

2. Make new fractions using the common denominator.

    For the first fraction, 5 goes into 40 eight times. Multiply the numerator by 8 to get the new numerator.

    $3 \cdot 8 = 24$

    For the second fraction, 8 goes into 40 five times. Multiply the numerator 1 by 5 to get the new numerator.

    $1 \cdot 5 = 5$

$$\frac{3 \, (\cdot \, 8)}{5 \, (\cdot \, 8)} = \frac{24}{40}$$

$$- \frac{1 \, (\cdot \, 5)}{8 \, (\cdot \, 5)} = \frac{5}{40}$$

$$\frac{19}{40}$$

Figure 2-16. *To subtract common fractions, first change them into fractions with a common denominator, and then subtract.*

Continued

3. Subtract the numerator of the second fraction from the numerator of the first, to get the numerator of the difference.

$$\frac{24}{40} - \frac{5}{40} = \frac{19}{40}$$

4. Therefore:

$$\frac{3}{5} - \frac{1}{8} = \frac{19}{40}$$

Finding the Smallest Common Denominator

smallest common denominator. The smallest number that all of the denominators in a problem will go into an even number of times.

When you add several common fractions, instead of multiplying all of the denominators together and ending up with an unwieldy number, you can combine the denominators and find the smallest denominator that can be used by all of the fractions.

If we want to add $\frac{1}{16} + \frac{2}{3} + \frac{1}{12} + \frac{5}{9} + \frac{3}{8}$, we could multiply all of the denominators together to get a denominator of 41,472. This number is entirely too large, and it is inconvenient to work with. There are some simple steps we can follow to find the least, or smallest, common denominator. We can follow this procedure in Figure 2-17.

| Problem: | $\frac{1}{16}$ | $+$ | $\frac{2}{3}$ | $+$ | $\frac{1}{12}$ | $+$ | $\frac{5}{9}$ | $+$ | $\frac{3}{8}$ | $=$ | |

STEP	Original Denominators					New Denominators
1.	16	3	12	9	8	4
2.	4	3	3	9	2	3
3.	4	1	1	3	2	2
4.	2	1	1	3	1	2
5.	1	1	1	3	1	3
	1	1	1	1	1	—

6. $4 \cdot 3 \cdot 2 \cdot 2 \cdot 3 = 144$

7. $\frac{1}{16} = \frac{9}{144}$ $\frac{2}{3} = \frac{96}{144}$ $\frac{1}{12} = \frac{12}{144}$ $\frac{5}{9} = \frac{80}{144}$ $\frac{3}{8} = \frac{54}{144}$

(9 + 96 + 12 + 80 + 54 = 251)

8. $\frac{251}{144} = 1\frac{107}{144}$

Figure 2-17. *Finding the smallest common denominator*

1. Make a horizontal list of all of the denominators. Find a number that will go evenly into two or more of the denominators. Four will go into 16, 12, and 8. Place the 4 to the right of the denominators.

   Divide 4 into each number it will go an even number of times, and write this number beneath the number it went into. If 4 does not go into one of the denominators an even number of times, bring the denominator itself down.

2. Find a number that will go evenly into two or more of the new denominators. Three will go into 3, 3, and 9. Place the 3 to the right of the denominators.

   Divide 3 into each number it will go an even number of times, and write this number beneath the number it went into. If 3 does not go into one of the denominators an even number of times, bring the denominator itself down.

3. Find a number that will go evenly into two or more of the new denominators. Two will go into both 4 and 2. Place the 2 to the right of the denominators.

   Divide 2 into each number it will go into an even number of times, and write this number beneath the number it went into. If 2 does not go into one of the denominators an even number of times, bring the denominator itself down.

4. Since we do not have any two numbers that can be divided by any one number, place 2 to the right of the new denominators and divide the 2 by it. Bring the other denominators down.

5. The new row of denominators contains one 3 and the rest are 1s. Place a 3 to the right of this row of denominators and divide. The new row of denominators will all be 1s.

6. Multiply all of the new denominators together to get the least common denominator. $4 \cdot 3 \cdot 2 \cdot 2 \cdot 3 = 144$

7. Rewrite the fractions with the new numerator and denominator. We do this by dividing the old denominator into the new common denominator and then multiplying that answer, the quotient, by the old numerator.

   $\frac{1}{16} = \frac{9}{144}$
   $\frac{2}{3} = \frac{96}{144}$
   $\frac{1}{12} = \frac{12}{144}$
   $\frac{5}{9} = \frac{80}{144}$
   $\frac{3}{8} = \frac{54}{144}$

8. Add all of the numerators: $9 + 96 + 12 + 80 + 54 = 251$

   The sum of these fractions is $\frac{251}{144}$. This is an improper fraction, because its numerator is larger than its denominator. We can change this into a mixed number by subtracting 144 from the numerator to get the sum of $1\frac{107}{144}$.

improper fraction. A common fraction in which the numerator is greater than the denominator.

mixed number. A number that contains both an integer and a fraction.

$$\frac{3}{8} \times \frac{2}{2} = \frac{6}{16} \qquad \frac{3}{8} = \frac{6}{16}$$

$$\frac{18}{36} \div \frac{18}{18} = \frac{1}{2} \qquad \frac{18}{36} = \frac{1}{2}$$

Figure 2-18. *The value of a fraction is not changed when both its numerator and denominator are multiplied or divided by the same number.*

$$\frac{27}{144} \div \frac{3}{3} = \frac{9}{48} \div \frac{3}{3} = \frac{3}{16}$$

Figure 2-19. *Reducing a common fraction to its lowest terms*

$$\frac{3}{8} \times \frac{1}{2} = \frac{3}{16}$$

Figure 2-20. *Multiplication of common fractions.*

Invert the divisor and multiply:

$$\frac{3}{5} \div \frac{2}{3} = \frac{3}{5} \times \frac{3}{2} = \frac{9}{10}$$

Figure 2-21. *Division of common fractions is done by inverting the divisor and multiplying.*

$$2\frac{7}{16} = \frac{32}{16} + \frac{7}{16} = \frac{39}{16}$$

Figure 2-22. *Changing a mixed number into an improper fraction.*

Reducing a Fraction to its Lowest Term

A fraction that contains large numbers in both its numerator and denominator can often be changed to one that is easier to work with by reducing it to its lowest term. For example, $^{18}\!/_{45}$ can be reduced to $^2\!/_5$.

The value of a fraction is not changed if both the numerator and denominator are multiplied or divided by the same number, as seen in Figure 2-18.

To reduce a fraction to its lowest term, divide both the numerator and denominator by any number that will go into both of them an even number of times. *See* Figure 2-19.

Multiplication of Common Fractions

Multiplication of common fractions is done by multiplying the denominators to find a new denominator, and then multiplying the numerators to find the new numerator. When common fractions are multiplied together, the value of the product will always be smaller than either of the original fractions. *See* Figure 2-20.

Division of Common Fractions

Division of common fractions is similar to multiplication, except we invert the divisor and then multiply. When one common fraction is divided by another, the quotient will always be larger than the dividend. In Figure 2-21, we see the way this is done.

Mixed Numbers

A mixed number is made up of a whole number and a fraction. An example of a mixed number is $1\frac{2}{3}$.

Addition, subtraction, multiplication, and division of mixed numbers is done by changing the mixed number into an improper fraction and then working with it just as you do with a proper fraction. A proper fraction is one in which the denominator is larger than the numerator, while in an improper fraction the numerator is larger than the denominator.

To change a mixed number into an improper fraction, follow these steps shown in Figure 2-22.

1. Change the whole number into a common fraction with the same denominator as the fractional part of the number.

2. Add the fractional part of the number to the whole number you have just made into a fraction.

3. The answer is an improper fraction.

Answers begin on Page 58. Page numbers refer to chapter text.

5. Find the sum of each of these common fractions:

    a. $\frac{1}{4} + \frac{5}{16} + \frac{3}{8} =$ _____

    b. $\frac{1}{2} + \frac{2}{3} + \frac{3}{5} =$ _____

    c. $\frac{1}{16} + \frac{5}{32} + \frac{1}{8} =$ _____

    d. $\frac{3}{64} + \frac{9}{16} + \frac{1}{4} =$ _____

    Page 25

6. Find the difference between each of these common fractions:

    a. $\frac{24}{32} - \frac{1}{8} =$ _____

    b. $\frac{9}{16} - \frac{1}{2} =$ _____

    c. $\frac{7}{16} - \frac{1}{3} =$ _____

    d. $\frac{1}{8} - \frac{1}{32} =$ _____

    Page 25

7. Find the smallest common denominator (SCD) of each of these common fractions:

    a. $\frac{1}{2}, \frac{1}{9}, \frac{1}{16}$ SCD = _____

    b. $\frac{3}{5}, \frac{7}{16}, \frac{1}{8}$ SCD = _____

    c. $\frac{1}{4}, \frac{1}{32}, \frac{1}{9}$ SCD = _____

    d. $\frac{1}{24}, \frac{1}{16}, \frac{1}{3}$ SCD = _____

    Page 26

8. Reduce these common fractions to their lowest terms:

    a. $\frac{526}{1274} =$ _____

    b. $\frac{24}{64} =$ _____

    c. $\frac{150}{900} =$ _____

    d. $\frac{98}{200} =$ _____

    Page 28

Continued

9. Multiply these common fractions and reduce your answer to fractions having their lowest terms:

    a. $\frac{1}{2} \cdot \frac{2}{3} =$ _____

    b. $\frac{3}{4} \cdot \frac{1}{8} =$ _____

    c. $\frac{1}{3} \cdot \frac{6}{18} =$ _____

    d. $\frac{3}{16} \cdot \frac{4}{10} =$ _____

    Page 28

10. Find the quotient of these common fractions:

    a. $24 \div \frac{1}{2} =$ _____

    b. $\frac{1}{16} \div \frac{3}{8} =$ _____

    c. $\frac{5}{8} \div \frac{5}{16} =$ _____

    d. $\frac{5}{16} \div \frac{5}{8} =$ _____

    Page 28

11. Change these mixed numbers to improper fractions:

    a. $1\frac{7}{8} =$ _____

    b. $3\frac{19}{64} =$ _____

    c. $4\frac{1}{2} =$ _____

    d. $9\frac{1}{8} =$ _____

    Page 28

12. Perform the arithmetic functions called for in each of these problems:

    a. $1\frac{1}{2} + 5\frac{5}{16} =$ _____

    b. $6\frac{2}{3} - 4\frac{1}{2} =$ _____

    c. $3\frac{1}{8} \cdot 1\frac{1}{2} =$ _____

    d. $5\frac{1}{16} \div 1\frac{1}{8} =$ _____

    Page 28

Decimal Fractions

Common fractions are awkward to work with, but a special type of fraction, called a decimal fraction, is used to make our work easier and more accurate. Precision measuring instruments work directly with decimal fractions, and almost all engineering dimensions are made with units in which the inch is divided into tenths and hundredths, rather than sixteenths, thirty-seconds, and sixty-fourths.

A decimal fraction is a special fraction whose denominator is divisible by ten. It is not written with the numerator above the denominator, but the value of the denominator is shown by the number of digits that are placed to the right of the decimal point. *See* Figure 2-23.

The value of a number containing a decimal fraction is not changed by adding zeros to the left of the whole number or adding zeros to the right of the decimal fraction. The value of 4.8 is the same as the value of 004.800. When writing a decimal fraction with no whole number, it is customary to place a zero to the left of the decimal point.

Addition of Numbers Containing Decimal Fractions

Decimal fractions and mixed numbers containing a whole number and a decimal fraction may be added in the same way as whole numbers. It is important that the decimal points all be kept in a straight vertical line. The decimal point in the answer will be directly below the decimal points in the numbers being added. *See* Figure 2-24.

Subtraction of Numbers Containing Decimal Fractions

Subtraction of numbers with decimal fractions is done by arranging the subtrahend below the minuend with the decimal points lined up. The decimal point in the difference will be below the decimal points in the numbers above it, as shown in Figure 2-25.

Multiplication of Numbers Containing Decimal Fractions

When multiplying numbers with decimal fractions, disregard the decimal point and multiply the numbers. The location of the decimal point in the answer is found by counting the number of places to the right of the decimal point in both the multiplicand and the multiplier, and adding these numbers. The decimal point in the answer will be this number of places from the right digit. This is illustrated in Figure 2-26.

1/10	= 0.1
1/100	= 0.01
1/1,000	= 0.001
1/10,000	= 0.000 1
1/100,000	= 0.000 01
1/1,000,000	= 0.000 001

Figure 2-23. *The value of the denominator of a decimal fraction is shown by the number of digits to the right of the decimal point.*

```
     0 | 36
    21 | 45
     0 | 125
+  136 | 75
-----------
   158 | 685
```

Figure 2-24. *When adding numbers with decimal fractions, keep the decimal points all in vertical alignment. The decimal point in the answer will be in line with the other decimal points.*

```
   36 | 67
+   8 | 45
----------
   28 | 22
```

Figure 2-25. *When subtracting numbers with decimal fractions, keep the decimal points all in vertical alignment. The decimal point in the answer will be in line the other points.*

The problem:	$26.35 \cdot 5.625 = 148.21875$	
The product disregarding the decimals: $2635 \cdot 5625 = 14821875$	Count the places to the right of the decimal points in the multiplicand and the multiplier. 2 in the multiplicand and 3 in the multiplier: $2 + 3 = 5$	Place the decimal point five places to the left of the last digit: 148.21875

Figure 2-26. *Multiplication of numbers containing decimal fractions*

Division of Numbers Containing Decimal Fractions

Division of numbers containing decimal fractions is done in the same way as long division of whole numbers.

Before starting the division problem, remove the fractional part of the divisor by moving the decimal point all of the way to the right. To keep from affecting the answer, move the decimal point in the dividend the same number of places to the right. *See* Figure 2-27.

The steps needed to divide 379 by 36.875 are:

1. Arrange the numbers as you do for long division of whole numbers.

2. Move the decimal point in the divisor over to the right until it follows the last digit. Place a caret (∧) after the last digit.

3. Move the decimal point in the dividend the same number of places to the right that the decimal point in the divisor was moved. In this case we had to add three zeros. Place a caret where the decimal point is now located.

4. Perform the division as is done with whole numbers.

5. The decimal point in the quotient will be above the caret in the dividend.

1. $36.875 \overline{)\ 379}$

2.
$$36.875_\wedge \overline{)\ 379.000_\wedge 00}\ \ ^{123}10.27$$
$$-3797\,5$$
$$102500$$
$$-\ 73750$$
$$287500$$
$$-\ 258125$$
$$29375\ ...$$

Figure 2-27. *Division by a number containing a decimal fraction*

caret. A small inverted "V" used to show the new location of the decimal in multiplication and division problems using decimal fractions.

Converting Common Fractions into Decimal Fractions

One of the handiest charts in a mechanics handbook is the conversion between common and decimal fractions. But sometimes you may not have such a chart, and you will need to convert them by dividing the numerator by the denominator.

To convert $^{19}/_{64}$ into its decimal equivalent, divide 19 by 64.

$^{19}/_{64} = 0.296875$

Converting Decimal Fractions into Common Fractions

To change a decimal fraction into a common fraction with its lowest terms, first move the decimal point to the right until you have a whole number. This is the numerator of the common fraction. The denominator is 1, followed by the same number of zeros as places you moved to make the numerator.

$0.5 = {}^{5}/_{10}$
$0.25 = {}^{25}/_{100}$
$0.125 = {}^{125}/_{1000}$

To reduce this common fraction to its lowest term, divide the numerator and denominator by the same number. You may need to divide this more than once to get a fraction in which the numerator and the denominator cannot be divided by the same number.

$$\frac{5}{10} \div \frac{5}{5} = \frac{1}{2}$$

$$\frac{25}{100} \div \frac{25}{25} = \frac{1}{4}$$

$$\frac{125}{1000} \div \frac{25}{25} = \frac{5}{40} \div \frac{5}{5} = \frac{1}{8}$$

STUDY QUESTIONS: DECIMAL FRACTIONS

Work these problems by hand, then check your answers with a calculator.
Answers begin on Page 58. Page numbers refer to chapter text.

13. Find the sum of each of these columns of numbers containing decimal fractions:
    Page 31

a.	b.	c.	d.
0.25	12.67	3.98	0.01
14.03	4.32	16.45	0.0025
130.65	44.05	4.06	0.018
5.33	9.45	199.74	0.0005

14. Find the difference between these numbers containing decimal fractions:
    Page 31

a.	b.	c.	d.
125.5	25.67	138.096	199.98
47.25	6.33	98.79	44.105

15. Find the product of these numbers containing decimal fractions:

a. $14.65 \cdot 8.21 =$ _____

b. $197.34 \cdot 0.25 =$ _____

c. $372.94 \cdot 0.0005 =$ _____

d. $47.5 \cdot 3984.21 =$ _____

Page 31

Continued

16. Find the quotient of these numbers containing decimal fractions:

    a. $126 \div 36.87 =$ _____

    b. $5,280 \div 6.09 =$ _____

    c. $973 \div 33.33 =$ _____

    d. $6 \div 0.75 =$ _____

      Page 32

17. Convert these common fractions into their decimal equivalent:

    a. $\frac{9}{16} =$ _____

    b. $\frac{17}{32} =$ _____

    c. $\frac{1}{2} =$ _____

    d. $\frac{7}{8} =$ _____

      Page 32

18. Convert these decimal fractions into common fractions with the lowest terms:

    a. $0.875 =$ _____

    b. $0.5625 =$ _____

    c. $0.625 =$ _____

    d. $0.125 =$ _____

      Page 32

ratio. A kind of fraction that shows the relationship between two values.

proportion. A statement of equality between two ratios.

Ratio and Proportion

Ratio

A ratio is a special kind of fraction that allows us to easily see the relationship between two values. It compares one value with another, and a ratio may be written A is to B, A : B, or A/B. For instance, the speed ratio of a gear train is the inverse ratio of the number of teeth on the input and output gears:

$$\frac{\text{input speed}}{\text{output speed}} = \frac{\text{output teeth}}{\text{input teeth}}$$

Two ratios that are familiar to aviation technicians are the compression ratio of a reciprocating engine and the aspect ratio of an airplane wing. The compression ratio is the ratio of the volume of the cylinder with the piston at the bottom of its stroke to the volume of the cylinder with the piston at the top of its stroke.

The aspect ratio of a wing is the ratio of its length, or span, measured from tip to tip, to its width, or chord, measured from the leading edge to the trailing edge. *See* Figure 2-28.

1. The wing in Figure 2-28 has a span of 36 feet and a chord of 72 inches.

2. To find the ratio, we must have both the span and the chord in the same terms, so we change the chord from inches to feet by dividing by 12.

3. Find the aspect ratio by dividing the span by the chord. This gives us a common fraction of $^{36}/_6$. Reduce this to its smallest term by dividing both the numerator and denominator by 6. The aspect ratio now becomes $^6/_1$, or as it is more commonly expressed, 6:1.

4. When a ratio is expressed as some number to 1, the 1 is usually dropped. The aspect ratio of 6 to 1 is expressed as 6:1, or just as an aspect ratio of 6.

Proportion

A proportion is a statement of equality between two ratios. The use of proportion allows us to solve problems involving one ratio when we know the other.

Proportion is written by making one ratio equal to the other:

A : B = C : D

The two outside terms, A and D, are called the extremes and the two inside terms, B and C are called the means. The product of the means is always equal to the product of the extremes. Consider the proportion in Figure 2-29.

We can find the amount of hardener we would need for 6 pounds of resin if we know that the desired resin-to-hardener ratio is 3:1. *See* Figure 2-30.

1. Multiply the two extremes together. $3 \cdot X$ pounds = 3X pounds

2. Multiply the two means together. $1 \cdot 6$ pounds = 6 pounds

3. Since 3X pounds = 6 pounds, X pounds = $6 \div 3$ = 2 pounds.

4. To keep a ratio of resin to hardener of 3:1, we must mix 2 pounds of hardener with 6 pounds of resin.

Aspect ratio = wing span ÷ wing chord

= 36 feet ÷ 72 inches

= 36 feet ÷ $^{72}/_{12}$ feet

= 36 feet ÷ 6 feet

= 6 : 1

= 6

Figure 2-28. *To find a ratio, put both values in the same terms and divide one by the other. Reduce both the numerator and denominator by the same value to get the lowest terms. If the denominator reduces to 1, it is usually omitted when the ratio is expressed.*

$3 : 9 = 12 : 36$ or $\dfrac{3}{9} = \dfrac{12}{36}$

The extremes are 3 and 36.
$3 \cdot 36 = 108$
The means are 9 and 12.
$9 \cdot 12 = 108$

Figure 2-29. *In a proportion, the product of the extremes always equals the product of the means.*

desired resin : desired hardener =
      actual resin : **actual hardener**

$3 : 1 = 6 : X$
$3X = 6$
$X = 2$

Figure 2-30. *A proportion problem*

19. If a wing span is 35 feet and the chord is 60 inches, the aspect ratio is _____ . *Page 35*

20. The volume of a cylinder with the piston at the bottom of its stroke is 90 cubic inches. With the piston at the top of its stroke, the volume is 15 cubic inches. The compression ratio is _____ . *Page 35*

21. An engine is using an air/fuel mixture ratio of 12:1 (12 parts of air to 1 part of fuel by weight). How many pounds of air would have to be taken into the engine to burn 1 gallon of gasoline? Gasoline weighs 6 pounds per gallon. _____ pounds. *Page 35*

22. A pinion gear with 14 teeth is driving a spur gear with 42 teeth at 140 RPM. The speed of the pinion gear is _____ RPM. *Page 35*

23. An airplane flying a distance of 875 miles uses 70 gallons of fuel. At this rate of fuel consumption, it will need _____ gallons to fly 3,000 miles. *Page 35*

24. If a propeller turns at ½ of the engine speed, how fast will the propeller be turning when the engine is turning at 1,800 RPM?
Propeller speed = _____ RPM. *Page 35*

25. If a drive shaft turns 9 revolutions when the driven shaft turns 16 revolutions, what will be the speed of the driven shaft when the drive shaft is turning at 150 RPM?
Driven shaft speed = _____ RPM. *Page 35*

26. If the maximum permissible landing weight of an airplane is ⅞ of its permissible takeoff weight, what is the maximum takeoff weight when the maximum landing weight is 38,000 pounds?
Maximum takeoff weight = _____ pounds. *Page 35*

27. The fuel for a certain two-cycle engine is mixed with a fuel/oil ratio of 24:1. Since there are 128 ounces in 1 gallon, _____ ounces of oil must be mixed with 1 gallon of gasoline. *Page 35*

Percentage

One Number Which is a Given Percentage of Another

A percentage is a fraction with 100 as the denominator. Percentages are useful in describing or determining parts of a whole. The whole is considered to be 100/100 or 100 percent, and is expressed as 100%.

To find a number which is a given percentage of another number, we change the percentage to a decimal fraction by moving the decimal point two places to the left. Then multiply as is done with decimal fractions.

To find 70% of 230 horsepower, multiply 230 by 0.70.

$$230 \cdot 0.70 = 161$$

70% of 230 horsepower is 161 horsepower.

The Percentage One Number is of Another

We can find what percentage 20 is of 80 by visualizing the relationship we see in Figure 2-31.

$$\frac{\text{number whose percentage is to be found}}{\text{original number}} = \frac{X\%}{100\%}$$

1. First set up the relationship that 20 is to 80 as X% is to 100%.
2. Cross multiply. $80X = 2000$
3. Divide 2000 by 80. $2000 \div 80 = 25$
4. 20 is 25% of 80

This procedure is made simpler by these steps:

1. Multiply the number whose percentage is known by 100.
2. Divide this by the known percentage.

   The problem in Figure 2-31 would then be worked as:

   $$20 \cdot 100 \div 80 = 25$$

Find the percentage that 20 is of 80.

$$\frac{20}{80} = \frac{X\%}{100}$$

$$80X = 2,000$$

$$X = \frac{2,000}{80}$$

$$X = 25$$

20 is 25% of 80

Figure 2-31. *Finding the percentage one number is of another number.*

A Number of Which a Given Percentage is Known

If 5% of a box of rivets weighs 2 pounds, what does the entire box of rivets weigh? We can find this by following these steps and referring to Figure 2-32.

$$\frac{5}{2} = \frac{100}{W}$$

$$5W = 200$$

$$W = 40 \text{ pounds}$$

Figure 2-32. *Finding a number of which a given percentage is known*

1. First set up the relationship that 5% is to 2 as 100% is to the weight we want to find, or W.

2. Cross multiply. $5 \cdot W = 2 \cdot 100$

3. Divide 200 by 5. $200 \div 5 = 40$

4. If 5% of the rivets weighs 2 pounds, the entire box of rivets weighs 40 pounds.

This procedure is made simpler by these steps:

1. Multiply the number whose percentage is known by 100.

2. Divide this by the known percentage.

$$\frac{2 \cdot 100}{5} = 40$$

STUDY QUESTIONS: PERCENTAGE

*Answers begin on Page 58. **Page numbers refer to chapter text.***

28. Find the required percentage of each of these numbers:

   a. 13% of 26 = _____
   b. 32% of 897 = _____
   c. 125% of 368 = _____
   d. 25% of 0.5 = _____
   Page 37

29. Find the percentage the first number is of the second:

   a. 30 is _____% of 240
   b. 927 is _____% of 5,275
   c. 75 is _____% of 6,200
   d. 350 is _____% of 50
   Page 37

30. Find the total amount when a partial amount and the percentage it represents are known:

   a. 4 is 16% of_____
   b. 320 is 50% of_____
   c. 75 is 125% of_____
   d. 350 is 35% of_____
   Page 38

AVIATION MAINTENANCE TECHNICIAN SERIES   GENERAL

Signed Numbers

Up to this point we have considered all numbers to be positive, or greater than zero. Positive numbers are considered to have a plus (+) sign in front of them, but this sign is generally omitted.

There are also numbers less than zero. These are called negative numbers, and they are preceded by a minus (-) sign.

There are rules we use to add, subtract, multiply, and divide signed numbers.

Adding Signed Numbers

When we want to add several numbers with different signs, we add all of the positive numbers and all of the negative numbers. Subtract the smaller from the larger and give the answer the sign of the larger.

To find the sum of +4 -9 +17 +5 -3, follow these steps:

1. Add all of the numbers which have a plus sign.

   +4 +17 +5 = +26

2. Add all of the numbers which have a minus sign.

   -9 -3 = -12

3. Subtract the smaller of these answers from the larger. The sign of the answer will be the sign of the larger.

   +26 -12 = +14

Subtracting Signed Numbers

When subtracting signed numbers, change the sign of the subtrahend and add. *See* Figure 2-33.

1. Change the sign of the subtrahend (the number that is being subtracted).

2. Add the two numbers. If the signs are different, subtract the smaller from the larger and give the answer the sign of the larger.

Multiplying Signed Numbers

When we multiply two signed numbers, we proceed as though the numbers had no sign. If the signs of the two numbers are the same, the sign of the answer is positive. If the signs of the two numbers are different, the sign of the answer is negative. *See* Figure 2-34.

1. Multiply the numbers, disregarding the signs.

2. If the signs of the two numbers are the same, the sign of the answer is positive. If the signs of the two numbers are not the same, the sign of the answer is negative.

signed numbers. Numbers marked to indicate whether they are larger or smaller than zero. Numbers smaller than zero are preceded with a minus (–) sign, and are called negative numbers

$$
\begin{array}{rr}
+36 & +36 \\
(-)\ \underline{-24} & (+)\ \underline{+24} \\
& 60 \\
\end{array}
$$

$$
\begin{array}{rr}
-128 & -128 \\
(-)\ \underline{-12} & (+)\ \underline{+12} \\
& -116 \\
\end{array}
$$

Figure 2-33. *Subtracting signed numbers*

$-14 \cdot -64 = +896$

$+8 \cdot -47 = -376$

Figure 2-34. *Multiplying signed numbers*

$$-125 \div -25 = +5$$

$$+36 \div -9 = -4$$

Figure 2-35. *Dividing signed numbers*

Dividing Signed Numbers

Signed numbers are divided by following the same rules as are used for multiplying. Disregard the signs and divide the dividend by the divisor. If the two numbers have the same sign, the sign of the quotient is positive; if the two numbers have different signs, the sign of the quotient is negative. *See* Figure 2-35.

1. Disregard the signs, and divide as though the numbers had no signs.

2. If the signs of the two numbers are alike, the sign of the answer is positive. If the signs of the two numbers are not alike, the sign of the answer is negative.

STUDY QUESTIONS: SIGNED NUMBERS

Answers begin on Page 58. **Page numbers refer to chapter text.**

31. Find the sum of these signed numbers:

   a. +24 + (-19) + (+8) + (+7) + (-13) = _____
   b. -9 + (-26) + (-7) + (+54) = _____
   c. +7 + (+32) + (-16) + (+41) = _____
   d. +6 + (+12) + (-18) + (-24) = _____
   Page 39

32. Find the difference between these signed numbers:

   a. +13 (–) +8 = _____
   b. -126 (–) -45 = _____
   c. +85 (–) -64 = _____
   d. -118 (–) +69 = _____
   Page 39

33. Find the product of these signed numbers:

   a. +5 · -16 = _____
   b. -9 · -36 = _____
   c. -24 · +8 = _____
   d. +75 · +5 = _____
   Page 39

34. Find the quotient of these signed numbers:

   a. +16 ÷ -5 = _____

   b. -36 ÷ -6 = _____

   c. -28 ÷ +4 = _____

   d. +70 ÷ +6 = _____

    Page 40

Powers and Roots

Powers

A power of a base number is the number of times it is multiplied by itself to give us the value we want. This power, or exponent, is written as a small number, above and to the right of the base number.

In the number 9^2, 9 is the base, and 2 is the exponent. The base 9 is raised to its second power, or 9 squared. $9^2 = 9 \cdot 9 = 81$. Any number raised to the zero power is equal to 1 ($4^0 = 1$), and any number raised to the first power is the same as the number itself ($4^1 = 4$). In Figure 2-36 we see how we find the value of 2^8.

2^8 is 2 raised to the eighth power

$2^8 = 2 \cdot 2 \cdot 2 \cdot 2 \cdot 2 \cdot 2 \cdot 2 \cdot 2$

$2^8 = 256$

Figure 2-36. *The power of a number tells how many times the number is multiplied by itself.*

Roots

The root of a number is that number which, when multiplied by itself an indicated number of times, will give us the number under the radical sign. The small number in the V of the radical sign tells how many times the number should be multiplied. If nothing is written in the V, a square root is indicated. *See* Figure 2-37.

There is a longhand method of extracting a square root that can be used, but this method involves a large number of steps. So, since there are tables of square and cube roots in most handbooks, and because most electronic calculators can extract square roots, we will not explain this method.

Powers and roots of a number other than squares and square roots are difficult to work by hand, but a hand calculator makes them very easy. For example, $\sqrt[4]{1296}$ means "find the fourth root of 1,296." To find such a root

$\sqrt{a}$ This is the square root of number *a*.

$\sqrt[3]{a}$ This is the cube root of number *a*.

Figure 2-37. *The root which is to be taken of a number is shown by the small number written above the radical sign.*

power of a number. The number of times a number is multiplied by itself.

root. A number which, when multiplied by itself a specified number of times, will give a specific number.

base. The number in an exponential expression that is multiplied by itself the number of times shown by the exponent.

Continued

we can raise the number to the power that is the reciprocal of the root that is called for. This is 1 divided by the number in the V of the radical, or ¼. In this way $\sqrt[4]{1296}$ becomes $1296^{1/4}$.

$$\sqrt[4]{1296}$$

$$1296^{1/4} = 6$$

To check this answer for accuracy, multiply 6 by itself 4 times.

$$6 \cdot 6 \cdot 6 \cdot 6 = 1,296$$

STUDY QUESTIONS: POWERS AND ROOTS

Answers begin on Page 58. Page numbers refer to chapter text.

35. Raise each of these numbers to their required power:

a. $6^2 =$ _____
b. $3^8 =$ _____
c. $5^5 =$ _____
d. $4^3 =$ _____
   Page 41

36. Find the indicated roots of these numbers:

a. The square root of 64 = _____
b. The square root of 96 = _____
c. The cube root of 71 = _____
d. The cube root of 48 = _____
   Page 41

scientific notation. A mathematical procedure in which very large or very small numbers are made more manageable by changing them to numbers between 1 and 10, raised to a power showing the number of places the decimal point was moved.

Scientific Notation

Scientific notation is a mathematical procedure in which very large or very small numbers are made more manageable by changing them to numbers between 1 and 10, raised to a power equal to the number of places the decimal point was moved. Scientific notation is also called "powers of ten."

Changing Numbers into Scientific Notation

The number 1,000 is written in scientific notation as $1 \cdot 10^3$, and 100,000 is written as $1 \cdot 10^5$. To change any number into scientific notation, move the decimal point until you have a number between 1 and 9. Count the number of places you have moved the decimal point to get the exponent of 10 (the small number above and to the right of the 10).

To change 1,542,000 into scientific notation, move the decimal point to the left 6 places. This gives $1.542 \cdot 10^6$. (Notice that we are able to drop the zeros, since they have no meaning when they follow the last nonzero digit to the right of the decimal point.)

The process of changing numbers smaller than 1 into scientific notation is similar. Move the decimal to the right until you have a number between 1 and 9. Count the number of places you have moved it. This is the exponent of 10 and is a negative number, so place a minus sign in front of it. To change 0.000 000 632 into scientific notation, move the decimal to the right 7 places. This gives $6.32 \cdot 10^{-7}$. We are able to get rid of zeros here too, because zeros before the first nonzero digit to the left of the decimal point have no meaning.

Changing Scientific Notation into Ordinary Numbers

A number greater than 1, written in scientific notation, can be changed into ordinary numbers by writing enough zeros after the decimal point to give as many digits as the value of the exponent.

To change $5.862 \cdot 10^9$ into ordinary numbers, move the decimal point 9 places to the right. To do this, we will have to add 6 zeros: 5,862,000,000 is the same as $5.862 \cdot 10^9$.

Numbers smaller than 1 that are written in scientific notation can be changed into ordinary numbers by moving the decimal point to the left as many digits as the value of the negative exponent.

To change $7.6 \cdot 10^{-5}$ into ordinary decimal fraction, we move the decimal point to the left 5 places. This gives the decimal fraction 0.000 076.

Adding Numbers Using Scientific Notation

When adding numbers written in scientific notation, move the decimal points in the numbers until they all have the same power of ten. Add the numbers as whole numbers with decimal fractions and attach the power of ten. We see this procedure in Figure 2-38.

1. Change all of the numbers so they have the same power of ten.

2. Add the numbers and attach the same power of ten.

3. To make a correct number in scientific notation, move the decimal point to the left to get a number between 1 and 9 and change the power of ten accordingly.

$$
\begin{array}{r}
8.45 \cdot 10^7 \\
6.50 \cdot 10^5 \\
+\ 3.65 \cdot 10^6 \\
\hline
8.88 \cdot 10^7
\end{array}
$$

$$
\begin{array}{r}
845.0 \cdot 10^5 \\
6.5 \cdot 10^5 \\
+\ 36.5 \cdot 10^5 \\
\hline
888.0 \cdot 10^5
\end{array}
$$

$$
\begin{array}{r}
84{,}500{,}000 \\
650{,}000 \\
+\ 3{,}650{,}000 \\
\hline
88{,}800{,}000
\end{array}
$$

Figure 2-38. *Adding numbers in scientific notation*

$$\begin{array}{r} 3.65 \cdot 10^6 \\ - \ \underline{4.50 \cdot 10^5} \\ 3.20 \cdot 10^6 \end{array}$$

$$\begin{array}{r} 36.5 \cdot 10^5 \\ - \ \underline{4.5 \cdot 10^5} \\ 32.0 \cdot 10^5 \end{array}$$

$$\begin{array}{r} 3,650,000 \\ - \ \underline{450,000} \\ 3,200,000 \end{array}$$

Figure 2-39. *Subtracting numbers in scientific notation*

$3.8 \cdot 10^5 \cdot 2.7 \cdot 10^2 = \underline{}$

$3.8 \cdot 2.7 = 10.26$

$10^5 + 10^2 = 10^7$

$10.26 \cdot 10^7 = 1.026 \cdot 10^8$

Figure 2-40. *Multiplying numbers in scientific notation*

$6.4 \cdot 10^7 \div 3.5 \cdot 10^6 =$

$(6.4 \div 3.5) \cdot 10^{7-6} =$

$1.83 \cdot 10^1 = 18.3$

Figure 2-41. *Dividing numbers in scientific notation*

Subtracting Numbers Using Scientific Notation

When subtracting numbers written in scientific notation, move the decimal points in the numbers until they all have the same power of ten. Subtract as you would with whole numbers with decimal fractions and attach the power of ten. We see this procedure in Figure 2-39.

1. Change all of the numbers so they have the same power of ten.

2. Subtract the subtrahend from the minuend and attach the same power of ten.

3. To make a correct number in scientific notation, move the decimal point to the left to get a number between 1 and 9 and use the correct power of ten.

Multiplying Numbers Using Scientific Notation

To multiply numbers using scientific notation, multiply the decimal fraction portions independent of the powers of ten. Then add the exponents of the powers of ten as signed numbers. This becomes the new power of ten. If the decimal fraction product is greater than ten, move the decimal point and change the power of ten to make the number proper in scientific notation. Follow the procedure illustrated in Figure 2-40.

1. Multiply the numbers as whole numbers with decimal fractions.

2. Add the powers of ten as signed numbers.

3. Apply the new power of ten to the answer.

Dividing Numbers Using Scientific Notation

To divide numbers using scientific notation, divide them as though they were whole numbers with decimal fractions. Subtract the powers of ten as signed numbers, and use the resulting power of ten for the answer. Follow the procedure in Figure 2-41.

1. Divide the numbers as whole numbers with decimal fractions.

2. Subtract the powers of ten as signed numbers.

3. Apply the new power of ten to the answer.

Raising Numbers to Powers Using Scientific Notation

When a number written in scientific notation is raised to a power, the number is raised to the required power; then the power of ten is multiplied by the power to which it is to be raised. As shown in Figure 2-42, square $4.5 \cdot 10^3$. First, square 4.5 and get 20.25. Then multiply the third power of 10 by the second power of 10 to find that 20.25 is to be raised to its sixth power ($3 \cdot 2 = 6$). Change this answer into proper scientific notation by moving the decimal point to the left to get a number between 1 and 9 and change the exponent to indicate this change.

$$(4.5 \cdot 10^3)^2 = \underline{\hspace{1cm}}$$
$$4.5^2 = 20.25$$
$$10^3 \cdot 10^2 = 10^6$$
$$20.25 \cdot 10^6 = 2.025 \cdot 10^7$$

Figure 2-42. *Raising scientific notation to a power*

STUDY QUESTIONS: SCIENTIFIC NOTATION

Answers begin on Page 58. Page numbers refer to chapter text.

37. Change these numbers into scientific notation:

    a. 6,800,000 = _____

    b. 5,872 = _____

    c. 0.000 000 000 874 = _____

    d. 0.000 2 = _____
    Page 42

38. Convert these scientific notations into ordinary numbers:

    a. $8.56 \cdot 10^6$ = _____

    b. $7.096 \cdot 10^4$ = _____

    c. $6.53 \cdot 10^{-14}$ = _____

    d. $9.431 \cdot 10^{-6}$ = _____
    Page 43

39. Find the sum of these numbers, using scientific notation:

    a. $4.7 \cdot 10^4 + 3.8 \cdot 10^6 + 9.58 \cdot 10^5$ = _____

    b. $9.6 \cdot 10^3 + 8.2 \cdot 10^2 + 8.13 \cdot 10^4$ = _____

    c. $2.1 \cdot 10^{-2} + 1.95 \cdot 10^{-3} + 7.6 \cdot 10^{-2}$ = _____

    d. $3.9 \cdot 10^4 + 2.7 \cdot 10^3 + 8.4 \cdot 10^2$ = _____
    Page 43

Continued

40. Find the difference in these numbers, using scientific notation:

    a. $3.8 \cdot 10^6 - 4.3 \cdot 10^5 =$ _____

    b. $7.4 \cdot 10^3 - 9.2 \cdot 10^2 =$ _____

    c. $3.4 \cdot 10^{-2} - 4.1 \cdot 10^{-3} =$ _____

    d. $5.9 \cdot 10^{-7} - 7.7 \cdot 10^{-9} =$ _____

    Page 44

41. Find the product of these numbers, using scientific notation:

    a. $4.8 \cdot 10^3 \cdot 2.7 \cdot 10^4 =$ _____

    b. $9.4 \cdot 10^5 \cdot 3.2 \cdot 10^{-4} =$ _____

    c. $7.3 \cdot 10^{-2} \cdot 6.3 \cdot 10^4 =$ _____

    d. $9.2 \cdot 10^{-2} \cdot 7.2 \cdot 10^{-3} =$ _____

    Page 44

42. Find the quotients of these numbers, using scientific notation:

    a. $9.4 \cdot 10^5 \div 3.6 \cdot 10^7 =$ _____

    b. $4.1 \cdot 10^2 \div 6.2 \cdot 10^{-2} =$ _____

    c. $8.3 \cdot 10^{-2} \div 2.6 \cdot 10^4 =$ _____

    d. $1.6 \cdot 10^{-4} \div 2.7 \cdot 10^{-6} =$ _____

    Page 44

43. Raise these numbers to the required powers, using scientific notation:

    a. $(3.6 \cdot 10^2)^2 =$ _____

    b. $(8.4 \cdot 10^1)^3 =$ _____

    c. $(6.2 \cdot 10^2)^{-3} =$ _____

    d. $(9.1 \cdot 10^{-2})^4 =$ _____

    Page 45

Trigonometry

One of the most useful tools in mathematics is trigonometry. Trig, as it is generally called, is a handy and fast way to work all kinds of vector problems such as those we encounter in navigation, electrical circuits, and stress analysis. In this section we will discuss the most generally used aspects of trig as they apply to the science of aviation.

Triangles

Trigonometry is the branch of mathematics that deals with the measurements of triangles, and is primarily concerned with the relationships between the lengths of the three sides of a triangle and the angles they contain. This basic study will deal primarily with right triangles, triangles that contain a 90° angle. Figure 2-43 shows a right triangle with the terms we will use in this study.

Angle A is the one we will begin to study. Side a is called the side opposite, and side b is called the side adjacent. Side c is opposite the right angle and it is called the hypotenuse. In any triangle, the sum of the angles is always 180°, and since in a right triangle, angle C is always 90°, angle A + angle B = 90°.

The basic tools of trigonometry are called the functions. These are six ratios that relate to the length of the three sides of a right triangle. By using these functions, when you know one of the acute angles and the length of one of the sides, or both of the acute angles, or the lengths of any two of the sides, you can find the value of any angle and the length of any of the sides. These trig functions are the sine, cosine, tangent, cosecant, secant, and cotangent. *See* Figure 2-44 on page 48.

Trig Function Table

Figure 2-45 (page 48) is a table of trigonometric functions. In the first column along the left side, starting at the top and going down, are the degrees of the acute angle. They start at 0° and go down to 45° in increments of one-half degree. In the sixth column, along the right side of the table, starting at the bottom and going up, are the degrees and half degrees of angles between 45° and 90°. Only the functions for 90° need to be considered since the functions between 0° and 90° are the same as those between 90° and 180°, 180° and 270°, and 270° and 360°.

In the second column, reading from top to bottom, and in the third column reading from bottom to top, are the sines of the angles. In the third column reading down, and in the second column reading up are the cosines of the angles. In the fourth column reading down and the fifth column reading up are the tangents of the angles, and in the fifth column reading down and the fourth column reading up are the cotangents of the angles.

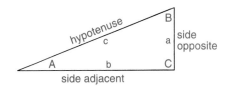

Figure 2-43. *A right triangle contains a 90°, or right angle.*

Trigonometric Functions

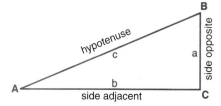

Tangent (tan) $= \dfrac{\text{side opposite}}{\text{side adjacent}}$

Sine (sin) $= \dfrac{\text{side opposite}}{\text{hypotenuse}}$

Cosine (cos) $= \dfrac{\text{side adjacent}}{\text{hypotenuse}}$

Cotangent (cot) $= \dfrac{1}{\tan} = \dfrac{\text{side adjacent}}{\text{side opposite}}$

Cosecant (csc) $= \dfrac{1}{\sin} = \dfrac{\text{hypotenuse}}{\text{side opposite}}$

Secant (sec) $= \dfrac{1}{\cos} = \dfrac{\text{hypotenuse}}{\text{side adjacent}}$

Figure 2-44. *The six basic trigonometric functions*

Figure 2-45. *Trigonometric functions*

Degrees		Sines	Cosines	Tangents	Cotangents		
0.00°		0.0000	1.0000	0.0000	—	90.00°	
	0.50°	0.0087	0.9999	0.0087	114.59		89.50°
1.00°		0.0175	0.9998	0.0175	57.290	89.00°	
	1.50°	0.0262	0.9997	0.0262	38.188		88.50°
2.00°		0.0349	0.9994	0.0349	28.636	88.00°	
	2.50°	0.0436	0.9990	0.0437	22.904		87.50°
3.00°		0.0523	0.9986	0.0524	19.081	87.00°	
	3.50°	0.0610	0.9981	0.0612	16.350		86.50°
4.00°		0.0698	0.9976	0.0699	14.301	86.00°	
	4.50°	0.0785	0.9969	0.0787	12.706		85.50°
5.00°		0.0872	0.9962	0.0875	11.430	85.00°	
	5.50°	0.0958	0.9954	0.0963	10.385		84.50°
6.00°		0.1045	0.9945	0.1051	9.5144	84.00°	
	6.50°	0.1132	0.9936	0.1139	8.7769		83.50°
7.00°		0.1219	0.9925	0.1228	8.1443	83.00°	
	7.50°	0.1305	0.9914	0.1317	7.5958		82.50°
8.00°		0.1392	0.9903	0.1405	7.1154	82.00°	
	8.50°	0.1478	0.9890	0.1495	6.6912		81.50°
9.00°		0.1564	0.9877	0.1584	6.3138	81.00°	
	9.50°	0.1650	0.9863	0.1673	5.9758		80.50°
10.00°		0.1736	0.9848	0.1763	5.6713	80.00°	
	10.50°	0.1822	0.9833	0.1853	5.3955		79.50°
11.00°		0.1908	0.9816	0.1944	5.1446	79.00°	
	11.50°	0.1994	0.9799	0.2035	4.9152		78.50°
12.00°		0.2079	0.9781	0.2126	4.7046	78.00°	
	12.50°	0.2164	0.9763	0.2217	4.5107		77.50°
13.00°		0.2250	0.9744	0.2309	4.3315	77.00°	
	13.50°	0.2334	0.9724	0.2401	4.1653		76.50°
14.00°		0.2419	0.9703	0.2493	4.0108	76.00°	
	14.50°	0.2504	0.9681	0.2586	3.8667		75.50°
15.00°		0.2588	0.9659	0.2679	3.7321	75.00°	
	15.50°	0.2672	0.9636	0.2773	3.6059		74.50°
16.00°		0.2756	0.9613	0.2867	3.4875	74.00°	
	16.50°	0.2840	0.9588	0.2962	3.3759		73.50°
17.00°		0.2924	0.9563	0.3057	3.2709	73.00°	
	17.50°	0.3007	0.9537	0.3153	3.1716		72.50°
18.00°		0.3090	0.9511	0.3249	3.0777	72.00°	
	18.50°	0.3173	0.9483	0.3346	2.9887		71.50°
19.00°		0.3256	0.9455	0.3443	2.9042	71.00°	
	19.50°	0.3338	0.9426	0.3541	2.8239		70.50°
20.00°		0.3420	0.9397	0.3640	2.7475	70.00°	
	20.50°	0.3502	0.9367	0.3739	2.6746		69.50°
21.00°		0.3584	0.9336	0.3839	2.6051	69.00°	
	21.50°	0.3665	0.9304	0.3939	2.5386		68.50°
22.00°		0.3746	0.9272	0.4040	2.4751	68.00°	
	22.50°	0.3827	0.9239	0.4142	2.4142		67.50°
23.00°		0.3907	0.9205	0.4245	2.3559	67.00°	
	23.50°	0.3987	0.9171	0.4348	2.2998		66.50°
24.00°		0.4067	0.9135	0.4452	2.2460	66.00°	
	24.50°	0.4147	0.9100	0.4557	2.1943		65.50°
25.00°		0.4226	0.9063	0.4663	2.1445	65.00°	
	25.50°	0.4305	0.9026	0.4770	2.0965		64.50°
26.00°		0.4384	0.8988	0.4877	2.0503	64.00°	
	26.50°	0.4462	0.8949	0.4986	2.0057		63.50°
27.00°		0.4540	0.8910	0.5095	1.9626	63.00°	
	27.50°	0.4617	0.8870	0.5206	1.9210		62.50°
28.00°		0.4695	0.8829	0.5317	1.8807	62.00°	
	28.50°	0.4772	0.8788	0.5430	1.8418		61.50°
29.00°		0.4848	0.8746	0.5543	1.8040	61.00°	
	29.50°	0.4924	0.8704	0.5658	1.7675		60.50°
30.00°		0.5000	0.8660	0.5774	1.7321	60.00°	
	30.50°	0.5075	0.8616	0.5890	1.6977		59.50°
31.00°		0.5150	0.8572	0.6009	1.6643	59.00°	
	31.50°	0.5225	0.8526	0.6128	1.6319		58.50°
32.00°		0.5299	0.8480	0.6249	1.6003	58.00°	57.50°
	32.50°	0.5373	0.8434	0.6371	1.5697		
33.00°		0.5446	0.8387	0.6494	1.5399	57.00°	56.50°
	33.50°	0.5519	0.8339	0.6619	1.5108		
34.00°		0.5592	0.8290	0.6745	1.4826	56.00°	55.50°
	34.50°	0.5664	0.8241	0.6873	1.4550		
35.00°		0.5736	0.8192	0.7002	1.4281	55.00°	54.50°
	35.50°	0.5807	0.8141	0.7133	1.4019		
36.00°		0.5878	0.8090	0.7265	1.3764	54.00°	53.50°
	36.50°	0.5948	0.8039	0.7400	1.3514		
37.00°		0.6018	0.7986	0.7536	1.3270	53.00°	52.50°
	37.50°	0.6088	0.7934	0.7673	1.3032		
38.00°		0.6157	0.7880	0.7813	1.2799	52.00°	51.50°
	38.50°	0.6225	0.7826	0.7954	1.2572		
39.00°		0.6293	0.7771	0.8098	1.2349	51.00°	50.50°
	39.50°	0.6361	0.7716	0.8243	1.2131		
40.00°		0.6428	0.7660	0.8391	1.1918	50.00°	49.50°
	40.50°	0.6494	0.7604	0.8541	1.1708		
41.00°		0.6561	0.7547	0.8693	1.1504	49.00°	48.50°
	41.50°	0.6626	0.7490	0.8847	1.1303		
42.00°		0.6691	0.7431	0.9004	1.1106	48.00°	47.50°
	42.50°	0.6756	0.7373	0.9163	1.0913		
43.00°		0.6820	0.7314	0.9325	1.0724	47.00°	46.50°
	43.50°	0.6884	0.7254	0.9490	1.0538		
44.00°		0.6947	0.7193	0.9657	1.0355	46.00°	45.50°
	44.50°	0.7009	0.7133	0.9827	1.0716		
45.00°		0.7071	0.7071	1.0000	1.0000	45.00°	
		Cosines	Sines	Cotangents	Tangents	Degrees	

The trig table in Figure 2-45 lists the angles in degrees and decimal parts of a degree, but sometimes you may need to work with degrees and minutes. To convert decimal parts of a degree into minutes, multiply by 60.

$0.25° \cdot 60 = 15'$
$0.5° \cdot 60 = 30'$
$0.75° \cdot 60 = 45'$

To convert minutes to decimals, divide them by 60.

$15' \div 60 = 0.25°$
$30' \div 60 = 0.5°$
$45' \div 60 = 0.75°$

Sometimes a number found in a problem is between two numbers in the trig table. For most practical problems it is accurate enough to choose the degree or half degree nearest this value. But there is a way to get a more accurate answer. For example if you find a sine value to be 0.2718, you can check in the sines column and find that this is between 0.2672 for 15.50° and 0.2756 for 16.00°. To find the exact value you can interpolate. To find the angle whose sine is 0.2718, follow these steps:

1. Find the difference between the sine of 16.00° and the sine of 15.50°.

    Sin 16°   0.2756
    – Sin 15.50°   0.2672
    _____
                 0.0084

2. Find the difference between the sine of the unknown angle, angle X, and the sine of 15.50°.

    Sin °X   0.2718
    – Sin 15.50°   0.2672
    _____
                 0.0046

3. Using a ratio, find the portion of a degree represented by 0.0046.

    If 0.0084 = 0.50°, 0.0046 = X°

    $$\frac{0.0084}{0.5} = \frac{0.0046}{X}$$

    $X = 0.27°$

4. Add the portion of a degree found in step 3 to 15.50°.

    $15.50 + 0.27° = 15.77°$

    The angle whose sine is 0.2718 is 15.77°

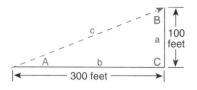

$$\text{Tan A} = \frac{100}{300} = 0.333$$

$$\text{Tan}^{-1} 0.333 = 18.5°$$

Figure 2-46. *Finding an angle using the tangent*

$$c = \sqrt{b^2 + a^2}$$

$$= \sqrt{300^2 + 100^2}$$

$$= \sqrt{90,000 + 10,000}$$

$$= 316 \text{ feet}$$

Figure 2-47. *Finding the length of the hypotenuse using the Pythagorean formula*

$$\text{Sin A} = \frac{a}{c}$$

$$0.3173 = \frac{100}{c}$$

$$c = \frac{100}{0.3173}$$

$$= 315 \text{ feet}$$

Figure 2-48. *Finding the length of the hypotenuse using the sine function*

Tangent

The tangent is the ratio of the length of the side opposite to the side adjacent. When we know these two lengths, we can find the value of the two acute angles and the length of the hypotenuse. In Figure 2-46 we have a problem that can be solved by using trigonometry.

An object has been moved 300 feet to the east, and then 100 feet to the north. We want to know the straight-line distance between the starting point and the ending point and the values of angles A and B.

The tangent of A is 0.333, and to find the value of angle A, we follow the fourth column of the trig table down to the number nearest to this, which is 0.3346. Follow the line on which this is located to the left and find that the angle whose tangent is 0.3346 is 18.50°. In Figure 2-46, we see the term Tan^{-1} 0.333. This term is the arctangent, which simply means the angle whose tangent is 0.333.

We find the distance c between A and B by using the Pythagorean formula, as seen in Figure 2-47; but since we are studying trigonometry, we will also solve it by using the sine function, as seen in Figure 2-48.

Sine

The sine of an angle is the ratio of the length of the side opposite to the length of the hypotenuse. Look in the second column opposite 18.50° and find that the sine of 18.50° is 0.3173. *See* Figure 2-48.

Distance Measuring Equipment (DME) is an electronic navigation system that measures the straight-line distance between the aircraft and the ground transmitting station. This presents the pilot with a direct reading of the length of the hypotenuse of the right triangle we see in Figure 2-49. The DME reads 35 nautical miles to the station when the aircraft is flying at an altitude of 36,000 feet, or approximately 6 nautical miles above the surface. We can find the actual distance on the ground to the station by using the sine and cosine functions.

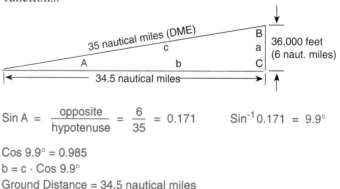

$$\text{Sin A} = \frac{\text{opposite}}{\text{hypotenuse}} = \frac{6}{35} = 0.171 \qquad \text{Sin}^{-1} 0.171 = 9.9°$$

Cos 9.9° = 0.985
b = c · Cos 9.9°
Ground Distance = 34.5 nautical miles

Figure 2-49. *Finding an angle using the sine function*

Vector Quantities

We will introduce vector quantities in this chapter because they are so closely related to the trigonometric functions. A practical discussion of vectors is included in Chapter 3 on Basic Physics.

One of the more important uses of the sine and cosine functions is in the solution of vector quantities. A vector is a quantity that has both magnitude and direction. In Figure 2-50 we have vector R that has a magnitude of 10 units and a direction of 30° clockwise from North. We normally think of this direction in aviation terms, as 030°, but for problem solving, we will omit any zeros to the left of the first nonzero digit.

Vector R is the hypotenuse of a right triangle made up of a horizontal component, called the *x* component, and a vertical component, called the *y* component. To best understand vectors, we will place the tail of vector R, the end without the arrowhead, at the intersection of a horizontal line representing the X-axis and a vertical line representing the Y-axis. The horizontal, or *x*, component of vector R is a line drawn from the tip of the vector, horizontally to the left until it intersects the Y-axis. This is the side opposite the 30° angle. The vertical, or *y*, component is the adjacent side of this triangle.

We know that the sine of 30° is the ratio of the length of the side opposite to the length of the hypotenuse, and by using the trig function chart, Figure 2-45, we see that the sine of 30° is 0.5000.

$$\text{Sine } 30° = \frac{\text{opposite}}{\text{hypotenuse}}$$

$$0.5000 = \frac{\text{opposite}}{10}$$

$$\text{opposite} = 0.5000 \cdot 10$$
$$= 5 \text{ units}$$

We can find the vertical component by using the cosine function. The cosine of 30° is the ratio of the length of the side adjacent to the hypotenuse, and the cosine of 30° is 0.8660.

$$\text{Cosine } 30° = \frac{\text{adjacent}}{\text{hypotenuse}}$$

$$0.8660 = \frac{\text{adjacent}}{10}$$

$$\text{adjacent} = 0.8660 \cdot 10$$
$$= 8.66 \text{ units}$$

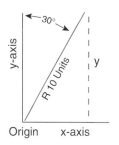

$$\text{Sin } A = \frac{x}{R}$$

$$0.500 = \frac{x}{10}$$

$$x = 0.500 \cdot 10 = 5$$

$$\text{Cos } 30° = \frac{y}{R}$$

$$\text{Sin } A = \frac{y}{10}$$

$$y = 0.866 \cdot 10 = 8.66$$

Figure 2-50. *Vector R has both direction, 30° clockwise from north, and magnitude, 10 units. This vector can be broken down into its horizontal, or x, component and its vertical, or y component.*

Vector R which has a magnitude of 10 units and a direction of 30° can be broken down into an *x* quantity of 5 units and a *y* quantity of 8.66 units. We can prove that this is correct by using the Pythagorean formula:

$$R = \sqrt{x^2 + y^2}$$

$$= \sqrt{5^2 + 8.66^2}$$

$$= \sqrt{25 + 75}$$

$$= 10 \text{ units}$$

Cotangent, Secant, and Cosecant

Now that we have seen the practical use of the sine, cosine, and tangent, we must realize that there are three other functions that are available, but are not used as often. The secant of angle A is the ratio of the length of the hypotenuse to the length of the side adjacent, and is the opposite of the cosine. The cosecant is the opposite of the sine and is the ratio of the length of the hypotenuse to the length of the side opposite. The cotangent is the opposite of the tangent and is the ratio of the length of the side adjacent to the length of the side opposite. *See* Figure 2-51.

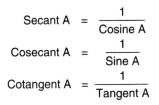

$$\text{Secant A} = \frac{1}{\text{Cosine A}}$$

$$\text{Cosecant A} = \frac{1}{\text{Sine A}}$$

$$\text{Cotangent A} = \frac{1}{\text{Tangent A}}$$

Figure 2-51. *Values of secant, cosecant, and cotangent*

STUDY QUESTIONS: TRIGONOMETRY

Answers begin on Page 58. **Page numbers refer to chapter text.**

44. Using the trig function table in Figure 2-45, find these values:

a. Sine 30°	
b. Cosine 30°	
c. Tangent 76°	
d. Secant 18°	
e. Cosecant 47°	
f. Cotangent 21°	

Page 48

45. A gas-filled balloon is anchored with a rope 200 feet long. The wind is blowing the balloon, so the rope is taut and it forms an angle of 50° with the ground. The balloon is _____ feet above the ground. *Page 51*

AVIATION MAINTENANCE TECHNICIAN SERIES   GENERAL

46. It is necessary to build a ramp from the ground to the side door of a cargo aircraft. The door is 10 feet above the ground, and to load the equipment, the ramp must not have an angle greater than 15°. The ramp must be _____ long. *Page 48*

47. A road from the bottom of a hill to the top is 800 feet long, and the top of the hill is 60 feet higher than the bottom. The angle of elevation of the road is _____ degrees. *Page 48*

48. The DME in an airplane indicates that the station is 85 nautical miles away, and the airplane is flying at an altitude of 5.7 nautical miles above the surface. The station is _____ nautical miles from a point directly below the airplane. *Page 48*

49. An airplane climbs out from an airport at an angle of 16°. Its elevation above the ground when it is 6 statute miles from the airport will be _____ feet. *Page 48*

50. A ladder 25 feet long is placed against the side of a building in such a way that it forms a 60° angle with the ground. The top of the ladder will touch the building _____ feet from the ground. *Page 48*

51. Find the horizontal and vertical components of these vectors. The directions of all the vectors are measured clockwise from vertical.

	Magnitude	Direction	Component magntitude	
			Horizontal	Vertical
a.	10	45°		
b.	25	60°		
c.	500	25°		
d.	50	0°		
e.	100	90°		

Page 48

Mathematical Sequence

A mathematical problem may include several of the operations studied in this chapter. To arrive at the needed value, you may have to multiply, divide, add and subtract all in one problem. Some operations must be worked before others or an incorrect final answer will result.

1. Clear any parentheses by working that part of the problem first.

2. Follow this sequence: first perform all multiplications, then all divisions, then all additions, and finally all subtractions.

STUDY QUESTION: MATHEMATICAL SEQUENCE

Answer to this question is on Page 58. Page number refers to chapter text.

52. Solve these problems, paying careful attention to the proper sequence of operations:

a. $[(4 \cdot -3) + (-9 \cdot +2)] \div 2 =$ _____

b. $(64 \cdot 3/8) \div 3/4 =$ _____

c. $(32 \cdot 3/8) \div 1/6 =$ _____

d. $2/4 \, (30 + 34) \, 5 =$ _____

e. $\dfrac{(-35 + 25)(-7) + (\pi)(16^{-2})}{\sqrt{25}} =$ _____

f. $\dfrac{125 \div 4}{-36 \div 6} =$ _____

g. $4 - 3[-6(2 + 3) + 4] =$ _____

h. $-6[-9(-8 + 4) - 2(7 + 3)] =$ _____

i. $(-3 + 2)(-12 - 4) + (-4 + 6) \cdot 2 =$ _____

j. $\dfrac{(-5 + 23)(-2) + (3^{-3})(\sqrt{64}\,)}{-27 \div 9} =$ _____

Page 54

Practical Measurements

Area

The area of a triangle is found by the formula:

$$A = \frac{b \cdot h}{2}$$

b = length of the base
h = height, or altitude

The area of a trapezoid is found by the formula:

$$A = h \cdot \frac{b_1 + b_2}{2}$$

h = height, or altitude
b_1 = length of one base
b_2 = length of the other base

The circumference of a circle is found by the formula:

$C = \pi \cdot D$

  = a constant, 3.1416
D = diameter

The area of a circle is found by the formula:

$A = \pi R^2$

  = a constant 3.1416 (the ratio of the length of the circumference of a
    circle to the length of its diameter)

R = radius of the circle

We normally know the diameter of a circle rather than its radius, and to prevent having to divide the diameter by 2, we can use the formula:

$$A = \frac{\pi D^2}{4}$$

We can divide   by 4 to get a new constant 0.7854, and this formula then becomes one that is convenient to use:

$A = 0.7854 \cdot D^2$

The surface area of a sphere is found by the formula:

$A = 4 (0.7854 \cdot D^2)$
D = diameter of the sphere

Force

To find the amount of force produced by a pressure acting on a surface, first find the area of the surface and multiply this by the amount of pressure.

$F = P \cdot A$

P = pressure acting on the surface in pounds per square inch
A = area of the surface in square inches

Volume

The volume of a cylinder is found by the formula:

$V = (0.7854 \cdot D^2) \cdot H$

0.7854 = a constant, $/4$
D = diameter of container
H = height of container

The volume of a rectangular container is found by the formula:

$V = L \cdot W \cdot D$

L = length of container
W = width of container
D = depth of container

The volume of a cone is found by the formula:

$$V = \frac{(0.7854 \cdot D^2)h}{3}$$

D = diameter of base
h = height of cone

The volume of a pyramid is found by the formula:

$$V = \frac{Bh}{3}$$

B = area of base
h = height of pyramid

The volume of a sphere is found by the formula:

$$V = \frac{\pi}{6} \cdot D^3$$

$= $ a constant 3.1416
D = Diameter of sphere

One U.S. gallon is equal to 231 cubic inches, or 0.1333 cubic foot. One cubic foot contains 7.5 U.S. gallons.

Answers begin on Page 58. **Page numbers refer to chapter text.**

53. The area of a trapezoid whose altitude is 2 feet, one base is 4 feet, and the other base is 6 feet, is _____ square feet. *Page 55*

54. A piece of sheet metal needed to make a cylinder 20 inches long and 8 inches in diameter is _____ by _____ inches. *Page 55*

55. The area of a right triangle with a base of 4 inches and an altitude of 3 inches is _____ square inches. *Page 55*

56. The area of a piston head having a diameter of 4 inches is _____ square inches. *Page 55*

57. The force exerted on a piston with an area of 1.2 square inches by a pressure of 850 psi is _____ pounds. *Page 56*

58. The force exerted on the side of a fuel tank measuring 12 by 24 inches, when the tank is pressure tested to 6 psi, is _____ pounds. *Page 56*

59. A rectangular fuel tank whose dimensions are 60 inches long, 30 inches wide, and 12 inches deep contains _____ cubic inches, _____ cubic feet, and will hold _____ U.S. gallons. *Page 56*

60. A brake master cylinder having a bore of 1.5 inches and a stroke of 4 inches displaces _____ cubic inches of fluid when the piston travels its full stroke. *Page 56*

61. A 4-cylinder aircraft engine has a bore of 3.78 inches and a stroke of 4.5 inches. Its total piston displacement is _____ cubic inches. *Page 56*

Answers to Chapter 2 Study Questions

1. a. 452
    b. 7,214
    c. 1,274
    d. 9,304
2. a. 262
    b. 709
    c. 491
    d. 21
3. a. 15,376
    b. 279,598
    c. 64,872
    d. 757,757
4. a. 40 rem 5
    b. 247 rem 13
    c. 2 rem 42
    d. 14
5. a. $^{15}/_{16}$
    b. $1\,^{23}/_{30}$
    c. $^{11}/_{32}$
    d. $^{55}/_{64}$
6. a. $^5/_8$
    b. $^1/_{16}$
    c. $^5/_{48}$
    d. $^3/_{32}$
7. a. 144
    b. 80
    c. 288
    d. 48
8. a. $^{263}/_{637}$
    b. $^3/_8$
    c. $^1/_6$
    d. $^{49}/_{100}$
9. a. $^1/_3$
    b. $^3/_{32}$
    c. $^1/_9$
    d. $^3/_{40}$
10. a. 48
    b. $^1/_6$
    c. 2
    d. $^1/_2$

11. a. $^{15}/_8$
    b. $^{211}/_{64}$
    c. $^9/_2$
    d. $^{73}/_8$
12. a. $6\,^{13}/_{16}$
    b. $2\,^1/_6$
    c. $4\,^{11}/_{16}$
    d. $4\,^1/_2$
13. a. 150.26
    b. 70.49
    c. 224.23
    d. 0.031
14. a. 78.25
    b. 19.34
    c. 39.306
    d. 155.875
15. a. 120.2765
    b. 49.335
    c. 0.186485
    d. 189,249.975
16. a. 3.417
    b. 866.99
    c. 29.193
    d. 8
17. a. 0.5625
    b. 0.53125
    c. 0.5
    d. 0.875
18. a. $^7/_8$
    b. $^9/_{16}$
    c. $^5/_8$
    d. $^1/_8$
19. 7
20. 6
21. 72
22. 420
23. 240
24. 900
25. 266.67
26. 43,428.57
27. 5.33

28. a. 3.38
    b. 287.04
    c. 460
    d. 0.125
29. a. 12.5
    b. 17.57
    c. 1.21
    d. 700
30. a. 25
    b. 640
    c. 60
    d. 1,000
31. a. 7
    b. 12
    c. 64
    d. -24
32. a. 5
    b. -81
    c. 149
    d. -187
33. a. -80
    b. 324
    c. -192
    d. 375
34. a. -3.2
    b. 6
    c. -7
    d. 11.67
35. a. 36
    b. 6,561
    c. 3,125
    d. 64
36. a. 8
    b. 9.79
    c. 4.14
    d. 3.63
37. a. 6.8×10^6
    b. 5.872×10^3
    c. 8.74×10^{-10}
    d. 2×10^{-4}

38. a. 8,560,000
    b. 70,960
    c. 0.000 000 000 000 065 3
    d. 0.000 009 431
39. a. 4.805×10^6
    b. 9.172×10^4
    c. 9.895×10^{-2}
    d. 4.25×10^4
40. a. 3.37×10^6
    b. 6.48×10^3
    c. $2.99 \; 10^{-2}$
    d. 5.823×10^{-7}
41. a. 1.29×10^8
    b. 3.01×10^2
    c. 4.60×10^3
    d. 6.62×10^{-4}
42. a. 2.61×10^{-2}
    b. 6.61×10^3
    c. 3.19×10^{-6}
    d. 5.93×10^1

43. a. 1.29×10^5
    b. 5.93×10^5
    c. 4.20×10^{-9}
    d. 6.86×10^{-5}
44. a. 0.500
    b. 0.8660
    c. 4.0108
    d. 1.0514
    e. 1.3672
    f. 2.6051
45. 153.2
46. 39
47. 4.3
48. 84.8
49. 9,083
50. 21.6
51. a. 7.07, 7.07
    b. 21.65, 12.5
    c. 211.31, 453.15
    d. 0, 50
    e. 100, 0

52. a. -15
    b. 32
    c. 72
    d. 160
    e. 14.00
    f. -5.208
    g. 82
    h. -96
    i. 20
    j. 11.90
53. 10
54. 20, 25.12
55. 6
56. 12.56
57. 1,020
58. 1,728
59. 21,600, 12.5, 93.5
60. 7.07
61. 201.99

BASIC PHYSICS

3

Continued

Basic Physics

3

Aviation technology is actually a branch of applied physics. Airplanes and their powerplants are designed to obey the basic laws of physics. Technicians must maintain and repair them in such a way that they continue to obey physical laws.

Physics is the natural science that deals with matter and energy and the relationships between the two. In this section we begin with a discussion of what matter is and then progress through such aspects as energy, force and motion, heat and temperature, the gas laws, and fluid mechanics, and conclude with a discussion of sound and light. Physics and mathematics are so closely related that it is impossible to gain a knowledge of physics without using math. In this section, we have used only simple math to the level that is covered in the previous section.

A knowledge of physics increases our understanding of the way reciprocating and turbine engines convert fuel into thrust, and the way wings and rotors moving through the air create lift. This knowledge allows us to troubleshoot systematically and efficiently, and to design structural repairs that restore the aircraft to its original condition of strength and rigidity.

In this section on physics, we treat the subject from a practical point of view. The U.S. Customary system of measurement is used for most problems rather than the metric system. The math involved in this study is all covered in the section on Mathematics, and study questions follow each section to allow you to verify your understanding.

Matter

Matter is anything that takes up space and has weight. The air we breathe, the food we eat, the clothes we wear, and even our own bodies are all matter. All matter we are familiar with exists in the form of chemical elements or compounds which are combinations of elements. Matter can exist in three physical states: solid, liquid, and gaseous. In this section we will consider both the chemical and physical natures of matter.

Chemical Nature of Matter

There are slightly more than 100 chemical elements which are the building blocks of which all matter is made. The smallest part into which an element can be broken by ordinary chemical means is an atom.

matter. Anything that takes up space and has weight.

energy. Something that changes, or tries to change, matter. There are two basic types of energy: potential and kinetic. Common forms of energy are: chemical, electrical, light, and heat.

atom. The smallest particle of a chemical element that can exist, either alone or in combination with other atoms. An atom is made up of a nucleus, which contains protons and neutrons, and electrons, which spin around the nucleus. In a balanced atom, there are as many electrons spinning around the nucleus as there are protons in the nucleus.

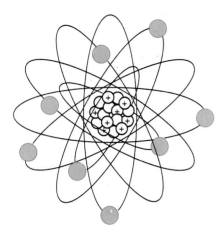

Figure 3-1. *An atom of oxygen is made of eight positive charges of electricity called protons and eight neutral charges called neutrons, all bound together in its nucleus. Spinning around the nucleus at great speed are eight electrons which are negative charges of electricity.*

Atoms of all of the elements are made up of many different kinds of particles. Here we are concerned with the more basic particles: protons, neutrons, and electrons.

Protons are positive charges of electricity, and neutrons are neutral, having no electrical charge. Protons and neutrons make up the nucleus in the center of an atom and are held by a strong force into a tight, compact group.

Electrons are negative charges of electricity. In a stable atom there are as many electrons spinning around the nucleus as there are protons in the nucleus. These electrons encircle the nucleus in a definite pattern. Electrons having the same energy level maintain a specific average distance from the nucleus and form a pattern called a shell. *See* Figure 3-1.

There can be as many as 7 shells of electrons in an atom, with these shells identified as *k, l, m, n, o, p,* and *q.* The shell nearest the nucleus, the *k* shell, can hold only 1 or 2 electrons. The *l* shell is full when it has 8 electrons. The *m* shell is full when it contains 18 electrons. The *n* shell can hold up to 32 electrons. The *o* shell could hold 50, but no atom has more than 32 in this shell. The *p* shell could hold up to 72 electrons, but no atom has more than 10 electrons here. The *q* shell is found around the atoms of only a few of the heaviest elements, and they contain only 1 or 2 electrons.

The electrons, protons, and neutrons in the atoms of all elements are the same. (*See* Figure 3-2.) It is the number of these particles that makes an atom of one element different from an atom of another. Made up of atoms with only one proton and one electron, hydrogen is the simplest of all known elements. It is a very light gas, and is the only element whose atoms have no neutrons.

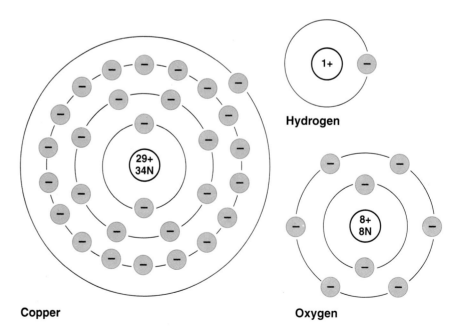

Figure 3-2. *All electrons, protons, and neutrons are the same, but atoms of each of the different chemical elements have different amounts of electrons, protons, and neutrons.*

Copper

Hydrogen

Oxygen

Note: An isotope of hydrogen is a special type of hydrogen atom that has one proton, one electron, and one or more neutrons. Because of these neutrons, its weight is different from a normal atom of hydrogen.

Oxygen is also a gas, but its nucleus contains 8 protons and 8 neutrons, and spinning around the nucleus are 8 electrons. Copper is a metal, with a nucleus of 29 protons and 34 neutrons. Spinning around this nucleus, in 4 shells, are 29 electrons.

A compound is a combination of elements that contains a specific number of atoms of each element. The characteristics of a compound are different from those of any one of the elements that make it up.

Water molecules are compounds made up of 2 atoms of hydrogen (H) and 1 atom of oxygen (O), both of which are elements. A glassful of water has the same chemical makeup as a spoonful, or even just a drop. A drop of water can be broken into smaller and smaller droplets, and if we continue to break the drops into smaller ones, we will finally get down to the smallest particle of water that can exist—a molecule of two atoms of hydrogen and one of oxygen. *See* Figure 3-3.

A molecule is the smallest particle of matter that can still remain the same substance, and it is far too small to see, even with a powerful microscope. A molecule of water can be broken down into hydrogen and oxygen atoms, the two elements it is made of, and the chemical formula for water is H_2O. *See* Figure 3-4.

Physical Nature of Matter

As we have just seen, a compound is a substance that is made of two or more chemical elements, and most compounds can exist in more than one physical form, or state. Compounds can exist as a solid, a liquid, or a gas, depending upon the amount of heat energy they contain.

At room temperature, water is normally in a liquid form. Pour it into a glass and it will take the shape of the glass, but it will not expand to completely fill the glass. When water gets cold enough, however, it freezes and becomes ice, which is water in its solid form. Remove the ice from a glass, and it will retain its shape, not spread out as liquid water does. When water gets hot, it evaporates and changes into a vapor, its gaseous form (sometimes called steam). Water vapor is lighter than air, and it will expand to fill the container in which it is held. *See* Figure 3-5 on page 68.

molecule. The smallest particle of a substance that retains the characteristics of the substance.

Water   Water

Figure 3-3. *Water is a chemical compound, and it is the same substance, whether it is a glassful or a drop.*

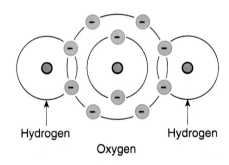

Hydrogen   Hydrogen

Oxygen

Figure 3-4. *A molecule of water is made of two atoms of hydrogen joined with one atom of oxygen.*

gas. The physical condition of matter in which a material takes the shape of its container and expands to fill the entire container.

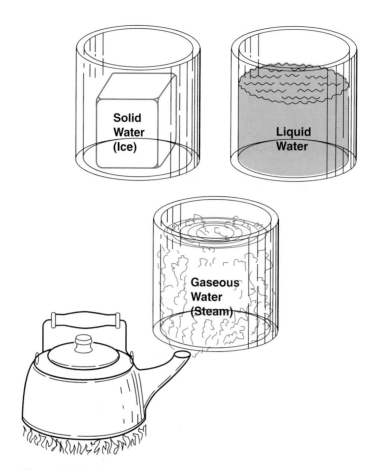

Figure 3-5. *Ice is water in its solid form. It holds its shape and does not take the shape of its container. Water is normally a liquid. It takes the shape of the container, but it does not expand to fill it. Steam is water in its vapor, or gaseous, form, and is lighter than air. Steam takes the shape of its container and expands to fill the entire container.*

While water can change from one physical form to another, the molecules do not change. The molecules of water in all three forms are made up of two atoms of hydrogen and one atom of oxygen.

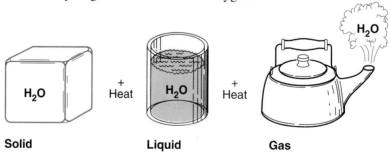

Figure 3-6. *When heat is added to a material such as water, it changes from a solid to a liquid. When more heat energy is added, it changes from a liquid into a gas.*

Answers are on Page 136. **Page numbers refer to chapter text.**

1. Anything that takes up space and has weight is called _____ .
    Page 65

2. The smallest particle of a compound is called a/an _____ .
    Page 67

3. A molecule of a compound is made up of atoms of some of the more than 100 _____ . *Page 67*

4. The three most important kinds of particles in an atom are: _____ , _____ , and _____ . *Page 66*

5. The nucleus of an atom is made of _____ and _____ .
    Page 66

6. Spinning around the nucleus of an atom are _____ which move in orbits, or rings.
    Page 66

7. The electrical charge of an electron is _____ (negative or positive). *Page 66*

8. The three physical forms in which a compound can exist are: _____ , _____ , and _____ . *Page 67*

9. Do molecules of a compound change when the compound changes from a solid to a liquid or to a gas? _____ (yes or no) *Page 68*

10. Water can exist in three forms. In its solid form we call it _____ , and when it is a gas we call it _____ . *Page 68*

11. The form of a compound that does not change its shape or its volume is called a _____ . *Page 68*

12. The form of a compound that changes its shape but not its volume is called a _____ . *Page 68*

Continued

13. The form of a compound that changes both its shape and volume is called a

_____ . *Page 68*

14. It is energy in the form of _____ that causes a compound to change its
form from solid, to liquid, to gas. *Page 68*

Weight and Mass

weight. A measure of the force of gravity
acting on a body.

mass. The amount of matter in an object.

The mass of an object is the amount of matter it contains. We consider mass
with such units as ounces and pounds in the U.S. system, and grams and
kilograms, in the metric system. Unfortunately, we measure weight with the
same units, and it is easy to think of weight and mass as being the same, but
they are not.

Weight is the force by which the earth attracts an object (this attraction
is called gravity). Actually, every particle of matter is attracted to every other
particle of matter, and the amount of attraction varies directly with the masses
of these particles. It also varies inversely with the square of the distance between the particles. In other words, the greater the masses of the objects, the
greater the attraction between them. And, the farther the objects are apart,
the less attraction there is between them. *See* Figure 3-7.

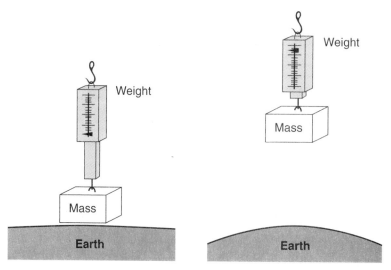

Figure 3-7. *An object is pulled toward the center of the earth by a force called gravity.
The amount of this pull is the weight of the object. The closer the object is to the center of
the earth, the more it weighs. If the object were in space beyond the pull of gravity, it
would not have any weight, but its mass would be the same.*

Since the earth has a great mass, the attraction between the earth and any object on or near it is very powerful. This attraction will pull an object toward the center of the earth with such a force that the object will speed up at a rate of 32.2 feet per second each second it falls. This speeding up is called acceleration due to gravity.

To find the weight of an object, multiply its mass by the acceleration due to gravity, 32.2.

Density

Density is a measure of the amount of matter in a certain volume of material. A block of lead weighs more than a block of wood which has the same dimensions, and the wood weighs more than the same size block of cork. All three blocks are of the same size, but the molecules of lead are much closer together. More molecules fit into the same space. The lead has the greater density, and therefore it weighs more. *See* Figure 3-8.

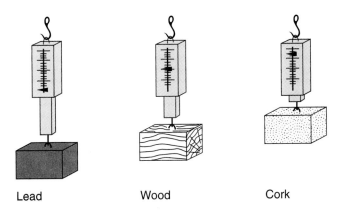

Lead   Wood   Cork

Figure 3-8. *Lead is more dense than wood or cork; therefore a block of lead weighs more than the same size block of wood or cork. Lead is the most dense of the three materials.*

Density is expressed in terms of pounds per cubic foot or pounds per cubic inch. Pure water has a density of 62.4 pounds per cubic foot, or 0.0361 pound per cubic inch.

Specific Gravity

A practical way to work with the density of a material is to use its specific gravity. The specific gravity of a material may be found by dividing the density of the material by the density of pure water.

acceleration caused by gravity. The change in speed of an object falling in a vacuum caused by the pull of gravity. The object will increase its speed 32.2 feet per second each second it falls.

specific gravity. The ratio of the density of a material to the density of pure water.

Material	Density (pounds/cubic inch)	Specific Gravity
Gold	0.697	19.3
Mercury	0.491	13.6
Lead	0.408	11.3
Copper	0.321	8.9
Iron	0.285	7.9
Aluminum	0.101	2.8
Sulfuric acid	0.0665	1.84
Sea water	0.0372	1.03
Pure Water	0.0361	1.00
Ice	0.0331	0.917
Jet engine fuel	0.0289	0.80
Gasoline	0.0260	0.72
Pine wood	0.0180	0.50
Air	0.0000469	0.0013
Hydrogen	0.00000325	0.00009

Figure 3-9. *Density and specific gravity of various materials*

In the table of Figure 3-9 we see that one cubic inch of pure water weighs 0.0361 pounds and has a specific gravity 1.0. Aluminum has a specific gravity of 2.8, and is 2.8 times as heavy as water. Jet engine fuel is lighter than water. Its specific gravity is 0.80, meaning that it weighs only 80% as much as water.

When any material has a specific gravity of less than 1.0, it weighs less than an equal volume of water, and it will float on the water. If its specific gravity is greater than 1.0, it will sink. *See* Figure 3-10.

Sulfuric acid is a liquid which is mixed with water in lead-acid aircraft batteries. It is heavier than water, having a specific gravity of 1.84. When sulfuric acid is poured into a container of pure water, it sinks and mixes with the water.

Solids are also compared with water to find their specific gravity. Aluminum has a specific gravity of 2.8. This means that one cubic inch of aluminum weighs 0.101 pound. Copper, with a specific gravity of 8.9, is heavier than aluminum, and gold with a specific gravity of 19.3 is even heavier.

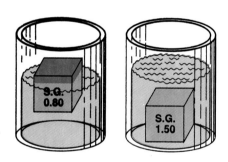

Figure 3-10. *If the specific gravity of a material is less than 1.0, it will float in water. If it is greater than 1.0, it will sink.*

STUDY QUESTIONS: WEIGHT AND MASS

Answers are on Page 136. **Page numbers refer to chapter text.**

15. **The amount of matter in an object is called the** _____ **of the object.** *Page 70*

16. **The amount of pull acting on an object caused by the force of gravity is called the** _____ **of the object.** *Page 70*

17. Which of the two, mass or weight, changes as the distance changes between the object and the center of the earth? _____ . *Page 70*

18. The measure of the mass of a given volume of material is called the _____ of the material. *Page 71*

19. The ratio of the density of a material to the density of pure water is called the _____ of the material. *Page 71*

20. A liquid having a specific gravity of 0.96 will _____ (float or sink) in pure water. *Page 72*

21. Aluminum has a specific gravity of 2.8. How many pounds will a block of aluminum weigh if its dimensions are 10 inches long, 10 inches high, and 5 inches wide? _____ pounds. *Page 72*

Energy

Almost all of the energy on earth comes from the sun This white-hot star continually releases an unbelievable amount of its energy which travels to us through space. When it reaches the earth, it changes into several different forms of energy we can use. Some is absorbed in plants and becomes chemical energy, some is changed directly into electricity, and some is available as heat and light. *See* Figure 3-11.

energy. Something that changes, or tries to change, matter. There are two basic types of energy: potential and kinetic. Common forms of energy are: chemical, electrical, light, and heat.

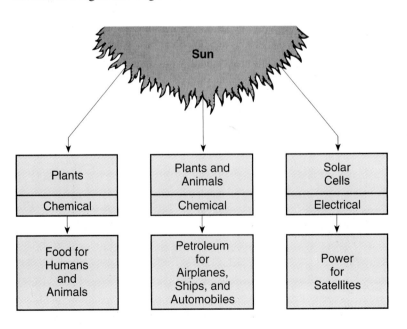

Figure 3-11. *The sun is our main source of energy. Plants absorb energy from the sun and furnish us with energy when we eat them. Plants and animals that absorbed energy from the sun millions of years ago have become petroleum and coal. We can convert solar energy directly into electricity with solar cells.*

Matter and energy are fundamentals of nature, and can be neither created nor destroyed. However, we can change energy into matter and matter into energy. In either change, the total of mass and energy remain the same.

When one chemical compound is changed into another, energy is either released or absorbed. When, for example, a gallon of gasoline is burned, it changes into water and carbon dioxide and releases energy in the form of heat and light.

Potential Energy

Energy that is possessed by an object because of its position, chemical composition, shape, or configuration is called potential energy, and this energy can be stored. Stored potential energy can be in a battery, in gasoline, in a compressed spring, or in compressed air. Potential energy does not do any work while it is stored, but it does perform work when it is properly released. *See* Figure 3-12.

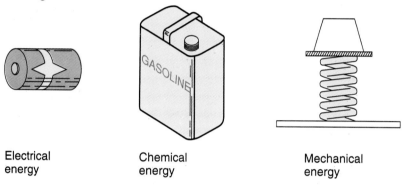

Electrical energy   Chemical energy   Mechanical energy

Figure 3-12. *Forms of potential energy*

Kinetic Energy

Potential energy may be released in such a way that it causes motion, and the energy produced by the motion is called kinetic energy.

In Figure 3-13 we see an example of the conversion between potential and kinetic energy. In 3-13A, a ball on a string is pulled back until it is raised to height h. The energy used to raise the ball to this height is now stored in the ball as potential energy.

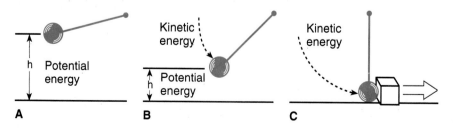

Figure 3-13. *The conversion of potential energy into kinetic energy*

In 3-13B, the ball is released, and gravity is pulling it down. It now has some kinetic energy because of its motion, and some potential energy because of its height. In 3-13C, the ball is at the bottom of its swing, and there is no more height, so all of its energy is kinetic energy. Then when it hits the block, this energy goes into the block and knocks it away in the direction shown by the arrow.

Exchanges Between Matter and Energy

Since energy can be neither created nor destroyed, the total amount of energy in a given situation remains constant. But we can convert potential energy into kinetic, and we can change matter into energy.

Aerodynamic Lift

Air flowing over the wing of an airplane or the rotor of a helicopter contains a given amount of total energy, which is the sum of potential energy from its pressure and kinetic energy from its velocity. When this air flows over the upper surface of the wing, as we see in Figure 3-14, the surface drops away, and the air is forced to speed up. The increased speed changes some potential energy into kinetic energy, and the pressure above the wing decreases. This decreased pressure pulls air down to the surface, and an equal force is created which pulls upward on the wing, creating aerodynamic lift. This is discussed in much more detail in the section on theory of flight in the Airframe section of this series.

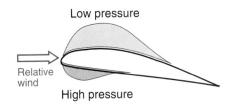

Figure 3-14. *Aerodynamic lift is produced when the air flowing over an airfoil speeds up. Some potential energy (pressure) is changed into kinetic energy (velocity). The lowered pressure on the top of the wing produces aerodynamic lift.*

Nuclear Energy

A new and important source of energy in use today is nuclear energy— energy that is released when the structure of certain atoms is changed. All matter is composed of atoms whose nuclei contains both protons and neutrons. And we have seen that energy is released or absorbed when matter changes from one form into another.

For example, when we burn a piece of coal, which is made of carbon and hydrogen atoms, these atoms join with oxygen atoms from the air and form carbon dioxide (carbon and oxygen) and water (hydrogen and oxygen). When these changes take place, energy that we can see and feel in the form of light and heat is released.

Heat may also be obtained in another way, through nuclear fission, in which an atomic nucleus splits and releases energy. All of the positive charges of electricity (the protons) in the nucleus of an atom push against each other and try to spread out, but they are held together by the force of the neutrons, which act like an adhesive. So, in most atoms, the nucleus remains in a very tight and compact bundle.

However the nuclei in some of the heavier atoms, such as uranium, have so many protons and neutrons that some of the neutrons do break away and strike other materials. They strike with such force that they actually combine with the nucleus of the atom they hit and change it into a different element. Each neutron that splits a nucleus releases many more neutrons so that they can split more nuclei in a chain reaction. When the nucleus of an atom is split, a tremendous amount of heat energy is released. *See* Figure 3-15.

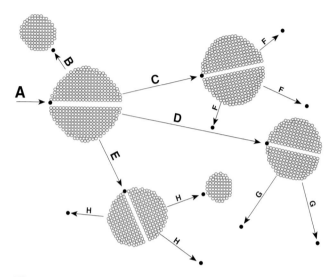

Figure 3-15. *When a neutron is shot into the nucleus of a uranium atom (A), the atom splits. This splitting releases other neutrons (B, C, D, E) which split other atoms (F, G, H). This chain reaction produces enormous amounts of heat.*

A nuclear reactor is used to produce heat from nuclear reactions. When releasing this heat, it is necessary to prevent the chain reaction from getting out of control and causing an explosion. For this reason, the lumps of the nuclear fuel, the uranium, inside the reactor are separated by blocks of graphite which slow the neutrons. There are also rods of cadmium metal, called control rods, that absorb some of the neutrons so they cannot strike the uranium fuel.

The heat produced when atoms are split is used to heat water to a high temperature. This water is held under pressure so it can absorb a great deal of the heat energy without turning into steam. The superheated water is taken from the reactor into a heat exchanger. Here it gives up some of its heat and pressure and becomes steam which is used to drive turbine-powered generators that produce electricity. *See* Figure 3-16.

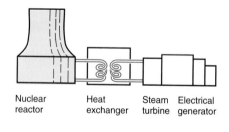

Nuclear   Heat   Steam   Electrical
reactor   exchanger turbine generator

Figure 3-16. *The tremendous amount of heat that is released when atoms are split is used to produce steam which drives generators, producing electrical power.*

Answers are on Page 136. Page numbers refer to chapter text.

22. Most of the energy we use on the earth comes from the _____ . *Page 73*

23. Energy stored in aircraft fuel, in a battery, or in a compressed spring are all forms of _____ (kinetic or potential) energy. *Page 74*

24. Energy that is released by the movement of an object is called _____ (kinetic or potential) energy. *Page 74*

25. Heat is released in a nuclear reactor when the _____ of an atom is split. *Page 76*

26. The cadmium rods in a nuclear reactor that are used to absorb some of the neutrons are called _____ rods. *Page 76*

27. The superheated water is taken out of a nuclear reactor and is run through a _____ where it gives up some of its heat energy to produce steam. *Page 76*

Work and Power

Work, power, and energy are all interrelated. Work is the amount of movement a given force causes; energy is the ability to do work, and power is the rate of doing work.

Work

In its technical sense, work is the product of force and distance, and work is done only when a force causes movement. We can see this by the formula:

Work = Force · Distance

We normally measure distance in feet or inches, and force in pounds or ounces. This allows us to measure work in foot-pounds or inch-ounces. To find the amount of work done when a 500-pound load is lifted for a distance of 6 feet, we can use the formula:

Work = Force · Distance
= 500 · 6
= 3,000 foot-pounds

work. The product of a force and the distance an object moves under the influence of the force. Work is measured in foot-pounds.

power. The time rate of doing work. It is found by dividing the amount of work done, measured in foot-pounds, by the time in seconds or minutes used to do the work.

force. Energy brought to bear on an object that causes or tries to cause change in its direction or speed of motion.

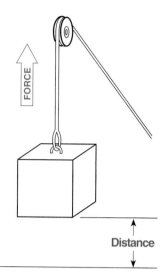

Figure 3-17. *Work is the result of energy used to produce a force that moves an object.*

horsepower. The unit of mechanical power that is equal to 33,000 foot-pounds of work done in one minute, or 550 foot-pounds of work done in one second.

It is important to understand that when there is no motion, no work is done. If we push against an object with a force of 100 pounds and it does not move, we use energy, but we do no work on the object. *See* Figure 3-17.

Power

In the U.S. system, the basic unit of power is the foot-pound per minute, and in the metric system, it is the watt.

In the United States, we normally use the watt as a measure of electrical power, and horsepower for measuring mechanical power. One horsepower is the amount of mechanical power used to do 33,000 foot-pounds of work in 1 minute, or 550 foot-pounds of work in 1 second, and 1 horsepower is equal to 746 watts of power.

To find the horsepower needed to lift a 500-pound weight 3 feet in 5 seconds, first find the number of foot-pounds of work done, then divide this by the time used to lift the weight.

$500 \cdot 3 = 1,500$ foot-pounds

$1,500 \div 5 = 300$ foot-pounds per second

To find the horsepower, divide this by 550, the number of foot-pounds per second in 1 horsepower.

$300 \div 550 = 0.545$ horsepower

STUDY QUESTIONS: WORK AND POWER

Answers are on Page 136. Page numbers refer to chapter text.

28. The amount of work done when a force of 25 pounds is used to lift an object 30 feet is _____ foot-pounds. *Page 77*

29. The number of foot-pounds per minute of power needed to pull a cart 30 feet in 3 minutes if a force of 12 pounds is required is _____ foot-pounds per minute. *Page 78*

30. The amount of power needed to lift a 12,500-pound airplane to a height of 3 feet in 1 minute is _____ horsepower. *Page 78*

Force and Motion

Force

Force is anything that tends to cause motion, change motion, stop motion, or prevent motion. This force acts on the mass of an object, so to be technically accurate, we should define it in terms of mass. But since this is a practical rather than theoretical text, we will consider the effect of gravity on the mass and use pounds and ounces of weight, rather than poundals of force.

Mechanical Advantage

Many mechanical devices allow us to work with the force we have and afford us a mechanical advantage in which we exchange distance for force or speed. The most widely used mechanical advantage devices are the lever, the pulley, the inclined plane, and the gear train.

When we have a flat tire on our car, we need some way to increase the amount of force we can produce with our arms so that it will be great enough to lift the car. We normally do this with a jack. If the jack allows us to raise 350 pounds of weight by pushing down on the handle with a force of 35 pounds, the jack gives us a mechanical advantage of 10.

$$350 \text{ Pounds} = \text{Force out}$$
$$35 \text{ Pounds} = \text{Force in}$$
$$350 \div 35 = 10$$

We increase the force we use 10 times, but we do not get something for nothing. Work is the amount of force times the distance the force acts, and we must put exactly the same amount of work into the jack that we get out of it. For each stroke of the jack handle to raise the car 1 inch, we must move the jack handle down 10 inches. The amount of work the jack does is 350 pounds times 1 inch, or 350 inch-pounds. We have done exactly the same amount of work on the jack handle: We have moved a force of 35 pounds through a distance of 10 inches, or we have done 350 inch-pounds of work on the jack handle.

There are several ways we can obtain mechanical advantage and nearly all machines use one or more. *See* Figure 3-18.

The Law of the Lever

The basic lever is a rigid arm supported on a fulcrum in such a way that a force can be applied to cause rotation. We see a basic lever in Figure 3-19. A force applied to one end of the lever, the force arm, causes the other end, the weight arm, to move in the opposite direction and lift the weight.

poundal. The unit of force in the foot-pound-second system of measurement that is required to accelerate a mass of 1 pound, 1 foot per second, per second.

mechanical advantage. The increase in force or speed produced by mechanical devices such as levers, pulleys, gears, or hydraulic cylinders.

Figure 3-18. *An automobile jack is a form of lever we use to get a mechanical advantage. A small force acting downward produces a much larger force acting upward.*

lever. A rigid bar, free to pivot, or rotate about a point called the fulcrum. An input force is applied at one point, and an output force is taken from the lever at another point.

arm. The distance on a lever between the fulcrum and the point of application of the force or the weight.

moment. A force that causes rotation of a lever. A moment is the product of a weight and its arm.

The arm of the lever is the distance between the fulcrum and the point where the force or weight is applied. The lever is balanced when the force moment, the amount of force times the length of the force arm, is equal to the weight moment, the weight times the length of the weight arm. Moments are usually expressed in pounds-feet.

Force · Arm = Force Moment
Weight · Arm = Weight Moment

Moments try to cause rotation, and in Figure 3-19, the force moment tries to rotate the lever in a clockwise direction and is called a positive moment. The weight moment tries to rotate the lever in the counterclockwise direction and is called a negative moment.

In Figure 3-19, we see one of the more important facts about the lever: The lever is balanced when the weight moment equals the force moment. Another way to express this is that the lever is balanced when the algebraic sum of the moments is zero.

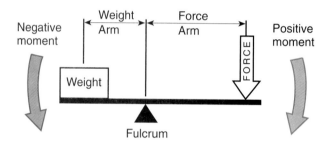

Figure 3-19. *When the lever is balanced, the sum of the moments about the fulcrum is zero.*

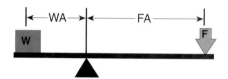

Figure 3-20. *First-class lever*

First-Class Lever

The lever in Figure 3-20 is a first-class lever, one whose fulcrum is between the force and the weight, with the weight moving in the direction opposite the direction of the force.

Second-Class Lever

A second-class lever is one in which the weight is between the fulcrum and the force, and the weight moves in the same direction as the force. A wheelbarrow is a good example of a second-class lever. *See* Figure 3-21.

The wheel of the wheelbarrow acts as the fulcrum, and the center of the handgrip is the point at which the force is applied. The load is the weight.

The same law of the lever applies to the second-class lever as applies to the first-class lever. The lever is balanced when the weight moment and the force moment are equal.

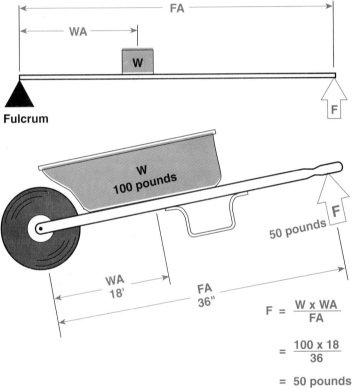

$$F = \frac{W \times WA}{FA}$$

$$= \frac{100 \times 18}{36}$$

$$= 50 \text{ pounds}$$

Figure 3-21. *Second-class lever*

Third-Class Lever

We sometimes want to move the weight a greater distance than the force can act, or we may want the weight to move faster. To do this, we can use a third-class lever in which the force is applied between the fulcrum and the weight, and the weight moves in the same direction as the force.

In the retractable landing gear in Figure 3-22, the weight of 500 pounds has an arm of 4 feet. This gives a weight moment of 2,000 pounds-feet. This must be balanced with a force whose arm is only 1 foot.

To raise the landing gear, we must apply a force of 2,000 pounds, but we can raise the wheel 4 feet by moving the point where the force is applied by only 1 foot.

This lever requires 4 times as much force as the weight it lifts, but it moves the weight 4 times as far as the force moves, in the same length of time.

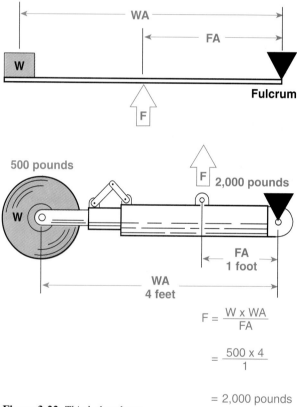

$$F = \frac{W \times WA}{FA}$$

$$= \frac{500 \times 4}{1}$$

$$= 2{,}000 \text{ pounds}$$

Figure 3-22. *Third-class lever*

The Inclined Plane

The inclined plane is one of the simple machines that is used to gain mechanical advantage. Suppose we want to load a drum of oil into a truck, but we do not have any form of hoist with which to lift it. We can use a long board as an inclined plane. Put one end on the bed of the truck and the other end on the ground. We can roll the drum up the board, with much less force than we would need to lift it straight up off the ground.

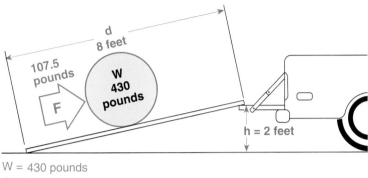

W = 430 pounds
h = 2 feet
d = 8 feet

$$F = \frac{W \times h}{d}$$

$$= \frac{430 \times 2}{8}$$

$$= 107.5 \text{ pounds}$$

Figure 3-23. *An inclined plane is used to gain a mechanical advantage.*

To find the amount of force needed to roll the drum into the truck, use the formula in Figure 3-23. A force of only 107.5 pounds is needed to roll the 430 pound drum into the truck. However, we will have to roll it 8 feet to raise it only 2 feet.

Ropes and Pulleys

One of the oldest methods of gaining mechanical advantage is by using ropes and pulleys, and we find the mechanical advantage by counting the number of sections of ropes that support the weight being lifted.

In Figure 3-24A the weight is supported by 1 section of rope. In order to lift a 100-pound weight, we need a force of 100 pounds; and if we raise the weight 1 foot, we will have to pull the rope 1 foot. The wheel, or pulley, changes the direction of the force, but it does not give any mechanical advantage.

If we attach the pulley to the weight and use 2 sections of rope to support it, as we have in Figure 3-24B, we have a mechanical advantage of 2. We need a force of only 50 pounds to lift it. But, we will have to pull 2 feet of rope to lift the weight 1 foot.

A group of pulleys, such as we see in Figure 3-24C, is called a block and tackle. Here we have four sections of rope supporting the weight. The force required to lift the load is only 25 pounds, but we must pull 4 feet of rope to raise the weight 1 foot.

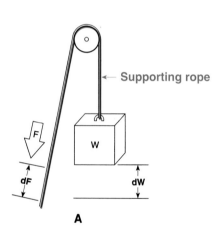

A. With one section of supporting rope, no mechanical advantage is gained.

Figure 3-24

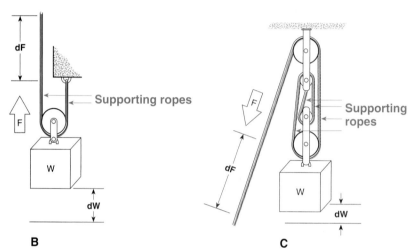

B. Two sections of supporting rope give a mechanical advantage of 2.

C. Four sections of supporting rope give a mechanical advantage of 4.

Gears

Gears are special wheels with notches and teeth on their outside edge. By meshing the teeth of one gear with the teeth on another, one gear can drive the other gear without slipping.

We can determine the mechanical advantage of a set of gears by counting the teeth of both gears. In the set of gears we see in Figure 3-25, the large drive gear has 90 teeth and turns in a counterclockwise direction. The smaller driven gear has 60 teeth and turns faster, and in the opposite, or clockwise, direction.

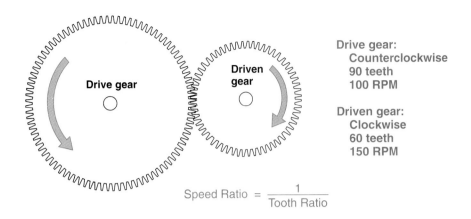

Drive gear:
  Counterclockwise
  90 teeth
  100 RPM

Driven gear:
  Clockwise
  60 teeth
  150 RPM

$$\text{Speed Ratio} = \frac{1}{\text{Tooth Ratio}}$$

Figure 3-25. *Gears are used to change the direction of rotation between shafts and to gain a mechanical advantage.*

To find the speed of the driven gear, find the ratio of the number of teeth in the two gears. The drive gear has 1.5 times as many teeth as the driven gear, and so the driven gear will turn 1.5 times as fast as the drive gear. When the drive gear turns at 100 RPM, the driven gear will turn at 150 RPM.

Motion

Motion is the action in which objects change their position. Motion requires energy and is an essential component of work. In this section, we will discuss the difference between speed and velocity, see the way vectors can be combined, and consider each of Newton's important laws of motion.

vector. A quantity which has both direction and magnitude.

Speed and Velocity

Speed is a rate of motion, and velocity is a rate of motion in a specified direction. Speed is normally measured in units such as feet per second, miles per hour, or knots, and does not take direction into consideration. If an airplane flies north at 120 miles per hour, its speed is 120 miles per hour, but its velocity is 120 miles per hour, to the north.

Change in Speed

When an object increases its speed, it accelerates, and acceleration is measured in feet per second, per second, or feet per second^2 (read as feet per second squared). When an object decreases its speed, it decelerates, and deceleration is negative acceleration. If an object falls freely in a vacuum, it is acted upon only by the force of gravity; and as it falls, it accelerates 32.2 feet per second each second it falls. This is called the acceleration due to gravity.

accelerate. To increase speed or to make an object move faster.

We use this value to find the mass of matter. We saw earlier that mass is the amount of matter in an object, and weight is the effect gravity has on the mass. We can find the mass of an object by dividing its weight, in pounds, by 32.2.

$$\text{Mass} = \frac{\text{Weight}}{32.2}$$

To find the amount of thrust a gas turbine engine is producing, first find the mass of the air flowing through the engine, then multiply this mass by the amount the air speeds up as it passes through the engine.

For example, assume that 100 pounds of air passes through an engine each second, and this air speeds up from zero feet per second to 900 feet per second. Find the amount of thrust by the formula:

$f = M \cdot a$

f = the pounds of thrust produced by accelerating the air as it passes through the engine

M = the mass of the air

a = the change in velocity of the air as it passes through the engine

$f = M \cdot a$

$$= \frac{100}{32.2} \cdot 900$$

$= 2,795.0$ pounds of thrust

Newton's Laws of Motion

Many of the properties of objects are explained by Newton's three laws of motion.

Newton's first law explains that when an object is at rest, it tries to remain at rest. But when it is moving, it tries to keep moving in a straight line and will not speed up, slow down, or turn unless it is acted upon by an outside force. This tendency of the object to remain in its original condition of motion is called inertia.

Newton's second law is called the law of acceleration: the amount of acceleration depends upon the mass of the object and the amount of force used. Acceleration is directly proportional to the amount of force that acts upon the object and inversely proportional to its mass.

Newton's third law is called the action-reaction law. It says that for every action, there is an equal and opposite reaction.

inertia. The characteristic of all matter that causes an object to remain in its present condition.

Circular Motion

When a bucket of water with a rope tied to its handle is swung in a circle, two interesting things happen. First, the water stays at the bottom of the bucket, which is now straight up and down, and it does not spill out. Also, the faster we swing the bucket, the heavier it becomes.

The bucket of water is obeying two of Newton's laws of motion, the first law which says that an object in motion will try to remain in motion in a straight line unless it is acted upon by an outside force; and the third law which says that for every action there is an equal and opposite reaction. *See* Figure 3-26.

When we start the bucket of water swinging, we put energy into it, and this energy tries to carry the bucket and the water away from us in a straight line. However, the bucket can go only as far from us as the rope allows. The rope holds it in a circular path around our body.

As the bucket is held in its circular path by the rope, it tries to travel in a straight line. The force trying to cause the bucket to travel in a straight line is opposed by the rope and is called centrifugal force. It is greater than the force of gravity that tries to pull the bucket and the water down, and it holds the water against the bottom of the swinging bucket.

As the bucket swings, centrifugal force causes the action that tries to pull it away from us. It is prevented from flying away by the force on the rope, which is the reaction. The faster the bucket swings, the greater the centrifugal force. The force on the rope opposing the centrifugal force is called centripetal force, and its magnitude is exactly equal to the centrifugal force.

Helicopter rotor blades droop when the helicopter is parked on the ramp and the rotor is not turning. This droop is caused by gravity pulling the blades down. But as soon as the rotor starts turning, centrifugal force becomes greater than the force of gravity, and it pulls the blades straight out. *See* Figure 3-27.

On some small helicopters, the centrifugal force acting on the rotor is about 20,000 pounds for each blade. For some of the larger helicopters, this force can be as much as 100,000 pounds for each blade. The hub and blade grips must be strong enough to withstand this great amount of force.

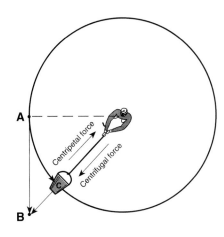

Figure 3-26. *The bucket of water is trying to obey Newton's first law and travel in a straight line from A to B. But the rope holds it along the curved path A to C. The resultant, C-B, is the centrifugal force, and this is the force that holds water in the bucket and makes the bucket heavier.*

magnitude. The amount of a force.

Figure 3-27. *When a helicopter rotor is not turning, gravity causes the blades to droop. But when the rotor is turning, centrifugal force holds the blades straight out.*

Answers are on Page 136. *Page numbers refer to chapter text.*

31. Anything that tends to cause motion, change motion, stop motion, or prevent motion is called a/an
_____ . *Page 79*

32. When a force acts on an object and causes it to move faster, the object has been caused to
_____ . *Page 85*

33. A lever acting as a jack has a force arm of 1 foot and a weight arm of 4 inches. In order to lift a weight of 600 pounds, a force of _____ pounds must be applied. *Page 80*

34. The distance between the fulcrum of a lever and the point at which the force is applied is called the force
_____ . *Page 80*

35. The value we find when we multiply the amount of force acting on a lever by the length of the arm of the force is called the force _____ . *Page 80*

36. A lever is said to be balanced when the sum of the force moments and the weight moments is equal to
_____ . *Page 80*

37. If the force arm of a lever is 10 times as long as the weight arm, the force will have to be only $\frac{1}{10}$ of the weight. But the force end of the lever will move _____ (how many) times as far as the weight end. *Page 80*

38. If we roll a 600-pound drum of oil up a 20-foot-long inclined plane onto a platform that is 4 feet high, we will have to apply a force of _____ pounds. *Page 83*

39. A block and tackle with 4 pulley wheels and 4 supporting ropes is used to lift a 250-pound weight. To lift the weight 3 feet, the rope will have to be pulled _____ feet. *Page 84*

40. If a geared drive uses a driven gear with 120 teeth and a drive gear with 60 teeth, the driven gear will turn 200 RPM when the drive gear is turning _____ RPM. *Page 85*

41. Fifty miles an hour to the north is a measure of _____ (speed or velocity). *Page 85*

42. An object which is falling freely will accelerate at a rate of 32.2 feet per second each second it falls. This acceleration is caused by _____ . *Page 85*

43. The force that tries to pull a helicopter blade out from the blade grips is called
_____ force. *Page 87*

44. The force that is exerted by the helicopter blade grips and opposes centrifugal force is called
_____ force. *Page 87*

Vectors

Discussions of velocity or force involve both magnitude (amount) and direction. Vectors encompass both concepts.

A vector is a quantity that indicates both direction and magnitude. The length of vector A in Figure 3-28 indicates its magnitude, and it is drawn in a direction that is measured in degrees clockwise from a certain reference line, and an arrowhead is attached to the line to show its direction.

We can add two or more vectors to get a resultant, which is a single vector with the same direction and magnitude as the other vectors would have if they were applied individually to the same object. Figure 3-29 shows vectors A and B and their resultant R. We measure the direction of the individual vectors in degrees clockwise from the vertical lines, which we will consider to be north.

Let's begin by plotting vector A, starting at the origin, point O. This vector has a direction of 90° clockwise from north, and it has a magnitude of eight units. Vector B has a direction of 180° clockwise from north, and its magnitude is six units.

If we roll a ball over our diagram, following the line we have drawn for vector A, and then turn and roll the ball along the line that has the direction and length of vector B, the ball will end up at point D, the destination.

The resultant, which is vector R, is a single vector between O and D. If the ball were to roll along vector R, it would end up at exactly the same place as it did when it followed vector A and then vector B. It is correct to say that the resultant, R, is the sum of vectors A and B. If we measure the length of vector R using the same scale we used for A and B, we find it to be 10 units long. And when we measure the direction of vector R, we find it to be 127° clockwise from north. *See* Figure 3-29.

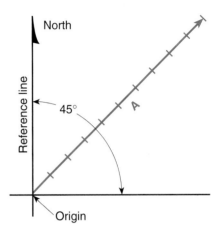

Figure 3-28. *Vector "A" shown here has a length, or magnitude, of 10 units, and its direction is 45° clockwise from north.*

vector. A quantity which has both direction and magnitude.

resultant vector. A single vector which is the sum of two or more vectors.

Figure 3-29. *The magnitude of vector A is 8 units, and its direction is 90° clockwise from north. Vector B is 6 units long, and its direction is 180° clockwise from north. The resultant of vectors A and B is 10 units long, and its direction is 127° clockwise from north.*

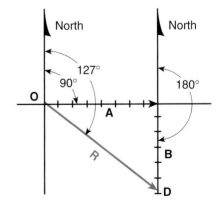

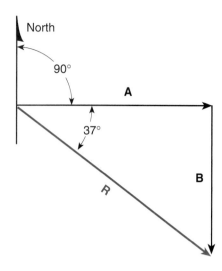

Figure 3-30. *The resultant, vector R, is the hypotenuse of a right triangle with vectors A and B as the two sides. The length of R is the square root of the sum of the squares of the lengths of A and B.*

Pythagorean formula. The length of the hypotenuse of a right triangle is equal to the square root of the sum of the squares of the lengths of the other two sides.

$$H = \sqrt{A^2 + B^2}$$

theta (Θ). The Greek symbol normally used to represent an unknown angle.

We can find the length and direction of resultant R without having to draw the triangle of vectors to scale. To do this, we can use the Pythagorean formula, $R = \sqrt{A^2 + B^2}$.

This very useful formula says that in a right triangle, one that contains a 90° angle, the length of the hypotenuse is always equal to the square root of the sum of the squares of the lengths of the other two sides.

$$
\begin{aligned}
R &= \sqrt{A^2 + B^2} \\
&= \sqrt{8^2 + 6^2} \\
&= \sqrt{64 + 36} \\
&= \sqrt{100} \\
&= 10 \text{ units}
\end{aligned}
$$

R = Length of the resultant vector

A = Length of vector A

B = Length of vector B

To find the number of degrees in the angle Θ between the reference line and vector R, we will use trigonometry. As we studied in the section on mathematics, the sine of an angle is the ratio of the length of the side of the right triangle opposite the acute angle (vector B) to the length of the hypotenuse (vector R). We know the length of vector R is 10 units, and the length of vector B is 6 units.

$$
\begin{aligned}
\text{Sin } \Theta &= \frac{\text{opposite}}{\text{hypotenuse}} \\
&= \frac{6}{10} \\
&= 0.60
\end{aligned}
$$

Refer to the chart of trigonometric functions in Figure 3-31 and find the angle whose sine is nearest to 0.60. The sine of 37° is 0.6018, and will be considered close enough for our answer in this problem. This is written $Sin^{-1}0.60 = 37°$. The term Sin^{-1} is the arcsine, which simply means the angle whose sine is 0.60.

Now add this 37° to the initial 90° direction of vector A to obtain the direction of the resultant vector R, which is 127° (90° + 37°) clockwise from our reference, north.

Trigonometric Functions

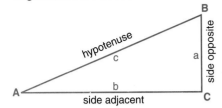

Tangent (tan) = $\dfrac{\text{side opposite}}{\text{side adjacent}}$

Sine (sin) = $\dfrac{\text{side opposite}}{\text{hypotenuse}}$

Cosine (cos) = $\dfrac{\text{side adjacent}}{\text{hypotenuse}}$

Cotangent (cot) = $\dfrac{1}{\tan}$ = $\dfrac{\text{side adjacent}}{\text{side opposite}}$

Cosecant (csc) = $\dfrac{1}{\sin}$ = $\dfrac{\text{hypotenuse}}{\text{side opposite}}$

Secant (sec) = $\dfrac{1}{\cos}$ = $\dfrac{\text{hypotenuse}}{\text{side adjacent}}$

Degrees	Sines	Cosines	Tangents	Cotangents	Degrees
0.00°	0.0000	1.0000	0.0000	—	90.00°
0.50°	0.0087	0.9999	0.0087	114.59	89.50°
1.00°	0.0175	0.9998	0.0175	57.290	89.00°
1.50°	0.0262	0.9997	0.0262	38.188	88.50°
2.00°	0.0349	0.9994	0.0349	28.636	88.00°
2.50°	0.0436	0.9990	0.0437	22.904	87.50°
3.00°	0.0523	0.9986	0.0524	19.081	87.00°
3.50°	0.0610	0.9981	0.0612	16.350	86.50°
4.00°	0.0698	0.9976	0.0699	14.301	86.00°
4.50°	0.0785	0.9969	0.0787	12.706	85.50°
5.00°	0.0872	0.9962	0.0875	11.430	85.00°
5.50°	0.0958	0.9954	0.0963	10.385	84.50°
6.00°	0.1045	0.9945	0.1051	9.5144	84.00°
6.50°	0.1132	0.9936	0.1139	8.7769	83.50°
7.00°	0.1219	0.9925	0.1228	8.1443	83.00°
7.50°	0.1305	0.9914	0.1317	7.5958	82.50°
8.00°	0.1392	0.9903	0.1405	7.1154	82.00°
8.50°	0.1478	0.9890	0.1495	6.6912	81.50°
9.00°	0.1564	0.9877	0.1584	6.3138	81.00°
9.50°	0.1650	0.9863	0.1673	5.9758	80.50°
10.00°	0.1736	0.9848	0.1763	5.6713	80.00°
10.50°	0.1822	0.9833	0.1853	5.3955	79.50°
11.00°	0.1908	0.9816	0.1944	5.1446	79.00°
11.50°	0.1994	0.9799	0.2035	4.9152	78.50°
12.00°	0.2079	0.9781	0.2126	4.7046	78.00°
12.50°	0.2164	0.9763	0.2217	4.5107	77.50°
13.00°	0.2250	0.9744	0.2309	4.3315	77.00°
13.50°	0.2334	0.9724	0.2401	4.1653	76.50°
14.00°	0.2419	0.9703	0.2493	4.0108	76.00°
14.50°	0.2504	0.9681	0.2586	3.8667	75.50°
15.00°	0.2588	0.9659	0.2679	3.7321	75.00°
15.50°	0.2672	0.9636	0.2773	3.6059	74.50°
16.00°	0.2756	0.9613	0.2867	3.4875	74.00°
16.50°	0.2840	0.9588	0.2962	3.3759	73.50°
17.00°	0.2924	0.9563	0.3057	3.2709	73.00°
17.50°	0.3007	0.9537	0.3153	3.1716	72.50°
18.00°	0.3090	0.9511	0.3249	3.0777	72.00°
18.50°	0.3173	0.9483	0.3346	2.9887	71.50°
19.00°	0.3256	0.9455	0.3443	2.9042	71.00°
19.50°	0.3338	0.9426	0.3541	2.8239	70.50°
20.00°	0.3420	0.9397	0.3640	2.7475	70.00°
20.50°	0.3502	0.9367	0.3739	2.6746	69.50°
21.00°	0.3584	0.9336	0.3839	2.6051	69.00°
21.50°	0.3665	0.9304	0.3939	2.5386	68.50°
22.00°	0.3746	0.9272	0.4040	2.4751	68.00°
22.50°	0.3827	0.9239	0.4142	2.4142	67.50°
23.00°	0.3907	0.9205	0.4245	2.3559	67.00°
23.50°	0.3987	0.9171	0.4348	2.2998	66.50°
24.00°	0.4067	0.9135	0.4452	2.2460	66.00°
24.50°	0.4147	0.9100	0.4557	2.1943	65.50°
25.00°	0.4226	0.9063	0.4663	2.1445	65.00°
25.50°	0.4305	0.9026	0.4770	2.0965	64.50°
26.00°	0.4384	0.8988	0.4877	2.0503	64.00°
26.50°	0.4462	0.8949	0.4986	2.0057	63.50°
27.00°	0.4540	0.8910	0.5095	1.9626	63.00°
27.50°	0.4617	0.8870	0.5206	1.9210	62.50°
28.00°	0.4695	0.8829	0.5317	1.8807	62.00°
28.50°	0.4772	0.8788	0.5430	1.8418	61.50°
29.00°	0.4848	0.8746	0.5543	1.8040	61.00°
29.50°	0.4924	0.8704	0.5658	1.7675	60.50°
30.00°	0.5000	0.8660	0.5774	1.7321	60.00°
30.50°	0.5075	0.8616	0.5890	1.6977	59.50°
31.00°	0.5150	0.8572	0.6009	1.6643	59.00°
31.50°	0.5225	0.8526	0.6128	1.6319	58.50°
32.00°	0.5299	0.8480	0.6249	1.6003	58.00°
32.50°	0.5373	0.8434	0.6371	1.5697	57.50°
33.00°	0.5446	0.8387	0.6494	1.5399	57.00°
33.50°	0.5519	0.8339	0.6619	1.5108	56.50°
34.00°	0.5592	0.8290	0.6745	1.4826	56.00°
34.50°	0.5664	0.8241	0.6873	1.4550	55.50°
35.00°	0.5736	0.8192	0.7002	1.4281	55.00°
35.50°	0.5807	0.8141	0.7133	1.4019	54.50°
36.00°	0.5878	0.8090	0.7265	1.3764	54.00°
36.50°	0.5948	0.8039	0.7400	1.3514	53.50°
37.00°	0.6018	0.7986	0.7536	1.3270	53.00°
37.50°	0.6088	0.7934	0.7673	1.3032	52.50°
38.00°	0.6157	0.7880	0.7813	1.2799	52.00°
38.50°	0.6225	0.7826	0.7954	1.2572	51.50°
39.00°	0.6293	0.7771	0.8098	1.2349	51.00°
39.50°	0.6361	0.7716	0.8243	1.2131	50.50°
40.00°	0.6428	0.7660	0.8391	1.1918	50.00°
40.50°	0.6494	0.7604	0.8541	1.1708	49.50°
41.00°	0.6561	0.7547	0.8693	1.1504	49.00°
41.50°	0.6626	0.7490	0.8847	1.1303	48.50°
42.00°	0.6691	0.7431	0.9004	1.1106	48.00°
42.50°	0.6756	0.7373	0.9163	1.0913	47.50°
43.00°	0.6820	0.7314	0.9325	1.0724	47.00°
43.50°	0.6884	0.7254	0.9490	1.0538	46.50°
44.00°	0.6947	0.7193	0.9657	1.0355	46.00°
44.50°	0.7009	0.7133	0.9827	1.0716	45.50°
45.00°	0.7071	0.7071	1.0000	1.0000	45.00°
	Cosines	Sines	Cotangents	Tangents	Degrees

Figure 3-31. *Trigonometric functions*

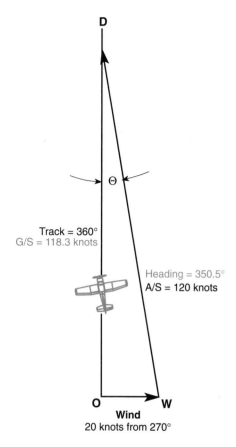

D

Track = 360°
G/S = 118.3 knots

Θ

Heading = 350.5°
A/S = 120 knots

O   W
Wind
20 knots from 270°

Figure 3-32. *Vector addition is used to find the heading required to fly a given track, and to find the ground speed when the airspeed, track and wind direction and velocity are known.*

In Figure 3-32, we have a wind triangle which is one of the common uses for vector addition in everyday flying, although flight computers do all of the plotting. One side of the wind triangle has a direction representing the track the airplane is flying over the ground, and its length represents the ground speed of the airplane. One side is the wind direction and velocity, and the other side is the heading of the airplane and the airspeed.

The pilot wants to fly from point O to D, which will give a track of 360° over the ground. There is a 20-knot wind blowing from the west that will force the pilot to crab, or head into the wind, to keep from being blown off of the track.

Vector O-D is drawn with a direction of 360° but its length is not considered at this time. The wind vector of 20 knots from 270° is drawn from the origin O to point W. A line whose length is the airspeed of the airplane is drawn from point W so that it touches the track line, and this forms the hypotenuse of the triangle. We know the length of the hypotenuse and the length of the side opposite the angle we want to find. Look at the trigonometric functions in Figure 3-31 and see that we need to use the sine function.

$$\text{Sin } \Theta = \frac{\text{opposite}}{\text{hypotenuse}}$$

$$= \frac{20}{120}$$

$$= 0.166$$

$$\text{Sin}^{-1} 0.166 = 9.5$$

To keep the wind from blowing him off his desired track, the pilot will have to head the airplane 9.5° to the left of the way he wants to go, or will have to hold a heading of 360° − 9.5° = 350.5°.

The ground speed is found by using the cosine function.

Angle Θ = 9.5°   Cosine of 9.5° = 0.986

$$\text{Cosine } \Theta = \frac{\text{side adjacent}}{\text{hypotenuse}}$$

$$\text{Side adjacent} = \cos \Theta \cdot \text{hypotenuse}$$

$$= 0.986 \cdot 120$$

$$= 118.3 \text{ knots}$$

For the airplane to cover a track of 360° from point O to D, the pilot will have to fly a heading of 350.5°. The airspeed of 120 knots will give a ground speed of 118.3 knots.

The nose of a vector is the end with the arrowhead, and the other end is the tail. Several vectors can be added tail to nose to find a single resultant vector that has a direction and magnitude that is equal to the sum of all of the individual vectors. Figure 3-33 shows the graphic representation of vectors A, B, and C, and the single resultant vector R that is the vector sum of the three.

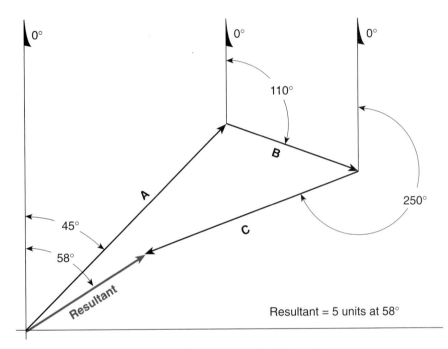

Resultant = 5 units at 58°

Figure 3-33. *Graphic addition of three vectors to find the resultant vector*

Rather than going to the trouble to draw these to scale, we can use trigonometry. Compile a chart such as the one in Figure 3-34.

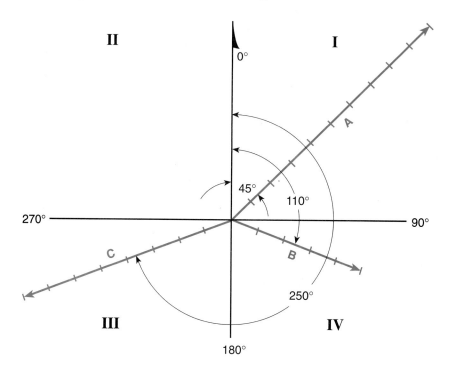

Figure 3-34. *Three vectors drawn from a common origin and measured from a common reference line.*

To find the length of the side opposite, we will use the sine function; and to find the length of the side adjacent, we will use the cosine function. *See* Figure 3-35.

A	10 units at 45° Sin 45° = 0.707 Cos 45° = 0.707	Side opposite = 10 x 0.707 = 7.07 units Side adjacent = 10 x 0.707 = 7.07 units
B	5 units at 110° (110° − 90° = 20°) Sin 20° = 0.3420 Cos 20° = 0.9397	Side opposite = 5 x 0.3420 = -1.71 units Side adjacent = 5 x 0.9397 = 4.69 units
C	8 units at 250° (270° − 250° = 20°) Sin 20° = 0.3420 Cos 20° = 0.9397	Side opposite = 8 x 0.3420 = -2.74 units Side adjacent = 8 x 0.9397 = -7.52 units

Figure 3-35. *Finding the vertical and horizontal components of the three vectors in Figure 3-34*

Now that we have the vertical and horizontal components of each of vectors A, B, and C, we can add them and find the vertical and horizontal components of the resultant vector R. This is shown in Figure 3-36.

Vector	Length	Direction from Horizontal Axis	Side Opposite (vertical)	Side Adjacent (horizontal)
A	10	45°	7.07	7.07
B	5	20°	-1.71	4.69
C	8	20°	-2.74	-7.52
R	5	31.7°	2.62	4.24

Figure 3-36. *Finding the resultant of the three vectors in Figure 3-34*

Notice that in Figure 3-34 the four quadrants are numbered I, II, III, and IV. Both the horizontal and vertical values for vectors in quadrant I are positive. In quadrant II the vertical values are positive, but the horizontal values are negative. In quadrant III both vertical and horizontal values are negative, and in quadrant IV, the horizontal values are positive, but the vertical values are negative.

Now that we know the horizontal and vertical components of the resultant vector R, we can find its angle from the horizontal axis by using the arctangent function. The arctangent of an angle, written $\tan^{-1}$, simply means the angle whose tangent is the number given.

$$\text{Tan} = \frac{\text{opposite}}{\text{adjacent}}$$

$$= \frac{2.62}{4.24}$$

$$= 0.618$$

$$\text{Tan}^{-1} 0.618 = 31.7°$$

The magnitude, or length, of the resultant vector is found by using the Pythagorean formula:

$$R = \sqrt{\text{opposite}^2 + \text{adjacent}^2}$$

$$= \sqrt{2.62^2 = 4.24^2}$$

$$= \sqrt{6.86 + 17.98}$$

$$= \sqrt{24.84}$$

$$= 4.98 \text{ units}$$

*Answers are on Page 136. **Page numbers refer to chapter text.***

45. A vector quantity must always consist of two things. They are _____ and
_____ . *Page 89*

46. Find the resultant of these two vectors:
Vector A: 10 units long with a direction of north.
Vector B: 5 units long with a direction of 90 degrees clockwise from north.

Resultant is _____ units long, and its direction is _____ degrees clockwise from north.
Page 93

47. Find the resultant of these two vectors:
Vector A: 12 units long, with a direction of 45° clockwise from north.
Vector B: 18 units long, with a direction of 180° clockwise from north.

Resultant is _____ units long, and its direction is _____ degrees clockwise from north.
Page 93

48. Find the resultant of these three vectors:
Vector A: 10 units long, with a direction of 100° clockwise from north.
Vector B: 15 units long, with a direction of 200° clockwise from north.
Vector C: 20 units long, with a direction of 300° clockwise from north.

Resultant is _____ units long, and its direction is _____ degrees clockwise from north.
Page 93

Stress and Strain

stress. A force set up within an object that tries to prevent an outside force changing its shape.

strain. A deformation or physical change caused by stress in a material.

In this section we will discuss the five basic stresses that can exist in an object and consider the factors involved in converting stress into strain.

Stress

Any time an outside force acts on an object, it causes another force inside the object called stress. When a helicopter rotor is turning, centrifugal force tries to pull the rotor blades out of the blade grips. This causes a stress inside the blade.

There are five types of stress: tension, compression, torsion, bending, and shear. But when we analyze these stresses, we find that they can all be broken down into the two basic stresses: tension and compression.

Tension

Tension is the stress that tries to pull an object apart. When a weight is suspended from a hoist by a chain, we have two forces in action. The weight tries to pull the end of the hoist down and, at the same time, the hoist is trying equally hard to hold the weight up. The chain has a tension, or tensile, stress in it that tries to stretch it or pull it apart. *See* Figure 3-37.

Compression

Compression is the other of the two basic stresses, and it is the stress that tries to squeeze the ends of an object together.

Riveting is one practical use of compressive forces. The rivet is slipped through a hole in the sheet metal, and one end is hammered with a rivet gun while a heavy steel bucking bar is held tight against the other end. The force between the rivet gun and the bucking bar compresses the rivet, making the middle of the rivet swell out and tightly fill the hole. The part of the rivet that sticks out of the sheet metal and is pushed against the bucking bar swells out to form the shop, or bucked, head. *See* Figure 3-38.

Torsion

The two basic stresses of tension and compression may be combined to form the other three stresses. Torsion is a stress inside an object that tries to twist it. In Figure 3-39, we see the way torsional stresses act in the shaft of a crank. When an external force rotates the shaft that is held in the block, it causes both a tensile stress and a compressive stress inside the shaft. These two stresses act at 45° to the axis of the shaft and at right angles to each other.

The rotor shaft in a helicopter has a great deal of torsional stress in it. One end of the shaft is turned by the engine and the other end is held back by the mass of the rotor.

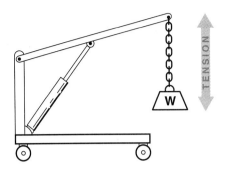

Figure 3-37. *When a weight is held up with a chain, the chain has a tensile stress in it.*

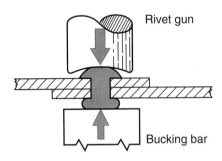

Figure 3-38. *When a rivet is driven with a compressive force on its ends, it expands to tightly fill the hole.*

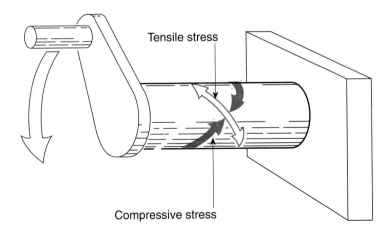

Figure 3-39. *Torsion is a combination of tension and compression. These two stresses act at right angles to each other and at 45° to the axis of the shaft.*

Bending

Another stress that is made up of tension and compression is bending. Bending tries to pull up or push down on one end of a beam, while the other end is held still.

The wings of an airplane are subjected to bending stresses. When the airplane is resting on its landing gear, the weight of the wing tries to bend the tips down. This places the top skin under a tensile stress and the bottom skin under a compressive stress. But when the airplane is flying, the opposite is true. As lift tries to bend the end of the wing up, the bottom skin has a tensile stress in it, and the top skin has a compressive stress. *See* Figure 3-40.

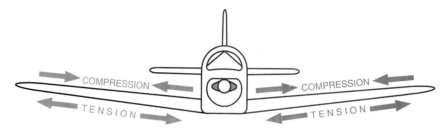

Figure 3-40. *The wing of an airplane is subjected to a bending stress. On the ground the top of the wing is under tension and the bottom is under compression. In flight, the opposite is true; the bottom is under a tensile stress and the top is under a compressive stress.*

Shear

The third stress that combines tension and compression is the shear stress, which tries to slide an object apart. Shear stress exists in a clevis bolt when it is used to connect a cable to a stationary part of a structure. A fork fitting, such as we see in Figure 3-41, is fastened onto one end of the cable, and an eye is fastened to the structure. The fork and eye are held together by a clevis bolt.

When the cable is pulled, there is a shearing action that tries to slide the bolt apart. This is a special form of tensile stress inside the bolt caused by the fork pulling in one direction and the eye pulling in the other.

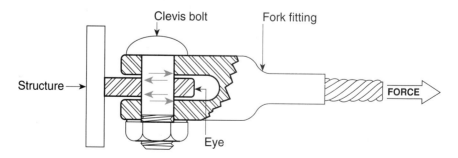

Figure 3-41. *A shear stress tries to slide the clevis bolt apart.*

Strain

Stress is a force inside an object caused by an external force. If this outside force is great enough to cause the object to change its shape or size, the object is not only under stress, but is also strained.

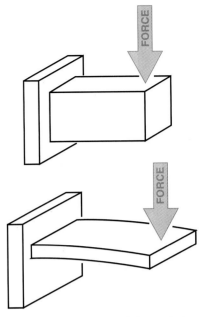

In Figure 3-42, we see two beams with the same amount of force applied to them. Both beams have the same bending stress in them, but the thick beam is of such a shape that it does not bend. The force is not great enough to strain it. But the thin beam cannot resist the stress, and it is strained.

The law concerning stress and strain is called Hooke's law. It tells us that the strain produced in an object is proportional to the applied stress until the elastic limit of the material is reached. At this point the material is permanently deformed and will not return to its original shape when the stress is removed.

As long as an excessive stress is not put on a material, we can double the force applied to it, and the amount of deflection will double. When we remove the force, the material will go back to its original size and shape.

Figure 3-43 shows the way a spring scale works. When there is no load on the hook, the spring is not strained and the scale reads zero. When a weight of 1 pound is put on the hook, the spring stretches and the indicator is opposite the 1-pound mark. When a weight of 2 pounds is put on the hook, the spring stretches twice as much; the indicator lines up with the 2-pound mark.

When all weight is removed from the hook, the scale returns to its original position, and the indicator again lines up with the zero mark. If there is too much strain for the material, however, it will not return to its original shape when the force is removed. The elastic limit of the spring has been reached, and the spring becomes deformed. *See* Figure 3-44.

Figure 3-42. *The physical shape of a beam determines the amount of stress it can withstand before it is bent, or strained.*

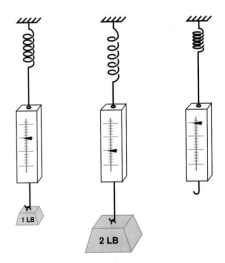

Figure 3-43. *If the elastic limit of the spring in the scale is not exceeded, it will stretch an amount proportional to the weight and will return to zero when the weight is removed.*

Hooke's law. The law which states that the strain within an object is directly proportional to the stress that causes it until the elastic limit of the material is reached.

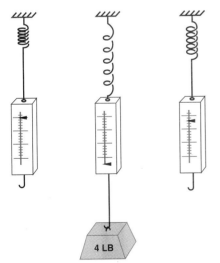

Figure 3-44. *If too much weight is put on a spring scale, the spring will be deformed, and the scale will not return to zero when the weight is removed.*

Answers are on Page 136. Page numbers refer to chapter text.

49. The five types of stress are:
    a. _____
    b. _____
    c. _____
    d. _____
    e. _____
       Page 96

50. The two basic stresses that may be combined to make up the others are:
    a. _____
    b. _____
       Page 96

51. The two stresses that make up a torsional stress act at _____ (how many degrees) to the axis of the shaft. *Page 97*

52. The upper skin of an airplane wing in flight has a _____ (tension or compression) stress in it. *Page 98*

53. When a force causes an object to change its shape or size, the object is said to be _____ (stressed or strained). *Page 99*

Heat and Temperature

heat. A form of energy that determines the speed of movement of molecules in a material.

temperature. A measure of the intensity of heat.

Heat and temperature are often thought of as being the same thing, but they are different. Heat is a form of energy that is associated with the movement of the molecules in a material, and temperature is a measurement of this energy.

Heat

Heat is one of the most important forms of energy because it is easily changed it into other forms and is used extensively to do practical work. In this section, we will see the effect of heat on various materials and study the way it may be transferred from one object to another.

Work Equivalent of Heat

Turbine engine fuel contains chemical energy which, when burned, changes into heat energy. This heat energy enters the air inside the engine, expands it, and produces the thrust that pushes the airplane through the air. In this way, heat energy does work.

Mechanical energy can be changed into heat. This happens when we use the brakes to stop an airplane after it has landed. Kinetic energy in the airplane keeps it rolling down the runway, and in order to stop it, we must use up this kinetic energy. We do this by applying the brakes. The brakes produce friction that makes the wheels hard to turn, and the energy used to turn the wheels against the friction becomes heat energy which causes the brake to get hot. It is not uncommon for the brakes on large jet airplanes to get red hot when the pilot makes an emergency stop.

In the U.S. system, the British thermal unit (Btu) is the basic unit of heat energy. One Btu is the amount of heat energy needed to increase the temperature of 1 pound of water 1°F, and 1 Btu can do 778 foot-pounds of work. In the metric system, the basic unit of heat energy is the calorie, which is the amount of heat energy needed to raise the temperature of 1 gram of water 1°C.

British thermal unit (Btu). The amount of heat energy needed to raise the temperature of 1 pound of pure water from 60° to 61°F.

calorie. A small calorie is the amount of heat energy needed to raise the temperature of 1 gram of water 1°C. A large calorie is the amount of heat energy needed to raise the temperature of 1 kilogram of water 1°C.

Physical Changes Caused by Heat

When heat energy is added to a material, it speeds up the movement of the material's molecules, and this increased movement usually causes the material to change some of its characteristics. Most materials expand when they absorb heat, and some change their form or shape. When ice absorbs enough heat, it melts, and when it absorbs yet more heat, it turns into steam.

Sensible Heat

Sensible heat is the heat that raises the temperature of a material without changing its physical state. The temperature of most materials increases when they absorb heat. For example, if we put a pan of cold water on a stove, heat from the stove enters the water and increases its temperature. The water remains liquid, and its temperature continues to rise until it reaches 100°C. It is sensible heat that causes the temperature of a material to increase without changing its physical state.

sensible heat. Heat that raises the temperature of a substance without changing its state.

Latent Heat

If we leave the pan of water on the stove after it reaches a temperature of 100°C and continue to add heat to it, the temperature of the water does not go any higher, but the water changes from a liquid into a gas and boils away, or evaporates. The heat that causes it to change its physical state but stay at the same temperature is called latent heat. *See* Figure 3-45.

When water evaporates, the latent heat remains in the water vapor. Then, when the vapor cools enough to change back into liquid water, the latent heat is released and warms the surrounding air.

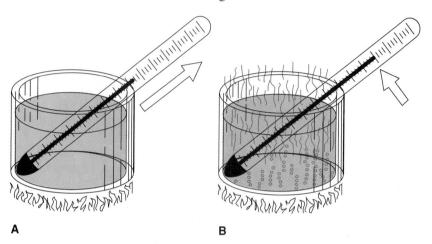

A   B

Figure 3-45
When sensible heat is added to water, its temperature increases, but the water does not change its physical state.

When latent heat is added to water, its temperature remains constant, but the water changes its state from liquid water into steam.

Dimensional Changes Caused by Heat

When heat energy is added to a material, the molecules increase their speed, and this actually causes the material to expand. This is called thermal expansion, and it takes place in almost all types of matter. Liquids expand the least and solids expand in different amounts. Gases expand the most. When the air inside a turbine engine is heated by the burning fuel, it expands a great deal, and this expansion produces thrust.

It is important when working with any kind of engine to understand the way different metals change their size when they are heated. Because of this change, many engine parts are assembled with what is called an interference fit. If a steel part is to be installed in a hole in an aluminum casting so it will not loosen when the parts get hot, the steel part is made slightly larger than the hole into which it is to fit. Then the aluminum casting is heated in an oven and the steel part is chilled with dry ice. The aluminum expands, making the hole larger, and the steel part shrinks. In this way, the two parts can be easily assembled. But when the two metals reach the same temperature, the aluminum shrinks around the steel and produces a tight fit that will not loosen when the parts both become hot during normal engine operation.

Specific Heat

Specific heat is the ratio of the amount of heat energy needed to raise the temperature of a specific mass of material 1°C, to the amount of heat energy needed to raise the temperature of the same mass of pure water 1°C. One gram of pure water requires 1 calorie of heat energy to raise its temperature 1°C, and water is given a specific heat value of 1.00.

Figure 3-46 shows the specific heat values of several commonly used materials, and since water has a specific heat of 1.00, it is used as a reference. Aluminum has a specific heat of 0.22. This means that the temperature of 1 gram of aluminum can be raised 1°C with less heat than we need for water. Only 0.22 calorie is needed.

Material	Specific Heat
Water	1.00
Alcohol	0.59
Ice	0.50
Aluminum	0.22
Glass	0.19
Iron	0.11
Copper	0.09
Silver	0.05
Mercury	0.03
Lead	0.03

Figure 3-46. *Specific heat of various materials*

Transfer of Heat

Energy can neither be created nor destroyed, but other forms of energy can be turned into heat, and heat can be turned into other forms of energy. We can also transfer, or move, heat from one object to another. There are three ways by which this can be done: conduction, convection, and radiation.

specific heat. The ratio of the amount of heat energy needed to raise the temperature of a certain mass of a material 1°C to the amount of heat energy needed to raise the temperature of the same mass of pure water 1°C.

convection. The method of heat transfer by vertical currents within a fluid.

Conduction

If we heat the end of a bar of metal with a flame and measure the temperature at different points along the bar, we find that the point nearest the flame will be hotter than points farther away from the flame (*see* Figure 3-47). This is because the heat energy from the flame forces the molecules in the metal into violent motion and raises the temperature of the metal. The molecules receiving the most heat touch other molecules and cause them to move faster. In this way, heat is conducted throughout the metal as each molecule affects the one next to it. The molecules farthest from the flame receive the least heat, and their motion is the least violent, so the temperature at that point in the metal will be the lowest. Most metals are good conductors of heat, but materials such as wood, cloth, paper, and most plastics are not; they are insulators.

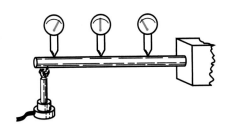

Figure 3-47. *When the end of the bar is heated with the flame, heat is transferred through the bar by conduction.*

Convection

Convection is a method of moving heat inside a gas or a liquid by means of vertical currents inside the fluid. When a pan of water is placed on a hot stove, the water at the bottom of the pan is heated by conduction, and the molecules of water that touch the metal absorb heat from the pan.

Then, as the movement of these molecules increases, the water becomes less dense and rises. The water that has not been heated is forced down to the bottom where it absorbs heat from the metal of the pan. *See* Figure 3-48.

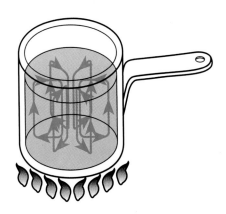

Figure 3-48. *When water in a container is heated by conduction, it becomes less dense and rises, forcing the cold water down to where it can be heated. This is heat transfer by convection.*

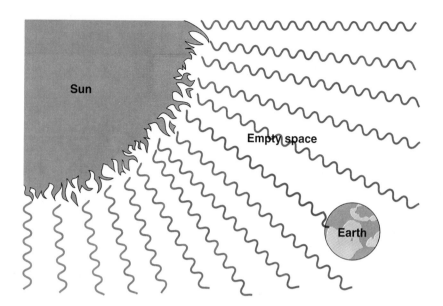

Figure 3-49. *Heat energy from the sun reaches the earth through the vacuum of empty space by radiation. Invisible heat energy passes through empty space in the same way as visible light energy.*

Radiation

radiation. The method of heat transfer by electromagnetic wave action.

Both conduction and convection depend upon direct physical contact with the source of heat. But heat can be transferred from one object to another without this direct contact. This method of heat transfer is called radiation. *See* Figure 3-49.

The heat energy we receive from the sun reaches us in the form of electromagnetic waves. Some of these waves have frequencies that make them visible, and this is the light we see. Others, with shorter wavelengths, are not visible, but they are able to penetrate solid substances. These are called cosmic rays.

Of primary interest are the waves of energy that are longer than those of visible light. When these waves strike the earth, they are absorbed by physical matter and release their energy into the molecules of the matter. This absorbed energy causes the matter to get hot.

All objects radiate energy, and the hotter the object, the more energy it radiates; and all objects absorb radiation. The only way an object can remain at the same temperature is for it to radiate exactly the same amount of energy as it receives.

Temperature

absolute temperature. Temperature measured from absolute zero. Absolute temperature is measured in degrees Kelvin or degrees Rankine.

absolute zero. The temperature at which all molecular movement inside a material stops. It is zero degrees on both the Kelvin and Rankine scales and -273°C and -460°F.

Heat is a form of energy that causes the molecules of a material to move around, and temperature is a measure of the amount of this motion. Normally, the molecules of a material are moving around all the time, and the hotter they are, the faster they move. There is a point, though, at which all of this molecular motion stops. This point is called absolute zero, and we use it as the reference point for absolute temperature measurement.

The two most commonly used systems for measuring temperature do not start with absolute zero but are based instead on two points, the freezing point and boiling point of pure water.

The Celsius, formerly Centigrade, scale sets the freezing point of pure water as 0° and the boiling point as 100°. The scale is continued in steps of equal size, both above and below the range between 0° and 100°. Absolute zero, or the point at which all molecular movement stops, is -273°C.

The Fahrenheit system uses the freezing temperature of a mixture of salt, ice, and water as its 0° mark. Pure water freezes at 32°F and boils at 212°F. The difference between boiling and freezing is divided into 180 equal divisions, and this scale is continued both below and above this range. On the Fahrenheit scale, all molecular movement stops at -460°F.

For temperature measurement in scientific calculations, there are two temperature scales based on absolute zero. The Kelvin scale uses the same divisions as the Celsius system, and 0°K is absolute zero. Pure water freezes at 273°K and boils at 373°K.

The other absolute temperature system is the Rankine system, and its divisions are the same size as those used in the Fahrenheit system. All molecular movement stops at 0°R, and pure water freezes at 492°R and boils at 672°R. *See* Figure 3-50.

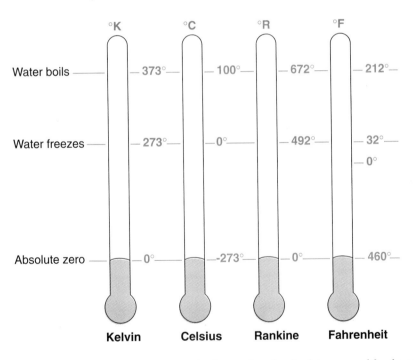

Figure 3-50. *The four temperature scales have values for absolute zero and for the points at which pure water freezes and boils.*

To change °C into °F, multiply °C by 1.8, then add 32.

$$°F = 1.8 (°C) + 32$$

Another way to do this is to multiply °C by 9 and divide by 5, then add 32.

$$°F = 9/5 (°C) + 32$$

To change °F into °C, subtract 32 from °F, and then divide by 1.8.

$$°C = (°F - 32) \div 1.8$$

Another way is to subtract 32 from the °F, and multiply this by 5 and divide by 9:

$$°C = (°F - 32) \cdot 5/9$$

We can change °C into °K by adding 273 to the °C.

$$°K = °C + 273$$

To change °K into °C, subtract 273 from the °K.

$$°C = °K - 273$$

We can also change °F into °R by adding 460 to the °F.

$$°R = °F + 460°$$

Or, to change °R to °F, subtract 460 from the °R.

$$°F = °R - 460°$$

*Answers are on Page 136. **Page numbers refer to chapter text.***

54. When heat energy is added to air, the air _____ (expands or contracts). *Page 101*

55. When brakes are used to stop an airplane, the kinetic energy from the motion of the airplane is converted into _____ in the brake. *Page 101*

56. The basic unit of heat energy in the metric system is the _____ . *Page 101*

57. The basic unit of heat energy in the U.S. system is the _____ .
    Page 101

58. Heat that is added to an object that changes its temperature but not its physical state is called _____ heat. *Page 101*

59. Heat that is added to an object that changes its physical state but not its temperature is called _____ heat. *Page 102*

60. It requires _____ (more or less) heat to raise the temperature of 1 pound of aluminum 10°C than it does to raise the temperature of 1 pound of water the same amount. *Page 103*

61. Three methods of heat transfer are:
    a. _____
    b. _____
    c. _____
    Page 103

62. The temperature at which all molecular motion stops is called absolute _____ . *Page 104*

63. Convert these temperatures into the systems called for:
    a. 62° F = _____ ° C.
    b. 62° C = _____ ° F.
    c. 200° F = _____ ° C.
    d. 200° C = _____ ° F.
    e. 500° C = _____ ° K.
    f. 500° K = _____ ° C.
    g. 500° F = _____ ° R.
    h. 500° R = _____ ° F.
    Page 106

Pressure

Pressure is the measure of the amount of force that acts on a given area of surface. It is usually expressed in such terms as pounds per square inch. Less familiar terms which are used sometimes include inches or millimeters of mercury, bars, millibars, and atmospheres. When we speak of pressure, we must have a reference from which to measure. There are three different references we can use, and the kind of pressure measured from each reference has its own name.

Absolute Pressure

Absolute pressure is measured from a vacuum, which is zero pressure, and it is used for indicating atmospheric pressure. One way of measuring absolute pressure is with a mercury barometer. A glass tube, about one meter long and closed at one end, is filled with mercury and turned upside down in a bowl of mercury with its open end below the surface. The mercury in the tube will drop down and leave a vacuum above it. The pressure caused by the atmosphere will push down on the mercury in the bowl and prevent any more mercury coming out of the tube.

The greater the pressure of the atmosphere, the higher the mercury will stay up in the tube, and when the atmospheric pressure decreases, the mercury in the tube drops. The standard pressure caused by the weight of the air surrounding the earth will hold the top of the mercury in the tube to a height of 29.92 inches, or 760 millimeters, above the mercury in the bowl. This pressure is equal to 14.69 pounds per square inch absolute, and is called one atmosphere of pressure. *See* Figure 3-51.

Atmospheric pressure may also be expressed in units of bars or millibars. One bar is a pressure of 29.53 inches of mercury. The pressures shown on weather maps and the reference pressures used on some aircraft altimeters are measured in millibars (one thousandth of a bar). Standard sea level pressure in this system is 1013.2 millibars.

One atmosphere of pressure can be expressed in any of the following terms:

760 millimeters of mercury
29.92 inches of mercury
14.69 pounds per square inch
1013.2 millibars

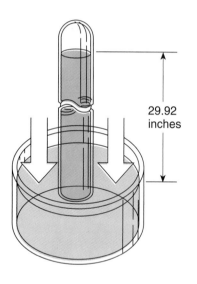

Figure 3-51. *Standard sea-level atmospheric pressure will support a column of mercury 29.92 inches, or 760 millimeters, high.*

Gage Pressure

When measuring the pressure produced by a pump on either a liquid or a gas, we generally measure it in terms of gage pressure, which is measured from the existing atmospheric pressure.

If the pressure shown on the dial of an oil pressure gage, as shown in Figure 3-52, is 40 pounds per square inch, it is called 40 psi, gage pressure, or 40 psig. The absolute pressure of this oil is 54.69 psia, but only 40 psi is available to force the oil through the engine. This is because the same atmospheric pressure, 14.69 psia, that is forcing the oil from the tank into the inlet of the pump is also trying to force the oil back into the pump at the pump outlet.

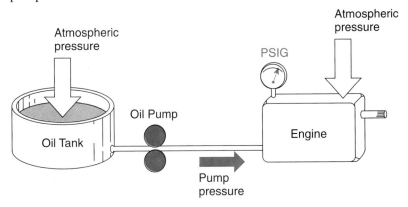

Figure 3-52. *Gage pressure is referenced from atmospheric pressure and is a measure of the amount of pressure rise caused by the pump.*

Differential Pressure

The difference between any two pressures is called differential pressure. Airplane cabins are pressurized to a certain differential pressure, or the difference between the pressure of the air inside and outside of the airplane.

Airspeed is determined by the difference between the ram air pressure produced by the aircraft moving through the air and the pressure of the still air through which the aircraft is flying. This special differential pressure is expressed in terms of miles per hour or knots. *See* Figure 3-53.

differential pressure. Pressure which is the difference between two opposing pressures.

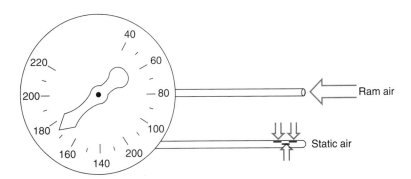

Figure 3-53. *An airspeed indicator measures the difference between ram air pressure and the pressure of the surrounding static air. It is a differential pressure.*

Answers are on Page 136. **Page numbers refer to chapter text.**

64. The amount of force acting on a given amount of surface area is called
_____ . *Page 108*

65. The pressure that is measured from zero pressure, or a vacuum, is called
_____ pressure. *Page 108*

66. Give the condition of standard sea-level barometric pressure in each of the following units:
    a. _____ millimeters of mercury
    b. _____ pounds per square inch
    c. _____ inches of mercury
    d. _____ millibars
    e. _____ atmosphere
       Page 108

Gas Laws

The gaseous state is the physical state in which matter is most active. A solid will try to keep its shape and size; a liquid, while changing its shape to fit its container, will keep its same volume. But a gas will change both its shape and its volume and will expand to fill its entire container.

Several chemical elements exist as gases at normal room temperature and pressure. These include hydrogen, helium, nitrogen, oxygen, fluorine, neon, chlorine, and argon. Also, some compounds, such as carbon dioxide and ammonia, are gases at ordinary room temperature and pressure.

Gases are made up of molecules that move about in space at a high rate of speed and continually collide with each other. When one molecule collides with another, it drives away the one that is hit and causes the mass of the gas to expand and mix with any other gas that is in the same area. If the gas is in a closed container, the molecules will strike against the walls and will produce a pressure.

Boyle's Law

Boyle's law is one of the basic laws concerning gases, and it explains the relationship between the pressure of a gas and its volume. This law tells us that the product found by multiplying the volume of a gas by its pressure remains constant.

If we keep the temperature of the gas in a container constant, any time we decrease its volume, we increase its pressure. Increasing the volume will decrease its pressure.

Figure 3-54 shows the way this works. With the piston near the end of the cylinder, the volume V_1 is large, but the pressure P_1 is low. When we push the piston into the cylinder, the volume V_2 becomes smaller, but the pressure P_2 becomes higher. We can see this relationship in the formula:

$$\frac{V_1}{V_2} = \frac{P_2}{P_1}$$

When V_1 is larger than V_2, P_2 will be greater than P_1.

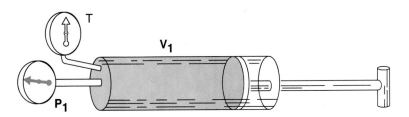

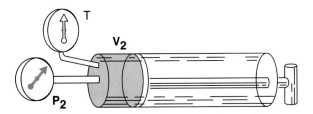

Figure 3-54. *If we hold the temperature of a gas constant, any change in its volume will cause an opposite change in its pressure.*

Charles's Law

Charles's law also explains the behavior of gases, and it shows what happens when the temperature of a gas changes and its pressure is held constant.

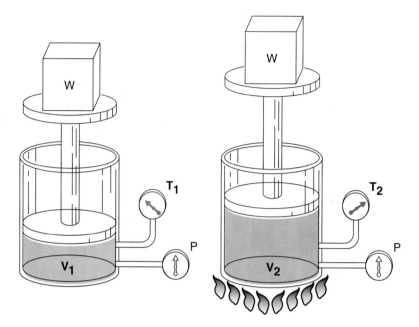

Figure 3-55. *When the pressure of the gas in a container remains constant, an increase in the temperature of the gas causes the volume of the gas to increase.*

The weight on the piston in the cylinder in Figure 3-55 keeps the pressure of the gas in the cylinder constant. When we increase the absolute temperature of the gas in the cylinder, the molecules of the gas collide with each other with a greater force, and they will push the piston up, increasing the volume of the gas.

This equation shows what is happening:

$$\frac{T_1}{T_2} = \frac{V_1}{V_2}$$

If the first absolute temperature, T_1, is lower than the second absolute temperature, T_2, the first volume, V_1, will be smaller than the second volume, V_2.

If the volume of a container of gas remains the same, and we add heat energy to the gas, the molecules will collide with each other and with the walls of the container with more force. So the pressure will go up with the absolute temperature (*see* Figure 3-56).

$$\frac{T_1}{T_2} = \frac{P_1}{P_2}$$

If the second absolute temperature, T_2, is higher than the first, T_1, the second pressure, P_2, will be greater than the first, P_1.

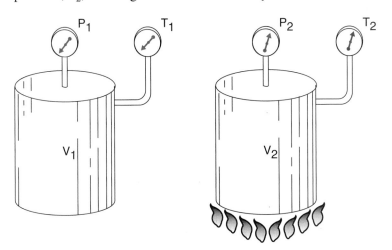

Figure 3-56. *When the volume of a container of gas remains constant, an increase in the absolute temperature of the gas causes its pressure to increase.*

General Gas Law

Since any change in the absolute pressure, absolute temperature, or volume of a gas affects the other two conditions, Boyle's law and Charles's law can be combined into the general gas law following the equation:

$$\frac{P_1 \cdot V_1}{T_1} = \frac{P_2 \cdot V_2}{T_2}$$

P_1 and V_1 are the first absolute pressure and volume of the gas, and T_1 is its first absolute temperature. P_2 and V_2 are the final absolute pressure and volume of the gas, and T_2 is its final absolute temperature.

Let's try some examples of the way this general gas law works. Suppose we have a closed 50-cubic-inch container of gas under an absolute pressure of 100 psia and an absolute temperature of 250° Kelvin. If we heat the gas in this container to a temperature of 400° Kelvin, what will its final pressure be?

This is worked out in Figure 3-57. If the volume of the gas is held constant and the absolute temperature is increased from 250°K to 400°K, the pressure will go up from 100 psia to 160 psia.

Next, we have a container that will hold a constant pressure of 50 psia on a gas, but allows the gas to change its volume. If we start with a volume of 100 cubic inches and a gas temperature of 400°K, what will the volume of the gas be if we lower its temperature to 300°K? *See* Figure 3-58.

When you lower the temperature of the gas, its molecular movement decreases. Since the pressure is held constant at 50 psia, the volume will decrease from 100 to 75 cubic inches.

This time, consider a cylinder with a piston in it that allows the volume of the gas to increase without increasing the pressure. We want to know how high the temperature of the gas will have to rise to increase the volume of the container from 50 to 100 cubic inches, without the pressure of the gas changing. In Figure 3-59, we see that we will have to double the absolute temperature if we double the volume without changing the absolute pressure.

P_1 = 100 psia $\qquad$ P_2 = <u>160</u> psia
V_1 = 50 cubic in. $\qquad$ V_2 = 50 cubic in.
T_1 = 250°K $\qquad$ T_2 = 400°K

$$\frac{P_1 \times V_1}{T_1} = \frac{P_2 \times V_2}{T_2}$$

$$P_2 = \frac{P_1 \times T_2}{T_1}$$

$$= \frac{100 \times 400}{250}$$

$$= 160 \text{ psia}$$

Figure 3-57. *Finding the change in pressure with a change in temperature when the volume remains constant*

P_1 = 50 psia $\qquad$ P_2 = 50 psia
V_1 = 100 cubic in. $\qquad$ V_2 = <u>75</u> cubic in.
T_1 = 400°K $\qquad$ T_2 = 300°K

$$\frac{P_1 \times V_1}{T_1} = \frac{P_2 \times V_2}{T_2}$$

$$V_2 = \frac{V_1 \times T_2}{T_1}$$

$$= \frac{100 \times 300}{400}$$

$$= 75 \text{ cubic in.}$$

Figure 3-58. *Finding the change in volume with a change in temperature when the pressure remains constant*

P_1 = 14.69 psia $\qquad$ P_2 = 14.69 psia
V_1 = 50 cubic in. $\qquad$ V_2 = 100 cubic in.
T_1 = 300°K $\qquad$ T_2 = <u>600</u> °K

$$\frac{P_1 \times V_1}{T_1} = \frac{P_2 \times V_2}{T_2}$$

$$T_2 = \frac{T_1 \times V_2}{V_1}$$

$$= \frac{300 \times 100}{50}$$

$$= 600°K$$

Figure 3-59. *Finding the change in temperature with a change in volume when the pressure remains constant.*

Dalton's Law

Chemists have found that when equal volumes of every kind of gas are held at an equal temperature and pressure, there are an equal number of molecules in each volume. This fact is expressed as Dalton's law.

In a mixture of gases in a container, the total pressure caused by these gases pushing against the walls of the container is the sum of the partial pressures caused by each of the gases in the mixture. The partial pressure, the amount of pressure caused by each type of gas, depends on how much of that particular gas is present.

The air we breathe is a mixture of gases that contains approximately 78% nitrogen and 21% oxygen. The other 1% is made up of traces of hydrogen, helium, neon, argon, krypton, and other gases. Under standard sea-level conditions, this air has a pressure of 29.92 of mercury. Now, according to Dalton's law, the nitrogen which makes up 78% of the volume of the gas also causes 78% of the pressure; the partial pressure of the nitrogen is 23.34 inches of mercury. The oxygen, which makes up 21% of the volume of the air, causes 21% of the pressure; its pressure is 6.28 inches of mercury.

Dalton's law. The gas law which states that there will always be the same number of molecules of gas in a container when the gas is held at a uniform pressure and temperature. Dalton's law explains the partial pressure of the gases which make up the air in our atmosphere.

partial pressure. The pressure caused by each of the gases in a mixture.

STUDY QUESTIONS: GAS LAWS

Answers are on Page 136. Page numbers refer to chapter text.

67. If we hold the absolute temperature of a gas constant while we decrease its volume, the pressure will _____ (increase or decrease). *Page 111*

68. If we hold the absolute pressure of a gas constant while we increase its absolute temperature, its volume will _____ (increase or decrease). *Page 112*

69. If we hold the volume of a gas constant while we increase its absolute temperature, its absolute pressure will _____ (increase or decrease). *Page 113*

70. The temperature we must use when working problems using the gas laws is _____ temperature. *Page 113*

71. We have this mixture: 30% nitrogen, 20% oxygen, and 50% hydrogen. If the mixture has a pressure of 29.92 of mercury, what is the partial pressure of each gas?
    a. Nitrogen = _____ inches of mercury
    b. Oxygen = _____ inches of mercury
    c. Hydrogen = _____ inches of mercury
    Page 115

Fluid Mechanics

Levers, inclined planes, pulleys, and gears all may be used to gain mechanical advantage. There is another way that is often used to achieve a mechanical advantage, and this is by fluid mechanics in the form of hydraulic or pneumatic systems.

Hydraulic systems transmit a force from one location to another by using an incompressible fluid, usually some form of oil. Hydraulic systems are used for operating the brakes in most airplanes, as well as for operating the retractable landing gear and many of the flight controls on large airplanes. Pneumatic systems use some form of compressible fluid such as air for transmitting force. Some airplanes use pneumatic systems to operate the brakes, flaps, and retractable landing gear.

Pressure Produced by a Fluid

The pressure produced by a column of fluid is determined by the density of the fluid and the height of the column.

The shape or volume of the container does not have any effect on the pressure. In Figure 3-60 we see several containers of different shapes. If we connect them all together at the bottom, the liquid in all of the containers will stay at the same height, h. The pressure shown on the gage is that caused by the height of the fluid.

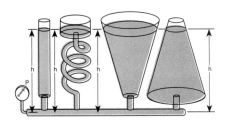

Figure 3-60. *The pressure at the bottom of a column of liquid is caused by the height of the liquid, and it is not affected by the quantity of the fluid or the shape of the container.*

The second thing that determines the pressure produced by a column of fluid is the density of the fluid. Pure water weighs 0.0361 pound per cubic inch, and since one gallon contains 231 cubic inches, a column of water 231 inches high will produce a pressure of 8.34 psi. Other liquids have different densities and specific gravities, and a column of the same height will produce a different pressure. Mercury has a specific gravity of 13.6, and a column of mercury 231 inches high will produce a pressure of 113.42 psi. The specific gravity of gasoline is only 0.72, so a column of gasoline 231 inches high will produce a pressure of 6 pounds per square inch. *See* Figure 3-61.

Material	Density (pounds cubic inches)	Specific Gravity
Mercury	0.4913	13.6
Pure water	0.0361	1.00
Jet engine fuel	0.0289	0.80
Gasoline	0.0260	0.72

Figure 3-61. *Density and specific gravity of various liquids*

We can find the pressure produced by a column of liquid by using the formula:

$$P = D \cdot h$$

P is the pressure in pounds per square inch. D is the density of the liquid in pounds per cubic inch, and h is the height of the column of liquid in inches.

We can use this formula to find the amount of pressure pushing on the bottom of a gasoline tank if the level of the fuel in the tank is 30 inches above the bottom. Gasoline has a density of 0.026 pound per cubic inch.

$$
\begin{aligned}
P &= D \cdot h \\
&= 0.026 \cdot 30 \\
&= 0.78 \text{ pounds per square inch}
\end{aligned}
$$

Pascal's Law

Pascal's law states that when there is an increase in pressure at any point in a confined fluid, there is an equal increase at every other point in the container.

If we have a container of liquid such as the one we see in Figure 3-62, the pressures shown on the gages P_1, P_2, and P_3 are the pressures caused by the height of the liquid above the gage. P_3 shows more pressure than either P_2 or P_1 because there is a greater height of liquid above it.

Put a piston in the container and put a load on it so that it pushes down on the liquid, the pressure will increase on each of the gages. All three gages will show the same amount of increase. *See* Figure 3-63.

Pascal's law. The law that states that when pressure is applied to a fluid in an enclosed container, the pressure is transmitted equally throughout all of the fluid, and it acts at right angles to the walls that enclose the fluid.

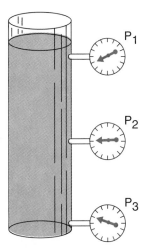

Figure 3-62. *The pressure produced by a liquid in a container is caused by the height of the liquid above the point at which the pressure is measured. The higher the liquid above the gage, the greater the pressure.*

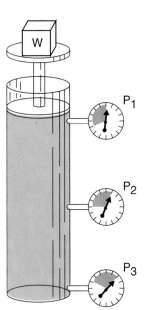

Figure 3-63. *When we apply pressure on the liquid in a closed container, the pressure rises the same amount in all parts of the container.*

In practical hydraulic systems, we do not consider the weight of the fluid in the system, but think only of the changes in pressure caused by the piston pushing on the fluid.

Figure 3-64 shows a practical hydraulic system that uses Pascal's law to give us a mechanical advantage. Here we have a cylinder with an area of 1 square inch connected to a cylinder having an area of 10 square inches. A piston in the smaller cylinder holding a weight of 1 pound balances the piston in the larger cylinder holding 10 pounds.

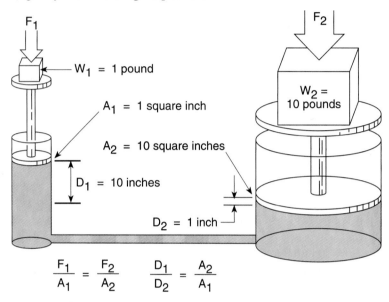

$$\frac{F_1}{A_1} = \frac{F_2}{A_2} \qquad \frac{D_1}{D_2} = \frac{A_2}{A_1}$$

Figure 3-64. *Hydraulic cylinders produce a mechanical advantage. A 1-pound force (F_1) can lift a 10-pound weight (W_2), but no work is gained. The work done by the small piston is the same as that done by the large piston.*

The 1-pound load on the 1-square-inch piston causes a pressure increase in the cylinder of 1 psi. And, according to Pascal's law, this pressure increase is carried to every part of the fluid and pushes up on the piston in the large cylinder.

The large piston has an area of 10 square inches, and the fluid pushes on every square inch with a force of 1 pound. So the fluid pushes up on the piston with enough force for it to hold 10 pounds.

This arrangement of two cylinders having unequal area gives a mechanical advantage in the same way a lever does. The force on the small piston (F_1), divided by the area of the small piston (A_1), is equal to the force on the large piston (F_2), divided by the area of the large piston (A_2).

$$\frac{F_1}{A_1} = \frac{F_2}{A_2}$$

Another way in which this hydraulic system resembles the lever is that the work which is done by the small piston is the same as that done by the large piston. When the piston in the small cylinder moves down 10 inches, it forces 10 cubic inches of fluid out of the small cylinder into the large one. This fluid spreads out over all 10 square inches of area and lifts the large piston only 1 inch. The work done by the small piston is the same as the work done by the large piston, 10 inch-pounds.

In our study of Mathematics, we introduced the formula for force: $F = P \cdot A$ (force = pressure times area). A convenient way to remember this formula and all of its possible rearrangements is by the use of the circle we see in Figure 3-65. The top half of the circle labeled F represents the force, and it is equal to the bottom half, labeled A and P, which represents area and pressure.

We can find the area needed to produce a specified force from the available pressure by dividing the top quantity (F) by the known bottom quantity (P). $A = F \div P$. We can also find the pressure required to produce a given amount of force when the area of the piston is known. We can do this by dividing the value represented by the top half of the circle (F) by the known value represented by one of the bottom parts of the circle (A). $P = F \div A$.

From the formula $F = P \cdot A$, we can see that the amount of force produced by a hydraulic system is equal to the amount of pressure in the system times the area of the piston that the pressure acts against. If we have a pressure of 100 psi acting on a piston whose area is 20 square inches, the force produced by the piston is 2,000 pounds. *See* Figure 3-65.

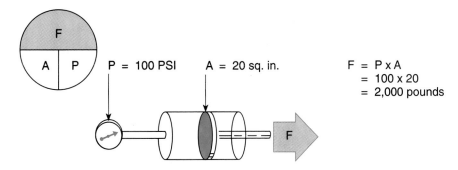

Figure 3-65. *The amount of force produced by the piston in a hydraulic cylinder may be found by multiplying the area of the piston by the amount of pressure inside the cylinder.*

Look at Figure 3-66 to find the area needed to give us a certain amount of force when we know the pressure in the system. In this example, we want to know how large the piston will have to be for it to produce 100 pounds of force with a pressure of 20 psi.

To do this, we divide the force of 100 pounds by the pressure of 20 psi, and find that we need a piston having an area of 5 square inches. *See* Figure 3-66.

We can also use our circle to find the amount of pressure that is built up in a cylinder when we know the area of the piston and the amount of force that is pushing on the piston. When a force of 40 pounds pushes on a piston whose area is 10 square inches, the pressure of the fluid in the cylinder increases by 4 psi, as shown in Figure 3-67.

This same kind of circle helps us visualize the relationship between the area of the piston, the distance the piston moves, and the amount of fluid that is forced out of the cylinder.

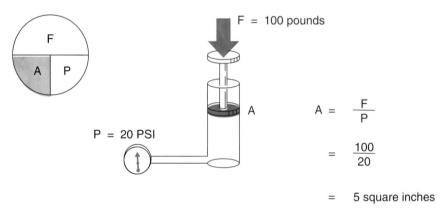

Figure 3-66. *The area of a piston needed to produce a given amount of force with a certain amount of pressure may be found by dividing the amount of force by the pressure.*

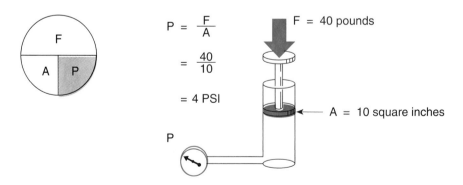

Figure 3-67. *The amount of pressure produced in a hydraulic cylinder may be found by dividing the amount of force on the piston by the area of the piston.*

In Figure 3-68, the shaded half of the circle shows that the volume of the fluid moved by a piston is equal to the area of the piston times the distance the piston moves. When a piston with an area of 2 square inches moves 4 inches into the cylinder, it pushes 8 cubic inches of fluid out of the cylinder.

This circle can also help us find the piston area needed to expel a given amount of fluid when it is moved a specified distance. In Figure 3-69, the piston moves 4 inches to force 8 cubic inches of fluid from the cylinder. By using the formula shown here, we see that the piston must have an area of 2 square inches.

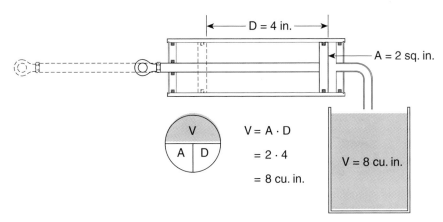

Figure 3-68. *The volume of fluid moved out of a cylinder by a piston may be found by multiplying the area of the piston by the distance the piston is moved.*

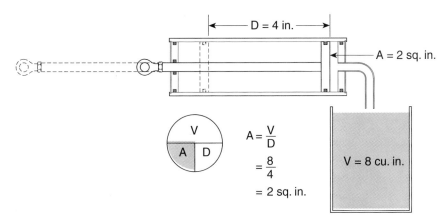

Figure 3-69. *The area of a piston needed to move a given volume of fluid when it moves a certain distance may be found by dividing the volume by the distance the piston is moved.*

And this circle also helps us find the distance a piston of a certain size will have to move in order to force a given amount of fluid out of the cylinder. The illustration in Figure 3-70 (page 122) shows a piston with an area of 2 square inches moving 8 cubic inches of fluid out of a cylinder. In order to do this, the piston must move for a distance of 4 inches.

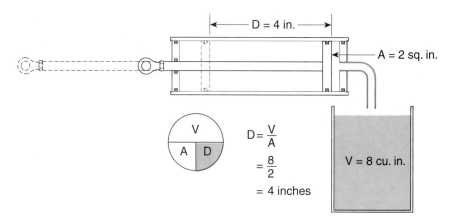

Figure 3-70. *The distance a piston must move to force a given amount of fluid out of a cylinder may be found by dividing the volume of the fluid by the area of the piston.*

Bernoulli's Principle

Energy exists in two forms: potential and kinetic. In fluid mechanics, pressure is a form of potential energy in a fluid, and the velocity of the fluid is its kinetic energy. In any flow of fluid, the total energy in the fluid is the sum of the kinetic and the potential energy.

Bernoulli's principle explains that if we neither add nor take away energy from a flow of fluid, any increase in the velocity (kinetic energy) of the flow will cause a corresponding decrease in its pressure (potential energy). This principle is extremely important in helping us understand the way an airplane wing or a helicopter rotor produces lift as it passes through the air. It also helps us understand the way in which paint spray guns operate.

A venturi is a specially shaped tube through which a fluid, either a liquid or a gas, flows. There is a restriction in the tube where the area gets smaller, and then it returns to its original size. *See* Figure 3-71.

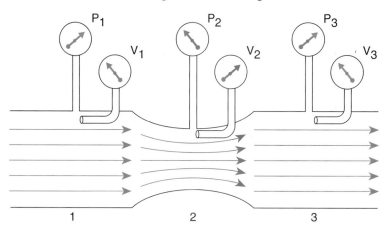

Figure 3-71. *When energy is neither added to nor taken from fluid in motion, any restriction that causes the fluid to speed up will cause the pressure to decrease.*

Fluid flows through this tube, and, at position 1, the pressure is the value P_1. The speed, or velocity, is shown as V_1. If we do not add or take away any energy from the fluid, it must speed up when it reaches the restriction to allow the same volume of fluid to move the same distance through the tube in the same length of time.

When it speeds up, the kinetic energy (velocity) increases. But since no energy was added, the potential energy (pressure) had to decrease. We see this on the gages P_2 and V_2. As soon as the tube returns to its original size, at 3, the fluid slows down so the same volume will move the same distance in the same time. When it slows down, the velocity decreases, but the pressure increases to the value it had originally.

In a spray gun, air is forced through a venturi, and a tube carries the liquid to the restriction point. Here the velocity is the greatest and the pressure is the lowest. Atmospheric pressure forces the liquid out of the tube into the area of low pressure, where it is broken up into tiny droplets by the high-velocity air. *See* Figure 3-72.

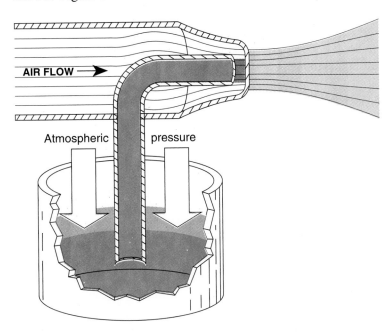

Figure 3-72. *An atomizer, such as is used in a spray gun, is a form of venturi. When the air flow is restricted, the pressure drops, and atmospheric pressure forces the liquid up so that it mixes with the high-velocity air and is broken up into tiny droplets. It is atomized.*

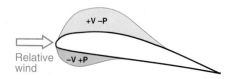

Figure 3-73. *Aerodynamic lift is produced by an airfoil when the kinetic energy (velocity) in the air flowing over its upper surface increases and its potential energy (pressure) decreases. Below the surface, the velocity decreases and the pressure increases.*

Bernoulli's principle also helps us understand the way aerodynamic lift is produced by an airplane wing and by a helicopter rotor.

The cross-sectional shape of a wing or a rotor is much like the one we see in Figure 3-73. As the air strikes the wing and flows over the top, it finds the surface dropping away from it. For the air to continue to cling to the surface, it must speed up. Energy is needed to speed up the air, and this energy comes from changing some of the potential energy, or pressure, into velocity, or kinetic energy. As the pressure over the top of the wing becomes less, it pulls air down to the surface, and a force equal to the weight of the air being pulled down pulls upward on the wing.

The air flowing below the wing encounters the bottom surface rising into its flow path, and it slows down. This loss of velocity increases its potential energy, or pressure, and this pressure pushes the wing up. The low pressure on top of the wing and the high pressure below the wing produce aerodynamic lift.

Buoyancy

There are two types of flying machines that allow us to overcome the force of gravity and rise into the air. Aerodynamic flying machines such as airplanes and helicopters depend upon movement through the air to produce lift. Aerostatic machines such as balloons rise in the air because of their buoyancy.

Balloons are filled with a gas, such as hot air, which is less dense than the colder air surrounding it. They rise because they displace a weight of air greater than their own weight.

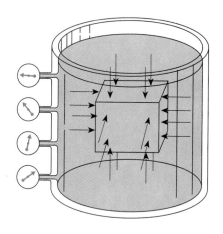

Figure 3-74. *The pressure exerted by the liquid in a container increases with the depth of the liquid, and the pressure is greatest at the bottom.*

When a block of material is submerged in the liquid, the pressure acts on all sides of the block, and since the pressure is greater on the bottom of the block than it is on the top, the liquid tries to force the block up. The block is said to be buoyed up by the liquid.

If we put a block of aluminum in a container of water, the pressure of the liquid pushes against its top, bottom, and sides. Since the forces on the sides are exactly equal, they cancel each other, but there is more force on the bottom of the block than there is on its top, and the water will try to force the block up. The amount of this force is exactly equal to the weight of the water the block displaces. *See* Figure 3-74.

A 10-inch cube of aluminum has a volume of 1,000 cubic inches, and since its specific gravity is 2.8, the block is 2.8 times as heavy as an equal volume of water.

Archimedes' principle explains the way buoyancy acts on an object that is immersed in a fluid, either a liquid or a gas. We can understand this principle if we support the block of aluminum with a spring scale, as in Figure 3-75, and lower it into a container of water so that some of the water is forced out of the container into another container on the scales.

buoyancy. The uplifting force that acts on an object when it is placed in a fluid.

The aluminum block weighs 101 pounds when it is outside of the water. And when we lower it into the water, it displaces some of the water. As the block pushes the water out, the water pushes up on the block and the scale reads less. When the block is completely submerged in the water, the scale reads 64.9 pounds, because we have forced 36.1 pounds of water out of the container. The aluminum block is buoyed up by the water with a force equal to the weight of the water that was displaced.

The same size block of wood, with a specific gravity of 0.50, weighs 18.15 pounds outside of the water; and when lowered into the water, it forces out only 500 cubic inches of water. The scale will read zero because the block has displaced its own weight of water and the water holds up the entire weight of the block. The block floats.

Hot air balloons rise into the air because the heated air inside the balloon is less dense than the surrounding cooler air. The balloon displaces a weight of air equal to the weight of the balloon with its basket and occupants.

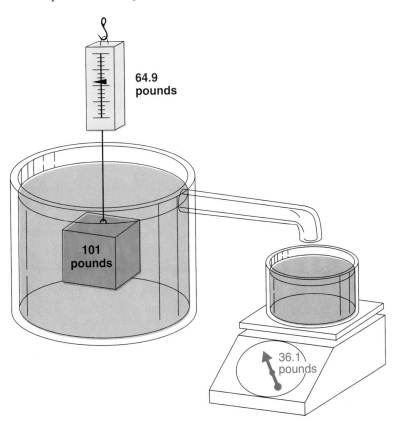

Figure 3-75. *Aluminum weighs 0.101 pound per cubic inch, so a 10 · 10 · 10 inch block of aluminum weighs 101 pounds. When the block is lowered into a container of water, it takes the place of 1,000 cubic inches of water, which weighs 36.1 pounds. The block is buoyed up by a force equal to the weight of the water it displaced, and it now pulls down on the spring scale with a force of only 64.9 pounds.*

*Answers are on Page 136. **Page numbers refer to chapter text.***

72. The fluid used in a hydraulic system is _____ (compressible or incompressible).
    Page 116

73. The fluid used in a pneumatic system is _____ (compressible or incompressible).
    Page 116

74. Two things that determine the amount of pressure produced by a column of fluid are:
    a. _____
    b. _____
       Page 116

75. Refer to Figure SQ-75. If piston area A_1 is 3 square inches, and A_2 is 30 square inches, weight W_1 must be _____ pounds in order to balance a weight W_2 of 100 pounds. *Page 118*

Figure SQ-75

76. Refer to Figure SQ-75. The small piston moves down a distance D_1 of 6 inches, to force the large piston up a distance D_2 of 0.5 inch. If the area of the large piston A_2 is 120 square inches, the area A_1 of the small piston must be _____ square inches. *Page 118*

77. Refer to Figure SQ-75. When a weight W_1 of 18 pounds pushes down on the small piston whose area A_1 is 9 square inches, the pressure inside the small cylinder is _____ psi. *Page 118*

78. Refer to Figure SQ-75. The small piston has an area A_1 of 8 square inches, and the large piston has an area A_2 of 32 square inches. In order to force the large piston upward for a distance D_2 of 0.5 inch, the small piston must move down a distance D_1 of _____ inches. *Page 118*

79. A piston whose area is 30 square inches, when moved 20 inches, will force _____ cubic inches of fluid from a cylinder. *Page 121*

80. The velocity of a moving fluid is a form of _____ (kinetic or potential) energy. *Page 121*

81. Pressure of a moving fluid is a form of _____ (kinetic or potential) energy. *Page 122*

82. If energy is neither added to nor taken from fluid in motion, when the velocity of the fluid increases, the pressure will _____ (increase or decrease). *Page 122*

83. When a 10-pound block of wood floats in a container of water, it displaces _____ pounds of water. *Page 125*

Vibration and Sound

Vibration is one of the major problems in aircraft design. All physical objects have a resonant frequency at which they will vibrate at the maximum intensity for a given amount of excitation. All moving parts of an aircraft and powerplant produce vibrations. It is important that no part of the aircraft structure is resonant at any frequency produced by the engine or any aerodynamic vibration.

We are mindful of sound because of the unusual things that happen when any part of an aircraft moves through the air at the speed of sound.

frequency. The number of complete cycles of a recurring event that takes place in one unit of time.

Vibration

Vibration is the up-and-down or back-and-forth movement of an object. Vibrations use up energy and cause wear. Vibration affects almost all mechanical devices, and airplanes and helicopters are especially affected, because they are built without the extra weight needed to absorb vibrations.

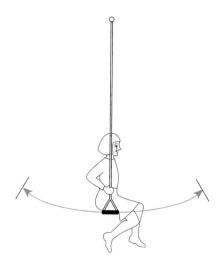

Figure 3-76. *A playground swing is a form of pendulum. Its period, or the time needed for one complete cycle, is determined by its length.*

resonance. The condition of a vibrating object that causes it to have the greatest amplitude of vibration for the amount of energy put into it.

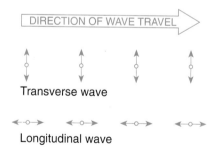

Figure 3-77. *In a transverse wave, the particles in motion rise above and drop below their original position, and the wave travels away from the point of disturbance. In a longitudinal wave, the particles in motion move back and forth parallel to the direction the wave is moving.*

Resonance

Every natural body has a frequency at which it vibrates most easily, and this is called its resonant frequency. Any time the body is disturbed, it vibrates at this particular frequency. Resonance is extremely important in aircraft design and maintenance because vibrations at the resonant frequency of an aircraft part can actually cause its destruction.

Think about a playground swing, which is a form of pendulum. A person weighing 100 pounds can be swung well above your head with only some very small pushes, but the pushes must be done at *exactly* the frequency at which the swing is resonant. *See* Figure 3-76.

If the swing is resonant at 30 cycles per minute, its period, or time required for one complete cycle, is 2 seconds. We must push the swing every 2 seconds exactly, to keep it swinging. We can start it swinging and keep it swinging at this frequency with very little energy, but we cannot make it swing any faster nor can it swing any slower and remain resonant.

When an aircraft is designed and the prototype is built, it is subjected to an intense series of vibration tests. Electronic transducers are connected to the aircraft structure, the structure is vibrated through a wide range of frequencies, and the amount of movement of the structure is measured. When the transducer produces the frequency at which the structure is resonant, the amplitude of vibration increases tremendously.

When the engineers identify the resonant frequencies of all the parts of the structure, and the frequencies of vibrations caused by the engines, the propellers, the exhaust systems, and disturbances of air flowing over the surface of the structure, revisions are made in the design that either change the resonant frequencies of the structure or eliminate the vibrations in these ranges. Helicopters are especially affected by vibration caused by the changing aerodynamic forces produced by the spinning rotors.

Sound

We normally think of sound as something we hear. But the human ear cannot hear all sound; that which we hear is only a small part of what is technically known as sound, a form of mechanical energy that is transmitted by longitudinal pressure waves.

There are two different kinds of waves that occur in nature, transverse and longitudinal waves. When we drop a stone into a pool of calm water, transverse waves form ripples. These ripples begin where the stone enters the water, and they move out in concentric circles. The particles of water rise and fall above and below the normal level of the water, and the wave motion moves away from the point of the disturbance. The ripples are the highest at the center and become smaller as they spread out. As the distance doubles from the point the stone struck the water, the wave height decreases to one fourth of its original height. *See* Figure 3-77.

Sound waves are a form of longitudinal wave. Rather than the particles of air moving up and down, they move back and forth parallel to the direction the wave is traveling. When we strike a tuning fork so its tines vibrate, sound is produced. This sound is caused by the tines of the fork alternately pushing and pulling on the air. When the fork moves toward us, it pushes on the air and moves the molecules of air closer together. Then, as it moves away from us, it pulls back on the molecules. This is called compressing and rarefying the air. When the air with this motion in it strikes our ears, our ear drums vibrate back and forth exactly as the tines of the tuning fork vibrate, and we hear the sound. *See* Figure 3-78.

The number of complete cycles of sound energy that take place in one second is called the frequency of the sound; and the amount of change in sound pressure is called the intensity of the sound.

Vibrations above the range we can hear, called ultrasonic vibrations, have a very important place in the technical world. They are used for such things as nondestructive inspection and parts cleaning, as well as for forcing bubbles out of some liquids.

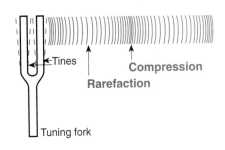

Figure 3-78. *When the tines of a tuning fork vibrate, they cause the particles of air to be alternately compressed and rarefied. This longitudinal wave affects our ear drums so we hear sound.*

tines. The prongs which extend from a fork-like object.

Sound Intensity

The basic unit for measuring sound intensity is the decibel, abbreviated dB. One dB is the smallest change in sound intensity the human ear can detect. The ticking of a small watch makes a sound of about one dB. Soft music used as a background in some homes and offices is around 60 dB, and very loud music can have as much as 100 decibels of sound energy. Any sound above about 130 decibels can vibrate ear drums enough to cause pain.

decibel (acoustic). The basic unit for measuring sound intensity. One decibel (dB) is the smallest change in sound intensity the normal human ear can detect.

Speed of Sound

Sound travels at different speeds in different materials. Some materials are good conductors of sound and others act as effective sound insulators. Air, like all gases, is a poor conductor of sound, liquids such as water are better conductors, and solids are the best conductors. Generally, the more dense the solid material is, the better it is as a conductor of sound.

Sound waves travel in air at approximately 761 miles per hour, depending on the temperature. In water, they travel much faster, and in iron or steel, they travel still faster.

The speed at which sound travels in the air has become of increasing importance in the field of aviation. This is because we are now able to build airplanes that can fly at the speed of sound and even much faster. When an airplane passes through the air, the air flowing over its surface is disturbed, and sound waves are set up that radiate out in all directions from the surface.

If the airplane itself moves as fast as the sound waves can travel in the air, these waves cannot go out ahead of it. Instead, they pile up in front of the aircraft, like the wave in front of a boat; and since the sound waves are waves of pressure, all of this pressure lies along a very thin line. We call this a shock wave, and it produces the familiar sonic boom (*see* Figure 3-79). When air flows through a shock wave, the velocity of the airflow decreases and its static pressure increases.

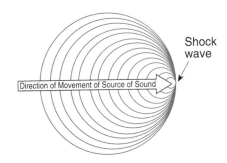

Figure 3-79. *When the source of sound moves at the speed of sound, the sound waves cannot move out ahead of the source. They pile up and form a shock wave that causes the familiar sonic boom.*

Shock waves form on an aircraft when air flows over the surface at the speed of sound. And the speed of sound is not constant; it varies with the temperature of the air.

At sea level, with a standard temperature of 15°C, the speed of sound is 661.2 knots. At 10,000 feet, the standard temperature of the air drops to -4.8°C, and the speed of sound is down to 638.0 knots.

At 20,000 feet the standard temperature is -24.6°C and the speed of sound is 614.1 knots. The temperature continues to drop until we reach an altitude of approximately 36,000 feet. At this altitude, the temperature is -56.2°C, and the speed of sound is 573.7 knots. It remains at this value even though the pressure of the air continues to drop, until an altitude of approximately 82,000 feet is reached. Above this altitude the temperature begins to rise and the speed of sound starts back up.

When an airplane is flying at the speed of sound, it is said to be flying at a speed of Mach one. When it is flying at a speed of 75% of the speed of sound, it is flying at a speed of Mach 0.75.

STUDY QUESTIONS: VIBRATION AND SOUND

Answers are on Page 136. Page numbers refer to chapter text.

84. The number of complete cycles of sound energy that take place in one second is called the
_____ of the sound. *Page 127*

85. Vibrations at a frequency higher than the human ear is capable of hearing are called
_____ vibrations. *Page 129*

86. The amount of change in the sound pressure is called the _____ of the sound.
Page 129

87. The smallest change in sound intensity the human ear can detect is called one
_____ of sound energy. *Page 129*

88. When an airplane travels faster than the speed of sound, the pressure waves from air disturbances on its surface cannot move out ahead of the airplane. These pressure waves pile up and form a
_____ wave. *Page 129*

89. The speed of sound varies with the _____ (pressure or temperature) of the air.
Page 129

90. The frequency at which any natural body vibrates most easily is called the _____ frequency of the body. *Page 128*

91. The resonant frequency of a pendulum is determined by its _____ . *Page 128*

Light

Visible light is a form of electromagnetic energy having a very limited frequency range. It is of extreme importance to us because it is light that enables us to see.

Natural Light

Like most of the energy on the earth, most light comes from the sun, in waves of electromagnetic radiation; but only an extremely small portion of this energy produces light that is visible to the human eye. Only electromagnetic waves whose wavelengths are in the range between 0.000 038 to 0.000 078 centimeter are visible, and rather than using such small terms when we speak of the wavelength of visible light, we use a system called angstroms. One angstrom, abbreviated A, is equal to 1/10,000,000 of a meter ($1 \cdot 10^{-10}$ or 0.000 000 000 1 meter). Using this system, the wavelength of visible light extends from about 3,800 A to about 7,800 A. *See* Figure 3-80.

angstrom. A convenient unit used to measure the wavelength of light. One angstrom, or A, is equal to 1/10,000,000 meter. The wavelengths of visible light are between about 3,800 and 7,800 angstroms.

color. The characteristic of light that is caused by the different wavelengths of electromagnetic energy that make up light. Violet light has the shortest wave lengths, and red has the longest.

	Wave length	Type of wave
Miles	1,000	
	100	
	10	
	1	
Feet	1,000	Radio waves
	100	
	10	
	1	
Inches	1	
	0.1	
	0.01	Infrared
	0.001	
		VISIBLE LIGHT
	1×10^{-6}	Ultraviolet
	1×10^{-9}	X-rays
	1×10^{-12}	and gamma rays

Figure 3-80. *Visible light makes up only a very small portion of the spectrum of electromagnetic radiation. We can see only the electromagnetic waves whose length is between 0.000 038 and 0.000 078 centimeters.*

Characteristics of Light

Light, like any other form of energy, obeys certain laws of physics, and while some of its characteristics can be changed, its basic energy can be neither created nor destroyed.

Light Travels in Straight Lines

Because we see shadows, we know that the waves of light energy leaving a source of light travel in straight lines. If we shine a spotlight on a light-colored wall in a dark room, it forms a circle of light on the wall. But if we hold the corner of a card between the light and the wall, part of the circle of light is blocked, and a shadow the shape of the part of the card in the beam shows up in the circle. Since the light is traveling in straight lines, it does not fill in the part of the circle that is blocked by the card. *See* Figure 3-81.

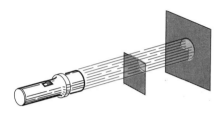

Figure 3-81. *Light travels from its source in a straight line. If a beam of light is interrupted, a shadow is formed.*

Light Spreads Out as it Leaves its Source

Light from a source such as the candle we see in Figure 3-82 travels out from the source in waves. If we hold a piece of cardboard with a hole in it in front of the candle, we can see the way light spreads out as it comes through the hole. The closer the cardboard is to the light, the more the light spreads.

Since the light spreads out as it travels away from the source, the amount of illumination decreases as the square of the distance from the source increases. In Figure 3-83, we have a candle 4 inches away from a card that has a hole cut in it. The hole is 1 inch square. If we hold a piece of white paper 4 inches from the card, we have doubled the distance between the source and the card, and the same amount of light that came through the 1-square-inch hole has now spread out to light up 4 square inches of area.

Each square inch of area that is lighted gets only ¼ of the light that passed through the hole in the card. Now, if we move the paper 12 inches away from the candle (3 times the original distance), the light passing through the hole in the card is spread out over 9 square inches of area. And each square inch gets only ⅑ of the light that came through the hole. When the paper is moved out 16 inches (4 times the original distance), each square inch will receive only ¹⁄₁₆ of the light.

This experiment demonstrates an important law of physics, called the Inverse Square Law: "The amount of light from a point source that falls on a surface is inversely proportional to the square of the distance between the source and the surface." *See* Figure 3-83.

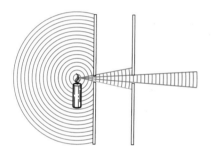

Figure 3-82. *When light passes through a hole, it spreads out. The closer the hole is to the source, the more the light spreads out.*

Inverse Square Law. The intensity of a physical quantity varies inversely with the square of the distance between the source and the point at which it acts.

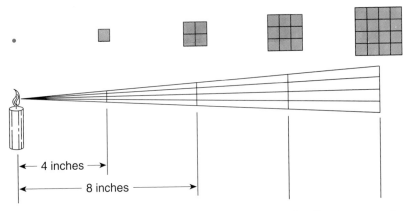

Figure 3-83. *Light obeys the Inverse Square Law. The light that illuminates a surface spreads out as it gets farther from the source. If we double the distance between the source of light and the surface on which it falls, the same amount of light that fell on one square unit of surface spreads out over 4 square units. Each square unit of surface receives one-quarter of the light.*

The Law of Reflection

If we have a point source of light that shines on a mirror, the light will be reflected, or bounced, off the surface, and it will travel in a special direction. In Figure 3-84 there is a line that is normal, or perpendicular to, the surface of the mirror, and the beam of light which strikes the mirror forms an angle with this normal line. This angle is called the angle of incidence. The reflection of the point source of light can be seen only along a line that extends up from the mirror at an angle (called the angle of reflectance) that is exactly the same as the angle of incidence. We can move the reflected spot of light wherever we want by changing the angle of incidence, which also changes the angle of reflectance.

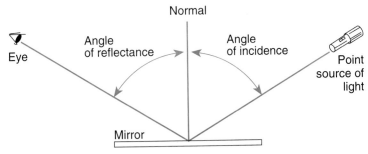

Figure 3-84. *The angle of reflectance of a light beam is always exactly the same as the angle of incidence.*

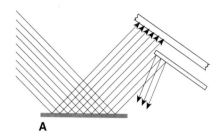

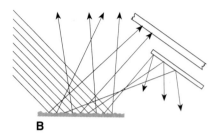

Figure 3-85

A. Light reflects from a smooth surface and causes sharp-edged shadows if it is blocked.

B. When light strikes a rough surface, it is diffused, or scattered. It does not cause sharp-edged shadows.

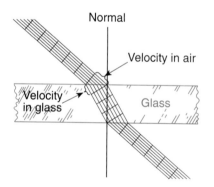

Figure 3-86. *The speed at which light travels through glass is less than its speed through air, so a beam of light is refracted (bent) as it passes through glass.*

Diffusion of Light

When parallel rays of light strike a smooth surface, all of them have the same angle of incidence and the same angle of reflectance; they leave the surface as a beam just like the beam from the source. Any object that interrupts the reflected beam causes a shadow, since none of the light can get behind the object.

If the parallel rays strike a rough, or irregular, surface, the reflected rays no longer form a beam. Instead, they bounce out in all directions. Any object that interrupts these reflected rays of light does not form a sharp shadow because some of the light gets behind it.

Most incandescent light bulbs used for home lighting are frosted, or have a rough surface on the inside. This rough surface diffuses the light leaving the bulb, and it produces a more even lighting than would be produced if the filament were inside a clear bulb. *See* Figure 3-85.

Speed of Light

Experiments have proven that light travels at an extremely fast speed, about 186,000 miles a second as it travels to Earth from the sun or from the stars through empty space. But the speed of light is different as it passes through different substances. For example, light in water travels 139,000 miles per second, and through glass, it is slowed down to 124,000 miles per second.

When a beam of light shines through a glass plate at an angle, such as we see in Figure 3-86, the light slows down. The beam changes its angle as it travels through the glass. The amount the angle changes is determined by the density of the glass. The denser the glass, the slower the light travels, and the more the beam is bent. When the beam leaves the glass, it speeds up and leaves at the same angle it entered.

Light is refracted, or bent, in camera lenses to make images appear larger or smaller, and in eyeglasses, light is refracted to correct any faulty refraction of light by the natural lenses in our eyes. A common example of refraction occurs when an object like a spoon is placed in a glass of water. *See* Figure 3-87.

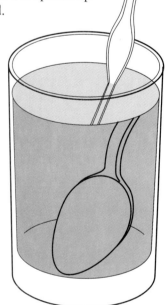

Figure 3-87. *The spoon appears to bend when a part of it is seen through air and a part is seen through the water. The shape of the glass and the water forms a lens that magnifies the spoon.*

*Answers are on Page 136. **Page numbers refer to chapter text.***

92. Our main source of natural light is the _____ . *Page 131*

93. When we double the distance between a source of light and the surface on which it falls, the amount of illumination on the surface decreases to _____ (what fraction) of the original illumination. *Page 133*

94. When a beam of light strikes a smooth surface and is reflected, the angle of incidence is always the same as the angle of _____ . *Page 134*

95. Light travels through empty space at the rate of _____ (how many) miles per second. *Page 134*

96. Light travels _____ (faster or slower) when it passes through glass than it does when it is passing through air. *Page 134*

Answers to Chapter 3 Study Questions

1. matter
2. molecule
3. elements
4. protons, neutrons, electrons
5. protons, neutrons
6. electrons
7. negative
8. solid, liquid, gaseous
9. no
10. ice, steam
11. solid
12. liquid
13. gas
14. heat
15. mass
16. weight
17. weight
18. density
19. specific gravity
20. float
21. 50.5
22. sun
23. potential
24. kinetic
25. nucleus
26. control
27. heat exchanger
28. 750
29. 120
30. 1.14
31. force
32. acceleration
33. 200
34. arm
35. moment
36. zero
37. 10
38. 120

39. 12
40. 400
41. velocity
42. gravity
43. centrifugal
44. centripetal
45. direction, magnitude
46. 11.18, 26.6
47. 12.75, 138.5
48. 13.86, 245
49. a. tension
    b. compression
    c. torsion
    d. shear
    e. bending
50. a. tension
    b. compression
51. 45
52. compression
53. strained
54. expands
55. heat
56. calorie
57. British thermal unit
58. sensible
59. latent
60. less
61. a. conduction
    b. convection
    c. radiation
62. zero
63. a. 16.67
    b. 143.6
    c. 93.3
    d. 392
    e. 773
    f. 227
    g. 960
    h. 40
64. pressure

65. absolute
66. a. 760
    b. 14.69
    c. 29.92
    d. 1013.2
    e. 1
67. increase
68. increase
69. increase
70. absolute
71. a. 8.98
    b. 5.98
    c. 14.96
72. incompressible
73. compressible
74. a. height of the column
    b. density of the fluid
75. 10
76. 10
77. 2
78. 2
79. 600
80. kinetic
81. potential
82. decrease
83. 10
84. frequency
85. ultrasonic
86. intensity
87. decibel
88. shock
89. temperature
90. resonant
91. length
92. sun
93. ¼
94. reflectance
95. 186,000
96. slower

BASIC ELECTRICITY

4

Continued

Continued

Continued

BASIC ELECTRICITY

4

By controlling the flow of electrons, which are tiny invisible charges of electricity, we can produce heat and light, and we can transmit voices and pictures all over the world at the speed of light. Electricity makes possible unbelievably complex data-handling and number-crunching computers. By controlling this powerful, invisible flow, we have built aircraft that allow us to go anywhere in the world in a matter of hours.

Because electricity is so vital to sustained flight, everyone involved in aviation must have a good understanding of electricity and the laws that govern it. This section of the *Aviation Maintenance Technician Series* furnishes the needed background.

An Introduction to Electricity

For years we did not know exactly what electricity was, only that it could be used to do work. Within the past six decades, however, we have learned much more about electricity, and the more we learn about it, the more practical uses we find for it.

Centuries ago, it was discovered that when a piece of hardened tree rosin, called amber, was rubbed with sheep's wool, the amber attracted tiny pieces of straw. But when the straw touched the amber, an invisible force pushed the straw away. Sometimes a spark would jump between the straw and the amber.

Because of these strange happenings, the theory was formulated that there was some kind of invisible fluid on the wool and the amber. The fluid was called "electrik," after the Greek word for amber. There were thought to be two conditions: a lack of fluid and an excess of fluid. When an object having an excess of this invisible fluid was touched by an object having a lack of it, the electrik left one object and went to the other, often causing a spark as it went. When both objects had an excess of fluid, or when both had a lack of fluid, they would repel, or push away, from each other. Lightning, the huge spark that jumps between clouds or from a cloud to the ground, seemed to prove this theory. Certain terms were developed to explain what was happening.

An object having an excess of fluid was said to be "positive," and, in written explanations, a plus sign (+) was used to show this condition. The object having a lack of fluid was called "negative," and this was shown by a minus sign (-). When the fluid passed from one object to the other, it was said that "current" flowed between them.

This theory and its explanation worked quite well, even though people did not know exactly what it was that flowed or what caused the flow. Today, we know that this flow is made up of invisible particles of matter called electrons, and that we can control this flow, making it perform work.

Electron Flow

The study of physics teaches that all matter is made up of just slightly more than one hundred different chemical elements whose smallest particles are called atoms.

The nucleus, or center, of an atom is made up of protons (positive electrical charges) and neutrons, which have the same amount of mass as a proton, but with no electrical charge. Spinning around the nucleus in rings, or shells, are negatively charged particles called electrons. The electron's mass is only about 1/1,846 that of a proton, but its negative electrical charge is exactly as strong as the positive charge of a proton. *See* Figure 4-1.

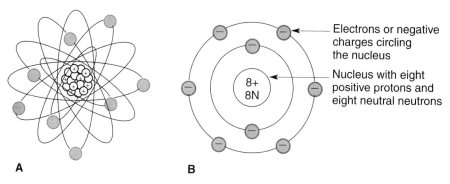

Electrons or negative charges circling the nucleus

Nucleus with eight positive protons and eight neutral neutrons

A   B

Figure 4-1

A. *Electrons circle the nucleus of an atom in shells, with all the electrons in each shell circling the nucleus the same distance from the center. This is an atom of oxygen, which has two electrons in its inner shell and six in its outer shell.*

B. *This type of diagram helps us see the way an atom of oxygen is constructed.*

Most atoms are electrically balanced. This means that there are exactly the same number of electrons circling around the nucleus as there are protons in the nucleus. All electrons and protons are exactly alike, and it is the number of protons and electrons in an atom that makes an atom of one element different from an atom of another element.

In Figure 4-2, we see that the diagrams of atoms of hydrogen, neon, sulfur, and copper, are all very different from each other. Hydrogen is a very active gas that combines readily with other elements; neon is an inert gas that does not combine with other elements; sulfur is a nonmetal that resists the flow of electricity; and copper is a metal and one of the best conductors of electricity.

Figure 4-1 shows that the electrons circle the nucleus in shells, with some atoms having as many as seven shells. Each shell can hold only a certain number of electrons. For example, the first shell can hold 2 electrons, the

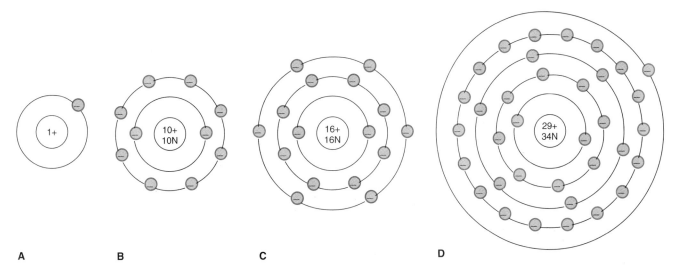

Figure 4-2. *The electrons in all of these atoms are exactly alike. Materials differ from each other because of the different number of electrons and protons in their atoms.*

A. Hydrogen is a very active gas.
B. Neon is an inert gas.
C. Sulfur is a nonmetal solid that opposes the flow of electrons.
D. Copper is a metal that is a very good conductor of electricity.

second shell can hold 8, the third can hold 18, and so on. Regardless of the number of electrons the inner shells can hold, the outer shell can never hold more than 8 electrons.

Valence Electrons

The outer shell of an atom is called the valence shell, and its electrons are called valence electrons. It is these valence electrons that are of interest to us in the study of electricity, as they are the ones that give an atom its electrical characteristics.

Chemical elements are classified by these characteristics into three categories: conductors, insulators, and semiconductors.

Conductors

An electrical conductor has between one and three electrons in its valence shell, and these electrons are easily attracted away from the atom by an outside electrical force. They then move freely through the material. Silver, gold, and copper have only one electron in the outer shell, and they are excellent conductors of electricity.

Insulators

Insulators are made of materials whose atoms have between five and eight electrons in their valence shell, and these materials do not readily give up any of their valence electrons. A strong electrical force is needed to pull any of the valence electrons from the atoms in these materials. Wood, glass, ceramic, and certain plastic materials are good insulators.

conductor. Any device or material that allows the flow of electrons under a reasonable amount of electrical pressure, or voltage.

semiconductor. A material whose electrical characteristics may be changed from that of a conductor to that of an insulator by changing its circuit conditions.

insulator (electrical). A material whose valence electrons are so tightly bound to the atom that they resist any force that tries to move them from one atom to another.

Two negative ions will repel each other.

Two positive ions will repel each other.

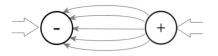

A positive and a negative ion will attract one another.

Figure 4-3. *Ions with like charges repel each other, while ions with unlike charges attract each other.*

Semiconductors

Semiconductors are a special group of elements that are neither always a conductor nor an insulator. They all have four electrons in their valence shell, and by alloying them with an insulator or with a conductor, they can be given extremely useful electrical characteristics. They will conduct under some conditions and act as an insulator under others.

The two most widely used semiconductors are silicon and germanium, and because of the importance of semiconductors in electronics, we will study these materials in detail later on.

Ions

Most atoms are balanced, meaning they have the same number of electrons as protons. But it is possible for an atom to either gain an electron or lose one, and when it does, the atom is no longer balanced—it has become charged. These charged atoms are called ions. For example, if an atom gains an electron, it has more negative charges than positive charges, and it becomes a negative ion. If a balanced atom loses an electron, it has lost some of its negative charge, and it becomes a positive ion. The nucleus of the atom does not change, but when an atom becomes an ion, its characteristics change and it behaves differently from a balanced atom. For example: two positive ions will repel, or push away from each other, as will two negative ions. But a positive and a negative ion will attract each other and will join, becoming neutral. *See* Figure 4-3.

Electrons can be made to flow and do useful work any time materials having different electrical charges are joined by a conductor. We will soon see that there are five ways in which electrons can be made to flow. Right here, however, we will think only about the way chemical energy forces them to flow.

In a common carbon-zinc flashlight battery, a chemical action takes place between the zinc and the ammonium chloride that causes some of the zinc atoms to lose electrons and become positive zinc ions. These positive ions give the paste a positive charge, and electrons are attracted away from the carbon rod to restore the electrical balance in the paste. This action leaves the zinc can with too many electrons (a negative charge) and the carbon rod with too few electrons (a positive charge). *See* Figure 4-4.

If a copper wire and a light bulb are connected between the zinc can and the carbon rod, the extra electrons in the zinc will flow to the carbon rod. This flow of electrons causes the bulb to give off light and heat. This is the work done by these electrons. *See* Figure 4-5.

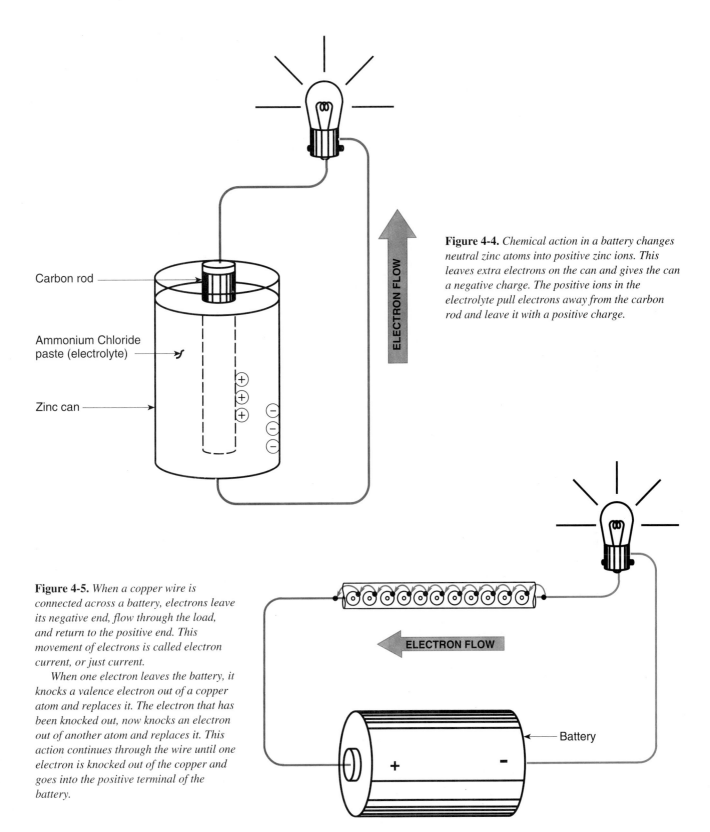

Carbon rod

Ammonium Chloride
paste (electrolyte)

Zinc can

ELECTRON FLOW

Figure 4-4. *Chemical action in a battery changes neutral zinc atoms into positive zinc ions. This leaves extra electrons on the can and gives the can a negative charge. The positive ions in the electrolyte pull electrons away from the carbon rod and leave it with a positive charge.*

Figure 4-5. *When a copper wire is connected across a battery, electrons leave its negative end, flow through the load, and return to the positive end. This movement of electrons is called electron current, or just current.*

When one electron leaves the battery, it knocks a valence electron out of a copper atom and replaces it. The electron that has been knocked out, now knocks an electron out of another atom and replaces it. This action continues through the wire until one electron is knocked out of the copper and goes into the positive terminal of the battery.

ELECTRON FLOW

Battery

Billions of electrons move in a conductor. Current flow does not consist of one electron leaving the zinc can and rushing through the wire directly to the carbon rod; instead, every time one electron enters the end of the wire at the zinc can, another electron leaves the end of the wire at the carbon rod. Electron movement between the time an electron enters one end of the wire until another electron leaves the other end, takes place at the speed of light—about 300,000,000 meters per second, or 186,000 miles per second.

Copper, as previously stated, is a very good conductor of electricity because each atom of copper has only one electron in its valence shell. In a piece of copper wire, there are billions of atoms, and each atom has one valence electron. When electrons leave the zinc and enter the copper wire, each of them knocks a valence electron out of a copper atom and takes its place. The electrons that are knocked out are called free electrons, and they knock electrons from the valence shell of other copper atoms. Exactly the same number of electrons leave the wire at the positive end of the battery as entered it at the negative end. As long as the wire joins the two ends of the battery, electrons flow, and it is this flow of electrons that makes the entire field of electricity and electronics possible.

Useful Work

When electrons flow through a conductor, they are capable of performing useful work. They have this capability because two very important things happen: heat is produced in the conductor, and a magnetic field surrounds the conductor. These two things are so important that we will study them both in detail.

Direction of the Flow of Electricity

One problem of concern in the study of electricity is the direction in which electricity flows. Benjamin Franklin and others who experimented with electricity in the early days thought that the "fluid" traveled from a high level, which they called positive, or plus, to a lower level, called negative, or minus. This flow was called current, and the assumption made about the direction of its flow was logical. Many textbooks on electricity have been written that define current as the flow of electricity that travels from the positive terminal of a source of electrical energy to its negative terminal.

As more was learned about atoms, with their protons and electrons, it was found, however, that it is actually the electrons that move in an electrical circuit, or path. And since electrons are negative charges of electricity, they actually flow toward the positive terminal, not away from it—just opposite of what was originally thought. This is referred to as the flow of electron current.

This new information increases our knowledge of electricity, but it causes some confusion because many of the symbols used in electrical circuits have arrows pointing in the wrong way. The electrons actually travel in the direction that is *opposite* to the direction in which the arrows point. *See* Figure 4-6.

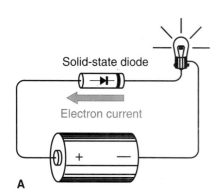

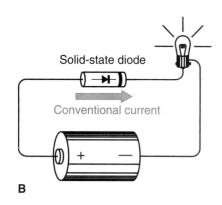

Figure 4-6

A. *Electron current flows from the negative terminal of a battery through the load (the light bulb), back to the positive terminal of the battery. This flow is opposite the arrowhead in the symbol for the solid-state diode.*

B. *Conventional current is an imaginary flow of electricity that is considered to flow from the positive terminal of a battery, through the load and the diode, to the negative terminal. This assumed flow is in the direction of the arrowhead in the solid-state diode symbol.*

It really makes no difference at all which direction we think when we consider flow in an electrical circuit; but we must be sure to think of it as going in the same direction all the time. We can follow the electron flow, which is from negative to positive; or, if we like to follow the direction of the arrows used in a circuit diagram, we can think of the flow as *conventional current*, from positive to negative. Although there is no actual flow in this direction, conventional current is often used by technicians when analyzing or troubleshooting electrical circuits.

In any study of electricity or electronics, it is important to understand clearly which direction the text uses. Throughout this text, the flow of electron current, from negative to positive, is used.

STUDY QUESTIONS: AN INTRODUCTION TO ELECTRICITY

Answers begin on Page 359. Page numbers refer to chapter text.

1. An atom is made up of a nucleus that contains positive charges called _____ and neutral charges called _____ . *Page 144*

2. Surrounding the nucleus and spinning in a series of rings, or shells, are negative electrical charges called _____ . *Page 144*

3. Electrons in the outer shell of an atom may be knocked out of their orbits, and they will travel to the next atom where they knock out and replace the electrons in its outer shell. This movement of electrons is called _____ . *Page 148*

4. Electron movement in a conductor is considered to be at the speed of _____ . *Page 148*

5. A material whose valence electrons are easily knocked out of their orbits is called a/an _____ . *Page 145*

6. A material whose valence electrons are tightly held in their orbits and are able to be dislodged only with a high electrical pressure is called a/an _____ . *Page 145*

Types of Electricity

There are two basic types of electricity: static and current. In static electricity, electrons accumulate on a surface and remain there until they build up a pressure high enough to force their way to another surface or device which has fewer electrons. Static electricity is uncontrollable and unpredictable; therefore it is a nuisance, and we take steps to prevent it or to get rid of it. Current electricity, on the other hand, is the type we most often use. We can produce and control both direct current (DC) and alternating current (AC). In DC the electrons always flow in the same direction and in AC the electrons periodically reverse their direction of flow.

Static Electricity

When we slide across the plastic seat covers of an automobile, the friction between our clothing and the seat cover causes our clothes to pick up an excess of electrons from the seat. This is exactly the same thing described earlier when a piece of amber was rubbed with sheep's wool.

If there is no conductor between our body and the car seat to make a path for these electrons to leak off, our body will hold the extra electrons. Our body is said to be charged because there is an electrically unbalanced condition between it and the car. But as soon as we touch or even come close to a bare metal part of the car, the extra electrons leave us and jump to the metal in the form of a spark. This accumulation and holding of electrical charges is called static electricity.

Lightning is just a big spark. Friction of the air moving up and down inside the clouds causes the water droplets in the clouds to become charged, and when enough electrons are concentrated in a cloud, the electrical pressure they produce forces them to flow through the air. These electrons jump between clouds having different charges or from a cloud to the ground. This is the gigantic spark called lightning.

As mentioned earlier, an object with an excess of electrons is negatively charged, and an object which has lost its electrons and wants to get them back is positively charged. Two positively charged or two negatively charged objects repel each other, while objects having opposite charges attract. When oppositely charged objects touch, the extra electrons travel from the negative object to the one with the positive charge. They become discharged, or electrically neutral.

alternating current. Electricity that continually changes its voltage and periodically reverses its direction of flow.

While static electricity has some uses, it is most often thought of as a nuisance. So we try to provide a path for the electrons to pass harmlessly from one charged object to another before the charges can build up enough pressure to spark.

In addition to giving us a mild shock when we touch the metal part of our car, static electricity can cause radio interference and can damage sensitive electronic components. It is possible, on a dry day, that just taking a few steps on a nylon carpet can build up more than 10,000 volts of static electricity on our body. This much charge can destroy delicate electronic circuit devices, and technicians should wear a grounded wrist strap to bleed off any static charge from their bodies before handling this type of equipment.

Many airplanes have static discharge points or wicks installed on the trailing edge of the control surfaces. These devices allow the static charges that build up on the control surfaces as air flows over them to discharge harmlessly into the air, thus preventing static interference in the radio equipment. *See* Figure 4-7.

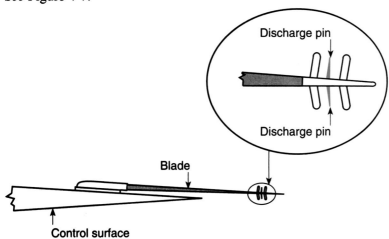

Figure 4-7. *Static discharge points are installed on the trailing edge of control surfaces to bleed off the static charges that are built up as air flows over the surfaces.*

Static electricity causes a serious fire hazard when aircraft are being fueled or defueled. The flow of gasoline or turbine fuel in the hose produces enough static electricity to cause a spark to jump and ignite explosive fumes. *See* Figure 4-8 on Page 152.

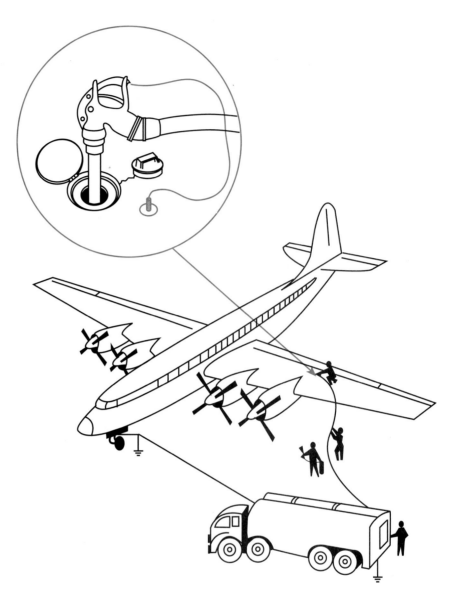

Figure 4-8. *Aircraft must be electrically grounded before they are fueled. Ground wires connect the aircraft and the fueling truck or pit together, and both of them are connected to the earth ground so that static charges that build up during fueling can pass harmlessly to the ground.*

Current Electricity

Current electricity is the form of electricity that has the most practical applications. A source of electrical energy such as a battery or generator acts as a pump that forces electrons to flow through conductors. This is the flow we call electron current. *See* Figure 4-9.

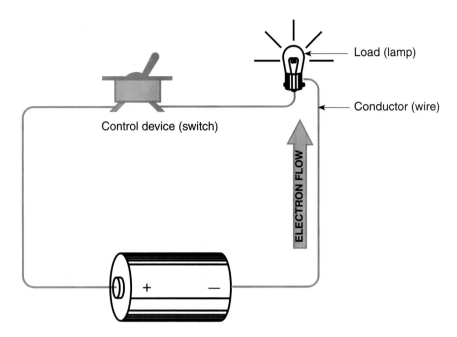

Load (lamp)

Conductor (wire)

Control device (switch)

ELECTRON FLOW

+ —

Figure 4-9. *This is a complete electrical circuit. When the switch is closed to complete the path, electrons are forced out of the battery by internal chemical action. Electrons move through the conductor to the lamp where they find so much friction, or opposition, that they get the filament white hot. After the electrons lose all of their pressure, they return to the positive terminal of the battery.*

In order for current to flow, there must be a complete path from one terminal of the source back to the other terminal. In Figure 4-9 observe the complete electrical circuit, with the battery as the source of electrical energy. Here, chemical energy is changed into electrical energy, and electrons are forced out of the negative terminal. Electrons flow through the conductor to the lamp, which acts as the load to change the electrical energy into heat and light. Then, the electrons continue through the conductor and the switch, which is the control device, back to the positive terminal of the battery. As long as the switch is closed, there is a complete path, electrons flow, and the lamp has energy to use.

The electrical pressure that forces the electrons to flow through the circuit is measured in volts, with the basic unit of electrical pressure being one volt. Electrical current is measured in amperes or, amps. One amp is the flow of one coulomb per second, and one coulomb is equal to 6.28 billion, billion (6.28 x 10^{18}) electrons. All conductors have some resistance which opposes the flow of electrons in much the same way that friction opposes mechanical movement. The basic unit of electrical resistance is the ohm. One volt of electrical pressure will force 1 amp of current to flow through 1 ohm of resistance.

ampere. A flow of current equal to one coulomb per second.

ohm (Ω). The basic unit of electrical resistance, or opposition, to current flow.

volt. The basic unit of electrical pressure. One volt is the amount of pressure required to force 1 ampere of current to flow through 1 ohm of resistance.

When current flows through a resistance, power is used and voltage is dropped. The voltage dropped across a resistor can be measured with a voltmeter in the same way as the voltage produced across the terminals of a battery. *See* Figure 4-10.

Electrical pressure caused by changing some other form of energy into electrical energy may be called an electromotive force, an EMF, a potential difference, or just a potential. Electrical pressure caused by current flowing through a resistance is not a source of electrical energy; it is a drop in the electrical pressure. This voltage is usually called a voltage drop or an IR drop. This is because the amount of drop may be found by multiplying the current by the resistance through which it flows. The terms voltage, potential, potential difference, electromotive force, EMF, and IR drop are often used interchangeably, and all of them use the volt as the basic unit of measurement.

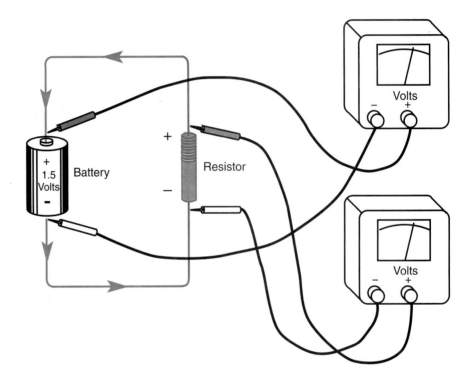

Figure 4-10. *A battery is a source of electrical pressure that may be spoken of as an EMF, electromotive force, potential, or potential difference. All are measured in volts, and all mean essentially the same thing.*

When current flows through the resistor, power is used and voltage is dropped. The voltage across a resistor can be measured with a voltmeter in the same way as the voltage produced by a battery. This voltage is caused by current (I) flowing through the resistor (R), and it is called an IR drop, or a voltage drop. The end of the resistor where the electron current enters is the negative end, and the end where it leaves is the positive end.

*Answers begin on Page 359. **Page numbers refer to chapter text.***

7. The accumulation and holding of electrical charges is called _____ electricity.
   Page 150

8. Electricity that makes use of the flow of electrons is called _____ electricity.
   Page 152

9. Electrons leave a source of electrical pressure at its _____ terminal and return at
   the _____ terminal. *Page 153*

10. The unit of electrical pressure is the _____ . *Page 153*

11. The unit of electrical current is the _____ . *Page 153*

12. The unit of electrical resistance is the _____ . *Page 153*

13. One _____ of electrical pressure will force one _____ of
    current flow through a resistance of one _____ . *Page 153*

Production of Electricity

Electricity is a form of energy, and we can neither create nor destroy it. But we can change other forms of energy into electricity, and we can also change electricity into these other forms.

Electricity from Heat

We can produce electricity with heat. A good example of this is the thermocouple system used to get an indication of the cylinder head temperature in an aircraft reciprocating engine. *See* Figure 4-11.

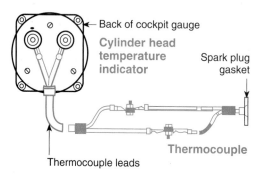

Figure 4-11. *A thermocouple made of two different kinds of wire produces electricity when one of its junctions is heated. The amount of current that flows is determined by the difference in the temperature between the hot and cold junctions, and by the resistance of the wires.*

A thermocouple is a loop made of two different kinds of wire welded together at one end to form a hot, or measuring, junction. The coil of a current-measuring instrument is connected between the wires at the other end to form a cold, or reference junction. This is seen in Figure 4-11. The hot junction is held against the cylinder head in the spark plug gasket, and a voltage is produced in the thermocouple whose amount is determined by the difference in temperature between the hot and cold junctions. This voltage difference causes a current to flow that is proportional to the temperature of the cylinder head.

Electricity from Chemical Action

Chemical energy can be changed into electricity. As we saw in the section on electron flow, a simple flashlight battery produces electricity in this way. A flashlight battery is made of a zinc can filled with a moist electrolyte paste, and a carbon rod is supported in the center of the paste so that it does not touch the can.

A chemical action between the electrolyte and the zinc changes the zinc into zinc chloride, and when this change takes place, electrons are released from the zinc. If a wire and an electric light bulb connect the zinc to the carbon rod, electrons will flow from the zinc to the carbon. The zinc can is the negative terminal of this battery, and the carbon rod is the positive terminal. *See Figure 4-12.*

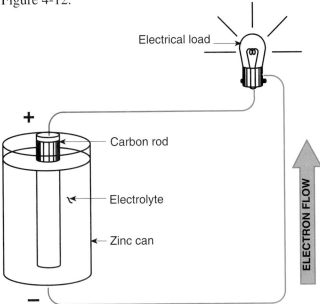

Figure 4-12. *A flashlight battery is a device that changes chemical energy into electricity. Chemical action changes the zinc of the can into zinc chloride, and when this change is made, electrons are released. When a wire connects the zinc can to the carbon rod, electrons flow from the can to the rod.*

Aircraft batteries are more complex, of course, than the simple flashlight battery. All of them are composed of secondary cells that can be recharged by forcing electrons from the engine-driven alternator or generator through them. Lead-acid and nickel-cadmium batteries are commonly used, and we will discuss both types of batteries at the appropriate point in this series.

Electricity from Pressure

When certain types of crystals are bent or distorted, an electrical pressure difference is built up across their opposite faces. This action is reversible, and pulses of electricity applied to the opposite faces of a crystal will cause it to distort. This is called a piezoelectric characteristic, and it allows crystals to be used in microphones and phonograph pickups. Because all physical bodies have a natural resonant frequency, a crystal having specific dimensions can be used to produce alternating current with an exact stable frequency for radio transmitters.

piezoelectric. The characteristic of certain materials that causes them to produce an electrical pressure when they are bent or twisted or when pressure is applied to them.

resonant frequency. The frequency of AC at which inductive and capacitive reactances are the same.

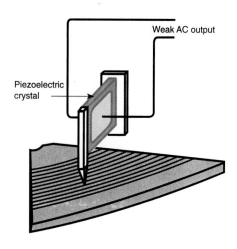

Figure 4-13. *A piece of crystal produces electricity when it is bent or twisted by the needle riding in the grooves of a phonograph record.*

Electrons move through the external circuit from one side of the crystal to the other. This weak flow of electrons is made stronger by an amplifier so that it can power a speaker.

Electricity is produced in a crystal phonograph pickup, as seen in Figure 4-13. A piece of quartz or Rochelle salt is mounted between two metal plates which hold the phonograph needle. These plates and the crystal are twisted or bent by the needle when it rides in the grooves of the phonograph record. When the crystal is bent, it forces electrons from one plate to the other.

Electrons travel through wires which carry them from one plate, through an outside circuit, back to the other plate as long as the crystal is being twisted. This current is very weak, and for practical use, must be amplified to increase the amount of current. Electricity produced by pressure is called piezo-electricity.

Electricity from Light

Light is another form of energy that can be changed into electricity. When certain chemical elements are exposed to light, they absorb energy from the light and release electrons. Photographic light meters use this type of energy exchange.

Today the space program has developed powerful solar cells that absorb light energy from the sun and release electrons used to power electrical devices. Solar cells can be activated by light from any source and are often used to power such devices as pocket calculators.

Electricity produced by light is called photoelectricity. *See* Figure 4-14.

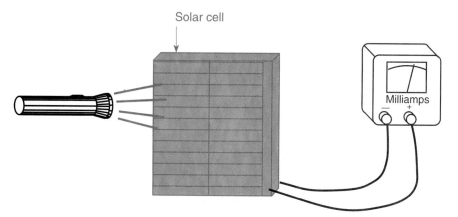

Figure 4-14. *When light strikes a solar cell, electrons are driven from it to produce a flow of current.*

Electricity from Magnetism

By far the most important exchange of energy is between magnetism and electricity. Invisible lines of magnetic force, called magnetic flux, pass between the poles of a magnet, and any time a conductor cuts across these lines of flux, electrons are forced to move through the conductor. *See* Figure 4-15.

Generators and alternators, driven by aircraft engines, rotate conductors through magnetic fields to produce electricity. Both produce alternating current, but in DC generators and alternators the AC is changed into DC before it leaves.

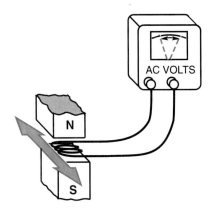

Figure 4-15. *When a coil of wire is moved back and forth so that it cuts across a magnetic field, electrons are forced to flow in the wire. This is the way almost all of the electricity used in aircraft electrical systems is produced.*

STUDY QUESTIONS: THE PRODUCTION OF ELECTRICITY

Answers begin on Page 359. Page numbers refer to chapter text.

14. Five forms of energy that can be converted into electricity are:
    a. _____
    b. _____
    c. _____
    d. _____
    e. _____
       Page 155

15. Electricity produced by chemical action is _____ (AC or DC). *Page 156*

16. Electricity produced by magnetism is _____ (AC or DC). *Page 158*

17. Electricity produced by pressure is _____ (AC or DC). *Page 157*

resistance (R). Opposition to the flow of electricity. Resistance is measured in ohms. It drops voltage, causes heat, and uses power.

power (P). The ability of an electrical device to produce work. The basic unit of electrical power is the watt, which is the product of current times the voltage that causes the current to flow.

watt (W). The basic unit of electrical power.

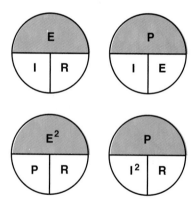

Figure 4-16. *Relationship between voltage, current, resistance, and power in an electrical circuit. The top quantity is equal to the product of the two bottom quantities, and one bottom quantity is equal to the top quantity divided by the other bottom quantity.*

Electrical Relationships

Voltage, current, resistance, and power are all characteristics of electricity, and one important law proposed by the German physicist Georg Simon Ohm, who lived between 1787 and 1854, shows how these characteristics are related. This law, known as Ohm's law, ties all of these characteristics together in such a way that when we know any two of the values, we can find the others.

Ohm's Law

Electrical pressure is measured in volts, current is measured in amps, and resistance is measured in ohms, and one volt of pressure will force one amp of current through one ohm of resistance.

Our main use of electricity is to perform work, and in order to do work, power is needed. The unit of electrical power is the watt, and one watt is the amount of power produced when one amp of current is pushed along by a pressure of one volt.

Mechanical power is the rate of doing work, and its basic unit in the U.S. system is the horsepower—the amount of power needed to lift 33,000 pounds of weight one foot in one minute, or 550 pounds of weight one foot in one second. Electrical power can be changed directly into mechanical power, since 746 watts of electrical power is equal to one horsepower.

To use these electrical values in formulas, letters are assigned to each of them. Voltage is represented by the letter E, which stands for electromotive force. The symbol for current is the letter I, which comes from the intensity of the current. R is used for the resistance, and P is used for power.

Ohm's law says that the current flowing in a circuit is directly proportional to the applied voltage—the more voltage, the more current. And inversely proportional to the resistance through which the current flows—the more resistance, the less current. This may be stated by the formula:

$$I = \frac{E}{R}$$

The Ohm's law relationships are easy to see with the circles in Figure 4-16. The value in the top half of each circle is equal to the two bottom values multiplied together, and either of the two bottom values may be found by dividing the top value by the other value on the bottom.

The four circles in Figure 4-16 produce twelve formulas, and if we know any two values and use these formulas, we can find any other value.

$E = I \cdot R$	$P = I \cdot E$	$E = \sqrt{P \cdot R}$	$P = I^2 \cdot R$
$I = E \div R$	$I = P \div E$	$P = E^2 \div R$	$I = \sqrt{P \div R}$
$R = E \div I$	$E = P \div I$	$R = E^2 \div P$	$R = P \div I^2$

Examples of Ohm's Law Problems

1. Find the voltage needed to force 10 amps through a resistance of 20 ohms. Use the formula:

    $E = I \cdot R$

    $= 10 \cdot 20$

    $= 200$ volts

2. Find the amount of current that 24 volts can force through a resistance of 144 ohms. Use the formula:

    $I = E \div R$

    $= 24 \div 144$

    $= 0.167$ amp

3. Find the amount of resistance needed to drop 6 volts when 3 amps is flowing. Use the formula:

    $R = E \div I$

    $= 6 \div 3$

    $= 2$ ohms

4. Find the amount of power used when 4 amps is being forced through 16 ohms of resistance. Use the formula:

    $P = I^2 \cdot R$

    $= 4^2 \cdot 16$

    $= 256$ watts

5. Find the voltage needed to produce 100 watts of power when 6 amps is flowing. Use the formula:

    $E = P \div I$

    $= 100 \div 6$

    $= 16.7$ volts

6. Find the amount of current that must flow under a pressure of 6 volts to produce 48 watts of power. Use the formula:

    $I = P \div E$

    $= 48 \div 6$

    $= 8$ amps

7. Find the amount of resistance in a circuit in which 100 volts is producing 200 watts of power. Use the formula:

    $R = E^2 \div P$

    $= 100^2 \div 200$

    $= 50$ ohms

8. Find the amount of power developed when 24 volts forces 6 amps to flow in a circuit. Use the formula:

    $P = I \cdot E$

    $= 6 \cdot 24$

    $= 144$ watts

9. Find the voltage needed to produce 100 watts of power when the resistance is 25 ohms. Use the formula:

    $E = \sqrt{P \cdot R}$

    $= \sqrt{100 \cdot 25}$

    $= \sqrt{2,500}$

    $= 50$ volts

10. Find the amount of current needed to produce 60 watts of power in a circuit having a resistance of 20 ohms. Use the formula:

    $I = \sqrt{P \div R}$

    $= \sqrt{60 \div 20}$

    $= \sqrt{3}$

    $= 1.73$ amps

11. Find the amount of resistance needed for 16 amps of current to produce 800 watts of power. Use the formula:

    $R = P \div I^2$

    $= 800 \div 16^2$

    $= 800 \div 256$

    $= 3.12$ ohm

Continued

12. Find the amount of power produced when 120 volts are applied to a resistance of 6 ohms. Use the formula:

$$P = E^2 \div R$$
$$= 120^2 \div 6$$
$$= 14{,}400 \div 6$$
$$= 2{,}400 \text{ watts}$$

13. Find the electrical power equivalent of 6 horsepower. Use the formula:

$$P = HP \cdot 746$$
$$= 6 \cdot 746$$
$$= 4{,}476 \text{ watts}$$

14. Find the electrical power required to produce 6 horsepower if the motor is 75% efficient. Use the formula:

$$P = (HP \cdot 746) \div \% \text{ efficiency}$$
$$= (6 \cdot 746) \div .75$$
$$= 5{,}968 \text{ watts}$$

Metric Prefixes

Up to this point, we have been working with basic units of electricity. But we will not always be dealing with these easy-to-handle numbers. We must often work with very small or very large numbers.

1,000,000,000,000	10^{12}	TERA
1,000,000,000	10^{9}	GIGA
1,000,000	10^{6}	MEGA
1,000	10^{3}	KILO
100	10^{2}	HECTO
10	10^{1}	DEKA
1	$\mathbf{10^{0}}$	**UNIT**
0.1	10^{-1}	DECI
0.01	10^{-2}	CENTI
0.001	10^{-3}	MILLI
0.000 001	10^{-6}	MICRO
0.000 000 001	10^{-9}	NANO
0.000 000 000 001	10^{-12}	PICO

Figure 4-17. *Scientific notation and metric prefixes*

Fortunately, we have methods of handling both of these extremes. We can use a form of metric prefixes, and as in all metric values, these prefixes work in multiples of ten. In Figure 4-17 we see the most commonly used prefixes and powers of ten.

Let's begin with numbers greater than one and see the way these prefixes work. When talking about a distance of 120,000 meters, it is convenient to call it 120 kilometers. The prefix kilo means thousand. In the same way, 250,000,000 hertz is called 250 megahertz, because mega means million. This works the same way with numbers smaller than one. One millimeter is 0.001 meter, 1 microfarad is 0.000 001 farad, 1 nanosecond is 0.000 000 001 second, and one picofarad is 0.000 000 000 001 farad.

kilo (k). The metric prefix meaning 1,000.

mega (M). The metric prefix meaning 1,000,000.

milli (m). The metric prefix meaning 1/1,000, or 0.001.

micro (μ). The metric prefix meaning 1/1,000,000, or 0.000 001.

STUDY QUESTIONS: ELECTRICAL RELATIONSHIPS

Answers begin on Page 359. Page numbers refer to chapter text.

18. Find the amount of power used by each of these components:
    a. A 12-volt motor requiring 8 amperes = _____ watts.
    b. Four 30-watt lamps in a 12-volt parallel circuit = _____ watts.
    c. Two lights requiring 3 amperes each in a 24-volt parallel system = _____ watts.
    d. A $\frac{1}{10}$-horsepower, 24-volt motor which is 75% efficient = _____ watts.
    Page 160

19. A circuit contains 5 lamps in parallel. Three lamps have a hot resistance of 6 ohms each, and 2 have a hot resistance of 5 ohms each. A 28-volt generator will have to supply _____ amps to this circuit. *Page 160*

20. The potential difference between two conductors insulated from each other is measured in _____ . *Page 153*

21. When .05 ampere flows through a 14-ohm resistor, _____ watts of power is dissipated. This is _____ milliwatts. *Page 160*

22. a. The basic measure of electrical pressure is the _____ .
    b. The basic measure of electrical power is the _____ .
    c. The basic measure of electrical current flow is the _____ .
    Page 153

Continued

23. The hot resistance of a 30-watt light bulb operating in a 28-volt electrical system is
_____ ohms. *Page 160*

24. Two things that affect the voltage drop across a conductor are:
   a. _____
   b. _____
   Page 160

25. Use the correct metric prefixes to express these terms:
   a. 1,000 hertz = 1 _____ hertz
   b. 476,000,000 hertz = 476 _____ hertz
   c. 0.01 meter = 1 _____ meter
   d. 0.009 watt = 9 _____ watt
   e. 0.000 004 farad = 4 _____ farad
   Page 163

Direct Current Electricity

Direct current, or DC electricity is of great importance to us because it is easy to generate and can be stored for future use. In DC electricity, the electrons flow in one direction all of the time, while in alternating current, or AC electricity, they periodically reverse their direction.

Electricity produced by chemical action, light, and heat are all direct current, while that produced by pressure and magnetism are alternating current.

Direct Current Circuits

One of the best ways to learn the practical applications of electricity is to study DC circuits. All complete circuits must have three things: a source of electrical power, a load to use this power, and conductors to connect the source to the load. In this study we will consider simple series circuits in which there is only one path for the electrons, parallel circuits which contain more than one path, and complex circuits that contain both series and parallel sections.

Series Circuits

A series circuit is one in which there is only one path for the current to flow from one terminal of the voltage source to the other. To understand a series DC circuit, we must be able to measure the values of voltage, current, resistance, and power in the circuit. This is normally done with a multimeter. This handy instrument is sometimes called a VOM because it measures volts, ohms, and milliamps. The multimeter does not measure power directly; rather it measures voltage, current, and resistance that allows power to be computed using an Ohm's law formula.

Assume a simple series circuit made up of two flashlight batteries in series as the power source, and a three-volt bulb as the load. The pictorial diagram of Figure 4-18A shows the way the connections are made, and the schematic diagram of Figure 4-18B shows the way circuits are usually drawn. The batteries are represented by a series of long and short lines, with the longer lines representing the positive terminal. The circle with the loop in it represents the lamp.

series circuit. An electrical circuit in which the components are arranged in such a way that there is only one path from one terminal of the power source to the other terminal.

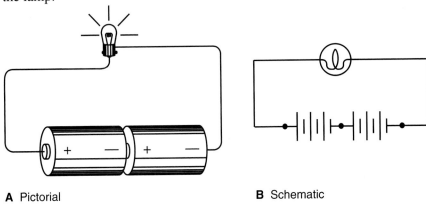

A Pictorial

B Schematic

Figure 4-18
A. A pictorial diagram of an electrical circuit
B. A schematic diagram of an electrical circuit

The multimeter has several scales for voltage, resistance, and current. When connecting the meter into the circuit, be sure to select a scale that is higher than the expected voltage or current. This prevents damage to the meter. When the meter is connected, turn the selector switch back to a range that allows the indicating needle to move up to about mid-scale, since this is where the meter is most accurate.

To measure the current we must open, or break, the circuit and use the meter leads to restore it. Select the highest current range, and connect the positive lead of the meter to the open end of the circuit connected to the positive terminal of the battery. Connect the negative lead of the meter to the bulb at the point the wire from the battery was connected. This is a series circuit, and the current has only one path through which it can flow, so the current can be measured at any point there is a break in the circuit.

We cannot measure the resistance of the bulb directly because it changes so much when it heats up. A measurement taken when the bulb is cold will not tell anything about its resistance when it is hot. So, to find the resistance, use Ohm's law.

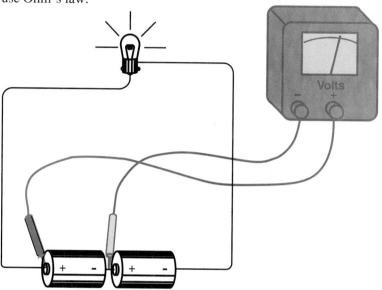

Figure 4-19. *Method of measuring voltage*

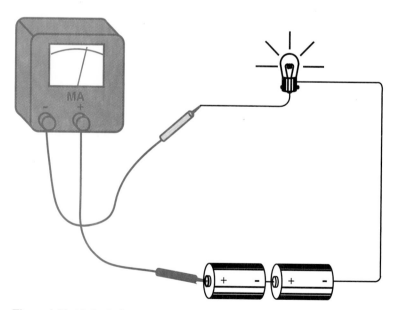

Figure 4-20. *Method of measuring current*

Assume that the 3 volts of electrical pressure in our batteries forces 0.46 amp (460 milliamps) of current through the bulb. According to Ohm's law the resistance of the bulb when it is hot is 6.52 ohms.

$$R = \frac{E}{I}$$

$$= \frac{3}{0.46}$$

$$= 6.52 \text{ ohms}$$

Compute the power used by the bulb by using this formula:

$$P = E \cdot I$$

$$= 3 \cdot 0.46$$

$$= 1.38 \text{ watt}$$

When the two batteries are in series, their voltages add, but they can supply only as much current as one battery.

Analysis of a Series Circuit

It is important in any study of electricity to be able to analyze electrical circuits. This means that we should be able to find the amount of current flowing through any resistance, the voltage dropped across any resistance, and the amount of power that is being used, or dissipated, by the resistance. We will look at several circuits to see the rules to follow when analyzing a circuit.

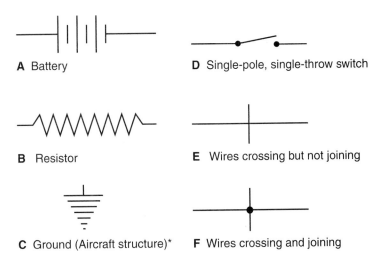

A Battery

D Single-pole, single-throw switch

B Resistor

E Wires crossing but not joining

C Ground (Aircraft structure)*

F Wires crossing and joining

* This is used to show that there is a return path for the current between the source of electrical energy and the load. Aircraft use the structure as a common ground.

Figure 4-21. *Typical symbols used in electrical schematic diagrams*

The symbols used here are the ones used in almost all electrical schematic diagrams. For the source of electrical energy, use the battery symbol which is a series of alternating long and short lines. There is no standard number of long and short lines to be used, but the long line always represents the positive terminal. The voltage of the source should be written beside the symbol.

For analysis of DC circuits, use a zigzag line, the symbol for a resistor, to represent the electrical load. Resistors oppose the flow of electrons, and they have a certain amount of resistance, measured in ohms. Since they use power when they oppose the flow of electrons, resistors get hot. We must know the amount of power that is used by each resistor to know the amount of power used in the entire circuit.

Figure 4-22 is a schematic diagram of a simple series circuit using a 6-volt battery as the source of electrical energy. This source supplies power to a 6-ohm, a 12-ohm, and an 18-ohm resistor connected in series. We want to find the total current flowing in the circuit, the amount of voltage dropped across each resistor, the amount of power used in each resistor, and the total amount of power used in the circuit.

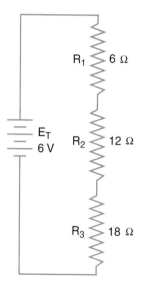

Component	Resistance Ohms	Voltage Volts	Current Amps	Power Watts
R_1	6	1	0.167	0.167
R_2	12	2	0.167	0.334
R_3	18	3	0.167	0.502
Total	36	6	0.167	1.000

Figure 4-22. *Analysis of a simple series DC circuit*

To make it easy to follow all of the steps in our circuit analysis, we will use subscripts. E_T, I_T, R_T, and P_T are the total values of voltage, current resistance and power. When a number is placed beside the letters E, I, R, or P it refers to these values as they apply to a specific resistor. For example E_3 is the voltage drop across resistor R_3, I_4 is the current through resistor R_4, and P_6 is the power dissipated in resistor R6.

Begin by finding the total resistance of the circuit. Unless it is specifically mentioned, do not consider the resistance of the wires used in the circuit or the resistance of the battery. The total resistance of the three resistors in series is the sum of the resistance of the individual resistors:

$$R_T = R_1 + R_2 + R_3$$
$$= 6 + 12 + 18$$
$$= 36 \text{ ohms}$$

We can find the total current by dividing the total voltage by the total resistance:

$$I_T = \frac{E_T}{R_T}$$

$$= \frac{6}{36}$$

$$= 0.167 \text{ amp}$$

This gives us a total current of 0.167 amp, or 167 milliamps, and since this is a series circuit, and there is only one path from the negative terminal of the battery back to the positive terminal, all the current flows through each resistor. Find the amount of voltage dropped across each resistor by multiplying the amount of current flowing through the resistor, measured in amps, by the resistance of the resistor, in ohms:

$$E_1 = I_T \cdot R_1 \qquad E_2 = I_T \cdot R_2 \qquad E_3 = I_T \cdot R_3$$
$$= 0.167 \cdot 6 \qquad = 0.167 \cdot 12 \qquad = 0.167 \cdot 18$$
$$= 1.0 \text{ volt} \qquad = 2.0 \text{ volts} \qquad = 3.0 \text{ volts}$$

One volt is dropped across resistor R_1, 2 volts are dropped across resistor R_2, and 3 volts are dropped across resistor R_3. The total voltage dropped across the 3 resistors is 6 volts, which is the same as the voltage of the battery.

This proves one of the laws of circuit analysis, Kirchhoff's voltage law, which tells us that the sum of the voltage drops around any complete circuit that joins one end of a battery with the other end is the same as the voltage of the battery.

Kirchhoff's voltage law. The sum of the voltage drops in a series circuit is equal to the voltage of the source.

We can find the amount of power used by each of the resistors by multiplying the value of the resistor in ohms, by the square of the current in amps flowing through the resistor:

$$P_1 = I^2 \cdot R_1 \qquad P_2 = I^2 \cdot R_2 \qquad P_3 = I^2 \cdot R_3$$
$$= 0.167^2 \cdot 6 \qquad = 0.167^2 \cdot 12 \qquad = 0.167^2 \cdot 18$$
$$= 0.167 \text{ watt} \qquad = 0.334 \text{ watt} \qquad = 0.502 \text{ watt}$$

Find the power used in the circuit by adding the amount of power used by each resistor. We can also find the total amount of power used in the circuit by multiplying the total circuit resistance by the square of the current, or by multiplying the total voltage by the total current.

$$P_T = P_1 + P_2 + P_3 \qquad\qquad P_T = I_T^2 \cdot R_T$$
$$= 0.167 + 0.334 + 0.502 \qquad = 0.167^2 \cdot 36$$
$$= 1.00 \text{ watt} \qquad\qquad = 1.00 \text{ watt}$$

$$P_T = I \cdot E$$
$$= 0.167 \cdot 6$$
$$= 1.00 \text{ watt}$$

If we know the resistance of all of the resistors in a series DC circuit and the voltage drop across any one resistor, we can find the total voltage and the power used in the circuit. Figure 4-23 shows this.

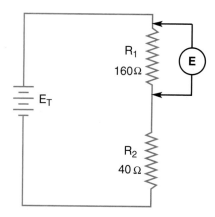

Component	Resistance Ohms	Voltage Volts	Current Amps	Power Watts
R_1	160	120	0.75	90
R_2	40	30	0.75	22.5
Total	200	150	0.75	112.5

Figure 4-23. *Finding the source voltage in a series DC circuit*

One hundred and twenty volts are dropped across the 160-ohm resistor R_1. By dividing this voltage by the resistance, we find the current through this resistor to be 750 milliamps. Since this is a series circuit, the total current is 750 milliamps. When this current flows through the 40-ohm resistor R_2, it will produce a voltage drop of 30 volts. The total voltage across this circuit is the sum of these two voltage drops, or 150 volts. The total power, found by multiplying the total current by the total voltage, is 112.5 watts.

$$I_1 = \frac{E_1}{R_1} \qquad E_2 = I_T \cdot R_2 \qquad E_T = E_1 + E_2 \qquad P_T = I_T \cdot E_T$$

$$= \frac{120}{160} \qquad = 0.75 \cdot 40 \qquad = 120 + 30 \qquad = 0.75 \cdot 150$$

$$= 0.75 \text{ amp} \qquad = 30 \text{ volts} \qquad = 150 \text{ volts} \qquad = 112.5 \text{ watts}$$

STUDY QUESTIONS: SERIES DC CIRCUITS

Answers begin on Page 359. Page numbers refer to chapter text.

26. When batteries are connected in series, the total voltage is the _____ of the individual battery voltages. *Page 165*

27. When connecting two batteries in series, the positive terminal of one battery is connected to the _____ terminal of the other. *Page 165*

28. The symbol for a battery is a series of alternate long and short lines. The long line identifies the _____ (positive or negative) terminal. *Page 168*

29. The resistance of a light bulb may be found by _____ (multiplying or dividing) the voltage across the bulb by the current through it. *Page 166*

30. The power used by a bulb may be found by _____ (multiplying or dividing) the voltage across the bulb by the current through it. *Page 167*

Parallel Circuits

There are two basic ways in which components in an electrical circuit can be connected: in series and in parallel. In a series circuit, there is only one path for the current to flow from one terminal of the voltage source back to the other terminal, but in a parallel circuit, there may be any number of paths the current can follow between the terminals of the voltage source. Of the two arrangements, there are a lot more practical circuits connected in parallel than in series. For instance, in an aircraft electrical system, the lights, radio, starter, and the alternator are all connected in parallel across the battery. *See* Figure 4-24.

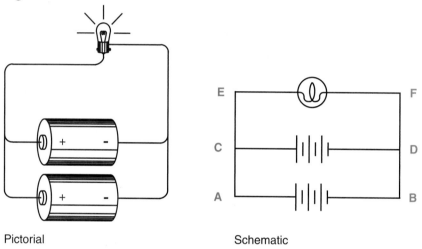

Pictorial   Schematic

Figure 4-24. *Pictorial and schematic diagrams of a parallel circuit.*

Let's begin our study of parallel circuits in the same way as the study of series circuits, by considering a circuit made up of two flashlight batteries and a bulb. This time, arrange the batteries in parallel. Connect the positive terminals of the batteries together, with the bulb connected in parallel with them.

Measure the voltage across the batteries, between points A and B, and between points C and D. Also measure it across the bulb at points E and F. Since this is a parallel circuit, the three voltage measurements will be the same.

The bulb will be very dim, compared with its brilliance when the batteries were in series. This is because there is only one-half the voltage needed to force the electrons through the filament of the bulb.

To measure the current, open the circuit at the bulb at either point E or F, and insert the test leads to complete the circuit. With the voltage and current both known, we can compute the resistance of the bulb and the power used in the circuit.

When batteries are connected in series, the voltage is the sum of the individual voltages, and all of the current must pass through each of the batteries. But, when the batteries are connected in parallel, the total voltage is the same as that of one battery. Each battery furnishes about half of the current. The total current is more than half of what it is when the batteries are in series, because the resistance of the bulb is less when the batteries are in parallel. The resistance of the bulb increases as it gets hot; and it gets hotter when more current is pushed through it.

Analysis of a Parallel Circuit

Before going to more complex DC circuits, let's analyze a simple parallel circuit. Here are some facts that will help when we study parallel circuits:

1. The voltage across all of the components in a parallel circuit is the same, and it is the same as the voltage of the source.

2. The total current is the sum of all of the currents that flow in the branches of the circuit.

3. The total resistance of the circuit is less than that of the smallest resistor that is connected in parallel.

Figure 4-25 shows a simple parallel circuit made up of a 12-volt battery with three 24-ohm resistors connected in parallel across it. The current through each resistor is found by dividing the battery voltage by the resistance of each resistor.

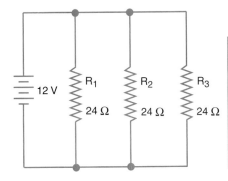

Component	Resistance Ohms	Voltage Volts	Current Amps	Power Watts
R_1	24	12	0.5	6
R_2	24	12	0.5	6
R_3	24	12	0.5	6
Total	8	12	1.5	18

Figure 4-25. *Analysis of a simple parallel circuit*

One-half amp, or 500 milliamps, flows through each resistor, therefore the total current through all three is 1.5 amps. Find the total resistance by dividing the battery voltage by the total current. This gives a total resistance of eight ohms which is less than the resistance of any of the three resistors.

$$I = \frac{E}{R}$$

$$= \frac{12}{24}$$

$$= 0.5 \text{ amp or } 500 \text{ milliamp}$$

One-half amp, or 500 milliamps, flows through each resistor, therefore the total current through all three is 1.5 amps. Find the total resistance by dividing the battery voltage by the total current. This gives a total resistance of eight ohms which is less than the resistance of any of the three resistors.

$$R = \frac{E}{I}$$

$$= \frac{12}{1.5}$$

$$= 8 \text{ ohms}$$

Find the power used in each resistor by multiplying the battery voltage by the current through each resistor. Six watts of power is used in each resistor. The total power is found by multiplying the battery voltage by the total current, and this is 18 watts.

$$P = I \cdot E$$
$$= 1.5 \cdot 12$$
$$= 18 \text{ watts}$$

When resistors are connected in parallel, they provide a path for the current through each resistor. And the total resistance is less than that of any one of the resistors in the combination. If all of the resistors have the same value, the total resistance may be found by dividing the resistance of one of the resistors by the number of resistors:

$$R_T = \frac{R}{n}$$

When there are two unequal resistors in parallel, their total resistance may be found by dividing the product of the two resistors by their sum:

$$R_T = \frac{R_1 \cdot R_2}{R_1 + R_2}$$

When the total resistance and the resistance of one of the two resistors are known, the value of the other resistor may be found by the formula:

$$R_1 = \frac{R_2 \cdot R_T}{R_2 - R_T}$$

The equivalent resistance of more than two resistors may also be found by combining them two at a time, using the product divided by the sum method:

$$R_A = \frac{R_1 \cdot R_2}{R_1 + R_2} \quad \text{and} \quad R_B = \frac{R_3 \cdot R_4}{R_3 + R_4}$$

Now, combine the two equivalent resistances to get the total equivalent resistance:

$$R_T = \frac{R_A \cdot R_B}{R_A + R_B}$$

The equivalent resistance of more than two resistors in parallel may also be found by the formula:

$$R_T = \frac{1}{\dfrac{1}{R_1} + \dfrac{1}{R_2} + \dfrac{1}{R_3} + \dfrac{1}{R_4}}$$

This last formula is somewhat awkward to work with, but if you have a calculator with the reciprocal key, a 1/x key, you can quite easily find the equivalent resistance of any number of resistors in parallel. Enter the problem into the calculator in this way:

$$(R_1)(1/x) + (R_2)(1/x) + (R_3)(1/x) + (R_4)(1/x) = (1/x)$$

By entering the problem into the calculator in this manner, you can find the total equivalent resistance of any number of resistors in parallel.

Answers begin on Page 359. Page numbers refer to chapter text.

31. The ohmmeter in the figure below reads _____ ohms. *Page 173*

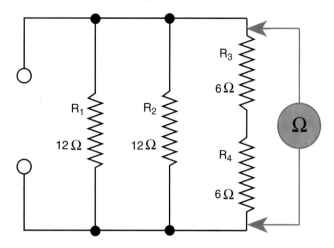

32. Fill in the missing values using the circuit in the figure below. *Page 175*

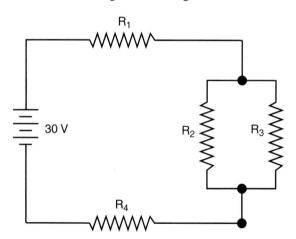

Volts	Ohms	Amps	Watts
$E_1 =$	$R_1 = 10$	$I_1 =$	$P_1 =$
$E_2 =$	$R_2 = 20$	$I_2 =$	$P_2 =$
$E_3 =$	$R_3 = 20$	$I_3 =$	$P_3 =$
$E_4 =$	$R_4 = 10$	$I_4 =$	$P_4 =$
$E_T = 30$	$R_T =$	$I_T =$	$P_T =$

33. When batteries are connected in parallel, the positive terminal of one is connected to the _____ (positive or negative) terminal of the other. *Page 172*

34. When two similar batteries are connected in parallel, the current supplied by each battery is approximately one-_____ of the total current. *Page 172*

35. Find the total resistance of each combination of resistors in series:
    a. R_T = _____ ohms.
    b. R_T = _____ ohms.
    c. R_T = _____ ohms.

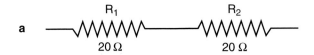

Page 173

36. Find the equivalent resistance of these resistors in parallel.
    a. R_T = _____ ohms.
    b. R_T = _____ ohms.
    c. R_T = _____ ohms.

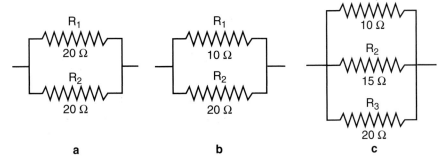

Page 175

Series-Parallel Circuits

If several resistors are connected in a complex arrangement, with some in parallel and others in series, we can find the current through each resistor, the voltage drop across each of them, and the power used in each resistor. To do this, combine series and parallel groups of resistors into their equivalent resistances. *See* Figure 4-26.

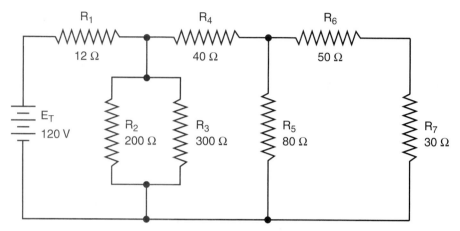

Figure 4-26. *Analysis of a complex circuit, with some resistors connected in series and others connected in parallel*

In order to find the voltage, current, and power associated with each resistor in Figure 4-26, find the equivalent total resistance of the circuit, then find the total current. When the total current is known, all of the other values can be found.

1. Combine R_6 and R_7 to find the equivalent series resistance R_{6-7}.

$$R_{6-7} = R_6 + R_7$$
$$= 50 + 30$$
$$= 80 \text{ ohms}$$

2. Combine R_{6-7} in parallel with R_5.

$$R_{5-6-7} = \frac{R_{6-7} \cdot R_5}{R_{6-7} + R_5}$$
$$= \frac{80 \cdot 80}{80 + 80}$$
$$= \frac{6400}{160}$$
$$= 40 \text{ ohms}$$

3. Add $R_{5\text{-}6\text{-}7}$ to R_4 in series.

$$R_{4\text{-}5\text{-}6\text{-}7} = R_4 + R_{5\text{-}6\text{-}7}$$
$$= 40 + 40$$
$$= 80 \text{ ohms}$$

4. Find the equivalent of R_2 and R_3 in parallel.

$$R_{2\text{-}3} = \frac{R_2 \cdot R_3}{R_2 + R_3}$$
$$= \frac{200 \cdot 300}{200 + 300}$$
$$= \frac{60,000}{500}$$
$$= 120 \text{ ohms}$$

5. Combine $R_{4\text{-}5\text{-}6\text{-}7}$ in parallel with $R_{2\text{-}3}$.

$$R_{2\text{-}3\text{-}4\text{-}5\text{-}6\text{-}7} = \frac{R_{2\text{-}3} \cdot R_{4\text{-}5\text{-}6\text{-}7}}{R_{2\text{-}3} + R_{4\text{-}5\text{-}6\text{-}7}}$$
$$= \frac{120 \cdot 80}{120 + 80}$$
$$= \frac{9600}{200}$$
$$= 48 \text{ ohms}$$

6. Add $R_{2\text{-}3\text{-}4\text{-}5\text{-}6\text{-}7}$ to R_1 in series. This is the equivalent total resistance, R_T.

$$R_T = R_1 + R_{2\text{-}3\text{-}4\text{-}5\text{-}6\text{-}7}$$
$$= 12 + 48$$
$$= 60 \text{ ohms}$$

7. Find the total current.

$$I_T = \frac{E_T}{R_T}$$
$$= \frac{120}{60}$$
$$= 2.0 \text{ amps}$$

8. Find the voltage drop across R_1.

$$E_1 = I_T \cdot R_1$$
$$= 2.0 \cdot 12$$
$$= 24 \text{ volts}$$

9. Find the current through R_1.

$$I_1 = \frac{E_1}{R_1}$$
$$= \frac{24}{12}$$
$$= 2.0 \text{ amps}$$

10. Find the voltage drop across R_2 and R_3.

$$E_{2\text{-}3} = E_T - E_1$$
$$= 120 - 24$$
$$= 96 \text{ volts}$$

11. Find the current through R_2.

$$I_2 = \frac{E_2}{R_2}$$
$$= \frac{96}{200}$$
$$= 0.48 \text{ amp}$$

12. Find the current through R_3.

$$I_3 = \frac{E_3}{R_3}$$
$$= \frac{96}{300}$$
$$= 0.32 \text{ amp}$$

13. Find the current through R_4.

$$I_4 = I_T - (I_2 + I_3)$$
$$= 2.0 - (0.48 + 0.32)$$
$$= 2.0 - 0.8$$
$$= 1.2 \text{ amps}$$

14. Find the voltage drop across R_4.

$$E_4 = I_4 \cdot R_4$$
$$= 1.2 \cdot 40$$
$$= 48 \text{ volts}$$

15. Find the voltage drop across R_5.

$$E_5 = E_T - (E_1 + E_4)$$
$$= 120 - (24 + 48)$$
$$= 120 - 72$$
$$= 48 \text{ volts}$$

16. Find the current through R_5.

$$I_5 = \frac{E_5}{R_5}$$
$$= \frac{48}{80}$$
$$= 0.6 \text{ amp}$$

17. Find the current through R_6 and R_7.

$$I_{6-7} = I_4 - I_5$$
$$= 1.2 - 0.6$$
$$= 0.6 \text{ amp}$$

18. Find the voltage drop across R_6.

$$E_6 = I_6 \cdot R_6$$
$$= 0.6 \cdot 50$$
$$= 30 \text{ volts}$$

19. Find the voltage drop across R_7.

$$E_7 = I_7 \cdot R_7$$
$$= 0.6 \cdot 30$$
$$= 18 \text{ volts}$$

20. Find the power used in each resistor.

$$P_1 = I_1^2 \cdot R_1$$
$$= 2.0^2 \cdot 12$$
$$= 48.0 \text{ watts}$$

$$P_2 = I_2^2 \cdot R_2$$
$$= 0.48^2 \cdot 200$$
$$= 46.1 \text{ watts}$$

$$P_3 = I_3^2 \cdot R_3$$
$$= 0.32^2 \cdot 300$$
$$= 30.7 \text{ watts}$$

$$P_4 = I_4^2 \cdot R_4$$
$$= 1.2^2 \cdot 40$$
$$= 57.6 \text{ watts}$$

$$P_5 = I_5^2 \cdot R_5$$
$$= 0.6^2 \cdot 80$$
$$= 28.8 \text{ watts}$$

$$P_6 = I_6^2 \cdot R_6$$
$$= 0.6^2 \cdot 50$$
$$= 18.0 \text{ watts}$$

$$P_7 = I_7^2 \cdot R_7$$
$$= 0.6^2 \cdot 30$$
$$= 10.8 \text{ watts}$$

21. The total power is equal to the sum of the power used in each resistor:

$$P_T = P_1 + P_2 + P_3 + P_4 + P_5 + P_6 + P_7$$
$$= 48.0 + 46.1 + 30.7 + 57.6 + 18.0 + 10.8$$
$$= 240 \text{ watts}$$

Kirchhoff's Laws

Two other laws besides Ohm's law are important when working with electrical circuits. These are Kirchhoff's voltage law and Kirchhoff's current law.

Kirchhoff's voltage law states that the algebraic sum of the voltages around any loop (or closed circuit) is equal to zero.

Study the circuit in Figure 4-27, and find the loops:

E_T, R_1, and R_2 is one loop, and $+120 + (-24) + (-96)$ is equal to zero.

E_T, R_1, and R_3 is another loop, and $+120 + (-24) + (-96)$ is equal to zero.

E_T, R_1, R_4, R_5 is another loop, and $+120 + (-24) + (-48) + (-48)$ is equal to zero.

The final loop is E_T, R_1, R_4, R_6, and R_7. In this loop, $120 + (-24) + (-48) + (-30) + (-18)$ is equal to zero.

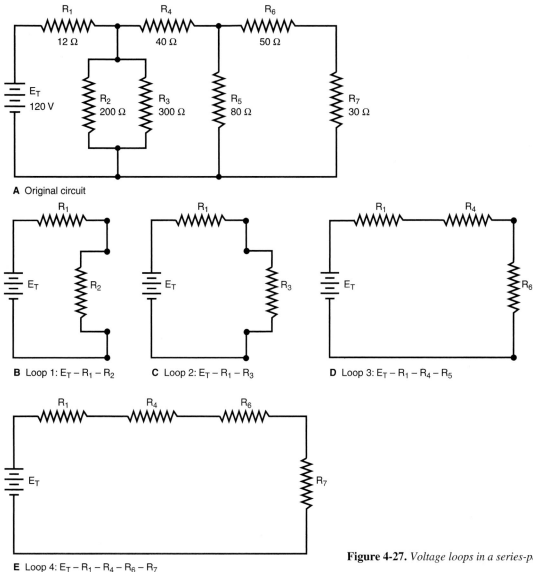

A Original circuit

B Loop 1: $E_T - R_1 - R_2$

C Loop 2: $E_T - R_1 - R_3$

D Loop 3: $E_T - R_1 - R_4 - R_5$

E Loop 4: $E_T - R_1 - R_4 - R_6 - R_7$

Figure 4-27. *Voltage loops in a series-parallel circuit*

Kirchhoff's current law says that the current leaving any point is equal to the current arriving at that point.

The two amps of current flowing through resistor R_1 splits and goes through R_2, R_3, and R_4. The 1.2 amps that flow through resistor R_4 from R_1 divides, with 0.6 amp flowing through R_5 and the 0.6 amp flowing through R_6. *See* Figure 4-28.

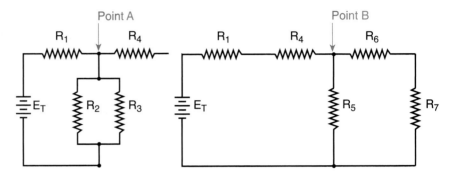

Figure 4-28. *Current branches in a series-parallel circuit.*
Point A: Current arriving = I_1 = 2.0 amps
*   Current leaving = $I_2 + I_3 + I_4$ = 0.48 + 0.32 + 1.2 = 2.0 amps*
Point B: Current arriving = I_4 =1.2 amp
*   Current leaving = $I_5 + I_{6-7}$ = 0.6 amp + 0.6 amp = 1.2 amps*

Circuits with Two Power Sources

Sometimes a DC circuit has two or more power sources, and we must find the current through, and the voltage drop across, the resistors that are connected across both sources. A common example of this type of circuit is the typical aircraft electrical system. The generator is the primary source of electrical power, but the battery is connected in parallel with the generator.

One of the simplest ways of finding the voltage, current, and power in a circuit with two power sources is:

1.   Imagine that source number 2 is replaced with a wire, and all of the voltages and currents are caused by source number 1 alone.

2.   Then, imagine that source 1 is replaced with a wire, and all of the voltages and currents are caused by source number 2 alone.

3.   Combine both sets of voltages and currents algebraically, by paying attention to the signs. In this way you can find the total current and the voltages that are caused by both power sources working at the same time.

In Figure 4-29(A) on page 184, we have a circuit with a 16-volt and a 40-volt battery supplying power to a group of 3 resistors. We want to find the amount of current through each resistor and the voltage across each of them.

Begin by assuming that battery E_2 is replaced with a piece of wire, and find the voltages and currents that are caused by battery E_1 alone. This is seen in (B). Without E_2, there is a simple series-parallel circuit that can be reduced to a single 40.3-ohm equivalent resistor across the 16-volt battery. This is seen in (D). The total current is 397 milliamps.

Now, looking at circuit (E), begin at point a, which is the negative terminal of the battery where the electrons leave. Follow the current through loops a-b-e-f and a-b-c-d-e-f. All 397 milliamps of the current flows through the 27-ohm resistor R_1 from right to left. And, according to Ohm's law, there is a voltage drop of 10.72 volts across this resistor; its end nearest the positive terminal of the battery is its positive end.

The battery has a voltage of 16 volts, and since 10.72 volts are dropped across R_1, the rest of the voltage (5.28 volts) must be dropped across resistors R_2 and R_3, which are in parallel. The ends of these resistors that are connected to the negative terminal of the battery are the negative ends.

Ohm's law formulas show that 104 milliamps of current flows through R_2, and 293 milliamps flow through R_3. This checks out according to Kirchhoff's current law, which says that all of the current arriving at point e must be the same as the current leaving that point. $104 + 293 = 397$.

The next step is to consider that battery E_1 is replaced with a wire. In (H), we find the total equivalent resistance of this circuit to be 35.65 ohms. Battery E_2 alone will cause 1.122 amps of electron current to flow. (I) shows the voltage drops and the polarity across each of the resistors caused by the current from E_2.

When we know the voltage drops across each of the resistors that would be caused by each of the batteries acting by themselves, we can find the actual voltage drop across each resistor. This is done by combining the voltage drops algebraically—that is, by paying attention to the polarities.

(J) shows the voltage drops caused by each battery alone, and (K) shows the voltage and current that are caused by both batteries acting at the same time. Resistor R_1 has a voltage drop of 9.084 volts across it, and the end nearest the positive end of battery E_1 is the negative end. Three hundred and thirty six milliamps of current is flowing through this resistor from left to right. Resistor R_2, has a voltage drop of 25.084 volts across it, and this causes 492 milliamps of current to flow through it. Resistor R_3 has a voltage drop of 14.916 volts across it and 828 milliamps of current flowing through it.

The current arriving at point e is exactly the same as the current leaving it, and the algebraic sum of the voltages around any of the loops is equal to zero.

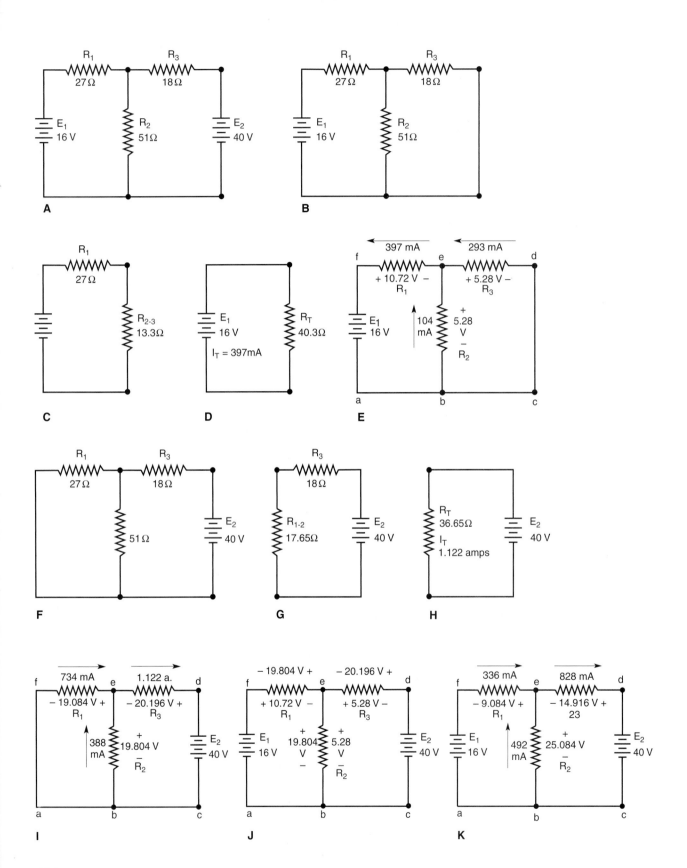

Figure 4-29 *(left facing page).*
A. *Original circuit with two power sources*
B. *Circuit with power source 2 shorted out*
C. *Circuit using power source 1 with resistors 2 and 3 combined*
D. *Circuit using power source 1 with all resistors combined into a single resistance*
E. *Current through resistors and voltage drops caused by power source 1 alone*
F. *Circuit with power source 1 shorted out*

G. *Circuit using power source 2 with resistors 1 and 2 combined*
H. *Circuit using power source 2 with all resistors combined into a single resistance*
I. *Current through resistors and voltage drops caused by power source 2 alone*
J. *Voltage drop across each resistor caused by each power source*
K. *Current through, and voltage across each resistor when both power sources are supplying power for the circuit*

Bridge Circuits

Bridge circuits are a special type of complex circuit often used in electrical measuring and controlling devices. Figure 4-30, shows a typical bridge circuit used to measure temperature. Resistor R_4 is a temperature probe, a coil of very fine wire whose resistance changes as its temperature changes.

When the bridge is connected across a battery, electrons find two paths through which they can flow. They can flow through resistors R_1 and R_2, or they can flow through resistors R_3 and R_4.

If the four resistors have values such that the ratio of the resistance R_1 to R_2 is the same as the ratio of R_3 to R_4, then the voltage at point C will be the same as the voltage at point D. Because there is no voltage drop (no voltage difference) across the indicator, no current will flow through it. In this condition, the bridge is said to be balanced.

Resistor R_4 is variable, and as it changes from the value that balanced the bridge, a voltage drop will be developed across the indicator that causes current to flow through it. As the resistance of R_4 goes up, current flows from D to C, and as the value of R_4 goes down below the balance value, current flows from C to D.

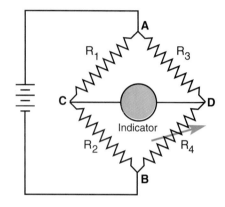

Figure 4-30. *Bridge circuits are used as measuring circuits. The current through the indicator varies as the resistance of R_4 changes.*

Finding the Equivalent Resistance of a Bridge Circuit

A bridge circuit cannot be changed into a simple series or parallel circuit as we have just been doing because of the resistor R_X seen in Figure 4-31 on Page 186. This resistor is the same as the indicator in Figure 4-30.

In order to change the bridge circuit into a series-parallel circuit that allows us to find a single equivalent resistance, we must take the delta-connected resistors (the resistors that are connected into the triangular-shaped pattern) R_X, R_Y, and R_Z into an equivalent Y-connected arrangement of resistors R_A, R_B, and R_C that we see in Figure 4-31.

Resistor R_A is the equivalent of R_Y and R_Z with R_X across them. Resistor R_B is equivalent to R_Y and R_X with R_Z across them, and resistor R_C has the same resistance as R_Z and R_X with R_Y across them.

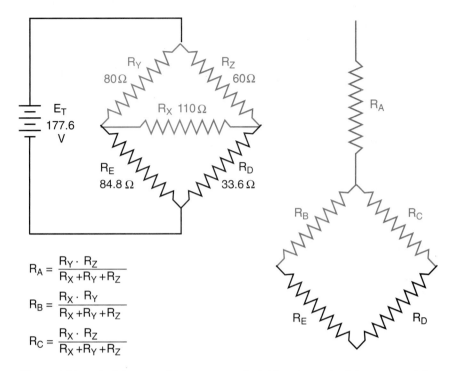

$$R_A = \frac{R_Y \cdot R_Z}{R_X + R_Y + R_Z}$$

$$R_B = \frac{R_X \cdot R_Y}{R_X + R_Y + R_Z}$$

$$R_C = \frac{R_X \cdot R_Z}{R_X + R_Y + R_Z}$$

Figure 4-31. *To find the equivalent resistance of a bridge circuit, the delta portion of the circuit, R_X, R_Y, and R_Z, must be converted into an equivalent Y-circuit, R_A, R_B, and R_C.*

Find the values of R_A, R_B, and R_C by using a form of the parallel resistance formula in Figure 4-31.

When we have found the equivalent Y-connected resistors, we can put them in place of the delta connection. Combine R_B and R_E in series, R_C and R_D in series, and then find the equivalent resistance of these two series values when they are connected in parallel.

Finally, add the value of R_A to this value to arrive at a single resistance that is the equivalent of all five resistors in the original bridge circuit.

If R_X = 110 ohms, R_Y = 80 ohms and R_Z = 60 ohms:

$$R_A = \frac{R_Y \cdot R_Z}{R_X + R_Y + R_Z}$$

$$= \frac{80 \cdot 60}{110 + 80 + 60}$$

$$= 19.2 \text{ ohms}$$

$$R_B = \frac{R_X \cdot R_Y}{R_X + R_Y + R_Z}$$

$$= \frac{110 \cdot 80}{110 + 80 + 60}$$

$$= 35.2 \text{ ohms}$$

$$R_C = \frac{R_X \cdot R_Z}{R_X + R_Y + R_Z}$$

$$= \frac{110 \cdot 60}{110 + 80 + 60}$$

$$= 26.4 \text{ ohms}$$

Replace the delta circuit with the Y-circuit you have just made, and find the total equivalent resistance of the parallel resistors:

$R_{B\text{-}E} = 35.2 + 84.8 = 120 \text{ ohms}$
$R_{C\text{-}D} = 26.4 + 33.6 = 60 \text{ ohms}$

The total resistance (R_T) of the bridge circuit is found by adding the resistance of R_A to the equivalent of the parallel resistance $R_{C\text{-}D}$ and $R_{B\text{-}E}$.

$$R_T = \left[\frac{R_{B\text{-}E} \cdot R_{C\text{-}D}}{R_{B\text{-}E} + R_{C\text{-}D}} \right] + R_A$$

$$= \left[\frac{120 \cdot 60}{120 + 60} \right] + 19.2$$

$$= 40 + 19.2$$

$$= 59.2 \text{ ohms}$$

Find the total amount of current flowing in the circuit:

$$I_T = \frac{E_T}{R_T}$$

$$= \frac{177.6}{59.2}$$

$$= 3.0 \text{ amps}$$

Find the voltage dropped across R_A.

$E_A = I_T \cdot R_A$
$= 3 \cdot 19.2$
$= 57.6 \text{ volts}$

Find the current through resistors R_C and R_D.

$$I_{C\text{-}D} = \frac{E_T - E_A}{R_{C\text{-}D}}$$

$$= \frac{177.6 - 57.6}{60}$$

$$= \frac{120}{60}$$

$$= 2.0 \text{ amps}$$

Find the current through resistors R_B and R_E.

$$I_{B\text{-}E} = \frac{E_T - E_A}{R_{B\text{-}E}}$$

$$= \frac{177.6 - 57.6}{120}$$

$$= \frac{120}{120}$$

$$= 1.0 \text{ amp}$$

Find the voltage drop across resistor R_D.

$$E_D = I_D \cdot R_D$$
$$= 2.0 \cdot 33.6$$
$$= 67.2 \text{ volts}$$

Find the voltage drop across resistor R_E.

$$E_E = I_E \cdot R_E$$
$$= 1.0 \cdot 84.8$$
$$= 84.8 \text{ volts}$$

Find the voltage drop across resistor R_X.

$$E_X = E_E - E_D$$
$$= 84.8 - 67.2$$
$$= 17.6 \text{ volts}$$

Find the current through resistor R_X.

$$I_X = \frac{E_X}{R_X}$$
$$= \frac{17.6}{110}$$
$$= 0.16 \text{ amps}$$

A Y-connected series of resistors can be converted into an equivalent delta connection by using the relationships seen in Figure 4-32.

$$R_X = \frac{(R_A \cdot R_B) + (R_B \cdot R_C) + (R_A \cdot R_C)}{R_A}$$

$$R_Y = \frac{(R_A \cdot R_B) + (R_B \cdot R_C) + (R_A \cdot R_C)}{R_B}$$

$$R_Z = \frac{(R_A \cdot R_B) + (R_B \cdot R_C) + (R_A \cdot R_C)}{R_C}$$

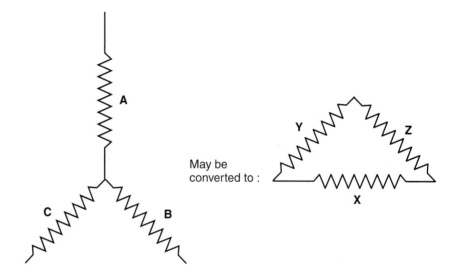

Figure 4-32. *A Y-circuit can be changed into an equivalent delta circuit.*

Answers begin on Page 359. Page numbers refer to chapter text.

37. Fill in the missing values using the circuit in the figure below.

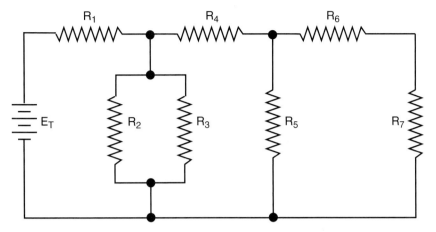

Volts	Ohms	Amps	Watts
$E_1 =$	$R_1 = 6$	$I_1 =$	$P_1 =$
$E_2 =$	$R_2 = 100$	$I_2 =$	$P_2 =$
$E_3 =$	$R_3 = 150$	$I_3 =$	$P_3 =$
$E_4 =$	$R_4 = 20$	$I_4 =$	$P_4 =$
$E_5 =$	$R_5 = 40$	$I_5 =$	$P_5 =$
$E_6 =$	$R_6 = 25$	$I_6 =$	$P_6 =$
$E_7 =$	$R_7 = 15$	$I_7 =$	$P_7 =$
$E_T = 60$	$R_T =$	$I_T =$	$P_T =$

Page 178

Continued

38. Fill in the missing values using the circuit in the figure below.

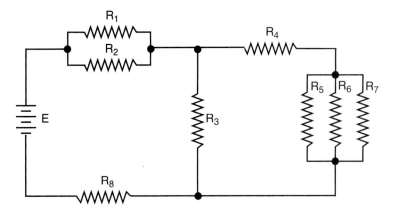

Volts	Ohms	Amps	Watts
$E_1 =$	$R_1 = 20$	$I_1 =$	$P_1 =$
$E_2 =$	$R_2 = 30$	$I_2 =$	$P_2 =$
$E_3 =$	$R_3 = 30$	$I_3 =$	$P_3 =$
$E_4 =$	$R_4 = 10$	$I_4 =$	$P_4 =$
$E_5 =$	$R_5 = 30$	$I_5 =$	$P_5 =$
$E_6 =$	$R_6 = 30$	$I_6 =$	$P_6 =$
$E_7 =$	$R_7 = 30$	$I_7 =$	$P_7 =$
$E_8 =$	$R_8 = 6$	$I_8 =$	$P_8 =$
$E_T = 30$	$R_T =$	$I_T =$	$P_T =$

Page 178

39. Fill in the missing values using the circuit in the figure below.

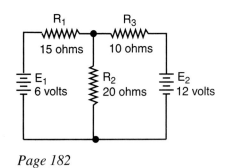

	Voltage volts	Current amps	Resistance ohms
R_1			15
R_2			20
R_3			10
E_1	6		
E_2	12		

Page 182

40. Fill in the missing values for each of these circuits in the figure below. *Page 185*

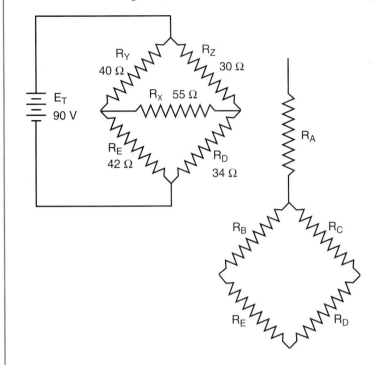

R_X =	55	ohms
R_Y =	40	ohms
R_Z =	30	ohms
R_D =	34	ohms
R_E =	42	ohms
E =	90	volts
R_A =		ohms
R_B =		ohms
R_C =		ohms
R_T =		ohms
I_T =		amps
E_X =		volt
I_X =		amp

Alternating Current Electricity

While DC electricity has the advantage that it can be stored, the difficulty with which its voltage can be changed makes it inferior to AC electricity when large amounts of electrical power are required. Most of the electrical power used in large aircraft is AC, and for applications where DC is needed, AC is changed into DC with a rectifier and used to charge the aircraft batteries.

Production and Use of Alternating Current Electricity

Remember in our discussion of the methods used to produce electricity that electricity produced by chemical methods, light, and heat are DC. All of the electrons leave the negative terminal of the source and flow in a steady stream, through the load back to the positive terminal of the source. But electricity produced by pressure on a crystal and by magnetism depends upon motion for its production, and they are both AC.

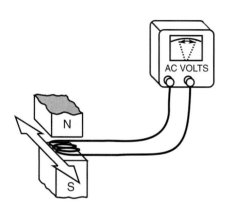

Figure 4-33. *The current produced by magnetism is alternating current. Electrons flow only as long as the coil of wire is moving in the magnetic field and cutting lines of magnetic flux.*

When a conductor is moved between the poles of a magnet, it cuts the lines of magnetic flux. When the lines are cut, they induce a voltage in the conductor that forces current to flow (*see* Figure 4-33). The direction of flow is determined by the position of the north and south poles of the magnet and the direction the conductor is moving. The intensity of the current is determined by the rate at which the lines of magnetic flux are cut. This rate is determined by the number of lines of flux there are between the poles and the speed with which the conductor is moved.

In AC, electrons begin to flow in one direction, reach a maximum, slow down, and stop. Then they reverse their direction. One complete sequence of events, starting and stopping the flow in both directions, is called one cycle, and the number of cycles that takes place in one second is called the frequency of the alternating current. Commercially produced AC in the United States has a frequency of 60 cycles per second and is called 60-hertz AC. Some foreign countries use 50-hertz AC. Most aircraft AC electrical systems use 400-hertz AC.

Alternating current has so many advantages that DC is used only when we must have some of its special features, features such as its ability to be produced by small batteries, to be stored, or to cause a flow of electrons in one direction only. Electric motors whose speed must be controlled are often DC motors.

AC is easier and less expensive to produce than DC, but even more important than its ease of production is the ease with which its voltage or current can be changed by simply passing it through a transformer.

When large amounts of electrical power must be moved over long distances, the voltage of the AC may be stepped up to several hundred thousand volts. Since electrical power is the product of the voltage and the current, stepping up the voltage allows the use of less current for the same amount of power. It is current that produces heat and uses power, so by decreasing the amount of current, we can move large amounts of electrical power with very small losses. When we are ready to use the electricity, passing it through another transformer lowers its voltage to a usable value and steps its current back up.

Alternating current can be produced with almost any wave shape we may need for special applications and with almost any frequency. High-frequency AC produces electromagnetic radiation that makes radio and television possible, and AC can be easily and efficiently changed into DC when it is needed to keep batteries charged and for other applications that require direct current. AC is so important in practical electricity and electronics that we will study it in detail.

Alternating Current Terms and Values

There are some terms unique to alternating current that we need to learn.

Amplitude

Later in this section of the *Aviation Maintenance Technician Series* we will cover electrical generators. We will discuss the way alternating current is produced, and you will see that when an armature rotates within a magnetic field, the voltage and current change in a very special way, and sine-wave alternating current is produced.

Figure 4-34 shows the shape of a single cycle of sine-wave voltage. It starts at zero, rises to a positive peak value, then drops back through zero as it continues to a negative peak value. The complete sequence of events seen here is one cycle, and the time needed for one cycle is called the period of the AC. One half of a cycle, either the positive or the negative half, is called an alternation. The reason this is called sine-wave AC is that the amplitude of the voltage or the current is directly related to the trigonometric sine of the angle through which the armature, or rotating portion of the generator, has turned from its zero-voltage position.

Let's review our trigonometry just a bit right here. For a complete review, refer to Chapter 2, Mathematics. For our purpose here, the sine of an angle is the ratio of the length of the side opposite the angle in a right triangle to the length of the hypotenuse. In this application, the length of the hypotenuse represents the maximum voltage the generator can produce. The length of the side of the triangle opposite the angle through which the armature has rotated is the value of the voltage being produced at the instant the armature is in this position. This is called the instantaneous value of the voltage. *See* Figure 4-35.

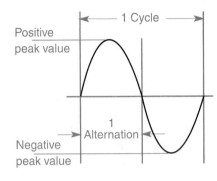

Figure 4-34. *A cycle of alternating current is one complete sequence of events. The voltage or current starts at zero, rises to a positive peak, and drops back to zero in one alternation. In the next alternation, it starts at zero, drops to the negative peak, and then returns to zero. One cycle of alternating current consists of two alternations.*

sine wave. The waveform of AC voltage and current produced by a rotary generator. The value of the voltage or current varies as the sine of the angle through which the armature has rotated.

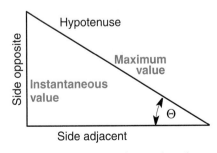

Figure 4-35. *The sine of an angle is the ratio of the length of the side opposite the angle to the length of the hypotenuse.*

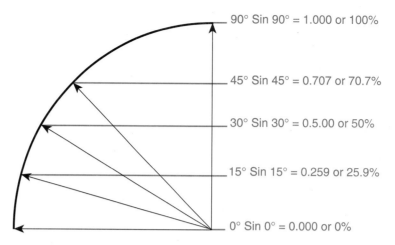

Figure 4-36. *The instantaneous value of sine-wave alternating current varies as the sine of the angle through which the generator armature has turned.*

The sine of 0° is 0, so in Figure 4-36, the value of voltage at 0° is plotted on the reference line. The sine of 15° is 0.259. This means that by the time the armature has rotated 15°, the windings are cutting enough lines of flux to produce 0.259 of the peak voltage. The sine of 30° is 0.500, so by the time the armature has rotated 30°, it is producing one half of the peak voltage. At 45°, it is producing 0.707 of the peak voltage, and at 90°, the winding is traveling at right angles to, or straight across, the flux, and it is cutting across the maximum number of lines. At this position it is producing the maximum, or peak, voltage. The side opposite the angle is now equal in length to the hypotenuse.

As the armature continues to rotate, the voltage drops according to the sine value to zero, and then it begins to rise, only this time the current is flowing in the opposite direction, and the voltage has the opposite polarity.

In the 0°-position, the coils move parallel with the lines of flux and cut, or cross, none of them. But as they rotate, they begin to cut more and more lines, until at the 90°-position, they cut the maximum number of lines. The instantaneous values of voltage are determined by the sine of the angle through which the coil has rotated from its 0°-position. *See* Figure 4-37.

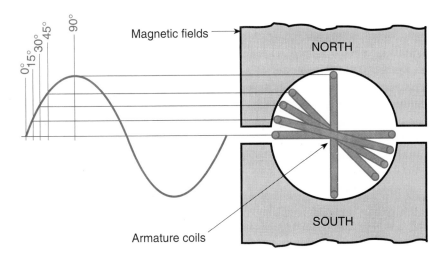

Figure 4-37. *When the coils of an AC generator rotate inside a magnetic field, they produce a voltage and current whose instantaneous values vary with the number of lines of magnetic flux the coils cut across.*

In DC electricity, the values of voltage and current remain relatively constant. But with alternating current, the amplitude of the voltage and current are continually changing, and the direction of the current periodically reverses so there are several different values that are important. The peak value is the maximum value, either positive or negative, that the current or the voltage reaches. Each cycle has a positive peak and a negative peak value. They are equal in magnitude, but opposite in polarity.

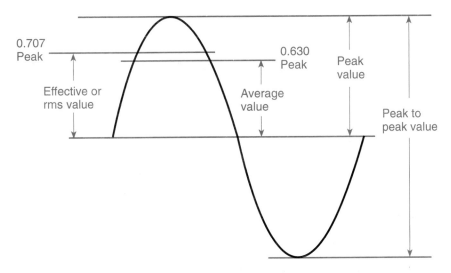

effective voltage. A measure of AC voltage that is 0.707 times the maximum instantaneous voltage. Effective voltage is also called rms (root mean square) voltage.

Figure 4-38. *The effective, or rms, value of sine wave AC is 0.707 times the peak value. The average value is 0.636 times the peak value, and the peak-to-peak value is twice the peak value.*

The peak-to-peak value of voltage or current is the maximum difference between the positive peak value and the negative peak value. Oscilloscopes and certain types of electronic voltmeters measure peak-to-peak voltage. This can be converted to peak value by simply dividing it by two.

If we could measure all of the instantaneous values of current or voltage in one alternation of sine-wave AC, add them together, and find their average, it would be 0.637 of the peak value. This is called the average value of the sine-wave AC.

Since the amount of current flowing in an AC circuit continually changes, AC having a peak value of 1 amp will not produce as much heat as 1 amp of DC. In order to find the amount of AC needed to produce a given amount of heat, we must use the effective value of the AC. The effective value of sine-wave AC is also called the rms, or root-mean-square, value. We can find this value by measuring an infinite number of instantaneous values of voltage or current, squaring each of them, and finding the average of the squares. Then find the square root of this average value.

The rms value is normally the most important current or voltage measurement and because it is, most AC meters are calibrated in rms values, even though the movement of the meter needle is usually proportional to the average current flowing through it. The rms, or effective, value of sine-wave AC is equal to 0.707 of the peak value. Another way of saying this is that the peak value of sine wave AC is 1.414 times its rms, or effective, value. The reciprocal of 0.707 is 1.414. It requires 1.414 amps of sine-wave AC to produce as much heat as 1.0 amp of DC.

Phase

When the switch is closed In a DC circuit, electrons begin to flow instantly, and the voltage rises immediately to the value of the source voltage. If we watch the rise and fall of the current and the voltage on an oscilloscope, we will see that they rise and fall together. The current and voltage are said to be in phase. *See* Figure 4-39.

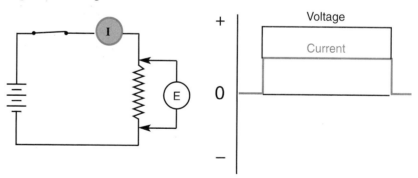

Figure 4-39. *When the switch is closed in a DC circuit, the voltage and the current rise at the same time. This means that the voltage and current are in phase.*

AVIATION MAINTENANCE TECHNICIAN SERIES   GENERAL

When AC flows through a resistor, as seen in Figure 4-40, the current and voltage rise and fall in phase. But when AC flows through a coil or into and out of a capacitor, something else happens. Figure 4-41 shows the current flowing into and out of a capacitor and the current must flow into it before the voltage can build up across it. The current is said to lead the voltage.

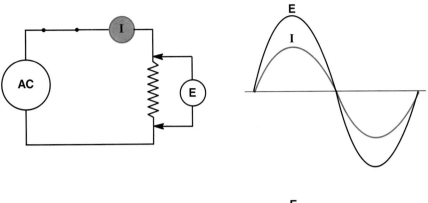

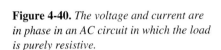

capacitance (C). The amount of electrical energy that can be stored in an electrostatic field in a capacitor. Capacitance is measured in farads, microfarads, or picofarads.

capacitor. An electrical component used to store electricity in the form of electrostatic fields.

Figure 4-40. *The voltage and current are in phase in an AC circuit in which the load is purely resistive.*

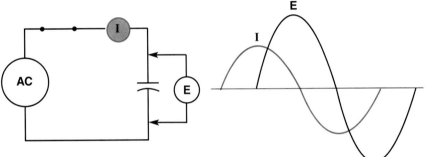

Figure 4-41. *If the load in an AC circuit is purely capacitive, the current must flow into the capacitor before the voltage can build up across it. The current LEADS the voltage.*

In Figure 4-42, AC is flowing through a coil, and when current begins to flow through a coil, a voltage is produced that opposes the voltage causing the current. There is opposition to the current only as long as the voltage is changing. In this type of circuit, the current is said to lag the voltage. The phase relationship between the current and the voltage in an AC circuit is so important that we will study it in detail.

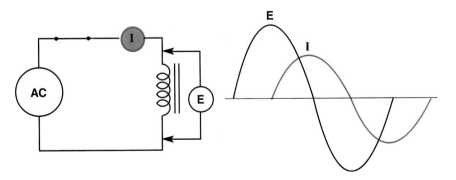

Figure 4-42. *If the load in an AC circuit is purely inductive, a change in the voltage produces a current that opposes the voltage change. The voltage change leads the current change, or we can say that the current LAGS the voltage.*

power. The ability of an electrical circuit to produce work. The basic unit of electrical power is the watt, which is the product of current times the voltage that caused the current to flow.

power factor. The percentage of current in an AC circuit that is in phase with the voltage. Power factor is found by dividing the circuit resistance by the circuit impedance. It is also the cosine of the phase angle.

Power

Power in a DC circuit and in an AC circuit in which all of the current and voltage are in phase, is the product of the current and the voltage.

$$P = E \cdot I$$

But, as we have just seen, there are certain kinds of AC circuits in which the current and voltage are not in phase. The true power, measured in watts, in this type of circuit is the product of the voltage and only that portion of the current that is in phase with the voltage. The percentage of current in phase with the voltage is called the power factor of the circuit. If all of the current is in phase with the voltage, as it is in a purely resistive circuit, the power factor is 100% or, more generally said, the power factor is one.

To find the true power in an AC circuit, multiply the current and the voltage together, and then multiply this product by the power factor.

$$P_T = E \cdot I \cdot PF$$

P_T = True power, expressed in watts

E = Voltage across the circuit, in volts

I = Current through the circuit, in amps

PF = Power factor

For example, if 3.0 amps of current flows in a 120-volt AC circuit with a power factor of 75%, the true power is 270 watts.

$$
\begin{aligned}
P_T &= E \cdot I \cdot PF \\
&= 120 \cdot 3.0 \cdot 0.75 \\
&= 270 \text{ watts}
\end{aligned}
$$

Answers begin on Page 359. Page numbers refer to chapter text.

41. Electricity produced by magnetism is _____ (AC or DC). *Page 192*

42. The intensity of current produced by a conductor moving through a magnetic field is determined by the _____ at which the lines of flux are cut. *Page 192*

43. One complete sequence of events in alternating current consisting of starting and stopping the current in both directions is called one _____ . *Page 193*

44. Which is easier and less expensive to produce, AC or DC? _____ . *Page 193*

45. When electricity is to be carried for long distances over a power line, its _____ (voltage or current) is stepped up to a high value. *Page 193*

46. One half of a cycle of alternating current is called a/an _____ . *Page 193*

47. The sine of an angle is the ratio of the length of the side opposite the angle in a right triangle to the length of the _____ . *Page 194*

48. The sine of 0° is _____ . The sine of 90° is _____ . *Page 194*

49. If sine wave AC has an effective value of 120 volts, it will have the following values:
    a. Peak value = _____ volts
    b. Peak-to-peak value = _____ volts
    c. Average value = _____ volts
       Page 195

50. AC having a peak value of 25 amps will produce the same amount of heat as _____ amps of DC. *Page 195*

51. Another name for the effective value of AC is the _____ value. *Page 195*

52. AC with a peak voltage of 141.4 volts has an effective voltage of _____ volts. *Page 196*

Continued

53. If an AC circuit contains only resistance, the current _____ (is or is not) in phase with the voltage.
    Page 197

54. If an AC circuit contains only capacitance, the current will _____ (lead or lag) the voltage.
    Page 197

55. If an AC circuit contains only inductance, the current will _____ (lead or lag) the voltage. *Page 197*

56. The percentage of the current in an AC circuit that is in phase with the voltage across the circuit is called the _____ of the circuit. *Page 198*

57. The power factor of a circuit that contains only resistance is _____ percent. *Page 198*

Effects of Capacitance in an AC Circuit

A capacitor is an electrical component made up of two conductors separated by an insulator. Electrical energy can be stored in a capacitor in the form of an electrical field. A capacitor blocks the flow of DC, but AC flows into and out of it and is not blocked. In an AC circuit, a capacitor drops voltage and shifts the phase of the current, but it does not use power nor produce heat.

Capacitive Reactance

reactance (X). The opposition to the flow of AC caused by both inductive and capacitive reactances.

In Figure 4-43, we see the basic relationship between current and voltage in a circuit that contains a battery, a switch, and a capacitor. When the switch is closed, current immediately begins to flow at its maximum rate because the capacitor appears to be a closed circuit between the two terminals of the battery. But as electrons enter the capacitor, they pile up on one of the plates because they cannot get across, and as they pile up, the voltage across the capacitor begins to rise. As the voltage rises, the current drops off, and when the capacitor is fully charged — that is, when the voltage across the capacitor is equal to the source voltage — no more current can flow. The capacitor now acts as an open circuit. From this example, it is easy to see that current must flow in a capacitive circuit before any voltage appears across the capacitor. In a purely capacitive AC circuit, the current must flow for 90 electrical degrees before the voltage across the capacitor begins to rise.

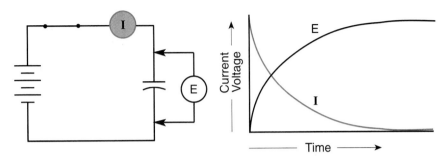

Figure 4-43. *At the instant the switch is closed, current begins to flow into the capacitor. As current flows into it, the voltage across it rises, and the current flow decreases.*

Alternating current is continually changing its amplitude and periodically reversing its direction of flow. If a capacitor is connected across a source of AC, current must flow into it before any voltage appears across it. At the 90°-position in Figure 4-44, the capacitor is fully charged. The voltage across it is at a maximum, and the current flow has dropped to zero. The capacitor now begins to discharge and current flows through the circuit in the opposite direction. As the current flow increases, the voltage drops off until at 180°, the current is maximum, and the voltage across the capacitor is zero. The current in a purely capacitive circuit leads the voltage by 90°.

In a DC circuit, the opposition to current flow is caused by resistance as it uses power by converting it into heat. In an AC circuit, opposition can also be caused by a capacitor which opposes the flow without using any power or producing any heat.

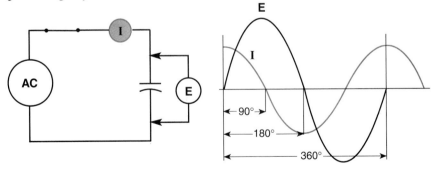

Figure 4-44. *When a capacitor is connected across a source of alternating current, the current must flow into it before the voltage builds up across it.*

Electrons do not flow through a capacitor, but rather they flow into it until it becomes charged, and then when, the polarity of the source voltage reverses, the electrons flow out of the capacitor. In Figure 4-44, as the voltage across the capacitor rises to oppose the source voltage, the current drops off, and when the capacitor is fully charged, the voltage across the capacitor is the same as the source voltage, and no more current flows.

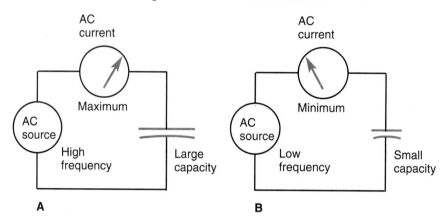

Figure 4-45
A. *When the frequency of the AC is high and/or the capacitor is large, the maximum amount of current will flow into and out of it. The opposition caused by the capacitor is low.*
B. *When the frequency of the AC is low and/or the capacitor is small, the capacitor becomes charged before the polarity of the AC reverses. When the capacitor is charged, no current flows, and the opposition caused by the capacitor is high.*

If the capacitor has a small capacity, it will charge quickly and no more current can flow until the polarity of the source voltage reverses. A small capacitor effectively opposes current flow. But if the capacitor is large, electrons can flow into it during the entire half cycle without completely charging it, and it will create very little opposition to the flow.

If the frequency of the alternating current is low—that is, the current flows in each direction for a long period of time—the capacitor will charge up and oppose current flow. But, if the frequency is high and the electrons flow in each direction for only a very short time, the capacitor does not have time to charge up completely. The voltage will not rise enough to oppose current flow.

From these two observations, we see that the opposition to AC caused by a capacitor is determined by the capacity of the capacitor and by the frequency of the AC. The larger the capacity, the less the opposition, and the higher the frequency, the less the opposition.

The opposition to the flow of AC caused by a capacitor is called capacitive reactance. It is represented by the symbol X_C, and it is measured in ohms. Capacitive reactance varies inversely as both the capacity of the capacitor and the frequency of the AC, and it may be found by the formula:

$$X_C = \frac{1}{2\pi fc}$$

X_C = Capacitive reactance in ohms

2π = A constant, 6.28

f = frequency of the AC in hertz

c = capacitance of the capacitor in farads

Since we have constants in both the numerator and the denominator, we can change this formula to:

$$X_C = \frac{159,200}{fc}$$

X_C = capacitive reactance in ohms

159,200 = a constant

f = frequency of the AC in hertz

c = capacitance of the capacitor in microfarads

The constant 159,200 in the numerator is found by dividing 1 by 2 times π ($1/2\pi$), and then multiplying it by 1,000,000. This allows us to use microfarads instead of farads for the capacitance.

Now, for a couple of examples. Let's find the amount of capacitive reactance that is caused by a 0.05-microfarad capacitor in a 1,000-hertz AC circuit:

$$X_C = \frac{159,200}{fc}$$

$$= \frac{159,200}{1,000 \cdot .05}$$

$$= \frac{159,200}{50}$$

$$= 3,184 \text{ ohms}$$

A 0.05-microfarad capacitor in a 1 kilohertz AC circuit will oppose the flow of the AC with an opposition of 3,184 ohms.

To find the capacitive reactance caused by a 315-picofarad capacitor in a 200-kilohertz circuit, first change the picofarads and kilohertz into microfarads and hertz by using scientific notation. Three hundred and fifteen picofarads is equal to 0.000 315 microfarads. This is 3.15×10^{-4} microfarads. Two hundred kilohertz is 200,000 hertz, and this is 2×10^5 hertz.

$$X_C = \frac{159,200}{200,000 \cdot 0.000\ 315}$$

$$= \frac{1.592 \cdot 10^5}{2 \cdot 10^5 \cdot 3.15 \cdot 10^{-4}}$$

$$= \frac{1.592 \cdot 10^4}{2 \cdot 3.15}$$

$$= 2,527 \text{ ohms}$$

By transposing the capacitive reactance formula, we can find the frequency at which a capacitive circuit will produce a specific amount of reactance, and also the capacity needed to produce a particular amount of reactance at a given frequency.

$$f = \frac{159,200}{X_C \cdot c}$$

$$c = \frac{159,200}{X_C \cdot f}$$

To find the frequency that will give us 2,000 ohms of capacitive reactance when there is a 200-picofarad capacitor in the circuit, we will use the formula:

$$f = \frac{159,200}{X_C \cdot c}$$

$$= \frac{159,200}{2,000 \cdot 0.000\ 200}$$

$$= \frac{159,200}{0.4}$$

$$= 398,000 \text{ hertz (398 kilohertz)}$$

To find the amount of capacitance needed to get 2,000 ohms of capacitive reactance in a circuit whose frequency is 400 hertz, we use the formula:

$$c = \frac{159,200}{X_C \cdot f}$$

$$= \frac{159,200}{2,000 \cdot 400}$$

$$= \frac{159,200}{800,000}$$

$$= 0.2 \text{ microfarads}$$

We will need 0.2 microfarads of capacitance to get 2,000 ohms of capacitive reactance in a circuit in which the frequency of the AC is 400 hertz.

Ohm's Law for Capacitive Circuits

In the study of Ohm's law as it applies to DC circuits, we saw that the current was directly proportional to the applied voltage and inversely proportional to the circuit resistance. In AC circuits, we have opposition caused by reactance as well as by resistance, and so we must modify our formula to include reactance.

First consider a circuit that has capacitance but no resistance. Of course, this cannot be, but for purposes of this explanation we will eliminate calculating resistance right now. Ohm's law can now say that the current in a capacitive circuit is directly proportional to the applied voltage and is inversely proportional to the capacitive reactance.

$$I = \frac{E}{X_C}$$

We can easily change this formula to find the voltage or the capacitive reactance when the other two are known:

$$E = I \cdot X_C$$

$$X_C = \frac{E}{I}$$

In reality, we cannot have a circuit that does not contain some resistance. Since the current and voltage are in phase through a resistor, but are 90° out of phase in a capacitor, we cannot simply add the resistance to the reactance. Rather we must add them as vector quantities, and vectors have both direction and magnitude. It might be a good idea, if your understanding of vectors is a little weak, to review the section on vectors in Chapter 3 on Basic Physics.

Series R-C Circuits

Begin by using the resistor-capacitor, or R-C circuit in Figure 4-46. A 1,000-ohm resistor is in series with a 2.5-microfarad capacitor. The circuit is powered with 120-volt, 60-hertz AC.

First, we must find the capacitive reactance produced by the capacitor:

$$X_C = \frac{159,200}{60 \cdot 2.5}$$

$$= \frac{159,200}{150}$$

$$= 1061.3 \text{ ohms}$$

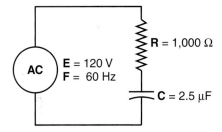

Figure 4-46. *In this circuit, the 1,000 ohms of resistance and the 1,061.3 ohms of capacitive reactance combine to form 1,458.2 ohms of impedance.*

There are two types of opposition in this circuit, resistance and capacitive reactance, and we want to find the total opposition to the current. This total opposition is called impedance, its symbol is Z, and it is the vector sum of the resistance and the reactance. We can find impedance graphically, but it is much faster to find it by using a formula:

$$Z = \sqrt{R^2 + X_C{}^2}$$
$$= \sqrt{1,000^2 + 1061.3^2}$$
$$= 1,458 \text{ ohms}$$

impedance (Z). The total opposition to the flow of AC. Impedance is the vector sum of resistance and reactance.

Since the current and voltage are in phase in a resistor and 90° out of phase in a capacitor, the resistance can be shown by one vector quantity and the capacitive reactance by a second vector quantity which is 90° out of phase with the first.

We can plot these two vectors to scale as they are in Figure 4-47B. The vector for the resistance is 1,000 units long and is drawn along the 0° line. The vector for the capacitive reactance is 1,061.3 units long and it is drawn along the 270° line because the current through the capacitor leads the current through the resistor by 90°. Since the vectors rotate counterclockwise, the 270° line is 90° ahead of the 360°, or 0° line. The resultant of these two vector quantities may be found by drawing lines perpendicular to the two axes at the ends of the vector arrows and then drawing the resultant arrow from the origin to the point where the two lines meet, as in Figure 4-47B. The length of this resultant is the amount of the total opposition, or the impedance, of the circuit, and the angle between this resultant and the horizontal reference line is the phase angle, or the number of degrees by which the current leads the voltage.

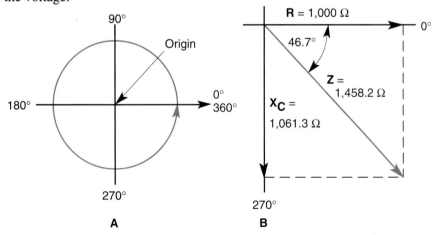

Figure 4-47.
A. Phase rotation in an alternating current circuit is considered to be counterclockwise from zero degrees. Zero degrees is drawn to the right of the origin.
B. Finding the impedance in a series R-C circuit using the graphic method.

We can also find the impedance by using the Pythagorean principle which states that the length of the hypotenuse of a right triangle is equal to the square root of the sum of the squares of the lengths of the two sides of the triangle. The resistance of 1,000 ohms is one side, and the capacitive reactance of 1,061.3 ohms is the other side. The vector sum of the resistance and the reactance is 1,458.2 ohms.

$$Z = \sqrt{R^2 + X_C^2}$$
$$= \sqrt{1,000^2 + 1,061.3^2}$$
$$= \sqrt{1,000,000 + 1,126,357.7}$$
$$= \sqrt{2,126,357.7}$$
$$= 1,458.2 \text{ ohms}$$

We can find the phase angle by measuring it with a protractor, but it is easier to use trigonometry. Looking at Figure 4-47B, we know the length of the resistance, 1,000 ohms, and the length of the reactance, 1,061.3 ohms. The resistance value forms the side adjacent to, or next to, the angle we want to find, and the reactance is the side opposite this angle. In trigonometry, the tangent of an angle is the ratio of the length of the side opposite the angle to the length of the adjacent side. In this case:

$$\text{Tan} = \frac{\text{opposite}}{\text{adjacent}}$$
$$= \frac{X_C}{R}$$
$$= \frac{1,061.3}{1,000}$$
$$= 1.06$$

The tangent of the angle is 1.06. With the chart of trigonometric functions, or by way of a calculator with trig functions, we can find the value of the angle. We want the arctangent of 1.06. The arctangent is the inverse function of the tangent, or simply, it is the angle whose tangent is 1.06. This is usually written as:

$$\text{Tan}^{-1}\ 1.06 = 46.7 \text{ degrees.}$$

A 2.5-microfarad capacitor in series with a 1,000-ohm resistor across a 120-volt, 60-hertz power source has a total opposition of 1,458 ohms, and the current leads the voltage by 46.7 degrees.

We can find the amount of current flowing in this circuit by using the formula:

$$I = \frac{E}{Z}$$

$$= \frac{120}{1,458}$$

$$= 0.0822 \text{ amp (82.2 milliamps)}$$

The voltage drops across the resistor and the capacitor are found by using the formulas:

$$E_R = I_T \cdot R \qquad\qquad E_C = I_T \cdot X_C$$
$$= 0.0823 \cdot 1,000 \qquad = 0.0823 \cdot 1061.3$$
$$= 82.3 \text{ volts} \qquad\quad = 87.3 \text{ volts}$$

Since this is a series circuit, the same current flows through both components. Notice that the sum of the voltage drops is greater than the source voltage. This, at first glance, appears to dispute Kirchhoff's voltage law which states that the sum of the voltage drops around a series circuit is equal to the applied voltage. But, remember that the current in the capacitor is not in phase with its voltage, and so we must add the voltages as *vector* quantities rather than as straight numbers.

Power in a Series R-C Circuit

There are two types of power to consider when working with AC circuits; true power and apparent power. The true power is the actual power consumed in the circuit, and it is measured in watts, just as it is in a DC circuit. It is found by the formula:

$$P = E \cdot I \cdot \text{Power Factor}$$

The power factor is the percentage of the current in phase with the voltage. There are two different ways the power factor may be found. One is by finding the ratio of the resistance of the circuit to its impedance:

$$PF = \frac{R}{Z}$$

$$= \frac{1,000}{1,458.2}$$

$$= 0.6857$$

true power. Power in an AC circuit that is the product of the circuit voltage and only that part of the current that is in phase with the voltage. It is measured in watts.

apparent power. The power in an AC circuit that is the product of the circuit voltage and all of the current. It is measured in volt-amps.

The power factor can also be found by trigonometry to be the cosine of the phase angle. We found the phase angle to be 46.7°, and using either a trig table or a calculator, we find the cosine of 46.7° to be 0.686. The power factor is 0.686. This means that 68.6% of the current is in phase with the voltage, and produces power.

The true power used in the circuit is:

$$P_T = E_T \cdot I_T \cdot PF$$
$$= 120 \cdot 0.0822 \cdot 0.686$$
$$= 6.77 \text{ watts}$$

The apparent power is simply the product of the total current and the source voltage and is expressed in volt-amps. In this circuit, the apparent power is:

$$P_A = E_T \cdot I_T$$
$$= 120 \cdot 0.0822$$
$$= 9.86 \text{ volt-amps}$$

In an R-C circuit, the only power actually used is that which causes heat in the resistor. We can also find the true power used in the circuit by the formula:

$$P_T = I_T^2 \times R$$
$$= 0.0822^2 \times 1,000$$
$$= 6.76 \text{ watts}$$

No power is used in the capacitor because the power put into the capacitor during one alternation is returned in the next.

Parallel R-C Circuits

If the capacitor and the resistor are connected in parallel rather than in series, the power used can be computed by a slightly different approach.

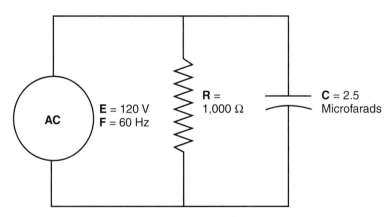

Figure 4-48. *To find the total current in a parallel R-C circuit, we add the current through the resistor and the current through the capacitor vectorially.*

In a parallel AC circuit as in a parallel DC circuit, the voltage across each component is the same as the source voltage. In the example in Figure 4-48, the resistor and capacitor both have 120 volts across them. Find the current through them by the formulas:

$$I_R = \frac{E_T}{R} \qquad\qquad I_C = \frac{E_T}{X_C}$$

$$= \frac{120}{1,000} \qquad\qquad\quad = \frac{120}{1,061.3}$$

$$= 0.120 \text{ amp} \qquad\qquad = 0.113 \text{ amp}$$

The total current is not simply the sum of the two currents, but like the voltage in a series circuit, the total current in a parallel circuit must be found by adding the two currents vectorially. We do this by using the Pythagorean formula:

$$I_T = \sqrt{I_R{}^2 + I_C{}^2}$$

$$= \sqrt{0.120^2 + 0.113^2}$$

$$= \sqrt{0.0144 + 0.0127}$$

$$= \sqrt{0.0271}$$

$$= 0.1648 \text{ amp}$$

Now that we know the total current in the circuit and the total voltage, we can find the total opposition, or the impedance.

$$Z = \frac{E}{I_T}$$

$$= \frac{120}{0.1648}$$

$$= 728 \text{ ohms}$$

Another way of finding the circuit impedance is to use the same type of formula we use for finding the total resistance of two resistors in parallel. The only difference is that the sum of the oppositions must be the vector sum.

$$Z = \frac{R \cdot X_C}{\sqrt{R^2 + X_C^2}}$$

$$= \frac{1{,}000 \cdot 1{,}061.3}{\sqrt{1{,}000^2 + 1{,}061.3^2}}$$

$$= \frac{1{,}061{,}300}{1{,}458.2}$$

$$= 728 \text{ ohms}$$

STUDY QUESTIONS: CAPACITANCE IN AN AC CIRCUIT

*Answers begin on Page 359. **Page numbers refer to chapter text.***

58. Find the capacitive reactance of a 50-microfarad capacitor in a 60-hertz AC circuit.
    $X_C =$ _____ ohms. *Page 203*

59. Find the capacitive reactance of a 5-microfarad capacitor in a 60-hertz AC circuit.
    $X_C =$ _____ ohms. *Page 203*

60. Find the capacitive reactance of a 50-microfarad capacitor in a 120-hertz AC circuit.
    $X_C =$ _____ ohms. *Page 203*

61. Find the capacitive reactance of a 350-picofarad capacitor in a 5-megahertz AC circuit.
    $X_C =$ _____ ohms. *Page 203*

62. At what frequency will a 0.03-microfarad capacitor cause a capacitive reactance of 1,000 ohms?
    $f =$ _____ hertz. *Page 205*

63. What size capacitor will be needed to cause a capacitive reactance of 2,000 ohms in a 900-hertz AC circuit?
    $c =$ _____ microfarad. *Page 205*

64. How much current flows in a circuit that has no resistance, but has a capacitive reactance of 200 ohms, and there is 120 volts across the circuit.
    $I =$ _____ amp. *Page 206*

65. How much voltage is dropped across a capacitor that produces a capacitive reactance of 425 ohms and has 250 milliamps of current flowing through it?

E = _____ volts. *Page 209*

66. How many ohms of capacitive reactance is needed to allow 500 milliamps of current to flow through a circuit that has 150 volts across it?

X_C = _____ ohms. *Page 203*

67. Find the values required for this circuit.

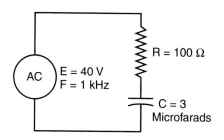

    a. Capacitive reactance = _____ ohms
    b. Impedance = _____ ohms
    c. Phase angle = _____ degrees
    d. The current _____ (leads or lags) the voltage
    e. Total current = _____ amp
    f. Voltage across the resistor = _____ volt
    g. Voltage across the capacitor = _____ volt
    h. Power factor = _____ percent
    i. Power used in this circuit = _____ watts.
      Page 206

68. Find the values required for this circuit.

    a. The current flowing through the resistor is _____ amp.
    b. The current flowing through the capacitor is _____ amp.
    c. The total current in the circuit is _____ amp.
    d. The impedance of the circuit is _____ ohms.
      Page 210

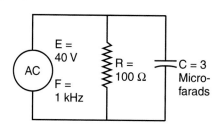

Effects of Inductance in AC Circuits

A coil, or inductor, installed in a DC circuit produces very little opposition, only the resistance that is produced by the resistance of the wires. But in an AC circuit, it opposes the flow of current without using any power or producing heat, and it shifts the phase of the current. Energy is stored by an inductor in its magnetic fields.

Self Induction

Any time electrons flow in a conductor, they cause a magnetic field to surround the conductor, and the direction the lines of flux encircle the conductor is determined by the direction the electrons flow. The distance the field extends out from the conductor is determined by the amount of current flow.

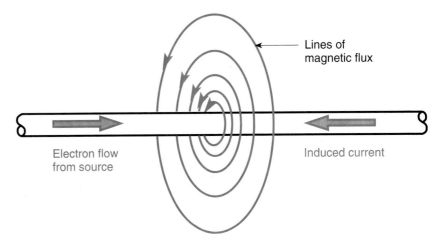

Figure 4-49. *Any time electrons flow in a conductor, a magnetic field surrounds the conductor. When the current flowing in the conductor changes, the magnetic field builds up or collapses, and as it does, it cuts across the conductor and induces, or creates, a current in it. This induced current flows in the direction opposite to that of the current which caused it.*

When flux lines cut across a conductor, a voltage is generated in it that causes current to flow. Lines of flux cut across a conductor any time current in the conductor changes. When alternating current flows in a conductor, the current is continually changing its flow rate and periodically reversing its direction, and so the magnetic field is also continually changing its strength and periodically reversing its direction.

The magnetic field begins at the center of the conductor; and when the current begins to flow, it expands outward through the conductor and into the space around it. Then it drops back into the conductor and finally decreases to zero as the current stops flowing. The magnetic field cuts back across the conductor with the lines encircling it in the opposite direction as it builds up in the next alternation. Each time the magnetic flux cuts across a conductor, voltage is generated that causes current to flow, and this voltage is produced by self induction.

An important law in the study of electricity explains what happens. Lenz's law tells us that current is induced in a conductor any time it is crossed, or cut, by lines of magnetic flux, and this current is always in the direction opposite that of the current that caused the magnetic field. This is illustrated in Figure 4-49. The magnetic field is built up by source current flowing from left to right, and the induced current flows from right to left. The result is that when current is induced into a conductor, the total current will be less than the source is capable of supplying. In other words, the source current sees an opposition. But, unlike resistance, this opposition neither uses power nor produces heat.

Inductive Reactance

As just described, when current flows in an inductive circuit, it produces a magnetic field which cuts across the turns of the inductor. This field generates a back voltage that opposes the voltage which caused the original current to flow. This back voltage decreases the voltage available to force electrons through the inductor. The result is an opposition to the flow of current that does not dissipate power nor produce heat. This opposition is called inductive reactance, it is measured in ohms, and is abbreviated X_L. Inductive reactance varies directly with the inductance, and since it is produced only when the current in the inductor is changing, it also varies directly with the frequency of the AC. In a DC circuit, there is no change in the current after it has started flowing, and so the inductive reactance for DC is zero. The formula for inductive reactance is:

inductive reactance. The opposition to the flow of AC caused by inductance. It drops voltage, but does not cause heat or use power.

$$X_L = 2\pi\, f\, l$$

X_L = Inductive reactance in ohms
2π = A constant, 6.28
f = Frequency of the AC in hertz
l = Inductance of the inductor in henries

We can change this formula to find the frequency or the inductance if the inductive reactance and the other variable are known.

$$f = \frac{X_L}{2\pi l} \quad \text{and} \quad l = \frac{X_L}{2\pi f}$$

Phase Shift in an Inductive Circuit

If a circuit has inductance, but no capacitance nor resistance, all of the opposition to the flow of current is caused by the inductive reactance which opposes the current by producing a back voltage, or counter EMF. This back voltage is produced only when the current is changing, and it is maximum when the current change is greatest. The greatest rate of current change occurs as the current passes through zero, going from the maximum flow in one direction to maximum flow in the opposite direction. Figure 4-50 shows the waveform of current, voltage, and back voltage in an AC circuit containing only inductance. Changes in the voltage occur 90° ahead of the changes in the current, meaning that the voltage leads the current by 90°. We can also think of this as the current *lagging* the voltage by 90°.

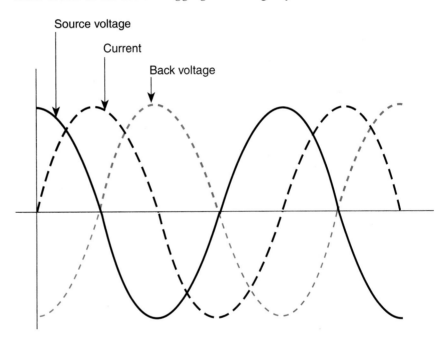

Figure 4-50. *The current in a purely inductive circuit lags 90° behind the voltage that causes it to flow. When the current changes, it induces, or causes, a back voltage to be produced in the circuit. This voltage is 180° out of phase with the source voltage.*

Ohm's Law for Inductive Circuits

In a DC circuit, Ohm's law deals with voltage, current, resistance, and power. In an inductive AC circuit it also deals with inductive reactance, which cause a voltage drop and shifts the phase of the current, but does not use power.

Series R-L Circuits

If a circuit contained only inductance, the voltage would lead the current by 90°, but it is impossible to have a practical circuit with no resistance. Since the current flowing through the resistor is in phase with the voltage, we must add the resistance and the inductive reactance as vector quantities to find the total circuit opposition.

The impedance of a series R-L circuit is found in the same way as the impedance of a series R-C circuit. Use the Pythagorean formula:

$$Z = \sqrt{R^2 + X_L^2}$$

The circuit in Figure 4-51 shows a 1,000-ohm resistor in series with a 2-henry inductor in a 120-volt, 60-hertz AC circuit. The inductive reactance is 753.6 ohms. When we add this vectorially to the 1,000-ohm resistance, we get an impedance of 1,252 ohms.

$$
\begin{aligned}
X_L &= 2\pi \ f \cdot 1 \\
&= 6.28 \cdot 60 \cdot 2 \\
&= 753.6 \text{ ohms}
\end{aligned}
$$

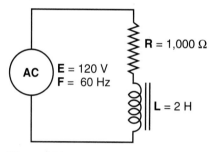

Figure 4-51. *Finding the impedance of a series R-L circuit*

$$
\begin{aligned}
Z &= \sqrt{R^2 + X_L^2} \\
&= \sqrt{1,000^2 + 753.6^2} \\
&= \sqrt{1,000,000 + 567,913} \\
&= \sqrt{1,567,913} \\
&= 1,252 \text{ ohms}
\end{aligned}
$$

The total current in this circuit is found by dividing the source voltage by the impedance:

$$
\begin{aligned}
I &= \frac{E}{Z} \\
&= \frac{120}{1,252} \\
&= 0.0958 \text{ amp}
\end{aligned}
$$

The voltage drop across each of the components is found by the formula:

$$E_R = I \cdot R \qquad\qquad E_L = I \cdot X_L$$
$$= 0.0958 \cdot 1{,}000 \qquad\qquad = 0.0958 \cdot 753.6$$
$$= 95.8 \text{ volts} \qquad\qquad = 72.19 \text{ volts}$$

You will notice that here, as in the series R-C circuit, the sum of the voltage drops is greater than the applied voltage. The reason is that the current flowing through the resistor is not in phase with the current flowing through the inductor.

Power in a Series R-L Circuit

To find the amount of power actually developed in a circuit, we must find the amount of current in phase with the voltage. Do this by finding the power factor which is the ratio of the resistance to the impedance.

$$PF = \frac{R}{Z}$$

$$= \frac{1{,}000}{1{,}252}$$

$$= 0.799 \text{ or } 79.9\%$$

The power factor may also be found by trigonometry since it is the cosine of the phase angle. We can find the phase angle, or the number of degrees the voltage leads the current in our circuit, by finding the angle whose tangent is the ratio of the inductive reactance to the resistance. This ratio is 0.7536 and the angle whose tangent is 0.7536 is 37°. The cosine of 37° is 0.799, which is the power factor of the circuit.

The true power of our circuit is found to be:

$$P_T = E \cdot I \cdot PF$$
$$= 120 \cdot 0.0958 \cdot 0.799$$
$$= 9.18 \text{ watts}$$

Since all of this power is used in the resistor, we could also find the amount of power by:

$$P_T = I^2 \cdot R$$
$$= 0.0958^2 \cdot 1{,}000$$
$$= 9.18 \text{ watts}$$

The apparent power in this circuit is the product of the voltage and the current, and it is 11.5 volt-amps.

$$P_A = E_T \cdot I_T$$
$$= 120 \cdot 0.0958$$
$$= 11.5 \text{ volt-amps}$$

Parallel R-L Circuits

When a circuit is arranged so the inductor and resistor are in parallel across the source voltage, the voltage will be the same across both components, but the current through them will be different.

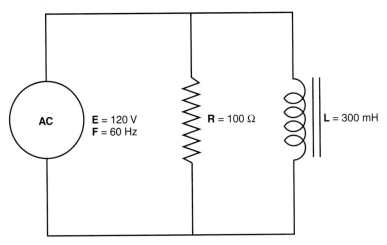

E = 120 V
F = 60 Hz

R = 100 Ω

L = 300 mH

Figure 4-52. *Finding the impedance of a parallel R-L circuit*

The currents through the two components are found by the formulas:

Inductive reactance:

$$X_L = 2\pi f l$$
$$= 6.28 \cdot 60 \cdot 0.3$$
$$= 113 \text{ ohms}$$

Current through the inductor:

$$I_L = \frac{E}{X_L}$$

$$= \frac{120}{113}$$

$$= 1.06 \text{ amp}$$

Current through the resistor:

$$I_R = \frac{E}{R}$$

$$= \frac{120}{100}$$

$$= 1.2 \text{ amp}$$

The total current in the circuit is the vector sum of the current through the resistor and that through the inductor.

$$I_T = \sqrt{I_R^2 + I_L^2}$$

$$= \sqrt{1.2^2 + 1.06^2}$$

$$= \sqrt{1.44 + 1.12}$$

$$= \sqrt{2.56}$$

$$= 1.6 \text{ amp}$$

The impedance of this parallel circuit is found by dividing the source voltage by the total current:

$$Z = \frac{E_T}{I_T}$$

$$= \frac{120}{1.6}$$

$$= 75 \text{ ohms}$$

This also could have been found by dividing the product of the resistance and the inductive reactance by the vector sum of these two oppositions.

$$Z = \frac{R \cdot X_L}{\sqrt{R^2 + X_L^2}}$$

$$= \frac{100 \cdot 113}{\sqrt{100^2 + 113^2}}$$

$$= \frac{11,300}{\sqrt{10,000 + 12,769}}$$

$$= \frac{11,300}{\sqrt{22,769}}$$

$$= \frac{11,300}{151}$$

$$= 74.9 \text{ ohms}$$

Answers begin on Page 359. Page numbers refer to chapter text.

69. Find the inductive reactance of a 0.75-henry inductor in a 120-hertz AC circuit.
    $X_L =$ _____ ohms. *Page 215*

70. Find the inductive reactance of a 50-millihenry inductor in a 2-kilohertz AC circuit.
    $X_L =$ _____ ohms. *Page 215*

71. Find the values required for this question:

    a. The inductive reactance = _____ ohms
    b. The circuit impedance = _____ ohms
    c. The total current = _____ amp
    d. The voltage across the resistor = _____ volts
    e. The voltage across the inductor = _____ volts
    f. The phase angle = _____ degrees
    g. The current is _____ (leading or lagging) the voltage
    h. The power factor = _____ percent
    i. The apparent power = _____ volt-amps
    j. The true power = _____ watts
       Page 217

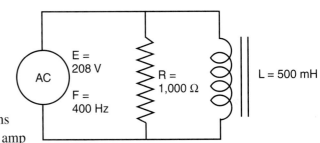

72. Find the values required for this question:

    a. The inductive reactance = _____ ohms
    b. The current through the resistor = _____ amp
    c. The current through the inductor = _____ amp
    d. The total current = _____ amp
    e. The circuit impedance = _____ ohms
       Page 219

Circuits with Resistance, Inductance, and Capacitance

A capacitor causes current to lead the voltage, an inductor causes it to lag the voltage, and a resistor has no effect on the phase. But when a circuit contains all three types of components, voltage is dropped, power is used, heat is generated, and the phase is shifted.

Series R-L-C Circuits

Now that we can find the impedance, the voltage drops, and the current flow in circuits that contain either resistance and capacitance or resistance and inductance, we can find these values in circuits that contain resistance and both capacitance and inductance.

Both capacitance and inductance cause phase shifts because the current in neither a capacitive nor an inductive circuit is in phase with the voltage that causes the current. In a purely capacitive circuit the current leads the voltage by 90°, and in a purely inductive circuit the current lags 90° behind the voltage. In a circuit that contains both capacitance and inductance, the two reactive currents are 180° out of phase with each other, and they cancel.

Note the series R-L-C circuit in Figure 4-53. In this circuit, there is a 200-ohm resistor in series with a 0.53-henry (530 mH) inductor and an 8.84-microfarad capacitor.

Begin the analysis of the circuit by finding the inductive reactance, which is 200 ohms, and the capacitive reactance, which is 300 ohms.

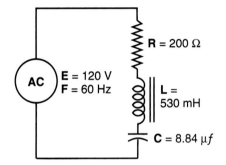

Figure 4-53. *Finding the characteristics of a series R-L-C circuit*

Since the current flowing in the capacitive part of the circuit is 180° out of phase with that which flows in the inductive part of the circuit, the two reactances oppose one another, and the total reactance is the difference between the two. In this example, the total reactance is 100 ohms. Since the capacitive reactance is greater than the inductive reactance, the total reactance is capacitive.

The impedance of this circuit is the vector sum of the 200-ohm resistance and the 100-ohm total reactance. Find the amount of impedance by finding the square root of the square of the resistance plus the square of the reactance.

$$Z = \sqrt{X^2 + (X_C - X_L)^2}$$
$$= \sqrt{200^2 + (300 - 200)^2}$$
$$= \sqrt{40,000 + 10,000}$$
$$= 223.6 \text{ ohms}$$

The total current in the circuit is found by dividing the voltage of the source by the circuit impedance.

$$I_T = \frac{E_T}{Z}$$
$$= \frac{120}{223.6}$$
$$= 0.537 \text{ amp}$$

This is a series circuit, so the total current flows through all three components, and we can find the voltage drops across each component by multiplying the total current by the resistance and by each of the reactances.

$$E_R = I_T \cdot R$$
$$= 0.537 \cdot 200$$
$$= 107.4 \text{ volts}$$

$$E_C = I_T \cdot X_C$$
$$= 0.537 \cdot 300$$
$$= 161.1 \text{ volts}$$

$$E_L = I_T \cdot X_L$$
$$= 0.537 \cdot 200$$
$$= 107.4 \text{ volts}$$

Find the phase angle, or the number of degrees the total current is out of phase with the voltage, by finding the angle whose tangent is the amount of the total reactance divided by the amount of resistance.

$$\text{Phase Angle} = \text{Tan}^{-1} \frac{X}{R}$$

$$= \text{Tan}^{-1} \frac{100}{200}$$

$$= \text{Tan}^{-1} 0.5$$

$$= 26.6 \text{ degrees}$$

The current in this circuit leads the voltage by 26.6 degrees. The power factor of this circuit is the percent of the current that is in phase with the voltage, and the power factor is the cosine of the phase angle. The phase angle is 26.6°, and the cosine of 26.6° is 0.89. Eighty-nine percent of the current is in phase with the voltage.

The apparent power in the circuit is found by multiplying the circuit voltage by the total current, and this gives us 64.4 volt-amps.

$$P_A = E_T \cdot I_T$$
$$= 120 \cdot 0.537$$
$$= 64.4 \text{ volt-amps}$$

The true power, measured in watts, is found by multiplying the apparent power by the power factor. When we multiply these two values, we get a true power of 57.3 watts.

$$P_T = P_A \cdot PF$$
$$= 64.4 \cdot 0.89$$
$$= 57.3 \text{ watts}$$

The only power used in this circuit is that used in the resistor, so the true power may also be found by multiplying the square of the total current by the resistance.

$$P_T = I_T^2 \cdot R$$
$$= 0.537^2 \cdot 200$$
$$= 57.6 \text{ watts}$$

In these two examples the answers should be exactly the same, but there is an error of 0.5%. This is caused by rounding off the numbers and an error this small is acceptable for all practical problems.

Parallel R-L-C Circuits

When the resistor, the capacitor, and the inductor are connected in parallel rather than in series, we must first find the current through the resistor, the capacitor, and the inductor, and then find the total current. *See* Figure 4-54.

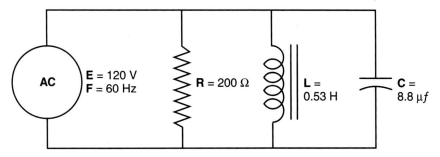

Figure 4-54. *Finding the characteristics of a parallel R-L-C circuit*

The current through the capacitor and the inductor are 180° out of phase with each other, so the total reactive current, I_X, is the difference between the two.

$$
\begin{aligned}
I_X &= I_L - I_C \\
&= 0.6 - 0.4 \\
&= 0.2 \text{ amp}
\end{aligned}
$$

The total current is the vector sum of the resistive current and the reactive current, and we find this by taking the square root of the sum of the square of the resistive current and the square of the reactive current.

$$
\begin{aligned}
I_T &= \sqrt{I_R{}^2 + I_X{}^2} \\
&= \sqrt{0.6^2 + 0.2^2} \\
&= \sqrt{0.36 + 0.04} \\
&= 0.632 \text{ amp}
\end{aligned}
$$

The circuit impedance, or the total opposition to the flow of current, is found by dividing the total voltage by the total current.

$$
\begin{aligned}
Z &= \frac{E_T}{I_T} \\
&= \frac{120}{0.632} \\
&= 189.9 \text{ ohms}
\end{aligned}
$$

The phase angle is the number of degrees the current is out of phase with the voltage, and we determine this by finding the angle whose tangent is equal to the amount of reactive current divided by the amount of resistive current.

$$
\begin{aligned}
\text{Phase Angle} \ &= \ \text{Tan}^{-1} \ \frac{I_X}{I_R} \\[2mm]
&= \ \text{Tan}^{-1} \ \frac{0.2}{0.6} \\[2mm]
&= \ \text{Tan}^{-1} \ 0.333 \\[2mm]
&= \ 18.4 \text{ degrees}
\end{aligned}
$$

The current in this circuit lags 18.4° behind the voltage. This is because the circuit is inductive; that is, there is more inductive current than there is capacitive current.

The true power used in this circuit is found by multiplying the total voltage by the current through the resistor. Do not consider the current through either the inductor or the capacitor because they do not use power nor produce heat.

$$
\begin{aligned}
P_T \ &= E_T \cdot I_R \\
&= 120 \cdot 0.6 \\
&= 72 \text{ watts}
\end{aligned}
$$

In order to find the apparent power in the circuit, we must first find the amount of reactive power. Reactive power, sometimes called wattless power, is the difference between the volt-amps in the inductor and the volt-amps in the capacitor.

$$
\begin{aligned}
P_L \ &= E_T \cdot I_L \\
&= 120 \cdot 0.6 \\
&= 72 \text{ volt-amps}
\end{aligned}
$$

$$
\begin{aligned}
P_C \ &= E_T \cdot I_C \\
&= 120 \cdot 0.4 \\
&= 48 \text{ volt-amps}
\end{aligned}
$$

$$
\begin{aligned}
P_X \ &= P_L - P_C \\
&= 72 - 48 \\
&= 24 \text{ volt-amps}
\end{aligned}
$$

When we know the amount of reactive power, we can find the apparent power by taking the square root of the sum of the squares of the true power and the reactive power.

$$P_A = \sqrt{P_T^2 + P_X^2}$$

$$= \sqrt{72^2 + 24^2}$$

$$= \sqrt{5{,}184 + 576}$$

$$= \sqrt{5{,}760}$$

$$= 75.9 \text{ volt-amps}$$

We can also find the apparent power by dividing the true power by the power factor (the cosine of the phase angle). The phase angle is 18.4° and its cosine is 0.948. Dividing the 72 watts of true power by 0.948 gives us 75.9 volt-amps.

STUDY QUESTIONS: CIRCUITS CONTAINING RESISTANCE, CAPACITANCE AND INDUCTANCE

Answers begin on Page 359. **Page numbers refer to chapter text.**

73. Find the indicated values:

a. The inductive reactance = _____ ohms.
b. The capacitive reactance = _____ ohms.
c. The total reactance = _____ ohms.
d. The circuit impedance = _____ ohms.
e. The total current = _____ amp.
f. The voltage across the resistor = _____ volts.
g. The voltage across the inductor = _____ volts.
h. The voltage across the capacitor = _____ volts.
i. The phase angle = _____ degrees.
j. The current is _____ (leading or lagging) the voltage.
k. The power factor = _____ percent.
l. The apparent power = _____ volt-amps.
m. The true power = _____ watts.

Page 222

R = 300 Ω
E = 208 V
F = 400 Hz
L = 0.2 H
C = 2 μf
AC

Continued

74. Find the indicated values:

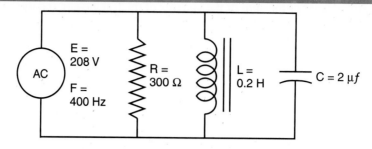

a. The inductive reactance = _____ ohms.

b. The capacitive reactance = _____ ohms.

c. The current through the resistor = _____ amp.

d. The current through the inductor = _____ amp.

e. The current through the capacitor = _____ amp.

f. The total reactive current = _____ amp.

g. The total current = _____ amp.

h. The circuit impedance = _____ ohms.

i. The phase angle = _____ degrees.

j. The current is _____ (leading or lagging) the voltage.

k. The true power = _____ watts.

l. The inductive power = _____ volt-amps.

m. The capacitive power = _____ volt-amps.

n. The reactive power = _____ volt-amps.

o. The apparent power = _____ volt-amps.

Page 225

Resonance

Capacitors and inductors are often used in an AC circuit to control the flow of current according to its frequency. It is possible to have a circuit that offers little opposition to the flow of AC above a certain frequency, while opposing the flow of DC or AC below that frequency. We can also have a circuit that opposes AC above a given frequency while passing DC and AC of a lower frequency.

Other commonly used circuits select certain bands of frequencies to either pass or reject them. Circuits that control current flow in this manner are called filters, and they work on the principle of resonance.

A capacitor in an AC circuit opposes the flow of current by its capacitive reactance. Figure 4-55A shows that as the frequency of the AC increases, the capacitive reactance decreases. For DC, whose frequency is zero, the capacitive reactance is infinite. As the frequency increases, the capacitive reactance becomes less.

The opposition caused by an inductor is called inductive reactance, and it also changes as the frequency changes, increasing as the frequency increases.

If a circuit contains both inductance and capacitance, there is a frequency at which the reactances are equal, and this frequency is called the resonant frequency of the circuit. The effect the inductor and the capacitor have on the current flow is determined by the way they are arranged in the circuit, in series or in parallel.

We can find the frequency at which a capacitor and an inductor are resonant by the formula:

$$f_r = \frac{1}{2\pi \sqrt{LC}}$$

f_r = Resonant frequency of the circuit in hertz
2π = A constant, 6.28
L = Inductance of the inductor in henries
C = Capacitance of the capacitor in farads

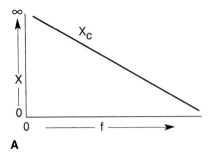

A

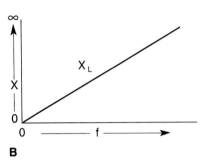

B

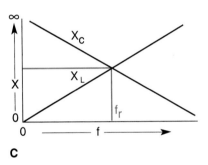

C

Figure 4-55.
A. *Capacitive reactance decreases as the frequency increases.*
B. *Inductive reactance increases as the frequency increases.*
C. *The resonant frequency of an AC circuit is the frequency at which the inductive reactance and the capacitive reactance are equal.*

The resonant frequency of an L-C circuit is that frequency at which the inductive reactance and the capacitive reactance are equal. We can find the amount of capacitance needed to resonate with a given inductance at a particular frequency by using the formula:

$$C = \frac{1}{(2\pi f_r)^2 \cdot L}$$

The amount of inductance needed to resonate with a capacitor at a given frequency can be found by using the formula:

$$L = \frac{1}{(2\pi f_r)^2 \cdot C}$$

For example, find the amount of capacitance for a 2-millihenry inductor to be resonant at 15 kilohertz.

$$C = \frac{1}{(2\pi f_r)^2 \cdot L}$$

$$= \frac{1}{(6.28 \cdot 15,000)^2 \cdot 0.002}$$

$$= \frac{1}{94,200^2 \cdot 0.002}$$

$$= \frac{1}{17,747,280}$$

$$= 5.63^{-8} \text{ farads} = 0.0563 \text{ microfarads}$$

We can also find the amount of inductance needed to go with a 0.001-microfarad capacitor to be resonant at 200 kilohertz.

$$L = \frac{1}{(2\pi f_r)^2 \cdot C}$$

$$= \frac{1}{(6.28 \cdot 20{,}000)^2 \cdot 0.000\,000\,001}$$

$$= \frac{1}{1.577 \cdot 10^{12} \cdot 1 \cdot 10^{-9}}$$

$$= \frac{1}{1.577 \cdot 10^3}$$

$$= 0.000\,64 \text{ henry} = 0.64 \text{ millihenry}$$

Series Resonance

If we have an AC circuit with a capacitor, an inductor, and a resistor all connected in series, the voltage across the inductor is 180° out of phase with the voltage across the capacitor, and the circuit impedance is the vector sum of the resistance and the total reactance. The circuit will act as it would if it had only one reactance.

In a series R-L-C circuit across a variable frequency AC power source, the capacitor will cause a large opposition to low frequencies, and the inductor will oppose all of the high frequencies. If we increase the frequency from zero (DC) to a high value, the current will increase with the frequency until the resonant frequency of the circuit is reached. Then the current will drop off as the frequency continues to increase.

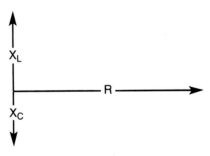

Figure 4-56. *Phase relationships in a series R-L-C circuit*

The current in a series circuit flows through all three components. This current is in phase with the voltage across the resistor, and shows along the horizontal line in Figure 4-56. But the current through the inductor lags 90° behind the applied voltage, so the voltage dropped across the inductor leads the current through it by 90°. Plot this vertically upward, since the phase rotation is counterclockwise.

The current into and out of the capacitor leads the voltage across the capacitor by 90°, so the voltage is 90° behind the current. Plot this voltage vertically downward. Figure 4-56 shows that the voltage across the capacitor opposes the voltage across the inductor, and at resonance, these two voltages are equal but of opposite polarity, so they cancel. At resonance, the only voltage in the circuit is that which appears across the resistor.

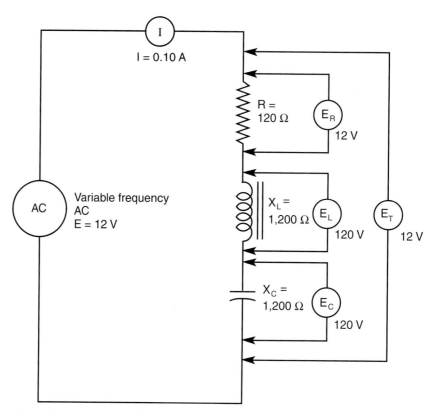

Figure 4-57. *Voltage distribution in a series R-L-C circuit at its resonant frequency*

Let's assume some values so we can better understand what is happening. At the resonant frequency, X_L and X_C are each 1,200 ohms, and all of the circuit resistance has been lumped into a single resistor, R, which equals 120 ohms. The voltage of the source is 12 volts. At resonance, the total current is 0.1 amp, or 100 milliamps.

$$I_T = \frac{E_T}{R}$$

$$= \frac{12}{120}$$

$$= 0.1 \text{ amp} = 100 \text{ milliamps}$$

Since this is a series circuit, the same 100 milliamps flow through the inductor and the capacitor, and each has a voltage drop of 120 volts.

$$
\begin{aligned}
E_L &= I_T \cdot X_L & \qquad E_C &= I_T \cdot X_C \\
&= 0.1 \cdot 1,200 & &= 0.1 \cdot 1,200 \\
&= 120 \text{ volts} & &= 120 \text{ volts}
\end{aligned}
$$

These voltages are both much higher than the source voltage, but since they are 180° out of phase with each other, their instantaneous polarities are opposite, and they cancel each other. Kirchhoff's voltage law applies to this circuit, as it says that the total voltage dropped around a series circuit is equal to the applied voltage.

$$
\begin{aligned}
E_T &= E_R + E_L + E_C \\
&= 12 + 120 - 120
\end{aligned}
$$

If the circuit resistance had been high—for example, if it had been 1,200 ohms instead of 120 ohms—the circuit current would have been only 10 milliamps, and the voltage drop across the inductor and the capacitor would have both been 12 volts rather than 120 volts. These voltage drops still cancel each other and the voltage across the resistor will still be 12 volts.

Since this is a series circuit, any one of the three components can control the amount of current that flows. At frequencies below resonance, the capacitive reactance is high and the capacitor opposes the flow of current. At frequencies above resonance, the inductive reactance is high and the inductor opposes the current. At the resonant frequency, the only opposition is that produced by the resistance, and at the resonant frequency, the current is maximum.

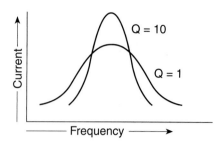

Figure 4-58. *The Q (quality factor) of an R-L-C circuit determines the steepness of the band pass curve.*

The steepness of the current rise and fall seen in Figure 4-58 is determined by the ratio of the reactance at resonance to the circuit resistance. This is called the Q of the circuit. In our example, we see the curves when the circuit resistance is 120 ohms, the circuit Q is 10:

$$Q = \frac{X}{R}$$

$$\frac{1{,}200}{120} = 10$$

When the circuit resistance is 1,200 ohms, the circuit Q is one:

$$\frac{1{,}200}{1{,}200} = 1$$

The higher Q provides a much steeper current rise and drop off, and this affects the width of the band of frequencies this type of circuit will pass.

Parallel Resonance

A series R-L-C circuit passes a band of frequencies near its resonant frequency because its impedance is minimum at resonance. A parallel R-L-C circuit acts in exactly the opposite way. Its impedance is maximum at its resonant frequency. It will block a band of frequencies near its resonant frequency, and will pass frequencies both above and below its resonant frequency.

Figure 4-59A shows a parallel R-L-C circuit, but for the moment, let's not consider the resistance. For low frequencies, the capacitive reactance is high and the inductive reactance is low. The current sees an easy path through the inductor, and the inductive current is high. But as the frequency increases, the inductive reactance increases, and it opposes the current, so the current flow decreases. In B, we see the way the current decreases as the frequency increases until the resonant frequency is reached, at which time the capacitive reactance and the inductive reactance are equal. The current through the circuit is minimum, and the circuit impedance is maximum. The current is essentially stopped. As the frequency increases above the resonant frequency, the capacitive reactance decreases and the current flow through the capacitor increases. At high frequencies, almost all of the current flows through the capacitor.

AVIATION MAINTENANCE TECHNICIAN SERIES   GENERAL

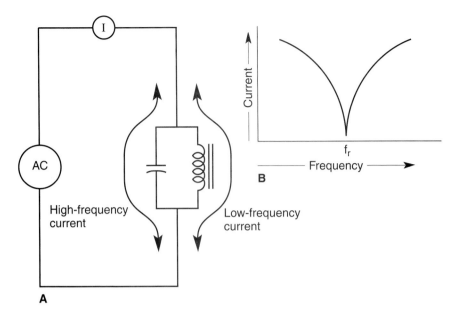

Figure 4-59

*A. In a parallel L-C circuit, most of the current at frequencies below resonance passes
through the inductive branch. At frequencies higher than the resonant frequency, most of
the current passes through the capacitive branch.*

B. At the resonant frequency, the circuit opposition is maximum, and the current is minimum.

A capacitor and an inductor, in parallel, form what is called a tank circuit.
This type of circuit is used as the frequency controlling portion of some
oscillators.

Look at Figure 4-60 on Page 236 to see the way this works. In this circuit, we have an inductor whose inductive reactance at the frequency of the
source is 100 ohms, and a capacitor whose capacitive reactance at this frequency is also 100 ohms. Assume that there is no resistance in the circuit.
The circuit is equipped with three switches making it possible to isolate or
combine components. Begin by opening switch B to remove the capacitor
from the circuit, and closing switches A and C so source current can flow
through the inductor. When the flow is established, and 120 milliamps of
current is flowing through the inductor, an electromagnetic field surrounds
the inductor and stores energy.

As soon as the current reaches its maximum flow rate, close switch B
and open switch A so no more energy will be supplied to the inductor from
the source. The magnetic field begins to collapse, and the voltage induced as
the field collapses forces electrons into the capacitor. Since there is no resistance in our hypothetical circuit, the current will flow into the capacitor as
long as the magnetic field around the inductor is collapsing. By the time the
electromagnetic field is completely gone, the electrostatic field across the
plates of the capacitor has built up to a maximum.

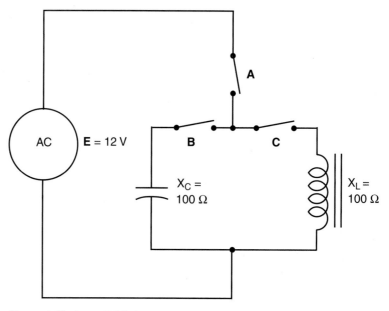

Figure 4-60. *A parallel L-C circuit is called a tank circuit. When the circuit is energized by alternating current at its resonant frequency, current will flow back and forth between the inductor and the capacitor as energy is alternately stored in electromagnetic and electrostatic fields.*

Now, all of the energy is stored in the capacitor and the inductor appears to be a short circuit across it, so the capacitor begins to discharge through the inductor. As current flows in the inductor, it builds up a magnetic field in which the energy is stored, and by the time the capacitor is fully discharged, this field will be at its maximum strength. If there were no resistance in the circuit, this interchange of energy between the electromagnetic field around the inductor and the electrostatic field across the capacitor could continue indefinitely even though switch A were open, isolating the tank circuit from the source of energy.

The current flow in the tank circuit is called circulating current, and if there were no resistance in the circuit, the current would be exactly the amount needed to produce sustained oscillation. But in the real world of electricity, we cannot have a circuit without some resistance. This resistance converts some of the energy being exchanged back and forth between the capacitor and the inductor into heat.

If there were no resistance in the circuit, the tank would, at its resonant frequency, act as an infinite opposition to source current. Since there is some resistance in the tank, some energy will be used and there will not be enough current flow to keep the fields at their original strength. The source must supply the energy used in the resistance. If the resistance in the tank circuit increases, the losses will increase and the source must supply more current.

L-C Filters

One of the more important uses for inductors and capacitors in electrical circuits is that of electronic filters. These circuits control the flow of current in the load as a function of the frequency of the alternating current. There are a number of types of filters in use, including the following four commonly used arrangements.

A low-pass filter offers a minimum of opposition to frequencies below its cutoff frequency, and it furnishes a path for the higher frequencies to bypass the load. Figure 4-61 shows such a filter. The inductive reactance of the inductor is less than the resistance of the load at frequencies below cutoff, and most of the voltage is dropped across the load. At frequencies above cutoff, most of the voltage is dropped across the inductor and only a small portion appears across the load. At these higher frequencies, the capacitive reactance of the capacitor is low and most of the current flowing through the inductor returns to the source through the capacitor.

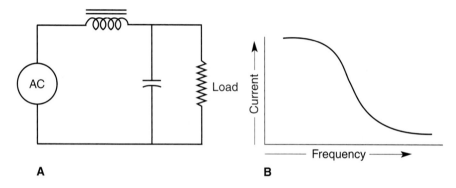

Figure 4-61
A. A low-pass filter
B. Current flow through a low-pass filter as frequency changes

A high-pass filter works in exactly the opposite way (*see* Figure 4-62). At frequencies below cutoff, the capacitive reactance is high enough that most of the voltage is dropped across the capacitor. The inductor across the load provides a low-impedance path back to the source for any current that flows beyond the capacitor so that it will not flow through the load.

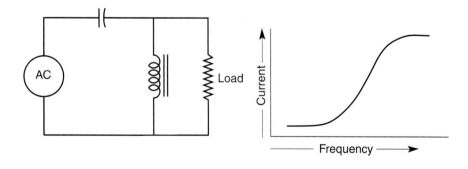

Figure 4-62
A. A high-pass filter
B. Current flow through a high-pass filter as frequency changes

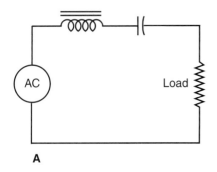

A

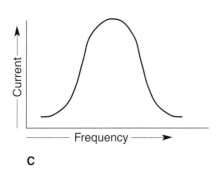

B

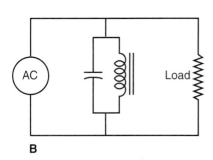

C

Figure 4-63.

A. *A series L-C bandpass filter*

B. *A parallel L-C bandpass filter*

C. *Current flow through a bandpass filter as frequency changes*

Figure 4-63 shows two types of band-pass filters. In A, we have an inductor and a capacitor in series between the source and the load. Below the resonant frequency, most of the voltage is dropped across the capacitor; above this frequency, most of it is dropped across the inductor. At the resonant frequency, the impedance of this series combination is lower than the resistance of the load and most of the voltage from the source is dropped across the load.

The filter in B uses a parallel L-C circuit across the load. At frequencies below resonance, the inductive reactance of the coil is less than the resistance of the load, and most of the current returns to the source through it. At frequencies above resonance, most of the current returns by way of the capacitor. At the resonant frequency of this tank circuit, its impedance is greater than the resistance of the load and most of the current flows through the load.

Figure 4-64 shows two configurations of band-reject filters. These filters pass current at frequencies on either side of a specific band of frequencies and they prevent current at frequencies in this band from reaching the load.

In A, the parallel L-C circuit is between the source and the load. Below the resonant frequency of the tank current flows through the coil to the load. Above the resonant frequency, current flows through the capacitor to the load. But at and near the resonant frequency, current to the load is blocked.

The filter in B uses a series L-C circuit across the load. Above the resonant frequency the coil blocks current flowing around the load and below the resonant frequency the capacitor blocks it. At the resonant frequency the impedance of the L-C circuit is minimum and the current bypass the load. The current through the load is minimum.

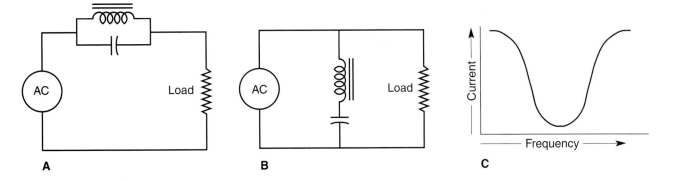

Figure 4-64
A. A parallel L-C band-reject filter
B. A series L-C band-reject filter
C. Current flow through a band-reject filter as frequency changes

Answers begin on Page 359. Page numbers refer to chapter text.

75. The capacitive reactance of a capacitor increases as the frequency of the AC _____
    (increases or decreases). *Page 230*

76. The inductive reactance of an inductor increases as the frequency of the AC _____
    (increases or decreases). *Page 230*

77. Find the resonant frequency of a circuit that contains a 25-microfarad capacitor and a 2-millihenry
    inductor.
    Resonant frequency = _____ hertz. *Page 230*

78. The value of a capacitor needed to install with a 4-millihenry inductor so they will be resonant at
    1 kilohertz is _____ microfarad. *Page 231*

79. The value of inductor that is needed to install with a 0.05-microfarad capacitor so they will be resonant at
    500 kilohertz is _____ millihenry. *Page 231*

80. The impedance of a series R-L-C circuit is _____ (maximum or minimum) at its
    resonant frequency. *Page 233*

81. Increasing the circuit resistance of a series resonant circuit will _____ (increase or
    decrease) the voltage across the capacitor. *Page 233*

Continued

82. Increasing the circuit resistance of a series resonant circuit will _____ (increase or decrease) the circuit Q. *Page 234*

83. The current through a series R-L-C circuit is _____ (minimum or maximum) at its resonant frequency. *Page 234*

84. The impedance of a parallel L-C circuit is _____ (minimum or maximum) at its resonant frequency. *Page 234*

85. A parallel L-C circuit is called a _____ circuit. *Page 235*

86. If the resistance of a parallel R-L-C circuit is increased, the impedance the circuit offers to the source current _____ (increases or decreases). *Page 233*

87. Identify each type of filter:

a. _____
b. _____
c. _____
d. _____

Page 237

Three-Phase Alternating Current Electricity

Much of the heavy-duty electrical equipment in aviation maintenance shops operates with three-phase alternating current. The generator that produces three-phase AC has three sets of windings that produce three independent voltage waves during each revolution.

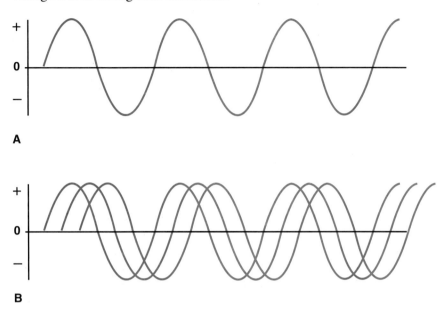

Figure 4-65
A. Single-phase alternating current
B. Three-phase alternating current

Refer to Figure 4-65A, to see the plot of the current in a single-phase AC circuit. At times, the current drops to zero and even though this happens at a high frequency, and for a very short period of time, the torque produced by a single-phase AC motor cannot be perfectly smooth. In B, we see the current plot for three-phase AC. Every 120 electrical degrees, the current in one of the phases begins to rise. There is no time when there is no current flowing in the circuit, and there is very little drop from peak current during its operational cycle. Three-phase motors are wound with three sets of windings and during almost any portion of the operational cycle, one of the phases is producing maximum torque.

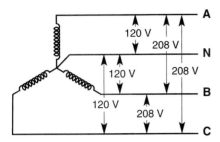

Figure 4-66. *Voltage between each phase winding and neutral in a Y-connected three-phase circuit*

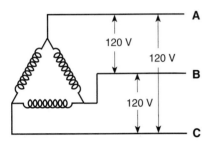

Figure 4-67. *Voltage across the three phases of a delta-connected three-phase circuit*

Three-phase power can be connected in such a way that it provides single-phase AC for circuits that require it. If the windings on a three-phase alternator are connected with a central tie point, the alternator is said to be Y-connected. Y-connected circuits normally have four leads, leads from the three windings identified as A, B, and C, and the neutral lead, N. *See* Figure 4-66.

Alternators that produce 120 volts in each of the phase windings do not produce twice this amount between two of the phase windings. This is because the voltages in the two windings are not 180° apart, they are only 120 electrical degrees apart, and the voltage between any two of the phase windings is 1.73 times the voltage across any one of the phases itself. The current between two of the phases is the same as that through a single phase. Commercial 60-hertz, three-phase, Y-connected AC has 120 volts across each phase and 208 volts between the phases. This power is brought into the maintenance shops from the power lines, and single-phase loads can be connected between the neutral and one of the phases. This type of connection provides 120-volt, single-phase AC. It is important, of course, that the loads on each of the three phases are kept well balanced.

Instead of all three windings being connected together at a single point, the ends of the three windings may be connected into a delta-connection. In this arrangement, the output voltage is the same as the voltage of a single phase, but the current is higher. Notice in Figure 4-67 that two of the windings are in series across the third winding. The total current is 1.73 times the current in a single winding.

STUDY QUESTIONS: THREE-PHASE ALTERNATING CURRENT

*Answers begin on Page 359. **Page numbers refer to chapter text.***

88. The current in one winding of a three-phase alternator is _____ electrical degrees out of phase with the current in the other winding. *Page 242*

89. If there is 120 volts across a single winding of a three-phase Y-connected alternator, the voltage across two of the phases is _____ volts. *Page 242*

Electrical Circuit Components

As already mentioned, a basic electrical circuit consists of a source of electrical energy, a load to use the energy, and conductors to connect the source to the load. In addition to these components, almost all practical circuits also contain circuit protection and control devices. These devices control the flow of electrons in the circuit and protect the conductors and components from too much current or from too high or too low a voltage. Knowing the way these electrical components function allows us to find the trouble when a system fails to work as it should.

Different types of electrical systems use different types of components. The components installed in an aircraft may appear similar, but are actually different from those used in boats and automobiles because of the stringent requirements of the Federal Aviation Administration.

Electrical Measuring Instruments
Voltmeters

Voltmeters are connected in parallel with the component whose voltage is to be measured. The (+) terminal of the voltmeter must be on the side of the component to which the positive terminal of the power source is connected (*see* Figure 4-68).

voltmeter. An electrical instrument used to measure voltage. Most analog voltmeters determine the voltage by measuring the current forced through a series of precision resistors.

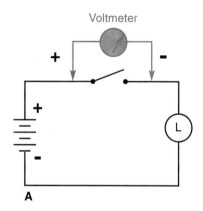

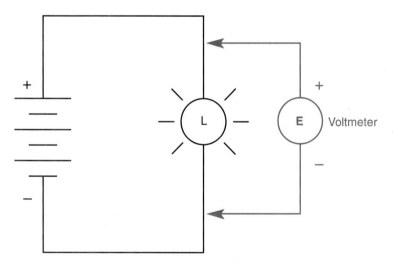

Figure 4-68. *A voltmeter must be connected in parallel with the voltage to be measured.*

When a voltmeter is connected across an open switch, a blown fuse, or an open component, it will read the system voltage. When it is connected across a closed switch or a good fuse, it will read zero voltage. *See* Figure 4-69.

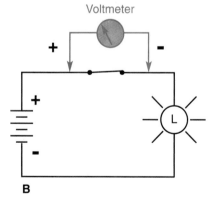

Figure 4-69
A. *A voltmeter across an open switch reads the system voltage.*
B. *A voltmeter across a closed switch reads zero voltage*

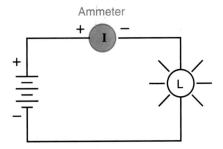

Figure 4-70. *Ammeters are connected in series with the load to measure the current flowing through the load.*

ammeter. A measuring instrument installed in series with an electrical load to measure the amount of current flowing through the load.

current (I). The flow of electricity. Current is measured in amperes.

ohmmeter. An instrument used to measure resistance in an electrical circuit or component. A known voltage is applied across the unknown resistance, and the resulting current is measured.

Ammeters

Ammeters are connected in series with the circuit whose current is to be measured (*see* Figure 4-70). The (+) terminal of the ammeter connects to the portion of the circuit to which the positive terminal of the power source connects.

Ammeters installed in an aircraft cockpit can measure the current flowing from the generator without routing the high-current cables through the cockpit. This is done by placing an ammeter shunt, a very low-resistance precision resistor, in the main generator output lead and measuring the voltage drop across it with a millivoltmeter calibrated in amps. The standard aircraft ammeter shunt has a 50-millivolt (0.05-volt) drop across it when the rated output current from the generator flows through it. *See* Figure 4-71.

Small amounts of current are measured with milliammeters, which measure current in increments of 0.001 amp, and microammeters, which measure current in increments of 0.000 001 amp.

Ohmmeters

Ohmmeters measure the resistance of a component by measuring the amount of current that flows through the component from the known voltage of a self-contained battery. They contain a battery and a variable resistor to adjust the voltage so it will furnish the correct amount of current to cause full-scale deflection of the meter when the test leads are shorted together.

There are several scales marked R x 1, R x 100, and R x 1,000 to give the meter a wide range of resistance it can measure. When determining the resistance being measured, multiply the reading on the dial by the multiplier value marked on the selector switch.

When using an ohmmeter to measure a circuit component, the component must be disconnected from all other components so the current from the ohmmeter will not flow through them and give an inaccurate indication. *See* Figure 4-72.

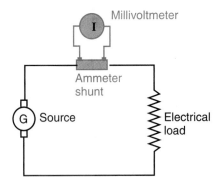

Figure 4-71. *Generator output current is determined by measuring the millivoltage drop across an ammeter shunt installed in the generator output lead. The millivoltmeter is calibrated in amperes.*

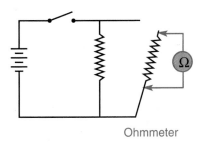

Figure 4-72. *Before the resistance of a component can be measured with an ohmmeter, the component must be isolated from the rest of the circuit.*

*Answers begin on Page 359. **Page numbers refer to chapter text.***

90. A voltmeter must be installed in _____ (series or parallel) with the component whose voltage is to be measured. *Page 243*

91. An ammeter must be installed in _____ (series or parallel) with the component whose current is to be measured. *Page 244*

92. Large amounts of current are measured by measuring the voltage drop across a/an _____ with a millivoltmeter whose dial is calibrated in amperes. *Page 244*

93. A/an _____ measures the resistance of a component by measuring the amount of current that flows through it from a self-contained battery of accurately known voltage. *Page 244*

Conductors

Any conductor in an aircraft electrical circuit must be able to carry all the current needed by the load without becoming too hot. Its resistance must be low enough that it will not cause an excessive voltage drop.

Most of the conductors used in aircraft circuits are made of copper wire because copper is a very good conductor of electricity. It has only one electron in its valence shell, and this electron can be knocked out and replaced by another electron with very little electrical pressure. Of all of the elements, only silver is a better conductor, but, of course, silver is much more expensive than copper. Figure 4-73, shows the relative resistance of several materials used as electrical conductors.

Material	Relative resistance
Silver	0.95
Copper	1.00
Gold	1.42
Aluminum	1.64
Brass	3.9
Iron	5.6
Constantan	28.45
Nichrome	65.0

Figure 4-73. *Relative resistance of electrical conductors*

The resistance of a conductor (its opposition to current flow) is measured in ohms, and the resistance depends upon four things: the material of which the conductor is made; its length; its cross-sectional area; and its temperature.

The longer the conductor the greater the distance the electrons must travel, and the more resistance it has. The larger the cross-sectional area, the more electrons can travel at the same time, and therefore the conductor has less resistance.

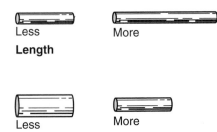

Length

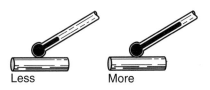

Cross-sectional area

Material

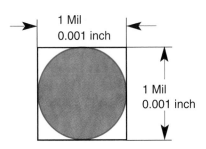

Temperature

Figure 4-74. *Factors affecting resistance*

Figure 4-75. *One circular mil is the area of a circle whose diameter is one mil (0.001 inch).*

The temperature of a conductor also affects its resistance. When metals are heated, the molecules move about much faster, and the free electrons find more opposition to their flow than they do when the metal is cold. *See* Figure 4-74.

Scientists have found that when the temperature of some metals is lowered to near absolute zero, the resistance of the metal drops so low that the metals act as though it were a superconductor. Some semiconductor materials act in exactly the opposite way, their resistance becomes less when they are heated. Semiconductor materials are used to make thermistors, which are special resistors whose resistance becomes less when its temperature increases. Thermistors are used in temperature-measuring instruments and for some types of electronic control devices.

Most practical conductors are made of round wire. Since the cross-sectional area of the wire determines its resistance, and thus the amount of current it can carry, we often need to know the area of the wire. There is a special type of measurement that makes it easy for us to find the area of round conductors. This measurement is the circular mil. One circular mil is the area of a circle whose diameter is one mil, or one one-thousandth of an inch. *See* Figure 4-75.

To find the area of a round conductor in circular mils, square its diameter. For example, a six-gage wire has a diameter of 0.162 inch. To change this diameter into mils, multiply it by 1,000. Its diameter is 162 mils. A diameter of 162 mils when squared gives an area of 26,244 circular mils.

Area (circular mils) = Diameter (in mils)^2

One circular mil is 0.7854 square mil, and so the square mil area of a round conductor can be found by multiplying its area in circular mils by 0.7854. Its area in square inches can be found by multiplying its area in circular mils by 7.854×10^{-7}.

The wires used for most electrical and electronic work are measured according to the American Wire Gage (AWG) system. Figure 4-76 shows a chart of the diameter, the cross-sectional area in circular mils, the resistance in ohms per thousand feet, and the feet per pound of several of the most generally used wire sizes.

Standard Annealed Copper Wire			
AWG Gage	Area Circular Mils	Ohms/ 1,000 Feet	Feet/ Pound
0	105,500	0.098	3.13
6	26,250	0.395	12.58
10	10,380	0.998	31.82
14	4,107	2.525	80.44
20	1,022	10.15	323.40

Figure 4-76. *Standard annealed solid copper wire*

When vibration is a problem, as it is when wires are installed in aircraft, stranded wire is normally used rather than solid wire. The most generally used conductors are made up of several small-diameter strands of tinned copper wire wrapped in a plastic. This type of stranded wire is often called a cable. Figure 4-77 is a chart showing the characteristics of some of the more generally used sizes of stranded wire cables.

Stranded Copper Wire Cable			
AWG Gage	Area Circular Mils	No. Wires	Ohms/ 1,000 Feet
0	104,118	19	0.114
6	26,813	7	0.436
10	10,433	7	1.10
14	3,830	7	2.99
20	1,119	7	10.25

Figure 4-77. *Stranded copper wire cable*

Answers begin on Page 359. Page numbers refer to chapter text.

94. Two things we must consider when we select a conductor for use in an electrical circuit are:

 a. _____

 b. _____

 Page 245

95. The two metals which are the best conductors of electricity are:

 a. _____

 b. _____

 Page 245

96. Four things that affect the resistance of a conductor are:

 a. _____

 b. _____

 c. _____

 d. _____

 Page 246

97. Some metals become superconductors when their temperature is very _____ (high or low). *Page 246*

98. The area of a piece of wire that has a round cross-sectional shape with a diameter of 0.040 inch is _____ circular mils. *Page 246*

99. The area of a circle whose diameter is one mil, or one thousandth of an inch, is one _____ . *Page 246*

100. Which wire has the larger area, a 20-gage wire, or a 10-gage wire? A _____-gage wire. *Page 247*

101. A _____ (solid or stranded) wire is used for installations where vibration is likely to be a problem. *Page 247*

Resistors

One of the most important operations in practical electricity is to control the flow of electrons so they will do the work we want them to. We can do this with mechanical switches, with semiconductor diodes or transistors, and with resistors that oppose the flow of electrons in much the same way friction opposes the flow of a fluid. Resistance in a circuit drops voltage, produces heat, and can be used to control the amount of current that flows in a circuit.

All conductors have some resistance, but the resistors we want to consider here are separate electrical components. Some are small cylinders of a carbon compound that have a wire lead extending out from each end. These resistors are made in several different sizes depending upon the amount of power they can dissipate, or get rid of, without overheating. One-eighth-, one-fourth-, one half-, one-, and two-watt sizes are commonly used.

Composition Resistor Color Code

Composition resistors are made in values from less than one ohm to several megohms (million ohms). The resistance of the resistor is marked according to colored bands around one end. The standard color code progresses from black, representing zero, to white, which signifies nine. *See* Figure 4-78.

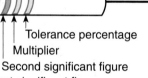

Tolerance percentage
Multiplier
Second significant figure
First significant figure

Color	First Band	Second Band	Third Band	Fourth Band
Black	0	0	0	
Brown	1	1	1	
Red	2	2	2	
Orange	3	3	3	
Yellow	4	4	4	
Green	5	5	5	
Blue	6	6	6	
Violet	7	7	7	
Gray	8	8	8	
White	9	9	9	
No color				±20%
Silver			0.01	±10%
Gold			0.1	± 5%

Figure 4-78. *The bands of color around a composition resistor show its resistance.*
The first band is the first digit, or number.
The second band is the second digit, or number.
The third band is the number of zeros to add to the first two digits. Silver and gold in this position are multipliers.
The fourth band, if one is used, shows the tolerance in percentage of the resistance value.

There are two exceptions in the third band: sometimes the third band is either silver or gold. When the third band is gold, the multiplier is 0.1, and if the band is silver, the multiplier is 0.01. A resistor marked brown, black, gold has a resistance of 1 ohm (10 x 0.1). One marked yellow, violet, silver has a resistance of 0.47 ohm (47 x 0.01). *See* Figure 4-79.

There is usually a fourth color band, and when it is used, it is either silver or gold. This is the tolerance band. When the fourth band is gold, the resistor has a tolerance of plus or minus 5% of the value shown by the first three bands. And when the fourth band is silver, the resistance tolerance is plus or minus 10% of the nominal value.

A resistor marked orange, orange, red, gold has a resistance of 3,300 ohms, plus or minus 5%, or an actual value somewhere between 3,135 and 3,465 ohms. If the resistor is marked orange, orange, red, silver, its resistance is within plus or minus ten percent of its marked value, and its actual resistance is between 2,970 and 3,630 ohms. If the resistor has only three color bands, its tolerance is plus or minus 20%, so a resistor marked orange, orange, red has a resistance between 2,640 and 3,960 ohms.

Tolerance		
5%	10%	20%
10	10	10
11		
12	12	
13		
15	15	15
16		
18	18	
20		
22	22	22
24		
27	27	
30		
33	33	33
36		
39	39	
43		
47	47	47
51		
56	56	
62		
68	68	68
75		
82	82	
91		
100	100	100

Figure 4-80. *Multipliers for preferred values for composition resistors*

1st Band	2nd Band	3rd Band	4th Band	Nominal Resistance	Tol. %	Resistance Range	
						Low	High
Yellow	Violet	Blue	Silver	47,000,000	10%	42,300,000	51,700,000
Brown	Black	Brown	Gold	100	5%	95	105
Red	Red	Orange		22,000	20%	17,600	26,400
Brown	Green	Brown	Silver	150	10%	135	165
Orange	Orange	Yellow		330,000	20%	264,000	396,000
Brown	Black	Green	Gold	1,000,000	5%	950,000	1,050,000

Figure 4-79. *Examples of resistance range of composition resistors*

Figure 4-80 lists the multipliers for values in which composition resistors are made. There is reason behind the seeming odd spacing between the resistance values. This is caused by the tolerances. For example, a 270-ohm resistor with a tolerance of plus or minus 5% could have a resistance between 256.5 and 283.5 ohms. The next smaller resistor, a 240-ohm resistor, could have a resistance as high as 252 ohms, and the next higher one, a 300-ohm resistor, could have a resistance as low as 285 ohms. With this spacing there are no overlaps. This makes the manufacturing of these resistors less costly. Resistors with 10% tolerance are made with fewer values than resistors with 5% tolerance, and there are even fewer made with 20% tolerance.

The multipliers in Figure 4-80 indicate, for example that there is a 13- and 130-, and 1,300-ohm 5% resistor but there are no 10% or 20% resistors whose values are multiples of 13 times 10.

AVIATION MAINTENANCE TECHNICIAN SERIES   GENERAL

Wire-Wound Resistors

When there is a need for a circuit to dissipate several watts of power, wire-wound resistors may be used. These are quite often made of bare nichrome wire wound on a ceramic tube. Nichrome is an alloy of nickel and chromium whose resistance is about 65 times as much as copper. Nichrome wire having the correct length and cross-sectional area for the resistance and power needed is wound around the tube, and the leads are attached to the end. The wire is then covered with a ceramic material, and it is fired in a furnace to protect the wire from damage and to insulate it. Some wire-wound resistors have one or more taps so that either the total resistance or only part of the resistance can be used.

A part of the wire may be left bare and a metal band, or strap is fastened around the resistor and held with a screw and a nut. The location of the band determines the amount of resistance. The band may be moved to get the exact amount of resistance needed, but when the screw is tightened, the band will not move.

Variable Resistors

There are two types of variable resistors commonly used in electrical and electronic equipment. A potentiometer is a variable resistor that has three terminals, one at each end of the resistance element, and one that is connected to the wiper. The wiper is moved around the resistor to change the amount of resistance in the circuit. Some potentiometers have a carbon material for their resistance element, and others have a length of resistance wire wound around a strip of insulating material. With either type, the position of the wiper determines the amount of resistance in the circuit.

A potentiometer places a constant amount of resistance across a voltage source, as seen in Figure 4-81A. Moving the wiper across the resistance changes the amount of voltage applied to the load. When the wiper is at the top of the resistor, all of the resistance is in parallel with the load, and the total source voltage is across the load. As the wiper is moved down the resistor, part of the resistance is in series with the load and part is in parallel with it, and the voltage across the load is less. When the wiper is at the bottom of the potentiometer, both ends of the load are connected to the negative end of the voltage source, and no current flows through the load.

A rheostat is a variable resistor that has only two connections. One connection is made to the end of the resistance element, and the other is made to the wiper. Most rheostats are wire-wound, and can dissipate several watts of power. A typical use of a rheostat is that of dimming lights by dropping voltage. In Figure 4-81B, a rheostat is in series with a light. When the wiper is

potentiometer. A variable resistor with three connections.

rheostat. A variable resistor with two connections.

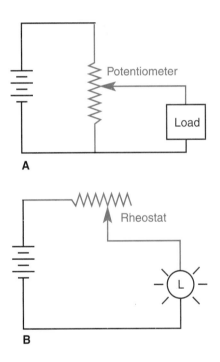

Figure 4-81
A. *Potentiometer is used to divide voltage.*
B. *A rheostat is used to drop voltage.*

positioned so it is at the end of the resistance element near the other connection, the least amount of resistance is in the circuit, and the lamp burns at full brilliance. When the wiper is moved across the resistor, more resistance is put into the circuit, and voltage is dropped across the resistor, so less voltage is available to force current through the lamp. With less current, the lamp burns dimly.

In an electrical schematic diagram, a resistor is shown as a zigzag line, as in Figure 4-82.

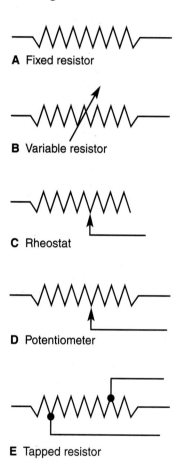

A Fixed resistor

B Variable resistor

C Rheostat

D Potentiometer

E Tapped resistor

Figure 4-82. *Symbols for various types of resistors*

STUDY QUESTIONS: RESISTORS

Answers begin on Page 359. Page numbers refer to chapter text.

102. Write in the value and tolerance for each of these composition resistors:

	Nominal Resistance	Tolerance ±%	1st Band	2nd Band	3rd Band	4th Band
a			Brown	Black	Green	Silver
b			Red	Red	Red	
c			Yellow	Violet	Violet	Silver
d			Orange	Orange	Gold	Silver
e			White	Brown	Black	Gold

Page 249

103. Give the proper color codes for these composition resistors:

	Nominal Resistance	Tolerance ±%	1st Band	2nd Band	3rd Band	4th Band
a	1,500	20				
b	6.8	5				
c	3,300,000	10				
d	390	10				
e	2,200	20				

Page 249

104. The amount of power a composition resistor can dissipate is determined by the ______________________________ of the resistor. *Page 249*

105. A variable resistor with three connections, one at either end of the resistor and one at the wiper is called a ______________________________ . *Page 251*

106. A variable resistor with only two connections, one at one end of the resistor and one at the wiper, is called a ______________________________ . *Page 251*

Continued

107. Identify the type of resistor represented by each of these symbols:

a.

b.

c.

d.

e.

Page 251

Switches

Switches are some of the simplest of electrical control devices, and there are many different kinds of switches for use in all kinds of applications. Switches are classified according to the number of circuits they control, and the number of circuit conditions they can select. Figure 4-83 shows the symbols used on electrical schematic diagrams for some of the different kinds of switches.

A single-pole, single-throw switch, abbreviated SPST, is used to control only one circuit, and it has only two conditions, ON and OFF. When the arm of the switch joins the two dots, the switch is closed, or ON, and when it is in the position shown, it is open, or OFF.

A single-pole, double-throw (SPDT) switch such as the one in B, controls one circuit, but it can select either of two conditions. Switches such as this are used to select high-speed or low-speed operation of a motor, or to open a valve when it is in one position and to close it when it is in the other position. The switch shown here has a center OFF position. Some SPDT switches, such as the one seen in C, are spring-loaded to one side, and may be switched to the other side momentarily. This kind of switch is used in a warning-light circuit. When it is moved to the momentary position, it completes a circuit through the light bulb to test it, and when it is released, the switch automatically moves back to complete the normal warning circuit.

In D, we see a double-pole, single-throw switch, a DPST. This kind of switch is used to open or close two circuits at the same time with the operator having to move only one control. The switch shown in E is a double-pole, double-throw switch, a DPDT. It controls two circuits, and can select either of two conditions.

When we must control more than 2 circuits, or when there are several conditions for each circuit, we can use a rotary wafer switch. With this type of switch, we have a selector knob on a shaft that rotates a switch blade between the contacts. A wiper contacts the switch blade so that it makes contact in all positions of the switch. By rotating the shaft with the knob, we can place the blade between any of the contacts.

The blades of a rotary wafer switch can be designed to control one or more circuits and to select up to approximately twelve conditions. As many wafers as are needed can be stacked on a single shaft. The rotary wafer switch is widely used for electronic communications equipment and for electronic test equipment.

A Single-pole, single-throw

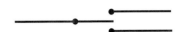

B Single-pole, double-throw, center OFF

C Single-pole, double-throw, spring-loaded to one side

D Double-pole, single-throw

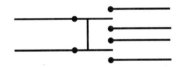

E Double-pole, double-throw

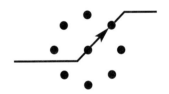

F Rotary-wafer

Figure 4-83. *Symbols for various types of switches*

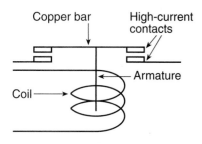

Figure 4-84.
Schematic of a solenoid switch

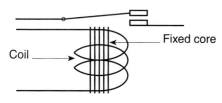

Figure 4-85. *Schematic of a relay switch*

Relays and Solenoids

We often need to control large amounts of current from a switch that is located some distance from the high-current circuit. When we need to do this, we can use a relay or a solenoid-type switch.

The starter for an aircraft engine is a good example of a circuit that uses a solenoid-type switch. Figure 4-84 shows such a switch. When the ignition switch, which can carry only a small amount of current because of its small size, is turned to the START position, current flows through it to the coil of the solenoid switch. This current causes a magnetic field to pull the iron armature down into the coil, and this pulls the copper bar down to make connections with the two copper contacts. A large amount of current can flow to the starter motor through this low-resistance circuit. When the ignition switch is released from the START position, the current stops flowing in the coil, and a spring pushes the copper bar up off of the contacts. No more current can flow to the starter motor.

A relay is a type of remotely controlled switch that functions in the same way as a solenoid switch, but it has a fixed iron core rather than a movable core. Non-electronic generator controls use relays to control the voltage, to limit the current, and to disconnect the generator from the battery when the generator output is lower than the battery voltage.

STUDY QUESTIONS: SWITCHES

*Answers begin on Page 359. **Page numbers refer to chapter text.***

108. A switch that can select either of two conditions for two circuits is called a
_____-pole, _____-throw switch. *Page 255*

109. When we need to control several circuits and have several conditions for each circuit, we can use a
_____ switch. *Page 255*

110. The difference between a relay and a solenoid is in the core. A solenoid has a
_____ (movable or fixed) core. *Page 256*

Circuit Protection Devices

Some type of device must be installed in most aircraft circuits to protect the wiring from an excessive amount of current in the event of certain kinds of malfunctions. These devices may be either fuses or circuit breakers. The only circuits that are not required to have one of these devices are the main circuits for starter motors and any other circuit in which no hazard is presented.

Fuses

One of the simplest devices used to protect a circuit is a fuse, which is a small strip of low-melting-point metal in series with the load. When too much current flows, the fuse link, as this metal strip is called, melts and opens the circuit. Fuses and circuit breakers are rated in amps to show the amount of current they will carry before they open the circuit.

Glass tubular fuses are often used in aircraft electrical systems and in electronic equipment, and some holders for tubular fuses have an indicator light in the cap that lights up when the fuse melts. When a fuse is melted, it is said to be "blown."

One special type of glass tubular fuse is the slow-blow fuse. Electric motors have a large inrush of current when they are starting, but as soon as they are turning at speed, the current drops to a much lower value. A regular fuse large enough to carry the starting current will not protect the motor from excessive current when the motor is running normally. To prevent the fuse blowing when the motor is starting, and still protect it from excess current during normal operation, a slow-blow fuse can be used. A slow-blow fuse has a large link that will carry the starting current without melting, but if more current than the fuse is designed to carry flows through it for a given length of time, the link will soften and a spring will pull it apart opening the circuit. *See* Figure 4-86.

Circuit Breakers

One of the main problems with using a fuse to protect a circuit is that you must have a new fuse available to replace one that is burned out. Most modern aircraft use circuit breakers rather than fuses to protect circuits. *See* Figure 4-87.

The most widely used type of circuit breaker is the thermal, or heat-operated type. The heart of this circuit breaker is a bimetallic conductor made of strips of two different kinds of metal welded together. These metals expand in different amounts when they are heated, and when too much current flows through the bimetallic strip, it warps and snaps the contacts apart, opening the circuit. When the strip snaps, it pushes the reset button out of the housing to show that the circuit is open. After allowing a few seconds for the bimetallic strip to cool down, the reset button may be pushed in to close the contacts and restore the circuit.

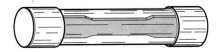

A

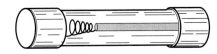

B

Figure 4-86.
A. Glass tubular fuse
B. Slow-blow fuse

fuse. A circuit protection device made of a strip of metal that melts when excessive current flows through it. When it melts, it opens the circuit.

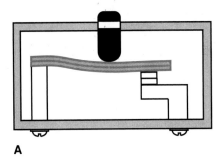

A

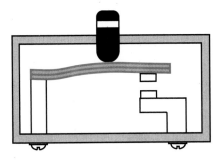

B

Figure 4-87.
A. Push-to-reset-type circuit breaker in its closed condition.
B. Excessive current has warped the bimetallic strip and snapped the contacts open.

Some circuit breakers have handles that allow them to be used as a switch as well as a circuit breaker. When the handle is down, the circuit is open, or OFF. When the handle is moved up, the circuit is closed, or ON. If too much current flows, the handle will trip to the center position and open the circuit. To restore the circuit, move the handle to the OFF position, and then back to the ON position.

Aircraft electrical systems are required to use trip-free circuit breakers. The operating handle of a trip-free circuit breaker will not close the contacts if a fault exists. This prevents a pilot from holding the circuit breaker closed and sending current into a short circuit that could cause a fire.

Some commercial electric motors have built-in automatic-reset circuit breakers to protect the motor windings. When the motor overheats, the circuit breaker opens the power lead to the motor. As soon as the windings cool down, the bimetallic strip snaps and restores the circuit and the motor starts again. Automatic-reset circuit breakers are not approved for use in aircraft electrical systems.

STUDY QUESTIONS: CIRCUIT PROTECTION DEVICES

*Answers begin on Page 359. **Page numbers refer to chapter text.***

111. A fuse that has a large link and a spring to pull it apart when it is softened by a sustained flow of current is called a _____ fuse. *Page 257*

112. Fuses and circuit breakers are rated in _____ . *Page 257*

113. A circuit breaker that cannot be closed into a fault regardless of the position of the operating control is called a/an _____ circuit breaker. *Page 258*

114. A circuit breaker that automatically resets itself after it has tripped because of excessive current _____ (is or is not) approved for use in an aircraft electrical system. *Page 258*

Capacitors

Capacitors are components used to store electrical energy in an electrostatic field. They are composed of two conductors, called plates, separated by an insulator, called the dielectric.

Energy Stored in Capacitors

All of the electric components studied up to this point are used to control the flow of electrons in a circuit. Conductors carry the electrons, resistors drop voltage and limit current, switches stop the flow of electrons or select parts of the circuit in which they are allowed to flow, and fuses and circuit breakers open a circuit when too much current flows.

Now, we want to study components that store electrical energy. Electrical energy can be stored in two ways: in electrostatic fields in a capacitor, and in electromagnetic fields in an inductor. First, we want to study capacitors and see the way they store energy.

A capacitor was at one time called a condenser. It is an electrical component made up of two conductors, called plates, separated by an insulator, called the dielectric. One common type of capacitor is the paper capacitor. The plates are made of two strips of metal foil separated by a strip of waxed paper which is the insulator, or dielectric. The two layers of foil and the waxed paper are stacked together in a sandwich, and the stack is rolled into a tight roll, with wires attached to the foil at either end. The entire roll is encapsulated, or molded, into a plastic cylinder with the lead wires sticking out of the ends.

When a capacitor is connected across a battery, electrons leave the negative terminal and flow onto one of the plates of the capacitor. They try to pass through the dielectric to the other plate and to the positive terminal of the battery, but, since they cannot flow through the dielectric, the electrons accumulate, or stack up, on the negative plate. The positive terminal of the battery attracts all of the electrons from the other plate, and leaves it with a shortage of electrons, or with a positive charge. The electrons flow from the negative terminal of the battery into the positive terminal only until the capacitor is charged; that is, until the voltage across the two plates of the capacitor is the same as the voltage across the two terminals of the battery. When the capacitor is charged, it acts as an open circuit, and no more electrons flow.

Disconnect the capacitor from the battery, and it will remain charged; that is, the negative plate will hold its excess of electrons, and the positive plate will continue to have a shortage of electrons. In this way, the capacitor stores electrical energy.

The amount of electrical energy a capacitor can store is called its capacitance, or capacity, and it is measured in farads. One farad of capacity can store 1 coulomb of electricity, 6.28 billion, billion electrons (6.28×10^{18} electrons) under a pressure of 1 volt. The farad is too large a unit for most practical work, and so, in electrical and electronic circuits, we normally use capacitors with capacity in microfarads (one millionth of a farad), or in picofarads (one millionth of a millionth of a farad). One microfarad is equal to 1×10^{-6} farad, and one picofarad is equal to 1×10^{-12} farad.

The amount of charge a capacitor can store can be found by the formula:

$$Q = C \cdot E$$

Q = Charge in coulombs
C = Capacity in farads
E = Voltage across the capacitor in volts

A 100-microfarad capacitor with 100 volts across its terminals will store a charge of 0.01 coulomb.

$$
\begin{aligned}
Q &= C \cdot E \\
&= 0.0001 \cdot 100 \\
&= 0.01 \text{ coulomb}
\end{aligned}
$$

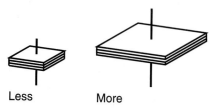

Less   More
Area of the plates

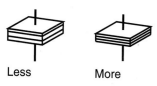

Less   More
Thickness of the dielectric

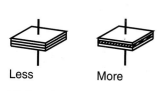

Less   More
Dielectric constant

Figure 4-88.
Factors affecting capacitance

Three things affect the capacity of a capacitor: the area of the plates, the separation between the plates, which is the thickness of the dielectric, and the dielectric constant of the material used for the dielectric. The greater the area of the plates, the greater the capacity; the closer the plates are together, the greater the capacity, and the higher the dielectric constant, the greater the capacity. *See* Figure 4-88.

We can find the capacity of a capacitor by using the formula:

$$C = \frac{0.2248 \cdot A \cdot K}{D}$$

C = Capacity of the capacitor in picofarads
0.2248 = A constant
A = Area of the plates, in square inches
K = Dielectric constant of the insulating material
D = Separation of the plates, or the thickness of the dielectric in inches

Typical values of the dielectric constant of some of the more commonly used insulating materials are:

Air = 1.0 (Air is used as the reference)
Turbine engine fuel = 2.0
Waxed paper = 3.0
Ceramic = 5.5
Mica = 7.0
Tantalum oxide = 11.0

Let's try a problem. Find the capacity of a capacitor whose plates have a total area of 10 square inches and whose separators are mica, each one with a thickness of 0.002 inch.

$$C = \frac{0.2248 \cdot A \cdot K}{D}$$

$$= \frac{0.2248 \cdot 10 \cdot 7}{0.002}$$

$$= 7{,}868 \text{ picofarads}$$

Electrical energy is stored not only in the stresses across the dielectric, but also by the distortion of the orbits of the electrons within the material itself. Usually, the better the insulating properties of a material, the higher its dielectric constant, and the stronger the electrostatic field for a given voltage. In a capacitor using air as the dielectric, and without changing anything else, if we fill the spaces between the plates with paper, the capacitance will increase. Electrical energy is stored in an electrostatic field between the plates. The closer the plates are together, the stronger the field, and therefore, more electrons can be stored with the same voltage. *See* Figure 4-89.

The strength of the dielectric determines the amount of voltage the capacitor can withstand, and this strength is expressed in terms of working voltage of the capacitor. The working voltage is the highest DC voltage that can be steadily applied to the capacitor without danger of the dielectric breaking down. A capacitor used in an AC circuit should have a working voltage at least 50% greater than the highest voltage that will be applied to it. The working voltage is determined by the type and thickness of the dielectric. Capacitors are also given a peak voltage rating, which is an AC voltage rating used to specify dielectric strength.

There are two basic types of capacitors used in electrical circuits: fixed and variable. We can further divide the fixed capacitors into electrolytic and non-electrolytic.

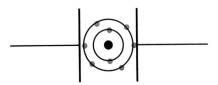

Plates are uncharged

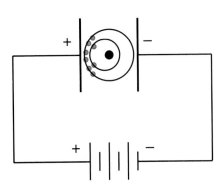

Plates are charged

Figure 4-89. *Uncharged plates do not affect the orbital pattern of the electrons in the dielectric. When a capacitor is charged, the orbits of the electrons in the dielectric are distorted, and electrical energy is stored in the distorted field.*

electrostatic field. An electrical force caused by an excess (negative field) or deficiency (positive field) of electrons.

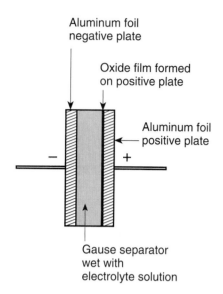

Figure 4-90. *An electrolytic capacitor has as its dielectric an extremely thin film of oxide deposited, or formed, on the aluminum foil plate.*

Electrolytic capacitors are polarized, which means that they can be used only in DC circuits. Electrons cannot flow from the oxide to the aluminum, but they can flow from the aluminum to the oxide.

An electrolytic capacitor is used to achieve large capacity in a low-voltage circuit. The dielectric in these capacitors is an extremely thin oxide coating on a plate of aluminum foil. Because the dielectric is so thin, the capacity is high, but because the thin insulation can be easily punctured by electrical pressure, the allowable DC working voltage must be carefully observed.

An oxide film deposited on a metal conductor, exactly the case in an electrolytic capacitor, makes an effective rectifier. It blocks any flow of electrons from the oxide into the metal. But if the capacitor is connected into the circuit with the metal on the negative side, or if it is installed in an AC circuit, electrons will flow from the metal through the oxide and puncture it. Then electrons can flow through the capacitor and produce enough heat to cause it to explode. *See* Figure 4-90.

Non-electrolytic capacitors normally use thin metal foil or metal film for their plates, and paper, mica, ceramic, or Mylar for the dielectric. For high voltage applications, oil is often used as the dielectric.

The capacity of variable capacitors may change by varying the amount the plates are meshed, by moving the plates closer together or farther apart, or by changing the dielectric between the plates.

Capacitors are rated according to their capacity, their working voltage, and by the peak voltage allowed across them. The working voltage is the maximum DC voltage that can be applied to the capacitor on a continuous basis. The peak voltage allowed, an AC voltage, is included in the rating to indicate the maximum strength of the dielectric.

One popular type of variable capacitor used in aircraft is the fuel tank probe used in capacitor-type fuel quantity indicating systems. Concentric metal tubes are used as the two plates of the capacitor, and the fuel or the air above the fuel is the dielectric. Air has a dielectric constant of one, and the fuel has a constant of approximately two. The capacity of the probe varies as the fuel level and the density of the fuel changes.

Series and Parallel Capacitors

When capacitors are connected in parallel, the total capacity is the sum of the individual capacitances. When you connect capacitors in parallel, you must be sure that the source voltage is not greater than the voltage rating of any individual capacitor.

$$C_T = C_1 + C_2 + C_3$$

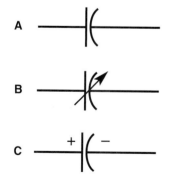

Figure 4-91. *Symbols for capacitors:*
A. Fixed nonelectrolytic capacitor
B. Variable capacitor
C. Fixed electrolytic capacitor

When capacitors are connected in series, their total capacity may be found in the same way as the total resistance of resistors connected in parallel. If there are several capacitors of the same size connected in series, the total capacitance is found by dividing the capacitance of one capacitor by the number of capacitors.

$$C_T = \frac{C}{n}$$

When two capacitors of unequal size are connected in series, the total capacity is found by dividing the product of the two capacitors by their sum.

$$C_T = \frac{C_1 \cdot C_2}{C_1 + C_2}$$

When more than two unequal capacitors are connected in series, the total capacity may be found by computing the capacity of each pair until you have only two equivalent capacitors left and then finding the capacity of this equivalent pair.

$$C_A = \frac{C_1 \cdot C_2}{C_1 + C_2}$$

then

$$C_B = \frac{C_3 \cdot C_4}{C_3 + C_4}$$

then

$$C_T = \frac{C_A \cdot C_B}{C_A + C_B}$$

You may use the reciprocal of the sum of the reciprocals formula and achieve the same answer:

$$C_T = \frac{1}{\dfrac{1}{C_1} + \dfrac{1}{C_2} + \dfrac{1}{C_3} + \dfrac{1}{C_4}}$$

If your calculator has a reciprocal key (1/x), you can solve this type of problem in a very short time. Be sure that all of the capacitances are in the same terms, either microfarads or picofarads, and your answer will come out in the same units.

$$(C_1)(1/x) + (C_2)(1/x) + (C_3)(1/x) + (C_4)(1/x) = (1/x)$$

Capacitive Time Constant

Electrons do not flow through a capacitor, but if a capacitor is connected across a source of DC voltage, as seen in Figure 4-92, electrons will begin to flow as soon as the switch is put into the charge position. As soon as the capacitor charges to the voltage of the battery, the current stops flowing, but the capacitor remains charged.

The time needed for a capacitor to reach a charge of 63.2% of the applied voltage is called the time constant (TC) of the circuit. This time, in seconds, may be found by multiplying the capacitance of the capacitor, in farads, by the circuit resistance, in ohms.

$$TC = R \cdot C$$

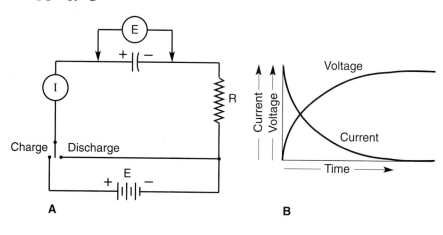

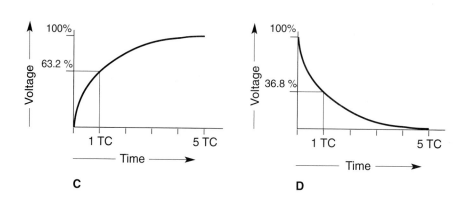

Figure 4-92

A. *When the switch is put into the charge position, electrons flow from the battery into the capacitor. The current flows rapidly at first and then tapers off as the voltage across the capacitor rises.*

B. *When the voltage across the capacitor reaches the voltage of the battery, no more current will flow.*

C. *Time constant when the capacitor is charging.*

D. *Time constant when the capacitor is discharging.*

Since the circuit capacitance is usually given in microfarads and the resistance in megohms, we can also find the time constant in seconds by multiplying the capacitance in microfarads (10^{-6}) by the resistance in megohms (10^6).

The capacitor will charge to 63.2% of the total voltage in one time constant, and it will reach the full voltage in approximately five time constants.

If the switch in Figure 4-92A is placed in the discharge position when the capacitor is fully charged, it will discharge through the resistor, and in one time constant the voltage across the capacitor will drop to 36.8% of the total voltage. The capacitor will be completely discharged in approximately five time constants.

STUDY QUESTIONS: CAPACITORS

*Answers begin on Page 359. **Page numbers refer to chapter text.***

115. Three factors that affect the capacity of a capacitor are:

    a. _____

    b. _____

    c. _____

    Page 260

116. The basic unit of capacity of a capacitor is called a/an _____ . *Page 260*

117. One millionth of a farad is called a/an _____ . *Page 260*

118. One millionth of a millionth of a farad is called a/an _____ . *Page 260*

119. The highest DC voltage that can be steadily applied to a capacitor without the danger of breaking down the dielectric is called the _____ voltage of the capacitor. *Page 261*

120. The working voltage of a capacitor should be at least _____% greater than the highest applied voltage. *Page 261*

121. Two things that affect the working voltage of a capacitor are:

    a. _____

    b. _____

    Page 261

Continued

122. Identify the type of capacitor represented by each of these symbols:

   a.

   b.

   c.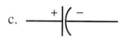

Page 262

123. One farad is the capacity needed to store one _____
under a pressure of one volt. *Page 260*

124. One farad = _____ microfarads or _____ picofarads. *Page 260*

125. One microfarad = _____ picofarads. *Page 260*

126. Find the capacity of a capacitor having a plate area of 25 square inches, using air as the dielectric, and
having a separation of 0.005 inch between the plates. C = _____ picofarads. *Page 260*

127. Increasing the thickness of the dielectric, with all else being the same, will
_____ (decrease or increase) the capacity of a capacitor. *Page 260*

128. Electrolytic capacitors _____ (should or should not) be used in an
AC circuit. *Page 262*

129. Capacitors that use oil as the dielectric usually have a high _____
(voltage rating or capacitance). *Page 262*

130. The peak voltage rating of a capacitor normally refers to _____
(AC or DC) voltage. *Page 262*

131. Find the equivalent total capacitance of these combinations:

    a. Three 0.5-microfarad capacitors in parallel:

       $C_T =$ _____ microfarads

    b. Five 350-picofarad capacitors in parallel:

       $C_T =$ _____ picofarads

    c. 0.05 microfarad, 0.10 microfarad, and 0.25 microfarad capacitors in parallel:

       $C_T =$ _____ microfarad

    d. 0.05-microfarad and 0.10-microfarad capacitors in series:

       $C_T =$ _____ microfarad

    e. 100, 150, and 300-picofarad capacitors in series:

       $C_T =$ _____ picofarads

    f. 4,500 picofarads, 0.007 microfarad, and 0.000 000 009 farad _____ capacitors in series:

       $C_T =$ _____ picofarads

    Page 263

132. The time constant of a circuit containing a 51,000-ohm resistor and a 25-microfarad capacitor is _____ seconds. *Page 264*

133. If an RC circuit has a time constant of 0.3 second, it will require _____ seconds to become fully charged. *Page 264*

Inductors

The energy stored in the electrostatic field in a capacitor is caused by the voltage that holds the electrons in the capacitor. Electrical energy can also be stored in an inductor in an electromagnetic field. The amount of energy stored in these fields depends upon the amount of current flowing in an inductor.

Self Induction

When electrons flow in a conductor, they cause a magnetic field to surround the conductor, and the direction the lines of flux encircle the conductor is determined by the direction the electrons flow. The distance the field extends out from the conductor is determined by the amount of current flowing in the conductor. *See* Figure 4-93.

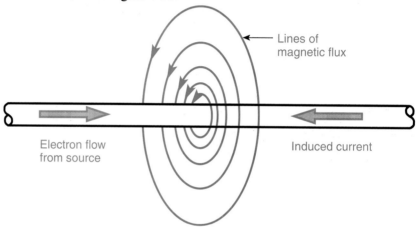

Lines of magnetic flux

Electron flow from source

Induced current

Figure 4-93. *Anytime electrons flow in a conductor, a magnetic field surrounds the conductor. When the current flowing in the conductor changes, the magnetic field builds up or collapses. As it does, it cuts across the conductor and induces, or creates, a current in it. This induced current flows in a direction opposite to that of the current which caused it.*

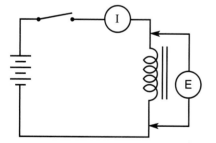

Figure 4-94. *As soon as the switch is closed, current begins to flow (it changes from zero flow to maximum flow). This changing current induces a voltage in the coil.*

When lines of magnetic flux cut across a conductor, a voltage is generated in the conductor that causes current to flow, and lines of flux cut across a conductor any time the current flowing in the conductor changes. If a coil is connected across a battery, as in Figure 4-94, the current will begin to flow as soon as the switch is closed.

Lenz's law tells us that an induced current is produced in a conductor any time the source current flowing in it changes. This current causes lines of magnetic flux to cut across the conductor. The direction of the induced current is always opposite to the direction of the source current, and the amount of induced current is determined by the rate at which the lines of flux cut across the conductor. This induced current is said to be produced by self induction.

The ability of a conductor to produce an induced current when lines of magnetic flux cut across it is called the inductance of the conductor, and it is measured in henries. One henry is the amount of inductance that will cause a change in current of 1 ampere per second to produce 1 volt of induced voltage. Most of the inductors in practical electrical circuits are in the millihenry (10^{-3}) range.

All conductors have some inductance, but if instead of the conductor being a straight wire, it is wound into a coil, the lines of flux will cut not only the conductor from its center outward, but it will also cut across the other turns of the coil. Much more voltage is induced in a coil than is induced in a simple straight wire. *See* Figure 4-95.

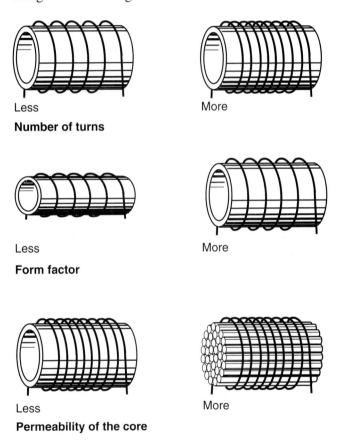

Less   More

Number of turns

Less   More

Form factor

Less   More

Permeability of the core

Figure 4-95. *Factors affecting inductance*

The inductance of a coil is determined by three things: the number of turns of wire in the coil, the form factor, which is the ratio of the diameter of the coil to its length, and the type of material used for the core of the coil.

Since the amount of induced voltage is determined by the rate at which the conductors are cut by the flux, we can increase the induced voltage by adding conductors. The easiest way to do this is by increasing the number of turns in the coil. With all else being equal, the more turns in a coil, the more inductance.

The form factor of a coil is the ratio of its diameter to its length. As the diameter is increased, the magnetic flux has a greater opportunity to affect the wire next to it. For example, in a coil whose diameter is one inch, each turn of wire is 3.14 inches long, and it has this distance to affect the turns next to it. If the diameter were two inches, each turn would be 6.28 inches long, and it would produce a greater number of lines of magnetic flux. With all else being equal, the larger the diameter of the coil, the greater will be its inductance.

Voltage is induced in a conductor only as lines of flux cut across it, and if we can make it easy for the flux to flow, the lines will concentrate in the coil and the inductance will increase. The permeability of the core material determines the amount the lines of flux will concentrate. Air is used as the reference, with a permeability of one. Some types of soft iron have permeabilities in the range of several thousand.

permeability. The ease with which a material conducts magnetic lines of force.

Mutual Induction

The form of induction we just studied is self induction, and it causes voltage to be produced in the inductor as the amount of current flowing through it changes. This induced voltage (or back voltage, as it is called) is caused by the expanding and collapsing magnetic field cutting across the turns of the inductor, or coil, itself. However, if another inductor is near enough the one through which the current is flowing and changing, the lines of flux will cut across it and induce a voltage into it, even though there is no electrical connection between the two. This voltage is produced by what is known as mutual induction. *See* Figure 4-96.

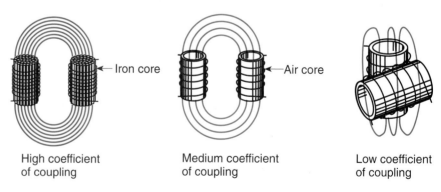

High coefficient of coupling   Medium coefficient of coupling   Low coefficient of coupling

Figure 4-96. *The amount of coupling between two coils is determined by the type of core used in the coils, by the distance the coils are apart, and by the angle between the two coils.*

The closer the inductors are together, the more lines of flux will link the two, and the more voltage will be induced. If all of the lines of flux link the two inductors, they have a coefficient of coupling of one (100%), but if none of the lines cut across the unenergized inductor, the coupling coefficient is zero. The closer the inductors are together, the higher the coefficient of coupling.

The angle between the two inductors also affects the coupling. If the coils are at right angles to one another, the flux lines will not cross in such a direction that they will induce a voltage, and even though they are close together, the coupling coefficient is nearly zero. We will see in the study of alternating current that a very handy electronic component is the transformer, which is basically two or more coils wound on a core made of laminations of highly permeable soft steel. The coils are usually wound, one on top of the other, to provide the maximum coefficient of coupling.

The formula for mutual induction is:

$$L_m = K\sqrt{L_1 \cdot L_2}$$

L_m = Mutual inductance in henries
K = Coefficient of coupling
L_1 = Inductance of first coil in henries
L_2 = Inductance of second coil in henries

Series and Parallel Inductances

If inductors, or coils, are connected in series in such a way that their magnetic fields aid one another, but they are separated so there is no coupling between them, the total inductance is equal to the sum of the individual inductances. *See* Figure 4-97.

$$L_T = L_1 + L_2 + L_3$$

We sometimes connect inductors in series close enough together that their magnetic fields cut cross each other, and in this case, mutual inductance must be considered. If the separate inductors are connected so their fields aid, and they are close enough together to have mutual inductance, the formula for total inductance is:

$$L_T = L_1 + L_2 + 2L_m$$

If the fields of the two inductors oppose one another, they still have the same self induction, but the mutual induction subtracts from the total induction. This is found by the formula:

$$L_T = L_1 + L_2 - 2L_m$$

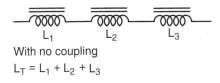

With no coupling
$L_T = L_1 + L_2 + L_3$

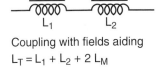

Coupling with fields aiding
$L_T = L_1 + L_2 + 2 L_M$

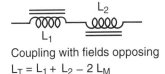

Coupling with fields opposing
$L_T = L_1 + L_2 - 2 L_M$

Figure 4-97. *Finding the total inductance of inductors connected in series.*

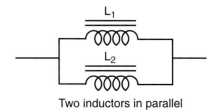

Two inductors in parallel

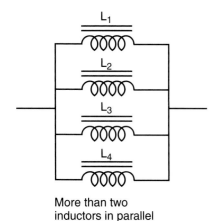

More than two
inductors in parallel

Figure 4-98. *Finding the total inductance of inductors connected in parallel*

The total inductance of inductors connected in parallel is found in the same way as the total resistance of resistors in parallel, or of capacitors in series (*see* Figure 4-98). For two unlike inductors with no coupling, the formula for total inductance is:

$$L_T = \frac{L_1 \cdot L_2}{L_1 + L_2}$$

If there are more than two inductors in parallel, the total inductance will be the reciprocal of the sum of the reciprocals of all of the individual inductances:

$$L_T = \frac{1}{\dfrac{1}{L_1} + \dfrac{1}{L_2} + \dfrac{1}{L_3} + \dfrac{1}{L_4}}$$

If your calculator has a reciprocal key (1/x), you can solve this in a short time. Be sure that all of the inductances are in the same terms, either henries or millihenries, and your answer will come out in the same units.

$$(L_1)(1/x) + (L_2)(1/x) + (L_3)(1/x) + (L_4)(1/x) = (1/x)$$

Inductive Time Constant

If we connect an inductor and a resistor into a DC circuit such as in Figure 4-99, and put the switch in position A, current will try to start flowing. But as soon as it begins to change, (as soon as it starts to rise from zero current) the magnetic field caused by the changing current begins to produce a voltage that opposes the source voltage and this opposing voltage keeps the current down to almost zero. When the switch is first closed, the induced voltage across the inductor is almost equal to the voltage of the battery, but it has the opposite polarity, and very little current flows through the resistor.

The small amount of current that flows through the resistor causes some voltage to be dropped across it. This voltage drop decreases the amount of voltage across the inductor, because the voltage across the resistor and the inductor, which are in series, must equal the battery voltage.

As the voltage across the inductor decreases, the battery is able to force more current through the circuit. The current through the L-C circuit rises, as seen in Figure 4-99B. In one time constant, the current rises to 63.2% of the maximum current the circuit will allow. The maximum current is limited by the combined resistance of the resistor and the inductor. As the voltage rises across the resistor, the change in the current decreases and there is less induced voltage produced by the inductor, and so the current through the circuit increases. After five time constants, the current stops changing, there is no more voltage induced in the inductor, and the current is limited only by the resistance of the circuit.

The inductive time constant, which is the time needed for the current in an R-L circuit to rise to 63.2% of the maximum current, may be found by the formula:

$$TC = \frac{L}{R}$$

TC = Time constant of the circuit, in seconds
L = Inductance of the circuit, in henries
R = Resistance of the circuit, in ohms

After five time constants, the current is no longer changing and it is at a maximum throughout the circuit. The magnetic field is maximum around the winding of the inductor, but the current through the inductor is steady, and since it is no longer changing, no voltage is being induced in the inductor.

When the switch is placed in position B, the magnetic field begins to collapse, and as it collapses, it cuts across the windings and produces a voltage that tries to prevent the current dropping off. It opposes the change, and instead of the current stopping immediately, it decreases according to the curve in Figure 4-99C. In one time constant, the flow drops off to 36.8% of the total flow, and in approximately five time constants, it drops to zero.

If we have a 5-henry inductor in series with a 5,000-ohm resistor, we can find the time constant by the formula:

$$TC = \frac{L}{R}$$

$$= \frac{5}{5,000}$$

$$= 0.001 \text{ second, or 1 millisecond}$$

Notice that the inductive time constant is different from the capacitive time constant. The amount of time needed for the voltage to build up across a capacitor is directly proportional to the amount of circuit resistance. Doubling the resistance doubles the time constant. However, the time needed for the current through an inductor to reach its maximum value is inversely proportional to the resistance of the circuit. The less resistance there is in the circuit, the faster the current through the inductor can change, and it is the rate of change of the current that produces the induced voltage. As the voltage across the inductor increases, the current flowing in the circuit increases at a slower rate.

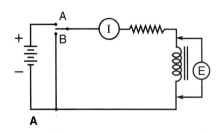

A

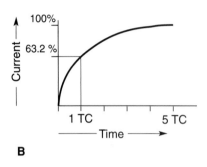

B

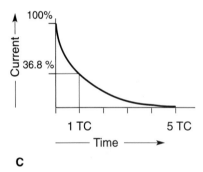

C

Figure 4-99
A. *Circuit used for measuring the time constant of an R-L circuit*
B. *Plot of current rise in an R-L circuit measured with time*
C. *Plot of current decay in an R-L circuit measured with time*

Decrease the circuit resistance to one half of the value it had in the problem just worked, and see that the time constant doubles. If the inductance remains at five henries, and the resistance changes to 2,500 ohms, the time constant will change to two milliseconds.

$$TC = \frac{L}{R}$$

$$= \frac{5}{2,500}$$

$$= 0.002 \text{ second, or 2 milliseconds}$$

Transformers

One of the major advantages of AC over DC is the fact that its current and voltage can easily be increased or decreased. We can do this with very simple components called transformers.

When alternating current flows in a coil, it produces expanding and collapsing magnetic fields that cut across the conductors of the coil itself as well as any other conductors that are near. The voltage generated within the conductor is produced by self induction, and the voltage produced in another conductor, one that is not electrically connected, is done by mutual induction. The amount of voltage produced by mutual induction is determined by the amount of coupling between the two conductors.

Most transformers have two or more coils of wire arranged so they have the maximum amount of coupling. The coil, or winding, as it may be called, that is connected to the power source is called the primary, and the winding connected to the load is called the secondary.

Most transformers used for power frequencies and audio frequencies are wound over cores of laminated sheet iron or steel. The laminations are thin and are coated with an insulating oxide or varnish that prevents, or at least minimizes, eddy current flow that would rob power and produce heat. Transformers used for radio frequencies usually have air cores and are wound over paper or plastic forms.

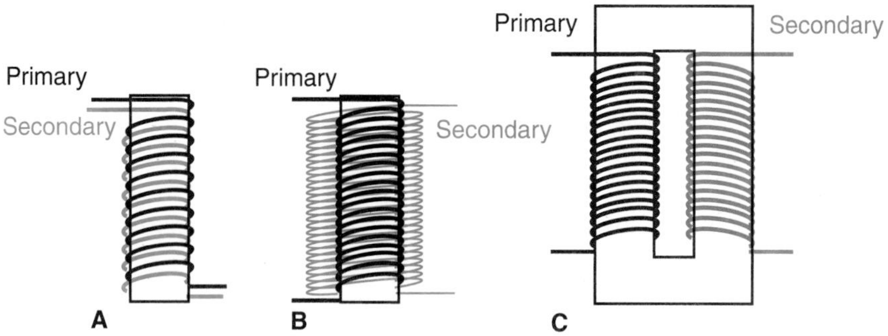

Figure 4-100
A. *Bifiliar winding provides almost 100% coupling.*
B. *Concentric winding provides a high degree of coupling with economy of construction.*
C. *The high permeability of the core gives this transformer good coupling.*

In Figure 4-100, we see some methods that are used to vary the amount of coupling between the primary and the secondary windings. In A, we have a bifiliar winding in which the primary and the secondary coils are wound side by side in the same direction. This provides essentially unity coupling, or 100% of the lines of flux from the primary cut across the winding of the secondary. In B, we have the more economical type of winding where one coil is wound over the core and the next coil is wound over the first one. In C, we have a transformer with one coil on one side of the core and the other winding on the other side. The highly permeable core concentrates the lines of flux and increases the coupling between the coils.

Types of Transformers

Transformers used in electrical and electronic equipment come in all shapes and sizes, and for use in almost all frequency ranges. One logical way to group transformers is to class them according to the frequency with which they are used. For our discussion, we will class them as power-frequency transformers, audio-frequency transformers, and radio-frequency transformers.

Power-frequency transformers are used to increase or decrease the voltage that comes into our homes and shops to a voltage that is correct for the equipment we are using. Power frequencies are usually 25-hertz, 50-hertz, 60-hertz, or 400-hertz. These transformers may either step up or step down the voltage and many of them have more than one secondary winding. *See* Figure 4-101.

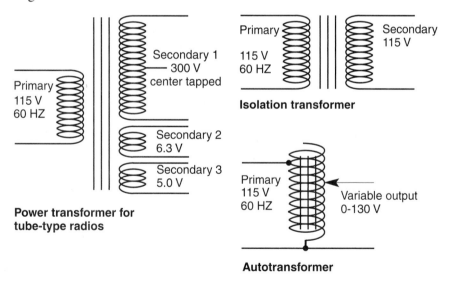

Figure 4-101. *Types of power-frequency transformers*

The chassis of some electrical equipment is connected directly to one side of the electrical power line, and users of this equipment are protected from electrical shock by the equipment being completely enclosed in a plastic cabinet. But when servicing it, there is a chance of getting a shock if you should touch the chassis. To prevent this danger, many electrical work benches have a power plug that is isolated from the power line by a 1:1 transformer. This is called an isolation transformer, and its secondary voltage and current are the same as those in the primary, but any device powered from its secondary winding is isolated from the line voltage.

Much of the single-phase alternating current in shops and homes in the United States has a nominal voltage of 120 volts, but we often need a higher or lower voltage. We can get it with an autotransformer which is a type of variable transformer. An autotransformer has a single winding, wound on a ring-shaped iron core. One side of the secondary is connected directly to one side of the primary, and the other side of the primary winding is tapped into the coil a short distance from the end. Contact for the other end of the secondary is made by a carbon brush that can be moved over a bare portion of the winding at the edge of the core. The turns ratio can be varied by moving the brush over the winding. When the brush is between the two primary connections, the transformer acts as a step-down transformer, but if the brush contacts the winding beyond the primary tap, the secondary voltage will be higher than the line voltage. This type of transformer uses less wire than a two-winding transformer, but it does not provide any isolation between the primary and the secondary winding.

Audio-frequency transformers usually have iron cores, and they operate with frequencies in the range of from about 15 hertz up to around 20,000 hertz. They are used primarily for impedance matching between the high output impedance of an amplifier and the low input impedance of a speaker. The fidelity of music that is amplified is dependent upon the coupling between the windings of the audio transformer. Some audio transformers are bifiliar wound in order to get the maximum amount of coupling.

Almost all radio-frequency transformers have air cores, but some have slugs of either powdered iron or copper. These may be moved up or down inside the winding to vary the inductance of the coil in order to change the frequency at which the transformer is resonant. Iron has a high permeability and it increases the inductance of the coil, while copper has a low permeability and it decreases the inductance of the coil.

Transformer Ratios

Transformers are used to change values of voltage, current, or impedance, but they cannot manufacture power. The ratio between the voltage in the primary winding of a transformer and that in its secondary winding is directly related to the ratio of the number of turns in the primary winding to the number of turns in the secondary.

If there are 100 turns in the primary winding and 1,000 turns in the secondary winding, the voltage in the secondary will be 10 times that in the primary, and this is called a step-up transformer. Since a transformer cannot produce power, any time the voltage is stepped up, the current must be stepped down in exactly the same ratio so the product of the voltage and the current in the secondary will be the same as the voltage times the current in the primary. The power in the two windings will not be exactly the same because of the transformer losses, but transformers are quite efficient and the output power will usually be around 95 to 98% of the input power.

The voltage ratio of a transformer is stated as:

$$\frac{E_S}{E_P} = \frac{N_S}{N_P}$$

E_S = Voltage across the secondary winding
E_P = Voltage across the primary winding
N_S = Number of turns in the secondary winding
N_P = Number of turns in the primary winding

If we know the turns ratio and the primary voltage, we can find the voltage across the secondary winding by changing the formula to:

$$E_S = \frac{E_P \cdot N_S}{N_P}$$

The current ratio is just the opposite of the turns ratio:

$$\frac{I_S}{I_P} = \frac{N_P}{N_S}$$

The current in the secondary can be found by the formula:

$$I_S = \frac{I_P \cdot N_P}{N_S}$$

One important function of a transformer is that of matching impedance. For the maximum amount of power to be transferred from a source to its load, the impedance of the two should be the same. And since this is not always the case, we can put a transformer between the source and load that will match their impedances.

Some electronic amplifiers are designed to operate most efficiently when their output circuit has an impedance of 1,000 ohms, but they may drive a speaker whose impedance is only eight ohms. For the amplifier to furnish enough current to effectively drive the speaker, an impedance-matching transformer must be installed between the two that will decrease the voltage and increase the current through the speaker. The impedance ratio of a transformer is equal to the square of the turns ratio:

$$\frac{Z_P}{Z_S} = \left(\frac{N_P}{N_S}\right)^2$$

In our example, we would need a transformer with a turns ratio of 11.2 to match the 8-ohm load to a 1,000-ohm source.

$$N_P = \sqrt{\frac{Z_P}{Z_S}}$$
$$= \sqrt{\frac{1,000}{8}}$$
$$= \sqrt{125}$$
$$= 11.2$$

This is a step-down transformer with 11.2 times as many turns in the primary as it has in the secondary. The voltage across the load is only 1/11.2 that of the source, but there is 11.2 times as much current in the secondary as there is in the primary.

Transformer Phase

Transformers change the voltage, current, and impedance, and they are also used in circuits to change the phase between the voltage in the primary and the voltage in the secondary. During the half cycle of AC in which the voltage in the primary winding is increasing, the voltage in the secondary is decreasing. *See* Figure 4-102.

A simple doorbell circuit gives a good illustration of the way a transformer operates. The primary winding of the doorbell transformer is connected across the power line with no switch. The bell is operated by closing a normally open pushbutton switch in the low-voltage secondary circuit. When the switch is open, no current flows in the secondary circuit, and in the primary circuit, the induced voltage is almost equal to the source voltage, but of opposite polarity, and almost no primary current flows. Only enough current flows to replace the power that is lost in the core in the form of heat and in the winding because of the primary resistance.

When the switch is closed, current flows through the bell, and this current creates a magnetic field around the secondary winding that cuts across the primary coil. This magnetic field induces a current in the primary whose

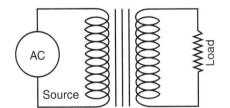

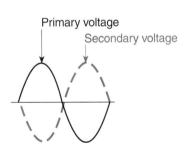

Figure 4-102. *The 90° phase shift between the voltage and current in the primary winding and the 90° phase shift between the current and voltage in the secondary winding cause the secondary voltage to be 180° out of phase with the voltage in the primary winding.*

direction is opposite to that of the current induced by the changing source voltage. When the induced current in the primary winding is opposed, it decreases, and the source current increases. Even though there is no electrical connection between the secondary and the primary winding in the transformer, any current flow in the secondary causes current to flow in the primary. *See* Figure 4-103.

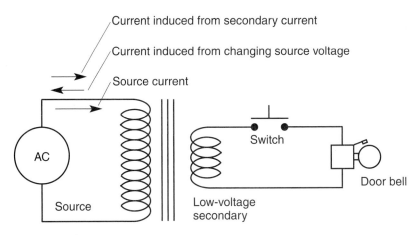

Figure 4-103. *No current flows in the primary winding of a doorbell transformer until the switch is closed, allowing secondary current to flow. This secondary current induces a current into the primary winding that cancels some of the current caused by the changing source voltage. This allows primary current to flow.*

Transformer Losses

The core of a transformer acts as a winding with only one turn, and when the primary current changes, it induces current into the core. The cross-sectional area of the core is large, and if its resistance were low, the current would be large. This core current increases the primary current by decreasing the opposing induced current, and it also wastes power because of the eddy currents that flow inside the iron core and produce heat. To minimize these losses, almost all transformer cores are made of stacks of thin laminations, or layers, of iron or steel. These laminations have a small cross-sectional area which gives them a high resistance, and they are insulated from each other by an oxide film or by a coating of insulating varnish.

Current flowing in the windings also causes a power loss in a transformer. These losses, which are proportional to the square of the current flow, may be minimized by using larger wire in the winding.

Answers begin on Page 359. **Page numbers refer to chapter text.**

134. The induced current in a conductor flows in the _____ (same or opposite) direction as the source current. *Page 268*

135. The unit of inductance is the _____ and this is the amount of inductance needed to produce one volt of electromotive force when the current through the inductor is changing at the rate of _____ per second. *Page 269*

136. Three variables that affect the inductance of a coil are:
    a. _____
    b. _____
    c. _____
       Page 269

137. Two inductors that are linked by all of the lines of magnetic flux surrounding them are said to have a coefficient of coupling of _____ . *Page 271*

138. Coils that are mounted at right angles to each other have a _____ (maximum or minimum) coefficient of coupling. *Page 270*

139. Find the mutual inductance of two coils, each having an inductance of 50 millihenries, if the coefficient of coupling is 0.6.
    L_m = _____ millihenries. *Page 271*

140. Find the total inductance of two inductors connected in series if the inductance of one is 20 millihenries and the inductance of the other is 35 millihenries. There is no coupling between the two inductors.
    L_T = _____ millihenries. *Page 271*

141. Find the total inductance of two inductors connected in parallel if the inductance of one is 20 millihenries and the other is 35 millihenries. There is no coupling between them.
    L_T = _____ millihenries. *Page 271*

142. Find the time constant of a 2.0-henry inductor whose resistance is 100 ohms.
    T C = _____ second. *Page 273*

143. The cores used in most power-frequency or audio-frequency transformers are made of _____ (air or iron). *Page 274*

144. Iron cores are used in some transformers to increase the coupling between the windings. Iron is used because it has a _____ (high or low) permeability. *Page 274*

145. A power transformer with a 1:1 turns ratio that is used to electrically separate the secondary winding from the power source is called a/an _____ transformer. *Page 275*

146. An autotransformer _____ (does or does not) isolate the secondary winding from the power source. *Page 275*

147. Most radio-frequency transformers have an _____ (air or iron) core. *Page 276*

148. What is the secondary voltage of a transformer that has 100 turns in the primary winding and 2,000 turns in the secondary, when the primary winding is connected across a 117-volt AC source?
_____ E_S = volts. *Page 277*

149. How much current flows in the secondary winding of the transformer described in question 148, when 1 amp of current flows in the primary winding?
I_S = _____ amp. *Page 277*

150. What is the turns ratio of an audio-frequency transformer that has a primary impedance of 2,500 ohms and a secondary impedance of 4 ohms?
Turns ratio = _____ :1.
Page 278

151. "The voltage in the secondary winding of a transformer is in phase with the voltage in the primary winding."
This statement is _____ (true or false).
Page 278

152. The iron core of most transformers is made of thin laminations of iron rather than solid iron to minimize power losses caused by _____ currents in the core. *Page 279*

rectifier. A device or circuit that changes alternating current into direct current.

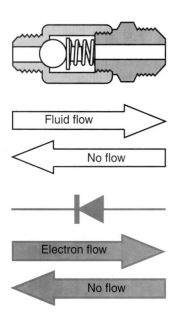

Fluid flow

No flow

Electron flow

No flow

Figure 4-104. *A diode controls electron flow in the same way a check valve controls the flow of hydraulic fluid.*

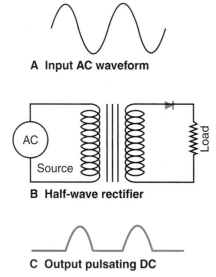

A Input AC waveform

B Half-wave rectifier

C Output pulsating DC

Rectifiers

Alternating current is easier and cheaper to make in the quantities needed for modern industry than direct current. But there are some functions that require DC, so we have devices called rectifiers that change AC into DC.

A rectifier acts as an electron check valve because it allows electrons to flow through it in one direction, but it blocks them so they cannot pass in the opposite direction. *See* Figure 4-104.

Figure 4-105A shows the input waveform of alternating current. Electrons flow in one direction, and then they reverse and flow in the opposite direction. In most aircraft electrical systems, we use 400-hertz AC in which the current changes its direction 800 times each second.

A rectifier in the AC circuit in Figure 4-105B allows electrons to flow in one direction only. Figure 4-105C, shows the output waveform of pulsating DC after it has passed through the rectifier. The positive half of the AC wave is just as it is in the input, but the negative half of the cycle has been cut off. A rectifier produces a pulsating, or interrupted, flow of electrons with all of them traveling in one direction. This is called pulsating DC.

There have been a number of types of rectifiers used to change AC into DC. Many of the early rectifiers were vacuum tubes which were large, produced a great deal of heat, and were easily damaged by vibration. Later metal-oxide rectifiers were used, but these were limited in their voltage-handling capability. Today, solid-state, semiconductor diodes are used for almost all rectifiers.

Because of the importance of semiconductor devices, we will study them later in detail.

Figure 4-105. *A half-wave rectifier*
A. Input waveform of AC in the
    transformer
B. Half-wave rectifier circuit
C. Output waveform of pulsating DC in
    the load

Terminal Strips

Aircraft electrical systems normally use a barrier-type terminal strip with studs
and nuts to attach the electrical wires. Any terminal strip carrying wires in
the electrical power circuit must use studs no smaller than size 10, but for
control circuits and electrical load circuits, studs as small as size 6 are used.

When connecting wires to a terminal strip, no more than four wires should
be connected to any single stud, and the terminals should be stacked as they
are shown in Figure 4-106 so they will all lie flat and provide the maximum
surface contact. When it is necessary to connect more than four wires to a
single point, two studs are connected with a jumper strap.

Solid-State Devices

One of the greatest developments in technology in the twentieth century is
that of solid-state electronics. The unusual electrical characteristics of certain chemical elements that have four valence electrons have opened an
entirely new field of electronics called solid-state electronics. Tiny, low-cost
solid-state diodes and transistors replace much larger and more costly vacuum
tubes with a far greater degree of reliability. Integrated circuits, much smaller
than a postage stamp and containing hundreds of diodes, transistors, and other
circuit elements have opened the amazing field of microelectronics.

Semiconductor Theory

The two most widely used semiconductor materials are germanium and silicon. Both have four valence electrons and act in much the same way, except
that silicon devices can operate over a much wider range of temperatures. In
our discussion we will talk about silicon, but almost everything also applies
to germanium.

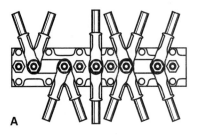

A

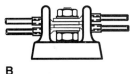

B

Figure 4-106. *A barrier-type terminal strip*
A. *When it is necessary to connect more
than 4 wires to a single point, 2 or more
studs are connected with a bus strap.*
B. *Correct method of stacking wire
terminals on a stud.*

terminal strip. A component in an aircraft
electrical system to which wires are
attached for the purpose of connecting
sections of the wire. Terminal strips are
normally installed in junction boxes.

solid-state electronics. Electronic circuits
which use semiconductor devices such as
diodes and transistors rather than
vacuum tubes.

A

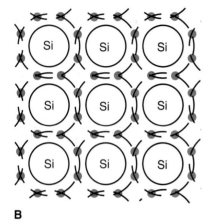

B

Figure 4-107

A. *Single atom of silicon has four electrons in its valence shell.*

B. *Atoms of silicon join with other silicon atoms to form a silicon crystal. Each atom shares electrons with four other atoms by the process called covalent bonding.*

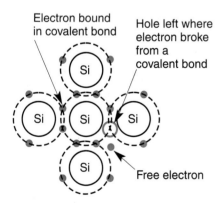

Electron bound in covalent bond

Hole left where electron broke from a covalent bond

Free electron

Figure 4-108. *Heat or a high voltage across a crystal of silicon can cause a few electrons to break out of their covalent bond and become free electrons. When an electron breaks out of its bond, it leaves a hole.*

A crystal of pure silicon is composed of atoms, all of which have four valence electrons. These valence electrons in one atom are shared with other atoms in such a way that the valence shell of each atom contains eight electrons, which is all they can hold. Atoms with a filled valence shell do not want to release any electrons, neither do they want to take on others. Pure silicon, therefore is an electrical insulator. *See* Figure 4-107.

While pure silicon is an insulator, heat or a high voltage across a silicon crystal will cause some electrons to break out of their covalent bond and become free electrons, leaving a hole (*see* Figure 4-108). The free electrons move through the silicon as negative electrical charges, and as they move from one atom to another, the holes they leave appear to move from one atom to another. Both electrons and holes move through the crystal, but they move in opposite directions. *See* Figure 4-109.

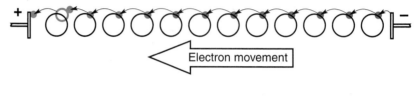

Electron movement

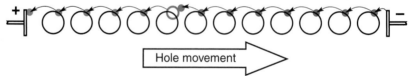

Hole movement

○ Silicon atom showing one of the electrons in its valence shell

◎ Silicon atom in which one electron has broken out of its valence shell and left a hole

○○ Electron moving from one silicon atom to another and leaving a hole

Figure 4-109. *When a piece of pure silicon is connected across a battery, some electrons will flow through it because of the electron-hole pairs that form when an electron breaks out of its covalent bond. The amount of current flowing through the silicon is determined by the temperature of the silicon and by the amount of voltage across it.*

If a few atoms of an element such as phosphorus, arsenic, or antimony which have five valence electrons are mixed with millions of silicon atoms, there will be some free electrons that have no place to go. All of the atoms have full valence shells and these electrons are left over. They will move through the material toward any positive electrical charge. Silicon that has been doped, as this process is called, with these elements is called N-type (negative-type) silicon because it has an excess of electrons. *See* Figure 4-110.

If a few atoms of an element such as boron, aluminum, or gallium which have three valence electrons are mixed with pure silicon, there will be some atoms that do not have a full valence shell, and the location where there is a missing electron is called a "hole." These holes act as positive charges and attract free electrons. Silicon that has been doped with these elements is called P-type (positive-type) silicon because it has a deficiency of electrons. *See* Figure 4-111.

Semiconductor Diodes

When a piece of N-type silicon is joined to a piece of P-type silicon, a junction between the two is formed, and this P-N junction demonstrates some very unusual and useful electrical characteristics.

The most widely used semiconductor device is the diode which acts as an electron check valve. The anode is represented in the diode symbol by the arrowhead, while the cathode is shown by the bar. *See* Figure 4-112 on Page 286.

When a junction is formed between a piece of N-silicon and a piece of P-silicon, some of the free electrons in the N-silicon cross the junction and fill the holes in the P-silicon that are right up against the junction. This leaves the N-silicon with a lack of free electrons, or an excess of positive ions beside the junction. The P-silicon has a lack of holes, or an excess of negative ions beside the junction.

The electrons in the N-silicon and the holes in the P-silicon are called majority carriers. The area on either side of the junction is called the depletion area, because it is depleted, or empty, of majority carriers.

When free electrons move across the junction and fill some of the holes, there are no free electrons left at the N-side of the junction and no more holes at the P-side. This leaves the material next to the junction in a charged condition. The N-side has a positive charge and the P-side has a negative charge. This voltage is called the barrier voltage, or barrier potential. *See* Figure 4-113 on Page 286.

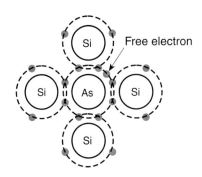

Figure 4-110. *When a few atoms of a pentavalent element such as arsenic are added to pure silicon and a crystal is produced, there are free electrons left after all of the covalent bonds have formed. Since there are more electrons than are needed for all of the covalent bonds, this is called N-type (negative-type) silicon.*

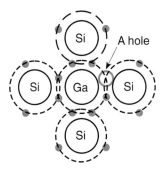

Figure 4-111. *When silicon is doped with a trivalent impurity such as gallium there are some places where covalent bonds cannot form, and these locations are called holes. Holes have no electrical charge, but since they are where there should be a negative charge, they act as though they are positive. Free electrons are attracted to holes, and they fill them.*

diode. A semiconductor check valve that allows current to flow in one direction, but blocks its flow in the opposite direction.

doping. The process of adding small amounts of certain chemical elements as impurities to a semiconductor element to alter its electrical characteristics.

pentavalent element. A chemical element that has five electrons in its valence shell. Nitrogen, arsenic, antimony, and bismuth are pentavalent elements.

trivalent element. A chemical element that has three electrons in its valence shell. Boron, aluminum, gallium, and indium are trivalent elements.

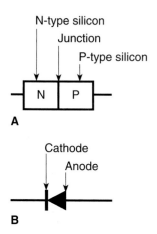

Figure 4-112
A. *A representation of a semiconductor to help us understand its operation.*
B. *Typical symbol used for a semiconductor diode used in electrical circuit diagrams.*

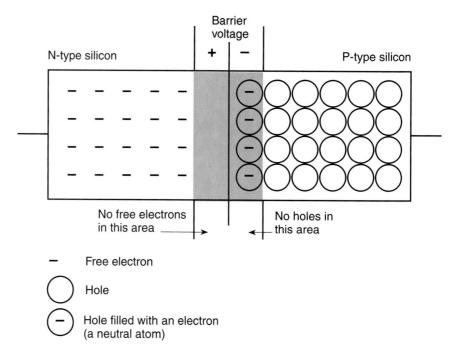

Figure 4-113. *A barrier voltage, or barrier potential, forms at the PN-junction when free electrons from the N-silicon combine with the holes in the P-silicon to form positive and negative ions.*

anode. The end of a semiconductor diode that is made of P-type material and is represented in the schematic symbol by the arrowhead.

cathode. The end of a semiconductor diode that is made of N-type material and is represented in the schematic symbol by the bar.

When a diode is installed in a circuit in such a way that it is forward biased, with its anode more positive than its cathode, current can flow through it. A forward-biased diode causes a voltage drop across it as the current flows, but unlike a resistor, this voltage drop does not change with the amount of current. A forward-biased silicon diode has a relatively constant voltage drop of approximately 0.7 volt across it, and the voltage drop across a germanium diode is about 0.3 volt.

When a diode is installed in a circuit in such a way that its anode is more negative than its cathode, it is reverse biased and the majority carriers are pulled away from the junction. The depletion area is wide, and the barrier voltage is high. The only current flowing is reverse current, I_R, caused by the minority carriers. The amount of this reverse, or leakage, current is determined by the temperature of the silicon and by the amount of voltage across the diode.

Ordinary silicon diodes are not designed to operate with a reverse bias voltage high enough to cause them to break down and conduct in their reverse direction. When this happens, the diode is normally destroyed. A special type of diode, the zener diode, is designed to operate with reverse current flowing.

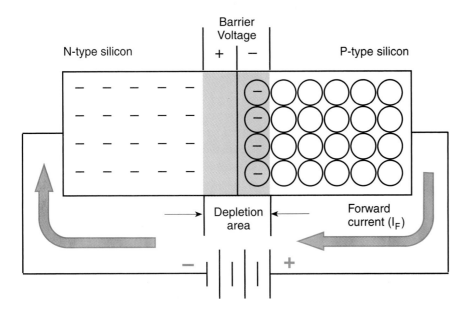

Figure 4-114. *When the negative terminal of a battery is connected to the cathode of a silicon diode, and the positive terminal is connected to the anode, the diode is forward biased and current flows through it. The depletion area is very narrow, and the barrier voltage is low.*

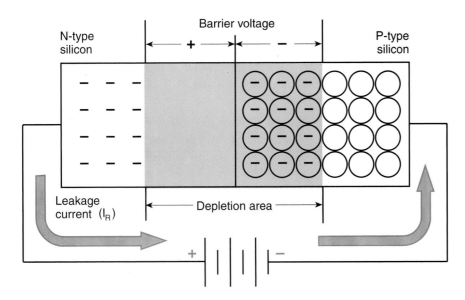

Figure 4-115. *When the positive terminal of a battery is connected to the cathode of a silicon diode, and the negative terminal is connected to the anode, the diode is reverse biased and only leakage current flows through it. The depletion area is very wide, and the barrier voltage is high.*

Figure 4-116. *A zener diode*

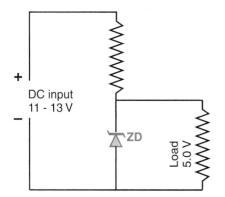

Figure 4-117. *A voltage regulator circuit using a zener diode as the voltage-sensing unit*

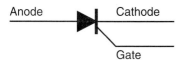

Figure 4-118. *A silicon controlled rectifier, or SCR*

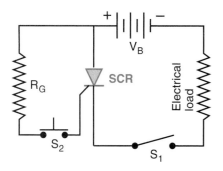

Figure 4-119. *An SCR acts in the same way as a holding relay. Momentarily closing switch S₂ triggers the SCR into conduction, and it continues to conduct until switch S₁ is opened.*

Zener Diodes

An ordinary diode can be destroyed when current flows through it in its reverse direction, but a zener diode is a special type of diode designed to have a specific breakdown voltage, and to operate with current flowing through it in its reverse direction.

A zener diode is used as the voltage sensing component in an electronic voltage regulator used with a DC alternator. In Figure 4-117, see the way a zener diode holds an output voltage constant as the input voltage changes. A 5-volt zener diode is installed in a 12-volt DC circuit in series with a resistor, so its cathode is more positive than its anode.

As soon as the voltage across the zener diode rises to 5 volts, it breaks down and conducts current to ground. Seven volts is dropped across the resistor, and the voltage across the zener diode and the electrical load remains constant at 5 volts. If the source voltage drops to 11 volts, the voltage drop across the zener diode will remain at 5 volts and the resistor will now drop 6 volts. If the input voltage rises to 13 volts, the voltage across the zener still remains at 5 volts, but the voltage across the resistor will rise to 8 volts.

A zener diode must always have a resistor in series with it to limit the current allowed to flow when it is conducting in its reverse direction, as its resistance drops to an extremely low value when it breaks down.

Silicon Controlled Rectifiers

A silicon controlled rectifier, an SCR, is a special type of solid-state device that acts much like a diode that can be turned on with a short pulse of current. *See* Figure 4-118.

The SCR has a cathode, an anode, and a gate. Current cannot flow through the SCR from the anode to the cathode, and no current can flow from the cathode to the anode until a pulse of positive current is sent into it through its gate. A positive pulse applied to the gate causes the SCR to conduct between its cathode and its anode.

Figure 4-119 shows the way an SCR works in a circuit. When switch S_1 is closed, voltage source V_B biases the SCR properly for it to conduct, but the SCR blocks all current until it is triggered by momentarily closing the switch S_2 in the gate circuit. When this switch is closed, current flows through the gate resistor R_G into the gate of the SCR. Only a very small current is needed to trigger the SCR into conduction. When the SCR conducts, a large current flows from the battery, through the load and the SCR, back into the battery. Switch S_2 can be opened as soon as the SCR begins to conduct, and load current will continue to flow until switch S_1 is opened to stop it. This action is the same as that of a holding relay.

An SCR can also act as a switch in an AC circuit. Figure 4-120 shows a simple circuit that allows a large amount of current to flow through the load R_L. This large load current can be controlled by a very small control current, which can be carried through a small wire and controlled with a small switch.

The input AC in the circuit shown in Figure 4-120B rises from zero to a peak value in one direction (+), and then it changes direction and goes through zero to a peak value in the opposite direction (-). Since an SCR blocks current flow in both directions before it is triggered, no current flows through the SCR as long as switch S_1 is open.

When switch S_1 is closed, diode D_1 allows current to flow to the gate during the half of the AC cycle when the current is positive. This small pulse of positive current triggers the SCR into conduction, and load current flows from the cathode to the anode during the entire positive half of the cycle. The SCR stops conducting as soon as the AC drops to zero. No current flows during the negative half cycle, but it starts to conduct again at the beginning of the positive half cycle. The current through the load looks like the plot in Figure 4-120C.

The intensity of a light and the speed of some types of electric motors can be controlled by using a large resistor in series with the light or motor, but this wastes electrical energy, produces a great deal of heat, and is heavy. A much simpler way to control alternating current is by using an SCR.

A circuit such as the one we see in Figure 4-121A, Page 290, serves as a very effective light dimmer or speed controller for a universal motor. A universal motor is an armature-type electric motor such as is used in a hand drill. It can run on either AC or DC and it produces a large amount of starting torque.

Figure 4-121B shows the input AC waveform. During the half cycle when the current flow is negative, it forward-biases diode D_2 and charges capacitor C with the top plate negative and the bottom plate positive. This charge puts a negative voltage on the anode of the diode D_1, so it cannot conduct and no current flows to the gate of the SCR. The SCR is shut off.

During the positive half cycle, capacitor C discharges through resistor R_1 and charges with the opposite polarity with the top plate positive and the bottom plate negative. As soon as the top plate of the capacitor becomes positive, current flows through diode D_1 and triggers the SCR so that it conducts.

Resistor R_1 is variable. The more resistance in the circuit, the longer it takes the capacitor to discharge and recharge, and the greater the portion of the positive half cycle is gone before the SCR begins to conduct. Figure 4-121C shows the way the load current looks when the wiper of resistor R_1 is at the top, so that it puts no resistance in the circuit. In Figure 4-121D there is enough resistance to decrease the amount of current flowing during the positive half cycle, and in Figure 4-121E and Figure 4-121F, more resistance has been added and the load current has been further decreased.

An SCR in a circuit such as this can control the load current without dissipating, or using, any power, so the control device using such a circuit can be made small and lightweight.

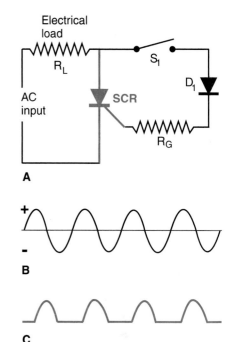

Figure 4-120

A. *An SCR installed in an AC circuit to act as a high-current switch. A small amount of current flows through switch S_1 and is rectified by diode D_1 to provide the positive pulse on the gate of the SCR to trigger it into conduction.*

B. *Waveform of the input AC.*

C. *Waveform of the pulsating DC flowing through the load.*

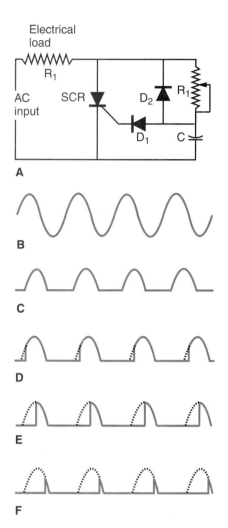

Figure 4-121

A. An SCR installed in an AC circuit to act as a current controller. Varying the resistance R_1 varies the time needed to charge capacitor C. The SCR is triggered into conduction when the voltage across the capacitor rises to a sufficiently high value.

B. Waveform of the input AC.

C. Waveform of the pulsating DC output when resistor R_1 is set to its minimum value.

D. Output waveform as resistance R_1 is increased.

E. Output waveform when resistance R_1 is further increased.

F. Output waveform as resistance R_1 is still further increased.

Triacs

An SCR blocks all current trying to flow from its anode to its cathode, but it allows current to flow from the cathode to the anode after it has been triggered into conduction. A triac is essentially the same kind of device as an SCR, but it conducts in either direction as long as a small amount of current flows into its gate. Triacs are used in AC circuits where a small amount of gate current is used to control a much larger flow of AC between its two main terminals, MT_1 and MT_2. *See* Figure 4-122.

Transistors

Perhaps the most important development that has been made in the field of electronics is the transistor, the tiny semiconductor device which takes the place of a much larger vacuum tube. It does the same job, but does it better, uses much less power, is more rugged, has a much longer life, and is far less expensive.

Bipolar Transistors

A bipolar transistor is made of a tiny sandwich of P- and N-doped silicon or germanium and has three connections; the emitter, the base, and the collector.

There are two types of bipolar transistors, the correct name for the common transistor, NPN and PNP. The difference between these two is the way they are made and the way they are installed in a circuit. In Figure 4-123, we see the symbols for these two types of transistors.

For an NPN transistor to conduct, the emitter, the part in the symbol with the arrowhead, is connected to the negative voltage, and the collector to the positive voltage. When the base is connected to a voltage more positive than the emitter, a very small current flows into the base, and this causes a large current to flow between the collector and the emitter. In Figure 4-124, when the switch is closed, the base is more positive than the emitter. A small current flows into the base and a much larger current flows through the load. When the switch is opened, no base current flows, and when there is no base current, there is no load current.

The symbol for a PNP transistor has the arrowhead pointing to the base, and it can be connected into the same kind of circuit as we have just seen with the NPN transistor, except that the battery must be reversed so that the emitter is positive and the collector is negative. When the switch is closed, a small amount of current flows from the base, and a much larger current flows between the emitter and the collector. When the switch is opened, no base current flows, and no load current flows.

A transistor can be used, not only as a switch as we have just seen, but also as a variable resistor. The switch circuit seen in Figure 4-124 can be replaced with a potentiometer across the voltage source, with the wiper connected to the base of the transistor through resistor R$_2$ (*see* Figure 4-125).

When the wiper is at the bottom of the resistance element, the base of the transistor is negative (this is an NPN transistor and its base must be positive for it to conduct). No current flows into the base, and no load current flows between the collector and the emitter. When the wiper is moved to the top of the resistance, the base is positive, and the transistor conducts the maximum amount of load current. The amount of load current can be controlled by moving the wiper across the resistance.

This kind of circuit is called an amplifier because a very small base current can control a much larger load current.

It is impossible to list all of the uses for transistors in modern aviation technology. They are used in voltage regulators, antiskid systems, autopilots, in all communications and navigation radio, and thousands of them are built into integrated-circuit chips used in the onboard computers.

Figure 4-122. *A triac acts much like an SCR except that it can be triggered with a pulse of either polarity.*

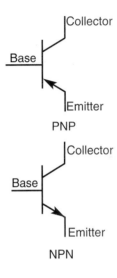

Figure 4-123. *Bipolar transistors*

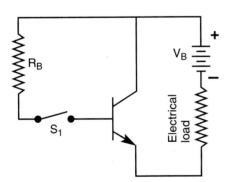

Figure 4-124. *A transistor acts much like a relay in an electrical circuit. When switch S₁ is closed, a small current flows in the base circuit of the transistor. This small current allows a much larger current to flow through the collector and emitter and the electrical load.*

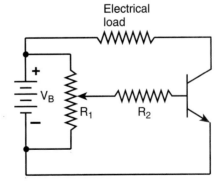

Figure 4-125. *A transistor acts as a variable resistor when its base current is varied. The greater the base current, the greater the load current.*

Field Effect Transistors

A bipolar transistor is turned on when a small amount of current flows between the base and the emitter. This small flow of current controls a much larger flow of current between the emitter and the collector. A bipolar transistor is called a low-impedance device because it has very little opposition (very little impedance) to current flow in its control, or base, circuit.

Many applications in electronics require a high impedance, or a large opposition to current flow, in the input to a device. When a high impedance is needed, a field effect transistor, or FET, is used.

An FET looks very much like a bipolar transistor, but its operation is different. An FET acts as a resistor whose resistance between its source and the drain is controlled by the voltage difference between the gate and the source. When there is no voltage on the gate, the resistance between the source and the drain is minimum, and the source-to-drain current, the load current, is maximum. When a negative voltage is placed on the gate of an N-channel FET, the load current decreases. Enough negative voltage can be placed on the gate to shut off the load current completely. It is the voltage on the gate that controls the load current, and virtually no gate current flows.

A P-channel FET works in the same way as an N-channel FET except that the polarity of the voltage sources is reversed. A positive voltage on the gate decreases the amount of current flowing between the source and the drain.

The FET just discussed is called a junction field effect transistor, JFET, and when there is no voltage on the gate, the load current is maximum. Increasing the voltage on the gate decreases the current. Enough voltage on the gate can completely shut off the load current. This type of operation is called operating in the depletion mode.

Another type of field effect transistor is widely used, especially in integrated circuits. This is the insulated-gate field effect transistor, IGFET, also called a metal-oxide semiconductor field effect transistor, MOSFET. The symbol

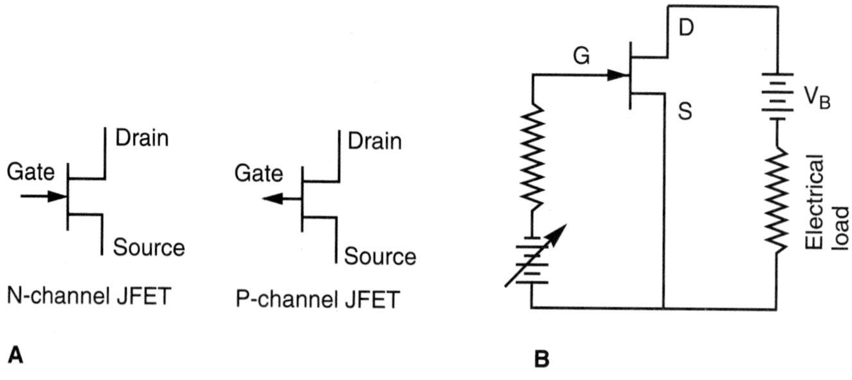

Figure 4-126

A. *Junction field effect transistors (JFETs)*

B. *The variable voltage source in the gate circuit controls the current flowing in the drain-source-load circuit. As the gate is made more negative than the source, the load current is decreased.*

N-channel JFET

P-channel JFET

A

B

for a MOSFET is seen in Figure 4-127. A MOSFET can operate in either the depletion mode (increasing the gate voltage decreases the load current) or in the enhancement mode (increasing the gate voltage increases the load current).

FETs are used in amplifiers, switches, and voltage-controlled resistors and are familiar to an aircraft mechanic in FET voltmeters. FET voltmeters have replaced the older vacuum-tube voltmeters for taking voltage measurements in circuits where the electrical load caused by a conventional voltmeter would cause an inaccurate reading.

Unijunction Transistors

The unijunction transistor, UJT, is not a true transistor because it cannot be used as an amplifier. It is a special type of three-terminal diode that acts as a voltage-controlled switch.

See in Figure 4-129 the way a UJT is used to send current through the electrical load when the voltage across the capacitor rises to a specified value. When switch S is closed, current flows through the resistor R_1 and charges capacitor C. As soon as the voltage across the capacitor rises to the trigger value for the UJT, it conducts between its emitter and base 1. This allows the capacitor to discharge through the load. As soon as the capacitor discharges, the UJT shuts off and the capacitor charges up again for another cycle.

UJTs are often used to trigger SCRs so that they will conduct as soon as a voltage rises to a specific value.

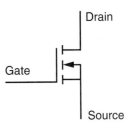

N-channel MOSFET

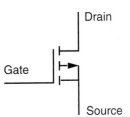

P-channel MOSFET

Figure 4-127. *Metal-oxide semiconductor field effect transistors*

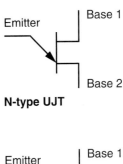

N-type UJT

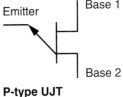

P-type UJT

Figure 4-128. *A unijunction transistor*

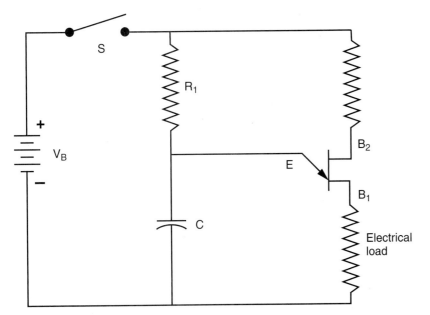

Figure 4-129. *This unijunction transistor sends a pulse of current through the load each time the voltage across the capacitor rises to the trigger voltage of the UJT.*

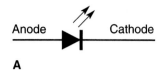

Anode   Cathode

A

B

Figure 4-130
A. Symbol for a light emitting diode, LED.
B. Seven LEDs arranged as a figure 8 are
*   used in digital numerical displays.*

Optoelectronic Devices

Light is a form of energy that is closely related to electrical energy. In certain materials the flow of electrons causes photons of light energy to be emitted, while in certain other materials striking photons cause electrons to flow. In this section of our text, we will look at both light emitting devices and light sensors.

Light Emitting Diodes

When electrical current passes through a junction of certain types of semiconductor materials, photons of light energy are released. This fact gives us a very important type of device known as light emitting diodes, or LEDs.

LEDs do not produce enough light for illumination, but they are widely used for indicator lights. One important use for LEDs is in digital displays in which seven LED bars are arranged in the form of a figure eight. By passing current through the correct bars, any number from zero through nine can be formed.

The color of light produced by an LED is determined by the semiconductor material used in its manufacture. Some LEDs produce red light, some green, and some yellow or orange, while others produce infrared light. LEDs that emit infrared light are used in various types of alarm and remote control devices.

Semiconductor Light Sensors
Photodiodes

A photodiode is a special type of semiconductor diode that allows current to flow from its cathode to its anode as any other type of diode does, but it blocks current from flowing from its anode to its cathode as long as it is dark. When light shines through a special lens onto the junction inside the photodiode, reverse current flows. The amount of reverse current is proportional to the amount of light reaching the junction.

Phototransistor

A phototransistor is similar to an ordinary bipolar transistor except that a lens is built into its housing that allows light to shine on the emitter-base junction. When light strikes this junction, electrons are released that furnish the base current. Load current then flows between the collector and the emitter. Some phototransistors have a base lead, and others do not. Phototransistors are much more sensitive to light than photodiodes.

Photofets

A photofet is a light-sensitive field effect transistor that is normally on, but is switched off when light strikes the gate-to-channel junction inside the device. A photofet is much more sensitive to light than an ordinary phototransistor.

Light-Activated Silicon Controlled Rectifier

A light-activated silicon controlled rectifier (LASCAR) is the highest current-carrying device of this type in popular use. When light shines on the gate-to-cathode junction, enough electrons are released to produce the required gate current and trigger the SCR into conduction.

Photoresistors

A photoresistor is a semiconductor device that acts as a variable resistor whose resistance is determined by the amount of light shining on it through a built-in lens. The resistance of a photoresistor decreases as the amount of light shining on it increases.

Solar Cells

A solar cell is a photo-voltaic semiconductor device, one that produces a voltage when light shines on the junction inside it. Solar cells are used to provide power to keep batteries charged on many remotely located radio transmitters and to operate many of our small, pocket-sized calculators. When light shines on the junction of the semiconductor materials inside the solar cell, electrons are released that form a usable current.

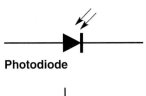

Photodiode

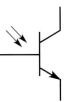

Phototransistor

Photofet

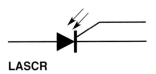

LASCR

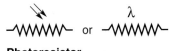

Photoresistor

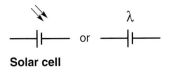

Solar cell

Figure 4-131. *Semiconductor light sensors*

Answers begin on Page 359. **Page numbers refer to chapter text.**

156. The voltage drop across a forward-biased semiconductor diode _____ (does or does not) change as the current flowing through it varies. *Page 286*

157. The voltage drop across a forward-biased silicon diode is approximately _____ volt. *Page 286*

158. A/An _____ is used as solid-state voltage sensor. *Page 288*

159. A zener diode is _____ (forward or reverse) biased when it is used as a voltage sensor. *Page 288*

160. A/An _____ is a solid-state component which acts in the same way as a holding relay. *Page 288*

161. Light intensity _____ (is or is not) controlled by an SCR in the same way it is controlled with a series resistor. *Page 289*

162. A/An _____ is a solid-state component which acts much like an SCR, but controls both halves of the AC cycle. *Page 291*

163. Load current _____ (does or does not) flow in a bipolar transistor circuit when no base current is flowing. *Page 291*

164. Emitter-collector current _____ (does or does not) flow in an NPN transistor when its base is negative with respect to its emitter. *Page 291*

165. Current _____ (does or does not) have to flow into or out of the gate of a field effect transistor for it to conduct. *Page 291*

166. A unijunction transistor is caused to conduct when a forward-bias voltage is applied to its _____ . *Page 293*

167. A light emitting diode produces light when it is _____ (forward or reverse) biased. *Page 294*

168. A phototransistor conducts the most current when it is in the _____ (dark or light). *Page 294*

Integrated Circuits

While the solid-state devices revolutionized electronics, the integrated circuit, or IC, chip has caused another revolution. These tiny chips of silicon contain many complete circuits consisting of transistors, diodes and capacitors. The availability of these ingenious little devices has allowed the entire field of digital electronics to develop.

Digital Integrated Circuits

For many years, all of the electronics used in communications and control systems were of the type we now call linear, or analog, electronics. Analog electrical signals vary in a continuous fashion from zero to the maximum signal. An amplifier, for example, reproduces all of the variations of the signal on its input into a signal that is identical, except for a higher amplitude, on its output. The reproduction of music in a radio and the control of motor speed as a function of the movement of a speed control knob are examples of analog changes.

Digital electronics is another form of electronics gaining popularity. Digital has become practical since the development of integrated circuits capable of housing thousands of gates, or switches, on a single chip of silicon.

In digital electronics, we consider only two electrical conditions in a circuit. We call these conditions by various terms; one and zero, high and low, on and off, yes and no, or true and false. Regardless of what we call them, the difference is actually in the level of voltage supplied to the components within the system, or within the chips. This text refers to these two conditions as "high" and "low."

In the same way that semiconductor diodes and transistors have replaced vacuum tubes, integrated circuits have replaced, to a great extent, discrete components. Instead of building a circuit with hundreds or thousands of separate transistors and diodes, almost all digital electronic equipment is built of integrated circuit, IC, chips. In this text, we are not concerned with what is inside an IC chip; rather we are interested in the symbols used for them and what they do in an aircraft electrical system.

The main building blocks used in digital electronics are the various types of gates as we see in Figure 4-132. A gate is a combination of diodes and transistors in a single chip that performs special functions. The gates and other integrated circuits we discuss here are some that are most generally found in aircraft electrical systems.

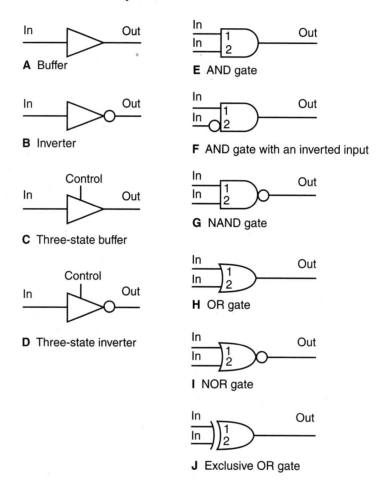

Figure 4-132. *Symbols for digital logic gates*

Buffer

A buffer is a device used to isolate circuits from one another. A buffer has the same signal on its output as it has on its input. Buffers are drawn in an electrical circuit with the point showing the direction the signal travels through the circuit.

Inverter

An inverter is similar to a buffer, except that the signal on its output is opposite to the signal on its input. Inverters, which are also called NOT gates, are used to change the output of other types of gates. The small circle at the point of the inverter symbol shows that the signal on the output is opposite to the signal on the input.

Three-State Buffer

A three-state buffer acts much like an electrically actuated switch. When the signal on the control is low, the three-state buffer acts as a regular buffer with the same signal on its output as is on its input. However, when a high signal is placed on the control, the buffer acts like an open switch, and there is essentially no connection between the input and the output.

Three-State Inverter

A three-state inverter acts like an electrically actuated switch in which the signal on its output is opposite to the signal on its input.

If there is a low on the input and on the control, there will be a high on the output. When the control is taken high, the three-state inverter acts like an open switch and there is no signal on the output, regardless of the signal on the input.

AND Gate

An AND gate is an integrated circuit that acts in the same way as two or more switches connected in series. A high signal can appear on the output only when every one of the inputs is high.

AND gates can be used in a landing gear indication system to turn on a single GEAR UP light only when all of the landing gears are up and locked in the wheel wells.

You may sometimes see an AND gate with a small circle on one of the inputs. This means that the input with the circle has an inverter in it that changes the condition of its signal before it is fed into the gate. In Figure 4-132F, input 2 of the AND gate has a circle on it. A high signal will be fed into the AND gate when input 2 has a low on it. The low is inverted and becomes a high before it goes into the gate.

AND gates may have as many inputs as are needed, but only one output.

NAND Gate

A NAND gate (NOT AND gate) is similar to an AND gate followed by an inverter. There is a high signal on the output only when all of the inputs have a low signal on them. NAND gates can be used in the same type of circuit as AND gates when a low signal rather than a high signal is needed on the output to actuate the subsequent stages.

OR Gate

An OR gate acts in the same way as two or more switches connected in parallel.

INCLUSIVE OR Gate

A high signal will appear on the output of an INCLUSIVE OR gate when there is a high signal on any of the inputs. An INCLUSIVE OR gate can be used in an overtemperature warning system to turn on the warning light if any of the sensors is providing a high signal because of an overtemperature condition.

OR gates can have as many inputs as are needed, but only one output.

EXCLUSIVE OR Gate

An EXCLUSIVE OR gate (XOR gate) has a high signal on its output when one, and only one of the inputs is high, but the output goes low when any of the other inputs goes high.

NOR Gate

A NOR gate (NOT OR gate) is similar to an OR gate followed by an inverter. There is a high signal on the output any time there is a low signal on any of the inputs. A NOR gate can be used in the same type of circuit as an OR gate when a low signal, rather than a high signal, is needed on the output to actuate the later stages.

Linear (Analog) Integrated Circuits

The gates we have just discussed all apply to digital electronics in which there are only two conditions. Analog electronics, on the other hand, deals with electronics in which values of voltage and current vary from zero to a maximum value in smooth changes rather than in steps.

Operational Amplifiers

Operational amplifiers, commonly called op-amps, are one of the most widely used linear integrated circuits. An op-amp has two inputs and a single output. The voltage on the output is an amplification of the difference between the voltages on the two inputs.

If the plus input is grounded and the signal to be amplified is put on the minus input, the phase of the output will be inverted from the phase of the input. If the minus input is grounded and the signal is put on the plus input, the output signal will have the same phase as that of the input. *See* Figure 4-133.

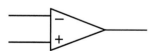

Figure 4-133.
Symbol for an operational amplifier

Answers begin on Page 359. Page numbers refer to chapter text.

169. The signal on the output of a buffer _____ (is or is not) the same as it is on its input.
     Page 298

170. The signal on the output of an inverter _____ (is or is not) the same as it is on its input.
     Page 299

171. A high signal on the control of a three-state buffer will cause it to act as a _____ (closed or open) switch. *Page 299*

172. A/An _____ (what type of two-input gate) must have a high on both of its inputs before it can have a high on its output. *Page 299*

173. A/An _____ (what type of two-input gate) can have a high on its output when either of its inputs has a high on it. *Page 299*

174. A/An _____ (what type of two-input gate) can have a high on its output when one, but only one, of its inputs is high. *Page 299*

Chemical Energy into Electricity

One of the more important devices used to produce electricity is the battery, or more accurately, the electrochemical cell.

As explained earlier, all of nature is composed of atoms which consist of a nucleus containing positive protons and neutral neutrons. Spinning around this nucleus in shells, or rings, are negatively charged particles of electricity called electrons. When atoms of some of the chemical elements react with atoms of other elements, electrons are released from one element and are attracted to the other. The force of attraction for these electrons is an electrical pressure we call voltage.

Simple Chemical Cell

We can see the way chemical energy is changed into electrical energy by studying the simple electrochemical cell in Figure 4-134 on Page 302.

A strip of zinc and a strip of copper in a solution of hydrochloric acid and water is an electrochemical cell.

The electrolyte (the acid and the water) contains positive hydrogen ions and negative chlorine ions. The zinc is an active chemical element, and it reacts, or combines, with the chlorine to form zinc chloride. When negative chlorine ions from the electrolyte combine with the zinc, the zinc becomes negative. The ions give it an excess of electrons.

If a conductor joins the zinc and the copper, the extra electrons will leave the zinc and travel to the copper where they attract positive hydrogen ions from the electrolyte. The hydrogen ions accept the electrons and become neutralized and form molecules of hydrogen gas. The zinc metal is eaten away, but electrons continue to flow through the conductor as long as there is any zinc left, and as long as the zinc and the copper are covered with the acid solution.

This zinc and copper cell is a primary cell, and the action of a primary cell is non-reversible. This means that it can convert chemical energy into electrical energy, but it cannot convert electrical energy back into chemical energy. When a primary cell is used up (in this case, when the zinc is eaten up or when the acid is neutralized) its energy cannot be restored.

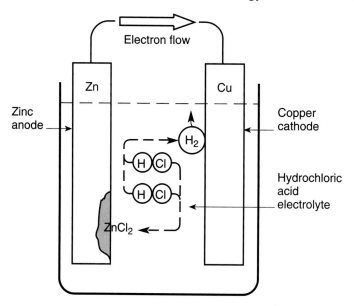

Figure 4-134. *In a simple electrochemical cell, the zinc reacts with chlorine ions from the hydrochloric acid to form zinc chloride. This reaction causes the zinc to release electrons which travel through the external circuit to the copper where they attract and neutralize hydrogen ions from the hydrochloric acid. Two atoms of hydrogen make one molecule of hydrogen gas which forms as bubbles on the copper.*

Primary Cells

The primary cells in most common use today are carbon-zinc cells, alkaline-manganese cells, mercury cells, silver oxide cells, and lithium cells. All of these cells release electrons when one of the active elements, the anode, is oxidized. When the anode is oxidized, electrons are released, and they travel through an electrical load to the other active element, the cathode. An electrolyte conducts electrical current between the active elements in the cell by the movement of ions, or charged atoms.

Carbon-Zinc Cells

Carbon-zinc cells have been used for years in flashlights and as a low-cost, low-voltage source of electrical power for portable radios. *See* Figure 4-135.

The case of a carbon-zinc cell is made of a can of zinc metal. This zinc is the anode of the cell, and it is the active element that is oxidized to release electrons. The zinc can is lined with a gummy separator paste made of starch and flour with small amounts of mercuric chloride mixed in it. This separator, which is saturated with electrolyte, allows ions from the electrolyte to migrate to the zinc can, but it prevents any direct contact between the cathode material and the zinc.

The cathode of the carbon-zinc cell, the active element that provides the oxygen to oxidize the anode, is a paste of manganese dioxide. Powdered manganese dioxide is mixed with powdered carbon, and it is packed around a solid carbon rod that acts as a current collector and is the positive terminal of the cell. This carbon rod is held upright in the can by the cathode material and is kept from touching the bottom of the can by a cardboard insulating washer.

The electrolyte of the carbon-zinc cell is a mixture of ammonium chloride and zinc chloride. It forms negative chloride ions, and ammonium and zinc ions. Both ions are positive. This electrolyte saturates the cathode material and the separator.

When the negative chloride ions from the electrolyte join with the zinc of which the can is made, electrons are forced out of the zinc and part of the zinc is changed into zinc chloride. The electrons that leave the zinc travel through the electrical load to the carbon rod which is packed in the manganese dioxide cathode material. These electrons attract and neutralize the positive ammonium ions left in the electrolyte.

Carbon-zinc cells are one of the oldest and least expensive portable sources of electrical energy, but they have a few drawbacks that have caused them to be replaced in most serious applications by the more powerful and longer life alkaline-manganese cells. The anode of a carbon-zinc cell is the zinc case that houses the moist separator and the electrolyte. As the zinc gives up electrons it changes into zinc chloride which is a form of corrosion. This corrosion can eat through the can and allow the electrolyte to leak out, damaging any device in which the battery is installed.

The voltage produced by an electrochemical cell is a function of the electrode potential difference of the chemicals that make up its active elements. The zinc and manganese dioxide that form the active elements in a carbon-zinc cell have an electrode potential difference of 1.5 volts, and regardless of the size of the cell, all carbon-zinc cells have an open-circuit voltage of 1.5 volts.

The amount of current a carbon-zinc cell can produce is determined by the amount of active ingredients that make up the cell. Cells range all of the way from the small AAA cells used in some small flashlights to the No. 6 dry cell that is used to power some door bells and to provide power for some emergency lighting systems.

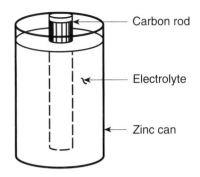

Figure 4-135. *Construction of a carbon-zinc cell*

electrolyte. The liquid in a battery. It is used to conduct the flow of electricity inside the battery.

When a carbon-zinc cell is being used, bubbles of hydrogen gas form on the carbon rod and these bubbles insulate the rod from the manganese dioxide cathode material. This insulation gives the cell a high internal resistance and drops its output voltage. The manganese dioxide absorbs the hydrogen and after the cell rests for a few minutes, the resistance between the carbon rod and the cathode material drops enough that the voltage rises.

The open-circuit voltage of a new carbon-zinc cell is 1.5 volts, but the voltage drops as the cell is used. The faster the rate of use, the greater the voltage drop.

Alkaline-Manganese Cells

Today we use thousands of small battery-operated, motor-driven devices such as clocks, tape recorders, VCR cameras, portable fans, and toys. These devices, as well as radios and portable audio systems, have brought about a demand for a battery that is inexpensive, yet more powerful and more durable than the carbon-zinc battery. The battery that is filling this need is the alkaline-manganese cell, usually called an alkaline battery.

The chemistry in an alkaline-manganese cell is similar to that in a carbon-zinc cell except that the electrolyte is an alkali rather than an acid.

The anode of an alkaline-manganese cell is made up of powdered zinc metal which has been mixed with a small amount of mercury. The cathode material is a mixture of graphite and manganese dioxide, and the electrolyte is a solution of potassium hydroxide and water.

The active cathode material is formed into a cylinder which is held inside a steel container. The container serves as the positive terminal of the cell, just the opposite of a carbon zinc cell in which the container is the negative terminal. A porous separator insulates the cathode materials from the anode materials. A zinc "nail" which serves as a negative current collector is embedded in the center of the anode material. This current collector contacts a metal cover that is insulated from the steel can, and it acts as the negative terminal of the cell.

The entire cell is insulated with a plastic sleeve and it is covered with a protective steel jacket. The metal cap that forms the positive terminal of the cell is raised so the outside of the alkaline-manganese cell has the same shape as a carbon-zinc cell. These more powerful cells can directly replace the older, less powerful ones.

Since the active elements in an alkaline-manganese cell are zinc and manganese dioxide, as they are in the older carbon-zinc cell, the open circuit voltage is the same in the two types of cells. The physical construction of the two cells gives the alkaline-manganese cell a much lower internal resistance and these cells hold a much higher voltage during their discharge.

Alkaline-manganese cells are available in the same sizes as the older carbon-zinc cells, as well as in several sizes of button cells for small devices. These cells are more expensive than the carbon-zinc cells, but since they have a longer operating life, their overall operating costs are lower.

Mercury Cells

Mercury cells have a large capacity and a long life for their small size, and they are manufactured in button, or disk, cases. These batteries are used in such devices as watches, calculators, hearing aids, and cameras.

The anode material in a mercury cell is pure powdered zinc and the cathode material is mercuric oxide. The electrolyte is a paste of potassium hydroxide in water.

The case of a mercury cell is nickel plated and it acts as the positive terminal, or cathode, of the cell. A button of powdered and compressed mercuric oxide, which is the source of the oxygen used to oxidize the zinc, is placed in the case and this button is covered with a porous separator. A button of powdered and compressed zinc metal is placed on top of the separator and the active elements are saturated with the potassium hydroxide electrolyte. The cell is covered with a metal cap that is insulated from the case by a blue nylon grommet.

The electrode potential difference of the active elements in a mercury cell give the cell an open-circuit voltage of 1.4 volts. One of the most important characteristics of this type of cell is that its voltage remains almost constant until the cell is practically used up.

Some mercury cells are designed for a much lower discharge rate, and these cells use a paste of sodium hydroxide and zinc oxide in water as the electrolyte. The low-discharge cells look the same as the high-discharge cells with the exception that the nylon insulator is yellow instead of blue.

Silver Oxide Cells

Mercury cells have been replaced for use in calculators and watches by silver oxide cells that cost somewhat more, but last longer, therefore their overall cost is lower.

Silver oxide cells are made in the same way as mercury cells except for the use of a different color nylon insulator between the case and the cap. The low-discharge-rate silver oxide cell has a clear nylon insulator. The insulator of a cell designed for a high discharge rate is green nylon.

The anode of a silver oxide cell is compressed powdered zinc, and the cathode is made of either silver oxide (Ag_2O) or silver peroxide (Ag_2O_2). The electrolyte used in the low-discharge-rate silver oxide cells is a paste of sodium hydroxide and zinc oxide in water. The electrolyte for the cells that are designed for a higher discharge rate is a paste of potassium hydroxide in water.

Silver oxide cells have an open-circuit voltage of 1.55 volts and this voltage drops very little until the cell is almost completely discharged.

The extremely long operating life and the wide range of temperatures in which the cell can operate has made silver oxide cells the most efficient type of power supply for hearing aids, calculators, and electronic watches. In these applications silver oxide cells will last about half again as long as a comparable mercury cell.

Lithium Cells

When looking at a list of the electrode potential values for the chemical elements, we find that lithium has the greatest voltage. Lithium is one of the alkaline-metal chemical elements and is the lightest metal known. Lithium cells have an open-circuit voltage of between 2.8 and 3.6 volts depending upon the type of cathode material used.

The anode for all lithium cells is high-purity lithium metal in the form of a grid or of solid metal. However, there are a number of different types of cathode material used in these cells. Thionyl chloride, which is also known as sulfur oxychloride, is sometimes used as both the cathode and the electrolyte. This cathode material produces a lithium cell with the highest output voltage. Some of the smaller button-type lithium cells use manganese dioxide or iodine as the cathode material.

Lithium cells have the longest shelf life of any primary cell, and even though there have been problems involving lithium cells installed in aircraft to power the emergency locator transmitters, these cells have the potential of becoming one of the most important types of primary cell.

STUDY QUESTIONS: PRIMARY CELLS

Answers begin on Page 359. **Page numbers refer to chapter text.**

175. Electrons are released in an electrochemical cell when one of the active chemical elements is _____ (oxidized or reduced). *Page 302*

176. The electrolyte in a carbon-zinc cell is a mixture of _____ and _____ . *Page 303*

177. The open-circuit voltage of a new carbon-zinc cell is _____ volts. *Page 303*

178. The voltage produced by a carbon-zinc cell _____ (does or does not) depend upon the size of the cell. *Page 304*

179. The anode material of an alkaline-manganese cell is _____ . *Page 304*

180. The cathode material of an alkaline-manganese cell is _____ . *Page 304*

181. The electrolyte of an alkaline-manganese cell is _____ and water. *Page 304*

182. The cathode of a mercury cell is _____ . *Page 305*

183. The anode of a mercury cell is _____ . *Page 305*

184. The open-circuit voltage of a mercury cell is _____ volts. *Page 305*

185. The nylon insulator used in a high-rate of discharge mercury cell is colored
_____ . *Page 305*

186. The nylon insulator used in a low-rate of discharge mercury cell is colored
_____ . *Page 305*

187. The open-circuit voltage of a silver oxide cell is _____ volts. *Page 305*

188. The nylon insulator used in a high-rate of discharge silver oxide cell is colored
_____ . *Page 305*

189. The nylon insulator used in a low-rate of discharge silver oxide cell is
_____ . *Page 305*

190. The anode of a lithium cell is high-purity _____ metal. *Page 306*

191. Two advantages of a lithium cell over other types of primary cells are:
a. _____
b. _____
Page 306

Secondary Cells

The electrochemical action in a primary cell is non-reversible, but in a secondary cell, the action is reversible. The cell is discharged by taking electrons from its negative plates. When these electrons leave, the active materials on the plates change, but they are not destroyed as they are in a primary cell. By putting electrons back into the cell in the direction opposite that which they left, the active material on the plates is changed back into its original condition and the cell is recharged.

The two most commonly used secondary cells are the lead-acid cell and the sintered-plate nickel-cadmium cell.

Lead-Acid Cells

Almost all automobiles and many aircraft use lead-acid batteries to store electrical energy for starting the engines.

The cells in a lead-acid battery are made of positive and negative plates covered by an acid electrolyte. The positive plates are made of a grid of a special lead alloy filled with lead dioxide (PbO_2). The grids of the negative plates are filled with porous, or spongy, lead. The positive and negative plates are held apart by a porous insulating material that keeps them from touching each other, but allows the electrolyte to reach all parts of the plates.

The electrolyte used in lead-acid batteries is a mixture of sulfuric acid and water, and it changes its chemical composition as the state of charge of the battery changes. As its composition changes, its specific gravity also changes. This allows the specific gravity of the electrolyte to serve as an indicator of the state of charge of the battery. When the cell is fully charged the specific gravity of the electrolyte is around 1.285, and when it is completely discharged, the specific gravity drops to approximately 1.150.

Chemical Changes During Discharge

When a lead-acid cell is fully charged, the electrolyte contains positive hydrogen ions and negative sulfate (SO_4) ions that are free to combine with other ions and form new chemical compounds. As soon as a conductor joins the two plates, electrons leave the negative plate and flow to the positive plate where they force the lead dioxide to break down into negative oxygen ions and positive lead ions. The negative oxygen ions join with positive hydrogen ions from the sulfuric acid and form water (H_2O). Negative sulfate ions join with positive lead ions in both plates and form lead sulfate ($PbSO_4$).

As the battery discharges, lead sulfate forms on both plates, and the electrolyte loses most of its positive and negative ions, with water taking the place of much of the acid.

The open-circuit voltage of a lead-acid cell is approximately 2.1 volts, and because of the internal resistance of the cell, the closed-circuit voltage is less than its open-circuit voltage. As the cell discharges, its internal resistance increases and the closed-circuit voltage drops.

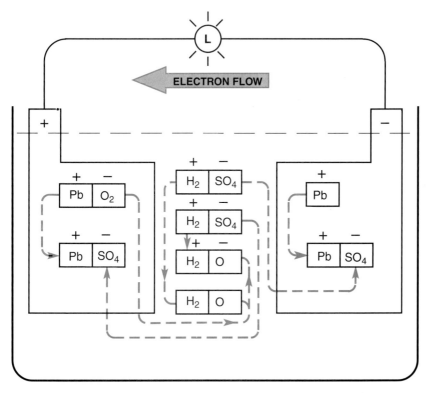

Figure 4-136. *Chemical changes in a lead-acid cell during discharge*

Chemical Changes During Charge

A lead-acid cell can be returned to its charged condition by connecting it to a battery charger so direct current can force electrons into the negative plate.

Electrons on the negative plate attract positive lead ions from the lead sulfate. This leaves negative sulfate ions which attract positive hydrogen ions from the water in the electrolyte to form sulfuric acid. The negative oxygen ions left from the water are attracted to the positive plate, where they join with the positive lead ions from the lead sulfate to form lead dioxide. As the battery charges and water is changed into sulfuric acid, the specific gravity of the electrolyte rises.

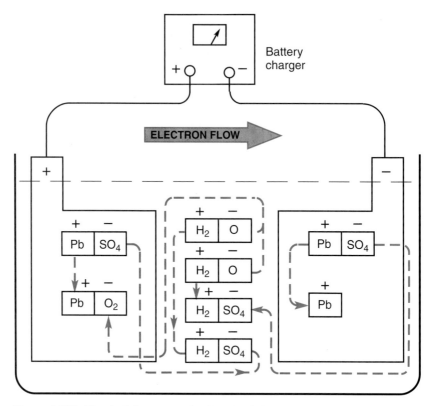

Figure 4-137. *Chemical changes in a lead-acid cell during charge*

Sintered-Plate Nickel-Cadmium Cells

Nickel-cadmium cells have the advantage that they can furnish high rates of current flow without the voltage drop associated with lead-acid batteries. They also can operate over an extremely wide range of temperatures.

Sintered-plate nickel-cadmium cells are made in many sizes and shapes, ranging all of the way from the heavy-duty cells used in batteries for aircraft and heavy equipment, to the smaller flashlight-type cells. These small cells are available from the AAA-size up to the D-size.

The active material in the positive plate of a nickel-cadmium cell is nickel hydroxide, and the active material in the negative plate is cadmium hydroxide. The positive and negative plates are separated with a thin strip of a special plastic material that allows the electrolyte to reach all parts of the plates. The electrolyte used in these batteries is a solution of potassium hydroxide and water.

The voltage of a nickel-cadmium cell is about 1.25 volts, which is lower than that produced by either a lead-acid secondary cell or carbon-zinc or alkaline-manganese primary cells, and the cell keeps this voltage until it is almost completely discharged.

When a nickel-cadmium cell is charged, the negative material loses some of its oxygen and becomes metallic cadmium, while the positive material absorbs more oxygen. The electrolyte does not enter into the chemical changes that take place when the cell is charged, therefore its specific gravity is not an indication of the state of charge of the cell.

When the nickel-cadmium cell discharges, the cadmium gains some of the oxygen and changes into cadmium hydroxide, and the active nickel material loses some of its oxygen and changes back into nickel hydroxide. Nickel-cadmium cells have two characteristics that make them different from other types of cells. They are subject to thermal runaway, and they have a "memory."

Thermal Runaway

If a nickel-cadmium cell is subjected to an excessively high charging rate, even though its internal resistance is low, it can become overheated. When this occurs, its internal resistance drops. The lower internal resistance allows the cell to take more current from the charger and more heat is generated. This condition is known as thermal runaway and it can destroy a cell. Sealed nickel-cadmium cells are vented to relieve the pressure that could build up to a dangerous level under thermal runway conditions.

The problem of thermal runaway is minimized by using a constant-current charger that limits the amount of current that can be put into the cell.

Cell Memory

Sintered-plate nickel-cadmium cells have a characteristic that causes them to lose capacity if they are repeatedly discharged and charged to only a small percentage of their capacity.

For example, if 20% of a cell's capacity is taken out of it and the cell is recharged repeatedly, the cell will lose some of its capacity and it will never accept a full charge.

A cell that has had its capacity decreased by repeated shallow charges can be restored to its full capacity by completely discharging it and overcharging it to approximately 140% of its rated ampere-hour capacity.

Cell Voltage Changes During Discharge

The characteristic of a nickel-cadmium cell to keep its full voltage until it is almost totally discharged is both good and bad. This characteristic allows electrical loads to have the full voltage until the cell is discharged, but the cell voltage gives no indication of the amount of charge still left in it.

The only way to know the amount of charge in a nickel-cadmium cell is to completely discharge it and then measure the amount of charge put back into it.

*Answers begin on Page 359. **Page numbers refer to chapter text.***

192. The two most widely used secondary cells are:

   a. _____

   b. _____

   Page 308

193. The active material in the negative plate of a lead-acid cell is _____ .
   Page 308

194. The active material in the positive plate of a lead-acid cell is _____ .
   Page 308

195. The electrolyte used in a lead-acid cell is a solution of _____ acid and water. *Page 308*

196. The specific gravity of the electrolyte in a lead-acid cell _____ (is or is not) an indication of the state of charge of the cell. *Page 309*

197. The open-circuit voltage of a lead-acid cell is approximately _____ volts. *Page 309*

198. The positive plate of a nickel-cadmium cell is made of _____ .
   Page 310

199. The negative plate of a nickel-cadmium cell is made of _____ .
   Page 310

200. The electrolyte used in a nickel-cadmium cell is _____ and water. *Page 310*

201. The open-circuit voltage of a nickel-cadmium cell is _____ volts. *Page 310*

202. Two problems inherent with nickel-cadmium cells are:

   a. _____

   b. _____

   Page 311

Aircraft Batteries

Lead-Acid Batteries

Lead-acid batteries are the most commonly used type of battery in light general aviation aircraft. They are made up of a number of cells which have an open-circuit voltage of about 2.1 volts.

Batteries are rated according to their voltage and ampere-hour capacity, which is their ability to produce a given amount of current for a specified length of time. One ampere-hour of capacity is the ability of the battery to produce a flow of 1 ampere for 1 hour. A 20-ampere-hour battery can produce 1 ampere for 20 hours, 20 amperes for 1 hour, or any combination of amperes and hours that produce 20. This relationship is not exactly true, because at the high rates of current drain, the battery produces less current than it does at lower rates due to losses within the battery.

Aircraft batteries are rated at their 5-hour, 20-minute, and 5-minute discharge rates. These ratings give the ampere-hour capacity of the battery when enough current discharges the battery to a closed-circuit voltage of 1.2 volts per cell in these specified times. A typical 24-volt battery may have a 5-hour rating of 17 ampere-hours, a 20-minute rating of 10.3 ampere hours, and a 5-minute rating of 6.7 ampere hours.

The open-circuit voltage of a lead-acid battery is about 2.1 volts, but the internal resistance of the battery causes a voltage drop as current flows, and the closed-circuit voltage is lower. As the battery discharges, its internal resistance increases and the closed-circuit voltage drops.

The internal resistance of a battery may be found by subtracting the closed-circuit voltage from the open-circuit voltage to find the voltage dropped across the battery. Then divide the voltage drop by the amount of current that caused the voltage drop.

For example, a 24-volt battery has an open-circuit voltage of 25.2 volts (12 cells x 2.1 volts per cell). The closed-circuit voltage when 10 amps is flowing through a load of 2 ohms is 20 volts.

Voltage drop across internal resistance = 25.2 – 20.0 = 5.2 volts
Internal resistance = 5.2 ÷ 10 = 0.52 ohms

Battery Charging

Batteries may be charged by the constant-current or constant-voltage method. In either method, the positive (+) lead of the charger is connected to the positive terminal of the battery and the negative (–) lead to the negative terminal.

An aircraft generator keeps the battery charged by the constant-voltage method. The generator output is slightly higher than the open-circuit battery voltage. This causes a high rate of charging current when the engine first starts, because the starter has used enough current to drop the battery voltage. As soon as the battery voltage rises, the charging current drops off to a much lower rate.

If the battery has an internal short in one or more of its cells, the aircraft ammeter will indicate a full charging rate, but the battery will never become fully charged.

Most aircraft maintenance shops charge batteries by the constant-current method. Several batteries may be connected in series across the charger and the charger voltage increased until the desired current flows. Batteries having different voltages may be charged at the same time, but all of them must have essentially the same ampere-hour capacity.

The state of charge of a lead-acid battery is indicated by the specific gravity of the electrolyte, and the specific gravity is affected by temperature. A correction must be applied for any temperature other than 80°F. For each 10° above 80°, add 0.004, and for each 10° below 80°, subtract 0.004.

For example, electrolyte with a specific gravity of 1.205 at 100°F will be less dense than at 80°F, so a correction of +0.008 point must be applied. The corrected specific gravity is 1.205 + 0.008 = 1.213.

The freezing temperature of a battery is determined by the specific gravity of the electrolyte. The higher the specific gravity, the lower the freezing temperature. The electrolyte in a fully discharged battery (SG = 1.100) will freeze at +19°F. If the battery were fully charged (SG = 1.300), its freezing temperature would be -90°F.

The sulfuric acid electrolyte from a battery will burn skin, eat holes in clothes, and cause severe corrosion in aircraft structure. Spilled electrolyte must be neutralized by a solution of baking soda (sodium bicarbonate) and water, and the battery box area of an aircraft should be protected by some type of chemical-resistant paint, such as bituminous (tar-based) paint or polyurethane enamel.

Battery Installation

When a battery is installed in an aircraft, it should be firmly secured in a clean, corrosion-free battery compartment. Connect the positive, or "hot," lead first so there will be no sparks if your wrench should contact the aircraft structure, then connect the ground lead.

Be sure that the battery box is adequately ventilated in the manner recommended by the aircraft manufacturer. If a sump jar is installed in the battery vent line, make sure its pad is saturated with a baking soda and water solution.

Nickel-Cadmium Batteries

Nickel-cadmium batteries are used in many aircraft because of their ability to produce large amounts of current for starting turbine engines. They are installed and serviced in ways similar to that of lead-acid batteries, but special precautions must be observed.

Because their chemistry is opposite, nickel-cadmium batteries must not be serviced in the same area used for servicing lead-acid batteries. They can easily contaminate each other. Tools used for servicing lead-acid batteries should not be used for servicing nickel-cadmium batteries.

Battery Construction

Nickel-cadmium batteries are made up of individual cells connected together with cell links and installed in an insulated steel case. Corrosion or loose links can cause overheating, resulting in burn marks on the hardware.

The positive plates of a nickel-cadmium battery are made of powdered nickel, called plaque, fused into a screen made of nickel wire mesh. This plaque is impregnated with nickel hydroxide.

The negative plates have the same type of base, but their plaque is impregnated with cadmium hydroxide.

The positive and negative plates are meshed together and are separated with porous nylon and cellophane. The cellophane acts as a barrier membrane that prevents the oxygen that forms on the positive plate during discharge from reaching the negative plate. If this oxygen were to combine with the cadmium, it would produce enough heat to cause a thermal runaway.

Chemical Changes During Discharge

The potassium hydroxide electrolyte in a nickel-cadmium battery does not enter into the chemical reaction that causes the movement of electrons. As the battery is discharged, hydroxide (OH) ions from the electrolyte combine with the cadmium on the negative plates to produce cadmium hydroxide and release electrons. While this is taking place, hydroxide ions from the nickel hydroxide on the positive plates go into the electrolyte and carry electrons with them.

The electrolyte does not change its chemical composition during discharge, and its specific gravity remains essentially constant during all battery operation.

Chemical Changes During Charge

When current is put into a nickel-cadmium battery with a battery charger, hydroxide ions are driven from the negative plates into the electrolyte, and hydroxide ions from the electrolyte combine with the nickel hydroxide on the positive plates increasing its oxidation.

After all the active material on the positive and negative plates is restored to charged condition, additional charging will decompose the electrolyte. Hydrogen gas will be released from the negative plates and oxygen gas from the positive plates.

Overcharging will increase the temperature of the cells and cause electrolyte to be spewed from the cell vents. This electrolyte will dry on the cell tops in the form of potassium carbonate, a white powder that must be cleaned off when the battery is serviced.

Battery Servicing

Nickel-cadmium batteries can be charged by either a constant-voltage or a constant-current charge. In the aircraft they get a constant-voltage charge, and in the shop, they are usually given a constant-current charge.

The constant-voltage produced by the aircraft electrical system keeps the battery fully charged, but may result in an excessive loss of electrolyte. Because of a condition known as cell memory, this continued partial charging will cause the cells to become unbalanced, some having a higher state of charge than others. This imbalance causes a loss of battery capacity and requires capacity reconditioning, or deep-cycling.

The electrolyte in a nickel-cadmium battery is a solution of potassium hydroxide and water whose specific gravity does not change as the state of charge of the battery changes. When the battery discharges, the plates absorb some of the electrolyte. The level of the electrolyte in the cell is the lowest when the cell is fully discharged. If water is added to a nickel-cadmium cell when the battery is not fully charged, some of the electrolyte will spew out when the battery is being charged.

Capacity Reconditioning

The only way to accurately know the state of charge of a nickel-cadmium battery is to discharge it completely and measure the amount of charge put back into it.

When cell imbalance occurs or when the capacity of the battery decreases, it should be given a capacity reconditioning. This consists of completely discharging the battery through a load bank, and when the cells are discharged, they are shorted out and allowed to remain in this shorted condition for a specific period of time. The shorting straps are removed and the battery given a constant-current charge to 140% of its ampere-hour rating.

The end-of-charge voltage of a nickel-cadmium battery depends upon the cell temperature and the method used for charging the battery. Be sure to follow the recommendations in the service manual for each battery.

Thermal Runaway

Nickel-cadmium batteries have a characteristic that can cause a serious problem unless proper precautions are taken. Their low internal resistance allows these cells to produce a high rate of current for engine starting, and they also take a high rate of charging current. However, this high current flow heats the cells, and the cells on the inside of the battery are not able to dissipate this heat. As a result, they overheat and more current flows through them, further increasing their temperature. This overheating continues until the battery is destroyed. Thermal runaways are prevented by monitoring the temperature of the inner cells and by monitoring the amount of charging current allowed to flow into the battery.

Answers begin on Page 359. **Page numbers refer to chapter text.**

203. The two most generally used ratings for aircraft batteries are:

    a. _____

    b. _____

    Page 313

204. A lead-acid battery with 12 cells connected in series has a no-load voltage of 2.1 volts per cell. If this battery furnishes 10 amps to a load having a resistance of 2 ohms, the internal resistance of the battery is _____ ohms. *Page 313*

205. Spilled electrolyte from a lead-acid battery is neutralized with a solution of _____ and water. After the area is neutralized, it should be flushed with clean water. *Page 313*

206. When measuring the specific gravity of battery electrolyte with a hydrometer, a correction for temperature is required if the electrolyte temperature is other than _____ degrees Fahrenheit. *Page 314*

207. If the electrolyte of a lead-acid has a temperature of 100°F when its specific gravity is measured, a correction of 0.008 should be _____ (added to or subtracted from) the hydrometer reading. *Page 314*

208. The freezing temperature of the electrolyte in a fully charged lead-acid battery is _____ (higher or lower) than it is for the electrolyte in a discharged battery. *Page 314*

209. Current flowing into lead-acid battery on a constant-voltage charge is greatest when the battery is _____ (fully charged or discharged). *Page 313*

210. Twelve-volt and 24-volt batteries can be charged at the same time with the same charger if the charger is of the constant-_____ (current or voltage) type. *Page 314*

211. If the ammeter in an airplane shows a continual charge, but the lead-acid battery does not become charged, one or more of the battery cells are probably _____ (open or shorted). *Page 314*

212. A nickel-cadmium battery installed in an aircraft is kept fully charged by the generator, which provides a constant-_____ (current or voltage) charge. *Page 315*

Continued

213. The electrolyte used in a nickel-cadmium battery is a solution of _____ and water. *Page 315*

214. Improperly torqued cell link connectors on a nickel-cadmium battery will cause a high-resistance connection. This can cause _____ on the hardware. *Page 314*

215. Excessive deposits of potassium carbonate on top of the cells of a nickel-cadmium battery are an indication of _____ . *Page 315*

216. The electrolyte in a nickel-cadmium cell is lowest when the cell is in a _____ (fully charged or discharged) state. *Page 316*

217. Two things that affect the end-of-charge voltage of a nickel-cadmium battery are:
    a. _____
    b. _____
    Page 316

218. When a nickel-cadmium battery is stored for a long period of time, the electrolyte level will _____ (drop or rise). *Page 316*

219. The specific gravity of the electrolyte of a nickel-cadmium battery _____ (does or does not) change with the state-of-charge of the battery. *Page 315*

220. Gassing of the cells of a nickel-cadmium battery occurs near the _____ (beginning or end) of the charge cycle. *Page 315*

Magnetism

When electrons flow in a conductor, two things happen: heat is produced as power is used, and a magnetic field surrounds the conductor. It is this magnetic field that is of interest to us now, because it is so useful. All electric motors depend upon this magnetic field for their operation. Many electrical measuring instruments use magnetism to make them work. Magnetic tapes and disks allow us to record and store speech, music, and data. But most important, it is by using magnetic fields that we produce most of our electricity.

Permanent Magnets

In order to more easily understand magnetism, let's begin with a permanent magnet, a piece of material that has magnetic characteristics all of its own.

Magnetism and magnetic fields have been observed since the fourth century B.C., when the characteristics known now as magnetism were mentioned by Plato who described the "magnetic virtue" as being divine.

As early as the 12th century A.D., natural magnets, called lodestones, were floated on a piece of wood in a pan of water and were used as crude magnetic compasses because the same part of the stone always pointed toward the north star. The reason it did this was that the earth itself is a huge magnet, and the lodestone lined up with the magnetism of the earth.

To begin a study of magnetism, we must think about the way all matter is made. Every atom has a nucleus, containing positive protons and electrically neutral neutrons, and spinning around this nucleus are negatively charged electrons. As the electrons circle the nucleus, they also spin around their own axes in much the same way the earth spins about its axis as it circles the sun. *See* Figure 4-138.

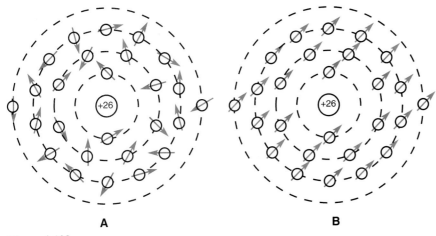

A   **B**

Figure 4-138.

A. In an atom of unmagnetized iron, the spin axes of the electrons point in different directions so the atom has no magnetic axis; it is magnetically inert.

B. When an atom of iron is magnetized, the spin axes of all of the electrons are lined up in the same direction, and the atom has a magnetic axis.

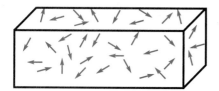

Figure 4-139. *Domain alignment in an unmagnetized material*

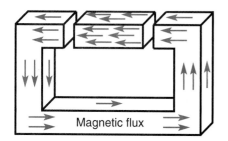

Magnetic flux

Figure 4-140. *The domains in a material may all be aligned in the same direction by holding the material in a strong magnetic field.*

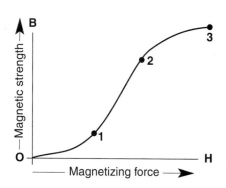

Figure 4-141. *The curve of magnetic strength (B) versus magnetizing force (H) of a piece of steel*

If the spin axes of the electrons in an atom are pointed in all different directions, the atom has no net magnetic axis, and it is magnetically inert. But, if the spin axes of all of the electrons in an atom are lined up in the same direction, the atom has a magnetic axis, and it will act as though it were a tiny gyroscope, continuing to spin in the same plane until it is acted on by some outside magnetic force. Millions of atoms that have the same spin axis within a material group themselves together in clumps called "domains," and when a magnetic force is applied to the material, an entire domain reorients at one time, rather than the individual atoms acting independently. *See* Figure 4-139.

Materials whose atoms line up easily and produce a magnetic polarity are said to be ferromagnetic, and nearly all of these materials contain iron. If the atoms line up their magnetic axes, but only weakly, the material is called a paramagnetic material. There are some materials that turn their axes across a magnetic force rather than aligning with it. These materials, such as bismuth, antimony, and zinc, are called diamagnetic materials.

When a ferromagnetic material such as iron is placed in a strong magnetic field, the magnetic axes of the spinning electrons in the iron all try to align themselves with the axes of the electrons in the magnetic source. *See* Figure 4-140.

If the magnetic field of the source is weak, some of the domains will line up with the field and magnetize the iron, but when the iron is taken out of the weak field, the domains will move out of alignment and the iron will again become unmagnetized. This magnetizing takes place within the reversible region of the magnetic strength versus magnetizing force curve, the B-H curve in Figure 4-141.

If the magnetizing force is increased beyond the reversible region, the number of domains that line up with the force will increase. Just a small increase in magnetizing force will give us a large increase in magnetic strength. See this as the portion of the B-H curve between points 1 and 2.

Increasing the magnetizing force after the upper knee of the curve is reached, above point 2, will cause the domains to rotate until they are lined up with the external force. The material is then said to be magnetically saturated and, regardless of the amount of increase in the magnetizing force, its magnetic strength cannot increase any more. If the magnetizing force is decreased after the saturation point, (point 3 in Figure 4-142), is reached, the magnetic strength will not decrease along the original curve, but the material will keep some of the magnetism. This is because the domains have rotated and cannot return to their original direction without some help. At point 4, the magnetizing force H has decreased to zero, but the material retains the magnetic strength shown.

If we reverse the magnetizing force, it becomes a demagnetizing, or coersive, force, and a force equal to that shown at point 5 is needed to completely demagnetize the material; that is, to destroy the alignment of all of its domains. If the demagnetizing force is increased to point 6, the material will be saturated in the opposition direction. All of the magnetic domains will be lined up, but now they are all in the direction opposite that at point 3.

The characteristic of a material that causes it to not follow its magnetizing curve when it is demagnetized is called the hysteresis of the material (*see* Figure 4-142). The curves shown in Figure 4-143 are called the hysteresis loops of the hard steel and soft iron.

A material such as hard steel has a very broad hysteresis loop. When the magnetizing force is removed, it retains a good deal of its magnetism, and a strong coersive, or demagnetizing, force is needed to get rid of this residual magnetism.

Soft iron has a very narrow hysteresis loop, because it loses its magnetism just as soon as the magnetizing force is taken away.

A bar of hard steel that has been exposed to a strong magnetizing force retains much of its magnetic properties after the magnetizing force is removed, and it becomes a permanent magnet.

Lay a piece of paper over a permanent magnet and sprinkle iron filings over the paper, and the filings will arrange themselves in a particular fashion. We can see from the way these filings line up that there are invisible lines of magnetism, called lines of magnetic force or magnetic flux, that travel from one end of the magnet to the other. These lines concentrate at the ends of the bar and spread apart near the middle. *See* Figure 4-144 on Page 322.

Let's consider some facts about a bar-shaped permanent magnet:

1. If we suspend the magnet from its center, it will swing until it lines up with the magnetic field of the earth. The end that points toward the earth's north pole is called the north-seeking pole or, more commonly, its north pole.

2. The lines of magnetic flux are invisible, and they travel from one pole of the magnet to the other. It has been decided and accepted by all who work with magnets that these lines leave the magnet at its north pole and enter it at its south pole, leaving and entering at right angles to its surface.

3. Each line of flux forms a complete loop, leaving at the north pole, entering at the south pole, and traveling through the magnet back to the north pole.

4. Lines of magnetic flux cannot cross one another.

Continued

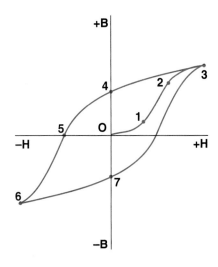

Figure 4-142. *The hysteresis loop of a piece of steel*

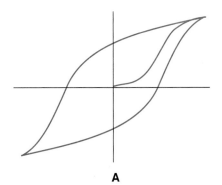

A

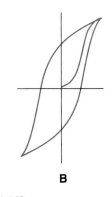

B

Figure 4-143.
A. *The hysteresis loop for hard steel*
B. *The hysteresis loop for soft iron*

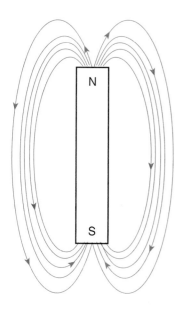

Figure 4-144. *Lines of magnetic flux surrounding a bar magnet*

5. Each loop of magnetic flux seeks the easiest path from one pole to the other.

6. The lines of magnetic flux repel each other, and they are highly concentrated as they enter and leave the poles; but they spread out, getting as far from the next one as they can. Their separation is determined by the balance of forces between the need to keep the loop as short as possible, and the repelling force trying to keep the lines next to each other as far apart as possible.

7. One line of magnetic force is called a maxwell, and a flux density of one line of flux per square centimeter is called one gauss.

8. A bar magnet will always have a north and a south pole, regardless of how small the pieces are into which we break the magnet.

Hold the south pole of one bar magnet near the north pole of another and the lines of flux will link the two magnets, as in Figure 4-145. The tendency for the lines of flux to form loops of the smallest possible size will cause a strong force of attraction that tries to pull the magnets together. The amount of this pull is affected by the strength of the magnet (the number of lines of flux) and the distance the two magnets are apart. If two magnets separated by one unit of space have a pull of one unit of force, increasing the separation to two units (doubling the separation) will cause the force to decrease to one fourth of a unit.

From what we have just seen, we can understand two of the fundamental laws of magnetism:

1. Unlike magnetic poles attract each other.

2. The attraction between unlike poles varies inversely as the square of the distance between the poles.

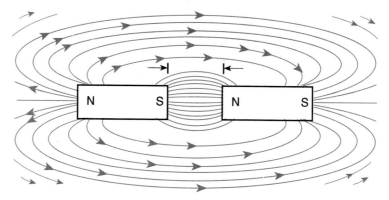

Figure 4-145. *Lines of magnetic force surrounding two bar magnets placed with their unlike poles next to one another*

Turn one of the magnets so the two north poles are together and they will push away from each other, as in Figure 4-146. Since the lines of flux must remain as complete loops and cannot cross one another, they will produce a force of repulsion. This force, like the force of attraction, follows the inverse square law. The closer the magnets are together, the stronger the repelling, or pushing, force, and this force decreases as the square of the separation between the magnets. This repelling action shows us another of the basic characteristics of magnets, that like poles repel each other.

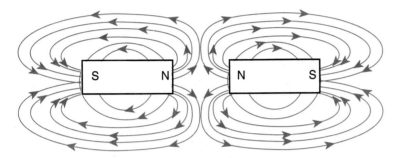

Figure 4-146. *Lines of magnetic force surrounding two bar magnets placed with their like poles next to one another.*

Not all substances conduct, or carry, lines of magnetic flux equally. The ability to conduct lines of flux is called the permeability of the material. Air, which is used as a reference, has a permeability of one, while some of the iron-nickel alloys have permeabilities of well over 100,000. This means that lines of magnetic flux find a much easier path through a material that contains iron than they find through air. The higher the permeability of a material, the easier the lines of magnetic flux can travel through it.

We can see the way a magnet attracts pieces of iron or steel by studying Figure 4-147 on Page 324. If a bar magnet is bent into the form of a horseshoe, the two poles will be near each other, and the lines of flux will pass between the poles by the easiest route possible to form complete loops. The loops act like rubber bands trying to keep themselves as short as possible.

Between the poles, the lines spread out and the loops become longer because the lines repel each other. Now, if we put a piece of iron that has a high permeability in the magnetic field, the lines of flux will pass through it, rather than through the air. Since the loops of force try to become as short as possible, they exert a physical pull on the iron and try to bring it up tight against the poles of the magnet. The force exerted by the magnet on the iron obeys the inverse square law. When the separation between the magnet and the iron is decreased to one half of its original value, the force acting on the iron is increased four times.

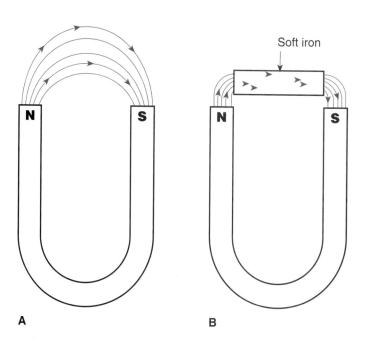

A

B

Figure 4-147.
A. Lines of magnetic flux passing through air repel each other and spread out.
B. Soft iron with a high permeability concentrates the lines of flux.

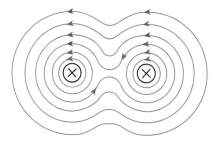

Figure 4-148. *If you hold a current-carrying conductor in your left hand with your thumb pointing in the direction of electron flow, your fingers will encircle the conductor in the same direction as the lines of magnetic flux.*

Figure 4-149. *The magnetic fields caused by current flowing in the same direction through parallel wires will pull the wires together.*

Electromagnets

When electrons flow through a conductor, the conductor's atoms are forced to line up their magnetic axes, and as the electrons spin and rotate about their nucleus, they create magnetic fields. When the magnetic axes of all of the atoms are lined up, the magnetic fields add, and they surround the conductor. The intensity of the field is proportional to the amount of current flowing in the conductor.

The direction in which the lines of flux circle around the conductor may be found by applying the left-hand rule: This says that if you hold a current-carrying conductor in your left hand with your thumb pointing in the direction of electron flow (from negative to positive), your fingers will encircle the conductor in the same direction as the lines of flux. *See* Figure 4-148.

Conductors carrying current behave much like the permanent magnet we have just studied. When two current-carrying conductors are parallel, and the current is flowing in the same direction in both conductors, as in Figure 4-149 (the cross represents the tail of the current arrow, and the dot the head), the magnetic fields loop both conductors and pull them together.

If the electrons flow in the opposite direction in the two conductors, as shown in Figure 4-150, the magnetic fields surrounding the conductors will pass in the same direction between the conductors. Since the lines of flux cannot cross over one another, they will crowd up between the conductors and force them apart.

The action of the magnetic fields surrounding current-carrying conductors is extremely important because it is upon this principle that all electric motors operate. There is an important relationship between electrical current and magnetism. When a conductor passes through a magnetic field, electrons are forced to flow in the conductor.

Figure 4-151 shows what causes this flow of electrons. When the conductor moves across the field, it cuts the lines of flux and they wrap around it, creating a magnetic field around the conductor. This magnetic field causes the electrons of the atoms within the conductor to align their magnetic axes, and if the conductor is formed into a complete loop, or circuit, electrons will move from one atom to the next and current will flow in the conductor.

The direction of current flow is determined by the direction the conductor is moving and the position of the north and south poles of the magnet. The intensity of flow is determined by the rate at which the lines of magnetic flux are cut. This rate is determined by the speed of movement of the conductor and the number of lines of flux between the magnetic poles.

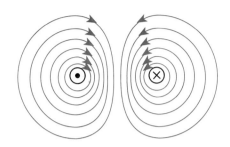

Figure 4-150. *The magnetic fields caused by current flowing through wires in the opposite direction will force the wires apart.*

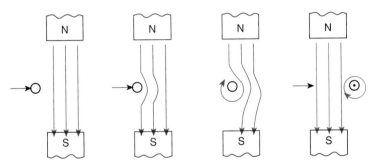

Figure 4-151. *Electrons are forced to flow in a conductor when lines of magnetic flux wrap around the conductor as it moves through a magnetic field.*

We should note here that it is the *relative* motion between the magnetic field and the conductor that is important. It does not make any difference if the conductor moves and the field stays still, or if the field moves and the conductor stays still. There is a third way to achieve relative motion, and this is a commonly used method. We can hold both the conductor and the magnetic field still and vary the strength of the field. This principle is used, as we will see, with alternating current.

The magnetic field surrounding a straight conductor is quite weak but the field's strength can be increased by winding the conductor into a coil. The field that surrounds the conductor in each turn acts in the same way as the fields around parallel conductors carrying current in the same direction. The effects of the fields build, and with all else being equal, the more turns in the coil, the stronger the resulting magnetic field.

The strength of an electromagnet, its magnetomotive force, is measured in ampere-turns, with one ampere-turn being the magnetomotive force produced when one amp of current flows through one turn of the coil. In the metric system, magnetomotive force is measured in gilberts, and one ampere turn is equal to 1.26 gilberts.

The strength of an electromagnet may be increased by concentrating the lines of flux. Remember these two things: (1) lines of flux must all form complete loops, and (2) lines of flux repel each other. If we fill the inside of the coil with some material that has a high permeability, the lines of flux will concentrate in this core and will produce a far stronger field than is produced by the same coil having an air core.

Permanent magnets have north and south poles, and electromagnets also have polarity. The polarity of an electromagnet is determined by the direction the electrons flow and the direction the coil is wound. If you hold a coil with your left hand in such a way that your fingers wrap around it in the same direction electrons flow in the conductor, from negative to positive, your thumb will point to the north pole of the electromagnet.

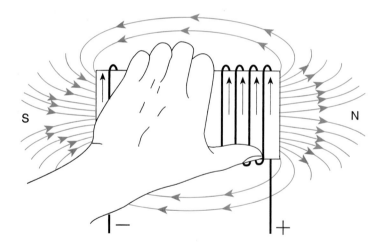

Figure 4-152. *If you hold an electromagnet in your left hand with your fingers encircling it in the same direction electrons flow through the conductor, your thumb will point to its north pole.*

*Answers begin on Page 359. **Page numbers refer to chapter text.***

221. What two things happen when electrons flow in a conductor?

    a. _____

    b. _____

    Page 319

222. The end of a suspended magnet that points toward the north star is called the

    _____ - seeking pole, or simply the _____ pole. *Page 321*

223. Lines of magnetic flux are said to leave the magnet at its _____ pole and enter the

    magnet at its _____ pole. *Page 321*

224. Fundamental laws of magnetism tell us that:

    a. _____ poles attract each other.

    b. _____ poles repel each other.

    Page 322

225. The strength of magnetic attraction or repulsion varies inversely as the _____ of the

    distance between the poles. *Page 322*

226. The ability of a material to conduct lines of magnetic flux is called the

    _____ of the material. *Page 323*

227. The _____ (higher or lower) the permeability of a material, the easier it will conduct

    lines of magnetic flux. *Page 323*

228. If you hold a current-carrying conductor with your _____ (left or right) hand with your

    thumb pointing in the direction of electron flow, your fingers will encircle the conductor in the direction

    of the lines of magnetic flux. *Page 324*

229. When current flows in the same direction in two parallel conductors, the magnetic fields surrounding the

    conductors will try to _____ (pull them together or

    separate them). *Page 324*

    Continued

230. Three ways of increasing the strength of an electromagnet are:

    a. _____

    b. _____

    c. _____

    Page 326

231. When a conductor cuts across a magnetic field, a field is set up around the conductor that causes current flow in the conductor. The amount of this current is determined by the rate at which the flux has been cut, and this rate is determined by:

    a. _____

    b. _____

    Page 325

232. Three ways of getting relative motion between a conductor and a magnetic field are:

    a. _____

    b. _____

    c. _____

    Page 325

233. The strength of an electromagnet is measured in the U.S. system in _____ and in the metric system in _____ . *Page 326*

Electric Motors

Direct Current Motors

Electric motors have become such a standard part of life that we are likely to take them for granted. They come in all sizes and power outputs, from the tiny motors that move the hands in analog wrist watches to the machines that drive ocean-going ships. Regardless of their size, all electric motors work on the same principle. One magnetic field reacts with another magnetic field to produce a physical force.

Figure 4-153 shows the basic way an electric motor works. The conductor in view A has no current flowing in it, and the lines of flux pass straight across the space from the north pole of the magnet to the south pole. When current flows in the conductor, as in B, the magnetic field caused by the current surrounds the conductor and reacts with the flux lines between the poles of the magnet. The flux concentrates on the right side of the conductor and produces a force that tries to move the conductor to the left.

The right-hand rule for motors helps us see this action. If we hold the fingers of our right hand as shown in Figure 4-154, with the forefinger pointing in the direction of the lines of flux (from the north pole of the magnet to the south pole) and the second finger pointing in the direction of electron flow in the conductor (from negative to positive), the thumb will point in the direction the conductor will move. The amount of force that acts on the conductor is determined by the strength of the two magnetic fields.

If a conductor is wound into a loop, as we see in Figure 4-155 on Page 330, with a battery forcing electrons to flow away from us in the conductor in front of the south pole and toward us in the conductor in front of the north pole, the reaction between the magnetic fields will be such that they will force the conductor on the left side to move down and the conductor on the right side to move up. If there were a shaft down the center of this loop, the loop would rotate.

The "motor" in Figure 4-155 is limited because it can rotate only until the conductors are outside of the field of the permanent magnet. We can improve on this so that the loop will turn continuously as long as power is supplied to it. We do this by connecting the battery to the armature (as the rotating loop is called) with brushes and a commutator.

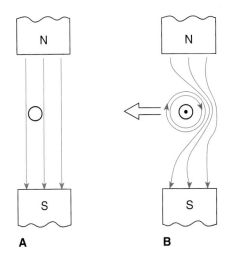

Figure 4-153. *The force that rotates the armature of an electric motor is caused by two magnetic fields reacting with each other.*

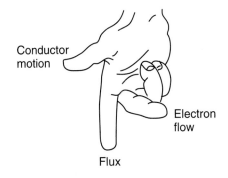

Figure 4-154. *If you hold your right hand with your forefinger pointing in the direction of the flux (north to south) and your second finger pointing in the direction of electron flow (negative to positive), your thumb will point in the direction the conductor will move.*

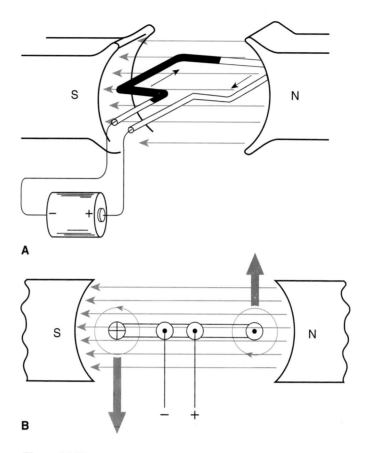

Figure 4-155

A. *When current from the battery flows through the loop of wire, the magnetic fields react and force the loop to rotate.*

B. *Diagram showing the magnetic force concentration above the wire in front of the south pole and below the wire in front of the north pole.*

If a metal ring is cut in half and one end of the loop of wire is connected to each of the halves, as in Figure 4-156, current from the battery will enter and leave the loop through carbon brushes that ride on the surfaces of the ring.

Figure 4-156 shows the way electrons from the battery flow through the left-hand brush and through the dark half of the loop from front to back, and through the light-colored half of the loop from back to front. The electrons leave through the right-hand brush and flow back to the positive terminal of the battery. The magnetic field caused by the current flowing in the loop reacts with the magnetic field of the permanent magnet and forces the loop to rotate until the left-hand brush contacts the half of the commutator that is connected to the light-colored half of the loop. The electrons flowing through this loop now reverse their direction of flow. Electrons still enter the left-hand brush, but now they flow through the light-colored half of the loop from

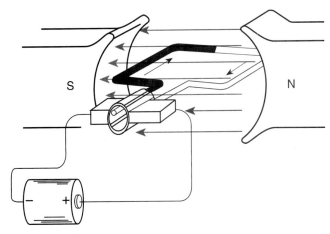

Figure 4-156. *The brush and commutator arrangement allows the direction of current flow to reverse in the armature coils so that it always flows in the same direction as the coil passes in front of a field magnet pole.*

front to back, and through the dark half from back to front. The important thing is that the electrons always pass from front to back through the half of the loop that is in front of the south pole of the permanent magnet, and that they always flow from back to front through the half of the loop that is passing in front of the north pole. By connecting the battery to the loop through the commutator, the torque, or the force that causes the loop to rotate, is always in the same direction, and the loop will rotate continuously.

Figure 4-157. *A typical armature for a small DC motor*

We have just described the basic operation of a DC motor, but such a motor would not be very practical. Figure 4-157, we see the actual armature of a DC motor. Instead of a single loop of wire, this armature uses a number of coils, each of which is made up of several turns of wire, and one end of each coil is connected to a copper commutator segment on which the brushes ride to carry electrons into and out of the coils.

The coils are wound in slots in an iron core mounted on the shaft. Iron has a very high permeability, and it concentrates the magnetic flux so that a maximum number of lines will pass through the armature and react with the flux caused by electrons flowing through the coils in the armature.

Any time electrons flow in a conductor, a magnetic field surrounds the conductor, and in a motor, this magnetic field reacts with a stationary magnetic field to produce a torque force that causes the armature to rotate.

Any time a conductor is moved through a magnetic field, a field is set up around the conductor that causes electrons to flow in it. This is called generator action. When electrons flow in the armature coils of an electric motor, the magnetic field surrounding the coils reacts with the field from the stationary magnet and causes the armature to rotate. As the armature rotates, the coils cut across the field of the stationary magnet, and a field is set up around the coils that tries to cause electrons to flow in the coil.

The important thing about this action is that it takes place any time the armature turns, and this induced current flows in the direction opposite that of the current causing the armature to rotate. The induced voltage that causes this opposing current is called back voltage, or counter electromotive force (counter emf, or CEMF), and the amount of this voltage is determined by the rate at which the lines of flux are cut by the conductors. The faster the conductor moves through the field, the greater the CEMF.

When the switch is first closed, connecting a DC motor to a battery, the electrons find very little opposition to their flow because the coils in the armature have low resistance, and the starting current is large. As soon as a field is set up around the coils, the armature begins to rotate and the coils cut across the magnetic field. A CEMF is produced in the coils that tries to force electrons through the coils in the direction opposite to that caused by the battery. This causes the current through the armature to decrease as the speed of the rotor increases.

Permanent Magnet DC Motors

The magnetic field in which the armature of a DC motor turns is one of the more important parts of the motor. This field can be produced by either a permanent magnet or an electromagnet.

Permanent-magnet motors have in the past been limited in their use to toys and other motors that must put out only a very small amount of torque. However, with the improvements that have been made in magnets, permanent-magnet motors are now finding many new applications.

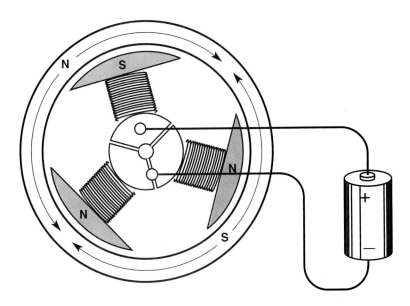

Figure 4-158. *A typical permanent-magnet DC motor such as is used in a cassette tape player*

One popular type of permanent-magnet motor is used for many of the small battery-operated cassette tape players and recorders. The field magnet for these motors is made in the form of a cylinder in which the rotor turns. The cylinder is magnetized so that its two poles are on opposite sides of the cylinder. The rotor used in these motors has three coils wound on a laminated steel frame that has three large pole faces.

Electrons from the battery enter the coils through brushes riding on the commutator in such a way that the rotor pole face moving toward the north pole of the permanent magnet has a south polarity, and the face moving toward the south pole has north polarity. By the time the poles of the rotor are almost lined up with the opposite pole of the field magnet, the brush moves to the next segment of the commutator, and this changes the polarity of the rotor. There is always a south pole of the rotor trying to line up with a north pole in the field, and a north pole in the rotor trying to line up with a south pole in the field.

A handy relationship exists in a permanent-magnet motor between the armature speed, the torque produced by the armature shaft, and the voltage applied to the armature. When the battery is first connected to the armature of a permanent-magnet motor, the armature current is high and the magnetic strength of the armature coils is high. Since the strength of the permanent magnet is constant, the locked-rotor, or starting, torque is high.

As soon as the armature begins to turn, its windings cut across the magnetic field of the permanent magnet and a CEMF is generated. This CEMF opposes the voltage that is supplied to the armature and the armature current decreases. The strength of the magnetism produced by the armature coils decreases, and so does the torque. When the voltage applied to the armature is increased, both the torque and the armature speed increase. The direction of rotation of a permanent-magnet motor can be reversed by reversing the polarity of the direct current applied to the armature.

Shunt-Wound DC Motors

If an electric motor uses an electromagnet for its field, the field may be connected either in series or in parallel with the armature. If the field is in parallel with the armature, the motor is called a shunt-wound motor.

Shunt-wound motors produce a relatively small amount of torque when they first begin to rotate, but they have a fairly constant operating speed. Shunt-wound motors are used for blowers and fans and for other types of loads that do not need a high starting torque.

Most of the smaller shunt-wound DC motors use an armature similar to the one in Figure 4-157, Page 331, and this armature is mounted in bearings inside a steel frame that holds the field poles. Carbon brushes carry the current into the copper segments of the armature.

The speed of a shunt-wound motor can be controlled by varying the field current. A rheostat can be placed in the field circuit, as in Figure 4-160, and increasing the resistance in the field circuit decreases the CEMF, allowing more armature current to flow. The increase in the armature current increases the armature speed.

Better control of the speed and torque of a shunt-wound motor is obtained by using separate power supplies for the armature and the field. By holding the field current constant and varying the armature current, both the armature speed and torque increase with an increase in armature current.

The direction of rotation of a shunt-wound motor can be changed by reversing the direction of current flow through either the armature or the field, but not both. Reversing the polarity of the DC that supplies the motor will not reverse its direction of rotation, because this reverses the polarity of both the armature and the field. The relationship between the two magnetic fields that produce the torque remain the same.

Series-Wound DC Motors

When an application demands high starting torque and the motor will continually operate into a mechanical load, a series-wound motor is the logical choice.

The field coil of a series-wound motor is wound of heavy wire because all the current that flows through the armature must also flow through the field windings. *See* Figure 4-161.

When the switch is first closed on a series-wound motor, a large amount of current flows, and the motor produces a correspondingly large amount of

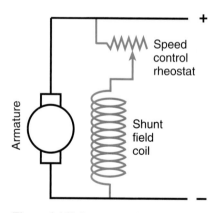

Figure 4-159. *Armature and coil arrangement of a shunt-field DC motor*

rheostat. A variable resistor with two connections.

Figure 4-160. *Increasing the resistance in the field circuit of a DC shunt-field motor increases the motor speed.*

torque. As soon as the armature begins to turn, a back voltage, or CEMF, is produced which decreases the series current and the torque. If the mechanical load slows the armature down, the CEMF will decrease and the current will increase, bringing the torque back up.

Series-wound motors must never be operated unless they are connected to a mechanical load. If a series-wound motor is operated without a load, the starting current will give it torque to start the armature turning. As soon as it starts to turn, the CEMF decreases the field current, and this in turn decreases the CEMF. As the CEMF decreases, more of the line voltage is applied across the motor and the speed increases. Since there is no load to slow the armature, it will increase its speed until it destroys itself.

A series-wound DC motor can have its direction of rotation changed by reversing the current flow through either the field or the armature, but not both. Most series-wound motors will operate on either AC or DC, because reversing the polarity of the power that supplies the motor does not change the relationship between the two magnetic fields that produce the torque in this type of motor.

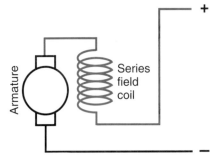

Figure 4-161. *Armature and field arrangement of a series-field DC motor*

Compound-Wound DC Motors

It is possible to get some of the good characteristics of both shunt-wound motors and series-wound motors by installing both a shunt and a series field (*see* Figure 4-162). By varying the relative effect of the two fields, the designer of a compound-wound motor can build one that has a good amount of starting torque and also a fairly good constant-speed operation with a changing load. Compound-wound motors are used when the amount of mechanical load changes. For example, they are used for raising and lowering the landing gear on some aircraft, and for operating electric generators and hydraulic pumps.

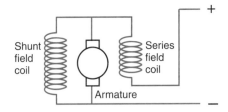

Figure 4-162. *A compound-wound DC motor has both a series and a shunt field.*

Answers begin on Page 359. Page numbers refer to chapter text.

234. The basic principle on which all electric motors operate is that a physical force is produced when two _____ react with each other. *Page 329*

235. The direction the current flows in the armature windings of a DC motor is reversed as the armature turns. This reversal is done by the brushes and the _____ . *Page 331*

236. The armature coils are wound in slots in a/an _____ (what material) core. This core concentrates the lines of magnetic flux that are produced by the field coils. *Page 331*

237. When the armature of a DC motor rotates, a voltage is produced in the armature windings. This voltage causes a current that is in the _____ (same or opposite) direction as the current used to run the motor. *Page 332*

238. When the switch used to control a DC motor is first closed, the current flow into the motor is _____ (higher or lower) than the normal running current. *Page 332*

239. Two kinds of magnetic fields that can be used for the stationary field of a DC motor are:
    a. _____
    b. _____
    Page 332

240. The torque that is produced by a permanent-magnet DC motor _____ (increases or decreases) as the speed of the motor increases. *Page 333*

241. DC motors that use an electromagnetic field may have the field connected to the armature in one of two different ways. These ways are:
    a. Connected in _____ with the armature
    b. Connected in _____ with the armature
    Page 334

242. A shunt-wound DC motor has _____ (high or low) starting torque. *Page 334*

243. Increasing the resistance in the field circuit of a shunt-wound DC motor will cause the armature speed to _____ (increase or decrease). *Page 334*

244. Both the speed and torque produced by a shunt-wound DC motor can be increased by holding the field current constant and increasing the amount of current flowing in the _____ . *Page 334*

245. Reversing the polarity of the DC power that is supplied to a shunt-wound DC motor _____ (will or will not) cause the direction of its armature to reverse. *Page 334*

246. A series-wound DC motor has a _____ (high or low) starting torque. *Page 334*

247. A series-wound DC motor _____ (is or is not) a constant-speed motor. *Page 335*

248. Reversing the polarity of the DC voltage supplied to a series-wound DC motor _____ (will or will not) reverse the direction the armature turns. *Page 335*

Alternating Current Motors

The continually changing magnetic field produced by alternating current makes it possible for AC motors to be made far simpler than DC motors. The vast majority of AC motors are of the induction type which require no electrical connections to the rotating element, or rotor. Only when speed control is needed do AC motors require commutators and brushes.

Universal Motors

Because the polarity of the current flowing into a series-wound DC motor does not affect the direction of rotation of the armature, a series-wound motor can operate on AC as well as DC. Series-wound motors that are specially designed to operate on AC are called universal motors. Most electric drill motors are universal motors, as are motors for many small appliances that require a significant amount of starting torque.

The operation of a universal motor is the same as that of a DC series-wound motor. The current flowing through the armature also flows through the field coils, and this produces the two magnetic fields needed to produce torque.

Universal motors always operate into some type of mechanical load. One of the disadvantages of this type of motor is that there is nearly always sparking at the brushes because of armature reaction.

Induction Motors
Single-Phase Induction Motors

The most widely used AC motor is the single-phase induction motor. These motors are used for fans, blowers, record players, tape players, and for such shop tools as drill presses and lathes. Just about any application that calls for a relatively constant speed, low to moderate starting torque, and low cost can be served with an induction motor. *See* Figure 4-163.

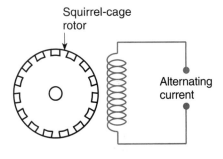

Figure 4-163. *Diagram of a single-phase AC induction motor*

An induction motor is often called a squirrel cage motor because of the construction of the rotor. The rotor is made up of a stack of circular soft-iron laminations with slots cut in them. Aluminum or copper end plates mount on each end of the stack, while aluminum or copper bars fit in the slots and weld to the two end plates. This entire assembly is mounted on a shaft which rides in bushings or ball bearings in the motor housing.

The field windings of an induction motor are usually of the distributed pole type in which they are wound in slots on the inside of the steel motor housing. These coils are connected directly to the alternating current supply and they provide a pulsing magnetic field across the rotor.

The pulsing magnetic field produced by the stator coils induces a voltage in the low-resistance bars in the rotor. This induced voltage causes a large amount of current to flow through these bars, and the current produces strong magnetic fields that react with the fields from the stator coils. As the polarity of the AC reverses, the polarity of the magnetic fields of both the rotor and the stator reverse, and the rotor, making a loud humming noise, remains stationary.

If you give the rotor of an induction motor a good spin by hand before the stator coils are connected to the AC power line, the rotor will continue to spin. It will accelerate until it reaches a constant speed and then will stabilize at this speed, which depends upon the frequency of the AC. The rotor of a single-phase induction motor operates equally well in either direction, depending upon the direction it was spun to start it. Spinning the rotor of an induction motor by hand is not an efficient way to start; there are better ways.

Split-Phase Induction Motors

One of the most popular ways of starting an induction motor is by the use of a separate start winding. The current flowing through the start winding is out of phase with the current flowing through the run winding because of the difference in the inductance of the two windings. The result is a split-phase induction motor, in Figure 4-164.

The run winding has a high inductance and a low resistance and the separate start winding has a low inductance and high resistance. When the motor is connected to the alternating current line, current flows through both the start winding and the run winding. The phase of the current flowing through the start winding is shifted slightly because of the low inductance and the high resistance of this winding, but the current flowing through the run winding lags behind its voltage because of its high inductance.

When current begins to flow through the two windings of the stator, two magnetic fields are set up, the magnetic strength of one field rises before the other, and as a result of these two out-of-phase fields, the rotor begins to turn. The two fields cause the rotor to speed up until it reaches a certain speed, at which time a centrifugal switch in the start winding circuit opens, and the motor continues to operate on just the run windings.

The direction of rotation of a split-phase, single-phase induction motor can be reversed by reversing the two connections on the start winding. *See Figure 4-164.*

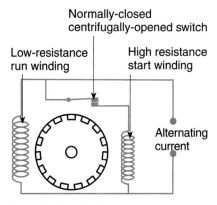

Figure 4-164. *Single-phase AC induction motor with a high resistance start winding*

Capacitor-Start Induction Motors

The split-phase induction motor does not have a large amount of starting torque, and when more torque is needed, a capacitor-start motor may be used. The phase of the current flowing through the start winding is shifted by a capacitor installed in series with the start winding.

When the motor is connected to the alternating current line, current flows through both the start winding and the run winding. Current flowing through the start winding charges and discharges the capacitor, and the current in this winding leads the voltage. The inductance of the run winding causes the current through it to lag behind the voltage.

When current begins to flow through the two windings of the stator, two magnetic fields are set up. The magnetic strength of one field rises before the other and, as a result of these two out-of-phase fields, the rotor begins to turn. The two fields cause the rotor to speed up until it reaches a certain speed, at which time a centrifugal switch in the start winding circuit opens and the motor continues to operate on just the run windings.

The direction of rotation of a capacitor-start single-phase induction motor can be reversed by reversing the two connections on the start winding.

Shaded-Pole Induction Motor

One very popular type of small alternating current motor is the shaded-pole induction motor. These motors are small, inexpensive to make, and require almost no service. Shaded-pole motors are used for record players, tape players, and for almost all small electric fans and blowers.

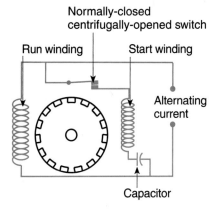

Figure 4-165. *Single-phase AC induction motor with a capacitor in its start winding circuit.*

The shaded-pole motor shown in Figure 4-166 on Page 340 is typical of the motors used in record players and small blowers. The frame is made of laminations of soft iron and the coil is made up of many turns of fine wire. The shorted turns are made of heavy-gage copper wire embedded in the frame in the upper right and lower left corners of the frame.

The rotor of this motor is a squirrel cage just like the one used in the larger induction motors. Copper bars embedded in slots in the laminated core are swaged to heavy copper end plates. The slots are skewed (cut at an angle) across the rotor to smooth the torque produced by this motor.

When the coil is connected across the alternating current line, the right half of the frame is magnetized with one polarity, and the left half of the frame is given the opposite polarity. If there were no shorted turns on the frame, the polarity of the frame would be that shown in view C (Figure 4-166, Page 340).

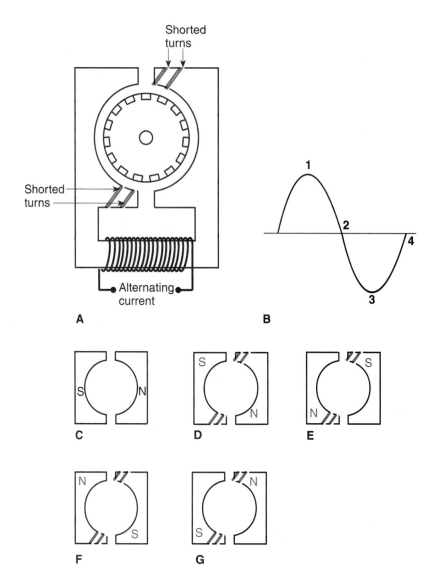

Figure 4-166

A. Single-phase, shaded-pole motor

B. Current through the coil of a shaded-pole motor

C. Polarity of motor frame with current at value 1 if there were no shading coils

D. Polarity of motor frame with current at value 1

E. Polarity of motor frame with current at value 2

F. Polarity of motor frame with current at valve 3

G. Polarity of motor frame with current at value 4

As the magnetic strength begins to build up in the frame with the current rising to the 90° point, a voltage is induced into the shorted turns and a large amount of current flows through the extremely low resistance of these heavy turns of wire. This current produces a magnetic field whose polarity is opposite to the magnetic field that produced it, and this induced magnetic field partially demagnetizes the part of the frame around which the shorted turn is wound. The effect of the magnetic field caused by the shorted turn moves the magnetic poles of the frame to the locations shown in D.

As the current in the coil drops off to zero at the 180° point, the magnetizing force from the coil drops off and the field that is produced by the shorted turns keeps the polarity of the frame as seen in E (Figure 4-166).

In F, the current in the coil is flowing at the full rate as shown at the 270° position, and the magnetic strength of the frame is concentrated at the corners away from the shorted turns.

In G, (Figure 4-166), the magnetic field caused by the shorted turns has sustained the magnetism in the frame as the current in the coil dropped back to zero.

The torque produced by a shaded-pole motor is low, but like all induction motors, a shaded-pole motor operates at a relatively constant speed determined by the design of the motor and the frequency of the AC used to power it.

Repulsion Motors

When high torque, reversibility, and speed control are needed, repulsion motors are often used.

A repulsion motor has a stationary field similar to that used in an induction motor, but its armature, or rotor, is wound in a manner similar to that used in a series motor. The two ends of each coil terminate at commutator segments across the armature from each other. *See* Figure 4-167.

Two brushes ride on the commutator, and these brushes are electrically connected together so they short out the ends of a coil, allowing current to flow through the coil to produce a magnetic field.

The changing magnetic field produced by the stator windings induces a voltage in the coil of the rotor whose ends are shorted by the brushes. This induced voltage causes current to flow in the coil and produce a magnetic field that reacts with the field in the stator.

When the brushes are placed at right angles to the stator field, no torque is produced, but by moving the brushes relative to the stator field, the armature can be caused to rotate in either direction, with its speed varying according to the position of the brushes.

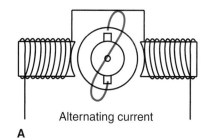

Figure 4-167

A. *Repulsion motor with brushes in the neutral position. The rotor will not turn with the brushes in this position.*

B. *When the brushes are moved around the commutator, a magnetic field is set up in the armature that is repelled by the pulsating stationary field. This causes the armature to spin.*

Three-Phase Induction Motors

Three-phase alternating current produces a rotating field in the stator of an induction motor. There is no need for extra starting windings or centrifugal switches.

Figure 4-168 shows the way a three-phase, delta-connected, and a three-phase, Y-connected induction motor are connected.

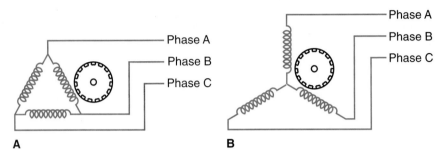

Figure 4-168.

A. Three-phase, delta-connected AC motor   B. Three-phase, Y-connected AC motor

---

STUDY QUESTIONS: AC MOTORS

Answers begin on Page 359. Page numbers refer to chapter text.

249. A series-wound electric motor that can operate on AC or on DC is called a/an
_____ motor. *Page 337*

250. A single-phase induction motor _____ (is or is not) a constant-speed motor.
Page 337

251. Two ways of getting a phase shift between the current flowing in the start winding and the run winding of a single-phase induction motor are:
a. _____
b. _____
Page 338

252. The rotating field in a single-phase, shaded-pole induction motor is produced by current induced into the
_____ on the frame of the motor. *Page 339*

253. The starting torque produced by a shaded-pole induction motor is _____
(high or low). *Page 341*

254. A repulsion-type AC motor has brushes that ride on the commutator mounted on the armature. These brushes _____ (are or are not) connected to the source of AC power. *Page 341*

255. The direction and speed of the armature of a repulsion-type AC motor is controlled by physically moving the _____ . *Page 341*

Electrical Generators

Earlier in this chapter we saw that it is possible to produce electrical energy in five ways; by chemical action, by heat, by light, by pressure, and by magnetism. By far the greatest amount of electricity used today is produced by using the relationship between electricity and magnetism.

In the study of electric motors, we saw that any time a conductor carries a flow of electrons, two things happen: heat is produced in the conductor, and a magnetic field surrounds the conductor. In an electric motor, the magnetic field surrounding the conductor reacts with another magnetic field and causes the conductor to move.

The action of an electric current causing a physical movement of the conductor is reversible. Any time a conductor is moved in a magnetic field, electrical current is forced to flow in the conductor.

Figure 4-169 shows the way this works. In A, we have a magnetic field in which the lines of flux travel in straight lines between the north and south poles. If we move a conductor across these lines of flux, some of the lines wrap around the conductor and cause electrons to flow in it.

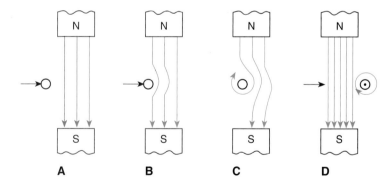

Figure 4-169

A. *Magnetic flux of the generator field.*

B. *Conductor moving into the magnetic field.*

C. *As lines of flux are cut, they encircle the conductor and induce a current in it.*

D. *The current is maximum when the greatest number of lines of flux are being cut.*

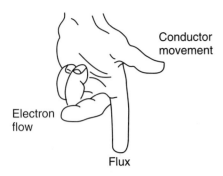

Figure 4-170. *If we hold our left hand so the forefinger points in the direction of the magnetic flux, with the thumb in the direction of conductor movement, the second finger will point in the direction of electron flow.*

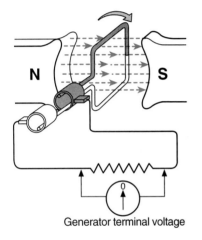

Figure 4-171. *Principle of a practical AC generator*

By using the left-hand rule for generators, we see that the electrons flow in the conductor in such a direction that they are moving off the page. We find this by holding our left hand as in Figure 4-170. Our forefinger points in the direction of the flux (from the north pole of the magnet to the south pole), our thumb points in the direction the conductor moved through the magnetic field, and our second finger points in the direction the electrons flow in the conductor.

The amount of electron flow produced in the conductor is determined by the rate at which the lines of flux are cut. This rate is determined by the number of lines of flux produced by the magnet, and by the speed at which the conductor is moved through the flux.

Figure 4-171 shows a more practical AC generator. The conductor is made in the form of a loop that can rotate inside of the magnetic field. The two ends of the loop are fastened to conductive rings, called slip rings, and carbon brushes ride on these rings. The electrical load is connected between the two brushes.

If we measure the voltage across the electrical load caused by the current flowing through it, we see that, as we rotate the conductor, the voltage rises from zero to a peak and then drops back to zero. It reverses its polarity and rises to a peak again, and then returns to zero.

In Figure 4-172, we see that as the conductors rotate, they produce a voltage whose value is the sine of the angle through which the conductor has moved from its zero position.

When the conductor has rotated 45° from its zero position, the voltage that is generated in the conductor is 0.707 time its peak value (0.707 is the sine of 45°). By the time the conductor has rotated 90°, it is cutting the maximum number of lines of flux for each degree of rotation and the voltage will be at its peak value. As the conductor continues to turn, the voltage drops to zero and the electrons begin to flow in the conductor in the opposite direction. When the conductor has rotated 270°, the voltage will again be peak, but this time the electrons will be traveling in the opposite direction, and the polarity of the voltage will be opposite to that which was produced at the 90° position.

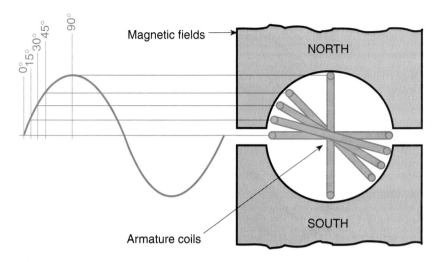

Figure 4-172. *The voltage produced by an AC generator varies with the number of degrees the armature coils have rotated from zero.*

Direct Current Generators

Figure 4-173 shows the way the alternating-current generator just studied can be changed into a direct-current generator.

Rather than connecting the ends of the conductor to two slip rings, the ends are connected to a single split ring called a commutator. In Figure 4-173, the left-hand brush is connected to the light-colored half of the coil, and the right-hand brush is connected to the dark-colored half. When the conductor is rotated in the direction shown by the arrow, electrons are forced from the conductor through the left-hand brush, out of the generator, and through the electrical load in the direction shown by the arrow, then back into the coil through the right-hand brush.

As the conductor continues to rotate, the half of the commutator connected to the light-colored half of the coil moves out from under the left-hand brush and makes contact with the right-hand brush. The dark-colored half of the coil moves upward in front of the north pole of the magnet, and electrons flow out of it through the left-hand brush and through the load in the same direction as before.

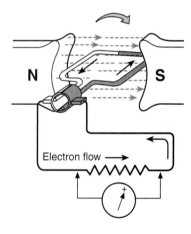

Figure 4-173. *Principle of operation of a direct-current generator*

Figure 4-174
Voltage output of a DC generator

The voltage produced by this generator is the same as that produced by the AC generator, but the commutator, as the split ring is called, has reversed the flow of electrons through the load during one half of the cycle, and the output is in the form of a pulsating direct current. The electrons travel through the load in the same direction all of the time, but the amount of flow is determined by the voltage produced by the generator, and this voltage varies, as shown in Figure 4-174.

STUDY QUESTIONS: GENERATORS

Answers begin on Page 359. **Page numbers refer to chapter text.**

256. The amount of current produced in the armature of a generator is determined by the
_____ at which the lines of magnetic flux are cut. *Page 344*

257. The _____ (what component) on the armature of a DC generator acts as a mechanical rectifier that changes the AC produced in the armature into DC before it leaves the generator. *Page 346*

Aircraft Electrical Circuits

Schematic diagrams used in aircraft maintenance manuals allow us to follow the flow of electricity through the circuit. The symbols show the placement of the components in the system, not as they are installed in the aircraft. *See* Figure 4-175 below and on Page 348.

To use a schematic diagram:

1. Start with the battery or the bus, and follow each wire completely through the system to the ground symbol; this is usually the zero-voltage position. No circuit is complete unless you can trace it all the way to ground.

2. When the circuit goes to the coil of a relay or solenoid, the contacts change position from that shown in the diagram. Make those changes, and follow the circuits that now go through the contacts.

3. When a circuit branches, follow one route all the way to ground, and then go back and follow the other route all the way to ground.

schematic diagram. A diagram of an electrical circuit in which the components are represented by symbols rather than drawings or pictures of the actual devices.

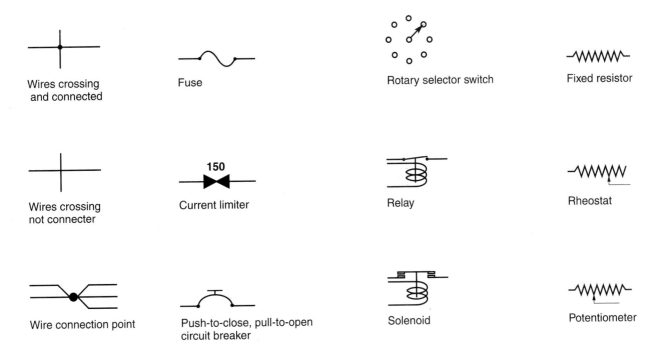

Wires crossing and connected

Fuse

Rotary selector switch

Fixed resistor

Wires crossing not connecter

Current limiter

Relay

Rheostat

Wire connection point

Push-to-close, pull-to-open circuit breaker

Solenoid

Potentiometer

Figure 4-175. *Commonly used symbols for aircraft electrical system schematic diagrams*

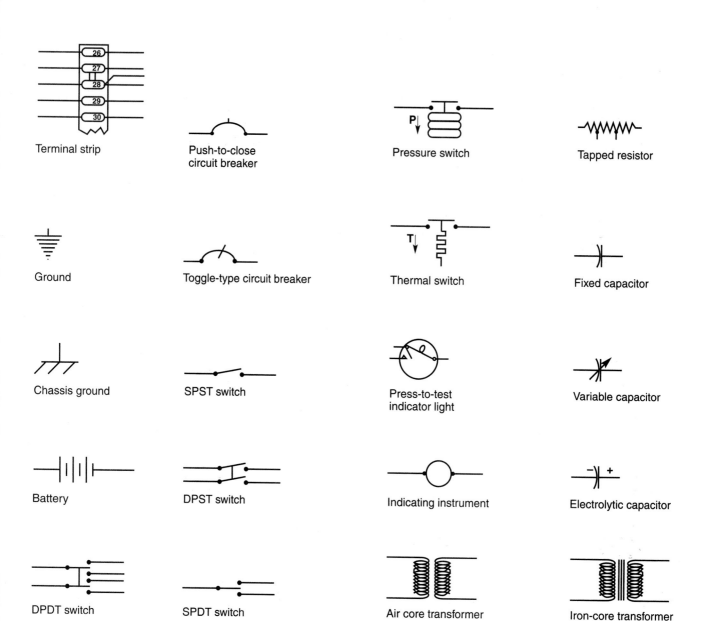

Terminal strip

Push-to-close circuit breaker

Pressure switch

Tapped resistor

Ground

Toggle-type circuit breaker

Thermal switch

Fixed capacitor

Chassis ground

SPST switch

Press-to-test indicator light

Variable capacitor

Battery

DPST switch

Indicating instrument

Electrolytic capacitor

DPDT switch

SPDT switch

Air core transformer

Iron-core transformer

Figure 4-175. *Continued*

Electrically Retractable Landing Gear

Figure 4-176 is a typical schematic diagram of an electrically retractable landing gear with its indicating system. This diagram shows the condition of the system when the landing gear is down and locked and the airplane is on the ground.

Trace the circuit through the 5-amp circuit breaker, wire #6, the nose-gear-down switch, wire #5, left-gear-down switch, wire #4, right-gear-down switch, wire #3, through the green indicator light, to ground.

In this condition, with the gear down, the landing gear motor cannot be actuated because the down-limit switch is open. This prevents current flowing through it to rotate the motor in the gear-down direction. The gear-up relay is also open which prevents current reaching the motor to rotate it in the gear-up direction.

The bulbs of both the red and green lights can be checked by pressing on their lenses. When the lens is pressed, a switch inside the light fixture closes, and current flows through the 5-amp circuit breaker, wire #7, wire #17 or #18, to ground through the bulbs.

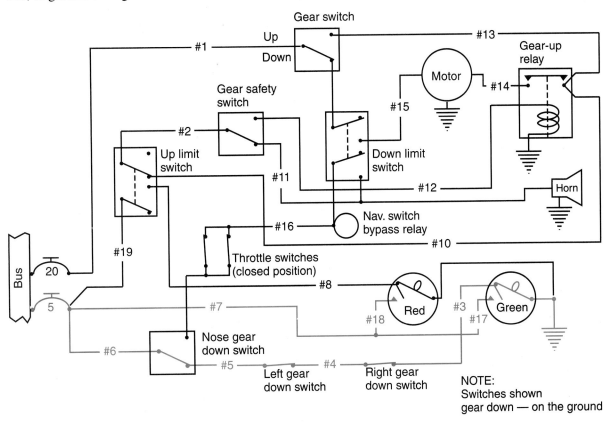

Figure 4-176. *Landing gear circuit with the airplane on the ground and the switches in the Gear Down position*

When the airplane is in the air with the weight off the landing gear, the gear switch can be moved to the Gear-Up position, and current can reach the motor to retract the gear. *See* Figure 4-177.

With the weight off the landing gear, the gear safety switch (squat switch) changes position, and when the gear switch is placed in the Gear-Up position, current can flow through the 20-amp circuit breaker, wire #1, the gear switch, wire #13, wire #10, the up-limit switch, the gear safety switch, and wire #12 to ground through the coil of the relay. With this coil energized, the relay closes, and current can flow through the relay contacts and wire #14 to ground through the motor, driving the landing gear to its down-and-locked position.

As soon as the landing leaves its locked-down condition, the nose-gear-, left-gear-, and right-gear-down switches change their position, the green light goes out, and the down-limit switch changes its position.

When the gear is down and locked, the up-limit switch changes its position, as we see in Figure 4-178.

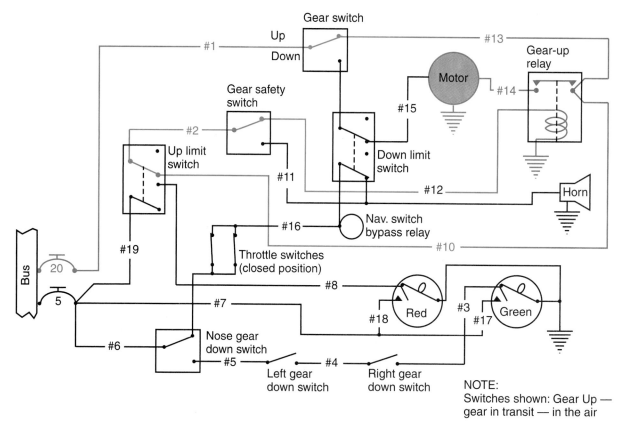

Figure 4-177. *Landing gear circuit with the airplane in the air, the switches in the Gear Up position, and the gear in transit*

Current flows through the 5-amp circuit breaker, wire #19, the up-limit switch, wire #8, to ground through the red light, showing that the gear is up and locked.

If either throttle is retarded while the landing gear is in any condition other than down and locked, current will flow through the 5-amp circuit breaker, wire #6, the nose-gear-down switch, the throttle switch, wire #16, the down-limit switch and wire #11 to ground through the horn, indicating an unsafe condition.

Other landing gear actuation circuits may be used. In Figure 4-179 on Page 352, we have one that requires the landing gear control valve to be placed in the Neutral position when the airplane is on the ground, to prevent the warning horn from sounding when either throttle is closed.

When the landing gear control valve switch is in the Neutral position and the landing gears are both down and locked, the green light will illuminate because it is grounded through both the right gear and left gear switches.

If the landing gears are both up and either throttle is retarded for landing, the warning horn will sound.

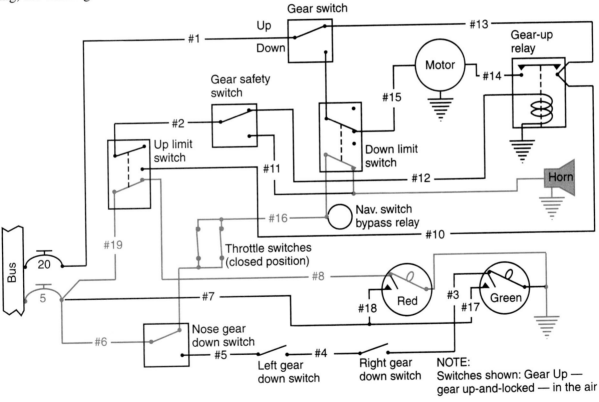

Figure 4-178. *Landing gear circuit with the airplane in the air, the switches in the Gear Up position, and the gear up and locked*

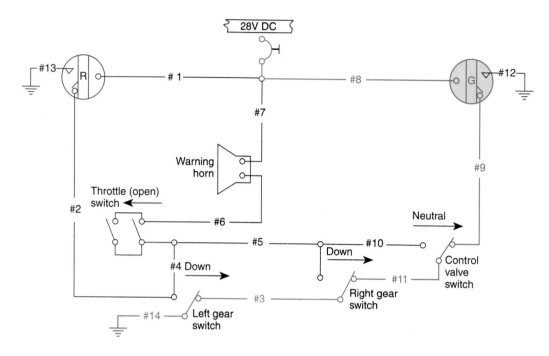

Figure 4-179. *Landing gear actuating circuit*

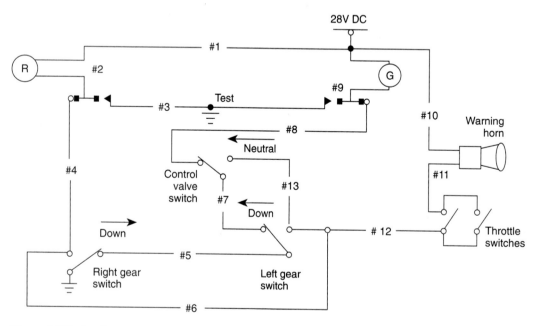

Figure 4-180. *Landing gear actuating circuit*

Still another type of landing gear actuating circuit is shown in Figure 4-180. This circuit shows a different symbol for the light test switches.

The red light is illuminated if either of the landing gears is not down and locked, and the green light illuminates when both gears are down and locked. The warning horn will sound if either throttle switch is closed and either of the landing gears is not down and locked. It will also sound when both gears are down and locked if the control valve switch is not in the Neutral position.

Electrically Operated Fuel Valves

Figures 4-181 through 4-184 depict an electrically operated fuel system. The fuel selector switch has these positions: Normal, Right-Hand Tank, Left-Hand Tank, and Crossfeed.

NORM — Follow Figure 4-181 to see what happens when the selector valve is in the NORM position.

Current flows from the bus through the left-hand 5-amp circuit breaker, through contacts 5, 7, 9, and 11, into the coil of relay PCC. This energizes the relay and opens contact 15.

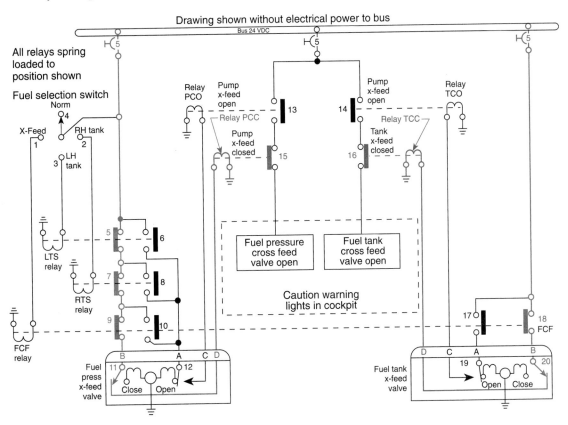

Figure 4-181. *Current flow when the fuel selector switch is in the NORM position*

Current flows through the right-hand 5-amp circuit breaker, through contacts 18 and 20, into the coil of relay TCC. This energizes the relay and opens contacts 16.

R H TANK — Follow Figure 4-182 to see what happens when the selector valve is in the R H TANK position.

Current flows from the bus, through the fuel selector switch RH TANK position, into the coil of the RTS relay. This relay energizes and changes the position of contacts 7 and 8.

Current flows from the bus, through the left-hand 5-amp circuit breaker, through contacts 5, 8, and 12, into the OPEN windings of the FUEL PRESSURE X-FEED VALVE. This valve opens, and contacts 11 and 12 change their position.

Current now flows through contacts 12 into the coil of relay PCO. This relay energizes and closes contacts 13. Current now flows from the bus, through the center 5-amp circuit breaker, through contacts 13 and 15, and illuminates the FUEL PRESSURE CROSSFEED VALVE OPEN light.

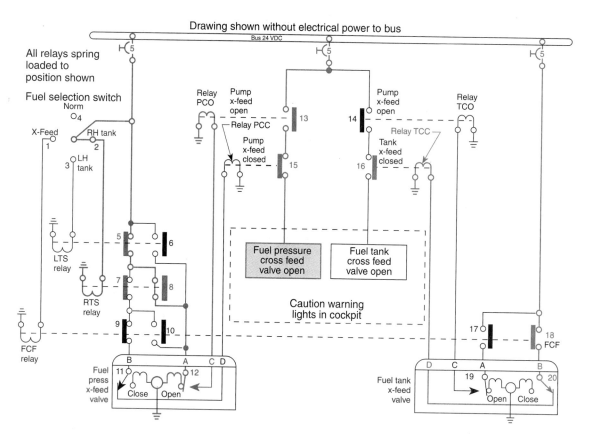

Figure 4-182. *Current flow when the fuel selector switch is in the R H TANK position*

All this time, current is flowing from the bus through the right-hand 5-amp circuit breaker, through contacts 18 and 20, into the coil of relay TCC, energizing this relay and holding contacts 16 open.

L H TANK — Follow Figure 4-183 to see what happens when the selector valve is in the R H TANK position.

Current flows from the bus through the left-hand 5-amp circuit breaker, through the fuel selector switch LH TANK position into the coil of the LTS relay. This relay energizes and changes the position of contacts 5 and 6.

Current flows from the bus, through the left-hand 5-amp circuit breaker, through contacts 6 and 12, into the OPEN windings of the FUEL PRESSURE X-FEED VALVE. This valve opens and contacts 11 and 12 change their position.

Current now flows through contacts 12 into the coil of relay PCO. This relay energizes and closes contacts 13. Current now flows from the bus, through the center 5-amp circuit breaker, through contacts 13 and 15, and illuminates the FUEL PRESSURE CROSSFEED VALVE OPEN light.

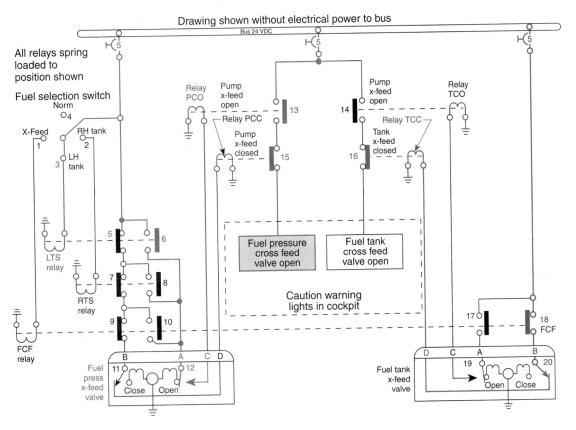

Figure 4-183. *Current flow when the fuel selector switch is in the L H TANK position*

All this time, current is flowing from the bus through the right-hand 5-amp circuit breaker, through contacts 18 and 20, into the coil of relay TCC, energizing this relay and holding contacts 16 open.

X-FEED — Follow Figure 4-184 to see what happens when the selector valve is in the X-FEED position.

Current flows from the bus through the left-hand 5-amp circuit breaker into the coil of FCF relay. This relay is energized and changes the position of contacts 9, 10, 17, and 18.

Current flows from the bus through the left-hand 5-amp circuit breaker, through contacts 5, 7, 10 and 12, into the OPEN windings of the FUEL PRESSURE X-FEED VALVE. This valve opens, and contacts 11 and 12 change their position.

Current now flows through contacts 12 into the coil of relay PCO. This relay energizes and closes contacts 13. Current now flows from the bus through the center 5-amp circuit breaker, through contacts 13 and 15, and illuminates the FUEL PRESSURE CROSSFEED VALVE OPEN light.

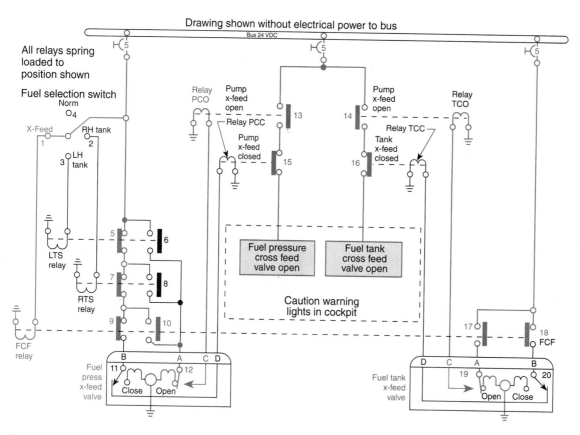

Figure 4-184. *Current flow when the fuel selector switch is in the X-FEED position*

Current is flowing from the bus, through the right-hand 5-amp circuit breaker, through contacts 17 and 19, into the OPEN winding of the FUEL TANK X-FEED VALVE. This drives the valve open and contacts 19 and 20 change positions. Current flows through contacts 19 into the coil of relay TCO, energizing this relay and closing contacts 14.

Current now flows from the bus, through the center 5-amp circuit breaker, through contacts 14 and 16, and illuminates the FUEL TANK CROSSFEED VALVE OPEN light.

STUDY QUESTIONS: AIRCRAFT ELECTRICAL SYSTEMS

Answers begin on Page 359. Page numbers refer to chapter text.

258. The zero voltage point in an electrical system is identified by a triangular-shaped series of parallel lines. This symbol is commonly called a _____ . *Page 348*

259. Refer to Figure 4-178. With the landing gear retracted, the red indicator light will not come on if there is an open in wire number _____ or _____ . *Page 351*

260. Refer to Figure 4-176. Neither the red nor the green light will test good when it is pressed in if there is an open in wire number _____ . *Page 349*

261. Refer to Figure 4-176. When the landing gear is down, the green light will not come on if there is an open in wire number _____ , _____ , _____ , or _____ . *Page 349*

262. Refer to Figure 4-179. When the landing gears are up and either throttle is retarded, the warning horn will not sound if there is an open in wire number _____ or _____ . *Page 352*

263. Refer to Figure 4-179. The landing gear warning horn will sound if either throttle is retarded when the landing gears are both down unless the control valve switch is placed in the _____ position. *Page 352*

264. Refer to Figure 4-180. When either throttle is retarded with only the right gear down, the warning horn will not sound if there is an open in wire number _____ . *Page 352*

265. Refer to Figure 4-183. When the Fuel Selector switch is in the Left-Hand Tank position, the Fuel Pressure Crossfeed Valve Open light will not illuminate if relay _____ fails to operate. *Page 355*

Continued

266. Refer to Figure 4-184. The TCO relay will operate if 24 volts DC is applied to the bus, and the fuel tank selector is in the _____ position. *Page 356*

267. Refer to Figure 4-182. When power is applied to the bus, and the fuel selector switch is in the Right-Hand Tank position, _____ (how many) relays are operating. *Page 354*

268. Refer to Figure 4-181. When the Fuel Selector switch is in the Norm position and power is applied to the bus, two relays are energized; these are _____ and _____ . *Page 353*

269. Refer to Figure 4-183. When the Fuel Selector switch is in the Left-Hand Tank position and power is applied to the bus, seven switches or sets of contacts will change position. These are

_____ , _____ ,

_____ , _____ ,

_____ , _____ , and

_____ .

Page 355

Answers to Chapter 4 Study Questions

1. protons, neutrons
2. electrons
3. electron current
4. light
5. conductor
6. insulator
7. static
8. current
9. negative, positive
10. volt
11. amp
12. ohm
13. volt, amp, ohm
14. a. heat
    b. chemical action
    c. pressure
    d. light
    e. magnetism
15. DC
16. AC
17. AC
18. a. 96
    b. 120
    c. 144
    d. 99.5
19. 25.2
20. volts
21. 0.035, 35
22. a. volt
    b. watt
    c. amp
23. 26.1
24. a. resistance of conductor
    b. amount of current
25. a. kilo
    b. mega
    c. centi
    d. milli
    e. micro

26. sum
27. negative
28. positive
29. dividing
30. multiplying
31. 4
32.

Volts	Ohms	Amps	Watts
$E_1 = 10$	$R_1 = 10$	$I_1 = 1.0$	$P_1 = 10$
$E_2 = 10$	$R_2 = 20$	$I_2 = 0.5$	$P_2 = 5$
$E_3 = 10$	$R_3 = 20$	$I_3 = 0.5$	$P_3 = 5$
$E_4 = 10$	$R_4 = 10$	$I_4 = 1.0$	$P_4 = 10$
$E_T = 30$	$R_T = 30$	$I_T = 1.0$	$P_T = 30$

33. positive
34. half
35. a. 40
    b. 30
    c. 45
36. a. 10
    b. 6.67
    c. 4.6

37.

Volts	Ohms	Amps	Watts
$E_1 = 12$	$R_1 = 6$	$I_1 = 2.0$	$P_1 = 24$
$E_2 = 48$	$R_2 = 100$	$I_2 = 0.48$	$P_2 = 23$
$E_3 = 48$	$R_3 = 150$	$I_3 = 0.32$	$P_3 = 15.4$
$E_4 = 24$	$R_4 = 20$	$I_4 = 1.2$	$P_4 = 28.8$
$E_5 = 24$	$R_5 = 40$	$I_5 = 0.6$	$P_5 = 14.4$
$E_6 = 15$	$R_6 = 25$	$I_6 = 0.6$	$P_6 = 9.0$
$E_7 = 9$	$R_7 = 15$	$I_7 = 0.6$	$P_7 = 5.4$
$E_T = 60$	$R_T = 30$	$I_T = 2.0$	$P_T = 120$

Continued

38.

Volts	Ohms	Amps	Watts
$E_1 = 12$	$R_1 = 20$	$I_1 = 0.6$	$P_1 = 7.2$
$E_2 = 12$	$R_2 = 30$	$I_2 = 0.4$	$P_2 = 4.8$
$E_3 = 12$	$R_3 = 30$	$I_3 = 0.4$	$P_3 = 4.8$
$E_4 = 6$	$R_4 = 10$	$I_4 = 0.6$	$P_4 = 3.6$
$E_5 = 6$	$R_5 = 30$	$I_5 = 0.2$	$P_5 = 1.2$
$E_6 = 6$	$R_6 = 30$	$I_6 = 0.2$	$P_6 = 1.2$
$E_7 = 6$	$R_7 = 30$	$I_7 = 0.2$	$P_7 = 1.2$
$E_8 = 6$	$R_8 = 6$	$I_8 = 1.0$	$P_8 = 6.0$
$E_T = 30$	$R_T = 30$	$I_T = 1.0$	$P_T = 30.0$

39.

	Voltage volts	Current amps	Resistance ohms
R_1	1.39	0.092	15
R_2	7.39	0.369	20
R_3	4.61	0.461	10
E_1	6		
E_2	12		

40.

$R_X =$	55 ohms
$R_Y =$	40 ohms
$R_Z =$	30 ohms
$R_D =$	34 ohms
$R_E =$	42 ohms
$E =$	90 volts
$R_A =$	9.6 ohms
$R_B =$	17.6 ohms
$R_C =$	13.2 ohms
$R_T =$	35.94 ohms
$I_T =$	2.5 amp
$E_X =$	1.4 volt
$I_X =$	0.0254 amp

41. AC
42. rate
43. cycle
44. AC
45. voltage
46. alternation
47. hypotenuse
48. 0, 1
49. a. 169.7
    b. 339.4
    c. 107.9
50. 17.7
51. rms
52. 100
53. is
54. lead
55. lag
56. power factor
57. 100
58. 53.06
59. 530.66
60. 26.53
61. 90.97
62. 5306.6
63. 0.088
64. 0.6
65. 106.25

66. 300
67. a. 53.07
    b. 113.2
    c. 27.95
    d. leads
    e. 0.353
    f. 35.3
    g. 18.7
    h. 88.3
    i. 12.47
68. a. 0.40
    b. 0.75
    c. 0.85
    d. 47.05
69. 565.2
70. 628
71. a. 1,256
    b. 1,605.5
    c. 0.129
    d. 129
    e. 162
    f. 51.4
    g. lagging
    h. 62
    i. 26.8
    j. 16.6
72. a. 1,256
    b. 0.208
    c. 0.166
    d. 0.266
    e. 781.9
73. a. 502.4
    b. 199
    c. 303.4
    d. 426.7
    e. 0.487
    f. 146.1
    g. 244.7
    h. 96.9
    i. 45.3
    j. lagging
    k. 70
    l. 101.3
    m. 70.9

74. a. 502.4
    b. 199
    c. 0.69
    d. 0.41
    e. 1.04
    f. 0.63
    g. 0.93
    h. 223.6
    i. 42.4
    j. leading
    k. 143.5
    l. 85.2
    m. 216.3
    n. 131.1
    o. 194.4

75. decreases

76. increases

77. 712

78. 6.3

79. 0.002

80. maximum

81. decrease

82. decrease

83. maximum

84. minimum

85. tank

86. decreases

87. a. band pass
    b. low pass
    c. high pass
    d. band reject

88. 120

89. 208

90. parallel

91. series

92. shunt

93. ohmmeter

94. a. current-carrying ability
    b. voltage drop

95. a. copper
    b. silver

96. a. length
    b. cross-sectional area
    c. temperature
    d. material

97. low

98. 1,600

99. circular mil

100. 10

101. stranded

102.

	Nominal Resistance Ohms	Tolerance ±%	1st Band	2nd Band	3rd Band	4th Band
a.	1,000,000	10	Brown	Black	Green	Silver
b.	2,200	20	Red	Red	Red	
c.	470,000,000	10	Violet	Yellow	Violet	Silver
d.	3.3	10	Orange	Orange	Gold	Silver
e.	91	5	White	Brown	Black	Gold

103.

	Nominal Resistance Ohms	Tolerance ±%	1st Band	2nd Band	3rd Band	4th Band
a.	1,500	20	Brown	Green	Red	
b.	6.8	5	Blue	Gray	Gold	Gold
c.	3,300,000	10	Orange	Orange	Green	Silver
d.	390	10	Orange	White	Brown	Silver
e.		20	Red	Red	Red	

104. size

105. potentiometer

106. rheostat

107. a. fixed resistor
    b. tapped resistor
    c. variable resistor
    d. rheostat
    e. potentiometer

108. double, double

109. rotary wafer

110. movable

111. slow-blow

112. amps

113. trip-free

114. is not

115. a. area of the plates
    b. thickness of the dielectric
    c. dielectric constant

116. farad

117. microfarad

118. picofarad

119. working

120. 50

Continued

121. a. type of dielectric
     b. thickness of the dielectric
122. a. variable capacitor
     b. fixed nonelectrolytic
        capacitor
     c. fixed electrolytic capacitor
123. coulomb
124. 1,000,000,
        1,000,000,000,000
125. 1,000,000
126. 1,124
127. decrease
128. should not
129. voltage rating
130. AC
131. a. 1.5
     b. 1,750
     c. 0.4
     d. 0.033
     e. 50
     f. 2,100
132. 1.275
133. 1.5
134. opposite
135. henry, 1 amp
136. a. number of turns
     b. form factor
     c. permeability of core
137. 1
138. minimum
139. 30
140. 55
141. 12.7
142. 0.02
143. iron
144. high
145. isolation
146. does not
147. air
148. 2,340

149. 0.05
150. 25
151. false
152. eddy
153. rectifier
154. check valve
155. pulsating
156. does not
157. 0.7
158. zener diode
159. reverse
160. silicon control rectifier
161. is not
162. triac
163. does not
164. does not
165. does not
166. emitter
167. forward
168. light
169. is
170. is not
171. open
172. AND
173. OR
174. EXCLUSIVE OR
175. oxidized
176. ammonium chloride, zinc
     chloride
177. 1.5
178. does not
179. powdered zinc
180. manganese dioxide
181. potassium hydroxide
182. mercuric oxide
183. powdered zinc
184. 1.4
185. blue

186. yellow
187. 1.55
188. green
189. clear
190. lithium
191. a. long shelf life
     b. high open-circuit voltage
192. a. lead-acid
     b. nickel-cadmium
193. spongy lead
194. lead dioxide
195. sulfuric
196. is
197. 2.0
198. nickel hydroxide
199. cadmium hydroxide
200. potassium hydroxide
201. 1.25
202. a. thermal runaway
     b. cell memory
203. a. voltage
     b. ampere-hour capacity
204. 0.52
205. baking soda
206. 80
207. added
208. lower
209. discharged
210. current
211. shorted
212. voltage
213. potassium hydroxide
214. burn marks
215. overcharging
216. discharged
217. a. method of charging
     b. cell temperature
218. drop
219. does not

220. end
221. a. heat is produced
     b. a magnetic field surrounds
        the conductor
222. north, north
223. north, south
224. a. unlike
     b. like
225. square
226. permeability
227. higher
228. left
229. pull them together
230. a. increase the number of
        turns of wire
     b. increase the current
     c. put high-permeability core
        in coil
231. a. number of lines of
        magnetic flux
     b. speed of movement of the
        conductor
232. a. move conductor
     b. move magnetic field
     c. use varying current to
        produce field

233. ampere turns, gilberts
234. magnetic fields
235. commutator
236. iron
237. opposite
238. higher
239. a. permanent magnet
     b. electromagnet
240. decreases
241. a. series
     b. parallel
242. low
243 increase
244. armature
245. will not
246. high
247. is not
248. will not
249. universal
250. is
251. a. high-resistance start
        winding
     b. capacitor in the start
        winding

252. shading coils
253. low
254. are not
255. brushes
256. rate
257. commutator
258. ground
259. 8, 19
260. 7
261. 3, 4, 5, 6
262. 4,14
263. neutral
264. 5
265. PCO
266. X-FEED
267. 3
268. PCC, TCC
269. 5, 6, 11, 12, 13, 15, 16

AIRCRAFT DRAWINGS

5

Continued

AIRCRAFT DRAWINGS

5

Before the first piece of metal is cut for the production of any airplane, thousands of drawings of all types are made. In the past all of these drawings were made on paper or Mylar film in pencil and reproduced as a paper print. These were blueprints with white lines on a dark blue background. Later these prints were made by a process that produced blue or brown lines on a white background.

The latest trend in aircraft drawings is the use of computers rather than drawing boards. A part is drawn in the computer using a graphics program. It is then entered into a data bank where it can be pulled up and used in various sections of the factory for design, manufacturing, and inspection. By using a single basic drawing that can be immediately updated, all company personnel have access to the same drawing, and the danger of using outdated information is therefore minimized. The vast amount of time saved by using computer-aided design has caused almost all aircraft manufacturers to replace the conventional drafting tables with computer work stations.

Mylar. A polyester film widely used as and electrical insulator and package material. Mylar film is used for making high quality ink drawings

Types of Aircraft Drawings

It has been facetiously said that an airplane design is complete when the weight of the drawings equals the weight of the airplane. There are drawings for every purpose; some describe the construction of a single part, others show how parts are assembled, and some show the way the part is installed in the aircraft. Some drawings are used for troubleshooting, and others are referred to when overhauling a component. In this section we will study the various types of drawings to understand their characteristics and uses and see examples of each type. The most important working drawings are: detail drawings, assembly drawings, and installation drawings.

Detail Drawing

A detail drawing is one that includes all of the information needed to fabricate the part. Figure 5-1 is a detail drawing of a simple bearing installation tool. All of the information needed to make this tool is on the drawing, including the type of material to be used, the dimensions of the tool, and, where necessary, the allowable tolerance.

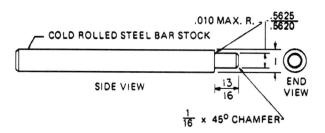

Figure 5-1. *A detail drawing includes enough information to fabricate the part.*

Assembly Drawing

An assembly drawing is handy for a technician servicing an aircraft or aircraft component. Figure 5-2A shows an assembly drawing of an aircraft alternator, and Figure 5-2B gives the part number of each component.

By studying an assembly drawing and keeping it handy as the part is repaired, you can be sure that all parts are installed in their proper place. Using the appropriate parts list will assure that only the correct parts are used.

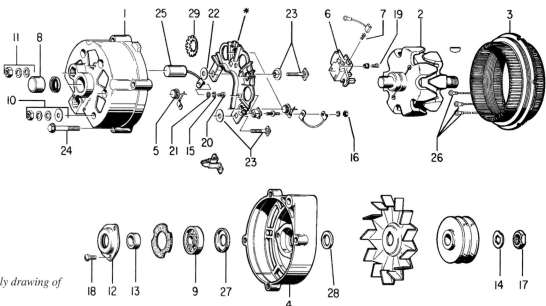

Figure 5-2A. *Assembly drawing of an aircraft alternator*

REF. NO.	PART NUMBER	DESCRIPTION 1 2 3 4 5	QTY. PER ENG.	MODEL USAGE
		ALTERNATOR ASSEMBLY		
	1100717	ALTERNATOR ASSEMBLY, 12V.-70Amp.	1	A
	1100718	ALTERNATOR ASSEMBLY, 24V.-50Amp.	1	B
1	1964858	FRAME, Slip ring end		A, B
2	1964512	ROTOR ASSEMBLY		A
	1964221	ROTOR ASSEMBLY		B
3	1961531	STATOR ASSEMBLY		A
	1959531	STATOR ASSEMBLY		B
4	1959917	FRAME, Diode end		A, B
5	1964354	DIODE		A, B
	1964353	DIODE		A, B
6	1965276	BRUSH HOLDER AND BRUSH ASSEMBLY		A, B
7	1964117	BRUSH, Spring		A, B
8	7451326	BEARING, Slip ring end		A, B
9	905920	BEARING, Diode end		A, B
10	1959832	TERMINAL PACKAGE (Battery)		A, B
11	1959833	TERMINAL PACKAGE (Ground)		A, B
11	1959834	TERMINAL PACKAGE (Diode junction)		A, B
12	1963213	BEARING RETAINER		A, B
13	1963211	COLLAR, Inside		A, B
14	1941978	LOCKWASHER, Shaft nut, diode end		A, B
15	9419392	LOCKWASHER, Diode junction terminal		A, B
	9419392	LOCKWASHER, Capacitor terminal screw		A, B
16	9418854	NUT, Diode junction terminal		A, B
17	1915172	NUT, Shaft, diode end		A, B
18	1961526	SCREW, Ball bearing retainer attaching		A, B
19	1961530	SCREW, Brush holder attaching		A, B
20	9418855	SCREW, Capacitor terminal		A, B
21	1959523	WASHER, Insul. capacitor screw		A, B
22	815540	WASHER, Capacitor terminal screw		A, B
23	1961521	BOLT, Thru, 2-1/8 in. long		A, B
24	1961522	BOLT, Thru, 3-13/32 in. long		A, B
25	1959455	CAPACITOR		A, B
26	1959532	CLIP, Stator lead terminal		A, B
27	1952244	RING, Collector, diode end		A, B
28	1961523	SPACER, Diode end		A, B
29	1960750	SPRING, Capacitor retaining		A, B

Figure 5-2B. *Part numbers of all components of the aircraft alternator*

Installation Drawing

When an assembly or group of assemblies is installed in an airplane, an installation drawing such as the one in Figure 5-3 is used.

An installation drawing shows the location of the parts and assemblies on the completed aircraft and identifies all of the detail parts used in the installation. An accompanying parts list shows the number of each part and the quantity of each that is required.

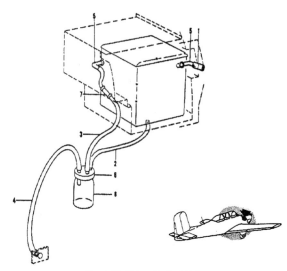

Figure 48. Battery Jar Installation

FIG. & INDEX NO.	PART NO.	1 2 3 4 5 6 7	DESCRIPTION	UNITS PER ASSY
48	45-361090		JAR INSTL,BATTERY /SEE FIG. 45 FOR NHA/	REF
- 1	45-361090-3		. TUBE,BATTERY JAR VENT	1
- 2	45-361090-7		. TUBE,BATTERY BOX DRAIN.	1
			/MAKE FR 114693-8-01112/	
- 3	114693-6-02400		. TUBE,BATTERY JAR.	1
- 4	45-361090-5		. TUBE,BATTERY JAR /MAKE FR 114693-8-04500/ . . .	1
- 5	9555		. ELBOW,BATTERY VENT /74144/.	2
- 6	45-369016		. COVER ASSY,BATTERY OVERFLOW SUMP JAR.	1
- 7	45-410236		. TUBE,BATTERY JAR.	1
- 8	NO NUMBER		. JAR,ONE PINT ROUND MASON.	1

Figure 5-3. *Installation drawing of a battery sump jar*

Sectional Drawing

A sectional drawing shows the way a component would appear if it were cut through the middle. Different types of sectional lines and cross-hatching show the different types of material used in the component.

The sectional drawing in Figure 5-4 shows the way an electronic cable connector would appear on the inside.

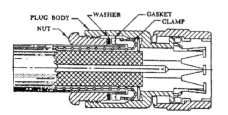

Figure 5-4. *Sectional view of an electronic cable connector*

Half-Sectional Drawing

It is sometimes helpful to show a part as it would appear in both a sectional view and a plain view. Figure 5-5 shows a half-sectional view of a hydraulic quick-disconnect coupling. In the upper half, we see the way the coupling would look if it were cut in two, and in the lower half, we see the way the outside of the coupling appears.

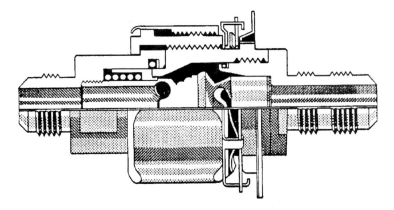

Figure 5-5. *Half-sectional view of a hydraulic quick-disconnect coupling*

Cutaway Drawing

In Figure 5-6, we see a cutaway drawing of a piston-type hydraulic pump. This type of drawing shows the outside of the pump with part of it cut away to show the parts on the inside. In the view of the valve plate, see phantom lines showing the passageways connecting the pump inlet and outlet to the pump cylinders.

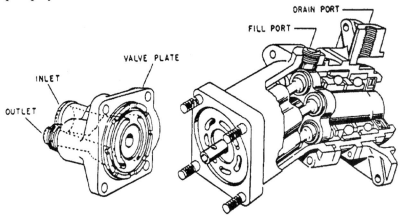

Figure 5-6. *Partial cutaway drawing of a piston-type hydraulic pump*

Exploded-View Drawing

Figure 5-7 is an exploded view of a two-way restrictor for a hydraulic system. The upper drawing shows a cross-sectional view of the restrictor, and the lower drawing shows all of the components spread out, or exploded, so you can see what each part looks like.

Exploded-view drawings are frequently used in illustrated parts manuals and service bulletins.

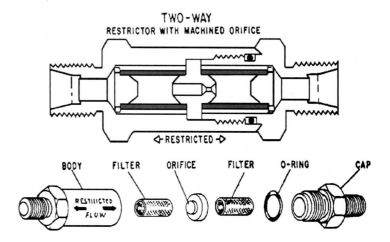

Figure 5-7. *Exploded view of a hydraulic restrictor*

Schematic Diagram

A schematic diagram shows the relative location of all of the parts in a system, but does not give the location of the parts in the aircraft. Figure 5-8 is a schematic diagram of an air conditioning system for a light airplane. This diagram shows the main components of the system and the direction the refrigerant flows. The different types of shading identify the pressure inside the lines.

Schematic drawings are of great help when troubleshooting a system.

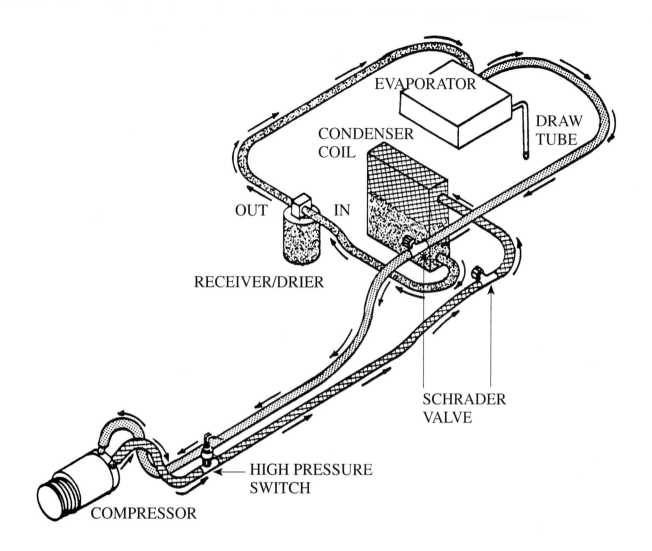

EVAPORATOR

DRAW TUBE

CONDENSER COIL

OUT   IN

RECEIVER/DRIER

SCHRADER VALVE

HIGH PRESSURE SWITCH

COMPRESSOR

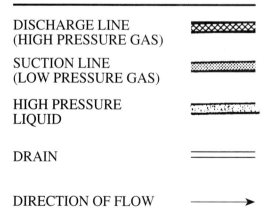

LEGEND

DISCHARGE LINE
(HIGH PRESSURE GAS)

SUCTION LINE
(LOW PRESSURE GAS)

HIGH PRESSURE
LIQUID

DRAIN

DIRECTION OF FLOW

Figure 5-8. *Schematic diagram of an aircraft air conditioning system*

Block Diagram

A block diagram, such as the one in Figure 5-9, shows the various functions of a system. These function blocks do not include any detail but rather indicate what happens. Lines connecting the blocks show the direction of flow of signals or other forms of information.

The main use of block diagrams is helping us understand the way a complex system works, and they are often used in troubleshooting.

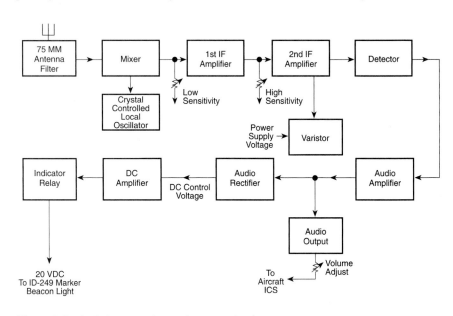

Figure 5-9. *Block diagram of an airborne marker beacon receiver*

Repair Drawing

Aircraft maintenance technicians are often required to repair an aircraft structure. Some maintenance manuals show methods recommended by the manufacturer for various types of repairs. Figure 5-10 is a repair drawing for a damaged nose rib. Since all damages are different, no dimension are given, but there is enough information provided that an experienced technician can make an airworthy repair.

Wiring Diagrams

Wiring diagrams show all of the wires in a particular section of an aircraft electrical system. The parts list with the drawing provides the wire size, wire number, and the part number of the terminals on each end of each wire. Figure 5-11 is an example of a wiring diagram of a battery circuit.

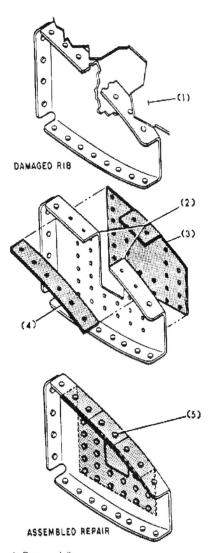

1. Damaged rib.
2. Damaged area smooth.
3. Patch prepared so that it will fit flush with the flange of the rib.
4. Reinforcement strip.
5. Assembled repair.

Figure 5-10. *Repair drawing of an aircraft nose rib*

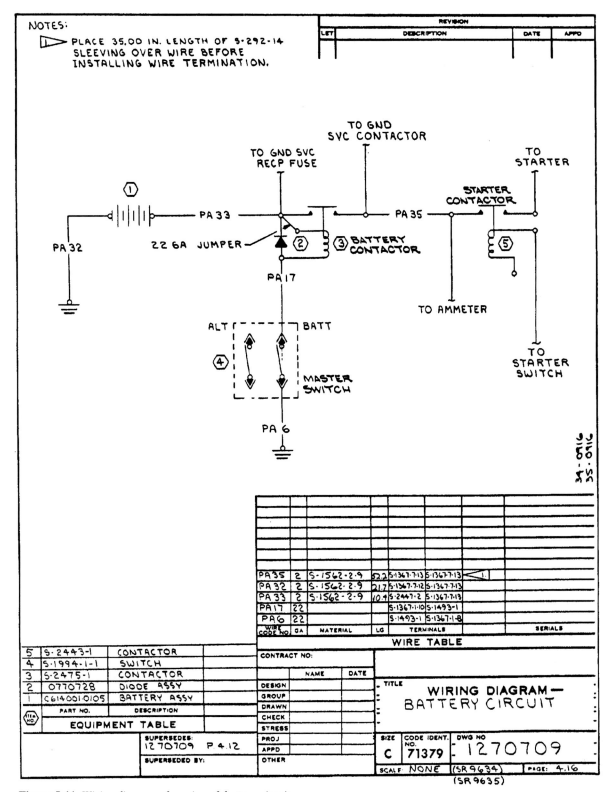

Figure 5-11. *Wiring diagram of an aircraft battery circuit*

Pictorial Diagrams

Pictorial diagrams show the components as they actually appear, rather than using conventional symbols. Figure 5-12 is a pictorial diagram of the electrical system of a small general aviation airplane.

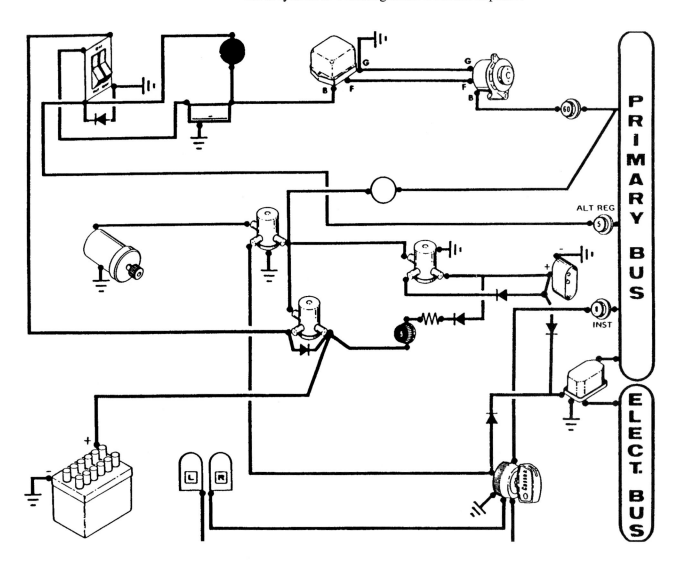

Figure 5-12. *Pictorial diagram of a light airplane electrical system*

Sketches

Sketches are rough drawings made without the use of instruments. They are used to convey only a specific bit of information and include the minimum amount of detail needed to manufacture the part.

We see the correct procedure for making a sketch in Figure 5-13:

1. Block in the space and basic shape used for the sketch.

2. Add details to the basic block.

3. Darken the lines that are to show up as visible lines in the finished sketch.

4. Add dimensions and any other information that will make the sketch more usable.

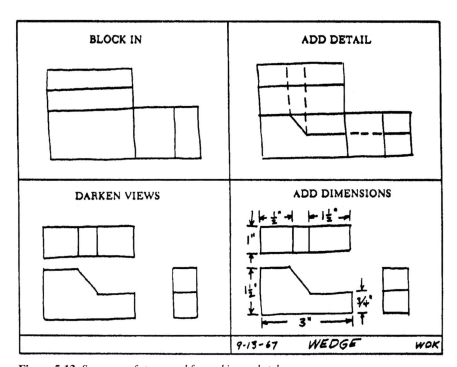

Figure 5-13. *Sequence of steps used for making a sketch*

Drawing Views

Perspective Views

Perspective views are used to make an object appear as it does in actual life. Lines that are parallel on the object actually converge at a vanishing point, as we see in Figure 5-14. Perspective views are difficult to make, and they are not normally used in maintenance and manufacturing drawings.

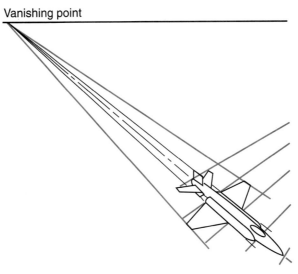

Vanishing point

Figure 5-14. *In a perspective view, parallel lines converge at a vanishing point off the drawing.*

Isometric Views

An isometric view is similar to a perspective view, except that the lines which are parallel on the object are also parallel in the isometric view. Vertical object lines appear vertical on the drawing and on a full size drawing are the true length. Horizontal lines are drawn at an angle of 30° to the horizontal in the view, and are also the true length. Any line which is neither vertical nor horizontal on the object is not drawn to its true length. Figure 5-15 is an isometric drawing of a solid object. All lines in this drawing are the true length except lines A and B.

Because one view shows three sides of the object, isometric views help us visualize the object. They may be used with adequate dimensions for simple components, but should not used for complex parts.

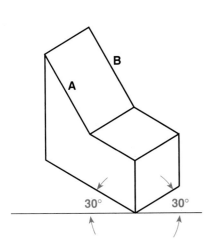

Figure 5-15. *Three surfaces of an isometric view are visible, and all lines in this drawing are true length except A and B.*

Orthographic Views

Most of the drawings used in aircraft construction and maintenance use orthographic views. A solid object can have six views: front, rear, left side, right side, top, and bottom.

Most orthographic drawings made for aircraft have one, two, or three views. Front, right side, and top are the most generally used views.

Figure 5-16 shows the way the six orthographic views of a solid object are made. Surfaces that are visible are drawn with solid lines, and surfaces that are not visible in the view are drawn with dotted lines.

orthographic projection. A method of showing all the sides of an object. There are six possible views of an object.

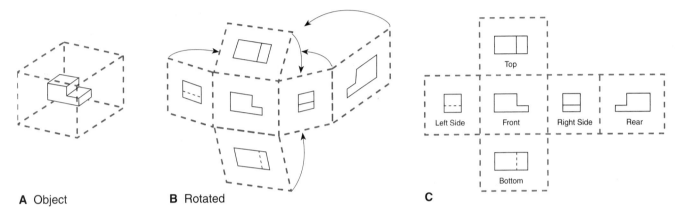

A Object   **B** Rotated   **C**

Figure 5-16. *An orthographic projection shows six possible views of an object.*

Auxiliary Views

It is possible to have six orthographic views, but sometimes it would be helpful to have a view that is not at right angles to one of the faces of an object. When we need this information, we make an auxiliary view, as in Figure 5-17.

auxiliary view. A view used on some aircraft drawings made at an angle to one of the three views of the main drawing.

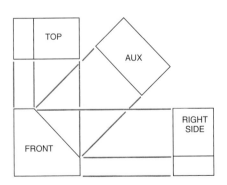

Figure 5-17. *Auxiliary views are used when the orthographic views do not convey the needed information.*

Answers are on Page 402. Page numbers refer to chapter text.

1. Refer to the figure below. The drawing which is correct for the view of the aileron weight pointed out by the arrow is shown as _____ . *Page 383*

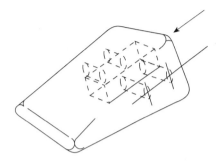

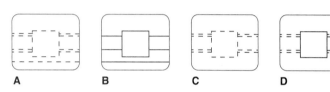

A   B   C   D

2. A drawing that includes enough information to allow a part to be fabricated is called a/an _____ drawing. *Page 368*

3. A drawing that shows the way various detail parts are put together to form an assembly or subassembly is called a/an _____ drawing. *Page 368*

4. Refer to the figure at right. Identify the orthographic views that show the top and bottom of the object.
   a. The top view is _____ .
   b. The bottom view is _____ .
      Page 379

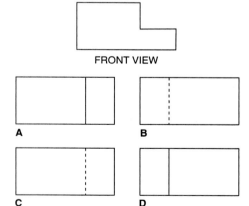

FRONT VIEW

A   B

C   D

5. An orthographic projection can show as many as six views of an object. List the three views that are most commonly used in aircraft drawings.
   a. _____
   b. _____
   c. _____
      Page 379

6. A drawing that shows the location of the components with respect to each other within the system, but not in the locations they appear on the aircraft, is called a/an _____ diagram.
Page 372

7. Refer to the figure below. The correct sequence of the steps for making a sketch of a component is: _____ _____ _____ _____ . *Page 377*

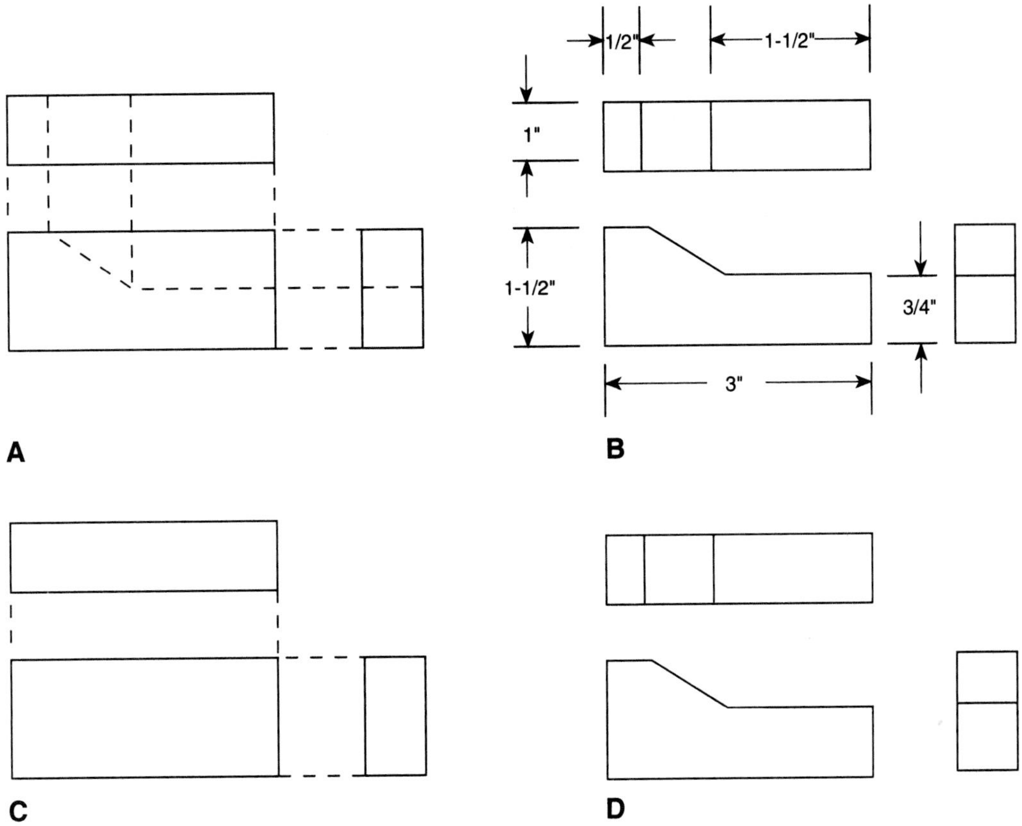

A

B

| 1/2" | 1-1/2" |

1"

1-1/2"

3/4"

3"

C

D

Continued

8. A simple, rough drawing that is made rapidly and without much detail, but which contains all of the necessary information to allow a part to be fabricated, is called a/an _____ .
Page 377

9. The three classes of working drawings are:
   a. _____ drawings
   b. _____ drawings
   c. _____ drawings
   Page 367

10. The type of drawing most helpful when troubleshooting a system is a/an _____ diagram. *Page 372*

11. The type of drawing most often used in illustrated parts manuals is the _____ drawing. *Page 372*

12. A drawing in which all of the parts and subassemblies are brought together is called a/an _____ drawing. *Page 368*

13. The type of drawing that specifies the wire size used in a particular electrical circuit is called a/an _____ diagram. *Page 375*

Drawing Practices

Line Types and Weights

Different types and weights of lines are used to make aircraft drawings. Figure 5-18 shows the most generally used lines.

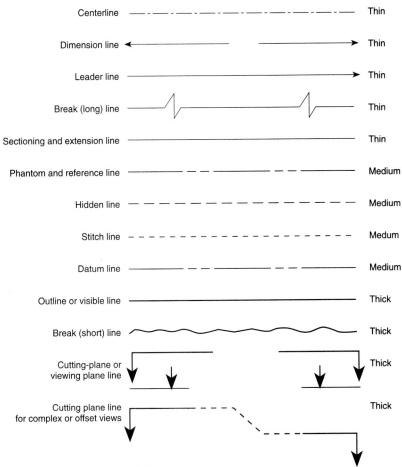

Figure 5-18. *Line characteristics and conventions*

A center line divides a part into symmetrical halves and is made of a thin line of alternate long and short dashes.

Dimension lines are thin lines with arrowheads on each end. The arrowheads touch the extension lines that locate the points from which the dimension is taken. Dimension lines are broken in their center, and the dimension is noted in the break.

A leader line is a thin line with an arrowhead. It joins a call-out on the drawing with the point to which the call-out is referring.

A short break line showing where a part is broken away from the view is a thick wavy line. Long break lines are thin straight lines that are broken, with zigzags inserted, to show that the line is not continuous.

Extension lines are thin lines used for dimensioning when it is not practical for the dimension line to touch the actual part from which the measurement is made. The arrowheads on the dimension lines touch the extension lines.

Phantom lines showing the location of a part that is used for a reference are made up of a medium-weight line of alternating one long and two short dashes.

The visible outline of a part is made with a thick solid line A hidden line, showing an edge of the part that is not visible in the view, is a medium-weight dashed line.

The alternate position of a part may be shown on a drawing by thin dashed lines. A cutting plane, or viewing plane, is a thick line with arrowheads showing the direction the part is viewed.

Section lines are used to identify the material of which a part is made. Figure 5-19 shows the section lines used to identify various materials.

When there are specifications showing the material of which a part is made, the section lines for cast iron (evenly-spaced diagonal lines) may be used regardless of the material.

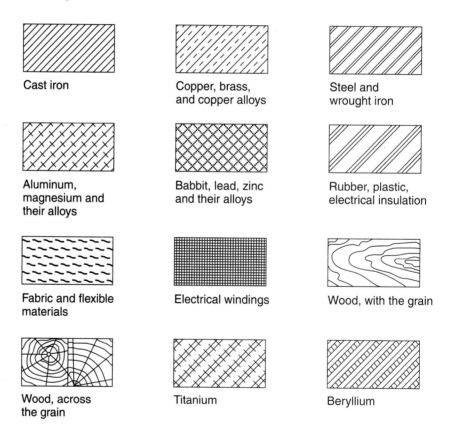

Figure 5-19. *Typical section lines used to identify materials*

Notes

Notes are used on a drawing for information that applies to more than one location or for information that cannot be conveniently placed at the point where it is needed. Notes which apply to the drawing in general are not specially marked. However, when a note applies to a specific component or area of the drawing, its identifying number is placed inside a triangle, square, hexagon, or some other distinctive shape. One commonly used method of identifying notes is to use a small numbered flag at the point the note is applicable and a similar flag at the note.

Figure 5-20 shows a typical note that refers to a capacitor installed across a generator. According to Note 1, this capacitor is part of the basic avionics kit. The number 8 inside the hexagon indicates that the part number of the capacitor is found in the bill of materials on the drawing, where it has the same numbered hexagon.

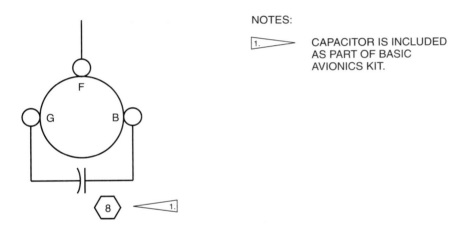

Figure 5-20. *Note flags are used to allow information to be placed on the drawing at some convenient location to prevent the drawing from becoming too cluttered.*

Dimensions and Tolerances

Dimensions should never be scaled from an aircraft drawing, because the paper shrinks or stretches in use.

Copy machines, which are sometimes used to reduce or enlarge sections of drawings, also may not reproduce the drawings to an exact scale. All measurements must be made using the dimensions marked on the drawing. Dimensions are placed in the break of a dimension line, between two extension lines, or, if the lines are too close together, the dimensions are placed outside the dimension line arrows.

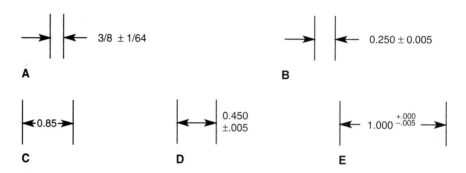

A Allowable dimensions between 23/64 and 25/64 inch
B Allowable dimensions between 0.245 and 0.255 inch
C No tolerance is specified
D Allowable dimensions between 0.445 and 0.455 inch
E Allowable dimensions between 0.995 and 1.000 inch

Figure 5-21. *Typical ways of showing allowable tolerances*

UNLESS OTHERWISE SPECIFIED		
LINEAR	.X	± .1
TOLERANCES	.XX	± .04
	.XXX	± .010
ANGULAR TOLERANCES	± 0° 30'	

Figure 5-22. *Tolerances may be specified by the number of digits following the decimal point in a dimension.*

tolerance. The difference between the extreme possible dimensions of a part.

Tolerances, which are the maximum differences between the extreme allowable dimensions, may be shown with the dimension, as shown in Figure 5-21.

Some tolerances are shown for the entire drawing and are indicated by the way the dimension is written. We see such a tolerance notation block in Figure 5-22. If a dimension is specified as 0.5 inch, it may have an actual dimension of between 0.4 and 0.6 inch. If the dimension is given as 0.50, its allowable dimensions are between 0.46 and 0.54 inch. If the dimension is given as 0.500, the allowable dimensions are between 0.490 and 0.510 inch.

Allowance is the difference between a nominal dimension and the upper or lower limit.

An angle specified as 15° could have an actual measurement between 14.5° (14° 30') and 15.5° (15° 30').

Examples of typical dimensioning practices are shown in Figure 5-23. In A, the way an isometric drawing is dimensioned. In B, the way angles are dimensioned; in C, the way circles are dimensioned; in D, the way holes are dimensioned; and in E, the way tapers are dimensioned.

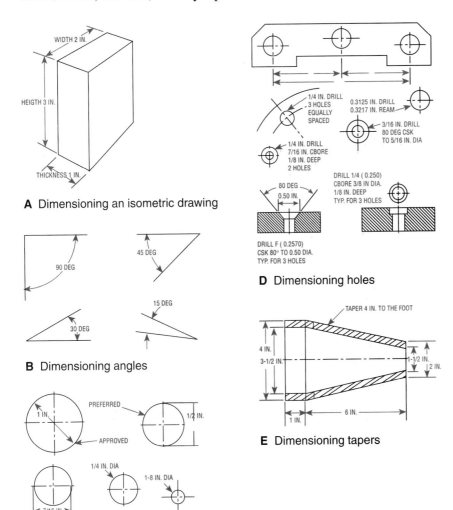

A Dimensioning an isometric drawing

B Dimensioning angles

C Dimensioning circles

D Dimensioning holes

E Dimensioning tapers

Figure 5-23. *Typical methods used for dimensioning*

Location Identification on an Aircraft

Longitudinal locations in an aircraft fuselage are identified with fuselage stations as we see in Figure 5-24. Fuselage station 0 is normally located at the datum, which in this airplane is 94 inches ahead of the nose. All fuselage station numbers are given in inches aft of the datum along the longitudinal axis of the aircraft. Some airplanes have the datum located behind their nose. When this is the case, stations ahead of FS 0 will have negative numbers. For example, FS -8 is located 8 inches ahead of FS 0.

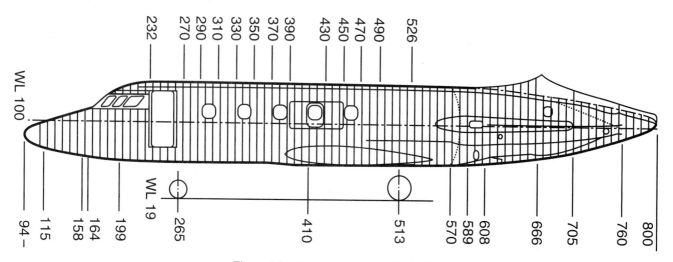

Figure 5-24. *Fuselage stations and waterlines on a typical multiengine airplane fuselage*

Vertical locations are identified with waterlines. Waterline zero may be the longitudinal axis of the aircraft or it may be at some other location chosen by the engineers that designed the aircraft. All locations above WL0 are positive, and all below it are negative. Waterline 16 is 16 inches above WL0.

Lateral locations are measured with buttock, or butt, lines which are measured in inches to the right or left of the fuselage center line. An object located at BL 6L is 6 inches to the left of the fuselage center line.

Wing and horizontal stabilizer stations are measured along their span, with their station zero being the center line of the fuselage.

Drawing Sizes

Aircraft drawings may be made on paper, vellum, or Mylar film in sizes that fold conveniently for storage in standard filing cabinets. The standard sizes are:

A-size = 8½ x 11 inches
B-size = 11 x 17 inches
C-size = 17 x 22 inches
D-size = 22 x 34 inches
E-size = 34 x 44 inches

Many drawings are far too large for a standard size sheet and they are made on a large roll of drawing paper, so the drawing may be longer than the drawing board. Drawings made on a roll are called R-size drawings and are 36 to 42 inches wide and are as long as is needed.

Zones

Large drawings contain so much information that a system of zones is necessary. Along the right-hand border of the drawing, starting at the title block and going upward, are a series of letters. Along the lower border of the print are a series of numbers, starting with 0 at the right edge and increasing to the left for the length of the drawing. If a note references a part on the drawing at location B-7, the part is located near the intersection of lines projected horizontally from zone B and vertically from zone 7.

zones. Numbers along the bottom and letters along the right side of a large drawing, used to aid in locating a part by defining a grid pattern on the drawing.

STUDY QUESTIONS: DRAWING PRACTICES

Answers are on Page 402. Page numbers refer to chapter text.

14. Refer to the figure below. Identify each of the types of lines pointed to in this drawing:

A is a/an _____ line.
B is a/an _____ line.
C is a/an _____ line.
D is a/an _____ line.

Page 383

Continued

15. Locations along the length of the fuselage measured from the datum or some other point specified by the manufacturer are called _____ . *Page 388.*

16. Locations laterally from the center line of the fuselage are identified by their _____ line. *Page 388*

17. Locations vertically from a given reference plane running through the fuselage are identified by their _____ line. *Page 388*

18. If the exact specification of a material is shown on the drawing, the symbol for _____ may be used for sectioning. *Page 384*

19. Refer to the figure below. Identify each of the section lines.

    A is _____ .
    B is _____ .
    C is _____ .
    D is _____ .
    Page 384

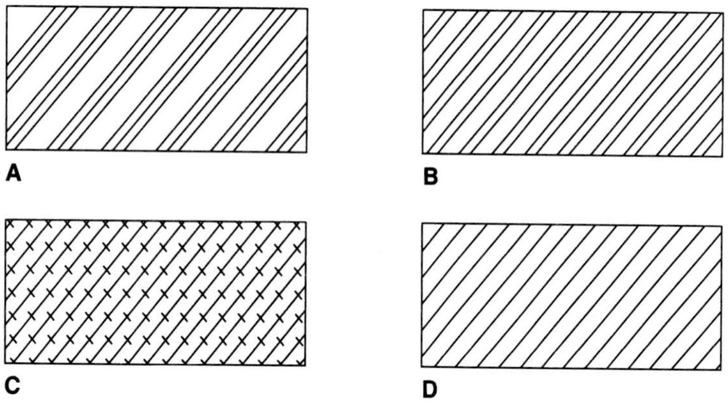

A

B

C

D

20. Refer to Figure SQ-20. The end of the cylindrical body of this clevis is chamfered at an angle of _____ degrees for a linear distance of _____ inch. *Page 387*

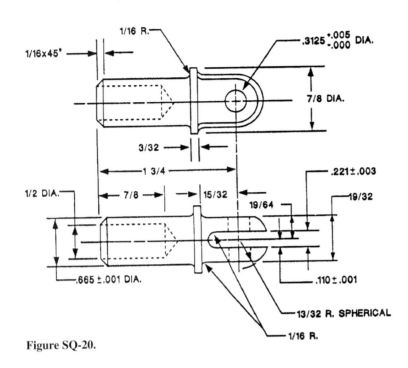

Figure SQ-20.

21. Refer to Figure SQ-20. The hole drilled in the cylindrical end of this clevis has a diameter of _____ inch and is drilled to a depth of _____ inch. *Page 387*

22. Refer to Figure SQ-20. The maximum allowable diameter of the hole in this clevis through which the clevis pin fits is _____ inch. The minimum diameter for this hole is _____ inch. *Page 386*

23. The allowable deviation from the dimensions of a part is called the _____ . *Page 386*

Continued

24. Refer to the figure below. The finished diameter of the two holes in this part is _____ inch. The finished diameter is made with a _____ . *Page 385*

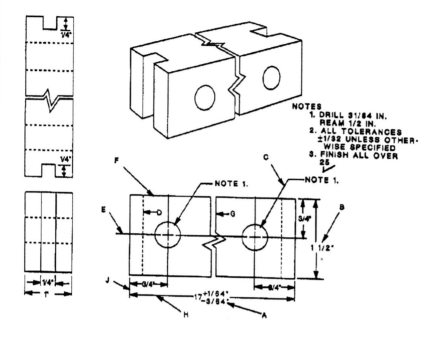

NOTES
1. DRILL 31/64 IN.
   REAM 1/2 IN.
2. ALL TOLERANCES
   ±1/32 UNLESS OTHER-
   WISE SPECIFIED
3. FINISH ALL OVER
   25

25. If the diameter of a part is dimensioned on a drawing as 4.387 +0.005 -0.002, its maximum diameter is _____ inches and its minimum diameter is _____ inches. *Page 386*

26. Refer to the figure below. The vertical distance from the top of the fitting and the bottom of the lowest $^{15}\!/_{64}$" hole is _____ inches. *Page 386*

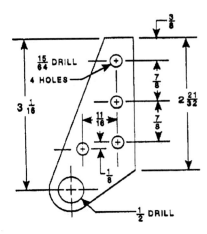

27. Measurements _____ (should or should not) be scaled from an aircraft drawing. *Page 386*

28. The difference between a nominal dimension and the upper or lower limit is called _____ . *Page 386*

Charts

Charts represent another form of aircraft drawings. However, instead of furnishing details for the manufacture or assembly of parts, charts are used to provide pictorial information regarding acceptable limits. Charts are used by both pilots and technicians to properly operate and maintain complex modern aircraft.

Brake Horsepower— Brake Mean Effective Pressure Chart

Refer to Figure 5-25 to find the BMEP when the BHP, the engine displacement, and engine speed are known:

1. From the given BHP, draw a line vertically downward until it intersects the diagonal line for the engine displacement.

2. From this point, draw a horizontal line to the right until it intersects the diagonal line for the engine speed.

3. From this point, draw a line vertically downward until it intersects the BMEP index.

To find the engine speed needed to produce a given BHP with a given BMEP:

1. From the given BHP, draw a line vertically downward until it intersects the diagonal line for the engine displacement.

2. From this intersection, draw a horizontal line all the way to the right edge of the chart.

3. Draw a line vertically upward from the given BMEP until it crosses the horizontal line you just drew.

4. The engine-speed diagonal line nearest to the intersection of the lines you just drew is the correct speed for these conditions.

Electric Wire Chart

The electric wire chart in Figure 5-26 on page 396 is drawn using these allowable voltage drops for a continuous load:

14-volt system – 0.5 volt
28-volt system – 1.0 volt
115-volt system – 4 volts
200-volt system – 7 volts

For an intermittent load, the allowable voltage drops are double those for continuous loads.

Brake Horsepower (BHP)

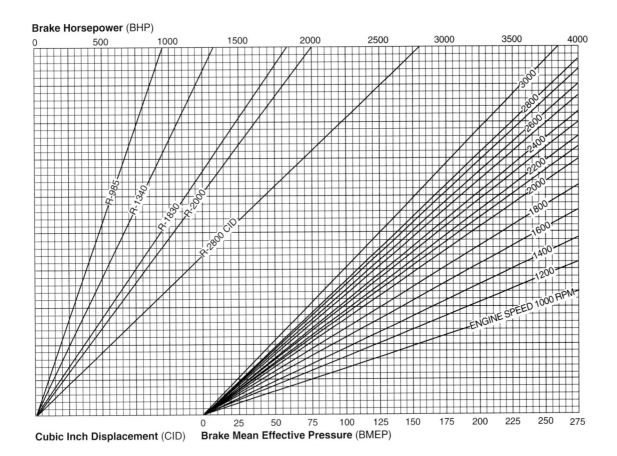

Cubic Inch Displacement (CID) **Brake Mean Effective Pressure** (BMEP)

Figure 5-25. *Brake Horsepower–Brake Mean Effective Pressure Chart*

When using the chart in Figure 5-26, any combination of current and wire size that intersects above curve 1 is satisfactory for a continuous load in a bundle or conduit.

Any combination of current and wire size that intersects between curves 1 and 2 is satisfactory for a continuous load, but the wire must be run in free air.

Any combination of current and wire size that intersects between curves 2 and 3 is allowable only for an intermittent load.

To find the correct wire size for a given current, allowable voltage drop, and wire length:

1. Follow the diagonal line for the amount of current down and to the left until it intersects a horizontal line for the wire length in the allowable voltage drop column.

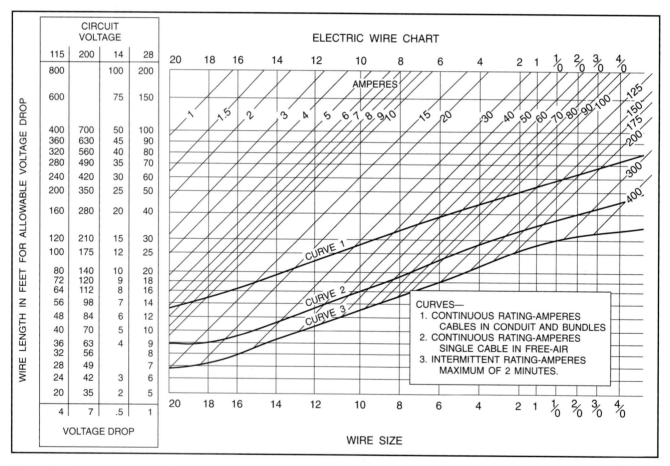

Figure 5-26. *Electric wire chart for determining the correct size wire to use when the total current and allowable voltage drop are known*

2. The nearest vertical line to the right of this intersection is the correct wire size for these conditions.

3. The placement of this intersection in relation to curves 1, 2, or 3 determines whether the load can be continuous or intermittent and whether the wire can be routed through a conduit or in a bundle.

To determine the maximum length of a given size wire that can be used to carry a given amount of current with a specified voltage drop:

1. Follow the diagonal line for the amount of current down and to the left until it intersects the vertical line for the given wire size.

2. From this intersection, draw a horizontal line to the left until it intersects the wire length index for the allowable voltage drop. This number is the maximum length of wire in feet that will not exceed the allowable voltage drop.

Control Cable Tension Chart

To find the correct cable tension (rigging load) when the cable size and type and the temperature are known, use the chart in Figure 5-27.

Continued

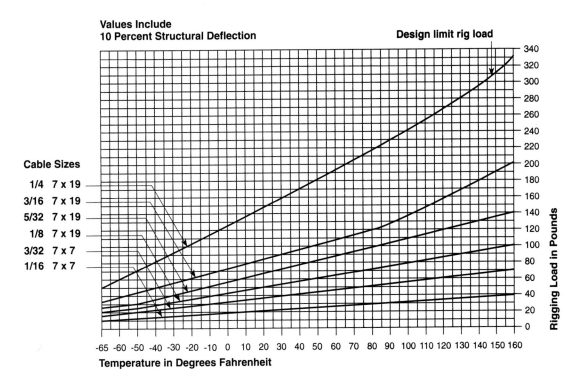

Figure 5-27. *Control cable tension chart*

1. From the existing temperature on the Fahrenheit temperature scale at the bottom of the chart, draw a line vertically upward until it intersects the curve for the size and type of cable being adjusted.

2. From this intersection, draw a horizontal line to the right until it intersects the rigging load. This is the desired cable tension in pounds.

Specific Fuel Consumption — Brake Horsepower Curve

To find the amount of fuel an engine will burn per hour when it is developing a specific horsepower, use the chart in Figure 5-28.

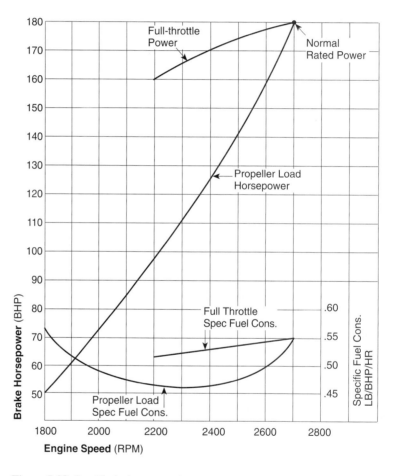

Figure 5-28. *Specific fuel consumption curve*

1. From the BHP index on the left side of the chart, draw a line horizontally to the right until it intersects the propeller load horsepower curve.

2. From this intersection, draw a line vertically downward until it crosses the propeller load SFC curve.

3. From this intersection, draw a line horizontally to the right until it intersects the SFC index. This number is the number of pounds of fuel burned per hour for each horsepower.

4. Multiply the SFC by the BHP to find the number of pounds of fuel burned per hour, and divide this by 6 to find the number of gallons per hour burned.

Answers are on Page 402. **Page numbers refer to chapter text.**

29. Refer to Figure 5-25. An engine with a displacement of 1,830 cubic inches develops 1,250 brake horse-power at 2,500 RPM. Its brake mean effective pressure is _____ psi. *Page 395*

30. Refer to Figure 5-25. An engine with a displacement of 2,800 cubic inches develops 2,000 brake horse-power with a brake mean effective pressure of 270 psi. It develops this power at a speed of _____ RPM. *Page 395*

31. Refer to Figure 5-26. A 28-volt electrical installation requires a 40-foot length of single cable routed in free air. The load is continuous at 15 amperes. The smallest wire that can be used without exceeding a 1-volt drop is a _____ -gage wire. *Page 396*

32. Refer to Figure 5-26. An electrical installation uses a 16-gage wire between the bus and the equipment in a 28-volt system. The load is 25-amps, intermittent, and the maximum allowable voltage drop is 1 volt. The longest wire that can carry this load without exceeding the allowable voltage drop is _____ feet. *Page 396*

33. Refer to Figure 5-26. A 28-volt electrical installation requires a 10-foot length of wire routed in a bundle. The load is continuous at 20 amperes. The smallest wire that can be used without exceeding a 1-volt drop or causing overheating in the bundle is a _____ -gage wire. *Page 396*

34. Refer to Figure 5-26. A 28-volt electrical installation has a continuous load of 20 amperes and uses a 12-gage wire routed singly in free air. The longest wire that can be used without exceeding a maximum of 1-volt drop is _____ feet. *Page 396*

35. Refer to Figure 5-27. The proper tension for a ³⁄₁₆-inch extra-flexible (7 x 19) control cable rigged at 87°F is _____ pounds. *Page 397*

36. Refer to Figure 5-27. The proper tension for a ¹⁄₈-inch extra-flexible (7 x 19) control cable rigged at -30°F is _____ pounds. *Page 397*

37. Refer to Figure 5-28. A reserve for 30 minutes flying time at 2,300 RPM will require _____ pounds of fuel. *Page 398*

38. Refer to Figure 5-28. When the engine is operating under cruise conditions at 2,350 RPM, it is developing _____ brake horsepower, and its fuel consumption is _____ pounds per hour. *Page 398*

Answers to Chapter 5 Study Questions

1. D

2. detail

3. assembly

4. a. A
   b. C

5. a. top
   b. front
   c. right side

6. schematic

7. C, A, D, B

8 sketch

9. a. detail
   b. assembly
   c. installation

10. schematic

11. exploded view

12. assembly

13. wiring

14. a. visible line or outline
    b. hidden line
    c. extension line
    d. center line

15. fuselage stations

16. buttock

17. water

18. cast iron

19. a. Rubber, plastic, and electrical insulation
    b. Steel and wrought iron
    c. Aluminum, magnesium, and their alloys
    d. Cast iron

20. 45, ¹⁄₁₆

21. ¹⁄₂, ⁷⁄₈

22. .3130, .3125

23. tolerance

24. ¹⁄₂, reamer

25. 4.392, 4.385

26. 2.367

27. should not

28. allowance

29. 217

30. 2,100

31. 10

32. 8

33. 12

34. 27

35. 128

36. 30

37. 25.3

38. 118, 55.5

WEIGHT AND BALANCE

6

Continued

WEIGHT AND BALANCE

6

Weight and balance is of such a critical nature that standard preflight operation requires the pilot to determine that his or her aircraft is loaded in such a way that its gross weight is not beyond the allowable limit and that the center of gravity is located within the prescribed limits for the actual weight of the aircraft.

For the pilot to know the actual weight and center of gravity location, the maintenance technician must provide accurate information on the empty weight of the aircraft and the location of the empty-weight center of gravity. In this chapter of the *Aviation Maintenance Technician Series — General*, we will consider the theory of weight and balance and study the application of these principles to aircraft from small single-engine general aviation airplanes through large multiengine jet transport aircraft.

Weight and Balance Theory

Regardless of how well an aircraft is designed and how well it is built, it is not safe to fly if it is loaded in such a way that its gross weight exceeds the limit allowed by its manufacturer, or if its center of gravity (CG) falls outside its allowable limits. If the weight is too great, too high a structural load can be placed on the aircraft during certain maneuvers or during flight through rough weather. If the CG is outside the allowable limits, the aircraft can become difficult or even impossible to control in certain flight conditions.

When the aircraft was first certificated, its empty weight, EW, and its empty weight center of gravity, EWCG, were determined by either actually weighing it or by using the average weight of aircraft of exactly the same configuration coming off the assembly line.

Private aircraft are not required to be weighed on any schedule, but it is the responsibility of the technician approving the aircraft for return to service after an inspection or maintenance to determine that the aircraft's empty weight and the empty weight CG are correctly recorded in the aircraft records.

The empty weight of an aircraft includes the weight of the airframe, engines and all items of operating equipment that have fixed locations and are permanently installed in the aircraft. It includes optional and special equipment, fixed ballast, hydraulic fluid, and unusable (residual) fuel. The empty weight of aircraft certificated under 14 CFR Parts 23 and 25 also includes all of the oil in the supply tank, but some aircraft include only the undrainable, or residual oil.

empty weight. The weight of the airframe, engines, and all items of operating equipment that have fixed locations and are permanently installed in the aircraft. It includes optional and special equipment, fixed ballast, full reservoirs of hydraulic fluid, and engine lubricating oil. It includes only unusable, or residual, fuel.

empty-weight center of gravity. The center of gravity of the aircraft as it is weighed. It includes all of the items required in aircraft empty weight.

useful load. The difference between the empty weight of an aircraft and its maximum allowable gross weight. Useful load is the weight of the pilot, copilot, passengers, baggage, fuel, and oil.

zero fuel weight. The weight of an aircraft without fuel. It is the basic operating weight of the aircraft plus the payload.

arm. The distance, in inches, between the center of gravity of an object and the reference datum. An arm ahead of the datum is negative, and an arm behind the datum is positive.

datum. An imaginary vertical reference plane or line chosen by the aircraft manufacturer from which all arms used for weight and balance computation are measured.

moment. A force that tries to cause rotation. In weight and balance, a moment is found by multiplying a weight by its arm. Moments are expressed in pound-inches. A moment that causes a nose-down condition is a negative moment, and one that causes a nose-up condition is a positive moment.

center of gravity (CG). The point in an aircraft at which all of the weight is considered to be concentrated. The algebraic sum of the moments about the center of gravity is zero. The center of gravity may be expressed in inches from the datum or in percent of the mean aerodynamic chord. The symbol for the location of the CG on an aircraft is ⊕.

The useful load of an aircraft is the difference between its empty weight and the maximum allowable gross weight. It includes the weight of the crew, passengers, fuel, and cargo.

The empty weight is recorded in the weight and balance information that must be carried in the aircraft, while the maximum allowable gross weight is found in the Type Certificate Data Sheets for the aircraft.

The zero fuel weight of an aircraft is the maximum allowable weight of the loaded aircraft without fuel. It includes the weight of the cargo, passengers, and crew.

The arm (lever arm) of a weight is the distance between the CG of the weight and the fulcrum. In aircraft weight and balance, the fulcrum is considered to be the datum, an imaginary vertical plane that can be located anywhere the manufacturer chooses.

The datum is often the center of the rotor mast of a helicopter, the leading edge of the wing of an airplane, or a specified number of inches ahead of some easily located point on the aircraft.

The arms of weights located behind the datum are positive, and those ahead of the datum are negative. When the datum is located ahead of the aircraft, all of the arms are positive and computational errors are minimized.

In aircraft weight and balance practice, weights are normally specified in pounds; arms, in inches from the datum; and moments, in pound-inches.

When a weight is removed from the aircraft, the weight removed is negative (−), and when weight is added, the weight added is positive (+).

An arm ahead of the datum is negative (−), and an arm behind the datum is positive (+).

- A positive weight and a positive arm produce a positive moment.
- A positive weight and a negative arm produce a negative moment.
- A negative weight and a positive arm produce a negative moment.
- A negative weight and a negative arm produce a positive moment.
- A positive moment produces a nose-up pitch, and a negative moment produces a nose-down pitch.

An aircraft is considered to be in balance if the average moment arm of the loaded aircraft falls within the approved CG range.

Specifications for some aircraft contain an empty-weight center of gravity range. If the CG for the empty weight of the aircraft falls within this range, it is not possible to legally load the aircraft in such a way that its loaded CG will fall outside its loaded CG range or limits.

Weight and balance of a helicopter are computed in the same way as for an airplane, but because of its limited control effectiveness, weight and balance of a helicopter are more critical and the CG range is more restricted than it is for an airplane.

Locating the Balance Point, or Center of Gravity (CG)

One of the easiest ways of understanding weight and balance is to consider a board with weights located at various locations. We can find the CG of the board and observe the way the CG changes as the weights are moved.

The CG of a board such as the one in Figure 6-1 on which three weights are located may be found by using these three steps:

1. Measure the arm of each weight from a datum point.

2. Multiply each arm by its weight to find the moment of each weight.

3. Add all the weights and all the moments. In this example, we will disregard the weight of the board.

4. Divide the total moment by the total weight to find the CG in inches from the datum point.

empty-weight center of gravity range.
The distance between the allowable forward and aft empty-weight CG limits. When EWCG limits are given for an aircraft, and the empty-weight CG falls within these limits, you cannot legally load the aircraft in such a way that its operational CG will fall outside its operational CG limits.

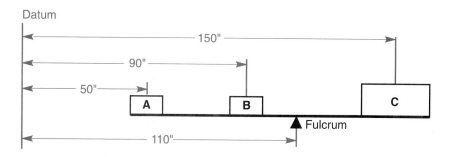

Figure 6-1. *Locating the balance point from a datum located off the board*

In Figure 6-1, we have the board with the three weights, and the datum located 50 inches to the left of the CG of Weight A. The first step in finding the CG of this board is to make a chart such as the one in Figure 6-2.

Weight A weighs 100 pounds and is 50 inches from the datum. Weight B weighs 100 pounds and is 90 inches from the datum. Weight C weighs 200 pounds and is 150 inches from the datum.

Item	Weight	Arm	Moment
Weight A	100	50	5,000
Weight B	100	90	9,000
Weight C	200	150	30,000
	400		44,000

Figure 6-2. *Chart for finding the CG of a board with three weights with the datum located off the board*

Find the CG by dividing the total moment by the total weight.

$$CG = \frac{\text{total moment}}{\text{total weight}}$$

$$= \frac{44,000}{400}$$

$$= 110 \text{ inches from the datum}$$

We can prove that this is the correct CG by finding the arm of each weight from this CG and making a new chart such as the one in Figure 6-3. If the CG is correct, the sum of the moments will be zero.

The new arm of Weight A is 110 – 50 = 60 inches. Since this weight is to the left of the CG, its arm is considered to be negative, or - 60 inches.

The new arm of Weight B is 110 – 90 = -20 inches.

The new arm of Weight C is 150 – 110 = 40 inches. Since it is to the right of the CG, this arm is positive.

Item	Weight	Arm	Moment
Weight A	100	-60	-6,000
Weight B	100	-20	-2,000
Weight C	200	40	8,000
			0

Figure 6-3. *Proof that the board balances at a point 110 inches to the right of the datum. The board is balanced when the sum of the moments is zero.*

The location of the datum used for finding the arms of the weights is not important; it can be anywhere. However, all of the measurements must be made from the same datum. In Figure 6-4 the datum is located at the center of gravity of Weight A.

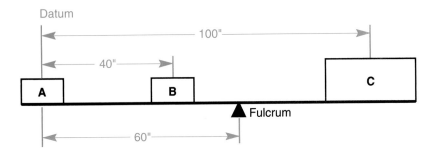

Figure 6-4. *Locating the balance point from a datum located at the CG of Weight A*

The chart in Figure 6-5 shows all of the arms measured from the CG of Weight A.

Item	Weight	Arm	Moment
Weight A	100	0	0
Weight B	100	40	4,000
Weight C	200	100	20,000
	400	60	24,000

Figure 6-5. *Chart for finding the CG of a board with three weights with the datum located at the CG of Weight A*

You will notice that the CG is in exactly the same location as it is in Figure 6-1; it is 20 inches to the right of Weight B.

Move the datum to the center of gravity of Weight C, and the arms will be as they are shown in Figure 6-6. The CG will be 40 inches to the left of this datum, but the CG is still located where it was before.

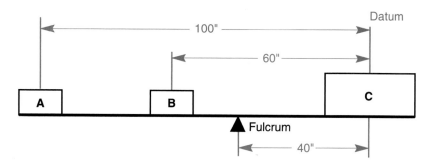

Figure 6-6. *Locating the balance point from a datum located at the CG of Weight C*

Item	Weight	Arm	Moment
Weight A	100	-100	-10,000
Weight B	100	-60	-6,000
Weight C	200	0	0
	400	-40	-16,000

Figure 6-7. *Chart for finding the CG of a board with three weights with the datum located at the CG of Weight C*

An airplane's center of gravity may be found in the same way as locating the CG of a board. The airplane is prepared for weighing and placed on three scales. Any tare weight is subtracted from the scale reading, and the net weight of the wheels is entered into a chart like the one in Figure 6-9. The arms of the weighing points are specified in the Type Certificate Data Sheets for the airplane in terms of fuselage stations, which are distances in inches from the datum. *See* Figure 6-8.

The empty weight of this aircraft is 5,862 pounds, and its empty-weight CG is located at fuselage station 151.1.

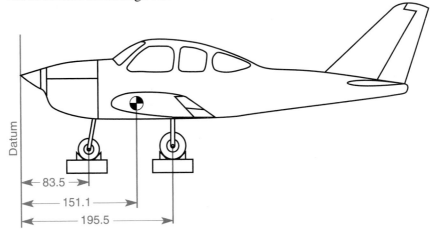

Figure 6-8. *Locating the CG of an airplane whose datum is ahead of the airplane*

Item	Weight	Arm	Moment
Main wheels	3,540	195.5	692,070
Nose wheel	2,322	83.5	193,887
	5,862	151.1	885,957

Figure 6-9. *Chart for finding the CG of an airplane whose datum is ahead of the airplane*

Shifting the CG

One common weight and balance problem involves shifting cargo from one cargo bin to another to move the CG to a desired location. We will begin to study this type of problem by using a board with three weights and will then see the way it is actually done on an airplane.

Solution by Chart

The CG of a board can be moved by shifting the weights. Consider Figure 6-10: as the board is loaded, it balances at a point 56 inches from the CG of Weight A.

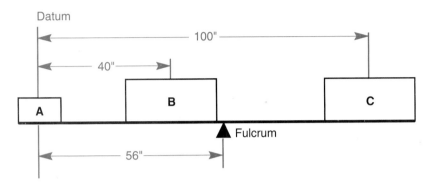

Figure 6-10. *Moving the CG of a board by shifting the weights*

Item	Weight	Arm	Moment
Weight A	100	0	0
Weight B	200	40	8,000
Weight C	200	100	20,000
	500	56	28,000

Figure 6-11. *Chart for shifting the CG of a board by moving one of the weights. This is the original condition of the board.*

To shift Weight B so the board will balance at its center, 50 inches from the CG of Weight A, we must find the arm of Weight B that will produce a moment causing the total moment of all three weights about this point to be zero. The moment of Weight B will have to be -5,000 pound-inches for the board to balance. *See* Figure 6-12.

Item	Weight	Arm	Moment
Weight A	100	-50	-5,000
Weight B			
Weight C	200	50	10,000
			5,000

Figure 6-12. *Finding the moment of Weight B needed to cause the board to balance about its center*

The arm of Weight B is found by dividing its moment, -5,000 pound inches, by its weight of 200 pounds. Its arm is -25 inches.

To balance the board at its center, Weight B will have to be placed so its CG is 25 inches to the left of the center of the board, as seen in Figure 6-13.

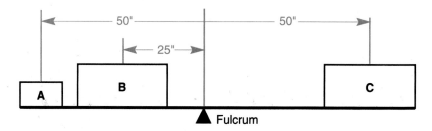

Figure 6-13. *Placement of Weight B to cause the board to balance at its center*

Item	Weight	Arm	Moment
Weight A	100	-50	-5,000
Weight B	200	-25	-5,000
Weight C	200	50	10,000
			0

Figure 6-14. *Proof that the board balances at its center. The board is balanced when the sum of the moments is zero.*

Solution by Formula

This problem can also be worked by using a formula. We want to find the new location of weight B that will shift the CG from 56 inches to 50 inches. The basic formula is:

$$\frac{\text{weight to be shifted}}{\text{total weight}} = \frac{\text{change in CG}}{\text{distance weight is shifted}}$$

We can rearrange this formula to find the distance the weight is to be shifted:

$$\text{distance weight is shifted} = \frac{\text{total weight x change in CG}}{\text{weight shifted}}$$

$$= \frac{500 \text{ x } 6}{200}$$

$$= 15 \text{ inches}$$

The 200-pound Weight B must be shifted 15 inches to the left for the board to balance about a point 50 inches to the right of the datum. Its original arm was 40 inches, and its new arm will be 40 −15 = 25 inches. The sum of the moments about the new CG will be zero. *See* Figure 6-13.

If we know the distance the weight is to be shifted, we can easily find the amount of weight to be shifted to move the CG to any location. To find the amount of weight that will have to be shifted from station 40 to station 25, to move the CG from station 56 to station 50, we can use this arrangement for a basic formula:

$$\text{weight shifted} = \frac{\text{total weight x change in CG}}{\text{distance weight is shifted}}$$

$$= \frac{500 \text{ x } 6}{15}$$

$$= 200 \text{ pounds}$$

If we shift 200 pounds from station 40 to station 25, the CG will move from station 56 to station 50.

Using the same information, we can find the distance the CG will be shifted when we move a 200-pound weight from station 40 to station 25 by using this rearrangement of the basic formula:

$$\text{CG} = \frac{\text{amount of weight shifted} \cdot \text{distance weight is shifted}}{\text{total weight}}$$

$$= \frac{200 \text{ x } 15}{500}$$

$$= 6 \text{ inches}$$

By shifting 200 pounds from station 40 to station 25, the CG of the board will shift 6 inches to the left.

*Answers are on Page 447. **Page numbers refer to chapter text.***

1. The distance between the center of gravity of an object and the fulcrum is called the lever
   _____ . *Page 406*

2. A force that tends to cause an object to rotate is called a/an _____ . *Page 406*

3. Moments are expressed in units of _____ . *Page 406*

4. When a weight is removed from a negative arm, the moment is _____
   (positive or negative). *Page 406*

5. When a weight is added at a negative arm, the moment is _____ (positive or negative).
   Page 406

6. When a weight is removed from a positive arm, the moment is _____
   (positive or negative). *Page 406*

7. When a weight is added to a positive arm, the moment is _____ (positive or negative).
   Page 406

8. The difference between the maximum allowable gross weight of an aircraft and its empty weight is called
   its _____ . *Page 406*

9. If a 40-pound generator has a moment of +1,400 pound-inches, its arm is _____ inches
   from the datum. *Page 407*

Weight and Balance Documentation

FAA-Furnished Information

Before an aircraft can be properly weighed and its empty weight center of gravity computed, certain information must be known. This information is furnished by the Federal Aviation Administration for every certificated aircraft in a form that is available to all technicians.

When the design of an aircraft is approved by the FAA, an Approved Type Certificate (ATC) and Type Certificate Data Sheets (TCDS) are issued. The TCDS includes all of the pertinent specifications for the aircraft, and at each annual or 100-hour inspection, it is the responsibility of the inspecting technician to ensure that the aircraft adheres to these specifications.

The weight and balance information on a Type Certificate Data Sheet includes the following:

Datum: The location of the datum is described in such terms as "Located 100 in. forward of front pressure bulkhead." All arms are measured from the datum, and when it is located ahead of the airplane all of the arms are positive.

Leveling means: A typical method is "Drop plumb line between leveling screws in cabin door frame rear edge." Other methods require a spirit level to be placed across leveling screws or leveling lugs in the primary aircraft structure.

CG range: This is given with the landing gear extended, and the moment change caused by retracting the landing gear is specified.

An example of the CG range is:

> (+135.2) to (+139.2) at 6725 lb.
> (+128.0) to (+139.2) at 5360 lb. or less
> Straight line variation between points given

When this information is given, there will be a chart similar to the one in Figure 6-15 on the TCDS. This chart allows you to visualize the CG range.

spirit level. An instrument used to determine when an object is level, or perpendicular to a line pointing directly toward the center of the earth. A curved glass tube partially filled with a liquid is mounted in a long, straight metal or wood bar. When the bar is perfectly level, the bubble in the liquid is in the center of the curve in the tube.

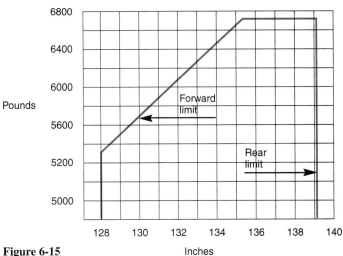

Figure 6-15

Empty weight CG range: When the EWCG is within this EWCG range, it is not possible to legally load the aircraft in such a way that its operational CG will fall outside the acceptable limits. If the aircraft has seats and baggage areas extending over a significant distance, the EWCG range will be listed as "None."

Maximum weight: The maximum allowable takeoff and landing weight and the maximum allowable ramp weight are given. This basic information may be altered by a note such as:

NOTE 5. A landing weight of 6435 lb. must be observed if 10 PR tires are installed on aircraft not equipped with 60-810012-15 (LH) or 60-810012-16 (RH) shock struts.

No. of seats: The number of seats and their arms are given in such terms as "4 (2 at +141, 2 at +173)."

Maximum baggage (structural limit): This is given as:

500 lb. at +75 (nose compartment)
655 lb. at +212 (aft area of cabin)

Fuel capacity: This important information is given in such terms as:

142 gal. (+138) comprising two interconnected cells in each wing, or
204 gal. (+139) comprising three cells in each wing and one cell in each nacelle (four cells interconnected)
See NOTE 1 for data on fuel system.

NOTE 1 will read something like:

NOTE 1. Current weight and balance data including list of equipment included in certificated empty weight and loading instructions when necessary must be provided for each aircraft at the time of original certification.

The certificated empty weight and corresponding center of gravity locations must include unusable fuel of 24 lb. at (+135).

Oil capacity (wet sump): The quantity of the full oil supply and its arm are given in such terms as "26 qt. (+88)."

Type Certificate Data Sheets are issued for aircraft that were certificated after January 1, 1958. Basically the same data on aircraft certificated before this date is included in Aircraft, Engine, or Propeller Specification Sheets.

Weight and balance information on aircraft of which there are less than 50 listed as being certificated is included in a book of Aircraft Listings.

Manufacturer-Furnished Information

When an aircraft is initially certificated, its empty weight and EWCG are determined and recorded in the weight and balance record. An equipment list is furnished with the aircraft that specifies all of the required equipment and all equipment that is approved for installation in the aircraft. The weight and arm of each item is included on the list, and all equipment installed when the aircraft left the factory is checked.

When a technician adds or removes any item that is on the equipment list, the weight and balance record is changed to indicate the new empty weight and EWCG, and the equipment list is changed to show what equipment is actually installed.

STUDY QUESTIONS: WEIGHT AND BALANCE DOCUMENTATION

Answers are on Page 447. Page numbers refer to chapter text.

10. The maximum certificated weight of an aircraft may be found in the _____ for the aircraft. *Page 415*

11. Required equipment that must be carried in an aircraft for it to maintain validity of its Airworthiness Certificate is found in the _____ for the aircraft. *Page 416*

12. The leveling means of an aircraft that must be used when weighing an aircraft may be found in the aircraft _____ . *Page 415*

Weighing the Aircraft

The manufacturer does not weigh every aircraft that comes off its assembly line, but one out of ten aircraft of the same configuration is weighed and its CG is computed. The average weight and CG of these aircraft are considered to be the basic weight and CG of that design, and this information is included in the initial weight and balance record.

When an aircraft has undergone extensive repair or major alteration, it should be weighed and a new weight and balance record started, using the current data specific to that particular aircraft.

Equipment for Weighing

There are two basic types of scales used to weigh aircraft; mechanical and electronic.

Most small general aviation aircraft are weighed with mechanical scales of the low profile type. The scales are placed under the wheels, and the aircraft is leveled both laterally and longitudinally. The weights of any devices such as chocks or tail wheel stands are considered tare weight and must be subtracted from the scale reading to get the actual weight of the aircraft.

A plumb bob is dropped from the datum, and the distances between the datum and the main wheels and the nosewheel or tail wheel weighing points are carefully measured to determine the arms of the weighing points.

Mechanical scales should be protected when they are not in use, and their accuracy should be checked periodically.

Large aircraft are all weighed with electronic weighing systems. These can be either in the form of a ramp-type wheel weigher onto which the aircraft wheel is rolled, or a load cell which is placed between the jack and the jack pad on the aircraft.

The measuring element in an electronic weighing system is a strain gage whose electrical resistance changes as a function of the weight applied to it. This change in resistance is measured with a sensitive bridge-type instrument which can provide a visual indication and/or a printout of the weight.

Preparation for Weighing

When an aircraft is prepared for weighing, it should be as free as possible of all mud and dirt. It should be checked to be sure that all of the required equipment is properly installed, and that no equipment is installed that is not included in the equipment list. Be sure that all required permanent ballast is in place and all temporary ballast is removed. The aircraft should be weighed in a closed hangar where wind cannot blow over the surface and produce a false scale reading.

Fuel should be drained from the tanks in the manner specified by the aircraft manufacturer. If there are no specific instructions, drain the fuel until the fuel quantity gauges read empty when the aircraft is in level-flight attitude. Any fuel remaining in the system is called residual, or unusable, fuel and is part of the aircraft empty weight.

If it is not feasible to drain the fuel, the tanks can be topped off to be sure of the quantity of fuel they contain and the aircraft weighed with full fuel. After the weighing is complete, the weight of the fuel and its moment are subtracted from those of the aircraft. To find the actual empty weight, the residual fuel as specified in the TCDS and its moment must be added. When computing the weight of the fuel, its specific gravity should be measured with a hydrometer because the weight of the fuel, especially jet fuel, varies appreciably with its temperature.

At one time, engine lubricating oil was not considered to be part of the empty weight, and it had to be drained before the aircraft was weighed. Now, 14 CFR Parts 23 and 25 both specify full oil as part of the empty weight. If the aircraft is certificated under any part of the regulations other than 23 or 25, be sure to check whether or not the oil should be drained.

The hydraulic fluid reservoir and all other reservoirs containing fluids required for normal operation of the aircraft should be full. Fluids not considered to be part of the empty weight of the aircraft are potable (drinkable) water, lavatory precharge water, and water for injection into the engines.

Consult the aircraft service manual regarding the position of the control surfaces for weighing. The main rotor of a helicopter must be in its correct position (as identified in its service manual) or it will cause an erroneous CG.

Before some aircraft are jacked for weighing, stress panels or plates must be installed to distribute the weight of the aircraft over the jack pad. Be sure that anytime an aircraft is jacked, the recommendations of the aircraft manufacturer are followed in detail.

STUDY QUESTIONS: WEIGHING AN AIRCRAFT

Answers are on Page 447. Page numbers refer to chapter text.

13. Which, if any, of these items is not considered to be part of the empty weight of an airplane certificated under 14 CFR Part 23: unusable fuel, engine oil, permanent ballast, lavatory water? _____ . *Page 418*

14. When preparing an aircraft certificated under 14 CFR Part 23 for weighing, the engine oil reservoir should be _____ (full or empty). *Page 418*

15. The weight of all the chocks used to prevent an aircraft rolling off the scales is called _____ weight, and it must be subtracted from the scale reading to get the actual weight of the aircraft. *Page 417*

16. Before some aircraft are jacked for weighing, _____ must be installed to distribute the aircraft weight over the jack pads. *Page 419*

Locating the Center of Gravity

We have seen the way to locate the CG of a board, and in this section, we will apply this knowledge to an airplane and locate the CG with respect to the datum and to the mean aerodynamic chord.

Location with Respect to the Datum

When all of the scales have been read and the tare weight subtracted, you are ready to find the center of gravity. There are four possible conditions for determining the CG. For tail wheel airplanes, the datum may be either ahead of the main wheels or behind them, and for nosewheel airplanes the same two conditions apply.

Tail Wheel Airplane with Datum Ahead of Main Wheels

Refer to Figure 6-16. If the datum is ahead of the main wheels, use the formula:

$$CG = D + \left(\frac{R \cdot L}{W} \right)$$

CG = Center of gravity in inches aft of the datum
D = Distance between the datum and the main wheel weighing point
R = Tail wheel net weight
L = Distance between main wheel and tail wheel weighing points
W = Total weight of the aircraft (main wheels + tail wheel)

Example:

Main wheels arm (D)	17.5 inches
Tail wheel to main wheels (L)	245.5 inches
Net weight main wheels	2,233.0 pounds
Net weight tail wheel (R)	217.0 pounds
Total weight of aircraft (W)	2,450.0 pounds

$$CG = D + \left(\frac{R \cdot L}{W} \right)$$

$$= 17.5 + \left(\frac{217 \cdot 245.5}{2,450} \right)$$

$$= 39.24 \text{ inches aft of the datum}$$

By subtracting the arm of the main wheels from the arm of the CG, we find that the CG is 21.74 inches aft of the main wheels.

$$39.24 - 17.5 = 21.74$$

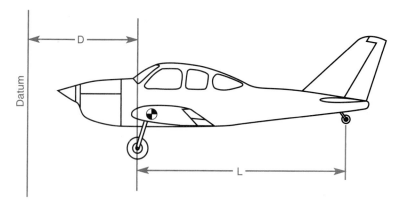

Figure 6-16. *Locating the CG of a tail wheel airplane with the datum ahead of the main wheels*

Tail Wheel Airplane with Datum Behind Main Wheels

Refer to Figure 6-17. If the datum is behind the main wheels, use the formula:

$$CG = -D + \left(\frac{R \cdot L}{W}\right)$$

CG = Center of gravity in inches aft of the datum
D = Distance between the datum and the main wheel weighing point
R = Tail wheel net weight
L = Distance between main wheel and tail wheel weighing points
W = Total weight of the aircraft (main wheels + tail wheel)

Example:

Main wheels arm (D)	30.5	inches
Tail wheel to main wheels (L)	245.5	inches
Net weight main wheels	2,233.0	pounds
Net weight tail wheel (R)	217.0	pounds
Total weight of aircraft (W)	2,450.0	pounds

$$CG = -D + \left(\frac{R \cdot L}{W}\right)$$

$$= -30.5 + \left(\frac{217 \cdot 245.5}{2,450}\right)$$

$$= -8.76 \text{ or } 8.76 \text{ inches ahead of the datum}$$

By subtracting the arm of the CG from the arm of the main wheels, we find that the main wheels are 21.74 inches ahead of the CG.

$$-30.5 - (-8.76) = -21.74$$

This is exactly the same location we found when we used the datum ahead of the main wheels.

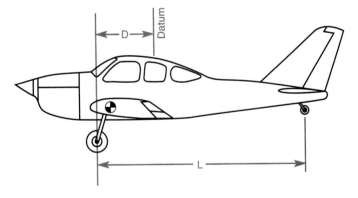

Figure 6-17. *Locating the CG of a tail wheel airplane with the datum behind the main wheels*

Nosewheel Airplane with Datum Ahead of Main Wheels

Refer to Figure 6-18. If the datum is ahead of the main wheels, use the formula:

$$CG = D - \left(\frac{F \cdot L}{W}\right)$$

CG = Center of gravity in inches aft of the datum
D = Distance between the datum and the main wheel weighing point
F = Nosewheel net weight
L = Distance between main wheel and nosewheel weighing points
W = Total weight of the aircraft (main wheels + nosewheel)

Example:

Main gear arm (D)	97.38	inches
Nosewheel to main wheels (L)	87.50	inches
Net weight main wheels	1,506.00	pounds
Net weight nose wheel (F)	122.00	pounds
Total weight of aircraft (W)	1,628.00	pounds

$$CG = D - \left(\frac{F \cdot L}{W}\right)$$

$$= 97.38 - \left(\frac{122 \cdot 87.5}{1,628}\right)$$

$$= 90.82 \text{ inches aft of the datum}$$

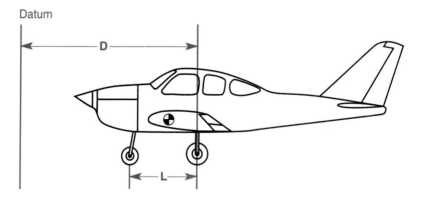

Figure 6-18. *Locating the CG of a nosewheel airplane with the datum ahead of the main wheels*

Nosewheel Airplane with Datum Behind Main Wheels

Refer to Figure 6-19. If the datum is behind the main wheels, use the formula:

$$CG = -\left(D + \frac{F \cdot L}{W}\right)$$

CG = Center of gravity in inches aft of the datum
D = Distance between the datum and the main wheel weighing point
F = Nosewheel net weight
L = Distance between main wheel and nosewheel weighing points
W = Total weight of the aircraft (main wheels + nosewheel)

Example:

Main gear arm (D)	12.5 inches
Nosewheel to main wheels (L)	87.5 inches
Net weight main wheels	1,506.0 pounds
Net weight nose wheel (F)	122.0 pounds
Total weight of aircraft (W)	1,628.0 pounds

$$CG = -\left(D + \frac{F \cdot L}{W}\right)$$

$$= -\left(12.5 + \frac{122 \cdot 87.5}{1,628}\right)$$

$$= 19.06 \text{ inches ahead of the datum}$$

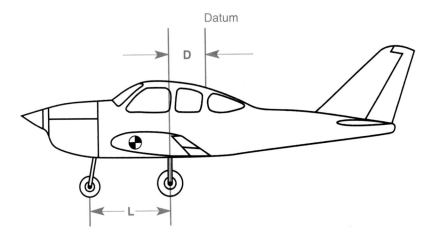

Figure 6-19. *Locating the CG of a nosewheel airplane with the datum behind the main wheels*

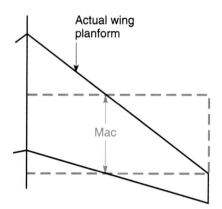

Figure 6-20. *The mean aerodynamic chord (MAC) may be thought of as the chord drawn through the geographic center of the plan area of the wing.*

Actual wing planform

Mac

mean aerodynamic chord. The chord of an imaginary airfoil that has the same aerodynamic characteristics of the actual airfoil. The length of the MAC is given for many aircraft, and the CG is expressed in percent of the mean aerodynamic chord (% MAC).

plan area. The area of a surface as viewed from the top.

LEMAC. Leading edge of the mean aerodynamic chord. When the CG of an airplane is given in % MAC, LEMAC is specified in inches from the datum to allow weight and balance computations to relate % MAC to the datum.

Location with Respect to the Mean Aerodynamic Chord

It means much more to a pilot, flight engineer, or dispatcher to know the location of the CG with respect to the mean aerodynamic chord (MAC) than it does to know its location relative to an arbitrary datum.

The MAC is the chord of an imaginary airfoil that has all of the aerodynamic characteristics of the actual airfoil. It can also be thought of as the chord drawn through the geographic center of the plan area of the wing.

It is important for reasons of stability that the CG of an aircraft be located within a certain percentage of the MAC, and the allowable CG ranges are expressed in terms of the % MAC.

In order to relate the % MAC to the datum, all weight and balance information includes two items: the length of MAC, in inches, and the location of the leading edge of MAC (LEMAC), in inches from the datum.

It is often necessary to shift cargo to move the CG to the proper location relative to the MAC. An example of such a move is given here.

Before the cargo change is made, the following information is known about the airplane:

Aircraft weight	175,000 pounds
CG position	29.5% MAC
MAC	Stations 860.2 to 1040.9

If 6,500 pounds of cargo is removed from an average location of station 1,170.0, what is the new CG position relative to MAC?

Work this problem by following these steps:

1. Find the CG in inches from the datum:

    Length of MAC = (1,040.9 − 860.2) = 180.7 inches
    CG = 29.5% MAC
        = LEMAC + 29.5% MAC
        = 860.2 + (180.7 x .295)
        = 913.5 inches aft of the datum.

2. Construct a chart such as the one in Figure 6-21 to locate the new CG in inches from the datum after the weight has been removed.

3. Divide the new total amount by the new total weight, and find that the new CG is 903.6 inches aft of the datum:

    152,257,500 ÷ 168,500 = 903.6 inches aft of the datum

4. Find the CG location in inches aft of LEMAC:

    903.6 − 860.2 = 43.4 inches aft of LEMAC

5. Find the CG in % MAC by using this formula:

$$CG \text{ in } \% \text{ MAC} = \frac{CG \text{ from LEMAC} \times 100}{MAC}$$

$$= \frac{43.4 \cdot 100}{180.7}$$

$$= 24.0\% \text{ MAC}$$

Item	Weight	Arm	Moment
Aircraft	175,000	913.5	159,862,500
Weight removed	- 6,500	1,170.0	-7,605,000
	168,500	903.6	152,257,500

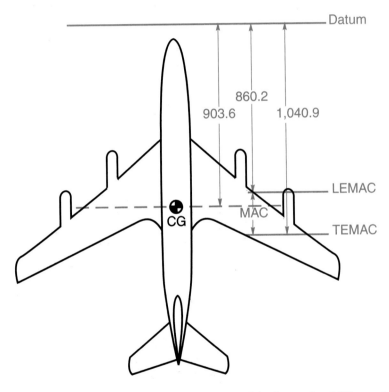

Figure 6-21. *Locating the new CG in inches aft of the datum after 6,500 pounds of cargo has been removed.*

Answers are on Page 447. Page numbers refer to chapter text.

17. An airplane is considered to be in balance when the average moment arm of the loaded aircraft falls within its center of gravity _____ . *Page 406*

18. The fuel used when computing the empty weight CG of an airplane is the _____ fuel. *Page 418*

19. Hydraulic fluid _____ (is or is not) part of the airplane empty weight. *Page 418*

20. An empty aircraft is weighed with a combined net weight at the main gear of 4,251 pounds with an arm of 190.3 inches. The nose gear has a weight of 2,446 pounds with an arm of 80.2 inches. The datum is forward of the nose of the aircraft. The empty weight of the aircraft is _____ pounds, and the empty weight CG is _____ inches from the datum. *Page 422*

21. Find the empty weight and empty weight CG of this airplane:

    Datum is 30.24 inches forward of the main gear center point.
    Actual distance between tail gear and main gear center points, 320.26 inches.
    Net weight at right main gear .... 9,980 pounds
    Net weight at left main gear .... 9,770 pounds
    Net weight at tail gear .... 1,970 pounds

    These items were in the aircraft when it was weighed:

    Lavatory water tank full .... (34 pounds at +352)
    Hydraulic fluid .... (22 pounds at -8)
    Removable ballast .... (146 pounds at +380)

    The airplane empty weight is _____ pounds, and the EWCG is _____ inches aft of the datum. *Page 420*

Single-Engine Aircraft
Weight and Balance Computations

The Pilot's Operating Handbook (POH) for many light single-engine airplanes includes a loading graph and a CG moment index envelope like those in Figures 6-22 and 6-24. These help the pilot determine whether or not the aircraft is loaded in such a way that its operating weight and operating CG fall within the allowable limits.

The Loading Graph

An airplane has an empty weight of 1,340 pounds and an EWCG of +38.5. It carries 40 gallons (240 pounds) of fuel, and the combined weight of the pilot and front seat passenger is 320 pounds. The total weight of two rear seat passengers is 300 pounds, and there is 60 pounds of baggage.

Begin by making a chart such as the one in Figure 6-22 to record the weight and moment index of each of the items. The moment index of the airplane is found by multiplying its weight by its arm and dividing this by the reduction factor of 1,000. Enter this in the chart.

Item	Weight	Arm	Moment/1,000
Aircraft	1,340	38.5	51.6
Front seat	320		11.2
Rear seat	300		21.0
Fuel	240		11.5
Baggage	60		6.7
	2,260		102.0

Figure 6-22. *Chart made by using the loading graph of Figure 6-23 on Page 428*

Find the moment index for the occupants, fuel, and baggage by using the graph in Figure 6-23 on Page 428.

1. For the pilot and front seat occupant, follow a horizontal line for 320 pounds to the right until it intersects the pilot and front seat diagonal. From this intersection, draw a line vertically downward to the moment/1,000 index. It touches this index at 11.2, which is 1,120 pound-inches. Record this in the chart.

Continued

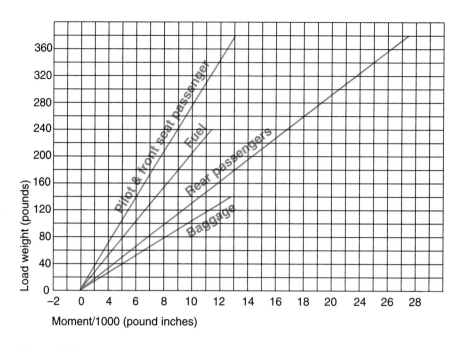

Figure 6-23. *Chart made by using the loading graph of Figure 6-22*

2. Follow a horizontal line for 300 pounds to the right until it intersects the rear seat diagonal. From this intersection, draw a line vertically downward to the moment/1,000 index. It touches this index at 21.0. Record this in the chart.

3. Follow a horizontal line for 240 pounds to the right until it intersects the fuel diagonal. From this intersection, draw a line vertically downward to the moment/1,000 index. It touches this index at 11.5. Record this in the chart.

4. Follow a horizontal line for 60 pounds to the right until it intersects the baggage diagonal. From this intersection, draw a line vertically downward to the moment/1,000 index. It touches this index at 6.7. Record this in the chart.

Add the weights and the moment indexes and refer to the CG moment index envelope chart of Figure 6-24. The total weight is 2,260 pounds, and the total moment index is 102.0 (102,000 pound-inches).

CG Moment Index Envelope

On the CG moment index envelope chart, Figure 6-24, draw a line horizontally to the left from 2,260 pounds on the weight index, and a line vertically upward from the 102 pound-inch/1,000 loaded aircraft moment index. These lines cross inside the Normal Category envelope, showing that the airplane, as loaded, is within the allowable weight and balance limits.

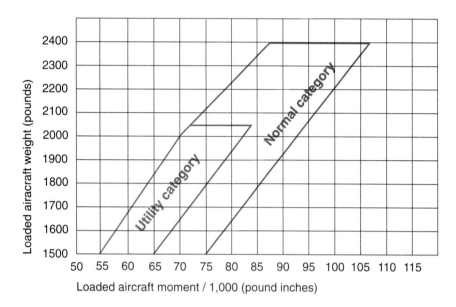

Figure 6-24. *CG moment envelope from Pilot's Operating Handbook*

Twin-Engine Airplane
Weight and Balance Computations

Datum: Forward face of fuselage bulkhead forward of rudder pedals

Location of main gear: +69.2
Location of nose gear: -28.0
MAC: 61.48 inches
LEMAC: +22.26

Seats

Front seat, pilot plus 1: +37.0
Rear seat, 3 occupants: +71.0

Fuel

2 Main tanks, 51 gallons each: +35.0
2 Auxiliary tanks, 20.5 gallons each: +47.0
Unusable fuel (not in fuel capacity) 12 pounds at +44.0

Oil

24 quarts (12 quarts in each engine): -3.3

Continued

Baggage

    Forward 100# limit: -15
    Aft 150# limit: +90

CG Range

    (+38) to (+43.1) at 5,200 pounds
    (+43.6) at 4,800 pounds
    (+32) to (+43.6) at 4,300 pounds or less.

    Straight line variation between points given.

Weighing conditions:

    Fuel: drained
    Oil: full
    Right wheel: 1,084 pounds, tare 8 pounds
    Left wheel: 1,148 pounds, tare 8 pounds
    Nosewheel: 1,196 pounds, tare 8 pounds

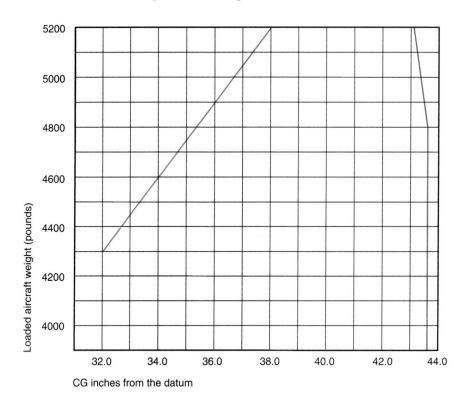

Figure 6-25. *Twin-engine airplane CG range envelope*

Finding the Empty Weight and Empty Weight Center of Gravity

There are two ways of finding the EW and EWCG: the chart method and the formula.

The Chart Method

Construct a chart such as in Figure 6-26.

Divide the total moment by the total weight to find the CG in inches from the datum: CG = 120,611.2 ÷ 3,416 = 35.3 inches aft of the datum.

Item	Weight	Arm	Moment
Right wheel	1,076	69.2	74,459.2
Left wheel	1,140	69.2	78,888.0
Nosewheel	1,188	-28.0	-33,264.0
Unusable fuel	12	44.0	528.0
	3,416	35.3	120,611.2

Figure 6-26. *Chart for finding the EWCG of a light twin-engine airplane*

The Formula Method

The information we are given states that the datum is the forward face of the fuselage bulkhead forward of the rudder pedals. With the datum in this location, we will use this formula:

$$CG = D - \frac{F \cdot L}{W}$$

$$= 69.2 - \frac{1188 \cdot (69.2 + 28.0)}{3,416}$$

$$= 69.2 - \frac{1188 \cdot 97.2}{3,416}$$

$$= 35.3 \text{ inches aft of the datum}$$

Finding the Operational CG

We want to consider loading the airplane in this way:

Pilot .... 170 pounds
Front seat passenger .... 120 pounds
Rear seat passengers
    1 at 120 pounds .... 120 pounds
    1 at 60 pounds .... 60 pounds
Fuel
    Full mains, 102 gallons .... 612 pounds
    Full auxiliaries, 41 gallons .... 246 pounds
Baggage
    Forward compartment .... 100 pounds
    Aft compartment .... 40 pounds

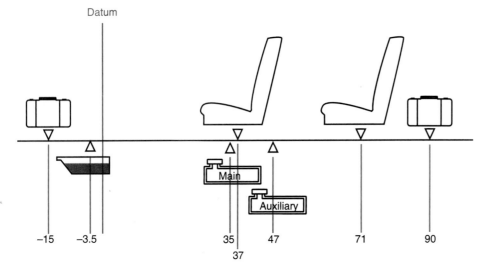

Figure 6-27. *Twin-engine airplane weight and balance diagram*

The Chart Method

Item	Weight	Arm	Moment
Airplane	3,416	35.3	120,585
Front seat	290	37.0	10,730
Rear seat	180	71.0	12,780
Main fuel	612	35.0	21,420
Auxiliary fuel	246	47.0	11,562
Forward baggage	100	-15.0	-1,500
Aft baggage	40	90.0	3,600
	4,884	36.7	179,177

Figure 6-28. *Chart for finding the operational center gravity of the airplane in Figure 6-27*

The operational weight under these conditions is 4,884 pounds, and the CG is located at 36.7 inches aft of the datum.

Plot these values on the CG range chart of Figure 6-25, and note that the weight and the CG are within the allowable limits.

CG in Percent of MAC

The operational CG is 36.7 inches aft of the datum.
The MAC is 61.48 inches long.
The LEMAC is located at station 22.26.
The CG is 36.7 – 22.26 = 14.44 aft of LEMAC.

$$\text{CG in \% MAC} = \frac{\text{CG in inches from LEMAC} \times 100}{\text{MAC}}$$

$$= \frac{14.44 \cdot 100}{61.48}$$

$$= 23.49 \text{ \% MAC}$$

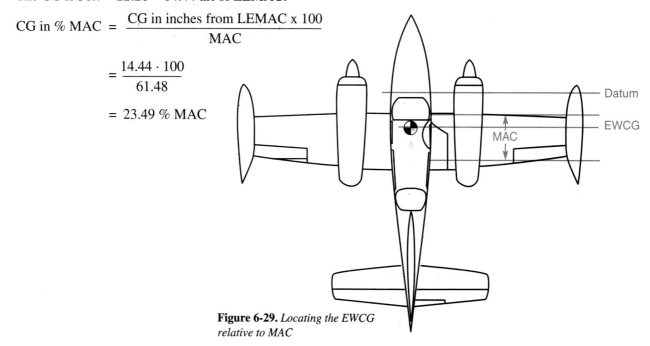

Figure 6-29. *Locating the EWCG relative to MAC*

Adverse-Loaded CG Checks

When an alteration has been made on an aircraft whose specifications do not list an empty-weight center of gravity range, it is wise to make an adverse-loaded CG check to determine whether or not it is possible to load the aircraft in such a way that its operational CG will fall outside of its allowable limits.

For an example of adverse-loaded CG checks, we will use this information:

Airplane EW and EWCG .... 1,340 pounds at +37.0
Engine METO horsepower 165
Maximum allowable gross weight .... 2,400 pounds
CG limits .... +35.6 to +47.5
Pilot .... 170 pounds at +34.5
Front seat passenger .... 170 pounds at +34.5
Rear seat passengers (2) .... 340 pounds at +71.5
Fuel
    Full tanks (40 gallons) .... 240 pounds at +48
    Minimum fuel (METO HP ÷ 2) .... 82.5 pounds at +48
Baggage (maximum) .... 60 pounds at +92

Forward CG Check

To conduct a forward CG check, make a chart that includes the EW and EWCG of the aircraft after the alteration, the pilot, and all passengers and equipment that would move the CG ahead of the forward CG limit. Do not include any passengers or equipment located behind the forward limit. Include full fuel in all tanks located ahead of the forward limit and minimum fuel in all tanks located behind the forward limit. Minimum fuel is no more than the quantity needed for one-half hour of operation at rated maximum continuous power, and is considered for this purpose as being $\frac{1}{12}$ gallon for each maximum except takeoff (METO) horsepower. Minimum fuel, in pounds, is found by dividing the METO horsepower by 2.

Under these conditions the most forward CG of +37.0 is behind the forward limit of +35.6, and is therefore an acceptable condition.

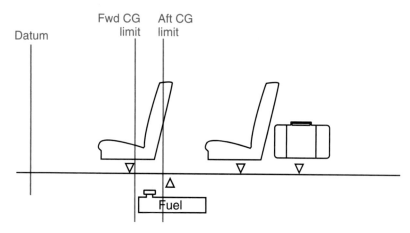

Figure 6-30. *Load conditions for adverse loaded CG checks*

Item	Weight	Arm	Moment
Airplane	1,340.0	37.0	49,580
Pilot	170.0	34.5	5,865
Front seat passenger	170.0	34.5	5,865
Minimum fuel	82.5	48.0	3,960
	1,762.5	37.0	65,270

Figure 6-31. *Chart for finding the most forward center of gravity*

Aft CG Check

To conduct an aft, or rearward, CG check, make a chart that includes the EW and EWCG of the aircraft after the alteration, the pilot, and all passengers and equipment that would move the CG behind the aft CG limit. Do not include any passengers or equipment located ahead the aft limit. Include full fuel in all tanks located behind the aft limit, and minimum fuel in all tanks located ahead of the aft limit.

Under these conditions the most rearward CG of +45.0 is ahead the rearward limit of +47.5, and is therefore an acceptable condition.

Item	Weight	Arm	Moment
Airplane	1,340	37.0	49,580
Pilot	170	34.5	5,865
Full fuel	240	48.0	11,520
Rear seat passengers	340	71.5	24,310
Baggage	60	92.0	5,520
	2,150	45.0	96,795

Figure 6-32. *Chart for finding the most rearward center of gravity*

Answers are on Page 447. **Page numbers refer to chapter text.**

22. No adverse-loaded CG checks are required if the empty-weight CG falls within the empty-weight _____ . *Page 434*

23. When computing the maximum forward-loaded CG of an aircraft, minimum weights, arms, and moments should be used for items of useful load that are located aft of the _____ (forward or aft) CG limit. *Page 434*

24. When computing the maximum rearward-loaded CG of an aircraft, minimum weights, arms, and moments should be used for items of useful load that are located forward of the _____ (forward or aft) CG limit. *Page 435*

Center of Gravity Change After Repair or Alteration

There is no requirement for periodic reweighing of a general aviation aircraft operated under 14 CFR Part 91, but it is the responsibility of any technician performing a repair or alteration that changes the empty weight and/or balance conditions to update the weight and balance information to reflect this change.

We want to find the new EW and EWCG after this alteration has been made.

1. Replace a 30-pound seat at +72 inches with a 20-pound seat whose arm is +73.5 inches.

2. Install a 30-pound radio at +30 inches

We start with the aircraft EW and EWCG found in the current weight and balance information; then construct a chart to compute the total moment and total weight after the alterations have been made. When the total moment and total weight have been found, divide the total moment by the total weight to find the new EWCG. *See* Figure 6-33.

The weight and balance information must be updated to change the EW from 1,800 pounds to 1,820 pounds, and the EWCG from 31.5 inches aft of the datum to 31.3 inches aft of the datum.

Item	Weight	Arm	Moment
Aircraft	1,800	31.5	56,700
Seat (remove)	-30	72.0	-2,160
Seat (install)	20	73.5	1,470
Radio	30	30.0	900
	1,820	31.3	56,910

Figure 6-33. *Chart for locating the center of gravity after a repair*

STUDY QUESTIONS: CG CHANGE AFTER REPAIR OR ALTERATION

Answers are on Page 447. **Page numbers refer to chapter text.**

25. An aircraft with an empty weight of 1,500 pounds and an empty weight CG of +28.4 was altered as follows:
    a. Two seats weighing 12 pounds each, located at +65.5, were removed.
    b. A structural modification increasing the weight by 28 pounds was made at +73.
    c. A seat and safety belt weighing 30 pounds were installed at +70.5.
    d. Radio equipment weighing 25 pounds was installed at +85.
    The new empty weight is _____ pounds, and the new empty weight CG is located _____ inches aft of the datum.
    Page 436

26. An aircraft with an empty weight of 2,100 pounds and an empty weight CG of +32.5 was altered as follows:
    a. A generator weighing 18 pounds, located at -8.0, was removed.
    b. A new propeller which weighs 17 pounds more than the old one was installed at -27.0.
    c. Radio equipment weighing 35 pounds was removed from +30.0.
    The new empty weight is _____ pounds, and the new empty weight CG is located _____ inches aft of the datum.
    Page 436

Determination of Needed Ballast

It sometimes becomes necessary to adjust the balance of an aircraft by adding ballast. This can be temporary ballast needed for certain flight conditions, or it can be permanent ballast needed to bring the EWCG into the allowable range after a repair or alteration has moved it outside its allowable limit.

Temporary ballast, in the form of bags of lead shot or lead bars, is often carried in the baggage compartments to adjust the balance for certain flight conditions. The bags are marked "BALLAST XX POUNDS — REMOVAL REQUIRES WEIGHT AND BALANCE CHECK." Temporary ballast must be secured so it cannot shift its location in flight, and the structural limits of the baggage compartment must not be exceeded.

An airplane whose empty weight is 1,205 pounds has been altered in such a way that its EWCG is +41.0. The forward EWCG limit is +43.2. In order to bring the EWCG into its allowable range, permanent ballast can be attached to a bulkhead at station 260.5. We can find the weight needed for permanent ballast by using this formula:

$$\text{ballast weight} = \frac{\text{aircraft weight x distance out of limits}}{\text{distance between ballast and desired CG}}$$

$$= \frac{1{,}205 \cdot (43.2 - 41)}{(260.5 - 43.2)}$$

$$= \frac{1{,}205 \cdot 2.2}{217.3}$$

$$= 12.2 \text{ pounds}$$

A lead weight weighing 12.2 pounds should be prepared, painted red, and marked as "PERMANENT BALLAST — DO NOT REMOVE." It should be attached to the structure in such a way that it does not interfere with any control action, and attached rigidly enough that it cannot be dislodged by any flight maneuvers or rough landing.

Answers are on Page 447. Page numbers refer to chapter text.

27. The weight of any installed permanent ballast _____ (is or is not) considered to be part of the empty weight of the aircraft. *Page 438*

28. An aircraft has a loaded weight of 4,954 pounds, its forward CG limit is at fuselage station 32.0, and its CG is located at +30.5.
    To move the CG into the allowable range, _____ pounds of ballast will have to be attached at fuselage station 162. *Page 438*

Large Aircraft Weight and Balance Computations

Finding the Maximum Payload

To determine the maximum amount of payload that can be carried, use these values:

Basic operating weight 150,000	pounds
Max. zero fuel weight 230,000	pounds
Max. landing weight 245,000	pounds
Max. takeoff weight 320,000	pounds
Fuel tank load 94,500	pounds
Estimated fuel burn en route 71,500	pounds

Basic Operating Weight (BOW). The weight of the aircraft, including the crew, ready for flight, but without payload and fuel. This term applies only to transport category aircraft.

zero fuel weight. The weight of an aircraft without fuel.

Solve this problem by using these steps:

1. Compute the maximum takeoff (T/O) weight for this trip:

   a. Start with the maximum landing weight of 245,000 pounds, and add the estimated fuel that will be burned en route. This will give the required trip takeoff weight.

   b. Compare the trip takeoff weight with the maximum takeoff weight and use the smaller value for the next step.

Maximum Limit		**Trip Limit**
245,000	landing weight	245,000
	+ trip fuel	+ 71,500
320,000	T/O weight	316,500

Continued

2. Our trip takeoff weight is smaller than the maximum allowed, so we will use it to find the zero fuel weight:

   a. Subtract the fuel load from the trip takeoff weight to find the zero fuel weight.

Maximum Limit		**Trip Limit**
320,000	T/O weight	316,500
	– fuel load	– 94,500
230,000	zero fuel weight	222,000

   b. Our trip zero fuel weight is smaller than the maximum zero fuel weight, so we will use it.

3. Subtract the basic operating weight from the trip zero fuel weight to find the maximum payload it is possible to carry.

Maximum Limit		**Trip Limit**
245,000	zero fuel weight	222,000
	– B.O.W.	– 150,000
	payload	72,000

We can carry 72,000 pounds of payload and a fuel load of 94,500 pounds without exceeding our maximum takeoff weight, landing weight, or zero fuel weight.

Determining Minutes of Fuel Dump Time

We will use this information to determine the number of minutes of dump time needed to reduce the airplane weight to its maximum allowable landing weight:

Three operating engines
171,000 pound cruise weight
142,500 pound maximum landing weight
3,170 lb/hr/engine average fuel flow during dumping and descent
19 minutes from start of dump to landing
2,300 lb/min fuel dump rate

Solve this problem by using these steps:

1. Find the needed weight reduction by subtracting the maximum landing weight from the cruise weight:

$$
\begin{array}{rl}
171,000 & \text{lb cruise weight} \\
- \ 142,500 & \text{lb maximum landing weight} \\
\hline
28,500 & \text{lb needed weight reduction}
\end{array}
$$

2. Find the total amount of fuel burned from beginning of dump to touch-down by multiplying the fuel flow per engine by the number of engines:

$$
\begin{array}{rl}
3,170 & \text{lb/hr/engine fuel flow} \\
\times \ 3 & \text{number of engines} \\
\hline
9,510 & \text{lb/hr (total fuel flow per hour)}
\end{array}
$$

Find the total fuel flow per minute by dividing the total fuel flow by 60:

9,510 lb/hr ÷ 60 = 158.5 lb/min

Multiply the fuel burned per minute by the number of minutes from start of dump to landing:

158.5 lb/min. x 19 min = 3,011.5 lb fuel burned after dumping started

3. Find the amount of fuel needed to dump by subtracting the amount of fuel burned after the dumping started from the needed weight reduction:

$$
\begin{array}{rl}
28,500.0 & \text{lb needed weight reduction} \\
- \ 3,011.5 & \text{lb fuel burned after dumping started} \\
\hline
25,488.5 & \text{lb = amount of fuel to dump}
\end{array}
$$

4. Find the time required to dump the fuel by dividing the amount of fuel to dump by the dump rate:

25,488.5 lb ÷ 2,300 lb/min = 11.08 minutes

STUDY QUESTION: LARGE AIRCRAFT WEIGHT AND BALANCE

Answer is on Page 447. **Page number refers to chapter text.**

29. The maximum allowable weight of a loaded aircraft without the fuel is called the _____ weight of the aircraft. *Page 439*

Weight and Balance Computations with an Electronic Computer

Weight and balance computations for large aircraft can be quite complex, and have for years been computed with slide rule-type devices called load adjusters. Modern electronic flight computers have weight and balance programs written into them that make computing weight and balance easy.

Consider these conditions:

Basic Operating Weight (BOW) = 70,500 pounds
BOW CG = 25.0% MAC
Length of MAC = 164.5 inches
LEMAC = 527.0 – 39.6 = Station 487.4
Cargo
    Compartment A Station 227.5 — 1,000 pounds
    Compartment B Station 317 — 2,000 pounds
    Compartment C Station 407 — 3,500 pounds
    Compartment D Station 497 — 3,500 pounds
    Compartment E Station 587 — 2,500 pounds
    Compartment F Station 677 — 2,500 pounds
    Compartment G Station 766.5 — 1,000 pounds

Fuel — Average location 555.0 — 30,000 pounds

Finding the CG in inches from the datum:

1. Length of MAC = 164.5

   CG = 25% MAC = 487.4 + (164.5 x .25) = 528.5 inches aft of the datum.

2. Construct a chart such as the one in Figure 6-34.

3. Find the CG in inches from the datum by dividing the total moment by the total weight:

   $61,861,250 \div 116,500 = 531$ inches aft of the datum

4. Find the CG location in inches aft of LEMAC:

   $531 – 487.4 = 43.6$ inches aft of LEMAC

Item	Weight	Arm	Moment
Aircraft	70,500	528.5	37,259,250
Fuel	30,000	555.0	16,650,000
Cargo A	1,000	227.5	227,500
Cargo B	2,000	317.0	634,000
Cargo C	3,500	407.0	1,424,500
Cargo D	3,500	497.0	1,739,500
Cargo E	2,500	587.0	1,467,500
Cargo F	2,500	677.0	1,692,500
Cargo G	1,000	766.5	766,500
	116,500	531.0	61,861,250

Figure 6-34. *Chart showing the effect of cargo and fuel on the center of gravity of a large aircraft using arms and moments*

Find the CG in % MAC:

$$\text{CG in \% MAC} = \frac{\text{CG from LEMAC} \cdot 100}{\text{MAC}}$$

$$= \frac{(531 - 487.4) \cdot 100}{164.5}$$

$$= \frac{43.6 \cdot 100}{164.5}$$

$$= 26.5 \text{ \% MAC}$$

The CX-1a Pathfinder electronic flight computer produced by ASA, Inc. (*see* Figure 6-35), handles this type of problem quickly and accurately by using the steps shown in Figure 6-36.

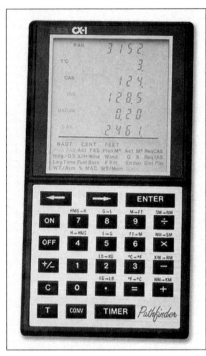

Figure 6-35. *CX-1a electronic flight computer can solve most complex weight and balance problems quickly and accurately.*

1. Press the [ON] button and the [left arrow] one time to enter the WT/Arm program.
2. Press [ENTER] and enter the aircraft weight of 70,500 pounds.
3. Press [ENTER] and enter the arm of the aircraft. This is 528.5 inches.
4. This problem uses very large numbers for the moment, and it would be convenient to use a reduction factor of 1,000. Press [ENTER] and enter the reduction factor of 1,000.
5. Press [ENTER] and enter the weight of the fuel. This is 30,000 pounds.
6. Press [ENTER] and enter the arm of the fuel. This is 555.0 inches.
7. Press [ENTER] and enter the weight of the cargo in compartment A. This is 1,000 pounds.
8. Press [ENTER] and enter the arm of the cargo in compartment A. This is 227.5 inches.
9. Press [ENTER] and enter the weight of the cargo in compartment B. This is 2,000 pounds.
10. Press [ENTER] and enter the arm of the cargo in compartment B. This is 317.0 inches.
11. Press [ENTER] and enter the weight of the cargo in compartment C. This is 3,500 pounds.
12. Press [ENTER] and enter the arm of the cargo in compartment C. This is 407.0 inches.
13. Press [ENTER] and enter the weight of the cargo in compartment D. This is 3,500 pounds.
14. Press [ENTER] and enter the arm of the cargo in compartment D. This is 497.0 inches.
15. Press [ENTER] and enter the weight of the cargo in compartment E. This is 2,500 pounds.
16. Press [ENTER] and enter the arm of the cargo in compartment E. This is 587.0 inches.
17. Press [ENTER] and enter the weight of the cargo in compartment F. This is 2,500 pounds.
18. Press [ENTER] and enter the arm of the cargo in compartment F. This is 677.0 inches.
19. Press [ENTER] and enter the weight of the cargo in compartment G. This is 1,000 pounds.
20. Press [ENTER] and enter the arm of the cargo in compartment G. This is 766.5 inches.
21. Press [ENTER] and the CG of 531.0 appears on the display. This is 531.0 inches aft of the datum.
22. Press [left arrow] to return to the menu and then press [right arrow] to enter the % MAC program.
23. Press [ENTER] and enter the length of MAC. This is 164.5 inches.
24. Press [ENTER] twice and enter LEMAC. This is 487.4 inches aft of the datum.
25. Press [ENTER] and 26.5 % MAC appears on the display. The CG is located at 26.5% MAC.

Figure 6-36. *Step-by-step solution for finding the center of gravity of a large aircraft in % MAC using an electronic flight computer*

The electronic flight computer can also be used if the information is given in terms of weight and moment index.

If the weight and balance information is furnished by charts or tables that list the weight and a moment index, use the steps on the CX-1a computer shown in Figure 6-38 on Page 446.

Item	Weight	Moment/1,000
Aircraft	70,500	37,259
Fuel	30,000	16,650
Cargo A	1,000	227
Cargo B	2,000	634
Cargo C	3,500	1,424
Cargo D	3,500	1,739
Cargo E	2,500	1,467
Cargo F	2,500	1,692
Cargo G	1,000	766
	116,500	61,861

Figure 6-37. *Chart showing the effect of cargo and fuel on the center of gravity of a large aircraft using weights and moment indices*

1. Press the [ON] button and the [left arrow] one time and the [right arrow] twice to enter the *WT/Mom* program.
2. Press [ENTER] and enter the aircraft weight of 70,500 pounds.
3. Press [ENTER] and enter the moment index of the aircraft. This is 37,259 pound-inches/1,000.
4. The reduction factor used to get the moment index is 1,000. Press [ENTER] and enter the reduction factor of 1,000.
5. Press [ENTER] and enter the weight of the fuel. This is 30,000 pounds.
6. Press [ENTER] and enter the moment index of the fuel. This is 16,650.
7. Press [ENTER] and enter the weight of the cargo in compartment A. This is 1,000 pounds.
8. Press [ENTER] and enter the moment index of the cargo in compartment A. This is 227.
9. Press [ENTER] and enter the weight of the cargo in compartment B. This is 2,000 pounds.
10. Press [ENTER] and enter the moment index of the cargo in compartment B. This is 634.
11. Press [ENTER] and enter the weight of the cargo in compartment C. This is 3,500 pounds.
12. Press [ENTER] and enter the moment index of the cargo in compartment C. This is 1,424.
13. Press [ENTER] and enter the weight of the cargo in compartment D. This is 3,500 pounds.
14. Press [ENTER] and enter the moment index of the cargo in compartment D. This is 1,739.
15. Press [ENTER] and enter the weight of the cargo in compartment E. This is 2,500 pounds.
16. Press [ENTER] and enter the moment index of the cargo in compartment E. This is 1,467.
17. Press [ENTER] and enter the weight of the cargo in compartment F. This is 2,500 pounds.
18. Press [ENTER] and enter the moment index of the cargo in compartment F. This is 1,692.
19. Press [ENTER] and enter the weight of the cargo in compartment G. This is 1,000 pounds.
20. Press [ENTER] and enter the moment index of the cargo in compartment G. This is 766.
21. Press [ENTER] and the CG of 531.0 appears on the display. This is 531.0 inches aft of the datum.
22. Press [left arrow] to return to the menu and then press [left arrow] to enter the % MAC program.
23. Press [ENTER] and enter the length of MAC. This is 164.5 inches.
24. Press [ENTER] twice and enter LEMAC. This is 487.4 inches aft of the datum.
25. Press [ENTER] and 26.5 % MAC appears on the display. The CG is located at 26.5% MAC.

Figure 6-38. *Step-by-step solution for finding the center of gravity of a large aircraft in % MAC with an electronic flight computer using moment indices*

Answers to Chapter 6 Study Questions

1. arm
2. moment
3. pound-inches
4. positive
5. negative
6. negative
7. positive
8. useful load
9. +35
10. Type Certificate Data Sheet
11. equipment list
12. Type Certificate Data Sheet
13. lavatory water
14. full
15. tare
16. stress plates
17. range
18. unusable
19. is
20. 6,697, 150.1
21. 21,540, +56.7
22. CG range
23. forward
24. aft
25. 1,559, +30.35
26. 2,064, +32.4
27. is
28. 57.16
29. zero fuel

MATERIALS AND PROCESSES

7

Continued

MATERIALS AND PROCESSES

7

The development of new "space age" materials for both aircraft structure and engines has made the vast progress of aviation possible. The basic structure of most of the earliest flying machines were made of strips of spruce or bamboo, and the lifting surfaces were covered with cotton or linen cloth. After World War I, welded steel tubing replaced the wooden truss used for the fuselage structure of most of the new airplanes. And it was during the 1920s that formed plywood became used for the primary structure of some of the most streamlined and high-strength aircraft of the time.

The technological developments made during World War II allowed the all-metal, stressed-skin, monocoque structure to replace the fabric-covered truss structure in the vast majority of aircraft. This technology was standard until the last few decades when resins reinforced with various types of composite materials have allowed us to build structural shapes that are superior to metals in strength, weight, and rigidity.

This section will consider some of the materials used in aircraft construction, and will look at some of the processes used to adapt these basic materials to aircraft use.

Materials

In this section we will consider both metallic and nonmetallic materials used in the construction of modern aircraft. In the study of metals, we will look at both ferrous and nonferrous metals and discuss the various methods of their heat treatment. In the discussion of nonmetals, we will discuss the natural materials, wood and fabric, and will also introduce some of the modern composite materials.

Metals

The basic classifications of metals for aircraft structure are ferrous and nonferrous. A ferrous metal is one that contains iron, and in this classification are the various types of steel. Nonferrous metals include aluminum, magnesium, titanium, and monel.

ferrous metal. A metal that contains iron.

Ferrous Metals

Most of the steel used in aircraft structure is classified according to the SAE four-digit numbering system that identifies its composition. In this system, the digits have the following meaning:

First digit: basic alloying element
Second digit: the percentage of the basic element in the alloy
Third and fourth digits: percentage of carbon in the alloy in hundredths of a percent

For example, SAE 1020 steel is low-carbon steel that contains 0.20% carbon.

Some of the most commonly used SAE steels are:

1xxx Carbon steel
Steels containing between 0.10% and 0.30% carbon (SAE 1010 and 1030) are classed as low-carbon steels and are used for making safety wire and certain secondary structural parts where strength is not critical.
Steels containing between 0.30% and 0.50% carbon (SAE 1030 and 1050) are medium-carbon steels and are used for machined and forged parts, especially where surface hardening is needed.
Steel containing between 0.50% and 1.05% carbon (SAE 1050 and 1150) are high-carbon steel and are used where extreme hardness is required. Springs are made of high-carbon steel.

2xxx Nickel steel
Between 3% and 3.75% nickel may be alloyed with carbon steel to increase its hardness, tensile strength, and elastic limit without appreciably decreasing its ductility. SAE 2330 steel is used for aircraft bolts, cable terminals, keys, clevises, and pins.

3xxx Nickel-chromium steel
Nickel gives toughness to steel, and chromium hardens it. Nickel-chromium steels such as SAE 3130 and 3250 are used for forged and machined parts where high strength, ductility, toughness, and shock resistance are needed.

41xx Chrome-molybdenum steel
Most aircraft structural steel is a chrome-molybdenum alloy that combines toughness and high strength with ease of welding and machining. SAE 4130 is one of the most popular alloys, and it is used extensively for welded steel structure such as fuselage frames, landing gear, and engine mounts. Engine cylinders and other highly stressed parts are often made of SAE 4130 steel.

6xxx Chrome-vanadium steel
Chrome-vanadium steels are used extensively for wrenches and other hand tools where extremely high strength and toughness are essential.

Corrosion-resistant steel, commonly called stainless steel, is not normally classified in the SAE system, rather it is identified by a three-digit system. The 300 series of stainless steel contains approximately 18% chromium and 8% nickel, and the 200 series contains some manganese. Both alloys are nonmagnetic and neither can be hardened by heat treatment. Aircraft fire-walls are usually made of 300 series stainless steel at least 0.015 inch thick.

The 400 series of stainless steel has gained popularity as knife blades and razor blades because it can be hardened by proper heat treatment, and it is magnetic.

Nonferrous Metals

Welded steel tubular trusses formed the primary structures of metal aircraft until advances were made with aluminum alloys. Pure aluminum is light-weight and corrosion resistant, but it lacks strength for use as a structural material. When other elements are mixed with it to increase its strength, it becomes susceptible to corrosion. Only when it became possible to protect aluminum alloys from corrosion did they become popular as an aircraft structural material—so popular, that today, most metal aircraft are made from aluminum alloys.

Aluminum Alloys

Most aluminum alloys used in aircraft structure are identified by a four-digit system. These digits have the following meaning:

First digit — Alloy type
Second digit — Modification of alloy
Third and fourth digits — Purity of aluminum*

*The last two digits are also used for the old designation of alloys in use before the adoption of the four-digit system.

Figure 7-1 lists the most generally used alloy types for aircraft structural aluminum.

Alloy 1100 is a low-strength, commercially pure aluminum that can only be used in non-structural applications where strength is not important. It has high thermal and electrical conductivity, good corrosion resistance, and is easy to work.

Alloy 2024 is the most popular structural aluminum alloy. Copper is its chief alloying agent and it can be hardened by solution heat treatment. Its strength is equivalent to that of mild steel, but it is susceptible to corrosion.

Alloy 3003 is similar to 1100 and is used for the same types of applications. Its chief alloying element is manganese. It is non-heat-treatable, but it can be hardened by cold working.

Alloy Type	Number Group
Aluminum 99+% pure	1xxx
Copper	2xxx
Manganese	3xxx
Silicon	4xxx
Magnesium	5xxx
Magnesium and silicon	6xxx
Zinc	7xxx

Figure 7-1. *Identification of aluminum alloys*

Alloy 5052 is used for welded applications such as fuel tanks and for rigid fluid lines. Magnesium is its chief alloying agent, and it cannot be heat treated, but it can be hardened by cold working. When it is exposed to temperatures above 150°F, or when it is excessively cold worked, its susceptibility to corrosion increases.

Alloy 6061 is a silicon and magnesium alloy and is used in applications where heat treatability, ease of forming, medium strength, and good corrosion resistance are needed.

Alloy 7075 is a zinc alloy with copper and chromium added. It is heat treatable and is used for high-strength structural requirements.

Pure aluminum is basically noncorrosive, but aluminum alloys are susceptible to corrosion. A standard structural material is clad aluminum in which a sheet of high-strength aluminum alloy has a coating of pure aluminum rolled onto its surfaces when the sheet is formed in the rolling mill. This material, called Alclad or Pureclad, has slightly less strength than an unclad sheet of the same thickness, but its corrosion resistance makes it a desirable material for aircraft skins that will not be protected with paint.

Magnesium Alloys

Magnesium is the lightest structural metal, weighing only about two thirds as much as aluminum. Pure magnesium does not have enough strength for use as a structural material, but when it is alloyed with aluminum, zinc, or manganese, its strength becomes sufficient.

Magnesium can be cast, forged, or rolled into thin sheets. It has two basic drawbacks as a structural material; it is highly susceptible to corrosion, and it has a tendency to crack when it is subjected to excessive vibration.

Under certain conditions magnesium can ignite and burn. Large sections have a high thermal conductivity and are difficult to ignite, but magnesium dust and fine chips are easily ignited. If a magnesium fire should occur, it should be extinguished by smothering it with dry sand or a dry-powder fire extinguisher. Water and foam type fire extinguishers should never be used because they can cause it to burn with a greater intensity.

Titanium

Titanium is a metal that has been developed within the past fifty years into an important aircraft structural material. It is lightweight and corrosion resistant, and has high structural strength which it retains to a high temperature. It is used in turbine engines, and for aircraft skins in areas where the temperature is high.

Titanium may be worked by methods similar to those used with stainless steel, but it requires some special techniques, and the tools used must be kept very sharp. It may be welded, but because it reacts with oxygen at high temperatures, it must be protected from the air with a blanket of helium or argon gas. For this reason, inert-gas arc welding is used.

clad aluminum. An aluminum alloy sheet that has a coating of pure aluminum rolled onto its surfaces. Aluminum alloys are corrosive, but pure aluminum is not. The pure aluminum cladding protects the core alloy sheet from corrosion.

Alclad. The registered trade name for clad aluminum alloy sheets.

Pureclad. A registered trade name for clad aluminum alloy sheets.

Monel

Monel is an alloy of nickel and copper with small amounts of iron and manganese. Monel is used for applications that demand high strength and high resistance to corrosion. Its low coefficient of expansion makes it useful in the exhaust systems for aircraft engines.

Nonmetal Materials

Very little metal was used in the first airplanes because wood and fabric were much lighter and the requirements for strength were not so great. But as aircraft speeds increased, so did their structural loads. Metal replaced wood and fabric, and for years, all-metal aircraft were considered to be state-of-the-art technology. Today plastic resins reinforced with fibers made of glass, aramid, carbon, and boron are proving to be superior in many applications to metals. Modern high-performance aircraft contain many of these composite materials.

Aircraft Wood

Sitka spruce is the reference wood for aircraft structures. It is straight grained, lightweight, and easy to work. It is used for wing spars and fuselage stringers in some of the older truss-type airplanes. Spruce has been replaced by extruded aluminum alloys in almost all applications and it is seldom used today in anything but amateur-built aircraft.

Propellers for low-horsepower engines were at one time made of strips of birch wood glued together in such a way that the grain of all of the layers ran in the same direction. This laminated wood was uniform in weight and its strength was concentrated along its length.

Plywood is made by gluing sheets of thin wood veneer together with the grain of alternate layers lying at 45° or 90° to that of the adjacent layers. Wood veneer can also be molded into complex-shaped plywood in special heated forms, or molds.

Mahogany plywood can be used for the outside skin for monocoque structure, and birch plywood is used to reinforce spruce wing spars at points where the spars take compressive loads.

Aircraft Fabrics

Long staple cotton fiber woven into a cloth with 80 threads per inch in both the warp and fill directions has been used as the standard covering material for truss-type airplanes for years. This material, known as Grade-A cotton, weighs approximately four ounces per square yard and has a tensile strength of 80 pounds per inch.

Irish linen, having approximately the same weight and strength, was approved for all applications that called for Grade-A cotton. Linen and cotton fabrics are both shrunk with dope.

Natural fabrics are being replaced with fabrics made of synthetic fibers. Polyester fibers woven into fabrics are available in three weights: 1.8-ounce-per-square yard material has a strength of 60 pounds per inch; 2.7-ounce material has a strength of 95 pounds per inch; and 3.7-ounce material has a strength of 130 pounds per inch.

Polyester fabric is shrunk onto the structure with heat and is finished with a special nontautening dope.

Composite Materials

Just as metal replaced wood and fabric, new generations of aircraft are being made of materials destined to replace much of the metal in aircraft structure. These materials are plastic resins reinforced with filaments of glass, carbon, Kevlar, and boron. Let's look first at the resins used as the matrix for these reinforcing fibers.

Plastic Resins

Plastics have replaced so many materials in our daily life that we take them for granted, and we sometimes fail to appreciate this family of truly wonderful materials. In this section we will consider the resins used in aircraft construction and the materials that are used to reinforce them. We can basically divide plastic resins into two groups: thermoplastic and thermosetting.

Thermoplastic Resins

Thermoplastic resins are those that can be softened by heat and will again become hard when they cool down. The most widely used application for thermoplastic resins in modern aircraft construction is for windshields and side windows.

Many of the earlier thermoplastic resins were made of cellulose, a derivative of cotton. Cellulose nitrate was one of the first thermoplastic resins, and it had the drawback of being highly flammable. Cellulose acetate has most of its characteristics and is less flammable.

Cellulose acetate was used for windshields and side windows on many of the very early lightplanes. When viewed along its edge, it has a slightly yellow tint, and when it is exposed to sunlight it becomes brittle, discolors, and shrinks. It will burn, and when it ignites it produces a smoky, sputtering flame and an unpleasant odor. Acetone will dissolve cellulose acetate material.

Acrylic resins sold under the trade names of Plexiglas, Lucite, and Perspex have almost completely replaced cellulose acetate resins in aircraft construction. Acrylics are more transparent, and are considerably stiffer than cellulose acetate.

Thermosetting Resins

A thermosetting resin will not soften when it is heated, and it will char and burn before it melts. The most important application for thermosetting resins in aircraft construction is as a matrix to hold filaments of glass, graphite, aramid, and other materials. These reinforced resins are widely used under the collective name of composites.

Polyester Resin

Polyester resins are popular for aircraft construction. Pure polyester is thick and unworkable, so it is mixed with another form of resin called styrene. If a mixture of polyester and styrene resins is allowed to sit for a time it will cure into a solid mass, so inhibitors are added to prevent this unwanted hardening. When you are ready to use the resin, add a catalyst that suppresses the inhibitors and allows the polyester molecules to join together and cure; the curing time may be decreased by adding a small amount of another chemical, called an accelerator.

Polyester resins cure when heat causes the individual molecules to join together to form chains. Part of this heat is produced within the resin by the chemical action between the catalyst and the accelerator. It is this internal heat that causes a thick layer of resin to cure more rapidly than a thin layer because the thick layer slows the escape of the heat.

Polyester resins shrink as they cure. This is helpful when bonding metal fittings into a fiberglass structure as the shrinkage tightens the grip on the metal. Care must be taken when applying long strips of fiberglass tape over a flat surface so that the shrinkage does not distort the base surface. To prevent this distortion, several short lengths of tape may be used rather than a single long piece.

Special care must be exercised when mixing polyester resins to use the exact procedure recommended by the resin manufacturer. Do not mix ingredients from different manufacturers. Use accurate scales and clean containers, and do not use polyesters when the temperature is lower than 65°F or higher than 85°F. Mix enough extra resin to make a test layup. If this test layup, made with identical resin and using identical procedures, gives the results you want, you may proceed confidently with the actual job.

Epoxy Resin

Epoxy resins are strong, resistant to moisture and chemicals and have extremely good adhesion characteristics. There are many different types of epoxy resins, and they are used as the matrix for many of the advanced composite materials.

Epoxy resins differ from polyester resins in that epoxy uses a curing agent rather than a catalyst. A typical mix of polyester resin calls for 64 ounces of resin and 1 ounce of catalyst to produce 64 ounces of catalyzed resin. A typical epoxy resin calls for mixing 1 part of curing agent with 4 parts of resin to produce 5 parts of material.

Reinforcing Materials

The resins just discussed are used only to bond fibers of various materials together. It is the fibers themselves that produce the strength and rigidity that make composite structures of such importance in aircraft construction. In this section we will discuss the fibers most widely used in aircraft construction.

Glass Fibers

Glass fibers were one of the first reinforcing materials for aircraft composite construction and they are still used for many applications even though they weigh more and have less strength than many of the other fibers.

There are two types of fiberglass cloth for use in aircraft construction: E glass is the original glass fabric, and S glass, which is stronger, tougher, and stiffer, and weighs slightly less than E glass.

Fiberglass is available in several forms. Fiberglass mat is a collection of fibers pressed loosely together with just enough polyester resin to hold them in place. Mat is used as a fill when low cost is more important than strength. Roving is similar to mat, but the fibers are formed into a long loose strand. Bidirectional cloth is woven of glass fibers with the major fiber bundles running in both the length of the fabric (warp threads) and width of the fabric (fill threads). Unidirectional cloth has all of the major fiber bundles running in the direction of the length of the fabric, and they are woven together with small cross fibers that do not carry any of the load.

Kevlar

Kevlar is an aramid fiber that is exceptionally well adapted for use in aircraft structure. It has high tensile strength and excellent stiffness, toughness, and resistance to impact, and it is lighter than either glass or graphite. It is available in both bidirectional and unidirectional cloths.

Graphite

Thin filaments of graphite, or carbon, are made into both bidirectional and unidirectional sheets. It is extremely stiff and strong, and is more brittle than Kevlar. It has the problem of being corrosive when it is bonded directly to aluminum alloys. By orienting several layers of unidirectional graphite fabric in the correct directions, aircraft structures can be made rigid enough to withstand flight loads not tolerated by more conventional types of aircraft construction.

Answers are on Page 524. **Page numbers refer to chapter text.**

1. The most generally used metal for aircraft firewalls is _____ . *Page 455*

2. Most welded steel aircraft structure is made of SAE steel _____ . *Page 454*

3. Clad aluminum alloy has a coating of _____ rolled onto its surfaces to improve its corrosion resistance. *Page 456*

4. SAE 1020 steel has a carbon content of _____ %. *Page 454*

5. Commercially pure aluminum is identified by the code number _____ . *Page 455*

6. Identify the series numbers for aluminum alloys that have the following major alloys:
   a. copper _____
   b. magnesium_____
   c. zinc _____
      Page 455

7. Titanium can be welded by using _____ electric arc welding. *Page 456*

8. The reference wood used for aircraft construction is _____ . *Page 457*

9. Grade-A cotton fabric has a tensile strength of _____ pounds per inch. *Page 457*

10. Polyester fabric is shrunk on an aircraft structure with _____ . *Page 458*

11. Resins that are reinforced with glass filaments to make aircraft structural components are _____ (thermoplastic or thermosetting) resins. *Page 459*

12. Catalysts are used with _____ (polyester or epoxy) resins to cause them to cure. *Page 459*

Continued

13. Curing agents are used rather than catalysts when mixing _____ (polyester or epoxy) resins. *Page 459*

14. Glass cloth that is woven with both warp and fill threads is called _____ (bidirectional or unidirectional) cloth. *Page 460*

15. Kevlar is _____ (lighter or heavier) than fiberglass fabric of equal strength. *Page 460*

Metal Heat Treatment

critical temperature of a metal. The temperature at which the internal structure of a metal takes on a crystalline form.

There is a direct relationship between the hardness of most metal alloys and their tensile strength. This allows a metal to be strengthened by hardening, or softened for ease of working, when its strength is not critical. In this section we will look at various methods of hardening and softening both ferrous and nonferrous metals.

Ferrous Metal Heat Treatment

A pure metal (a single chemical element) does not appreciably change its structure as it is heated and cooled. If it is heated to a temperature above its critical temperature and allowed to cool to room temperature, it will return to its original structure.

This is not true, however, for most alloys, because when they are heated, the alloying elements go into a solid solution with the base metal, and the structure of the metal changes.

Hardening

steel. An alloy of iron that usually contains between 0.1 and 1.5% carbon with other elements used to give it desirable characteristics.

The internal structure of steel determines its hardness. At room temperature, carbon in the steel exists in the form of iron carbide scattered throughout the basic iron structure, which is called ferrite. The number of these iron carbide particles, their size, and their distribution within the ferrite determine the hardness of the steel at room temperatures.

iron carbide. The form in which carbon exists in steel. The amount of iron carbide and its distribution in the metal determine the hardness of the steel.

The hardness of heat-treated steel can be controlled by the rate of cooling through the critical range, and this rate is determined by the quenching (soaking) liquid used. The fastest quench, using brine, produces the hardest steel. Water produces slightly less hardness, and oil produces the least.

ferrite steel. Alpha iron into which some carbon has been dissolved. It exists at temperatures below its critical temperature.

Normalizing

Normalizing is a method of strain-relieving steel parts. When a steel part is forged or welded, or after certain types of machining, stresses are left in the metal that can cause distortion or cracking. To relieve these stresses, the metal is heated to a temperature above its critical temperature and allowed to cool in still air. Normalizing removes stresses and improves the grain structure, toughness, and ductility of the metal.

Annealing

Annealing of steel is accomplished by heating the metal to just above the upper critical point, soaking it at this temperature, and then cooling it very slowly in the furnace. Annealing produces a fine-grain, soft, ductile metal without internal stresses or strains. In the annealed state, steel has its lowest strength.

Figure 7-2 lists the temperature ranges for hardening, normalizing, and annealing of various steel alloys.

SAE Alloy	Temperature °F			Quenching Medium
	Hardening	Normalizing	Annealing	
1020	1,575 - 1,675	1,650 - 1,750	1,600 - 1,700	Water
2330	1,450 - 1,500	1,475 - 1,525	1,425 - 1,475	Oil
3140	1,475 - 1,525	1,600 - 1,650	1,500 - 1.550	Oil
4130	1,575 - 1,625	1,600 - 1,700	1,525 - 1,575	Oil
6150	1,550 - 1,625	1,600 - 1,650	1,525 - 1,575	Oil

Figure 7-2. *Temperature ranges for heat treating steel alloys*

Tempering

After steel is hardened, it can be tempered to remove some of the internal stresses and brittleness. Tempering is done by holding it at an elevated temperature as seen in Figure 7-3 for a period of time and then allowing it to cool in still air.

SAE Alloy	Tempering Temperature in °F for Tensile Strength in PSI				
	100,000	125,000	150,000	180,000	200,000
1020					
2330	1,100	950	800		
3140	1,325	1,075	925	775	700
4130		1,050	900	700	575
6150		1,200	1,000	900	800

Figure 7-3. *Tempering temperatures for various steel alloys to obtain the indicated tensile strength*

Small tools such as screwdrivers, punches, and chisels must be tempered after they are hardened to remove some of the hardness and brittleness. Since few shops have access to sophisticated temperature measuring instruments, you can accurately indicate the temperature by watching the color of oxides that form on the steel.

To properly temper a tool, first harden it by heating it to a cherry red and then quenching it in oil or water. Then, polish the hardened steel and reheat it until the correct color of oxide forms on the polished surface. The first oxides that form are pale yellow, and they progress through darker yellow, brown, purple, and shades of blue. When the correct color of oxide forms, quench the tool again. *See* Figure 7-4.

Tool	Oxide color	Temperature	
		°F	°C
Scribers, scrapers & hammer faces	pale yellow	428	220
	straw	446	230
Center punches & drills	golden yellow	469	243
Cold chisels & drifts	brown	491	255
	brown with purple spots	509	265
Screwdrivers	purple	531	277
	dark blue	550	288
	bright blue	567	297
	pale blue	610	321

Figure 7-4. *Tempering of small tools by observing the color of the oxides that form when the steel is heated*

case hardening. A type of metal heat treatment in which the surface of the metal is hardened and made brittle while the core of the material remains strong and tough.

Case Hardening

Case hardening, both nitriding and carburizing, produces a hard, wear-resistant surface on the metal, and leaves the core strong and tough. Steels most suitable for case hardening have a low carbon content. Low-alloy steels are best suited for case hardening, because some alloying elements tend to interfere with the absorption of the carbon into the surface.

nitriding. A method of case hardening steel by heating it in an atmosphere of ammonia. The nitrogen in the ammonia reacts with the surface of the steel to form extremely hard nitrides.

Nitriding is a form of case hardening for steel in which the surface of the steel is changed into a layer of a nitride.

The steel part is heated in a retort in which there is an atmosphere of ammonia, a compound of nitrogen and hydrogen. Aluminum, an alloying element in the steel, combines with the nitrogen and forms an extremely hard aluminum nitride surface on the steel. Nitriding does not change the dimension of the part, and it causes less distortion than other types of case hardening.

Carburizing is a case hardening process in which additional carbon is infused into the surface of a low-carbon steel. This gives the steel a high-carbon surface that can be hardened to a depth ranging from 0.01 to 0.06 inch, while the low-carbon center remains relatively soft and tough.

One method of carburizing is to heat the steel in a furnace whose atmosphere contains a great deal of carbon monoxide. The carbon in the gas combines with the gamma iron surface of the steel to form the high-carbon surface. A more common method, called pack carburizing, is done by placing the steel part in a container and packing it with charcoal and other materials rich in carbon. The container is sealed with fire clay and placed in a furnace where it is heated to 1,700°F and soaked at this temperature for several hours. Carbon monoxide gas forms inside the container and combines with the gamma iron in the surface of the steel to form the high-carbon surface.

Nonferrous Metal Heat Treatment

Heat treatment of aluminum, magnesium, and titanium alloys differs in some ways from heat treatment of ferrous metals.

Aluminum and Magnesium Alloys

Several of the aluminum and magnesium alloys may be hardened by solution heat treatment. Unlike ferrous metals, these alloys are not hard when they are first removed from the quenching medium, rather they gain their full strength and hardness by natural aging over a period of a few days. To further strengthen these alloys, they may be artificially aged by a process called precipitation heat treatment.

Solution Heat Treatment

Some aluminum alloys may be hardened by heating them in a furnace until they have reached a specified temperature throughout and immediately quenching them in water. The metal does not have its full hardness immediately after it is quenched, but it gains hardness and strength over a period of several days through the process of aging.

During the aging process, precipitation of the soluble constituents from the supersaturated solid solution of the alloy occurs, and as precipitation progresses, the strength of the material increases. The submicroscopic particles that are precipitated provide the keys, or locks, between the grains that resist internal slippage and distortion when a load of any type is applied.

In the process of heat treating 2017 and 2024 aluminum alloys, the grain size is reduced when the metal is hot, and it grows as the metal cools. For maximum strength the metal must be quenched immediately after it is taken from the oven so it will have the smallest grain size possible. If there is a delay between the time the metal is removed from the oven and the time it is quenched, the grains will grow large enough for the metal to become susceptible to intergranular corrosion that forms along the grain boundaries within the metal.

gamma iron. The molecular arrangement of iron at temperatures between 911°C and 1,392°C.

artificial aging. A method of aluminum alloy heat treatment in which the part is heated and quenched (solution heat-treated) and then held at a slightly elevated temperature for a period of time. The metal gains additional strength by this process. Artificial aging is also called "precipitation heat treatment."

aging. The characteristic of certain aluminum alloys that causes them to gain hardness over a period of time after they have been heated in a furnace and quenched.

intergranular corrosion. Corrosion that forms along the grain boundaries in a piece of metal.

Aluminum alloy sheets can be repeatedly heat treated, but it is possible for clad aluminum alloy sheets to be damaged by repeated heat treatment. These sheets have a core of high-strength aluminum alloy onto which a thin layer of pure aluminum has been rolled. When clad sheets are heated in the process of heat treatment, some of the pure aluminum diffuses into the core alloy and weakens the sheet. The manufacturer of the aluminum specifies the number of times clad sheets can be heat treated. Typically, they may be heat treated only one to three times.

Precipitation Heat Treatment

When an aluminum alloy has been solution heat treated, it gains its full hardness and strength by natural aging, but this strengthening process may be speeded up and increased by returning the metal to the oven and heating it to a temperature much lower than that used for solution heat treatment. It is held at this temperature for up to 24 hours and then removed from the oven and allowed to cool in still air. This precipitation hardening, or artificial aging, greatly increases the strength and hardness of the metal, but it decreases the ductility; the metal becomes more difficult to bend and form. This procedure has no effect, however, on its corrosion resistance.

Annealing

Certain aluminum alloys can be hardened by heat treatment while others can be hardened only by cold working. Both types of alloys can be annealed, or softened, by heating them in an oven to a specified temperature and then cooling them slowly in the furnace or in still air. Annealing leaves the metal soft, and in its weakest condition.

	Solution Heat-Treatment			Precipitation Heat-Treatment		
Alloy	Temp. °F	Quench	Temper desig.	Temp. °F	Time of aging	Temper desig.
2017	930-950	Cold water	T4			T
2117	930-950	Cold water	T4			T
2024	910-930	Water	T4			T
6061	960-980	Water	T4	315-325	18 hr	T6
				345-355	8 hr	T6
7075	870	Water		250	24 hr	T6

Figure 7-5. *Typical temperatures for heat treatment of various aluminum alloys*

Heat Treatment of Rivets

Aluminum rivets of 2117 alloy may be driven as they are received, but rivets made of 2017 and 2024 alloys are called icebox rivets, and they must be heat treated before they are driven. After these rivets are removed from the oven and quenched, they remain soft enough to be driven for about 10 minutes to one hour, depending on the alloy. But, if they are stored in a refrigerator at a temperature lower than 32°F immediately after quenching, they will remain soft enough for driving for several days.

Aluminum Alloy Temper Designations

The temper, or condition of hardness, of an aluminum alloy is indicated by a letter that follows the alloy designation, as we see in Figure 7-6. One of the most popular alloys used in aircraft construction is 2024-T3. This particular alloy has been solution heat treated and strain hardened by passing it through rollers in the process of its fabrication.

F — The metal is left as fabricated. There has been no control over its temper.
T — The metal may be heat treated.
    T3 — solution heat treatment, followed by strain hardening. A second digit, if used, indicates the amount of strain hardening.
    T4 — solution heat treatment, followed by natural aging at room temperature.
    T6 — solution heat treatment, followed by artificial aging (precipitation heat treated).
    T7 — solution heat treatment, followed by stabilization.
    T8 — solution heat treatment, followed by strain hardening and then artificial aging.
    T9 — solution heat treatment, followed by artificial aging and then strain hardening.
H — The metal cannot be heat treated, but can be hardened by cold working.
    H1 — strain hardened by cold working.
        H12 — strain hardened to its 1/4 hard condition.
        H14 — strain hardened to its 1/2 hard condition.
        H18 — strain hardened to its full hard condition.
        H19 — strain hardened to its extra hard condition.
    H2 — strain hardened by cold working and then partially annealed.
    H3 — strain hardened and stabilized.
        H36 — strain hardened and stabilized to its 3/4 hard condition.
O — The metal has been annealed.

Figure 7-6. *Temper designations of aluminum alloys*

Titanium Alloys

Titanium alloys can be given four types of heat treatment: they may be stress relieved, annealed, hardened, and case hardened.

Stress Relieving

When titanium is cold formed or machined, stresses may be trapped within the metal and cause distortion or warping. To relieve these stresses, the metal is heated to a temperature between 650°F and 1,000°F and held at this temperature for a specified time depending on its thickness. After this soaking period, the metal is removed from the furnace and allowed to cool in still air. The heat causes a scale, or discoloration, to form on the surface of the metal which may be removed with a nitric and hydrofluoric acid pickling bath.

Annealing

Titanium and titanium alloys may be made easier to work by annealing them. Not only does the annealing make them easier to form, but it also gives toughness and ductility at room temperature, and dimensional and structural stability at elevated temperatures. Annealing is done by heating the metal to a temperature of between 1,200°F and 1,650°F and holding it for a specified time depending upon its thickness; then allowing it to cool in still air. Annealing usually results in the formation of enough scale that it must be removed by a caustic descaling bath.

Thermal Hardening

Pure titanium cannot be hardened by heat, but many of the titanium alloys used in aircraft construction can be hardened by heating them until they reach a temperature of around 1,450°F throughout and then quenching them in water. After quenching, the metal is again heated, this time to around 900°F, and held at this temperature for several hours. This treatment hardens the metal, but it also causes the loss of some of its ductility.

Case Hardening

The surface of titanium can be hardened without affecting the internal condition by nitriding or carburizing. Case hardening produces a wear-resistant surface for a depth of between 0.0001 and 0.0002 inch.

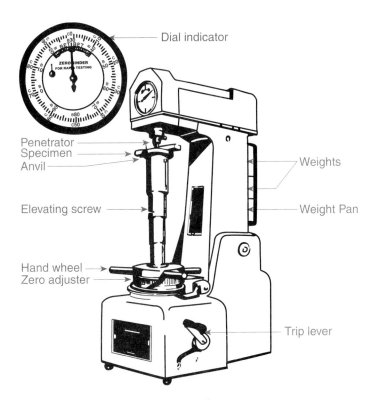

Dial indicator

Penetrator
Specimen
Anvil

Weights

Elevating screw

Weight Pan

Hand wheel
Zero adjuster

Trip lever

Figure 7-7. *Rockwell hardness tester*

Hardness Testing

Since the strength of most metals varies with hardness, an aviation maintenance technician is often required to measure the hardness of a metal. The two
most widely used methods of hardness measurement are the Rockwell and
Brinell methods.

Rockwell Hardness Testing

The Rockwell hardness tester measures the hardness of a metal by measuring
the depth of penetration of a special penetrator under a specified load. Figure
7-7 shows a typical Rockwell hardness tester.

Two types of penetrators are used to give the Rockwell tester a wide range of
applications. For soft metals a hardened steel ball is used, and for hard metals,
a diamond cone is used. The metal to be tested is placed on the anvil of the
tester, and it is raised up with the hand wheel until it rests against the
penetrator. A minor load of 10 kilograms is applied to the penetrator and the
indicator is zeroed, then a major load is applied, using the trip lever. The depth
the penetrator is forced into the metal is measured with the dial indicator on
the tester, and this depth indicates the hardness of the metal.

The indicator on the Rockwell tester has four scales, A, B, C, and D. The A and D scales are seldom used. The B scale uses a $\frac{1}{16}$-inch-diameter ball penetrator with a 100 kilogram major load to test soft materials. The C-scale is the most widely used for measuring the hardness and strength of steel. It uses a 120° diamond penetrator and a 150-kilogram major load. Figure 7-8 shows the relationship between the Rockwell C hardness number and the tensile strength of steel in thousands of pounds-per-square-inch increments.

Rockwell C-scale hardness number	Approximate tensile strength 1,000 psi	Rockwell C-scale hardness number	Approximate tensile strength 1,000 psi
60		40	186
59	326	39	181
58	315	38	176
57	305	37	172
56	295	36	168
55	287	35	163
54	278	34	159
53	269	33	154
52	262	32	150
51	253	31	146
50	245	30	142
49	239	29	138
48	232	28	134
47	225	27	131
46	219	26	127
45	212	25	124
44	206	24	121
43	201	23	118
42	196	22	115
41	191	21	113

Figure 7-8. *Relationship between the hardness of steel in Rockwell numbers and its tensile strength*

Brinell Hardness Testing

Brinell hardness testing is done on a machine such as the one we see in Figure 7-9. The hardness of the material is measured by the diameter of the impression made by a 10-mm-diameter hardened steel ball forced into the material by a hydraulic cylinder. A load of 3,000 kilograms is used for testing ferrous metals, and a 500-kilogram load is used for nonferrous metals.

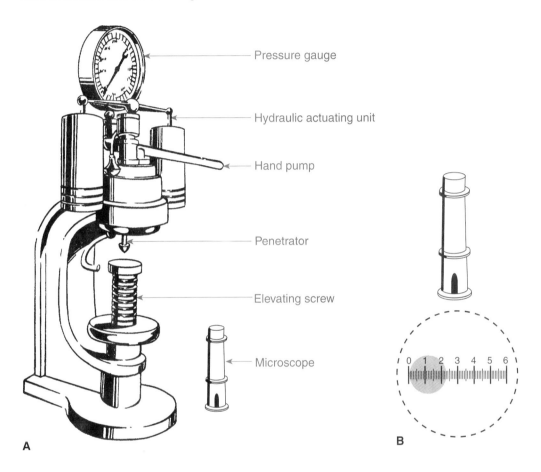

Figure 7-9
A. Brinell hardness tester
B. Microscopic view of impression made by a Brinell tester

The material to be tested is placed on the anvil and is moved up against the penetrator with the elevating screw, and a specified amount of pressure is built up by the hand pump that forces the penetrator into the material being tested. The pressure is maintained for a specified period of time and the material is then removed. The impression made by the penetrator is observed with a special microscope to measure its diameter. This diameter is converted into the Brinell number, using a chart on the tester.

Figure 7-10 lists the Brinell numbers for the various hardness tempers of aluminum alloys used in aircraft construction.

Alloy number	Hardness temper	Brinell number 500 kg load 10 mm ball
1100	O	23
	H18	44
3003	O	28
	H16	47
2014	O	45
	T6	135
2017	O	45
	T6	105
2024	O	47
	T4	120
5052	O	47
	H36	73
6061	O	30
	T4	65
	T6	95
7075	T6	135

Figure 7-10. *Brinell hardness number for various aluminum alloys*

STUDY QUESTIONS: METAL HEAT TREATMENT

Answers are on Page 524. Page numbers refer to chapter text.

16. A pure metal, as distinguished from an alloy, _____ (is or is not) normally hardened by heat treatment. *Page 462*

17. The form of heat treatment that hardens the surface of a metal while leaving the core relatively soft and tough is called _____ . *Page 464*

18. The form of heat treatment that softens a metal is called
_____ . *Page 463*

19. The form of heat treatment that relieves strains in a metal is called
_____ . *Page 463*

20. The form of heat treatment that removes some of the hardness from hardened steel is called
_____ . *Page 463*

21. Two methods of case hardening steel are:
    a. _____
    b. _____
       Page 464

22. A steel part is nitrided by heating it in an atmosphere containing _____ gas.
    Page 464

23. Aluminum alloy is softened by heating it in an oven and cooling it _____ (rapidly or slowly). *Page 466*

24. When an aluminum alloy part is heated in an oven and then quenched, it is said to be _____ heat treated. *Page 465*

25. Artificial aging is done by holding a heat-treated aluminum alloy part at an elevated temperature for a specified length of time. This process is called _____ heat treating.
    Page 466

26. When an aluminum alloy part is removed from the heat treatment oven and quenched, it is relatively soft. Over a period of a day or so, it increases its hardness and strength. This process is called _____ . *Page 465*

27. Steel is hardened by heating it to a specified temperature and then quenching it in oil, water, or brine. The hardest and most brittle steel is obtained by quenching it in _____ .
    Page 462

28. A steel part may be made less brittle by heating it to a temperature quite a way below its critical temperature and allowing it to cool in still air. This procedure is called _____ . *Page 463*

29. Fill in the code letter that is used to identify each of the following treatments for aluminum alloy:
    a. As fabricated with no control over its temper _____ .
    b. Annealed _____ .
    c. Solution heat treated _____ .
    d. Strain hardened _____ .
       Page 467

Continued

30. Icebox rivets are aluminum alloy rivets that must be heat treated and stored in a subfreezing refrigerator until they are driven. Two alloys of which icebox rivets are made are _____ and _____ . *Page 467*

31. An aluminum alloy sheet that has a coating of commercially pure aluminum rolled onto its surface is called _____ aluminum. *Page 466*

32. The aluminum alloy rivet that may be driven as it is received from the manufacturer without having to be heat treated is made of alloy _____ . *Page 467*

33. When a steel tubular fuselage is first welded, there are strains trapped in the structure. To relieve these strains, the structure is heated to a temperature above its critical temperature and allowed to cool in still air. This procedure is called _____ . *Page 463*

34. If too much time elapses between the removal of a piece of aluminum alloy from the heat treatment oven and the time it is quenched, there is danger of _____ corrosion forming inside the part. *Page 465*

Nondestructive Inspection (NDI)

As the name implies, nondestructive inspection is the inspection of an aircraft or aircraft component in such a way that neither the airworthiness nor structural integrity is damaged. The advanced age and high utilization of many aircraft in the airline fleets are making nondestructive inspection and corrosion control two major elements of modern aviation maintenance. In this section we will begin with the more complicated NDI systems and end with visual inspections.

Radiographic Inspection

radiographic inspection. Inspection of the interior of a structure by passing radiographic energy through the structure and either exposing a photographic film or exciting a fluorescent screen. Faults appear because their density is different from that of sound material. X-rays and gamma rays are used in radiographic inspection.

Radiographic (X-ray and gamma-ray) inspection is a satisfactory type of nondestructive inspection for checking the inside of a wing structure, as it does not require major disassembly. It is not recommended as an exploratory type of inspection, but is most profitably used when examining an area for a type of damage whose characteristics are known from previous experience.

X-Rays

X-rays are a form of high-energy, short-wavelength, electromagnetic radiation. When an electron emitted from the cathode in an X-ray tube and accelerated to a high speed strikes a target made of an element containing many electrons, it collides with electrons from the target and loses energy. As the electron loses energy, it emits X-rays.

Because of their high frequency, X-rays are able to pass through many materials that are opaque to visible light. As the X-rays pass through, they are absorbed in an amount that is dependent upon the density of the material. After passing through a material, the X-rays still have enough energy to expose a piece of photographic film.

The amount of current used to boil the electrons off the cathode determines the intensity of the X-ray beam. The greater the current, the more intense the beam, and more radiation is available for exposure of the film.

The voltage supplied to the anode of the X-ray tube determines the amount of energy the beam contains. The higher the voltage, the more energy there is in the X-rays, and the more the rays will penetrate the material being inspected. Low-powered X-rays are called soft X-rays, and those that are produced by high voltage are called hard X-rays. Soft X-rays are used to inspect for corrosion.

Gamma Rays

Gamma rays are composed of high-energy photons emitted by the nucleus of certain chemical isotopes such as Cobalt, Cesium, Iridium, and Thulium that are in the process of disintegration. Unlike X-rays, gamma rays cannot be shut off or controlled so the source of these rays must be kept in a radiation-proof container shielded with lead. When gamma rays are needed for an exposure, the equipment is set up and the active isotopes are exposed.

The penetrating energy of X-rays and gamma rays passes through the material being inspected and exposes a sheet of photographic film or causes a fluorescent screen to glow. Discontinuities or faults within the material alter its density and thus the amount of radiation that is allowed to pass. The more dense the material, the less radiation passes through, and the less the film is exposed. *See* Figure 7-11.

After a sheet of film is exposed to the radiation, it is developed and fixed as with any other photographic film, and its indication is interpreted by an experienced inspector. Damage and faults are detected by comparing the image on the developed film with the known indication of a sound structure.

Radiographic inspection is more costly, requires more elaborate equipment, and requires more safety considerations than other types of nondestructive inspection. Its advantage is that it can be used to inspect the inside of complex structures without having to disassemble them.

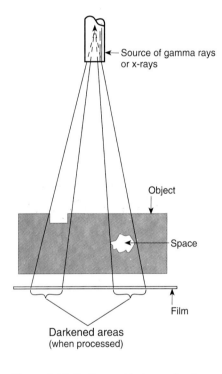

Figure 7-11. *Radiographic inspection is done by electromagnetic energy that passes through the material being inspected. Discontinuities within the material change its overall density, which varies the amount of energy allowed to strike the photographic film.*

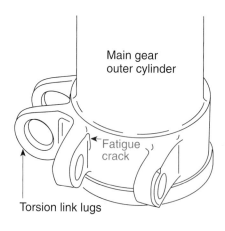

Figure 7-12. *Fatigue cracks normally appear at locations of high stress and are often found where the cross-sectional area of the part undergoes a drastic change.*

The factors of radiographic exposure are so interdependent that it is necessary to consider all factors for any particular inspection. These factors include, but are not limited to:

1. Material thickness and density
2. Shape and size of the object
3. Type of defect to be detected
4. Characteristics of X-ray machine used
5. The exposure distance
6. The exposure angle
7. Film characteristics
8. Type of intensifying screen, if one is used

Radiation from X-rays and radioisotope sources produce changes in living tissue through which they pass, and personnel must keep outside the high energy beam at all times. When this radiation strikes the molecules of the body, the effect may be no more than to dislodge a few electrons, but an excess of these changes can cause irreparable harm. The degree of damage depends on which of the body cells have been changed. This is determined by the amount of radiation received and by the percentage of the total body exposed.

Anyone who works with radiation equipment should wear a radiation-monitor film badge, which is developed at the end of a given period to determine the amount of radiation the wearer has absorbed. As a further precaution against radiation damage, anyone working with this equipment should have periodic blood-count tests.

Magnetic Particle Inspection

Magnetic particle inspection is used to detect flaws in ferromagnetic material on the surface or subsurface faults near the surface. When the part is magnetized, these flaws form north and south magnetic pole s. When iron oxide particles suspended in a fluid are flowed over the part, they are attracted to and held by the magnetism, where they outline the flaw.

Discontinuities are any interruption in the normal physical structure or configuration of a part. They may or may not affect the usefulness of a part.

Inclusions are a form of discontinuity caused by impurities trapped inside a piece of metal when it was cast. When the part is inspected by magnetic particle inspection, inclusions do not show up as clearly defined faults, but their indications are fuzzy. Rather than sharply defined poles, there are several sets of poles that cause the oxide to form in a series of parallel lines.

Fatigue cracks usually show up in areas that have been subjected to high concentrations of stresses, and they are likely to form where the cross-sectional area of the part changes abruptly. Fatigue cracks cause the greatest buildup of oxide particles, and these particles give a definite indication of the extent of the damage. *See* Figure 7-12.

AVIATION MAINTENANCE TECHNICIAN SERIES   GENERAL

A steel part is magnetized by holding it in a strong, steady magnetic field that aligns all of the magnetic domains in the material. Two methods of magnetization are used for magnetic particle inspection; these are the continuous and residual methods.

In the continuous method, the magnetic field is continually produced while the part is being inspected. This produces the strongest fields and is generally used for large parts.

In the residual method, the part is magnetized and then removed from the magnetizing force for inspection. Steel parts that have been heat treated for high-stress applications have a high retentivity and are normally inspected by the residual method.

When parts are magnetized for inspection, the type of magnetization determines the orientation of the faults that will be detected.

Circular magnetization is used to detect lengthwise cracks in the material. It is put into the metal by passing current through the material while it is held between the heads of the machine.

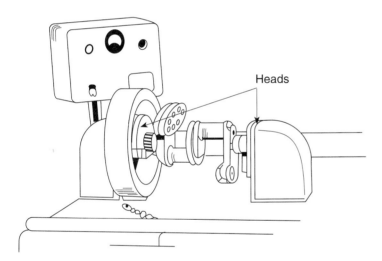

Figure 7-13. *Circular magnetization is put into a large object, such as a crankshaft, by passing the direct current through it while it is firmly clamped between the heads of the machine.*

continuous magnetic particle inspection. Magnetic particle inspection in which the part is inspected while the magnetizing current flows either through the material or through a coil, or solenoid, wrapped around the part.

residual magnetic particle inspection. Magnetic particle inspection in which the part is magnetized and removed from the magnetizing field. The inspection is made with the magnetism that is retained in the material.

retentivity. The ability of a material to retain magnetism.

circular magnetization. Magnetization of a part in which the magnetic field extends across the material. Circular magnetism is used to detect faults along the length of the part.

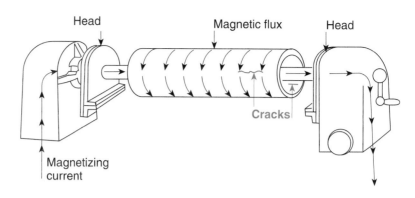

Figure 7-14. *Circular magnetization is put into a small object, such as a wrist pin, by passing the current through a rod inserted through the hollow pin. The rod is clamped firmly between the heads of the machine.*

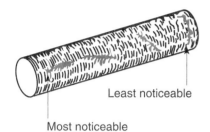

Figure 7-15. *Circular magnetization produces a magnetic field encircling the part. North and south poles are formed across a fault, and the oxide particles show up faults that extend along the length of the part.*

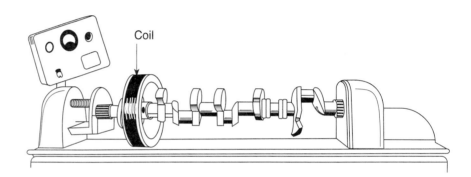

Figure 7-16. *Longitudinal magnetization is put into a part by passing the magnetizing current through a coil which surrounds it. The part becomes the core of an electromagnet, and the lines of flux extend lengthwise through the part.*

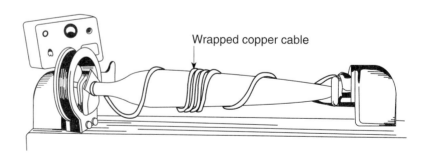

Figure 7-17. *Large parts, such as steel propeller blades, can be longitudinally magnetized by passing the magnetizing current through a heavy insulated copper cable wrapped around the blade.*

Longitudinal magnetization is used to detect cracks that extend across the material. It is put into the metal by passing current through a coil, called a solenoid, wrapped around the part.

Cracks that are oriented at 45° to the material can be detected by either circular or longitudinal magnetization. For a complete inspection that will show up all possible defects, the part must be magnetized twice, once longitudinally and once circularly, and given two separate inspections.

The iron oxides used in magnetic particle inspection can be applied as a dry powder, but more often they are mixed with a light oil and flowed over the surface as the part is being inspected. These oxides are often treated with a fluorescent dye that causes them to glow as a green mark when an ultraviolet (black) light shines on them.

After a part has been inspected, it must be thoroughly demagnetized. This is done by holding it in a magnetic field that continually reverses its polarity and decreases its strength. This reversing field causes the domains to continually change their orientation, and the decreasing field strength allows them to remain in a disoriented condition.

The demagnetizing force is usually created by alternating current, but some systems use pulses of reversing-polarity direct current, which have a carefully programmed decrease in intensity.

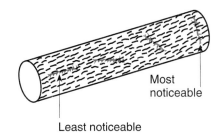

Figure 7-18. *Longitudinal magnetization produces a magnetic field that extends lengthwise through the part. North and south poles form along the part, and the oxide particles show up faults that extend across the part.*

longitudinal magnetization. Magnetization of a part in which the magnetic field extends lengthwise in the material. Longitudinal magnetization is used to detect faults across the part.

Eddy Current Inspection

Eddy current inspection checks for faults inside a metal that change its conductivity and is an especially good method for detecting intergranular corrosion. An electromagnetic field induced into the metal causes a given amount of free electron drift. This is the eddy current. Sound material allows a given amount of current for a specified electromagnetic field. The amount of eddy current is determined by four things: the conductivity, permeability, and mass of the material, and the presence of any faults or voids.

The conductivity of a metal is a function of its alloy type, its grain size, the degree of heat treatment, and its tensile strength. A comparison-type eddy current test can be used to sort metals according to any of these characteristics. The test probe is placed on a metal that is known to be good and the meter is zeroed. When the probe is placed on another metal of the same type the meter will zero, but if the metal is different, or if there are any faults within the metal, a different amount of current will be induced and the meter will read a different amount.

The mass of sound material is changed when corrosion is present on the opposite side of the structure being inspected. The probe of the eddy current tester is held against a part of the structure that is known to be free of corrosion, and the meter is zeroed. The probe is then moved over the portion of the

eddy current inspection. Inspection of a material by inducing eddy currents into it. The amount of eddy current induced in the material varies as the physical condition of the material changes, and it is affected by the presence of faults.

structure that is being inspected, and if corrosion is present on the opposite side of the skin, the meter will move off zero.

The ease with which eddy current inspection can be conducted and its inherent accuracy make it the ideal way of checking aircraft wheels for cracks in the bead seat area that close up when all of the stress is off the wheel, but which can become dangerous when the tire is installed and inflated.

Figure 7-19. *Eddy current inspection being used to check for cracks in the blade root radius on a ram air turbine. (Photo courtesy Dowty-Rotol, Inc.)*

Ultrasonic Inspection

Ultrasonic waves are vibrations at frequencies between about 200 kilohertz and 25 megahertz (200,000 and 25,000,000 hertz). In this frequency range, these waves are not perceptible to the human ear, but in all other ways they behave in the same way as vibrations we can hear.

A transducer is a piezoelectric crystal device that vibrates when it is excited by AC electrical energy from an oscillator. The transducer also has the characteristic that when it is vibrated, it will produce an AC voltage. The transducer is held against the structure being inspected and is excited by AC of the proper frequency. The crystal sends pulses of energy into the structure where it travels until it reaches the back surface of the material or until it strikes a fault, then it is reflected back to the transducer.

ultrasonic inspection. Inspection by vibrating the part with ultrasonic energy. The physical condition of the material and the presence of faults affect the passage of the energy through the part.

The indicator can be a cathode ray tube (CRT) such as the one in Figure 7-20. A pip is produced on the base line to represent the front surface of the test specimen, and a second pip represents the back surface. If there is a fault within the material, some of the energy will be reflected before it reaches the back surface, and it will form a third pip, this one between the other two. This type of indication in Figure 7-21.

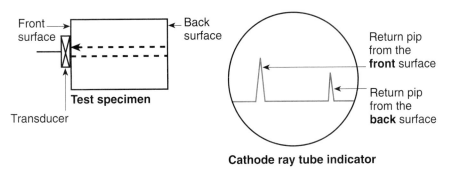

Figure 7-20. *Vibrations from the transducer pass through the test specimen and reflect off of the back surface. This produces two pips on the CRT screen, one for the front surface and one for the back surface.*

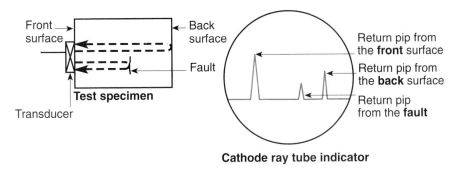

Figure 7-21. *A fault within the material being inspected by the ultrasonic method will reflect enough energy to form a pip between the front and back surface pips.*

Penetrant Inspection

Dye-penetrant and fluorescent-penetrant inspection can be used to detect faults in ferrous and nonferrous metals, and in nonmetals. One of the main limitations of this type of inspection is that it can only detect faults that extend to the surface of the part.

The basic steps to be taken when performing a penetrant inspection are:

1. Thoroughly clean the surface of the part to remove all contaminants that would prevent the penetrant soaking into any faults. Abrasive blasting is not recommended for cleaning, as it is likely to close up small faults that extend to the surface.

dye-penetrant inspection. Inspection of a material by soaking it in a penetrating liquid. After the liquid has soaked into any surface faults, it is washed off, and the surface covered with a developer powder which pulls the penetrant from the fault. The fault shows up as a vivid line or mark.

fluorescent penetrant inspection. A type of penetrant inspection in which the penetrating liquid pulled from a surface fault glows, or fluoresces, when it is inspected under an ultraviolet light.

2. Apply the penetrant. This can be done by immersing the part in a vat of the penetrant and by allowing it to soak for a given length of time.

    When looking for very small cracks, heat the part (but not enough to cause the penetrant to evaporate from the surface), and allow the penetrant to stay on the surface for a longer than normal time before washing it off. The amount of penetrant that enters a fault depends upon the temperature of the part and the length of time it remains in the penetrant.

    The penetrant can be applied to small parts that are inspected on the aircraft by applying it to the surface from an aerosol spray can and allowing it to remain for the required period of time.

3. Remove the penetrant with a remover-emulsifier or cleaner. This step removes the penetrant from the surface but does not remove any that has seeped into any existing faults. Porous materials are specially difficult to inspect by the penetrant method because of the difficulty in removing all of the penetrant from the surface.

4. Dry the part.

5. Apply the developer. The developer is a form of chalk that covers the surface and draws the penetrant from any faults into which it has seeped.

    Large parts are placed in a container of dry powder which is agitated so it covers the part. The powder adheres to any penetrant it contacts. Small parts are covered by spraying on a developer which is suspended in an aerosol. The developer forms a white porous coating over the surface and absorbs any penetrant it contacts.

6. Inspect and interpret the results.

    The penetrant used for large parts normally contains a fluorescent dye, and these parts are inspected in the dark under an ultraviolet light. Penetrant pulled from the faults shows up as a bright green light. The penetrant used with sprayed-on developer contains a bright red dye, and this shows up on the white developer surface as a bright red mark.

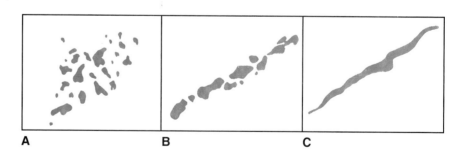

A   B   C

Figure 7-22. *Typical faults detected with dye-penetrant inspection:*
A. Pits of porosity
B . Tight crack or partially welded lap
C. Crack or similar opening

Bonded Structure Inspection

Delaminations in bonded honeycomb material may be detected by tapping the surface of the material with the edge of a coin or other metallic object. If the tapping produces a ringing sound, the material is probably good, but if the sound is a dull thudding noise, there is a possibility of delamination.

Welding Inspection

When a part is welded, it has expanded and been fused to another part. When it cools, stresses within the part try to warp it out of shape. If it is cooled too rapidly, cracks are likely to develop adjacent to the weld.

After the welding is completed, the part may be normalized by heating it red hot and allowing it to cool slowly in still air to room temperature. This relieves the stresses in the metal, and the part is not so likely to crack in service. *See* Figure 7-23.

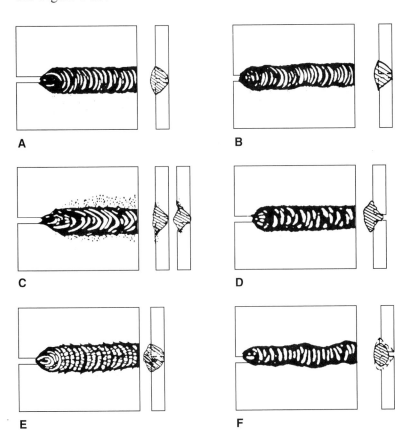

Figure 7-23. *Typical weld beads*

A. *Good weld: The bead shows good penetration and good fusion and is uniform and straight. It has a slightly crowned surface that tapers-off smoothly into the base metal.*

B. *Good weld*

C. *Weld made too rapidly with an excessive amount of heat or an oxidizing flame*

D. *Weld with improper penetration and cold laps caused by insufficient heat*

E. *Weld made with a flame having an excess of acetylene. There are bumps along the center of the bead and craters at the finish of the weld.*

F. *Bad weld with irregular edges and considerable variation in the depth of penetration.*

When making a weld, the heat should be concentrated in the area being welded. The oxides that form on the base metal give an indication of the amount of heat put into it. Oxides formed for a distance of much more than ½ inch from the weld show that too much heat was put into the metal, and it may have been weakened.

If a weld has blow holes and projecting globules in the bead, it is a poor weld. All of the old weld bead should be removed and the material rewelded.

Types of welds:

Lap welds are made along the edge of a sheet of metal that has lapped over another sheet. A single-lap has a bead along one edge, and a double-lap has beads along both edges.

Butt welds are made when the edges of the sheets of metal butt against each other without overlapping. A weld with a bead on one side is a single-butt weld, and a weld with beads on both sides is called a double-butt weld.

Fillet welds are made when one sheet is perpendicular to the other and the bead is made at their intersection. A properly made fillet weld has a penetration of 25% to 50% of the thickness of the base metal.

Edge welds are made when two sheets of metal are laid side by side and the bead is made along their common edges.

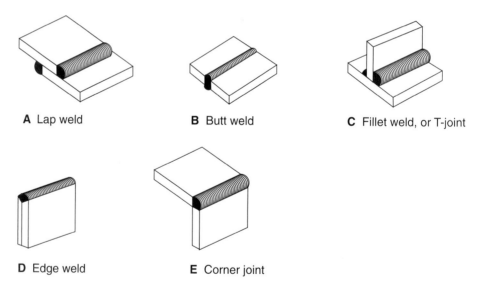

A Lap weld   **B** Butt weld   **C** Fillet weld, or T-joint

D Edge weld   **E** Corner joint

Figure 7-24. *Types of welds*

Answers are on Page 524. Page numbers refer to chapter text.

35. The method of nondestructive inspection that allows the inside of a structure to be inspected without requiring extensive disassembly is _____ inspection.
    Page 474

36. Two types of radiographic inspection are:
    a. _____
    b. _____
       Page 474

37. X-rays produced by low power are called _____ X-rays. *Page 475*

38. Anyone working with X-ray equipment should wear a _____
    film badge. *Page 476*

39. A fault that does not extend to the surface _____ (can or cannot) be detected by magnetic particle inspection. *Page 476*

40. Magnetic particle inspection can only be used to detect flaws in metals containing
    _____ . *Page 477*

41. When the strongest possible magnetic field is required to inspect for a fault, the
    _____ (continuous or residual) method of inspection is used. *Page 477*

42. Small parts made of heat-treated steel are usually inspected by the _____
    (continuous or residual) method of magnetic particle inspection. *Page 477*

43. A part that is magnetized by holding it in a coil, or solenoid, is magnetized
    _____ (circularly or longitudinally). *Page 478*

44. A part that is magnetized by passing magnetizing current through it is magnetized
    _____ (circularly or longitudinally). *Page 477*

45. When inspecting for faults that extend parallel to the length of the part, the part should be
    magnetized _____ (circularly or longitudinally). *Page 478*

Continued

46. When inspecting for faults that extend across a part, the part should be magnetized _____ (circularly or longitudinally). *Page 479*

47. Two types of magnetic medium that may be used to detect faults by the magnetic particle inspection method are:
    a. _____
    b. _____
       Page 479

48. A part is magnetized by holding it in a strong electromagnetic field produced by _____ (AC or DC). *Page 477*

49. A part is demagnetized by holding it in a decreasing magnetic field produced by _____ (AC or DC). *Page 479*

50. An indication of a fault detected by the magnetic particle inspection method that shows up as a rather fuzzy series of parallel lines is probably a/an _____ . *Page 476*

51. The type of crack that gives the strongest indication in a magnetic particle inspection is a/an _____ crack. *Page 476*

52. For a fault to be detected by the penetrant inspection method, it _____ (does or does not) have to extend to the surface. *Page 481*

53. After the penetrant has been applied to the surface of a part and allowed to soak in, the surface of the part is washed and dried, and a/an _____ is applied. *Page 482*

54. Dye-penetrant inspection _____ (can or cannot) be used to detect faults in nonmetallic materials. *Page 481*

55. Faults are detected when using the fluorescent-penetrant inspection method by examining the part under a/an _____ light. *Page 482*

56. A porous material _____ (is or is not) suited for inspection by the dye-penetrant method. *Page 482*

57. Abrasive blasting _____ (is or is not) a good way to clean a part that is to be inspected by the dye-penetrant method. *Page 481*

58. One of the most effective methods for inspecting a part for intergranular corrosion is the _____ method. *Page 479*

59. The metallic ring test is used when inspecting bonded structure for indications of _____ . *Page 483*

60. After a structure is welded, it may be heated above its critical temperature and allowed to cool in still air. This procedure is used to _____ . *Page 483*

61. If a welded joint is to be rewelded, all of the old weld bead must be _____ . *Page 484*

62. Too rapid cooling of a weld can cause it to contract unevenly and stresses will remain in the metal. These stresses cause the metal to _____ . *Page 483*

63. Heat should be concentrated in the area being welded, and oxides that form on the base metal give an indication of the amount of heat put into the weld. When too much heat is used, the oxide will form out to a distance of more than _____ inch from the weld. *Page 484*

64. A properly made fillet weld has a penetration of _____ to _____% of the thickness of the base metal. *Page 484*

Continued

65. Refer to the figure below. Identify the illustration for each of these types of welds:

a. Cold weld with no penetration _____

b. Bad weld with variations in penetration _____

c. Weld that was made too rapidly _____

d. Weld made with an excess of acetylene _____

Page 483

A

B

C

D

Aircraft Hardware

An aircraft, more than almost any other type of vehicle, must be lightweight and must have sufficient strength to preclude structural failure under the most adverse conditions. For this reason, all of the hardware used in construction must be of the highest quality and must meet rigid standards. Three sets of specifications are used for aircraft hardware: the National Aerospace Standards (NAS), Air Force-Navy Aeronautical (AN), and Military Standard (MS).

Hardware manufactured under any of these standards is approved for use in aircraft structure, and the engineering departments of aircraft and engine manufacturers have access to all of the detailed information on each item manufactured under these standards. The illustrated parts lists for each aircraft specify, by part number, the exact hardware that must be used. The use of any hardware other than that specified can compromise the safety of the aircraft and violate Federal Aviation Regulations.

Threaded Fasteners

Threaded fasteners in the form of bolts, nuts, and screws are important devices in aviation maintenance. The maintenance technician must understand the importance of choosing the correct fastener and installing it with the correct torque. In this section, we will discuss the types of fasteners and their proper installation.

Thread Fit

The relative tightness between the nut and the bolt is called the fit of the threads.

A class-1 fit is a loose fit. This is used for coarse-thread stove bolts fitted with square nuts.

A class-2 fit is a free fit. It is used for some machine screws.

A class-3 fit is a medium fit. It is used for almost all standard aircraft bolts.

A class-4 fit is a close fit, that requires a wrench to turn the nut onto the bolt.

The Importance of Torque

For any bolted joint to develop maximum strength, the fastener must have enough torque applied to it to load the bolt to a value greater than will be applied to it in its anticipated use. For example, if a load of 5,000 pounds will be applied to a bolt, it should be torqued to a value greater than this so it will not loosen when the load is applied to it. The engineering departments of the aircraft and engine manufacturers have conducted extensive tests and have listed the amount of torque that should be used on each bolt.

If a threaded fastener does not fail when it is being properly torqued, it will probably not fail in service. When the fastener is being torqued, it is subjected to both torsional and tensile stresses. After installation is completed, the fastener is subjected only to the tensile stress.

There are three methods of specifying torque so the maintenance technician can duplicate the torque recommended by the manufacturer. These methods are: the use of a torque wrench, the nut-rotation method, and the bolt-stretch method.

The nut-rotation and bolt-stretch method of preloading a joint do not consider the friction between the nut and the bolt. Some manufacturers specify that the nut should be tightened until it is snug, then turned $1/3$ to $2/3$ turn. In the bolt-stretch method, as is used with some connecting rod bolts, the length of the bolt is measured before torque is applied, and the nut is tightened until the bolt is stretched a specified amount.

For the desired torque to be duplicated with a torque wrench, the threads must be in good condition and must be completely clean and dry unless the overhaul or service manual calls for lubrication. If lubrication is specified, the exact type and amount called for must be used.

To get the correct torque on the bolt, run the nut down until it nearly contacts the washer or bearing surface and measure the amount of torque required to turn the nut. This is called the friction-drag torque and it must be added to the amount of torque recommended for the fastener. The torque values seen in Figure 7-25 are typical and may be used for steel nut and bolt combinations if specific values are not given in the maintenance instructions for the job you are doing.

Steel Nuts & Bolts in Tension			Aluminum Nuts & Bolts in Tension	
Fine Thread Series				
Nut-bolt size	Torque limits in pounds		Torque limits in pounds	
	Minimum	Maximum	Minimum	Maximum
8 - 36	12	15	5	10
10 - 32	20	25	10	15
$1/4$ - 28	50	70	30	45
$5/16$ - 24	100	140	40	65
$3/8$ - 24	160	190	75	110
$7/16$ - 20	450	500	180	280
$1/2$ - 20	480	690	280	410
$9/16$ - 18	800	1,000	380	580
$5/8$ - 18	1,100	1,300	550	670
$3/4$ - 16	2,300	2,500	950	1,250
$7/8$ - 14	2,500	3,000	1,250	1,900
1 - 14	3,700	4,500	1,600	2,400
$1 1/8$ - 12	5,000	7,000	2,100	3,200
$1 1/4$ - 12	9,000	11,000	3,900	5,600
Coarse Thread Series				
8 - 32	12	15		
10 - 24	20	25		
$1/4$ - 20	40	50		
$5/16$ - 18	80	90		
$3/8$ - 16	160	185		
$7/16$ - 14	235	255		
$1/2$ - 13	400	480		
$9/16$ - 12	500	700		
$5/8$ - 11	700	900		
$3/4$ - 10	1,150	1,600		
$7/8$ - 9	2,200	3,000		
1 - 8	3,700	5,000		
$1 1/8$ - 8	5,500	6,500		
$1 1/4$ - 8	6,500	8,000		

Figure 7-25. *Recommended torque values for nut and bolt combinations. Values are for clean and dry threads.*

It is sometimes necessary to use an extension on a torque wrench that changes its lever length. When this is necessary, the formulas seen in Figure 7-26 are used. Use the formula in (A) when the extension adds to the length of the wrench, and the formula in (B) when the extension shortens the lever length. Most cylinder base wrenches which are used for access to the hold-down nuts on the cylinder base flange do not change the lever length and do not require this calculation.

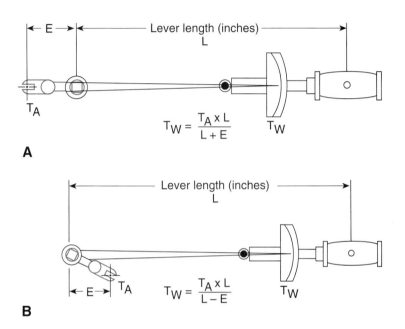

$$T_W = \frac{T_A \times L}{L + E}$$

A

$$T_W = \frac{T_A \times L}{L - E}$$

B

T_W = Torque indicated on the wrench
T_A = Torque applied at the adapter
L = Lever length of torque wrench
E = Arm of the adapter

Figure 7-26. *When an extension is used with a torque wrench, a correction must be applied to the indication on the wrench to get the actual torque on the fitting.*
A. The extension adds to the length of the wrench.
B. The extension subtracts from the length of the wrench.

When castellated nuts are torqued onto bolts, the cotter pin holes may not line up with the slots in the nuts at the minimum recommended torque plus the friction drag. If the hole and nut castellations do not line up, change washers, or nuts, or both, and try again. Exceeding the maximum recommended torque is not allowed.

In aviation maintenance, we generally measure torque in inch-pounds, but there are other units. Figure 7-27 is a conversion chart between the different torque units.

Inch Grams	Inch Ounces	Inch Pounds	Foot Pounds	Centimeter Kilograms	Meter Kilograms
7.09	0.25				
14.17	0.5				
21.26	0.75				
28.35	1.0				
113.40	4.0	0.25			
226.80	8.0	0.50			
453.59	16.0	1.00	0.08	1.11	
	96.0	6.00	0.50	6.92	
	192.0	12.00	1.00	13.83	0.138
	384.0	24.00	2.00	27.66	0.277
	576.0	36.00	3.00	41.49	0.415
	768.0	48.00	4.00	55.32	0.553
	960.0	60.0	5.00	69.15	0.692
		72.0	6.00	82.98	0.830
		84.0	7.00	96.81	0.968
		96.00	8.00	110.64	1.106
		108.00	9.00	124.47	1.245
		120.00	10.00	138.31	1.383

Figure 7-27. *Torque conversions*

Aircraft Bolts

The marks on the head of a bolt signify the material of which the bolt is made or tell the kind of bolt it is. A cross or asterisk shows that the bolt is made of nickel steel, a single dash identifies a corrosion-resistant steel bolt, and two dashes indicate aluminum alloy. A triangle surrounding the cross or asterisk shows that the bolt is a close-tolerance bolt. If there is no marking on the head, the bolt is probably a low-strength bolt, and it is not approved for use in an aircraft. *See* Figure 7-28.

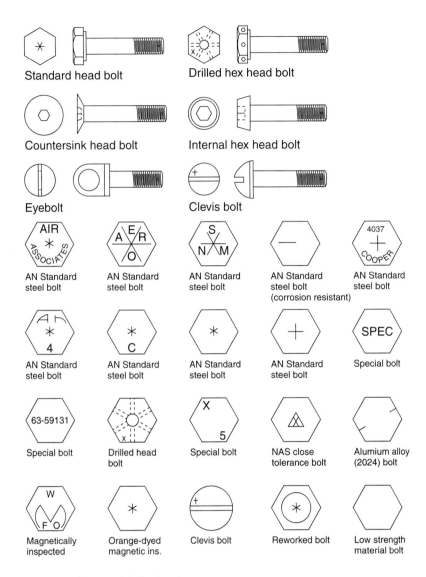

Figure 7-28. *Aircraft bolt identification*

The grip length of a bolt is the length of the unthreaded portion of the shank. The grip length should be the same as the thickness of the material being fastened with the bolt. *See* Figure 7-29.

When bolts are installed in an aircraft structure, unless some reason dictates otherwise, the heads should be upward, in a forward direction, or outboard. The reason for installing bolts in this way is that they are less likely to fall out if the nut should ever back off.

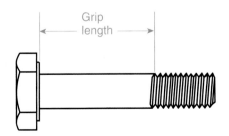

Figure 7-29. *Grip length of a bolt*

Figure 7-30. *A clevis bolt is designed to take shear loads only, and should never be used where a tensile load is imposed.*

Clevis Bolts

A clevis bolt, such as the one in Figure 7-30, should be used only where the load to which the bolt is applied is a shear load. It is not designed to take any type of tensile load.

The threaded portion of a clevis bolt is short, and there is a groove between the threads and the shank. The head has a screwdriver slot rather than flats for the use of a wrench.

Clevis bolts are normally installed so that they are loose and free to rotate. When rotation is possible, a shear castle nut should be installed and a cotter pin should be used to secure the nut to the bolt.

When a clevis bolt is used to secure a fork-end cable terminal, a shear castle nut should be used on the clevis bolt. The nut should be tightened until it is snug, but there must be no strain on the fork. The nut is secured to the clevis bolt with a cotter pin.

Aircraft Nuts

In Figure 7-31, we see several of the more commonly used aircraft nuts. The castle nut is used on drilled shank aircraft bolts that are subjected to tensile loads. Castle nuts are locked on the bolt with a cotter pin. Shear castle nuts are used on clevis bolts. They have very few threads and are to be used for shear loads only.

Plain nuts are used for tensile loads and must be secured with either a lock washer or a check nut. Light hex nuts are similar to plain nuts, but are thinner. They are used for light tension requirements, and must be locked with a lock washer or check nut.

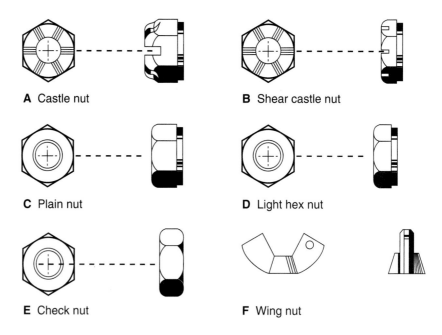

A Castle nut   **B** Shear castle nut

C Plain nut   **D** Light hex nut

E Check nut   **F** Wing nut

Figure 7-31. *Commonly used non-self-locking aircraft nuts*

A check nut is used to lock either the plain nut or the light hex nut. It is tightened down on top of the other nut to prevent the main nut from loosening.

Wing nuts are used where finger tightening is adequate and where the nut must be frequently removed.

Fiber-type lock nuts are held firmly on the threads of a bolt by pressure from an unthreaded fiber insert locked into a recess in the end of the nut. When the bolt is screwed through the nut, it forces its way through the unthreaded fiber. The fiber grips the threads and applies a downward force between the threads in the nut and those on the bolt. This force prevents the nut vibrating loose. *See* Figure 7-32.

Since there is no mechanical lock between the nut and the bolt, the FAA recommends that fiber-type self-locking nuts not be used in any installation in which the fastener is subject to rotation. These nuts should be discarded if the fiber insert ever wears to the point that the nut can be turned on the bolt without the use of a wrench.

Fiber-type self-locking nuts have a temperature limit of about 250°F. For applications at temperatures above this, other types of self-locking nuts must be used.

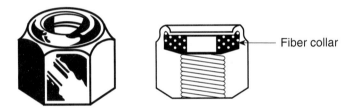

Fiber collar

Figure 7-32. *A fiber-type self-locking nut*

It is often necessary to have nuts inside a structure where there is no access to hold them when installing the bolt or screw. For these applications, an anchor nut such as that in Figure 7-32A or a channel containing several nuts is riveted to the structure as in Figure 7-32B. Channel nuts fit loosely in the channel so that they allow for slight misalignment when installing the screws.

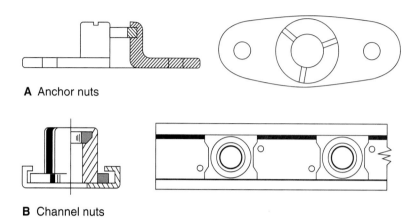

A Anchor nuts

B Channel nuts

Figure 7-33

Inspection covers in light aircraft structure are often held in place with sheet metal screws. Repeated inserting and removing them in the thin aluminum alloy skin would enlarge the holes and require the use of a larger screw. To prevent damage to the hole, a spring steel Tinnerman speed nut, such as the one seen in Figure 7-34, is slipped over the hole and the screw is driven into it. The springing action of the nut holds the screw tight so it will not vibrate loose.

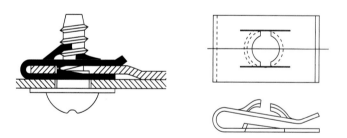

Figure 7-34. *A Tinnerman speed nut*

Washers

Plain washers are used under nuts and under the head of bolts that are turned to screw them into a tapped hole in the structure to provide a smooth bearing surface, and to act as a shim to get the correct grip length for a bolt and nut combination. They are also used under lock washers to prevent damage to the surface material. Most plain washers are made of cadmium-plated steel, but where dissimilar metal corrosion could be a problem in an aluminum or magnesium structure, aluminum alloy washers may be used.

Lockwashers, both the split type and spring type seen in Figure 7-35, are used in applications where self-locking or castellated nuts are not appropriate. There are several conditions under which lockwashers should not be used on aircraft structure. These are:

1. With fasteners to primary or secondary structure.

2. With fasteners on any part of the aircraft where failure might result in damage or danger to the aircraft or personnel.

3. Where failure would permit the opening of a joint to the airflow.

4. Where the screw is subject to frequent removal.

5. Where the washers are exposed to the airflow.

6. Where the washers are subject to corrosive conditions.

7. Where the washer is against soft material without plain washer underneath to prevent gouging the surface.

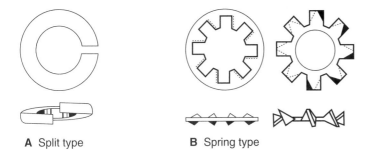

A Split type   **B** Spring type

Figure 7-35. *Lockwashers*

Aircraft Screws

The basic difference between a bolt and a screw is the fact that most screws have no unthreaded section, the threads extend all the way to the head. Also, a screw is turned with a screwdriver rather than with a wrench. There are three basic types of screws used in aircraft construction: structural screws, machine screws, and self-tapping screws.

Structural screws are made of heat-treated alloy steel and may be used in place of standard aircraft bolts. These screws have an unthreaded shank,

A 100° Flat-head machine screw

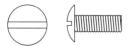

B Button-head machine screw

C 100° Flat-head structural
machine screw

Figure 7-36. *Machine screws*

and are manufactured with both fine and coarse threads. Structural screws are made with round heads, button heads, 100° countersunk heads, and washer heads.

Machine screws are made with round heads and countersunk heads and are made of low-carbon steel, corrosion-resistant steel, and brass. They are not used in primary structure, but are most generally used for such applications as instrument mounting and for the attachment of fairings and inspection covers in nonstressed locations. Machine screws are manufactured in sizes from 0-80 up through 3/8-16. *See* Figure 7-36.

Self tapping screws, also called PK or Parker Kalon screws, are available with round heads and 82° countersunk heads (*see* Figure 7-37). They are used for temporarily assembling sheet metal parts before they are riveted and for attaching fairings and inspection covers in nonstressed areas. These screws cut their own threads, and when used in thin sheet metal, pull the sheets tightly together. In applications where the screws are removed frequently from an aluminum alloy sheet, a spring steel Tinnerman speed nut is slipped over the hole so the screw enters the nut rather than wearing away the soft aluminum alloy.

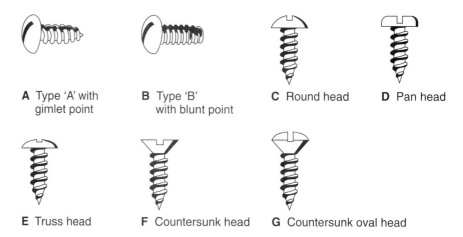

A Type 'A' with gimlet point   **B** Type 'B' with blunt point   **C** Round head   **D** Pan head

E Truss head   **F** Countersunk head   **G** Countersunk oval head

Figure 7-37. *Self-tapping screws*

Cowling Fasteners

Aircraft cowling and inspection doors that must be frequently opened are often installed with turnlock fasteners such as the Dzus, the Camlock, and the Airloc fasteners in Figures 7-38, 7-40, and 7-41.

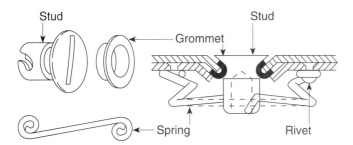

Figure 7-38. *Dzus fastener installation*

Figure 7-39. *Dzus fastener identification*

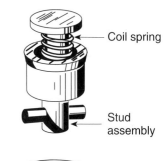

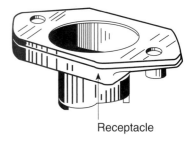

Figure 7-40. *Camlock fastener: exploded view*

With the Dzus fastener, holes are drilled in both the fixed and detachable parts and a spring is riveted over the hole in the fixed part, on the inside of the structure. The stud is slipped through the hole in the detachable part, and it is prevented from falling out by a metal grommet swaged into a groove just below the head. To use this fastener, the cam-shaped slot in the stud is slipped over the spring, and the stud is turned one quarter turn. This pulls the spring up in the slot and it locks in place.

Dzus fasteners are identified by a series of numbers and letters on the head of the stud as in Figure 7-39. The letter F indicates that this is a flush-head fastener. There are also W for wing-type heads and O for oval heads. The 6-1/2 means that the body diameter is 6-½ sixteenths, or 0.406 inch. The .50 is the length of the stud. It is 0.5 inch long, measured from the head to the bottom of the spring hole.

The Camlock and Airloc fasteners are similar to the Dzus, but both of them have a pin through the stud that passes through a slot in a receptacle riveted to the fixed part of the structure. Turning the stud a quarter turn locks the fastener. The stud of the Camlock fastener is held tight against the receptacle by a coil spring in the stud assembly, and the stud in the Airloc fastener is held tight by the spring action of the spring steel receptacle.

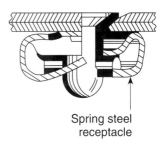

Figure 7-41. *Airloc fastener: assembly view*

Aircraft Control Cable

Many aircraft controls are actuated by steel cables routed through the structure. The direction of a cable is changed by passing the cable over a pulley, and the cable is held away from the structure with fairleads.

Control cables are made of preformed corrosion-resistant steel or preformed galvanized steel. There are three basic types of cable, and their use depends upon the type of installation. These types are: nonflexible, flexible, and extraflexible. Control cables are available in sizes from $\frac{1}{32}$-inch through $\frac{1}{2}$-inch diameter with primary flight controls normally operated with cables from $\frac{1}{8}$-inch through $\frac{1}{4}$-inch diameter. Cables smaller than $\frac{1}{8}$-inch cannot be used in the primary control system, but cable smaller than this can be used for trim tab actuation in certain applications. *See* Figure 7-42.

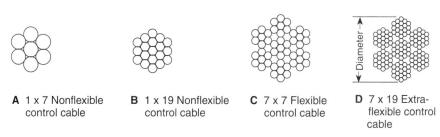

A 1 x 7 Nonflexible control cable   **B** 1 x 19 Nonflexible control cable   **C** 7 x 7 Flexible control cable   **D** 7 x 19 Extra-flexible control cable

Figure 7-42. *Control cables*

Nonflexible Control Cable

Nonflexible cable is used for straight runs where it does not have to pass over a pulley. There are two types of nonflexible cable. The 1 x 7 cable is made seven individual wires, and the 1 x 19 cable is made of 19 individual wires.

Flexible Control Cable

Flexible cable is made of six stands each containing seven wires that are preformed into a spiral. These strands are wound around a straight center strand containing seven wires. Flexible cable, called 7 by 7 cable, is primarily used for engine controls and trim tab controls. It may have its direction changed by pulleys, but it is not subjected to the extreme flexing that is encountered by the cables in the primary flight controls.

Extraflexible Control Cable

Primary flight controls are normally operated by extraflexible cables made up of 7 strands, each containing 19 individual wires. These cables are preformed so they will not spring apart when they are cut for installation of terminals.

Control Cable Terminals

Almost all of the cables installed in modern aircraft have swaged terminals such as those in Figure 7-43. These terminals are made of stainless steel and have a hole into which the cable fits. The cable is inserted into the hole and the terminal is placed between the dies in a special swaging tool such as the one in Figure 7-44. The handles are squeezed together to decrease the diameter of the terminal and force the metal tight around the wires of the cable. A properly swaged terminal has the full strength of the cable.

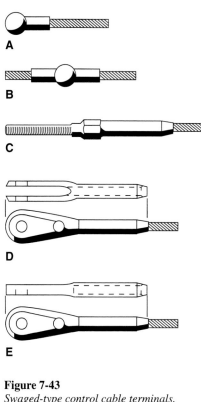

Figure 7-43
Swaged-type control cable terminals.
A. AN664 Single shank ball end
B. AN663 Double shank ball end
C. AN666 Threaded cable terminal
D. AN667 Fork end cable terminal
E. AN668 Eye end cable terminal

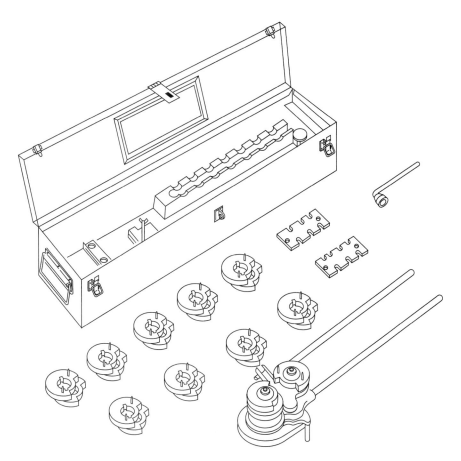

Figure 7-44. *Control cable swaging tools with dies*

To determine that a control cable terminal is properly installed, it must be measured both before and after the swaging operation as we see in Figure 7-45. Before the terminal is installed, its diameter must be great enough that it does not fit through the hole in the gage. After it is swaged, the diameter must be reduced enough that it fits through the slot.

As an aid to inspection, a spot of paint is placed at the end of the terminal and on the cable. If the cable should ever slip in the terminal, the paint will break, indicating that the cable has slipped.

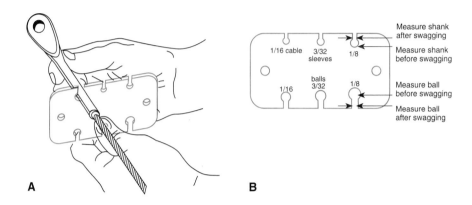

Figure 7-45
A. *Gaging a swaged-on control cable terminal to determine that it has been properly swaged.*
B. *Typical terminal gage*

The control cables in some of the older small aircraft are terminated with thimble-type eye splices such as the one seen in Figure 7-46. When installing a fitting of this type, a copper sleeve is slipped over the end of the cable and the cable is wrapped around a steel thimble. The end is put back through the sleeve with about $\frac{1}{16}$-inch of cable sticking out of the sleeve when it is pulled tight around the thimble. Using the special crimping tool, the sleeve is crimped three times; the first time in the center, then next to the thimble, and finally at the opposite end. A gage such as the one in Figure 7-46B is used to check that the sleeve has been properly compressed. A properly installed terminal of this type has 100% of the strength of the cable.

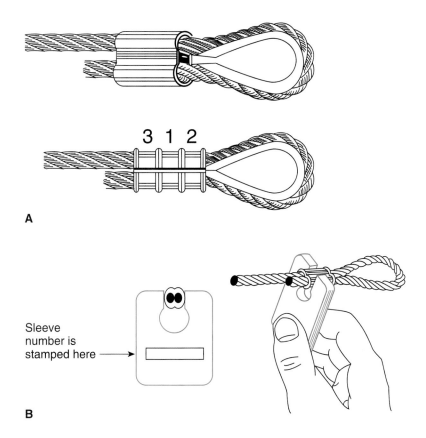

Figure 7-46
A. *Installation of Nicopress-type sleeves on a control cable.*
B. *Typical Nicopress gage*

Sleeve number is stamped here →

A

B

Turnbuckles

Control cable tension is adjusted by using turnbuckles such as the one in Figure 7-47. The bronze barrel has right-hand threads in one end and left-hand threads in the other end. The cable terminal ends are screwed into the barrel and as it is turned, it pulls the ends into it. To be sure that the terminals are screwed into the barrel enough to produce full strength, there must be no more than three threads exposed on either end of the barrel.

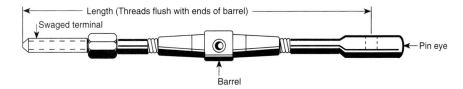

Length (Threads flush with ends of barrel)
Swaged terminal
Pin eye
Barrel

Figure 7-47. *Typical control cable turnbuckle*

When the cable tension is properly adjusted, safety the turnbuckle with the methods shown in Figure 7-48. Figure 7-49 is a guide for selecting the method and size safety wire to use.

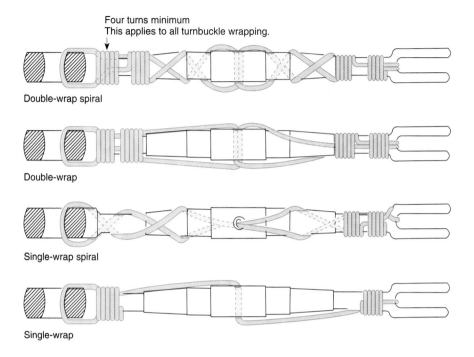

Four turns minimum
This applies to all turnbuckle wrapping.

Double-wrap spiral

Double-wrap

Single-wrap spiral

Single-wrap

Figure 7-48. *Turnbuckle safetying methods*

Cable size inch	Type of wrap	Safety wire diameter	Safety wire material
1/16	Single	0.040	Copper or brass
3/32	Single	0.040	Copper or brass
1/8	Single	0.040	Stainless steel
1/8	Double	0.040	Copper or brass
1/8	Single	0.057	Copper or brass
5/32	Double	0.040	Stainless steel
5/32	Single	0.057	Stainless steel
5/32	Double	0.051	Copper or brass

Figure 7-49. *Turnbuckle safetying guide*

Some turnbuckles are made for special locking devices such as the one in Figure 7-50. The cable tension is adjusted with the turnbuckle, and it is safetied by inserting the long end of the MS21256 wire locking clip into the groove cut into the inside of the barrel and the terminal ends. The clip is locked in place by passing its end into the hole in the side of the barrel. Notice that there is a groove around one end of the turnbuckle barrel in Figure 7-50. This groove identifies the end of the barrel that has the left-hand threads.

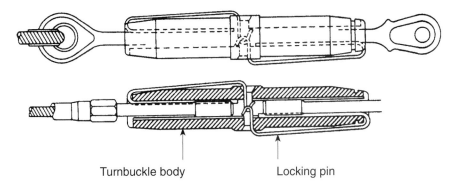

Turnbuckle body   Locking pin

Figure 7-50. *Clip type locking device for turnbuckles*

Aircraft Rivets

The greater part of a modern all-metal aircraft structure is held together with solid aluminum alloy rivets. It is the responsibility of an aviation maintenance technician to be able to inspect riveted joints and to remove damaged rivets and replace them with the correct type of rivet. In Chapter 2 of the *Airframe* textbook (Volume 1) in this *Aviation Maintenance Technician Series*, the actual methods of selection, inspection, installation, and removal of solid aircraft rivets are discussed.

Rivet Material Specifications

Since so many rivets are used in an aircraft structure, and since they are so small, some method must be used to allow a technician to know exactly what type of rivet is used. The material of which a rivet is made is indicated by marks on its head. These marks and their meaning are shown in Figure 7-51.

Material	Head Marking	Material Code
1100	No marks	A
2117T	Recessed dot	AD
2017T	Raised dot	D
2024T	Raised double dash	DD
5056T	Raised cross	B
7075T73	Raised three dashes	
Corrosion resistant steel	Raised dash	F
Copper	No marks	C
Monel	No marks	M

Figure 7-51. *Material specifications for aircraft solid rivets*

Rivet Head Style

In the past, there have been a large number of rivet head styles, but these have evolved until now there are two that are used in most modern construction. Figure 7-52 shows the old rivet number and the number of the modern rivet that has replaced it.

Old Rivet	Replaced by
AN 426 100° countersunk head	MS 20426 100° countersunk head
AN 430 Round head	MS 20470 Universal head
AN 442 Flat head	MS 20470 Universal head
AN 455 Brazier head	MS 20470 Universal head
AN 456 Modified brazier head	MS 20470 Universal head

Figure 7-52. *MS rivet replacement for AN rivets*

Rivet Identification

The part number of a rivet identifies its head shape, its material, its diameter, and its length. The head shape is specified by its AN or MS number; its material is specified by the material code letter; its diameter in $\frac{1}{32}$-inch increments is given by the first dash number; and its length, in $\frac{1}{16}$-inch increments is given by the second dash number. Examples of rivet identification numbers are shown in Figure 7-54.

The length of a rivet is measured from the bottom of the head of a protruding-head rivet to the end of the shank, and from the top of a countersunk-head rivet to the end of its shank, as in Figure 7-55.

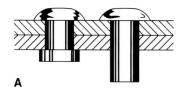

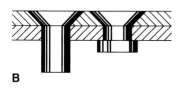

Figure 7-53
A. *MS20470 universal head rivet*
B. *MS20426 100° countersunk head rivet*

Part Number	Head Style	Material	Diameter (inch)	Length (inch)
MS 20426AD4-6	100° csk	2117	$1/8$	$3/8$
MS 20470DD6-8	Universal	2024	$3/16$	$1/2$
MS 20470D8-10	Universal	2017	$1/4$	$5/8$
AN 430A4-4	Round	1100	$1/8$	$1/4$

Figure 7-54. *Examples of rivet identification*

Special Rivets

Solid rivets are used for most of the riveted joints in an aircraft structure, but there are locations where a bucking bar cannot reach the end of the rivet and special "blind" rivets must be used.

Friction-Lock Self-Plugging Rivets

These rivets, seen in Figure 7-56, are installed by slipping them through the hole in the sheet metal, attaching a pulling tool to the stem, and pulling. When the stem is pulled, the tapered mandrel portion of the stem expands the end of the shank, which pulls the sheets tightly together and forms an upset head inside the structure. Continued pulling causes the stem to snap off at a predefined breakoff groove. Friction holds the bottom end of the stem inside the hollow shank, which increases the shear strength of the rivet. Friction-lock rivets are not generally approved for direct size-for-size substitution for solid rivets, but may often be used if they are one size larger than the solid rivet they replace.

It is important when using friction-lock rivets that the correct grip length be selected. The end of the shank should protrude through the skin between $3/64$ and $1/8$ inch, as in dimension B in Figure 7-57.

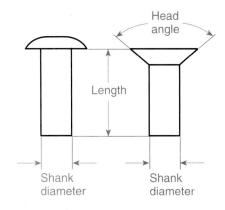

Figure 7-55. *Method of measuring solid rivets*

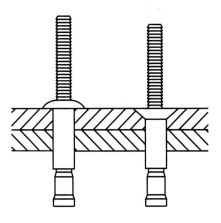

Figure 7-56. *Friction-lock self-plugging rivets*

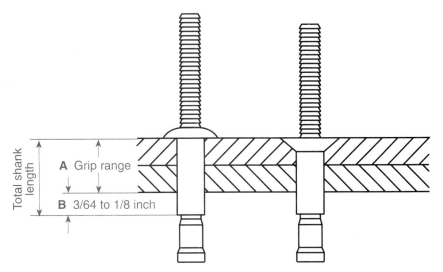

Figure 7-57. *Determining the length of friction-lock rivets*

Pop Rivets

Pop rivets are used in many commercial devices where speed of installation is important. They are not used for structural applications in certificated aircraft, but are used in many applications for amateur-built aircraft.

Mechanical-Lock Self-Plugging Rivets

Cherrylock® mechanical-lock rivets are similar in installation to friction-lock rivets, but have the advantage that the stem is locked in the hollow shank to increase the strength of the rivet. When the stem is pulled up into the shank, a collar is forced tightly into a groove in the shank. It locks the shank in place, and the final pull produced by the tool snaps the end of the stem off flush with the rivet head. These rivets can be used to replace solid rivets on a size-for-size basis. *See* Figure 7-58.

The shank diameter of mechanical-lock self-plugging rivets is measured in increments of $\frac{1}{32}$ inch and the grip length is measured in $\frac{1}{16}$-inch increments. To determine the correct grip length a special grip gage such as the one seen in Figure 7-59 is used. In this example the gage indicates a -4 grip length, which is usable for material thickness between $\frac{3}{16}$ and $\frac{1}{4}$ inch.

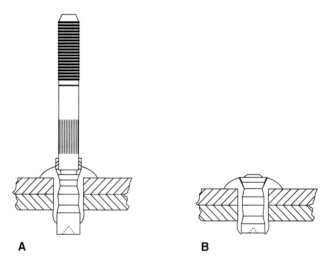

A   B

Figure 7-58. *Cherrylock® mechanical-lock self-plugging rivet*
A. The stem has been pulled up into the shank, the shank has expanded to tightly fill the rivet hole, and the locking groove has been pulled up into the rivet head.
B. The locking collar has been swaged into the groove in the stem, and the stem has been snapped off flush with the rivet head.

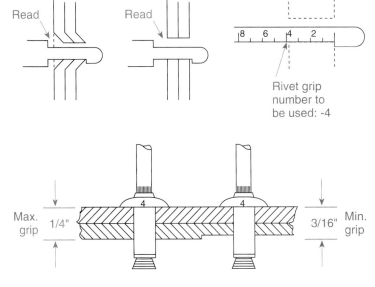

Rivet grip
number to
be used: -4

Max.
grip   1/4"

3/16"   Min.
grip

Figure 7-59. *Using a grip gage to determine the grip length of a mechanical-lock self-plugging rivet*

Figure 7-60. *Countersunk head Rivnut installed in a piece of thin sheet metal*

Rivnuts

It is often necessary to install a threaded fastener in a piece of thin sheet metal. A practical solution to this problem was found many years ago by the B.F. Goodrich Company for the installation of their rubber deicing boots on the leading edges of wings and empennages.

A hole of the correct size is drilled and a keyway is cut in the edge of the hole. If the Rivnut is to be a flush type, the hole is dimpled. The Rivnut is screwed onto the installation tool and is inserted in the hole with the key in the keyway. The installation tool pulls the Rivnut tight enough to form a head on the inside of the structure and squeezes the Rivnut tight enough around the skin to prevent it turning when it is used as a nut.

Hi-Shear Pin Rivets

There are locations in an aircraft structure where the strength of a steel bolt is required, but there is no need for the fastener to be removed in normal maintenance operations. For these applications, a high-strength pin rivet may be used. Figure 7-61 shows such a fastener. A steel pin with a flat head on one end and a groove around the other end is slipped through the hole in the structure. An aluminum alloy collar is slipped over the grooved end and a special swaging tool is used to swage the collar into the groove. Hi-Shear rivets have sufficient strength to replace structural steel bolts on a size-for-size basis. *See* Figure 7-61.

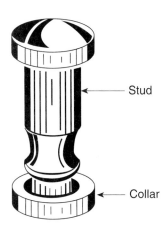

Stud

Collar

Figure 7-61. *A Hi-Shear pin rivet with collar*

Answers are on Page 524. Page numbers refer to chapter text.

66. The threads for most aircraft structural bolts have a class-_____ fit. *Page 489*

67. Torque values listed for aircraft bolts normally consider the threads to be clean and _____ (dry or lubricated). *Page 490*

68. The accepted rule of thumb for installing bolts in an aircraft structure is to have the bolt head _____ (up or down), _____ (forward, or rearward), and _____ (inboard or outboard). *Page 493*

69. A fiber-type self-locking nut should never be used on a bolt if the fastener is subject to _____ . *Page 495*

70. Identify the material of which the bolt is made when its head is marked with a/an:
    a. cross or asterisk _____
    b. single dash _____
    c. two dashes _____
        Page 493

71. A bolt whose head is identified with an asterisk enclosed in a triangle is a _____ bolt. *Page 493*

72. A steel bolt with no marking on its head is made of _____ steel and _____ (is or is not) approved for use in aircraft structure. *Page 492*

73. The length of the unthreaded portion of a bolt shank is called the _____ of the bolt. *Page 493*

74. Clevis bolts are designed to be used for _____ loads only. *Page 494*

75. Extraflexible control cable is made up of _____ individual strands of wire. *Page 500*

76. A swaged control cable terminal grips the cable with a strength equal to _____% of the strength of the cable. *Page 501*

77. To be sure that the terminal ends are screwed into a turnbuckle barrel enough to produce the maximum strength, there must be no more than _____ (how many) threads showing on either end of the barrel. *Page 507*

78. When safetying a turnbuckle, the ends of the safety wire must be wrapped around the terminal end for at least _____ (how many) turns. *Page 504*

79. Identify the material of which solid rivets are made which have the following head markings:
    a. raised dot _____
    b. recessed dot _____
    c. raised double dash _____
    d. raised cross _____
       Page 506

80. Give the diameter and length of these solid rivets:
    a. MS20470AD4-4   Diameter _____ in.   Length _____ in.
    b. MS20426DD4-6   Diameter _____ in.   Length _____ in.
    c. MS20470D6-8   Diameter _____ in.   Length _____ in.
    d. MS20426AD6-10   Diameter _____ in.   Length _____ in.
       Page 507

81. Friction-lock self-plugging rivets _____ (are or are not) approved for replacement of solid rivets on a size-for-size basis. *Page 507*

82. When it is necessary to provide a threaded hole in a piece of thin sheet metal, a _____ may be used. *Page 509*

83. Hi-Shear pin rivets _____ (may or may not) be used to replace steel aircraft bolts on a size-for-size basis. *Page 509*

Measuring Devices

Here we have a brief introduction to measuring devices, and a more comprehensive discussion of these and other tools are covered in Chapter 14, beginning on Page 729.

During the operational life of an aircraft, its moving parts undergo dimensional changes. As a maintenance technician, you must have a working knowledge of the basic precision measuring devices, know how to use them properly and how to read them correctly. Finally, you must be able to compare the measurements you have made with the manufacturer's recommended service limits to determine the continued airworthiness of the component.

Dial Indicators

Dial indicators are precision measuring instruments used to measure such things as crankshaft runout, gear backlash, end-play in a shaft or axle, and radial play in such components as turbosupercharger rotors.

To measure shaft end-play, clamp the dial indicator to a rigid part of the structure and push the shaft to one extreme of its travel. Move the indicator until its arm presses against the end of the shaft, and rotate the dial until the needle indicates zero.

Move the shaft to the opposite end of its travel, and read the dial of the indicator to see the distance, in thousandths of an inch, the shaft has moved. This movement is the shaft end-play.

Crankshaft runout (the amount the crankshaft wobbles as it turns) is also measured with a dial indicator. Place the crankshaft in V-blocks and mount a dial indicator so its arm presses against the crankshaft at the point the runout measurement is to be taken.

Rotate the shaft until the lowest reading is shown, and zero the gage at this point. Rotate the crankshaft for one full revolution, and record the amount the indicator needle travels.

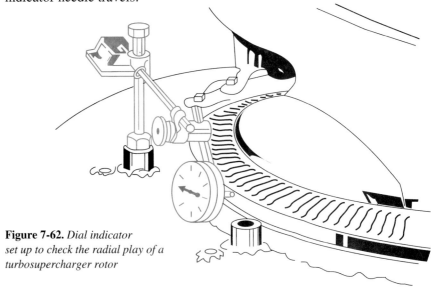

Figure 7-62. *Dial indicator set up to check the radial play of a turbosupercharger rotor*

Micrometer Calipers

Micrometer calipers, such as the one in Figure 7-63, are used for measuring outside dimensions for wear or out-of round conditions. They may also be used with small-hole gages and telescoping gages to measure inside dimensions.

Micrometer calipers are checked for accuracy by using gage blocks. A 0-to-1-inch micrometer is checked for its proper zero indication with the thimble screwed down against the anvil. For its 1-inch indication, it is checked with a 1-inch gage block. A 1-to-2-inch micrometer uses a 1-inch and a 2-inch gage block, and a 2-to-3-inch micrometer uses a 2-inch and a 3-inch gage block.

A micrometer caliper is used to measure a crankpin and a main bearing journal for an out-of-round condition. Make two measurements at right angles to each other; the difference between the two readings is the amount the shaft is out-of-round.

A standard micrometer caliper can be read directly to three decimal places; that is, to one thousandth of an inch (0.001 inch). A vernier micrometer caliper can be read directly to one ten thousandth of an inch (0.0001 inch).

gage block. A precision ground block of hardened and polished steel used to check the accuracy of micrometer calipers. Their dimensional accuracy is normally measured in millionths of an inch.

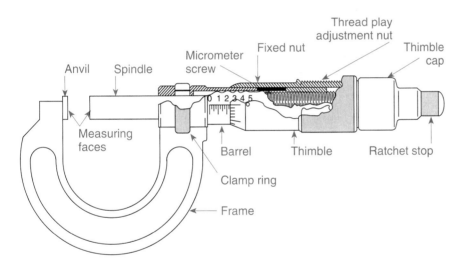

Figure 7-63. *Nomenclature of an outside micrometer caliper*

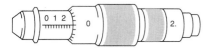

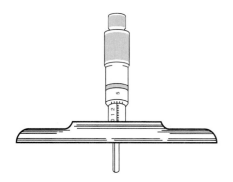

Figure 7-64. *An inside micrometer caliper*

Figure 7-65. *A depth micrometer caliper*

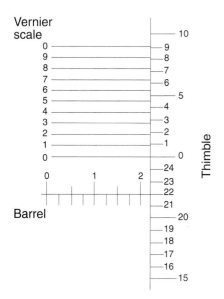

Figure 7-66. *Vernier micrometer caliper*

The inside diameter of a large hole is measured with an inside micrometer caliper such as the one in Figure 7-64. The diameter of a small hole is measured with a telescoping gage or a small-hole ball-gage, such as those seen in Figure 7-69. After these gages have been adjusted to the exact diameter of the hole, they are removed and measured with a micrometer caliper.

The depth of a groove in a machined part is measured with a depth micrometer (*see* Figure 7-65). The end of the spindle is flush with the bar when the instrument reads zero, and as the thimble is turned outward, the spindle extends from the bar.

To read the vernier micrometer caliper in Figure 7-66, follow these steps:

1. Adjust the thimble until the object to be measured exactly fills the space between the anvil and the spindle.

2. Read the number of graduations on the barrel beyond which the thimble has moved. The thimble has moved out beyond the 2 mark on the barrel but not quite to the first mark beyond it.

3. Read the number on the thimble that has just moved past the horizontal line on the barrel. In this case it is the number 22.

4. Find the line on the vernier scale that exactly lines up with one of the marks on the thimble. In this case the lower 0 line is exactly aligned with one of the marks on the barrel, the 0 mark.

5. Add the number of ten thousandths of an inch (the number of the line on the vernier scale) to the number of thousandths of an inch from the barrel and thimble.

6.

Barrel	0.2000
Thimble	0.0220
Vernier scale	+ 0.0000
Total reading	0.2220 inch

To read the metric vernier caliper in Figure 7-67, follow these steps:

1. Adjust the thimble until the object to be measured exactly fills the space between the anvil and the spindle.

2. Read the number of graduations on the barrel beyond which the thimble has moved. The thimble has moved out beyond the 8 mark below the horizontal line on the barrel and beyond the 0.5 mark above the horizontal line.

3. Read the number on the thimble that has just moved past the horizontal line on the barrel. In this example the number is 25.

4. Find the line on the vernier scale that exactly lines up with one of the marks on the thimble. In this example, the line beside number 6 is exactly in line with one of the marks.

5. Add the number of thousandths of a millimeter (the number of the line on the vernier scale) to the number of millimeters and hundredths of a millimeter from the barrel and thimble.

6. Barrel   8.50   mm
   Thimble   0.25   mm
   Vernier scale   + 0.006 mm
                   ──────────
   Total reading   8.756 mm

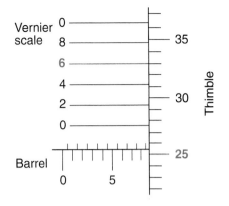

Figure 7-67. *Metric vernier micrometer caliper*

Vernier Calipers

A vernier caliper is a precision measuring instrument used to make inside or outside measurements with an accuracy in the range of $\frac{1}{1,000}$ inch or $\frac{1}{50}$ millimeter. They are more versatile than a standard micrometer caliper because of their greater range. Vernier calipers come in various sizes and with special jaws for special types of measurements. The most widely used machinist caliper measures from 0 to 6 inches. Figure 7-68 shows a typical vernier caliper with the scale enlarged.

The movable jaw of the vernier caliper moves a vernier scale next to the main scale. The distance between the end marks on the vernier scale is divided into one more space than the same distance on the main scale.

To read the vernier caliper in Figure 7-68, follow these steps:

1. Read the inches, tenths, and hundredths of an inch on the main scale opposite the zero on the vernier scale. The zero is past the 1-inch mark, past the 1.1-inch mark, and past the third mark beyond this. This is a total of 1.175 inches.

2. Find the line on the vernier scale that exactly lines up with one of the marks on the main scale. The 20 line on the vernier scale lines up with one of the marks on the main scale, so we add 0.020 to the reading found in step 1.

3. The final reading is 1.175 + .020 = 1.195 inches.

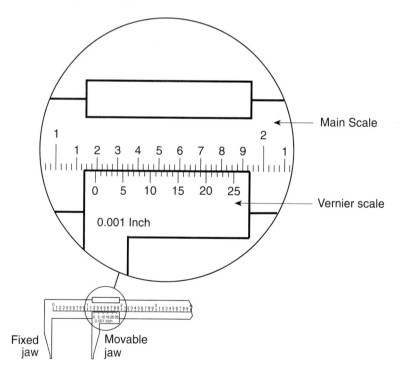

Figure 7-68. *A vernier caliper*

Small-Hole Gages and Telescoping Gages

The diameter of a small hole may be measured by placing a ball-type small-hole gage, Figure 7-69A, in the hole and expanding it until its outside diameter is exactly the same size as the inside diameter of the hole. Remove the gage from the hole, and measure its outside diameter with a micrometer caliper.

The diameter of larger holes that are too small to use an inside micrometer may be measured with a T-shaped telescoping gage, such as the ones in Figure 7-69 B. Select a gage having the right range and place it across the hole and release the locking handle. This releases the inside of the telescoping head, and a spring forces it against the walls of the hole. Hold the gage straight across the hole and lock the head by twisting the handle. Remove the gage and measure the length of the head with a micrometer caliper.

A dimensional inspection of a bearing in a rocker arm can be made by expanding a telescopic gage inside the bushing (bearing) until its length is exactly the same as the inside diameter of the bushing. Remove the gage and measure it with a micrometer caliper.

Measure the rocker arm shaft with the same micrometer caliper; the difference between the diameter of the shaft and that of the hole is the fit of the shaft in its bushing.

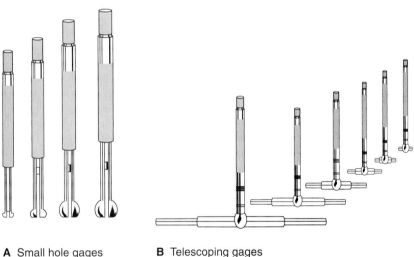

A Small hole gages   **B** Telescoping gages

Figure 7-69. *Gages*

Dividers and Calipers

Dividers are used to transfer a measurement from a device to a scale to determine its value. Place the sharp points at the locations from which the measurement is to be taken. Then place the points on a steel machinist's scale and read the distance between them. Do not measure from the end of the scale, but put one of the points on the 1-inch mark and measure from there.

Inside calipers, Figure 7-70A, are similar to dividers except that the tips are blunt and are turned outward. Place the tips of the calipers inside the hole to be measured, and turn the knurled knob so the spring can force the tips outward until they exactly match the inside diameter of the hole. Remove the calipers and measure the distance between the tips with a steel scale or with a vernier caliper.

Outside calipers, Figure 7-70B, are similar to inside calipers except that the tips are turned inward. The knurled knob is adjusted until the tips fit exactly across the part being measured. The distance between the tips is then measured with a steel scale or a vernier caliper.

Hermaphrodite calipers, Figure 7-70C, are used to scribe a line a specified distance from the edge of a part which has a radius on its edge. Hermaphrodite calipers are not used for precision measurements.

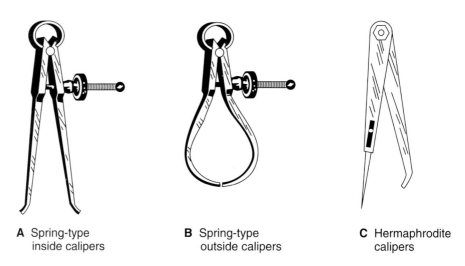

A Spring-type inside calipers

B Spring-type outside calipers

C Hermaphrodite calipers

Figure 7-70. *Calipers*

Thickness Gages

Thickness gages, or feeler gages, are precision-ground steel leaves, used to measure the clearance, or space, between parts. The number stamped on the thickest leaf that will fit between the parts is the separation between the parts in thousandths of an inch.

A thickness gage is used to measure the side clearance of a piston ring in its ring groove. The ring is installed in the groove, and its outside edge is held flush with the side of the piston. A thickness gage is placed between the side of the piston ring and the edge of the ring groove to measure the amount of clearance between the ring and the groove. *See* Figures 7-71 and 7-72.

Figure 7-71. *A set of thickness gages*

Combination Set

A combination set, Figure 7-73, consists of a steel scale with three heads that can be moved to any position on the scale and locked in place.

The three heads are: a stock head that measures 90-degree and 45-degree angles, a protractor head that can measure any angle between the head and the blade, and the center head that uses one side of the blade as the bisector of a 90° angle.

The center of a shaft can be found by using the center head. Place the end of the shaft in the V of the head and scribe a line along the edge of the scale. Rotate the head about 90° and scribe another line along the edge of the scale. The two lines will cross at the center of the shaft.

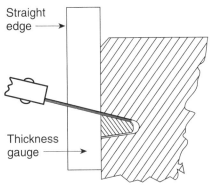

Figure 7-72. *Thickness gage being used to measure piston ring side clearance*

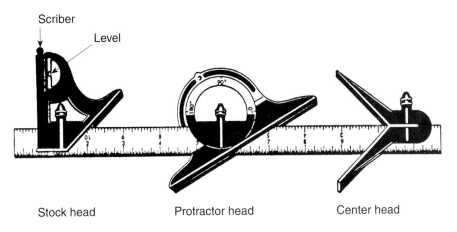

Scriber

Level

Stock head

Protractor head

Center head

Figure 7-73. *A combination set*

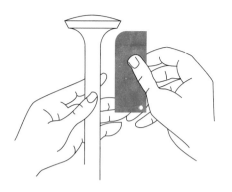

Figure 7-74. *A valve stretch gage*

Valve-Stretch Gage

A valve-stretch gage is used to determine whether or not a poppet valve has stretched. It is a flat metal precision tool with an accurate radius on one corner. The gage is held against a valve stem, and if the valve is stretched, the radius between the stem and the head will not be the same as the radius of the gage.

Connecting Rod Twist Fixture

Connecting rod twist is measured by fitting an arbor in each end of the rod and placing the arbors across parallel bars on a precision-ground surface plate. A feeler gage, or thickness gage, is passed between the ends of the arbors and the parallel bars to measure the amount of twist in the rod.

Figure 7-75. *Arbors, parallel bars, and thickness gages are used to measure the amount of twist in a connecting rod.*

Answers are on Page 524. **Page numbers refer to chapter text.**

84. Axle end-play can be measured with a/an _____ . *Page 512*

85. Refer to the figure below. This vernier micrometer caliper reads _____ inch. *Page 514*

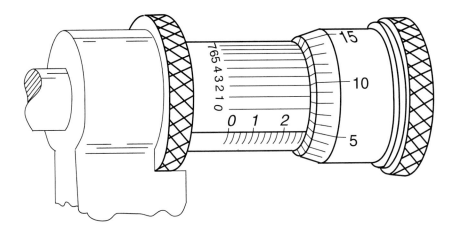

86. Refer to the figure below. This vernier caliper reads _____ inches. *Page 516*

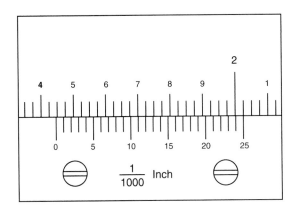

87. A part may be checked for flatness by using a surface plate and a _____ . *Page 519*

88. The vernier scale on a vernier micrometer caliper is used to give an indication of _____ inch of spindle movement. *Page 514*

Continued

89. A tool used to find the center of a shaft or other circle is the _____ head of a combination set. *Page 519*

90. The diameter of a small hole is measured with a _ _____ . *Page 517*

91. Refer to the figure below. This vernier micrometer caliper reads _____ inch. *Page 514*

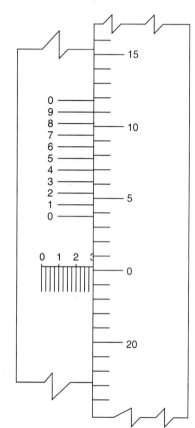

92. The distance between the points of a pair of dividers is measured with a/an
_____ . *Page 518*

93. The accuracy of a micrometer caliper may be checked and calibrated by using
_____ . *Page 513*

94. An engine crankpin may be measured for out-of-round by using a/an
_____ . *Page 513*

95. The side clearance and end-gap clearance of a piston ring in a piston are measured using a/an
_____ . *Page 519*

96. Crankshaft runout of a reciprocating engine may be measured with a/an
_____ . *Page 512*

97. A dimensional inspection of the bushing in a rocker arm can be measured with
a/an_____ and a/an _____ . *Page 517*

98. A reciprocating engine poppet valve can be measured for stretch by using a/an
_____ gage. *Page 520*

Answers to Chapter 7 Study Questions

1. stainless steel
2. 4130
3. pure aluminum
4. 0.20
5. 1100
6. a. 2XXX
   b. 5XXX
   c. 7XXX
7. inert gas
8. sitka spruce
9. 80
10. heat
11. thermosetting
12. polyester
13. epoxy
14. bidirectional
15. lighter
16. is not
17. case hardening
18. annealing
19. normalizing
20. tempering
21. a. carburizing
    b. nitriding
22. ammonia
23. slowly
24. solution
25. precipitation
26. aging
27. brine
28. tempering
29. a. F
    b. O
    c. T
    d. H
30. 2017, 2024
31. clad
32. 2117
33. normalizing
34. intergranular

35. radiographic
36. a. X-ray
    b. gamma-ray
37. soft
38. radiation monitor
39. can
40. iron
41. continuous
42. residual
43. longitudinally
44. circularly
45. circularly
46. longitudinally
47. a. dry powder
    b. oxide suspended in a
       light oil
48. DC
49. AC
50. inclusion
51. fatigue
52. does
53. developer
54. can
55. ultraviolet
56. is not
57. is not
58. eddy current
59. delamination
60. relieve stresses
61. removed
62. crack
63. ½
64. 25, 50
65. a. B
    b. D
    c. A
    d. C
66. 3
67. dry
68. up, forward, outboard

69. rotation
70. a. nickel steel
    b. corrosion-resistant steel
    c. aluminum alloy
71. close-tolerance
72. low-strength, is not
73. grip length
74. shear
75. 133
76. 100
77. 3
78. 4
79. a. 2017T
    b. 2117T
    c. 2024T
    d. 5056T
80. a. ⅛, ¼
    b. ⅛, ⅜
    c. ³⁄₁₆, ½
    d. ³⁄₁₆, ⅝
81. are not
82. Rivnut
83. may
84. dial indicator
85. 0.2792
86. 1.437
87. thickness gage
88. 0.0001
89. center
90. small-hole gage
91. 0.3009
92. machinist's scale
93. gage blocks
94. micrometer caliper
95. thickness gage
96. dial indicator
97. telescoping gage, micrometer
    caliper
98. valve stretch

CLEANING AND CORROSION CONTROL

Corrosion Control *(Continued)*

CLEANING AND CORROSION CONTROL

8

Cleaning

Aircraft fly more hours than ever before, and there are many old airplanes in the sky. These high-time aircraft have been given the name "the aging fleet," and keeping them free of corrosion is one of the big challenges faced by today's aviation maintenance technician. In this chapter, we will study the various types of corrosion, their causes and appearance, and learn of the ways to control corrosion.

Aircraft Cleaning

The most fundamental and important rule for corrosion control is to keep the aircraft clean. When it is clean and free of grease and dirt, there is nothing to hold the corrosion-forming moisture in contact with the aluminum alloy surface. Also, a clean aircraft is easy to inspect for the first indication of corrosion. In this section, we will consider the ways of cleaning both metal and nonmetal components.

Exterior Cleaning

A clean aircraft is easy to inspect for corrosion. Grime, dirt, exhaust residue, and deposits of dried oil and grease can be removed with a water emulsion-type cleaner that meets MIL-C-43616 specifications. The aircraft should be parked in an area where it can be hosed down and preferably in an area where the sun will not dry the surface before the cleaner has had time to penetrate the film.

Before washing the aircraft, install covers over the engine inlets and pitot tubes to prevent damage. Special care should be exercised when washing the windshield and windows to prevent their being exposed to harmful cleaners or scratched. Antiglare paint used on the top of the fuselage ahead of the pilot should be cleaned with special care, as it is easy to damage.

Dilute the cleaner with water to a ratio between 1:5 and 1:3 for cleaning most of the exterior of the aircraft. Brush or spray the cleaner on the surface and allow it to stand for a few minutes, then rinse it off with a high-pressure stream of warm water.

Wheel well areas and the engine cowling usually have grease and oil deposits in them that this treatment will not remove. To get rid of these deposits, soak them with a 1:2 dilution of the emulsion cleaner. After allowing the cleaner to soak for a few minutes, scrub the deposits with a soft bristle

emulsion-type cleaner. A chemical cleaner which mixes with water or petroleum solvent to form an emulsion (a mixture which will separate if it is allowed to stand). Emulsion-type cleaners are used to loosen dirt, soot, or oxide films from the surface of an aircraft.

brush to completely loosen the film. Then rinse the area with a high-pressure stream of warm water.

Exhaust stains are usually difficult to remove, but you can use a 1:2 dilution of the emulsion cleaner with varsol or kerosine. Mix the cleaner into a creamy emulsion and brush or spray it on the surface. Let it stand for a few minutes and work all of the loosened residue with a bristle brush, then hose it off with a high-pressure stream of warm water. If you do not get all of the stains off with the first application, repeat the treatment.

Aluminum and magnesium alloys are reactive metals, and many caustic cleaning products react with them to form salts of corrosion. Because of this, use only cleaning materials known to be safe for these metals.

It is important when chemically cleaning a structure that the faying surfaces, the parts of a structure that are covered in lap joints, be protected so that corrosive materials do not seep between the sheets. This would cause corrosion to form in an area where it is hard to detect.

Aliphatic naphtha is a petroleum product between gasoline and kerosine in its characteristics and is a good general cleaning agent for removing oily deposits from a painted surface. Aromatic naphtha, which is a derivative of coal tar, should not be used because it is toxic and it attacks acrylics and rubber products.

Other chemicals that can be used for exterior cleaning are trichloroethane (methyl chloroform), methyl-ethyl-ketone (MEK), and a dry-cleaning solvent such as Stoddard solvent. All traces of oil and grease may be removed from an aircraft surface prior to doping or painting by wiping it with dope thinner or acetone.

Nonmetal Cleaning

Transparent plastics such as acrylics are soft and easily scratched, and a scratched windshield can interfere with the pilot's vision. When cleaning a windshield, first flush the surface with plenty of fresh water to dissolve any salt deposits and wash away any dirt or dust particles. Remove any oil and grease by wiping it with a rag dampened with aliphatic naphtha. Then wash it with a mild soap and water, using your hand so you can feel any abrasive particles. Rinse the surface with fresh water and dry with a chamois or absorbent cotton. When the surface is completely clean, it can be protected with a coat of wax.

Aircraft tires can be damaged by allowing engine oil to drip on them and remain there. Oil and grease should be wiped off with a dry rag or one dampened with aliphatic naphtha. Then the tire should be washed with mild soap and water and dried with compressed air.

When preparing a metal or fabric-covered surface to be painted, remove every trace of oil or grease, as even the oil from a fingerprint can prevent dope or paint adhering to the surface. The final cleaning can be done by wiping it down with a rag dampened with dope thinner or acetone.

fayed surface (faying surface). The metal that is covered in a lap joint.

aliphatic naphtha. A petroleum product similar to gasoline and kerosine. It is used as a cleaning agent to remove grease from a surface prior to painting.

aromatic naphtha. A coal tar derivative that is used as an additive in certain reciprocating engine fuels, but is not used for cleaning aircraft parts.

Powerplant Cleaning

Grease and dirt on an air-cooled aircraft engine can interfere with the cooling and can hide cracks and other defects. To effectively clean an engine, remove all of the cowling, and beginning at the top of the engine, wash it down with a fine spray of kerosine and an emulsion cleaner. A bristle brush may be used on some of the difficult deposits. After the engine is cleaned and dried with compressed air, all of the control rods, bellcranks, and moving parts should be lubricated by the method specified by the aircraft manufacturer.

The propeller should be washed with soap and fresh water and dried, then protected with a thin coating of fresh engine oil. Propeller blades should be carefully checked for any evidence of pitting caused by sand or water. All pits should be carefully removed by the procedure described in the section on propellers in the Powerplant section of this textbook series

Paint Removal

After the structure is completely cleaned, if corrosion does exist, the damage must be assessed and a decision made on what action to take. All corrosion products must be removed as soon as they are discovered because corrosion will continue as long as these products are allowed to remain on the surface.

Corrosion that has formed beneath a coat of paint cannot be thoroughly inspected without first removing all of the paint. Before using any paint remover with which you are not completely familiar, first test it on a piece of metal that is similar to that from which you will be removing the paint. If the remover does not have any adverse effects on the test metal, it is safe to use.

Mask off all areas that are not to be stripped with a good quality masking paper and tape, to keep the stripper from accidentally coming into contact with any of the finish that you do not want removed.

Water-rinsible paint removers that have the consistency of a heavy syrup are best for aircraft surfaces. Apply the remover by daubing it on the surface with a brush rather than by brushing it on. Cover the surface with a heavy coating and allow it to stand until the old paint swells and wrinkles up. This breaks the bond between the surface and the finish.

Cover the surface that has the paint remover on it with polyethylene sheeting to prevent the solvents in the remover from evaporating. This will allow the remover to remain active long enough to penetrate the old finish. If the first application does not loosen all of the finish, it may be necessary to use a second coating. Scrape all of the residue away with a plastic or aluminum scraper and apply the second coating of remover. By getting rid of all of the loosened finishing materials and putting on a second coating, the active chemicals can get to the lower layers and break them away from the metal. After all of the finish has swelled up and broken away from the surface, rinse it off with hot water or steam. A stiff bristle brush will most probably be needed to get rid of all of the residue from around rivet heads and along the seams.

Caution must be used any time you are working with a paint remover because many solvents attack rubber and synthetic rubber products. Tires, hoses, and seals must be protected to keep the paint remover away from them.

The solvents used in paint removers are usually quite toxic, and you should take special care to not get them on your skin or in your eyes. If you should get any of it on your skin, flush it off with water immediately. If you get any in your eyes, flush them out with clean water and get medical attention as soon as possible.

STUDY QUESTIONS: CLEANING

Answers are on Page 578. **Page numbers refer to chapter text.**

1. Dirt, grime and exhaust residue can be removed from an aircraft structure by using a/an
   _____ type cleaner. *Page 529*

2. Stubborn exhaust stains can be removed from an aircraft by scrubbing the area with an emulsion cleaner
   mixed with _____ or _____ . *Page 530*

3. All traces of oil and grease may be removed from an aircraft surface prior to doping or painting by wiping
   it with dope thinner or _____ . *Page 530*

4. If a tire is covered with engine lubricating oil, all of the excess oil should be removed by wiping it with a
   dry cloth, then scrubbing it with a solution of _____ . *Page 530*

5. Oil and grease may be removed from acrylic plastics and rubber by wiping them with a rag dampened with
   _____ . *Page 530*

Corrosion Control

Modern aircraft are made of lightweight metals that are highly sensitive to contaminants in the atmosphere. Salt air from coastal regions and industrial contaminants from urban areas attack aluminum and magnesium alloy structures. Corrosion damage caused by these attacks cost the aviation industry billions of dollars each year. The advanced age of many airliners and military aircraft has made corrosion detection and removal one of the most important aspects of modern aircraft maintenance.

Corrosion is a complex electro-chemical action that transforms a strong metal into a powdery chemical salt that has no strength. While it is quite complex in its nature, corrosion's actual mechanics are relatively simple and straight forward.

In order for corrosion to form on or in a metal, three requirements must be met:

1. There must be an electrical potential difference (a voltage difference) within the metal.

2. There must be a conductive path between the areas of potential difference.

3. There must be some form of electrolyte, or electrically conductive liquid or gas, covering the areas of potential difference.

A carbon-zinc battery is an example of a corrosion cell. When there is a complete circuit between the terminals of the battery, as seen in Figure 8-1, electrons flow from the negative zinc can to the positive carbon rod. When the electrons leave the zinc, negative chloride ions from the electrolyte replace them and change some of the zinc metal into zinc chloride, a powdery salt. When the battery is producing current, the can is being corroded, or eaten away.

Corrosion is a natural process that is almost impossible to prevent, but it can be controlled in any of three ways:

1. We can minimize the electrical potential difference that exists within the metal.

2. We can eliminate the conductive path by placing an insulating barrier between the areas of electrical potential difference.

3. We can cover the surface of the metal with some form of oxide or organic coating to keep the conductive electrolyte from covering the areas in the metal that have a difference in potential.

By controlling the conditions that are necessary for corrosion to form, we can increase the longevity of aircraft and decrease the cost of maintenance.

Keeping the surface clean is one of the best ways to control corrosion. When moisture is held in contact with a metal surface by an accumulation of

corrosion. An electrochemical attack on metal that changes some of the metal into its salts. Corrosion destroys the strength of the metal.

electrolyte. A chemical, either a liquid or a gas, which conducts electrical current by releasing ions that unite with ions on the electrodes.

ion. An atom of a chemical element that does not have the same number of electrons spinning around it as there are protons in its nucleus. A positive ion has fewer electrons than protons, and a negative ion has more electrons than protons.

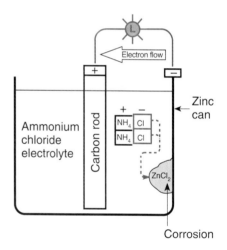

Figure 8-1. *When electrons leave the zinc can, chloride ions from the electrolyte replace them and change some of the zinc into zinc chloride, a salt of corrosion.*

electrical potential. A voltage that exists between different metals and alloys because of their chemical composition. An electrode potential causes electrons to flow between these materials when a conductive path is provided.

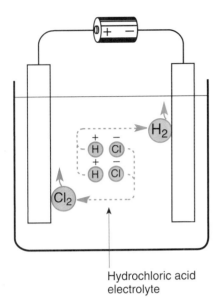

Hydrochloric acid
electrolyte

Figure 8-2. *A simple electrochemical cell breaks the hydrochloric acid down into its two chemical elements.*

Figure 8-3. *Electrochemical series for metals*

dirt or grease, corrosion is sure to start. If the surface can be kept clean and dry, corrosion has very little chance of getting started. The essence of corrosion control is therefore prevention rather than removal.

Once corrosion has formed, all we can do is to remove every trace of it and treat the cleaned surface so it will form a protective, non-porous oxide film. Complete the job by restoring the protective and decorative finish.

If the damage is too extensive, all we can do is replace the affected skin or component.

The Chemistry of Corrosion

To understand corrosion, we must understand the basics of electro-chemistry; corrosion is simply an electro-chemical action.

All matter is made up of atoms and molecules. An atom is the basic unit of a chemical element, while a molecule is a cluster of two or more atoms which make up the smallest identifiable unit of a chemical compound. For example, sodium (Na) is a metallic chemical element, and there are atoms of sodium. Chlorine (Cl) is another chemical element, a gas, and there are atoms of chlorine.

One atom of sodium can combine with one atom of chlorine to form one molecule of a well known chemical compound, sodium chloride (NaCl), common table salt. The characteristics of the molecule of sodium chloride are entirely different from the characteristics of either the metallic sodium or the gaseous chlorine.

An atom of any chemical element has a nucleus that contains protons with positive electrical charges, and neutrons with no electrical charge. Spinning around this nucleus, in a series of shells, are negatively charged electrons. It is the electrons in the outside shell of an atom that can be pulled loose and caused to flow in an electrical circuit, and it is these electrons, called valence electrons, that give an atom its distinctive chemical characteristics.

A balanced atom has exactly the same number of electrons spinning around its nucleus as there are protons in the nucleus, and a balanced atom has no tendency to either gain additional electrons nor lose any of its electrons. However, if an atom is unbalanced, it will try to combine with another unbalanced atom so they can both become balanced. An unbalanced atom is called an ion, and an ion with more electrons than protons is a negative ion, while one with fewer electrons than protons is a positive ion.

A molecule of liquid hydrochloric acid (HCl) is made up of positive hydrogen ions and negative chlorine ions. Figure 8-2 shows two metal bars in a container of hydrochloric acid and a battery connected to the bars. The bar that is connected to the negative terminal of the battery is called the cathode of the cell, and it attracts the positive hydrogen ions. The bar that is connected to the positive terminal of the battery, called the anode of the cell, attracts the negative chlorine ions.

Each hydrogen ion picks up an electron from the cathode and becomes a balanced, or electrically neutral, hydrogen atom. Pairs of these hydrogen atoms join together to form molecules of hydrogen gas that bubble up from the surface of the cathode.

The negative chlorine ions are attracted to the positive anode, and they give up their electrons to the anode which has a deficiency of electrons. When a negative chlorine ion loses its electron, it becomes a neutral chlorine atom, and two of these chlorine atoms join up to form a molecule of chlorine gas that bubbles up from the surface of the anode.

What has happened here is that the hydrochloric acid electrolyte has broken down into its two chemical elements, hydrogen and chlorine. While this was taking place, the solution remains electrically neutral because the same number of molecules of hydrogen gas and chlorine gas are formed.

The amount of chemical action that takes place is determined by the activity of the elements that are involved. Figure 8-3 lists a group of familiar metals arranged according to their chemical activity. The metals at the top of the list are the most anodic and they give up electrons most readily, while those at the bottom of the list are cathodic and do not readily give up their electrons. As we will see, when any two of these metals are involved in a corrosion cell, the metal nearer the top of the list will be corroded while the one below it will not.

If we take a piece of copper and a piece of aluminum and join them with a wire and place them in a solution of hydrochloric acid, we have a battery as in Figure 8-4. This battery forces electrons to flow through the wire, and the aluminum will be corroded, or eaten away.

The hydrochloric acid electrolyte forms positive hydrogen ions and negative chlorine ions. The aluminum, which is more active than the copper, dissolves in the hydrochloric acid, and as it dissolves, it releases electrons. The aluminum metal that has lost the electrons attracts the negative chlorine ions from the electrolyte, and aluminum chloride, a salt, forms where there was originally pure aluminum metal.

The electrons that left the aluminum flow through the wire to the copper, where they attract the positive hydrogen ions from the electrolyte. The hydrogen ions accept the electrons from the copper and become neutral hydrogen atoms. Two hydrogen atoms join together to form a molecule of hydrogen gas, and this gas bubbles to the surface of the electrolyte.

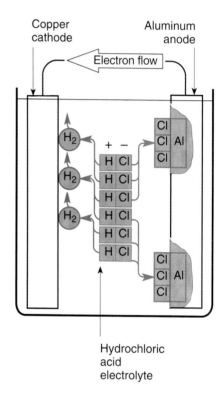

Figure 8-4. *A simple cell consisting of an aluminum anode, a copper cathode, and an electrolyte of hydrochloric acid. When electrons flow from the aluminum to the copper, negative chlorine ions from the electrolyte combine with positive aluminum ions to form aluminum chloride, which is a salt and is the product of corrosion.*

An airplane sitting outside in the industrial atmosphere surrounding most of our modern cities is a fair candidate for major corrosion. The aluminum of which the airplane is made corrodes in the same way as the aluminum in the battery.

Pure aluminum does not corrode readily, but it has very little strength, and for this reason it is not used for aircraft structure. But by alloying aluminum with other metals such as copper, zinc, manganese, and magnesium, we can make a metal that is both light weight and has high strength. However when we alloy the aluminum with these other metals we create the ideal conditions for corrosion to form.

Alloy 2024 is the main structural aluminum alloy that is used in the manufacture of aircraft. It contains 4.5% copper, 0.6% manganese, and 1.5% magnesium. A sheet of 2024 alloy may be protected from the environment by coating its surface with a layer of pure aluminum, by forming a hard film of oxide, or by covering it with a solid film of paint. When it is thus protected, it is relatively resistant to corrosion, but, if it is not properly protected, it will soon dissolve into a dry powder and become worthless as a structural material.

Since we have just seen the way the aluminum electrode of a battery is corroded when it is placed in an electrolyte of hydrochloric acid, let's look at the way an aircraft skin made of 2024 aluminum alloy corrodes when it sits, unprotected, in an industrial atmosphere. *See* Figure 8-5.

Hydrochloric acid is a common pollutant present in industrial haze. When dew forms on an aircraft surface on a cool morning, this hydrochloric acid mixes with it and forms an effective electrolyte that covers the metal. Inside the aluminum alloy are both aluminum and copper, and the aluminum, which is more active than the copper, dissolves in the electrolyte and releases electrons. Now, we have all three requirements for corrosion, and are on the way to losing a perfectly good aircraft.

The extremely weak hydrochloric acid solution dissolves a tiny bit of the aluminum, and as it dissolves, it releases electrons. These freed electrons flow through the metal to some of the copper grains. The area where the electrons left now has a positive charge and is the anodic area. The area to which the electrons have gone has a negative charge and is the cathodic area.

alloying agent. A metal, other than the base metal in an alloy.

anodic area. An area inside a piece of metal that has lost some of its electrons. This leaves a net positive charge which attracts negative ions from the electrolyte. Positive metallic ions and negative ions from the electrolyte unite to form the salts of corrosion.

cathodic protection. Another name for sacrificial corrosion. A material that is more anodic than the material being protected is attached to or plated on the material. This becomes the anode and is corroded, while the part that is being protected is the cathode and it is not damaged.

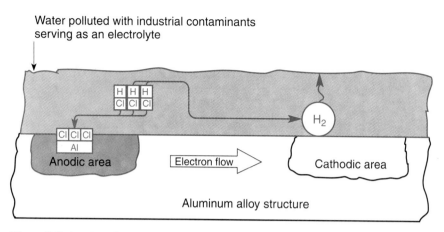

Figure 8-5. *An aircraft exposed to contaminated industrial atmosphere forms an electrochemical cell, and corrosion eats away the skin.*

The electrolyte on the surface of the metal contains some positive hydrogen ions and some negative chlorine ions. The negative chlorine ions are attracted to the anodic area of the metal, and the positive hydrogen ions are attracted to the cathodic area. The hydrogen ions unite with these freed electrons and become neutral hydrogen atoms. Two of these atoms join together to form a molecule of hydrogen gas, which leaves the metal without doing any damage.

At the anodic part of the metal, the negative chlorine ions are attracted to the positive aluminum ions, and when they join, they form a molecule of the salt, aluminum chloride. When the metallic aluminum changes into this powdery salt, strength is lost.

Corrosion that forms in this way is known as pitting corrosion. When an aircraft is left outside for a long period of time, the surface of the metal becomes dull and little bubble-like blisters appear on the surface. Take a pocket knife and pick these blisters to see that they are full of a dull gray powder. These blisters are the anodic area in the metal, and the powder is the salt of corrosion.

To protect aircraft from this type of damage, we must keep the surface of the metal from being covered with an electrolyte. We can do this by covering the alloy with a thin coating of pure aluminum, called cladding; we can cover the surface with a hard, airtight oxide film, called anodizing; or we can paint the surface with a good primer and a film of enamel or lacquer.

chemical salt. The result of the combination of an alkali with an acid. Salts are generally porous and powdery in appearance, and they are the visible evidence of corrosion in a metal.

Alclad. The registered trade name for high-strength sheet aluminum alloy that is protected from corrosion by a thin coating of pure aluminum rolled onto its surfaces.

cladding. A method of protecting aluminum alloys from corrosion by rolling a coating of pure aluminum onto the surface of the alloy. Cladding is done in the rolling mill, and because the pure aluminum coating is weaker than the alloy sheet, cladding reduces the strength of the material somewhat.

anodizing. A method of preventing corrosion of aluminum alloy parts. A hard oxide film is formed on the surface of the metal by an electrolytic process. This film prevents oxygen reaching the surface of the metal.

Answers are on Page 578. **Page numbers refer to chapter text.**

6. The smallest particle of a chemical element is a/an _____ . *Page 534*

7. The smallest particle of a chemical compound is a/an _____ . *Page 534*

8. An atom which has more electrons spinning around its nucleus than there are protons in the nucleus is a _____ (positive or negative) ion. *Page 534.*

9. The white powder which forms on the surface of aluminum when it corrodes is a chemical _____ . *Page 537*

10. The chief alloying agent in 2024 aluminum alloy is _____ . *Page 536*

11. In an alloy of aluminum and copper, the _____ will be eaten away by corrosion. *Page 536*

12. The three basic requirements for the formation of corrosion are:
    a. _____
    b. _____
    c. _____
    Page 533

13. Three steps that can be taken to minimize damage from corrosion are:
    a. _____
    b. _____
    c. _____
    Page 533

14. Arrange these metals, cadmium, copper, iron, and magnesium in the proper order of their electrochemical activity. Place the most active metal first.
    a. _____
    b. _____
    c. _____
    d. _____
    Page 534

15. When electrolytic or galvanic corrosion occurs between an aluminum structure and a steel bolt, the _____ (aluminum or steel) will be the metal that is corroded. *Page 534*

Types of Corrosion

There are several types of corrosion to be familiar with. Some types, like iron rust, continue to eat the metal until it is all gone, but others, like aluminum, form a dense film that prevents oxygen reaching the metal, and the corrosive action almost stops.

Figure 8-6 explains the type and appearance of corrosion on various types of metals.

Oxidation

One of the simplest forms of corrosion is "dry corrosion," or by its more common names, oxidation or rust.

When aluminum is exposed to the oxygen in the air, a chemical reaction takes place at the surface between the metal and the oxygen. Two atoms of aluminum unite with three atoms of oxygen to form one molecule of aluminum oxide, a white powder that gives the surface of the aluminum a dull, rough appearance.

When a ferrous metal is exposed to the air, two atoms of iron unite with three atoms of oxygen to form a molecule of iron oxide, or rust. The iron oxide is a porous film, and the iron will continue to react with the oxygen in the air until it is completely changed into rust.

Aluminum oxide and iron oxide are quite different. The oxide that forms on the aluminum is unbroken and is air tight. Once it forms, any further reaction between the aluminum and the oxygen continues at a greatly reduced rate or almost stops.

Aluminum alloy may be protected from oxidation by electrolytically or chemically forming a hard oxide film on its surface. This airtight film prevents any air or moisture reaching the metal, and the oxide itself will not continue to react with the oxygen in the air. The formation of this film is discussed in detail in methods of corrosion treatment under the heading, Oxide Film Protection.

To protect iron from rust, oxygen must be prevented from coming into contact with the metal. This can be done temporarily by covering it with oil or grease, or the surface can be permanently protected by a plating of cadmium or chromium, or by covering the surface with a good coat of paint.

oxidation. The chemical action in which a metallic element is united with oxygen. Electrons are removed from the metal in this process.

Alloy	Type of Attack to Which Alloy is Susceptible	Appearance of Corrosion Product
Magnesium	Highly susceptible to pitting	White, powdery, snowlike mounds and white spots on the surface
Low alloy steel	Surface oxidation and pitting, surface, and intergranular	Reddish-brown oxide (rust)
Aluminum	Surface pitting, intergranular, exfoliation, stress-corrosion and fatigue cracking, and fretting	White to gray powder
Titanium	Highly corrosion resistant; extended or repeated contact with chlorinated solvents may result in degradation of the metal's structural properties at high temperature	No visible corrosion products at low temperature. Colored surface oxides develop above 700°F (370°C)
Cadmium	Uniform surface corrosion; used as sacrificial plating to protect steel	From white powdery deposit to brown or black mottling of the surface
Stainless Steels (300 - 400 series)	Crevice corrosion; some pitting in marine environments; corrosion cracking; intergranular corrosion (300 series); surface corrosion (400 series)	Rough surface; sometimes a uniform red, brown stain
Copper-base brass, bronze	Surface and intergranular corrosion	Green powdery deposit
Chromium (plate)	Pitting (promotes rusting of steel where pits occur in plating)	No visible corrosion products; blistering of plating due to rusting and lifting
Silver	Will tarnish in the presence of sulfur	Brown to black film
Gold	Highly corrosion-resistant	Deposits cause darkening of reflective surfaces
Tin	Subject to whisker growth	Whisker-like deposits

Figure 8-6. *Appearance of corrosion on various metals*

Surface Corrosion

Anytime an area of unprotected metal is exposed to an atmosphere that contains industrial contaminants, exhaust fumes, or battery fumes, corrosion will form on the entire surface and give it a dull appearance. Contaminants in the air react with the metal and change microscopic amounts of it into the salts of corrosion. If these deposits are not removed and the surface protected against further action, pits of corrosion will form at localized anodic areas. Corrosion may continue in these pits until an appreciable percentage of the metal thickness is changed into salts, and in extreme cases, the corrosion may eat completely through the metal.

Pitting corrosion shows up as small blisters on the surface of the metal. When these blisters are picked with the sharp point of a knife, they are found to be full of a white powder.

Intergranular Corrosion

Aluminum alloys are made up of extremely tiny grains of aluminum and the alloying elements, and they may be hardened by heating them in an oven to the temperature at which the alloying elements go into a solid solution with the aluminum metal. When this temperature is reached, the alloy is taken from the oven and immediately quenched in cold water to lock all of these alloying elements to the tiny grains of the aluminum.

When the metal is removed from the oven and begins to cool, the grains begin to grow. If quenching is delayed, for even a few seconds, these grains will reach a size that will produce the anodic and cathodic areas needed for corrosion to form.

It is possible for corrosion that has started on the surface to reach the boundaries of some of these enlarged grains. When this happens the action will continue inside the metal. The electrolyte for this action travels from the

intergranular corrosion. Corrosion within a metal along the grain boundaries.

quenching. Rapid cooling of a metal as part of the heat treating process. The metal is removed from the furnace and it is submerged in a liquid such as water, oil, or brine.

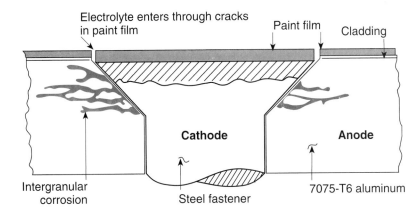

Figure 8-7. *Intergranular corrosion can start on the surface and progress through the metal, following the grain boundaries.*

surface through the porous salts of corrosion and along the grain boundaries as intergranular corrosion continues. *See* Figure 8-7 on the previous page.

Spot welds and seam welds can also cause the grain structure inside an aluminum alloy to grow until they are large enough for the metal to be susceptible to intergranular corrosion. The corrosive elements travel between the skins and around the weld spots and enter the metal through pits to reach the boundaries of the enlarged grains. *See* Figure 8-8.

Intergranular corrosion is difficult to detect because it is inside the metal, but it often shows up as a blister on the surface. If this blister is picked with the sharp point of a knife blade, it will show to be a thin covering of metal over a cavity that is filled with white powder. The fact that there is no surface blisters does not assure you that there is no intergranular corrosion.

Ultrasonic or X-ray inspection is needed for a good inspection for intergranular corrosion. Once intergranular corrosion is found, usually the only sure fix for it is the replacement of the part.

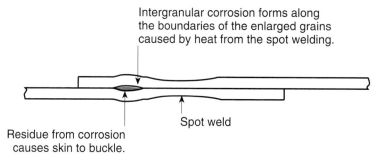

Intergranular corrosion forms along the boundaries of the enlarged grains caused by heat from the spot welding.

Spot weld

Residue from corrosion causes skin to buckle.

Figure 8-8. *Intergranular corrosion can form between sheets of aluminum alloy that are spot welded together.*

Exfoliation Corrosion

Exfoliation corrosion is an extreme case of intergranular corrosion that occurs chiefly in extruded materials such as channels or angles where the grain structure is more layer-like, or laminar, than it is in rolled sheets or in castings.

Exfoliation corrosion occurs along the grain boundaries, and causes the material to separate or delaminate. By the time it shows up on the surface, the strength of the metal has been destroyed.

Stress Corrosion

Stress corrosion is a form of intergranular corrosion that forms in a metal when it is subjected to a tensile stress in the presence of a corrosive environment.

The stresses that cause stress corrosion may come from improper quenching after the metal has been heat treated, or from a fitting that has been pressed into a structural part with an interference fit. Cracks caused by stress corrosion grow rapidly as the corrosive attack concentrates at the end of the crack, rather than along its sides as it does in other types of intergranular corrosion.

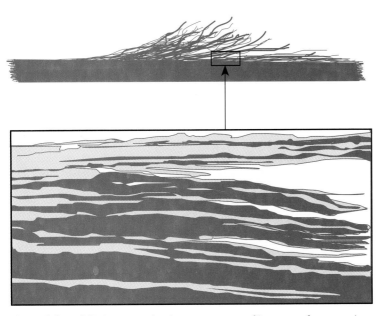

Figure 8-9. *Exfoliation corrosion is a severe case of intergranular corrosion that forms in extruded materials. The corrosion deposits force the metal to separate in layers.*

exfoliation corrosion. An extreme case of intergranular corrosion in an extruded metal part. The corrosion causes the metal to separate in layers.

delaminated. A condition caused by exfoliation corrosion in which the layers of grain structure in a metal extrusion separate from one another.

stress corrosion. A form of intergranular corrosion that forms in metals that are subject to a continuous tensile stress. The tensile stress separates the metal along the internal grain boundaries, and the corrosion acts at the apex of the cracks that form.

interference fit. A fit between two parts in which the part that is being put into a hole is larger than the hole itself. In order to fit them together, the hole is expanded by heating, and the part is shrunk by chilling. When the two parts are assembled and they reach the same temperature, they will not separate. The area around the hole is subjected to a tensile stress, and it is thus vulnerable to stress corrosion.

Stress corrosion often forms between rivets in a stressed skin, around pressed-in bushings, and around tapered pipe fittings. Careful visual inspection may reveal some cases of stress corrosion, but to find the actual extent of the damage, you must use some of the more effective types of non-destructive inspection such as dye penetrant, eddy current, or ultrasonic inspection. *See* Figure 8-10.

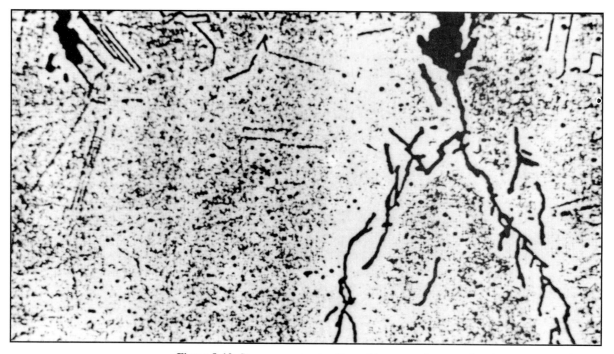

Figure 8-10. *Stress corrosion is a form of intergranular corrosion that progresses along the grain boundaries in a material that is under a constant tensile stress.*

dissimilar-metal corrosion. Corrosion that forms where two different metals are in contact with each other. The severity of the corrosion is determined by the relative location of the metals in the electrochemical series.

Galvanic Corrosion

Galvanic corrosion occurs any time two dissimilar metals make electrical contact in the presence of an electrolyte. The rate at which corrosion occurs depends on the difference in activities of the two metals.

Galvanic corrosion can form where dissimilar metal skins are riveted together, and where aluminum alloy inspection plates are attached to the structure with steel screws as in Figure 8-11.

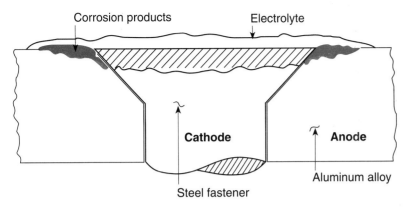

Figure 8-11. *Galvanic corrosion attacks an aluminum alloy skin adjacent to a steel screw.*

Figure 8-12 is a chart of metals grouped according to their electrochemical activity. When metals in the same group are joined together, there is little tendency for galvanic corrosion to form, but metals in one group will corrode when they are held in contact with metals in another group. The further apart the groups, the more active the corrosion will be.

The material in the lower number group will be the anode, and it will be the one that is corroded. When a steel screw from Group III is used to hold a 2024 aluminum alloy (Group II) inspection plate in place, the aluminum alloy which is in the lower numbered group will form the anode and is the metal that is corroded. If, on the other hand, a sheet of 2024-T3 aluminum alloy (Group II) is riveted to a piece of magnesium alloy from Group I, the magnesium will be corroded because it is in a lower numbered group than the aluminum alloy.

galvanic action. Electrical pressure within a substance which causes electron flow because of the difference of electrode potential within a material.

> **Group I**
> Magnesium and magnesium alloys
> **Group II**
> Aluminum, aluminum alloys, zinc, cadmium, and cadmium-titanium plate
> **Group III**
> Iron, steel (except stainless steel), lead, tin and their alloys
> **Group IV**
> Copper, brass, bronze, copper-beryllium, copper-nickel, chromium, nickel, nickel-base alloys, cobalt-base alloys, graphite, stainless steels, titanium, and titanium alloys

galvanic grouping. An arrangement of metals in a series according to their electrode potential difference.

Figure 8-12. *Galvanic grouping of metals.*

Concentration Cell Corrosion

There are two types of concentration cell corrosion that affect aircraft structure. Low oxygen concentration cell corrosion attacks areas where oxygen is kept from the surface. These areas are in the space where skins overlap for riveted joints, under the ferrules on aluminum alloy tubing; and under name plates and decals on aluminum alloy components. High metal ion concentration cell corrosion attacks areas in the open along lap joints in aircraft skins. Generally both types of corrosion occur at the same time in the same general areas of an aircraft structure.

Low Oxygen Concentration Cell Corrosion

Low oxygen concentration cell corrosion forms when water covers an aluminum airplane skin, and some of it seeps into the cracks between the lap joints of the sheets.

Water in an open area readily absorbs oxygen from the air, and in the process of two molecules of water (H_2O) combining with one molecule of oxygen (O_2), as in Figure 8-13, they take four electrons from the aluminum metal that is covered with the oxygen-absorbing water and become four negative hydroxide (OH) ions.

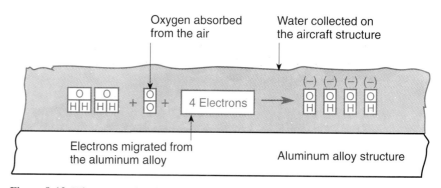

Figure 8-13. *When two molecules of water absorb one molecule of oxygen from the air, they attract four electrons from the metal and form four negative hydroxide ions.*

Water can seep between the sheets of metal in a lap joint, but there is not enough air between the sheets to furnish the oxygen needed to make the hydroxide ions. The electrons leave this area to go to the open area where hydroxide ions can be formed. When the electrons leave the area between the sheets, they leave positive aluminum ions, and this area becomes the anode of a corrosion cell. The positive aluminum ions attract the hydroxide ions that have formed in the open water, and when the aluminum ions and the hydroxide ions combine, they form aluminum hydroxide, which is the salt of corrosion. The metal back inside the lap joint where there is a deficiency of oxygen corrodes. *See* Figure 8-14.

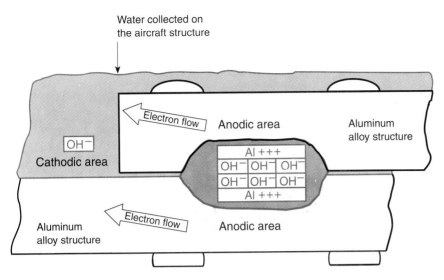

Figure 8-14. *Low oxygen concentration cell corrosion forms in areas where there is not enough oxygen for the formation of hydroxide ions. Electrons migrate from this area and leave it anodic. The positive aluminum ions attract negative hydroxide ions from the water and form corrosion.*

Low oxygen concentration cell corrosion can form on aluminum alloy, magnesium alloy, and ferrous metals. It forms under marking tape, under the ferrules that are installed on aluminum tubing, under loosened sealer inside an integral fuel tank, and under bolt and screw heads.

When dirt or other contaminants collect on a metal surface that is protected by a passive oxide film such as anodizing, they prevent oxygen reaching the surface. If the oxide film is scratched, low oxygen concentration cell corrosion can form and prevent the protective film from reforming on the surface.

High Metal Ion Concentration Cell Corrosion

An electrical potential can exist inside a metal because of the different metals that make up the alloy. A potential can also be built up on the surface of the metal when it is covered by an electrolyte that has a differing concentration of metal ions in it.

When water covers the surface of an aircraft, it absorbs oxygen from the air and takes electrons from the metal to form negative hydroxide ions. When electrons are taken from the aluminum, positive aluminum ions are left. *See Figure 8-15.*

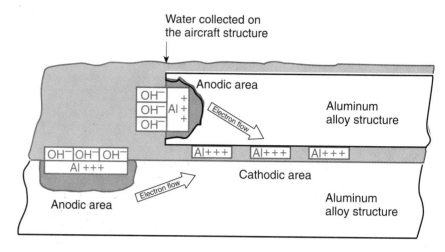

Figure 8-15. *High metal ion concentration cell corrosion forms in areas where the electrolyte contains a concentration of negative hydroxide ions. The area between the sheets contains a high concentration of positive metal ions, and it is the cathodic area of the corrosion cell.*

In the open areas of the skin, the water continually carries the aluminum ions away, but in the areas where the skins lap over each other, they cannot be carried away. These positive aluminum ions concentrate in the space between the skins and form a positively charged cathodic area. This positive area attracts electrons from the open areas of the skin, and anodic areas form along the edges of the sheets and on the surface of the skin near the lap joints.

As electrons are pulled from these anodic areas, they leave positive aluminum ions that attract negative hydroxide ions from the water on the open surface. The hydroxide ions and the aluminum ions combine to form aluminum hydroxide, or corrosion.

Fretting Corrosion

Fretting corrosion forms between two surfaces which fit tightly together, but which move slightly relative to one another. These surfaces are not normally close enough together to shut out oxygen, so the protective oxide coatings can form on the surfaces. However, this coating is destroyed by the continued rubbing action.

When the movement between the two surfaces is small, the debris between them does not have an opportunity to escape, and it acts as an abrasive to further erode the surfaces. Fretting corrosion around rivets in a skin is

fretting corrosion. Corrosion that forms between close-fitting parts that have a very slight amount of relative movement between them.

indicated by dark deposits streaming out behind the rivet heads. These dark deposits give the appearance of the rivets smoking.

By the time fretting corrosion appears on the surface, enough damage is usually done that the parts must be replaced.

Filiform Corrosion

Filiform corrosion consists of threadlike filaments of corrosion that form on the surface of metals coated with organic substances such as paint films. Filiform corrosion does not require light, electrochemical differences within the metal, or bacteria, but it takes place only in relatively high humidity, between 65% and 95%.

The threadlike filaments are visible under clear lacquers and varnishes, but they also occur under opaque paint films such as polyurethane enamels, especially when an improperly cured wash primer has left some acid on the surface beneath the enamel.

filiform corrosion. A thread- or filament-like corrosion which forms on aluminum skins beneath a dense paint film.

STUDY QUESTIONS: TYPES OF CORROSION

Answers are on Page 578. Page numbers refer to chapter text.

16. Corrosion that forms in riveted joints where there is a slight relative movement is called _____ corrosion. *Page 548*

17. A green corrosion film forms on _____ . *Page 540*

18. An extreme case of intergranular corrosion that forms in extruded metal in which the metal separates in layers is called _____ corrosion. *Page 543*

19. Another name for dry corrosion is _____ . *Page 539*

20. The oxide film that forms on aluminum alloy is _____ (porous or nonporous). *Page 539*

21. The oxide film that forms on iron is _____ (porous or nonporous). *Page 539*

22. Surface corrosion on aluminum alloy shows up in the form of _____ . *Page 541*

23. Corrosion that forms inside a metal along the grain boundaries is called _____ corrosion. *Page 541*

Continued

Answers are on Page 578. Page numbers refer to chapter text.

24. One of the primary causes for intergranular corrosion is
_____ . *Page 541*

25. Intergranular corrosion may often be detected by either of two types of nondestructive inspection, these are
_____ and _____ inspections. *Page 542*

26. Exfoliation corrosion usually develops in _____ metal parts. *Page 543*

27. If an unplated copper bonding braid is attached to an aluminum alloy structure and is not protected, the
_____ will corrode. *Page 545*

28. Low oxygen concentration cell corrosion forms _____ (between, or at the edge of) lap joints in the aircraft skin. *Page 546*

29. Stress corrosion occurs when a part is under a _____ (tensile or compressive) stress in a corrosive environment. *Page 543*

30. Fretting corrosion _____ (can or cannot) form if there is no relative motion between the surfaces. *Page 548*

Causes of Corrosion

For corrosion to form on a piece of metal, three requirements must be met: there must be areas of electrical potential difference, there must be a conductive path within the metal between these areas, and the areas of potential difference must be covered by an electrolyte. In this section, we will discuss the various types of electrolytes to which an aircraft is exposed.

Air

Airborne salts and other chemical compounds settle onto the surface of an airplane and attract moisture from the air to form an electrolyte, which is one of the prerequisites for corrosion.

Air can be kept away from the aluminum alloys by a tight coating of pure aluminum, an airtight oxide film, or a good continuous film of paint.

Water

Even pure water will react with metals to cause corrosion or oxidation, but water that holds a concentration of salts and other contaminants will cause corrosion to form much more rapidly.

Seaplanes, especially those that operate on salt water, are highly vulnerable to the formation of corrosion, and every precaution must be taken to prevent its formation or to remove it as soon as it forms. Seaplane ramps are often located in areas where the water has a concentration of industrial wastes. When a seaplane is taken out of the water it should be hosed down with large volumes of fresh water to get every trace of salt and other contamination off of the structure.

The bottom of floats and the hulls of flying boats are subject to the abrasive effect of high-velocity water each time they take off or land, and this abrasion damages the natural protective oxide film. Seaplanes must be carefully inspected to detect any damage which would allow water to reach the base metal of the structure.

Salts

The atmosphere around the ocean and the air above some of the industrial areas contains a large concentration of different types of salts which precipitate out of the air and settle on aircraft. These salts then attract water and form an electrolyte on the surface of the metal. Magnesium is especially subject to corrosive attack from these salt solutions.

Perspiration, or human sweat, contains salts, and if an unprotected metal part is touched with hands that are wet with sweat, enough of this effective electrolyte will be left on the surface to cause pitting.

Acids and Alkalis

Most acids and alkalis react with metals to form the metallic salts of corrosion, but some have more effect than others. Sulfuric acid from batteries is a main cause of corrosion in an aircraft.

While acids do cause corrosion, some can actually be used to prevent corrosion on aluminum and magnesium. A weak solution of chromic or phosphoric acids, for example, will form an airtight oxide film that keeps oxygen away from the metal. This film also roughens the surface of the metal enough that paint will bond tightly to it.

Ferrous metals are damaged almost equally by acids or alkalis, but aluminum may be damaged more by a strong alkaline solution than by an acid. An aluminum structure, for example, can be severely corroded if it is allowed to remain on a bare concrete floor. Water on the floor will leach, or dissolve, enough lime from the cement to form an alkaline solution that will cause the aluminum to corrode.

acid. A chemical substance that contains hydrogen, has a characteristically sour taste, and reacts with a base, or alkali, to form a salt.

alkali. A chemical substance, usually a hydroxide of a metal. An alkali has a characteristically bitter taste, and it reacts with an acid to form a salt.

Mercury

Mercury is not commonly found in large quantities around aircraft, but there is a possibility that mercury could be spilled in an aircraft, and if it is, the structure will be severely damaged. Mercury attacks an aluminum alloy along the grain boundaries, and in an exceedingly short time, completely destroys the metal.

Extreme care must be used when removing spilled mercury because it is "slippery," and it will flow through even a tiny crack to get to the lowest part of the structure where it can cause extensive damage.

Not only does mercury damage aircraft structure, but mercury and mercury vapors are also dangerous to people. If mercury is spilled, remove every particle with a vacuum cleaner that has a mercury trap in the suction line, or with a rubber suction bulb or medicine dropper. Never attempt to remove mercury from an aircraft structure by blowing it with compressed air. The air will scatter the mercury and spread the damage.

Mercury is especially damaging to brass. If a brass control cable turnbuckle barrel has been discolored by mercury, it must be replaced.

Organic Growths

Water that condenses in the fuel tank of a reciprocating-engine-powered aircraft causes few problems. Small perforated metal containers of potassium dichromate crystals change any water trapped in the tank into a mild chromic acid solution which prevents corrosion attacking the metal.

Jet aircraft fuel has a higher viscosity than gasoline and it holds more water in suspension. Jet airplanes also fly much higher than reciprocating-engine-powered aircraft, and in the high-altitude, low-temperature flight conditions, water entrained in the fuel will condense out and collect in the bottom of the tanks. This water contains microbes and bacteria, microscopic animal and plant life that live in the water and feed on the hydrocarbon fuel. The inside of the fuel tank is dark, which provides the ideal environment for these tiny organic creatures to multiply and form a scum inside the tank. This scum holds water in contact with the tank structure and allows concentration cell corrosion to form. If the scum forms along the edge of the sealant inside an integral fuel tank, the sealant will pull away from the structure and cause the tank to leak. This kind of leak requires an expensive resealing operation.

It is almost impossible to prevent this scum if bacteria and microbes are allowed to live in the fuel, so most jet fuels contain a biocidal additive which kills these "bugs" and prevents the formation of the corrosion-forming scum.

In addition to its biocidal action, this same fuel additive acts as an antifreeze agent by lowering the freezing temperature of the water that condenses out of the fuel.

bacteria. Microscopic plant life that lives in the water that is entrapped in fuel tanks. The growth of bacteria in jet fuel tanks forms a film of scum which holds water against the aluminum alloy surfaces and causes corrosion to form. *See also* microbes.

microbes. Extremely small living plant and animal organisms that include bacteria, mold, and algae. The term microbes is more generally replaced with the term micro-organisms.

biocidal action. The function of certain fuel additives which kill microbes and bacteria living in the water that accumulates inside aircraft fuel tanks. Biocidal action prevents the formation of scum, thus preventing corrosion in these tanks.

Answers are on Page 578. **Page numbers refer to chapter text.**

31. Aluminum alloys left in contact with a concrete floor are likely to corrode because of the
_____ (acid or alkali) that leaches out of the concrete. *Page 551*

32. If mercury comes into contact with an aluminum alloy, it will cause the aluminum to
_____ . *Page 551*

33. The scum that forms inside the fuel tanks of some jet aircraft is caused by _____ and
_____ in the fuel. *Page 552*

34. An additive may be used in jet fuel to help prevent corrosion inside the fuel tanks. This additive kills the
_____ and _____ . *Page 552*

Locations Susceptible to Corrosion

Any corrosion can degrade the strength of an aircraft structure. Therefore one of the most important functions performed by an aviation maintenance technician on an annual or 100-hour inspection is to check the entire structure for any indication of corrosion. Almost all parts of an aircraft are subject to corrosion damage, but corrosion is more likely to form in certain areas than in others.

External Skin Seams and Lap Joints

One of the first places corrosion appears on the surfaces of an aircraft is along the seams and lap joints. It is here that both types of concentration cell corrosion form. In clad skins, it is here that the sheared edges expose the alloy without the protection of the pure aluminum. There is also a danger of water or cleaning solvents becoming trapped in the lap joints and acting as an effective electrolyte.

Spot-welded seams are likely locations for corrosion to start because of the possibility that the spot-welding process may have caused the grain structure in the metal to become enlarged. Spot-welded seams are susceptible to further corrosion when moisture seeps between the skins. Check carefully for bulging along the spot welds. Hold a straightedge along the row of spots. If there is corrosion in the seams, the skin will bulge between the spots and show up as a wavy skin. Corrosion in a seam can progress to such a degree that the spots actually pull apart. *See* Figure 8-16.

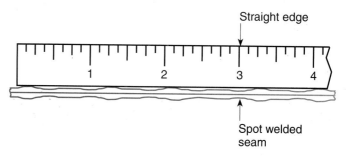

Figure 8-16. *Corrosion in a spot-welded seam causes the skin to buckle between the spots.*

Control Surface Recesses

Corrosion has an opportunity to start and progress in almost any place that is difficult to inspect. Some aircraft have areas in the wing or empennage where movable surfaces recess back into the fixed surface. Hinges are buried back in these cavities and are difficult to lubricate. Special attention must be paid when inspecting these areas to remove every trace of corrosion, and to provide drains for any water that might collect. A thin film water-displacing lubricant may be used to protect the skin lap joints in these recesses.

Piano Hinges

Piano hinges installed on control surfaces and access doors offer ideal conditions for the start and development of corrosion. The hinge body is made of aluminum alloy and the pin is hard carbon steel. These are the dissimilar metals, and dirt and dust hold moisture between the pin and the hinge body. This serves as the electrolyte. The pin may rust and seize in the hinge, even breaking off and becoming impossible to remove. *See* Figure 8-17.

Piano hinges should be kept as clean and as dry as possible. They should be lubricated with a spray that displaces water and leaves an extremely thin film of lubricant that will not form gum or attract dust.

Engine Inlet Areas

One of the most vital parts of a jet aircraft is directly in front of the engine where air is taken in. This inlet area is usually quite large, and air rushes into the engine at a high velocity. Abrasion by this high-velocity air and by contaminants that are carried in the air tend to remove any protective coating on

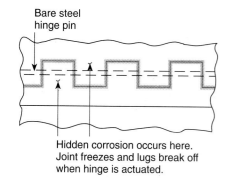

Figure 8-17. *Piano hinges are a prime location for corrosion. They contain dissimilar metals and trap moisture which acts as the electrolyte.*

the skin. Abrasion strips are often installed along the leading edges of intake ducts to help protect these areas. Engine inlets must be carefully inspected, and any damaged finish must be restored to prevent corrosion.

Engine Mount Structure

All of the current used by the starter must return to the battery through the engine mount. This current flowing through joints in an aluminum alloy mount creates the potential difference that is needed for corrosion, and corrosion is likely to form. Inspect built-up engine mounts carefully, and spray the inside of these mounts with a heavy coating of a water-displacing lubricant.

Protect the inside of welded steel tube engine mounts from corrosion by filling each tube with hot linseed oil or other type of tubing oil. Allow as much oil as possible to drain out of the tube, then plug the hole with a drive screw or with a self-tapping sheet metal screw.

Engine Exhaust Area

The exhausts of both reciprocating and turbine engines contain all of the ingredients needed to make a potent electrolyte for the formation of corrosion. Because these gases are so hot, corrosion can form all the more rapidly.

Lap joints and seams in the skin in the exhaust track are prime areas for corrosion to form. Fairings between the nacelles and the wings, and the hinges and fasteners on inspection doors all contain crevices which invite the formation of corrosion (*see* Figure 8-18). All of the area over which the exhaust gases flow must be carefully inspected, and all of the exhaust residue must be removed before corrosion has a chance to start.

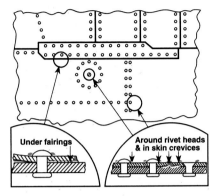

Figure 8-18. *Corrosion is likely to form around rivet heads, in skin crevices, and under fairings in the exhaust trail area of both reciprocating and turbine engine aircraft.*

Landing Gear Boxes

The fixed landing gear in many modern aircraft is attached to the structure through a strong, heavy-gage aluminum alloy box. This structure is under the cabin floor where it is accessible for inspection only through relatively small access holes. Water can collect in this area especially if the drain holes in the outer skin become plugged.

The landing gear boxes should be carefully inspected, all drain holes should be opened, and the entire enclosed area sprayed generously with a water-displacing lubricant film.

Wheel Wells and Landing Gear

There is probably no other location on an aircraft that is subjected to as much hard service as the wheel well. On takeoff and landing, debris from the runway surface may be thrown into it, and this can be especially troublesome in the wintertime when chemicals are used on runways for ice control. These chemicals may remove the protective lubricants and coatings from the structure. Water and mud can freeze in the wheel wells and damage the structure.

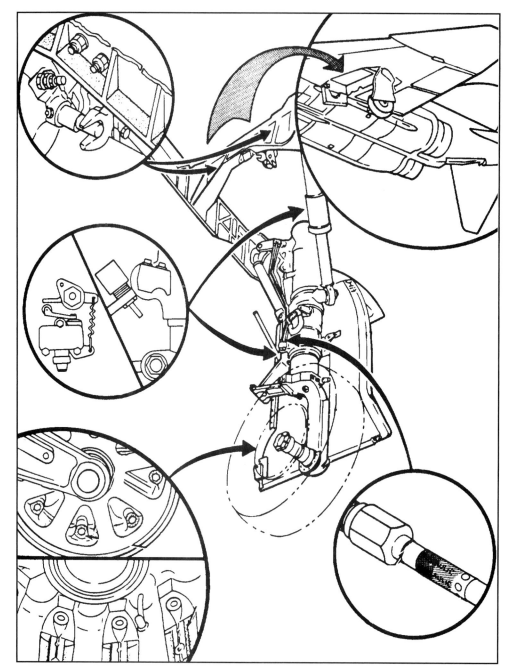

Figure 8-19. *Likely locations for the formation of corrosion in an aircraft landing gear*

Corrosion can take place in any of the electrical components such as the antiskid sensors, squat switches, and limit switches. Bolt heads and nuts on magnesium wheels are susceptible to galvanic corrosion, and concentration cell corrosion can form under the marking tape on aluminum tubing.

Special care must be taken to search out any area where water can be trapped. The drain holes that are located in these areas must be kept open.

Figure 8-19 shows some of the most likely locations for corrosion to form on landing gear.

Fuel Tanks

One of the most difficult areas to inspect, and yet one that is highly susceptible to corrosion, is the integral fuel tank in an aircraft. Integral tanks are actually a part of the structure that is sealed so it can hold fuel, and all of the seams in the structure are covered with a resilient sealant.

Jet engine fuel has a high enough viscosity that it can hold water entrained, or held in suspension. When the temperature of the fuel drops, some of the water precipitates out of the fuel and collects in the tank. Bacteria and microbes live in this water and feed on the hydrocarbon fuel. They multiply to such an extent that they form a scum inside the tank that breaks down the bond between the sealant and the tank structure and allows water to be held against the metal, causing low oxygen concentration cell corrosion. Corrosion inside the fuel tanks is difficult to detect and is usually found with X-ray or ultrasonic inspection from the outside of the wing.

Battery Compartments and Vents

All modern aircraft have an electrical system that uses a battery for starting and for backup power. These batteries store electrical energy by converting it into chemical energy and are therefore active chemical plants complete with environment-polluting exhausts.

Aircraft that use lead-acid batteries must have their battery boxes protected by some type of material that resists sulfuric acid fumes. Aircraft that use nickel-cadmium batteries must have the area around their battery boxes protected with a finish that resists alkaline fumes. These areas have been protected by an acid- or alkaline-resistant paint, usually a tar-base, or bitumastic, paint. Most modern aircraft protect this area with chemical-resisting polyurethane enamel.

On an inspection, these areas must be carefully checked, especially under the battery, and if any trace of corrosion is found, it must be removed and the area refinished.

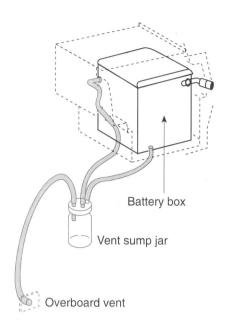

Battery box

Vent sump jar

Overboard vent

Figure 8-20. *Battery boxes are vented to the outside air through a sump jar that contains a porous pad moistened with a neutralizing agent. Bicarbonate of soda is used for lead-acid batteries, and boric acid is used for nickel-cadmium batteries.*

bilge. The lowest part of an aircraft structure where water, dirt, and other debris collect. Corrosion is likely to form in the bilge areas.

Both lead-acid and nickel-cadmium battery installations use a vent sump jar that contains a porous pad kept moist with a neutralizing agent — bicarbonate of soda is used for lead-acid batteries, and a boric acid solution is used for nickel-cadmium batteries. These sump jars should be checked to see that the pads are moist and that the jars are not leaking. All of the vent openings should be clear, and the intake and exhaust tubes must be free and open. *See* Figure 8-20.

If battery electrolyte spills when a battery is being serviced, the spill must be cleaned up immediately and the area neutralized. Flush the entire area with water and neutralize battery acid with bicarbonate of soda. The electrolyte from a nickel-cadmium battery is neutralized with a boric acid solution or with vinegar.

You can check the area with litmus paper to be sure that it has been completely neutralized. Blot the water on the surface with a piece of litmus paper. If the paper turns pink, the area is still acidic, or if it turns blue, the area is still alkaline. If the area is completely neutralized, as it should be, the paper will not change its color.

Bilge Areas

Bilges are in the bottom of the fuselage, below the floor boards. They are ideal locations for the formation of corrosion because water and all forms of liquid and solid debris accumulate in these areas. Dissimilar metals in the bilges are constantly exposed to an electrolyte, and because of their inaccessibility, corrosion can often go undetected until it has caused major damage.

All areas that are likely to accumulate water have drain holes, but since dirt and other debris also collect with the water, these holes may become clogged. It is important on every inspection to determine that all of the drain holes are clear, and to carefully inspect any area where water might stand. Air-powered vacuum cleaners may be used to remove any dirt or water that has collected in these areas.

A water-displacing liquid spray will form a thin film on the surface of the metal and prevent further contact between the metal and the electrolyte.

Control Cables

Some of the cables used in aircraft controls systems are made of carbon steel. If water enters them, they will corrode, and the corrosion will be difficult to detect. If corrosion is suspected, release the tension on the cable and open the strands by twisting them against the lay so you can see between the strands. If a cable has any indication of corrosion, it should be replaced.

Corrosion may be prevented by spraying the cable with a water-displacing lubricant. If the cable is used in a seaplane or exposed to agricultural chemicals, it should be coated with a waxy grease such as Par-al-ketone.

Lavatories and Food Service Areas

Organic materials such as food and human waste are highly corrosive to aluminum surfaces, and the areas where this type of material may be spilled must be carefully inspected.

Galleys, or food service areas, are especially troublesome as there is a possibility that some of the food particles can get into cracks under or behind the galley. While this material may not in itself be corrosive, if it is not removed, it can hold water against the metal and cause it to corrode.

The lavatory, or toilet, area is an especially important location to check for corrosion. Human wastes are usually corrosive and they promote corrosion in a hurry if they are allowed to remain on the skin or to get into cracks or seams in the structure. Disinfectants used in this area may even cause further damage. Check any disinfectant that is carried in the aircraft to be sure that is it is not of a type that is harmful to aluminum.

Aircraft that have relief tubes must have the area around and behind the discharge of the tube carefully inspected for indication of corrosion. The area where discharge contacts the aircraft skin must be painted with an acid-proof paint.

Welded Areas

Aluminum welding requires the use of a flux to keep oxygen away from the molten metal, and this flux may contain lithium chloride, potassium chloride, potassium bisulphide, or potassium fluoride. All of these chemicals are extremely corrosive to aluminum, and all traces of the flux must be removed after the welding is completed. Scrub the area with hot water and a brush that has nonmetallic bristles.

Spot welds and seam welds are susceptible to intergranular corrosion because the heat used in the welding can cause the grain structure in the spots and seams to enlarge. The corrosion can usually be detected by evidence of buckling between the sheets.

Answers are on Page 578. **Page numbers refer to chapter text.**

35. A type of finish used to protect the inside of a battery box against corrosion is
    _____ enamel. *Page 557*

36. A solution of _____ and water is used to neutralize fumes from a lead-acid
    battery. *Page 558*

37. A solution of _____ and water is used to neutralize fumes from a nickel-
    cadmium battery. *Page 558*

38. If blue litmus paper turns pink when it is placed in water which has been used to rinse out a battery box,
    the area is _____ . (acidic or alkaline). *Page 558*

39. The type of corrosion that is likely to form in a spot welded seam is _____
    corrosion. *Page 554*

40. Corrosion in a spot-welded seam will cause the metal between the spots to _____ .
    Page 554

41. A piano hinge should be lubricated with a _____ lubricant. *Page 554*

42. Engine mount structures are specially prone to corrosion attack because they carry the
    _____ from the starter. *Page 555*

43. The inside of a welded steel tube engine mount is protected from corrosion by coating the inside of the
    tube with _____ . *Page 555*

44. Steel control cables can be protected from corrosion by spraying them with a
    _____ lubricant. *Page 558*

45. Steel control cables installed in a seaplane can be protected from corrosion by a heavy grease such as
    _____ . *Page 558*

46. Welding flux may be removed from aluminum by scrubbing it with hot water and a
    _____ bristle brush. *Page 559*

Detecting Corrosion

The first step in corrosion control is finding it and determining its extent. In this section we will consider the most generally used inspection methods.

Visual Inspection

Elaborate inspection equipment is used in aircraft maintenance to make the work of the technician more efficient, but the well-trained and experienced eye is still the most effective tool for inspection.

Corrosion of aluminum and magnesium appears as a white or gray powder along the edges of skins, around rivet heads, and in small blisters that show up under the finish on painted surfaces. Since the salts of corrosion take up more space than sound metal, bulges along the lap joints of a skin are an indication that corrosion has formed between the faying surfaces.

We should make use of magnifying glasses, mirrors, borescopes, fiber optics, and other tools that allow us to see inside the structure and around corners so we can be assured of giving the aircraft a good visual inspection.

Penetrant Inspection

Stress corrosion cracks are sometimes difficult, if not impossible, to detect by a simple visual inspection. However, these and other cracks may be found by using dye penetrants which are usable for both ferrous and nonferrous metals.

All of the surface dirt must be removed from the material to be inspected before the penetrating liquid is sprayed on the surface. This liquid contains a bright red dye, and it has a very low surface tension, so it will seep deep into any crack that extends to the surface. After this penetrating liquid has been left on the surface long enough for it to seep into all cracks, it is wiped off. A developer is then sprayed over all of the surface. This developer is a white chalky powder that completely covers the surface and acts as a blotter to draw penetrant out of any cracks in the material that extend to the surface. Cracks show up as a bright red line on the white background of the developer.

Another type of penetrant inspection uses a fluorescent penetrant, and the part is inspected under an ultraviolet, or "black," light. This special light causes the cracks show up as green lines on the surface.

The limitation of dye penetrant inspection is that it will not show up cracks that are so full of corrosion product that the dye cannot penetrate. Also if the cracks are filled with oil or grease, the penetrant cannot get in, and there will be no indication of a flaw.

It is almost impossible to get all of the penetrant off of porous or rough surfaces, and this type of surface should not be inspected by either of the penetrant inspection methods.

Ultrasonic Inspection

There are two types of ultrasonic inspection that may be used for corrosion detection; the pulse-echo method and the resonance method. In both methods, pulses of high-frequency vibration, similar to sound waves, only at frequencies far above the audible range, are introduced into the aircraft structure. The frequency of these vibrations is usually from about 0.5 megahertz (500,000 cycles per second) to 25 megahertz (25,000,000 cycles per seconds).

In the pulse-echo method, a pulse of ultrasonic vibrations is sent into the structure with a transducer. These vibrations travel through the material to the opposite side and then bounce back. The cathode ray display such as we see in Figure 8-21 shows a pip that represents the front of the material, and another pip represents the back side. If there should be a hidden crack or a flaw such as may be caused by intergranular corrosion, a third pip will show up on the cathode ray screen. The position of this pip relative to those caused by the front and back surfaces of the material gives an indication of the position of the fault within the material. *See* Figure 8-21.

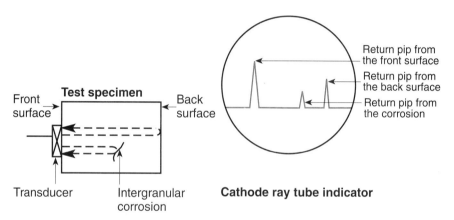

Figure 8-21. *Intergranular corrosion in an aircraft structure may be detected by ultrasonic inspection. The first pip represents the front side of the structure, the third pip represents the back side of the structure, and the pip in the middle represents the location of the corrosion within the structure.*

The resonance method of ultrasonic inspection operates on the basis that for a given thickness of material, there is one specific frequency of vibratory energy that will cause the material to vibrate with the greatest amplitude.

Ultrasonic energy having a variable frequency is fed into the material being tested, and the amount the material vibrates is measured. The relative amount of vibration is shown either on a meter or by a tone in a pair of headphones. When the frequency of the ultrasonic energy is the same as the resonant frequency of the material being inspected, the meter will read the highest value, or the tone heard in the phones will be the loudest.

If the metal has been eaten away by corrosion, its resonant frequency will be different from that of undamaged metal, and the meter reading will be different or the tone will have a lower volume.

False returns can easily disguise a fault, and an indication of a fault found by an ultrasonic inspection is not absolute proof of corrosion. Further inspection should be made to verify the actual presence and determine the extent of the corrosion that is indicated by ultrasonics.

Radiographic Inspection

Radiographic inspection is more difficult and more costly than many other types of nondestructive inspection, but it has the great advantage that the structure does not have to be disassembled for the procedure.

X-rays and gamma rays both produce extremely high frequency electromagnetic radiation that is able to pass through the structure being inspected and expose a photographic film. After the film is exposed, it is developed just as any other photographic negative.

At locations where the density of the structure is the greatest, less energy passes through, and this area shows up on the film as a light area. Areas of less density allow more energy to pass through and the exposure is greater. These areas show up dark on the film. The real value of a radiographic inspection is determined to a great extent by the experience and expertise of the person interpreting the image shown on the film.

The use of radiographic equipment involves some danger because exposure to the electromagnetic radiation used in this process may cause burns, damage to the blood, and in extreme cases, even death. Persons who work around radiographic equipment should wear a radiation monitor film badge which can be developed after a period of exposure to measure the amount of radiation the wearer of the badge has absorbed. A blood count should also be made at periodic intervals for persons who are involved in radiographic inspections.

The amount an X-ray penetrates a structure is determined by the amount of voltage applied to the X-ray tube. This voltage may range from about 8 kilovolts to as much as 200 kilovolts. The lower power X-rays are called "soft" X-rays, and they are used when inspecting for corrosion.

*Answers are on Page 578. **Page numbers refer to chapter text.***

47. The three steps that are used in the dye penetrant method of inspection are:

    a. _____

    b. _____

    c. _____

    Page 561

48. Penetrant inspection _____ (can or cannot) detect subsurface faults. *Page 561*

49. Penetrant inspection _____ (can or cannot) be used on a steel part to detect a surface crack.
    Page 561

50. Two methods of ultrasonic inspection appropriate for detecting corrosion are:

    a. _____

    b. _____

    Page 562

51. In an X-ray inspection, areas of corrosion damage show up as a _____ (light or dark) area on the photographic negative. *Page 563*

52. Technicians who work around radiographic equipment should wear _____ film badges. *Page 563*

53. The amount an X-ray penetrates the structure is determined by the amount of _____ applied to the X-ray tube. *Page 563*

54. X-rays used for corrosion inspection are _____ (low or high) power. *Page 563*

Removing and Treating Corrosion

When corrosion is discovered on an aircraft structure, all traces of it must be removed, and the surface treated to prevent the formation of more corrosion. In this section we will consider some of the methods of removing the corrosion deposits and treating the surface.

Corrosion Treatment of Aluminum Alloys

Since most of the metal in an aircraft structure is aluminum alloy, it is important to understand the best way of treating it to prevent the recurrence of corrosion.

Mechanical Corrosion Removal

After all of the paint has been removed from the surface, you must remove all traces of the corrosion products. Mild corrosion may be removed by scrubbing the affected area with a nylon scrubber such as a "Scotch-Brite" pad, or by using a household abrasive cleaner that does not contain any chlorine.

More severe corrosion can be removed with aluminum wool or with an aluminum wire brush. Be sure that you do not use a steel wire brush or steel wool, because little pieces of the steel will break off and embed themselves in the aluminum. These tiny bits of steel will cause severe corrosion. You can also blast the surface with glass beads smaller than 500 mesh to remove the deposits from pitting corrosion.

After brushing or abrasive blasting, examine the cleaned surface of the metal with a 5- to 10-power magnifying glass to be sure that all traces of the corrosion have been removed.

More drastic treatment is required to remove the corrosion from severely corroded aluminum alloys. Rotary files or power grinders using rubber wheels impregnated with aluminum oxide may be used to grind out every trace of corrosion damage. Watch carefully to see that only the minimum amount of material is removed, but that all of the damage is cleaned out. After an examination with a 5- or 10-power magnifying glass shows that no trace of corrosion remains, remove about two thousandths (0.002) of an inch more material to be sure that you have cleaned out beyond the ends of any intergranular cracking. Sand the cleaned-out area smooth, first with 280-grit sandpaper, then with 400-grit paper. Finally, clean the area with solvent or an emulsion cleaner, and then treat the surface with a corrosion-inhibiting conversion coating such as Alodine.

Chemical Treatment

After removing all of the corrosion products possible, treat the surface with a five percent solution of chromic acid to neutralize any traces of the corrosion salts that might possibly remain. After the acid has been on the surface for at least five minutes, wash it off with water and blow the surface dry.

abrasive. A material containing minute particles of some hard substance which when rubbed on a surface will wear away that surface.

Alodine treatment that conforms to MIL-C-5541 specification may also be used. It not only neutralizes the corrosion residue, but it also forms a protective film on the surface of the metal.

Protective Coatings

After all of the corrosion deposits have been removed and the surface of the metal neutralized, the surface must be covered to prevent air or moisture from reaching the unprotected metal. There are several methods used to keep electrolytes away from the surface.

Oxide Film Protection

When aluminum is exposed to the air, an oxide film forms on its surface that resists further oxidation and protects the aluminum from corrosion.

Using this principle, metallurgists have devised oxide films that are hard, decorative, waterproof, and airtight. There are two ways in which these films may be formed: chemically and electrolytically. Electrolytically deposited films, called anodizing, are most generally formed in the factories while the aircraft are being built, and the chemically deposited films are formed in the field.

Electrolytically Formed Oxides

The part to be treated is cleaned in a hot water bath with a special noncaustic soap solution. Then, it is made the anode in an electrolytic process with chromic acid and water as the electrolyte. After the oxide film forms, the part is washed in hot water and is air dried.

Anodizing does not appreciably change the tensile strength, weight, or dimensions of a part. The anodic film on aluminum alloy is normally light gray, but it varies to a darker gray on some of the alloys. Some aluminum alloy parts, such as fluid line fittings, are dyed for identification. When the film first forms, it is a soft, porous aluminum hydroxide which can absorb dyes, but as it changes into aluminum oxide, it becomes hard, airtight, and nonabsorbent, and it forms the protective film that is needed to shield the metal from moisture and to prevent the formation of corrosion.

The anodic film on aluminum alloys is an electrical insulator, and it must be removed before any electrical connection is made to the aluminum. Electrical bonding straps are often attached directly to an anodized aluminum alloy part. Therefore the anodic film must be removed by sanding or scraping before the straps are attached.

Chemically Formed Oxides

Anodizing is normally applied in the factory, but when small parts are made in the field, or when the anodizing film has been damaged or removed, the part may be protected by a film applied by a chemical conversion coating rather than by electrolysis.

This process uses a chemical such as Alodine 1201, or if an invisible film is desired, Alodine 1001. These are two proprietary products which meet MIL-C-5541 specification.

Alodine can be applied to a surface after all traces of corrosion have been removed. The surface should be chemically cleaned until it supports an unbroken water film. Any breaks in the film of rinse water show that there is some wax, grease, or oil on the surface, and further cleaning must be done.

Brush or spray a liberal coating of the Alodine chemical on the surface while it is still wet with rinse water. Allow it to stand for two to five minutes, and then rinse it off. Work on an area of a size that can be kept wet, and keep it wet all the time the chemical is working. If it is allowed to dry, streaks will appear and the film will not be adequately protective. After the chemical has been on the surface for the time specified by its manufacturer, flush it from the surface with a spray of fresh water, taking particular care not to damage the film, which is quite soft while it is wet. After the surface is completely dry, it is ready to paint.

A satisfactory coat of Alodine produces a uniform yellowish-brown iridescent film or a transparent film, depending on the particular treatment. If a powder appears on the surface after the material has dried, it is an indication of poor rinsing or a failure to keep the surface wet during the time the Alodine was working. If such a powder shows up, the part must be re-treated.

Rags or sponges that dry with the Alodine chemical in them can constitute a fire hazard. They should be kept wet or be washed thoroughly before they are discarded.

Organic Finishes

A simple corrosion control device is a good coat of paint. Paint adheres readily to most porous surfaces, but it may be difficult to get it to stick to some metals. Clad aluminum surfaces must be roughened so the paint will adhere. This can be done with a mild chromic acid etch or by either anodizing or Alodining. All of these chemical treatments provide a good base for the primer to which the paint film will adhere.

The surface may also be mechanically roughened by carefully sanding it with 400-grit sandpaper, but when this is done, it is imperative that every bit of the sanding dust be removed by using a rag dampened with lacquer thinner before applying the primer.

Zinc chromate primer has been used for decades for topcoat systems of lacquer or enamel. Zinc chromate is an inhibiting type of primer whose film is slightly porous so water can penetrate it and cause some of the chromate ions to be released and held on the surface of the metal. This ionized surface prevents electrolytic action, and it inhibits the formation of corrosion. Zinc chromate primer conforms to specifications MIL-P-8585A, and it may be either yellow-green or dark green. It is thinned for spraying with toluol or with some of the proprietary reducers that are made especially for zinc chromate.

zinc chromate primer. A primer that releases chromate ions and inhibits the formation of corrosion on the surface of aluminum alloys.

inhibitive film. A film of material on the surface of a metal which inhibits the formation of corrosion. It does this by providing an ionized surface which will not allow the formation of corrosive salts on the metal.

The surface to be painted is checked to see that it is absolutely free of fingerprints or any traces of oil, and a thin, wet coat of zinc chromate is applied with a spray gun. The synthetic resin base of zinc chromate primer provides a good bond between the finish and the metal and it is dope proof, meaning that aircraft dope will not cause it to lift.

A significant help to the aircraft mechanic has been the availability of zinc chromate in aerosol cans already mixed and ready to spray. When a repair is made or a part is fabricated, it can be given a coat of zinc chromate primer to prevent corrosion before it gets a chance to start.

Some of the newer finishes such as acrylic lacquers and polyurethane enamels are often applied over a wash primer which is a two-part material that consists of a resin and an alcohol-phosphoric acid etchant. Spray the primer on the surface with a light tack coat and then apply a full-bodied wet coat. Allow the primer to dry for at least four hours and apply the top, or finish coat, within 48 hours.

Because of the complexity of these new finishes, you should always follow the recommendations of the paint manufacturer in detail and not make any changes to those directions.

Corrosion Treatment of Magnesium Alloys

Magnesium is one of the most active of the commonly used metals for aircraft construction, but, because of its light weight for its strength, designers accept its corrosiveness. The special procedures described in this section help overcome the limitation caused by its susceptibility to corrosion.

Mechanical Corrosion Removal

Magnesium corrosion takes up more space than the pure metal it replaces, so when corrosion forms under a film of paint, it raises the paint; when it forms between skins, it swells the joints. When it is discovered, all traces must be removed and the surface treated to inhibit the formation of further corrosion.

Since magnesium is anodic to almost all of the metals used for corrosion removal tools, the corrosion cannot normally be removed with metallic tools. They are likely to leave contaminants embedded in the metal, and these contaminants will cause further damage.

Stiff nonmetallic brushes or nylon scrubbers may be used to remove corrosion from the surface or from shallow pits. Deep pits must be cut out with very sharp steel or carbide-tipped cutting tools or scrapers. Carborundum wheels or paper must not be used because it will contaminate the surface and cause galvanic corrosion.

If abrasive blasting is used, use only glass beads that have been used for nothing but magnesium, since scale that is left in the abrasive from other metals can be embedded in the magnesium and cause further damage.

Magnesium alloys do not naturally form a protective film on the surface the way aluminum does, so special care must be taken that any chemically or electrolytically deposited film is not destroyed.

Chemical Treatment

After all of the corrosion has been removed from the surface and the surface cleaned, a chromic acid pickling solution which conforms to MIL-M-3171A, Type I (Dow No. 1), should be applied to neutralize any remaining corrosion products.

If this particular chemical is not available, use a solution made by adding about fifty drops of sulfuric acid to a gallon of 10% chromic acid solution. Apply this solution to the surface with rags and let it remain for 10 to 15 minutes and then rinse it thoroughly with hot water.

A dichromate conversion treatment such as Dow No. 7, which conforms to MIL-M-3171A, Type IV, forms a more protective film. It is applied to the metal and allowed to stand until an oxide film of uniform golden brown appears on the surface. Rinse the surface with cold water and dry it with an air blast. The oxide film that is left by this treatment is very soft when it is wet, and it must be protected from excessive wiping or touching until it dries and hardens. This film is continuous, and it protects the magnesium from corrosion by keeping all electrolytes away from the surface.

An electrolytically deposited film similar to that used on aluminum alloys may be formed on magnesium. Anodizing magnesium by the Dow No. 17 process produces a hard surface oxide film, a good base for further protection with a paint finish.

Magnesium is such an active metal, and magnesium skins are usually so thin that it is absolutely vital that only the proper solutions and proper procedures be used for the treatment of corrosion. For this reason, rather than mixing your own pickling and conversion coating solutions, you should use prepared chemicals that meet the appropriate MIL specifications, and you should follow the manufacturer's recommended procedures in detail.

Corrosion Treatment of Ferrous Metals

Unlike aluminum, the oxide film that forms on ferrous metals is porous, and it will hold moisture and continue to convert the metal into corrosion or rust. For this reason, all rust, as this oxide is called, must be removed as soon as it forms and additional rust must be prevented from forming.

Mechanical Cleaning

Abrasive papers, as well as hand brushes and power-driven wire brushes, may be used on steel surfaces, but the most effective way of getting every bit of corrosion from unplated steel parts is by abrasive blasting which gets to the very bottom of the corrosion pits. Sand, aluminum oxide, and glass beads are all effective types of abrasives for cleaning steel parts. If a steel part has been plated with either cadmium or chromium, you must take special care that the plating is not abraded away since the plating is difficult to restore in the field.

pickling. The treatment of a metal surface with an acid to remove surface contamination.

dichromate solution. A solution of potassium or sodium dichromate used to form a hard, airtight film on the surface of magnesium parts to prevent corrosion.

ferrous metal. Iron or any alloy that contains iron.

cathodic area. An area within a piece of metal to which electrons from the anodic area have migrated.

noble. Inactive or inert. In the electro-chemical series of metals, the metal in a combination that does not corrode is the more noble.

sacrificial corrosion. A method of corrosion protection in which a surface is plated with a metal that is less noble than the metal itself. Any corrosion that occurs will attack the plating rather than the base metal.

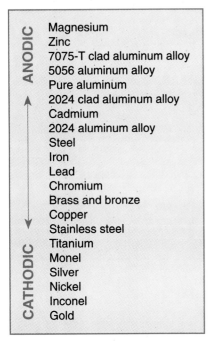

Figure 8-22. *Electrochemical series to determine the chemical activity of various metals*

Corrosion must be removed from highly stressed steel parts with extreme care. Any rust or corrosion on these parts should be eliminated immediately by removing the absolute minimum amount of material. A fine abrasive stone, fine abrasive paper, or pumice may be used. Wire brushes should not be used since they cause minute scratches. These scratches are likely to cause stress concentrations to develop and weaken the part. If abrasive blasting is used, it must be done with caution, using only very fine-grit abrasive or glass beads.

After all of the corrosion has been removed, the rough edges of any pits or damage must be faired smoothly into the surface with a fine stone or 400-grit abrasive paper. Apply a primer such as zinc chromate to the surface as soon as possible, since a clean, dry surface is an ideal setting for new rust to form.

Surface Treatment for Steel

After all traces of corrosion have been removed, the surface must be treated by one of the methods described here to permanently prevent air and moisture reaching the metal.

Cadmium Plating

Almost all aircraft hardware is cadmium plated because of its effectiveness in protecting the surface from corrosion. Cadmium plating protects the steel by the process of sacrificial corrosion.

Figure 8-22 lists cadmium above steel in the electro-chemical series. This means that if these two metals are involved in an electrolytic action, corrosion will take place in the anodic material. The cadmium will be corroded while the cathodic material, the steel, will not be damaged.

Cadmium, which is a soft, silvery-gray metal, is electroplated onto steel parts to a minimum thickness of 0.005 inch. The plating gives the part an attractive finish as well as protection against corrosion.

When the cadmium plating on a part is scratched through to the steel, galvanic action takes place in which the cadmium corrodes. The oxides which form on the surface of the cadmium are similar to those which form on aluminum. They are dense, airtight, and watertight. No further corrosive action can take place once the initial film has formed. This type of protection is known as sacrificial corrosion.

Nickel or Chrome Plating

Steel parts may be electroplated with either nickel or chromium to form an airtight coating over the metal. This coating excludes air and moisture from the base metal and keeps it from corroding.

There are two types of chrome plating used on aircraft parts: decorative chrome and hard chrome. Decorative chrome is used primarily for its appearance and surface protection, but hard chrome is used to make parts such as the piston rods of hydraulic actuators wear resistant. The cylinder walls of many reciprocating engines are treated with a special type of hard chrome, porous chrome, whose surface contains thousands of tiny cracks that hold lubricating oil.

Worn cylinder barrels of aircraft engines can be ground undersize and then plated back to standard size with hard porous chrome.

Galvanizing

Some steel parts such as fire walls are galvanized by coating them with zinc. Galvanizing protects the steel in the same way as cadmium plating, by sacrificial corrosion. When the zinc is scratched through to the steel, a corrosion cell is formed between the steel and the zinc with the zinc being the corroding anode. As it corrodes, it forms an airtight oxide film that stops the action and keeps any further corrosion from forming.

A steel sheet is galvanized by passing it through a vat of molten zinc, then sending it through a series of steel rollers.

Metal Spraying

Cylinders on some reciprocating engines are protected from corrosion by coating their external surfaces with molten aluminum sprayed onto the surface. The steel to be coated is prepared by sand blasting until it is perfectly clean. Aluminum wire is fed into an acetylene flame, and as it melts, it is blown onto the steel by a high-pressure stream of compressed air.

Sprayed-on aluminum protects the steel by sacrificial corrosion in much the same way that steel is protected by cadmium plating or by galvanizing.

Organic Finishes

Paint is an effective and widely used corrosion protection system, and its effectiveness is maintained by not allowing the film to break down. For the paint to bond properly, the surface must be perfectly clean and slightly roughened with a chemical etchant, abrasive paper, or abrasive blasting. After the surface is thoroughly clean and dry, spray on a thin wet coat of primer and allow it to dry. Then apply the finish topcoats, following the instructions of the paint manufacturer.

Cadmium-plated parts must normally have their surfaces etched with a five-percent solution of chromic acid before the primer will adhere.

electroplating. An electrochemical method of depositing a film of metal on some object. The object to be plated is the cathode, the metal which is to be deposited on the cathode is the anode. Both the cathode and the anode are covered with an electrolyte which forms ions of the plating metal.

galvanizing. The application of a coating of zinc on steel by dipping the steel in a vat of molten zinc.

Assessment of Corrosion Damage

Removing all of the corrosion products and forming an inhibitive oxide film on the surface will stop corrosion, but after this has been done, you must carefully examine the structure to be sure that there is enough material left to give the structure its required strength.

All pits which have been ground out of the surface should have their edges feathered to leave a shallow depression whose width is at least twenty times the depth of the cleaned-out area.

If there are several pits close together, they should be blended into one smooth repair without any surface irregularities or waviness. Extra-fine sand paper should be used for the final sanding, and the depression should be polished with fine rouge or pumice to get rid of any scratches that could possibly cause stress concentrations or hold moisture.

Extreme care must be taken when removing corrosion products from internal areas where there are stiffeners. These areas are usually difficult to reach, and as a result it is easy to grind into the stiffener or to form a pocket between the stiffener and the skin in which new corrosion can form. *See* Figure 8-26.

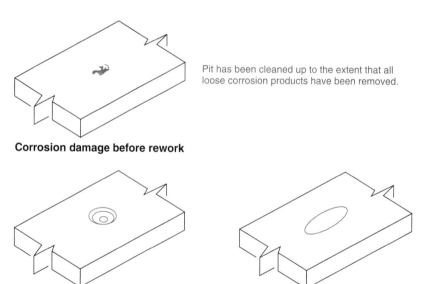

Pit has been cleaned up to the extent that all loose corrosion products have been removed.

Corrosion damage before rework

Rough edges have been smoothed and all corrosion has been removed. However, depression has not been shaped.

Dish-out after blending

Extent of rework

Figure 8-23. *Blending out a single pit in a corroded area*

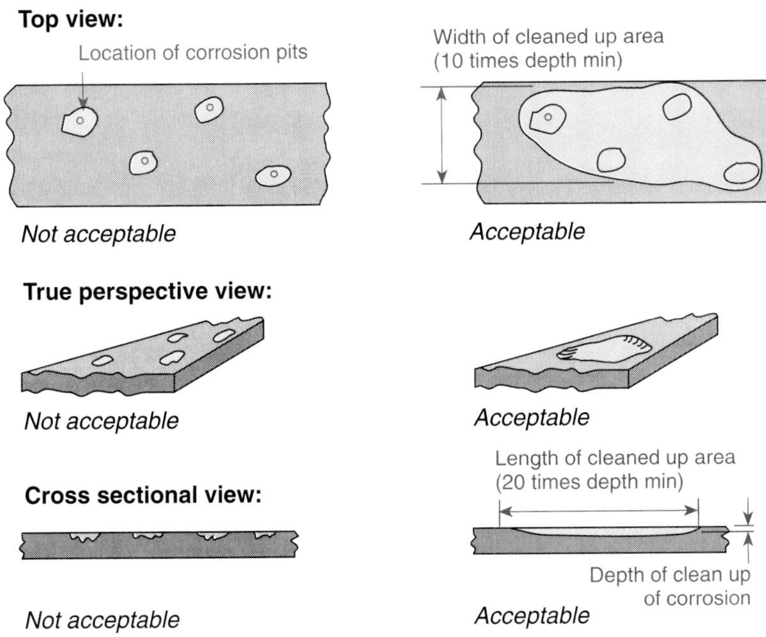

Top view:

Location of corrosion pits

Not acceptable

Width of cleaned up area
(10 times depth min)

Acceptable

True perspective view:

Not acceptable

Acceptable

Length of cleaned up area
(20 times depth min)

Cross sectional view:

Not acceptable

Acceptable

Depth of clean up
of corrosion

Figure 8-24. *Corrosion pits should be worked out with the length of the cleaned-up area at least 20 times its depth.*

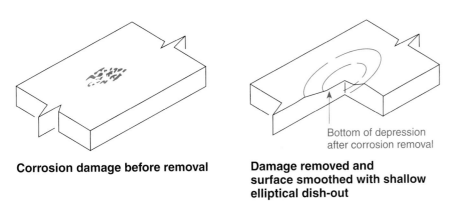

Corrosion damage before removal

Damage removed and surface smoothed with shallow elliptical dish-out

Bottom of depression after corrosion removal

Figure 8-25. *Blending out multiple pits in a corroded area*

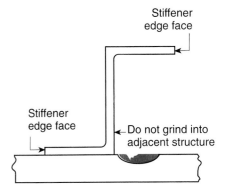

Stiffener edge face

Stiffener edge face

Do not grind into adjacent structure

Figure 8-26. *Special care must be exercised when reworking a corroded area near a stiffener to prevent damaging it.*

It is important when removing corrosion from the structure inside an integral fuel tank, where the joints are covered with a sealing compound, that none of the sealant is damaged. If any sealant is damaged, or if corrosion forms under it, every bit of the affected sealant must be removed and replaced with new compound.

After all of the rework has been finished, the depth of the cleaned-out area or the amount of material that is left must be determined. The manufacturer should be consulted if there is any question regarding the strength of the repaired structure.

For thin skins, any damage in a critical area which is caused by the removal of an appreciable percentage of skin thickness usually calls for the replacement of the affected skin.

Corrosion Control, A Summary

Corrosion is the most damaging natural phenomenon that the aircraft technician must contend with. The thin, highly reactive metals of which modern airplanes are made make them especially vulnerable to corrosion's attack. Once corrosion has started in a structure, it opens the way for more, and the corrosion spreads until the structure is destroyed.

Corrosion cannot be prevented totally, but it can be controlled by eliminating one or more of the basic requirements for its formation.

1. We can prevent the electrical potential difference within the metal.

2. We can insulate the conductive path between areas of potential difference.

3. We can eliminate any electrolyte which could form a conductive path on the surface of the metal.

While corrosion itself is highly complex, its control is mainly a matter of paying attention to detail. The structure must be kept clean and dry, and any breaks in the finish must be repaired immediately. Any corrosion that is found must be promptly removed, and the surface from which the corrosion was removed must be treated to neutralize any residue and inhibit further corrosion.

Some of the modern surface treatments, sealers, and finishes are complex, and they will not tolerate any improper procedures in their mixing or application. For this reason, it is imperative that the technician understand and follow in detail the specific instructions from the manufacturer of these products.

Answers are on Page 578. **Page numbers refer to chapter text.**

55. Corrosion may be removed from aluminum surfaces by scrubbing them with a/an
_____ . *Page 565*

56. Corrosion may be removed from a highly stressed steel part by the use of fine-grit
_____ . *Page 570*

57. The products of corrosion should be removed from magnesium parts by scrubbing them away with a stiff
_____ brush. *Page 568*

58. The oxide film produced by anodizing is _____ (airtight or porous). *Page 566*

59. A damaged anodized coating may be repaired in the field by using a chemical conversion coating material. One well-known treatment of this type is called _____ . *Page 567*

60. Mild corrosion can be removed from an aluminum alloy surface by scrubbing with a household abrasive that does not contain _____ . *Page 565*

61. Severe corrosion can be removed from an aluminum alloy structure by blasting it with
_____ . *Page 565*

62. A chemically deposited oxide film on an aluminum surface is called _____ .
Page 567

63. An electrolytically deposited oxide film on an aluminum surface is called a/an
_____ . *Page 566*

64. A fully formed anodized film is _____ (hard or soft). *Page 566*

65. An anodized film is an electrical _____ (conductor or insulator). *Page 566*

66. The surface of clad aluminum surface be _____ to allow better adhesion for the primer. *Page 567*

67. A self-etching primer used under acrylic lacquer finishes is called a _____ primer. *Page 568*

Continued

68. One of the best methods for removing the corrosion products from rusted steel parts is a/an
_____ . *Page 569*

69. Highly stressed steel parts should not be cleaned by scrubbing them with a wire brush because of the danger of scratches causing _____ . *Page 570*

70. Cadmium plating protects a steel part from corrosion by a process known as
_____ . *Page 570*

71. Galvanizing is a method of protecting steel with a coating of _____ . *Page 571*

72. Before paint will stick to a cadmium-plated surface, the surface should be etched with a solution of
_____ . *Page 571*

73. The oxides that naturally form on a magnesium surface _____ (do or do not) protect the surface from further oxidation or corrosion. *Page 568*

74. Corrosion which cannot be mechanically removed from a piece of magnesium may be neutralized by pickling the surface with _____ . *Page 569*

Answers to Chapter 8 Study Questions

1. water emulsion
2. varsol, kerosine
3. acetone
4. soap and water
5. aliphatic naphtha
6. atom
7. molecule
8. negative
9. salt
10. copper
11. aluminum
12. a. must have an electrode potential difference within the metal
    b. must have a conductive path between the areas of potential difference
    c. must be covered with an electrolyte
13. a. minimize potential difference
    b. eliminate conductive path
    c. prevent electrolyte contacting the metal
14. a. magnesium
    b. cadmium
    c. iron
    d. copper
15. aluminum
16. fretting
17. copper
18. exfoliation
19. oxidation or rust
20. nonporous

21. porous
22. pits or blisters
23. intergranular
24. improper heat treatment
25. ultrasonic, X-ray
26. extruded
27. aluminum
28. between
29. tensile
30. cannot
31. alkali
32. corrode
33. microbes, bacteria
34. microbes, bacteria
35. polyurethane
36. bicarbonate of soda
37. boric acid
38. acidic
39. intergranular
40. bulge
41. water-displacing
42. return current
43. hot linseed oil
44. water-displacing
45. par-al-ketone
46. nonmetallic
47. a. clean the area to be inspected
    b. apply the penetrant
    c. wash off surface penetrant and apply developer

48. cannot
49. can
50. a. pulse-echo
    b. resonance
51. dark
52. radiation monitor
53. voltage
54. low
55. nylon scrubber
56. abrasive
57. nonmetallic
58. airtight
59. Alodine
60. chlorine
61. glass beads
62. Alodine film
63. anodizing
64. hard
65. insulator
66. roughened
67. wash
68. abrasive blast
69. stress concentrations
70. sacrificial corrosion
71. zinc
72. chromic acid
73. do not
74. chromic acid

FLUID LINES AND FITTINGS

FLUID LINES AND FITTINGS

9

Fluid Lines

Fluid lines are an important part of an aircraft structure. In the airframe, hydraulic fluid under pressure, vast amounts of fuel, fire extinguishing agent, and compressed air are all moved through rigid lines and flexible hoses. The aviation maintenance technician must be able to determine the condition of these lines. When it is necessary to repair or replace them, he or she must understand the proper procedures and be able to determine the correct line for replacement.

Fluid lines in the engine pods or nacelles must meet all of the requirements of the lines installed in the airframe, and in addition many of them must also be protected from heat with fire sleeves.

Rigid Fluid Lines

Fluid lines installed in an aircraft where there is no relative motion between the line and the aircraft are normally made of aluminum alloy or corrosion-resistant steel tubing. Fuel lines, engine oil lines, and lines that carry instrument air may be made of half-hard 1100 or 3003 aluminum alloy. Lines installed in medium-pressure hydraulic systems may be made of 2024-T or 5052-O aluminum alloy. In the past, fluid lines in these types of installations were made of copper, but copper has the disadvantage that vibration can harden it and cause it to crack. Most of the low- and medium-pressure fluid lines are fitted with flared fittings.

Lines that carry high-pressure (3,000-psi and higher) hydraulic fluid, and lines that are in an exposed location where they are vulnerable to damage are usually made of annealed or 1/4-hard corrosion-resistant steel. These lines are fitted with either MS flareless fittings or swaged fittings.

Metal fluid lines are sized according to their outside diameter, which is given in increments of sixteenths of an inch, as in Figure 9-1. These metal lines are available with various wall thicknesses. The inside diameter of a metal line is found by subtracting two times the wall thickness from the outside diameter. For example, a piece of number 10 aluminum alloy tubing with a wall thickness of 0.065 inch has an inside diameter of: 0.625 – 2(0.065) = 0.495 inch.

Fluid Line size	Outside Diameter inch
4	¼
6	⅜
8	½
10	⅝
12	¾
16	1

Figure 9-1. *Relationship between fluid line size and its outside diameter*

Tube Cutting

It is important that metal tubing be cut with a square end that is free of burrs. A fine-tooth hacksaw blade can be used, but it is much better if a special tubing cutter such as the one seen in Figure 9-2 is used. Place the tubing in the cutter and turn the knob on the handle to bring the cutting wheel up snugly against the tubing at the location the tubing is to be cut. Rotate the cutter around the tubing and then turn the knob to move the cutting wheel in. Continue to rotate the cutter around the tubing, advancing the cutter in with each rotation until the tubing is cut. Be careful not to screw the cutting wheel in too tightly, as it will deform the tubing or cause an excessive burr to form inside.

After the tubing is cut, carefully use a knife or the deburring blade on the cutter to remove any burrs or raised metal resulting from the cutting operation. If the tubing is to be flared, the cut end should be polished with fine abrasive paper to remove any sharp edges that could cause the tubing to crack.

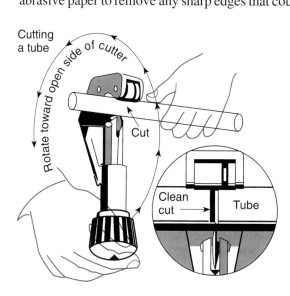

Figure 9-2. *A wheel-type tubing cutter cuts the end of a metal tube smooth and square.*

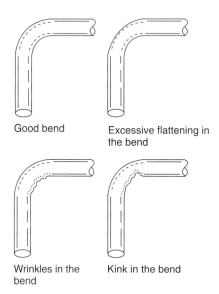

Figure 9-3. *Correct and incorrect tubing bends*

Tube Bending

Thin-wall tubing must be bent carefully to prevent it collapsing in the bend. Figure 9-3 shows an example of a good bend and three examples of bends that are not satisfactory. The tubing in the bend is often deformed, and the bend is not satisfactory if its small diameter is less than 75% of the outside diameter of the straight tubing.

Thin-wall tubing that is to be bent with many complex bends is often filled with a special metal alloy that melts at a temperature lower than that of boiling water to prevent it collapsing in the bends. After the tubing is bent, it is placed in a vat of boiling water, and the metal melts out and is used again. In the event the special alloy is not available, the tubing can be filled with clean sand and the ends plugged with wooden plugs. When using sand, it is extremely important, of course, that every trace of the sand be removed before the tubing is installed in the aircraft.

Tubing with an outside diameter of ¼-inch or less may be bent by hand without collapsing in the bend, and soft aluminum alloy and copper tubing may be bent by placing it in a special coil of spring steel that prevents flattening.

Aircraft maintenance shops often have large table-mounted benders that prevent the tubing from collapsing in the bend by placing a mandrel, or smooth, round-end bar, inside the tubing in such a way that it is always at the point the bend is being made. The tubing is bent around a radius block so that the bend is smooth and has the correct radius.

Tubing up to ¾-inch in diameter may be bent with hand benders such as the one in Figure 9-4. Choose the proper size bender and raise the slide bar upward. Place the tubing in the radius block with the location of the beginning of the bend at the 0° mark, and drop the clip over the tubing to hold

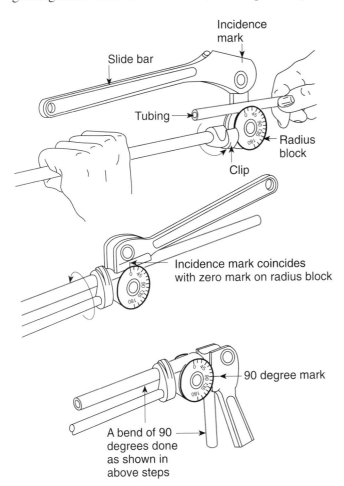

Figure 9-4. *Hand-operated tubing benders can bend thin-wall tubing up to ¾-inch diameter without the walls collapsing.*

it securely while the bend is being made. Rotate the slide bar down over the tubing, and the incidence mark on the bar will coincide with the 0° on the radius block. Force the tubing around the radius block with the slide bar until the incidence mark aligns with the degree mark on the radius block for the desired degrees of bend.

Thin-wall tubing installed in aircraft fluid systems must not be bent with a bend radius smaller than that shown in Figure 9-5. The bend radius shown in this table is that measured to the center line of the tubing.

Tubing OD	Minimum Bend Radius (inches)	
inches	Aluminum Alloy	Steel
1/8	3/8	
3/16	7/16	21/32
1/4	9/16	7/8
5/16	3/4	1 1/8
3/8	15/16	1 5/16
1/2	1 1/4	1 3/4
5/8	1 1/2	2 3/16
3/4	1 3/4	2 5/8
1	3	3 1/2

Figure 9-5. *Minimum bend radius for aluminum alloy and steel tubing*

Tubing Beading

When sections of metal tubing are subjected to vibration, they are joined with pieces of flexible hose. In many older aircraft, the ends of the metal tubing were beaded, and a section of rubber hose was slipped over the ends of the tubes and secured with hose clamps, as in Figure 9-6.

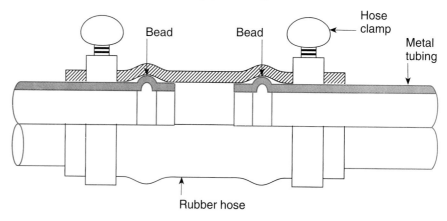

Figure 9-6. *Ends of metal tubing may be beaded and joined with a section of rubber hose and two hose clamps.*

Tubing Flaring

Most of the metal tubing used in modern aircraft is connected to other tubing or to components by flaring its ends and using flare-type fittings. When flaring tubing for installation in aircraft, be sure to use the correct flaring tool. Fluid lines in automobiles have a 45° flare angle, but those used with AN or AC fittings in aircraft must be flared with a 37° angle.

Double Flare

Tubing made of 5052-O and 6061-T aluminum alloy in sizes from ⅛ to ⅜ inch OD should be flared with a double flare, such as that seen in Figure 9-7. Double flares are smoother than single flares and are more concentric. Also, the extra metal makes the flare resistant to the shearing effect when the fittings are torqued.

Figure 9-8 illustrates the correct way to form a double flare. Cut the end of the tubing square and polish it, then slip the nut and sleeve onto the tube. Push the end of the tube into the flaring block until it contacts the stop pin, then clamp the block tightly in a vise to prevent the tube moving when it is being flared. Upset the end of the tubing by inserting the upsetting tool and striking it with a hammer. Finally, form the flare by inserting the flaring cone and striking it with a hammer.

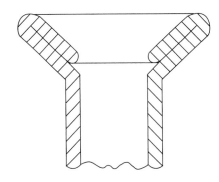

Figure 9-7. *A double flare on a piece of metal tubing provides extra metal to prevent damage when the fitting is torqued.*

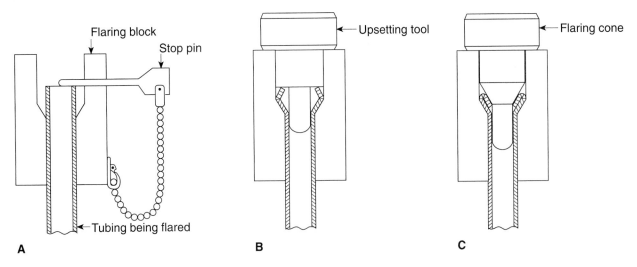

Figure 9-8. *Forming a double flare on a piece of tubing*
A. Insert the tube in the flaring tool until it contacts the stop pin.
B. Insert the upsetting tool and strike it with a hammer.
C. Insert the flaring cone and strike it with a hammer.

Single Flare

Single flares are produced on the end of a piece of tubing with either an impact-type flaring tool such as the one seen in Figure 9-9, or a tool in which the flaring cone is forced into the end of the tubing with hand-operated screw.

When using the impact-type flaring tool, follow these steps:

1. Slip the nut and sleeve on the tube.

2. Place the tube in the proper size hole in the flaring block.

3. Center the plunger, or flaring pin, over the tube.

4. Project the end of the tube slightly from the tip of the flaring tool, about the thickness of a dime.

5. Tighten the set screw securely to prevent slippage.

6. Strike the plunger several light blows with a lightweight hammer or mallet, and turn the plunger one-half turn after each blow.

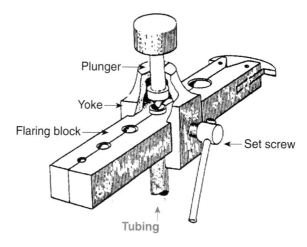

Figure 9-9. *An impact-type flaring tool for making single flares on rigid fluid lines*

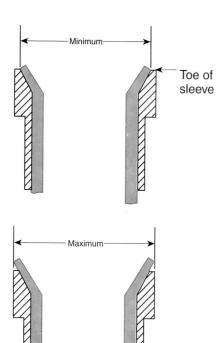

Figure 9-10. *Proper flare dimensions*

The minimum outside diameter of a properly made flare should be at least as large as the inside diameter of the toe of the sleeve. The maximum outside diameter should be no larger than the outside diameter of the sleeve. See these limits in Figure 9-10.

Flared Tube End Fittings

There are two types of nuts that may be used on a flared tube; the single-piece AN817 nut and the two-piece AN818 nut and AN819 sleeve, both seen in Figure 9-11.

The AN817 nut cannot be used on tubing where there is a bend near the end. The AN818 nut and AN819 sleeve combination is the preferred type of connector because it lessens the possibility of reducing the thickness of the flare by the wiping or ironing action when the nut is tightened. With the two-piece fitting, there is no relative motion between the fitting and the flare when the nut is being tightened.

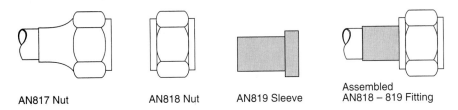

AN817 Nut   AN818 Nut   AN819 Sleeve   Assembled AN818 – 819 Fitting

Figure 9-11. *Flared tubing end fittings*

MS Flareless Fittings

The fluid lines used in some of the high-pressure hydraulic and pneumatic systems are so hard they are difficult to flare without cracking, so a system of flareless fittings has been developed. These fittings, such as the one seen in Figure 9-12, consist of a body, a sleeve, and a nut. The actual seal is between the outside of the sleeve and the inside of the body.

MS flareless fittings are attached to the end of the metal tubing by presetting the sleeve on the tube. Presetting puts enough pressure on the fitting to deform the sleeve and cause it to cut into the outside of the tube.

Presetting is done following these steps. *See* Figure 9-13 (page 588).

1. Cut the tubing to the correct length, with the ends perfectly square. Deburr the inside and outside of the tube. Slip the nut on first, and then slide the sleeve over the end of the tube.

2. Lubricate the threads of the presetting tool and nut with hydraulic fluid. Place the tool in a vise, and hold the tubing firmly and squarely on the seat of the tool. The tube must bottom firmly in the tool. Tighten the nut until the cutting edge of the sleeve grips the tube. This point is determined by slowly turning the tube back and forth while tightening the nut. When the tube no longer turns, the nut is ready for its final tightening.

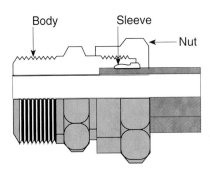

Figure 9-12. *MS flareless fitting for rigid fluid lines*

3. Final tightening depends upon the tubing. For aluminum alloy tubing up to and including ½-inch OD, tighten the nut from 1 to 1⅙ turns. For steel tubing and aluminum alloy tubing over ½-inch OD, tighten from 1⅙ to 1½ turns.

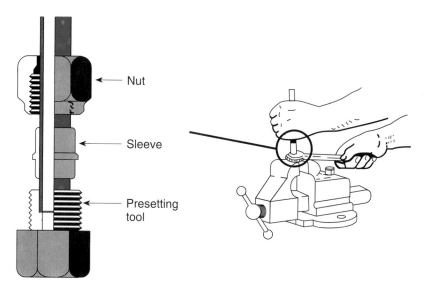

Figure 9-13. *Presetting a flareless tube fitting on a rigid fluid line*

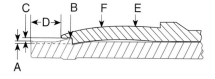

Figure 9-14. *Characteristics of a properly preset sleeve*

A properly preset sleeve should have these characteristics: *See* Figure 9-14.

1. The cutting lip of the sleeve should be embedded into the tube OD between 0.003 and 0.008 inch, depending upon the material (A).

2. A lip of material will be raised under the pilot (B).

3. The pilot of the sleeve should contact or be quite close to the outside diameter of the tube (C).

4. The tube projection from the sleeve pilot (D) should be between ⁷⁄₆₄ inch for No. 2 tubing to ⁹⁄₃₂ for No. 32 tubing.

5. The sleeve should be bowed slightly (E), and the sleeve may rotate on the tube and have a maximum lengthwise movement of ¹⁄₆₄ inch.

6. The sealing surface (F) of the sleeve which contacts the 24° angle of the fitting body seat should be smooth and free from scores. There should be no evidence of any lengthwise or circular cracks.

When installing the fitting in an aircraft hydraulic system, tighten the nut by hand until resistance is felt, and then turn it ⅙ to ⅓ of a turn (one hex to two hexes) with a wrench. Overtightening a fitting to stop a leak will damage the fitting and will probably cause the leak to become worse.

Swaged Tube Fittings

Modern high-performance aircraft that have high-pressure hydraulic and pneumatic systems often use swaged fittings on the rigid tubing used in these systems. To join two tubes with a swaged fitting, the ends of the tubes are cut square and the swaged fitting is slipped over them. The fitting is swaged, or forced into the tube, by hydraulic pressure acting on dies. Portable swaging tools are available that allow a technician to make permanent repairs to fluid lines installed in the aircraft by cutting out the damaged section and splicing in a new section with swaged fittings.

Installation of Rigid Fluid Lines

When a fuel or hydraulic line is routed through a compartment parallel with an electrical wire bundle, the fluid line should be installed below the wire bundle to prevent a leak wetting the wires.

Fluid lines must be installed in such a way that they are supported and protected from physical damage. They should be installed in such a way that they cannot be used as a hand hold or a step.

Each section of rigid tubing should have at least one bend in it to absorb vibration and the dimensional changes that occur when the tubing is pressurized, and the tubing should fit squarely against the fitting before the nut is started. Pulling a tube to the fitting with the nut will deform the flare and can cause a flare to fail.

Metal fluid lines are installed in an aircraft with bonded cushion clamps. These clamps have a strip of metal inside the cushion that electrically connects the tubing to the aircraft structure. When installing a bonded clamp, remove all of the paint and the anodized oxide film from the location to which the clamp is fastened. This will provide a good electrical connection between the tubing and the aircraft structure. Figure 9-16 gives the maximum distance between supports for rigid tubing installed in an aircraft.

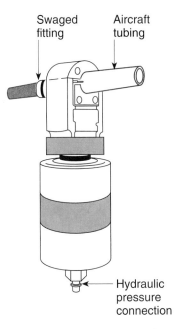

Figure 9-15. *Swaging tool used to swage fittings onto rigid fluid lines*

Tube OD	Distance Between Supports (inches)	
(inches)	Aluminum Alloy	Steel
1/8	9½	11½
3/16	12	14
1/4	13½	16
5/16	15	18
3/8	16½	20
1/2	19	23
5/8	22	25½
3/4	24	27½
1	26½	30

Figure 9-16. *Maximum distance between supports for rigid fluid lines*

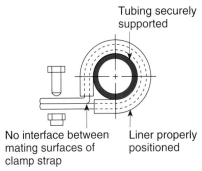

Tubing securely supported

No interface between mating surfaces of clamp strap

Liner properly positioned

Correct

Figure 9-17.
Correct and incorrect ways of installing the clamps to hold fluid lines

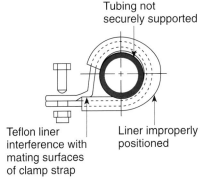

Tubing not securely supported

Teflon liner interference with mating surfaces of clamp strap

Liner improperly positioned

Incorrect

Repair of Rigid Fluid Lines

Scratches and nicks that are no deeper than 10% of the wall thickness of a piece of metal tubing can be repaired by burnishing, provided the damage is not in the heel of a bend. Tubing containing damage in the heel of a bend must be replaced.

Dents that are less than 20% of the tube diameter are not objectionable unless they are in the heel of the bend. Dents can be removed by pulling a bullet-shaped forming tool of the correct diameter through the tube. This can be done by using a length of cable.

Damage in a section of tubing may be repaired by cutting out the damaged area. Then, insert a new piece of tubing and join the ends with the proper nuts and unions as shown in Figure 9-18.

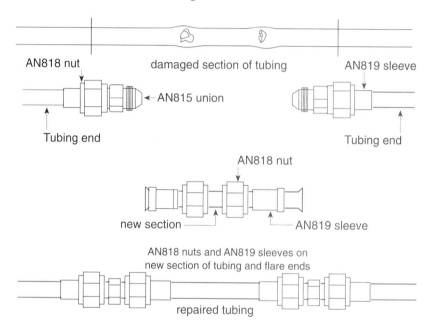

Figure 9-18. *Metal tubing may be repaired by removing the damaged area and splicing in a new section using the appropriate nuts, sleeves, and unions.*

Swaged fittings may also be used to make a permanent repair on a damaged fluid line. Figure 9-19A shows the way a pinhole leak or circumferential crack can be repaired with a single swaged fitting; Figure 9-19B shows how more extensive damage is repaired by splicing in a new section of tubing.

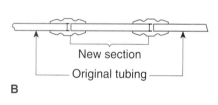

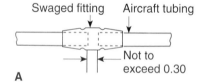

Figure 9-19. *Tubing repair using swaged fittings*

A. *A pinhole leak may be repaired with a single swaged fitting.*

B. *An extensively damaged tube may be repaired by cutting out the damaged area and splicing in a new section of tubing using two swaged fittings.*

Identification of Fluid Lines

Rigid tubing is marked with colored tape and symbols to identify its contents. The most commonly used symbols are shown in Figure 9-20.

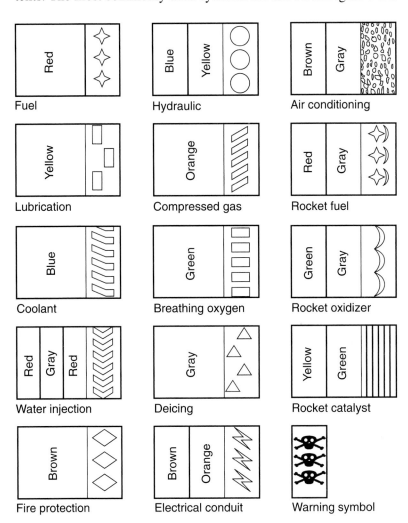

Red — Fuel	Blue / Yellow — Hydraulic	Brown / Gray — Air conditioning
Yellow — Lubrication	Orange — Compressed gas	Red / Gray — Rocket fuel
Blue — Coolant	Green — Breathing oxygen	Green / Gray — Rocket oxidizer
Red / Gray / Red — Water injection	Gray — Deicing	Yellow / Green — Rocket catalyst
Brown — Fire protection	Brown / Orange — Electrical conduit	Warning symbol

Figure 9-20. *Rigid tubing identification*

In addition to the colored bands and symbols, fluid lines carrying hazardous materials are marked with tape carrying an abbreviation which identifies the hazard. These abbreviations and typical fluids are seen in Figure 9-21.

Tubing that must be handled with special care because of its contents is marked with a warning symbol, which is a white band with black skull and crossbones.

Abbreviation	Meaning	Typical fluids
PHDAN	Physically dangerous	Air under pressure, carbon dioxide, Freon, gaseous oxygen, liquid nitrogen, liquid oxygen
FLAM	Flammable fluids	Alcohol, jet fuel, oils and greases
AAHM	Anesthetics and harmful materials	Trichlorethylene

Figure 9-21. *Identification of fluid lines carrying hazardous fluids*

STUDY QUESTIONS: RIGID FLUID LINES

Answers are on Page 604. Page numbers refer to chapter text.

1. The largest soft aluminum tubing that may bent by hand is _____ -inch outside diameter. *Page 583*

2. A piece of ¾-inch 5052 aluminum alloy tubing with a wall thickness of 0.070-inch has an inside diameter of _____ inch. *Page 581*

3. The flare angle to be used with an AN fitting is _____ degrees. *Page 585*

4. Rigid fluid lines for use in 3,000-psi hydraulic systems should be made of annealed or ¼-H _____ . *Page 581*

5. The largest aluminum tube that should be flared with a double flare has an outside diameter of _____ inch. *Page 585*

6. When rigid fluid lines are installed in an aircraft, each section of the tubing _____ (should or should not) have bends in it. *Page 589*

7. If the flare in a rigid fluid line almost reaches the flare cone of the fitting, it
_____ (is or is not) permissible to pull the flare tight against the fitting by
tightening the fitting nut. *Page 587*

8. When rigid fluid lines are attached to an aircraft structure with cushion clamps, the clamps should be of the
_____ type. *Page 589*

9. A fluid line that carries a fluid that is physically dangerous to personnel must be marked with the
abbreviation _____ . *Page 592*

10. Colored tape is used to identify the contents of the tubing installed in an aircraft. Fill in the blanks with the
colors used to identify the tubing for each of these applications:

a. air conditioning   _____   _____   _____

b. breathing oxygen   _____   _____   _____

c. compressed gas   _____   _____   _____

d. coolant   _____   _____   _____

e. deicing   _____   _____   _____

f. electrical conduit   _____   _____   _____

g. fire protection   _____   _____   _____

h. fuel   _____   _____   _____

i. hydraulic fluid   _____   _____   _____

j. lubrication   _____   _____   _____

k. rocket fuel   _____   _____   _____

l. rocket oxidizer   _____   _____   _____

m. water injection   _____   _____   _____
   Page 591

11. A fluid line that must be handled with special care is marked with a warning symbol. This symbol is a
series of black _____ on a white background. *Page 591*

12. If a fuel line is routed through a compartment parallel with an electrical wire bundle, the fuel line should be
installed _____ (above or below) the wire bundle. *Page 589*

Flexible Fluid Lines

Flexible fluid lines are used in an aircraft in locations where a rigid line must be connected to a component that has motion relative to the aircraft structure, and in installations in which the line must be frequently connected and disconnected.

A flexible hose may be used in any part of an aircraft fluid system where the aircraft manufacturer has proven that it meets all of the FAA requirements. It must not only pass the required fluid flow, but it must do so without an excessive pressure drop. It must also be able to carry the required system pressure and withstand the vibration of the aircraft.

When a particular hose is specified in an aircraft parts list or service manual, only that hose or an approved substitute may be used when the hose is replaced.

The size of flexible hose is approximately its inside diameter in $\frac{1}{16}$-inch increments. This refers to the outside diameter of a rigid tube that has the equivalent flow characteristics. For example, a -8 hose has flow characteristics equivalent to a piece of -8, or $\frac{1}{2}$ inch ($\frac{8}{16}$) rigid tubing. The inside diameter of the hose is not exactly $\frac{1}{2}$ inch; it is slightly smaller to allow for the tube wall thickness.

Flexible hoses have a linear stripe, called a lay line, running along their length. Its purpose is to help the mechanic prevent twisting the hose during installation. If this line spirals around the hose, the hose has been twisted.

Low-Pressure Hose

Low-pressure hose conforming to MIL-H-5593 specifications is made up of a synthetic rubber inner liner, a cotton braid, and a synthetic rubber outer cover. It is approved for a maximum pressure of 300 psi and is primarily used for instrument installations.

Low-pressure hose is identified by a broken yellow lay line. The letters LP, and the manufacturer's code number and date marking.

Medium-Pressure Hose

Medium-pressure hose conforming to MIL-H-8794 specifications has a seamless synthetic rubber inner liner, a synthetic rubber-impregnated cotton braid reinforcement, and a steel wire braid reinforcement. All of this is encased in a rough synthetic rubber-impregnated cotton braid. Medium-pressure hose is suitable for carrying fluids under pressures of up to 1,500 psi.

High-Pressure Hose

High-pressure hose, conforming to MIL-H-8788 specifications has a seamless synthetic rubber inner tube and either two or three carbon steel wire braid reinforcements. This hose is covered with a smooth synthetic rubber cover and is suitable for operating with pressures between 1,500 and 3,000 psi.

Extra-High-Pressure Hose

Extra-high-pressure hoses are used for pressures in the 3,000 to 6,000 psi range. These hoses are reinforced with layers of spiral-wound stainless steel wire encased in a special synthetic rubber. They can withstand temperatures up to 400°F.

Teflon Hose

Tetrafluoroethylene, also known as TFE or Teflon, is a material that is used for the inner liner of hoses that are required to carry fluids at temperatures up to 400°F. TFE is chemically inert, and it maintains its strength at these high operating temperatures.

Medium-pressure TFE hose has the TFE inner liner covered with a stainless steel braid, and high-pressure TFE hose has the TFE inner liner covered with several layers of spiral-wound stainless steel wire and one or more layers of stainless steel braid. The amount of reinforcement varies with the size of the hose.

TFE hose is unaffected by any fuel, petroleum, or synthetic-base oils, alcohol, coolants, or solvents commonly used in aircraft. Although it is highly resistant to vibration and fatigue, its principal advantage is its high operating strength, even at elevated temperatures. One problem with TFE hose, however, is its characteristic of taking a permanent set after it has been in service. If such a hose is temporarily removed from an aircraft, it must not be straightened out. To prevent inadvertent straightening, its ends should be held with a support wire, as seen in Figure 9-22.

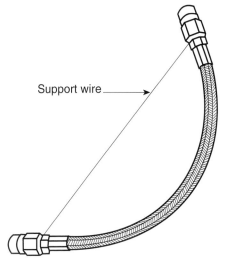

Support wire

Figure 9-22. *A support wire should be used to prevent a preformed tube or one that has taken a permanent set from being inadvertently straightened when it is removed from the aircraft.*

Installation of Flexible Hoses

Figure 9-23 shows the right and wrong way of installing flexible hose in an aircraft fluid system.

Flexible hoses should be approximately 5% to 8% longer than the distance between the fittings. This slack allows for contraction as the line expands its diameter and shortens its length when it is pressurized. See this in view A of Figure 9-23.

In B, we see an example of using the correct type of elbow fittings to prevent fluid lines from making sharp bends. In C, we see the correct way to connect a movable actuator into the aircraft hydraulic system. The hose must be of sufficient length, and installed in such a way that it is not crimped in any position of the actuator.

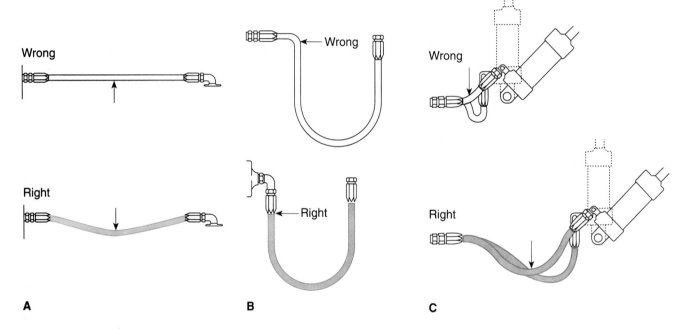

Figure 9-23. *Correct and incorrect installation of flexible hose*
A. Flexible hose should be 5% to 8% longer than the distance between the fittings to prevent straining the fittings.
B. Elbow fittings should be used to keep flexible hose from having to bend at a sharp angle.
C. Flexible hose should be installed on a movable actuator in such away that the hose is not crimped in any position of the actuator.

Flexible Hose End Fittings

Flexible hoses may be equipped with either swaged or replaceable end fittings. If a hose having swaged fittings is damaged, the entire hose must be replaced with one carrying the same part number or one that is approved by the aircraft manufacturer as a replacement.

Replaceable end fittings consist of three pieces: a nut, a nipple, and a socket, as in Figure 9-24. Clamp the hose in a vise and cut it to the correct length with the ends cut off square, using a fine-tooth hacksaw blade or a cutoff wheel. Remove the outer cover of the hose that goes into the socket, and twist the socket onto the hose, twisting in a counterclockwise direction. Place the nipple in the nut and screw the nut onto a fitting and tighten it securely. Lubricate the inside of the hose and the threads on the nipple, using mineral-base hydraulic fluid for hoses that will be used with this fluid, or with vegetable soap for hoses that will be used with Skydrol fluid. Screw the nipple into the socket until it bottoms, and then back it off until there is a clearance of between 0.005 and 0.031 inch between the nut and the socket. Remove the fitting from the nut and be sure the nut turns freely on the nipple.

When the fittings are installed, the hose must be installed on a hydraulic test stand and pressurized to 200% of the operating pressure of the hose. Hold this pressure for at least 30 seconds, but not more than five minutes. There should be no leaks at the fittings while the pressure is being. After the test is completed, drain the hose and seal the ends with the proper plugs until the hose is installed on the aircraft.

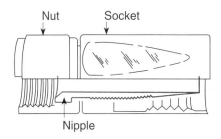

Figure 9-24. *Replaceable sleeve-type fitting for flexible fluid lines*

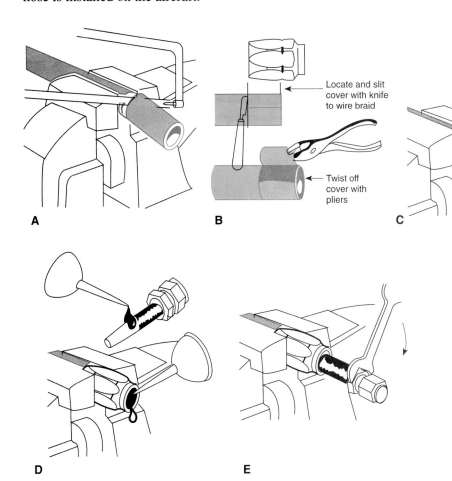

Figure 9-25. *Installation of end fitting on a high-pressure hose*

A. *Cut the hose to the correct length with a fine-tooth hacksaw blade or a cutoff wheel.*

B. *Cut the outer cover with a knife and slit it so it can be twisted off to expose the outer braid for the distance that will be inserted into the socket.*

C. *Twist the socket onto the end of the hose, twisting in a counterclockwise direction.*

D. *Lubricate the inside of the hose and the threads on the nipple.*

E. *Screw the nipple into the socket until it bottoms, and then back it off until there is a slight clearance between the nut and the socket.*

Answers are on Page 604. **Page numbers refer to chapter text.**

13. The maximum distance between end fittings to which a straight hose assembly is to be connected is 50 inches. The minimum hose length to make such a connection should be _____ inches. *Page 596*

14. A permanent impression left in a flexible hose by the pressure of hose clamps or supports is called _____ . *Page 596*

15. Damaged swaged-end fittings on a piece of flexible hydraulic hose _____ (can or cannot) be replaced. *Page 596*

16. Flexible hose has a stripe running along its length. This is called a lay line and is used to determine whether or not the hose has been _____ during installation. *Page 594*

17. The size of a flexible hose is determined by its _____ (inside or outside) diameter. *Page 594*

18. The type of flexible fluid line that is used when high operating strength and resistance to solvents are required is _____ hose. *Page 595*

Fluid Line Fittings

The size of fittings used with fluid lines is indicated by the dash numbers following the AN number of the fitting. These dash numbers are in $\frac{1}{16}$-inch increments for the outside diameter of the rigid tube the fitting matches. For example, a -6 fitting is for a $\frac{3}{8}$-inch tube.

The size of pipe fittings relates to the inside diameter of an iron pipe that has these threads on its outside.

Pipe Fittings

Many of the fittings that connect a fluid line to a component such as a pump or valve have tapered pipe threads on the end that screw into the component. Figure 9-26 shows an AN816 nipple. One end has tapered pipe threads and the other end has the standard flare cone and threads that fit an AN818 nut.

When installing a fitting having pipe threads, start the fitting into the hole for about one turn, and then put a small amount of thread lubricant on the second thread from the end. Screw the fitting into the hole and tighten it snugly. If the fitting is being screwed into an aluminum casting, it is possible that overtightening can cause the tapered threads to crack the casting.

Figure 9-26. *This AN816 nipple has tapered pipe threads on the end that screws into the component. The other end has a flare cone and threads that fit an AN818 nut.*

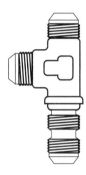

Figure 9-27. *AN804 Universal fitting. This is also called a bulkhead fitting.*

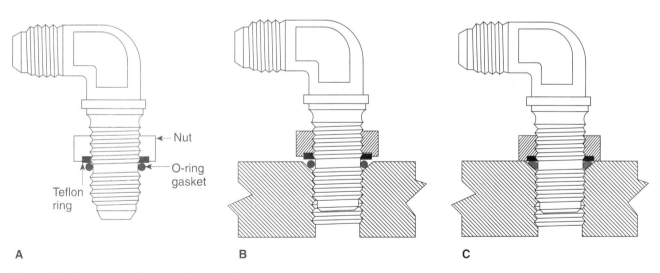

A   B   C

Figure 9-28. *Proper installation of a Universal fitting*
A. Screw the nut onto the upper threads and slip a Teflon ring and an O-ring gasket over the end threads into the groove.
B. Screw the fitting in until the O-ring contacts the housing.
C. Align the fitting with the connecting lines and screw the nut down until it contacts the housing. The compressed O-ring forms the fluid-tight seal.

Universal, or Bulkhead Fittings

Some components, such as selector valves and actuator cylinders, use fittings with double threads such as those seen on the AN804 Tee in Figure 9-27. An AN924 nut is screwed onto the fitting above the cutout portion of the threads. A Teflon ring and an O-ring gasket are slipped over the end threads and into the groove. The fitting is screwed into the housing until the O-ring contacts the housing and then screwed an additional amount needed to properly align the fitting with the lines that are to connect with it. Hold the fitting and turn the nut down until it contacts the housing. This will force the O-ring into the chamfered edge of the hole to provide the fluid-tight seal. *See* Figure 9-28 on Page 599.

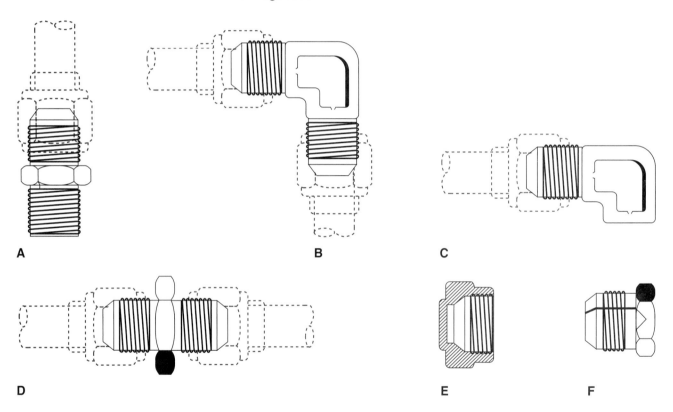

Figure 9-29. *AN flared tube fittings*

A. *AN816 Nipple, flared tube to pipe thread*

B. *AN821 Elbow 90°, flared tube*

C. *AN914 Elbow 90°, flared tube to internal pipe thread*

D. *AN815 Union, flared tube*

E. *AN820 Cap, flared tube*

F. *AN806 Plug, flared tube*

AN and AC Flared Tube Fittings

Flared tube fittings are available in many configurations. Figure 9-29 shows several typical fittings. The AN816 nipple and AN822 elbow are used to connect a flared tube or a flexible hose to a component with tapered pipe threads. The AN821 elbow and AN815 union are used to join flared tubes or flexible hose. The AN820 cap and AN806 plug are used to seal lines and fittings to keep dirt and contaminants out of the system.

Many of the airplanes built during World War II used AC fittings which are similar to the AN fitting. However, there is enough difference that they are not interchangeable (*see* Figure 9-30). AN fittings have a short shoulder between the end of the flare cone and the beginning of the threads. The older AC fittings do not have this recess. Steel AN fittings are colored black, and aluminum alloy AN fittings are colored blue. AC fittings are colored either gray or yellow.

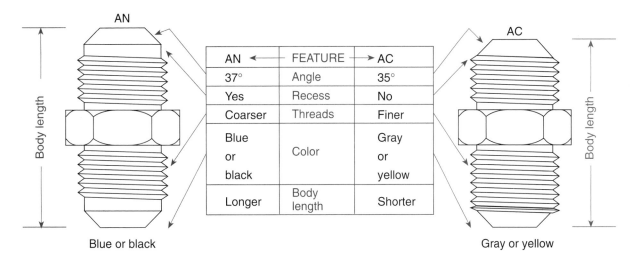

AN	FEATURE	AC
37°	Angle	35°
Yes	Recess	No
Coarser	Threads	Finer
Blue or black	Color	Gray or yellow
Longer	Body length	Shorter

Figure 9-30. *AN and AC flare-type fittings*

*Answers are on Page 604. **Page numbers refer to chapter text.***

19. An AN818-8 nut will fit a tube with an outside diameter of _____ inch. *Page 601*

20. AN fittings made of steel are colored _____ . *Page 601*

21. AN fittings made of aluminum alloy are colored _____ . *Page 601*

22. The flare-type fitting that has a short unthreaded section between the flare cone and the beginning of the threads is an _____ (AC or AN) fitting. *Page 601*

23. When presetting an MS flareless fitting, tighten the nut by hand until resistance is felt and then, using a wrench, turn _____ to _____ turns. *Page 587*

24. When installing a fluid line equipped with MS flareless fittings, tighten the nut by hand until resistance is felt, and then turn it _____ to _____ turn with a wrench. *Page 587*

Answers to Chapter 9 Study Questions

1. ¼
2. 0.61
3. 37
4. corrosion-resistant steel
5. ⅜
6. should
7. is not
8. bonded
9. PHDAN
10. a. brown, gray
    b. green
    c. orange
    d. blue
    e. gray
    f. brown, orange
    g. brown
    h. red
    i. blue, yellow
    j. yellow
    k. red, gray
    l. green, gray
    m. red, gray, red

11. skull and crossbones
12. below
13. 52½
14. cold flow
15. cannot
16. twisted
17. inside
18. Teflon
19. ½
20. black
21. blue
22. AN
23. 1, 1½
24. ⅙, ⅓

GROUND OPERATION AND SERVICING

10

Continued

GROUND OPERATION AND SERVICING

10

One of the important functions of an aviation maintenance technician is that of operating aircraft on the ground. This involves servicing it with the proper fuel and lubricants. In this section of the text, we will discuss safety procedures in the shop and on the flight line. We will also discuss the various fuels and the precautions to be observed when fueling an aircraft. Finally, since moving aircraft and running their engines are important parts of an aviation maintenance technician's work, we will discuss the basic procedures for starting both reciprocating and turbine engines, and the precautions to be observed when moving aircraft on the ramp and in the hangar.

Fire Protection

Aircraft carry huge quantities of fuel, and because of the large amount of electrical wiring and equipment, fire is always a potential danger. It must be guarded against at all times by the maintenance technician. This not only means taking safety precautions on the actual aircraft, but also in the hangar area and the maintenance shops.

All combustibles must be kept in the proper type of containers and stored in areas specially approved for them. Many combustible materials such as lacquer, dope, and paint thinners must be stored in an area where there is adequate ventilation.

Spilled gasoline presents a special fire hazard, and it must not be swept with a dry broom, as static electricity can be generated that will cause a spark and ignite the fumes. A small amount of gasoline can be picked up by covering it with an industrial absorbent and carefully disposing of the material in a manner approved by the local fire department. Large amounts of gasoline spilled around an aircraft should be flushed away from the aircraft with water and the local fire department notified.

Paint spray booths that have been used for spraying lacquer and dope often have dried overspray on the floor. Do not dry-sweep such a spray booth, as the friction can produce static electricity and ignite the flammable dried overspray. Always wet the floor before sweeping it.

Rags that are wet with oil, paint solvents, thinners, and certain chemicals such as Alodine and other conversion coatings must not be kept in a pile. These materials combine with oxygen in the air and generate heat, which if not allowed to escape will raise the temperature inside the pile high enough

flammable. Easily ignited. Flammable replaces the older term "inflammable" which can be misinterpreted to mean "not flammable."

Figure 10-1. *Three things are required for a fire: fuel, oxygen, and heat. If any one of the three is missing there can be no fire.*

spontaneous combustion. Ignition of a material without an external source of heat. The heat that causes the ignition is provided by oxidation, and if it is not allowed to escape, the temperature will rise to the combustion temperature of the material.

Piles of oily rags, or rags containing certain chemicals are subject to spontaneous combustion.

kindling point. The temperature to which a material must be heated for it to combine with oxygen from the air and burn.

halogenated hydrocarbon. A chemical compound containing hydrogen and carbon and one of the halogen-family elements such as fluorine, chlorine, or bromine.

The vapors of halogenated hydrocarbons are particularly effective as fire extinguishing agents as they chemically prevent the combination of the oxygen with the fuel.

to cause them to ignite spontaneously and burn. The chemicals should be washed out and the rags allowed to dry in a ventilated area. Oily rags should be stored in airtight safety containers.

Nature of Fire

Fire is the product of a chemical reaction in which a material, called a fuel, combines with oxygen and releases heat and light. The fuel is usually changed into carbon which unites with some of the oxygen to form carbon dioxide and carbon monoxide.

Three things are required for a fire: There must be fuel, there must be oxygen, and the temperature of the fuel must be raised enough for it to combine with the oxygen. Fire prevention consists of keeping these three constituents separated. Fire extinguishing is done by cooling the fuel or excluding oxygen from it.

Classification of Fires

Fires are classified into four categories that allow us to better understand them and choose the correct method for extinguishing them. Extinguishers suited for each classification of fire are marked with the classification letter designation and distinctive mark recommended by the National Fire Protection Association. *See* Figure 10-2.

Fire Classes	Letter Designation	Symbol
Ordinary combustibles	A	Green triangle
Flammable liquids	B	Red square
Energized electrical equipment	C	Blue circle
Combustible metals	D	Yellow star

Figure 10-2. *Classification of fires*

Fire Extinguishing Agents

Fire extinguishing agents are chosen for the class of fire on which they are effective, and they should be clearly marked with the appropriate class symbol.

Class A fires, with such fuels as paper, cloth, or wood, can be extinguished with a spray of water which cools the fuel to a temperature below its kindling point.

Class B fires are best put out with an extinguisher that excludes the oxygen from the burning fuel. Carbon dioxide, or CO_2, extinguishers blanket the fire and exclude the oxygen. Dry powder extinguishing agents, in the presence of heat break down to produce carbon dioxide that displaces the oxygen. Halogenated hydrocarbons such as Halon 1211 and Halon 1301 are highly effective for these fires, as they form a chemical reaction that prevents the oxygen and the fuel uniting. Water should not be used on a Class B fire because many of the burning fuels will float on the water and spread the fire.

Class C fires should be handled with special care because of the danger of contacting dangerously high voltages. Water should not be used because it will conduct the electricity. Dry powder, while effective on Class C fires, is not the best choice because the residue it leaves makes cleanup difficult. Carbon dioxide, when sprayed through a nonmetallic horn is very effective, but the best extinguishers are the halogenated hydrocarbons, the halons.

Class D fires should never have water sprayed on them as the water only intensifies the fire, and it can, in extreme cases, cause an explosion. Dry powder, which excludes oxygen from the flame, is the choice for extinguishing metal fires.

Toxicity Group	Extinguishing Agent
6 (least toxic)	Halon 1301 (Bromotrifluoromethane)
5a	Carbon dioxide
5	Halon 1211 (Bromochlorodifluoromethane)
4	Halon 1202 (Dibromodifluoromethane)
3	Halon 1011 (Bromochloromethane)
2	Halon 1001 (Methyl bromide)

Figure 10-3. *Fire extinguishing agents arranged according to their toxicity. The higher the number, the less toxic the agent.*

Fire Extinguishers

All fire extinguishers are not equally effective on all types of fires. The size of the extinguisher and the extinguishing agent it contains must be chosen for the classes of fires that are most likely to occur at the location the extinguisher is mounted. The class of fire for which the extinguisher is suited is marked near or on the extinguisher with the symbols described in Figure 10-2.

Water Fire Extinguishers

Small metal containers of water and an antifreeze agent may be mounted in brackets in the aircraft cabins to extinguish class A fires. The seal in a small CO_2 cartridge in the handle of these extinguishers is pierced when the handle is twisted. The released CO_2 pressurizes the water and sprays it out so it can effectively lower the temperature of the fuel and extinguish the fire. *See Figure 10-4.*

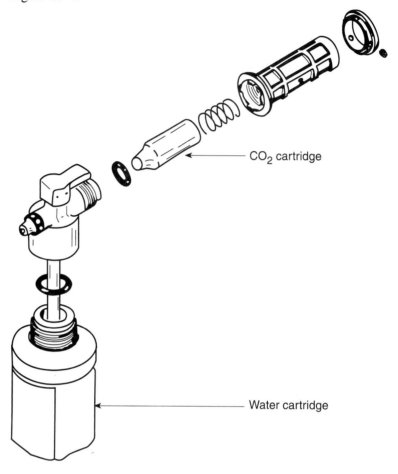

CO₂ cartridge

Water cartridge

Figure 10-4. *When the handle of this fire extinguisher is twisted, the seal on the CO_2 cartridge is broken and the water in the cylinder is pressurized and sprays out to extinguish the fire.*

Halon 1211 and 1301 Fire Extinguishers

Halon 1211 and 1301 are two of the most effective fire extinguishing agents available for use on class B and C fires and are also effective on Class A fires. They are colorless, noncorrosive liquids that evaporate rapidly and leave no residue, and they do not harm fabrics, metals, or other materials they contact. Halon 1211 and 1301 extinguish fires by producing a heavy blanketing mist that eliminates air from the fire, and their chemical action inhibits oxygen combining with the fuel.

Halon 1211 and 1301 extinguishers meet the requirements of 14 CFR §135.155 for installation in aircraft engaged in air taxi operation and are available in small, medium, and large sizes. The small size is capable of extinguishing fires of up to one square foot in area, the medium extinguisher is effective on fires of up to two square feet, and the large extinguisher is effective on fires up to five square feet. Halon 1211 uses nitrogen to propel the agent from the extinguisher but Halon 1301 does not require a separate propelling agent. All of these extinguishers are equipped with gages to indicate the pressure of the extinguishing charge.

Carbon Dioxide Fire Extinguishers

CO_2 is an inert gas that is stored in a steel container under pressure. When it is released it expands and its temperature drops. It blankets the fire and excludes oxygen so the fire goes out. CO_2 extinguishers are available in sizes ranging from small 2-pound units for installation in aircraft cabins and cockpits to the large wheel-mounted extinguishers for use in maintenance shops and on flight lines.

The state of charge of a CO_2 fire extinguisher is determined by weighing it and comparing its weight with the weight stamped on the extinguisher housing. If the weight is less than that stamped on the housing, the extinguisher must be returned to a service facility for recharging.

Dry-Powder Fire Extinguishers

Dry powder fire extinguishing agents such as bicarbonate of soda, ammonium phosphate and potassium bicarbonate are effective against class B, C, and D fires. When the agent is heated, it releases carbon dioxide and excludes oxygen from the fire. Dry powder fire extinguishers are not applicable for cockpit fires because of the reduced visibility they cause. They are, however, most effective for brake fires which involve burning metal.

The dry powder extinguishing agent is propelled from the container by a charge of compressed dry nitrogen, and the condition of the charge is indicated by a pressure gage built into the extinguisher.

Answers are on Page 647. Page numbers refer to chapter text.

1. Three things that are necessary for a fire are:
   a. _____
   b. _____
   c. _____
      Page 608

2. A fire involving paper as a fuel is a class- _____ fire. *Page 608*

3. A fire involving a flammable liquid as a fuel is a class- _____ fire. *Page 608*

4. A fire involving an energized electrical system is a class- _____ fire. *Page 608*

5. A fire involving combustible metals is a class- _____ fire. *Page 608*

6. A fire extinguisher suitable for use on a Class-A fire is identified by a
   _____ . *Page 608*

7. A fire extinguisher suitable for use on a Class-B fire is identified by a
   _____ . *Page 608*

8. A fire extinguisher suitable for use on a Class-C fire is identified by a
   _____ . *Page 608*

9. A fire extinguisher suitable for use on a Class-D fire is identified by a
   _____ . *Page 608*

10. A fire extinguishing agent with a toxicity rating of 2 is _____ (more or less) toxic than one with a rating of 6. *Page 609*

Safety in the Shop and on the Flight Line

Shop and flight line safety are extremely important parts of a technician's responsibility, and we must make safety awareness a way of life. Maintenance shops contain both visible and invisible hazards which must be recognized and guarded against.

Good housekeeping dictates that we immediately wipe up any liquids spilled on the floor and that we properly dispose of dirty and oily rags. Waste containers should be emptied frequently to prevent the accumulation of unnecessary flammable materials in the shop.

All power tools such as saws, sanders, grinders, and power shears should be kept clean and free of obstructions that make their operation awkward. And no one should be allowed to operate any power tool until he or she is properly checked out and aware of all of its safety features and requirements.

We should even be aware of such seemingly insignificant things as the proper disposition of used safety wire. These sharp pieces of wire can cut a person, and if they fall into an electrical junction box can cause an electrical malfunction or, even worse, a fire. If they fall into an engine or other mechanical device, they can cause expensive damage.

The time pressure under which we often work can cause us to be careless with our tools. It is an exceptionally good idea, when working on an aircraft to know exactly which tools we have with us and, when the job is complete, to account for each tool. Some operators even require a written tool list for on-the-aircraft work to minimize the chance of a tool being left in an aircraft structure or in an engine. Tools left in an aircraft control system or engine can cause serious accidents.

The welding area in a shop should receive special attention because of the flammable gases stored under pressure and the presence of sparks and flying particles of molten metal. When welding or cutting is done outside of the designated welding area, special care must be taken to prevent the flame or sparks igniting any flammable materials. Adequate fire extinguishers must always be available when welding or cutting is being done.

Safety Involving Compressed Gases

Most aviation maintenance shops use various gases under pressure that must be properly handled to insure safety. Some basic rules to observe when handling compressed gases are:

1. Use special caution when moving a bottle of compressed gas. Always have a cap installed over the valve, and strap the bottle to the cart to prevent it rolling off.

Continued

2. Always use some sort of eye protection when working with compressed gases, and do not direct any compressed gases toward a person. When using compressed air to blow dust and dirt away, be sure that the pressure is low enough that the flying particles cannot injure anyone.

3. Do not use oil or grease on an oxygen cylinder or regulator, as the pure oxygen can cause the petroleum product to spontaneously ignite.

Hearing Protection

The high noise level of rivet guns, air drills, metal saws, and operating turbojet engines requires that everyone in aircraft maintenance shops and on the flight lines use some form of hearing protection.

When a person is exposed to the noise for a relatively short period of time or in locations where the noise level is relatively low, small protectors that fit into the auditory canal of the ear are quite effective. One very popular type of protector consists of small plugs of sponge plastic that are formed into cones and inserted into the ear. When inside the ear, they expand to form a perfect fit in the auditory canal and decrease the sound pressure reaching the ear drum.

When working on a noisy flight line, most technicians use a hearing protector that resembles a large set of cushioned earphones and is held over the ears with a spring steel band. This is comfortable and provides a large degree of protection. *See* Figure 10-5.

Eye Protection

Our eyes are two of our most valuable assets and we should protect them against all types of hazards. One common type of eye protection for persons who wear prescription eye glasses is the use of special safety lenses with transparent plastic side shields. Another type of eye protector is safety glasses made of a soft but strong transparent plastic material that cover the eyes and are held on the head with an elastic band. The sides of these glasses fit snugly against the face to prevent injury from the side, and the sides are ventilated to keep the lenses from fogging.

Full-cover face shields that are mounted on an adjustable head band and wrap around the face should be used when working on air conditioning systems and when charging liquid oxygen systems to prevent injury from the extreme cold if any liquid refrigerant or oxygen is splashed on the face.

Respiratory Protection

There are two types of airborne contaminants that can be injurious to our lungs: solid particles and vapors; and we must protect our lungs from both of them.

Disposable paper or cloth masks are often used to protect against solid contaminants and should be used when sanding or grinding composite materials.

Spraying paints, lacquers, and enamels produce solid contaminants in the air as well as harmful vapors. You should use a mask that has a pre-filter to remove the solid contaminants and then a chemical cartridge to provide protection against the vapors. When it is necessary to work in an environment containing a heavy concentration of toxic vapors, an airflow-type respirator should be worn. This respirator covers the entire head and upper part of the body and is supplied with a constant flow of compressed air that prevents fumes entering the mask.

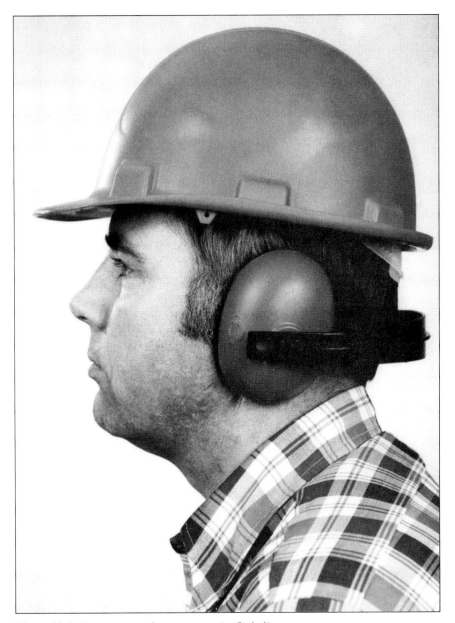

Figure 10-5. *Ear protectors for use on a noisy flight line.*

Shop and Flight Line Safety Summary

Operating jet engines act as huge vacuum cleaners and pick up loose objects on the ground, and many have been seriously damaged by sucking up bolts, pieces of sheet metal, safety wire, and tools. Many flight lines and aircraft parking ramps have containers for any debris you may find on the ground and for any litter you may need to dispose of. Make it a habit to pick up any litter and properly dispose of it.

A good technician not only cleans up after completing a task, but is always alert to any potentially dangerous situation that may have been left by someone else. Safety is really as much an attitude as it is an action.

Aviation Fuels

Reciprocating-Engine Fuels

Aviation gasoline is a blend of hydrocarbons obtained from crude petroleum by the process of fractional distillation. It has a nominal heat energy content of 20,000 Btu per pound, and it weighs approximately six pounds per U.S. gallon.

Aviation gasoline does not burn in its liquid state, but it readily changes from a liquid into a vapor, and these vapors combine with oxygen from the air to form a combustible mixture. The vapor pressure of a fuel is the pressure that must be maintained above the liquid to prevent it releasing vapors. The vapor pressure of aviation gasoline is carefully controlled to assure that it vaporizes easily enough for the engine to start in cold weather, but not so easily that it will cause a vapor lock in the fuel lines.

Aviation gasoline is required to have a vapor pressure of 7 psi or less, at 100°F. If it vaporizes too readily, its vapor pressure will be high and when a bubble forms in a fuel line, the pressure of the vapors in the bubble will prevent fuel flowing to the engine and the engine will not run. This condition is called a vapor lock, and it forms when the fuel gets too hot or when the aircraft goes high enough that the air pressure above the fuel drops enough to allow the fuel to release vapors, or boil.

One of the limits to the development of high-powered reciprocating engines has been the detonation characteristics of the available fuel. Detonation is an uncontrolled burning, or explosion, of the fuel-air mixture inside the cylinder of a reciprocating engine. The mixture ignites and burns normally, but as it burns, it compresses and heats the mixture ahead of the flame front. When the heated and compressed mixture reaches its critical pressure and temperature, it explodes, or releases its energy almost instantaneously. These explosions inside the cylinder increase the cylinder-head temperature and cylinder pressure and decrease the engine power. Severe detonation can destroy an aircraft engine.

The antidetonation characteristics of aviation gasoline are indicated by an octane number or performance number, and the FAA specifies in the Type

vapor pressure. The pressure of the vapor above a liquid required to prevent the liquid releasing additional vapors.

vapor lock. A condition in a fuel system in which the fuel has vaporized and formed pockets of gas in the fuel line. Vapor lock prevents liquid fuel flowing to the engine.

detonation. An explosion-like uncontrolled burning of the fuel-air mixture inside the cylinder of a reciprocating engine when the fuel-air mixture reaches its critical pressure and temperature. Detonation causes a rapid rise in cylinder pressure, excessive cylinder head temperature, and a decrease in engine power.

Certificate Data Sheets (TCDS) for each engine the minimum grade of fuel approved for that engine. If fuel of a lower grade than is approved for the engine is used, there is a serious danger of detonation, and it is a violation of the Federal Aviation Regulations to service an aircraft with fuel having an octane rating lower than the minimum specified in the TCDS.

Aviation gasoline is dyed to identify its octane rating or performance number, and these colors and their meanings are listed in Figure 10-6.

Grade	Color	Max. TEL (Ml/gal)	Notes
80	Red	0.5	Being phased out
82 UL	Purple	Unleaded	
100	Green	4.0	
100LL	Blue	2.0	
Jet fuel	Colorless		

Figure 10-6. *Identification of grades of aviation gasoline*

The octane rating or performance number of a gasoline is determined by burning the fuel in a special variable-compression ratio laboratory test engine, called a CFR (Cooperative Fuel Research) engine, and comparing its performance with that of a reference fuel made up of iso-octane and normal heptane. Iso-octane is a flammable, colorless hydrocarbon liquid that has a high critical pressure and temperature. It is used as the high reference and has been assigned a rating of 100. Normal heptane is another hydrocarbon liquid, but it has poor antidetonation characteristics and is used as the low reference and assigned a rating of zero.

The test engine is operated with a standard reference fuel (usually iso-octane) with operating conditions adjusted to standard day conditions. This produces a standard knock, and a knockmeter that measures peak combustion pressure is adjusted to a midscale setting of 50 to 55. The sample fuel with an unknown octane rating is now introduced into the induction system and the fuel-air ratio is adjusted to produce maximum knock. The compression ratio is then adjusted to return the knockmeter to the same reading as previously noted. The new compression ratio is checked in a reference table to determine the approximate octane rating of the fuel. This rating is verified by using a fuel composed of a mixture of iso-octane and normal heptane, with the percentage of iso-octane the same as the rating found in the CFR engine. This fuel should have the same knock characteristics as the sample fuel produced.

Gasoline with an octane rating of 100 has the same antidetonation characteristics as iso-octane, but some gasoline has better characteristics, and it is rated with performance numbers determined by using a reference fuel comprised of iso-octane containing controlled amounts of tetraethyl lead.

You will sometimes see a dual-number rating for aviation gasoline. This system gives the antidetonation rating for the fuel when it is operating with

Type Certificate Data Sheets (TCDS). The official specifications of an aircraft, engine, or propeller issued by the Federal Aviation Administration.

TCDS for an engine lists the minimum grade of fuel approved for its use.

fuel grade. A system of rating aviation gasoline according to its antidetonation characteristics. This is based on the older system of octane rating or performance number in which the higher the number, the more resistant the fuel is to detonation.

performance numbers. An antidetonation rating system for aviation gasoline whose performance characteristics are better than those of iso-octane, which is used as the top value in the octane rating system. Aviation gasoline ratings above 100 are called performance numbers.

iso-octane. The hydrocarbon fuel used as the high reference when rating the antidetonation characteristics of aviation gasoline.

standard day conditions. Conditions chosen by scientists and engineers that allow all test data to be corrected to the same conditions. These conditions include:
Temperature: 15°C or 59°F
Sea level pressure: 29.92 inches of mercury, or 1013.2 millibars
Acceleration due to gravity: 32.2 feet per second, per second
Specific weight of air: 0.07651 pounds per cubic foot
Density: 0.002378 slug per cubic foot
Speed of sound: 661.7 knots, or 761.6 miles per hour

both a lean and a rich mixture. A fuel rated as 100/130 has an octane rating of 100 when the engine is operating with a lean, or cruise, mixture, and a performance number of 130 when it is operating with a rich mixture, such as would be used for takeoff.

Tetraethyl lead (TEL), a heavy, oily, poisonous liquid [Pb(C$_2$H$_5$)$_4$] is added to aviation gasoline to improve its antidetonation characteristics by raising its critical pressure and temperature. This allows the engine to operate with higher cylinder pressures without the fuel-air mixture detonating. But TEL has the problem of leaving lead deposits inside the cylinders that foul spark plugs and cause corrosion. The maximum amount of TEL allowed in the various grades of aviation gasoline is seen in Figure 10-6.

In order to get rid of the lead residue from the TEL, ethylene dibromide is mixed with the gasoline. When the gasoline burns, the ethylene dibromide combines with the lead to form volatile lead bromides that go out with the exhaust gases instead of forming solid contaminants inside the cylinder.

The decline in the number of low horsepower engines in the general aviation fleet has caused such a decrease in the demand for grade 80 gasoline that it is often unavailable. When an engine designed to operate on grade 80 fuel must operate on grade 100 or 100LL there is too much lead, and spark plug fouling is likely to occur even with the ethylene dibromide. Another compound, trichresyl phosphate [(CH$_3$C$_6$H$_4$O)$_3$PO], commonly called TCP, may be added to the fuel. TCP changes the lead deposits into a nonconductive lead phosphate which is easier to eliminate from the cylinder than the lead bromide.

The critical pressure and temperature of a fuel may be increased by blending aromatic additives such as benzoil, toluene, xylene, and cumene with the fuel. These additives, first commonly used during World War II, allow the engine to use a higher manifold pressure and thus produce a higher horsepower without the danger of detonation. They do have the drawback that they soften certain rubber products. Because of this softening action, most of the hoses and diaphragms used in aircraft fuel systems are made of rubber compounds that are not affected by aromatic additives.

We have mentioned that the use of a fuel with an octane rating or performance number lower than that approved by the FAA can lead to detonation and engine damage or destruction. A condition more dangerous than using aviation gasoline with too low an octane rating results if the gasoline is contaminated with jet fuel. Jet fuel is not designed to burn under the pressures encountered in a reciprocating engine, and it takes only a small amount of jet fuel to lower the critical pressure and temperature of the fuel to such a level that catastrophic detonation can occur. If any tanks on a reciprocating-engine aircraft have been serviced with jet fuel, they should be drained, and all of the lines, valves, and strainers flushed. If the engine has been operated on the contaminated fuel, the cylinders should be inspected with a bore-scope to check for internal damage, and the engine should be given a compression check. The oil should be changed and the oil filters inspected for any indication of contaminants that could result from detonation.

The decrease in availability and increase in price of grade 80 aviation gasoline has caused many aircraft owners and operators to consider the use of automotive gasoline. Some aircraft have been operated safely with automobile gasoline without the approval of the FAA, but within the last few years the FAA has issued supplemental type certificates (STCs) that allow the use of automobile gasoline in certain aircraft under specific conditions. Aircraft and engine manufacturers and the major oil companies have advised against the use of automobile gasoline in aircraft engines because its production, storage, and handling requirements are not as rigid as those imposed on aviation gasoline. Automobile gasoline often has vapor pressures as high as 15 psi at 100°F, and this can cause vapor lock at high altitudes. The additives in automobile gasoline may be incompatible with the seals and diaphragms in aircraft fuel systems. Also, the lack of stringent government controls may allow the characteristics of automobile gasoline to vary from one batch to another.

As the cost of aviation gasoline continues to rise and as more experience is gained using automotive gasoline, its use and acceptance will surely increase. Under the present conditions, be sure, when servicing an aircraft with automotive fuel, that the aircraft and engine are covered by a valid STC and all of the requirements of the STC are followed in detail. Servicing an aircraft with automotive gasoline without the proper STC is a violation of the Federal Aviation Regulations.

Jet Fuels

There are two basic types of fuel used in turbine engines: Jet A and A1 and Jet B. The designations used to identify these fuels do not relate in any way to the performance of the fuel in the engine.

Jet A is a special blend of kerosine and is the most widely used fuel for civilian jet aircraft. Jet A1 is a special type of Jet A that contains additives that make it usable at extremely low temperatures. Navy JP-5 fuel is similar to Jet A fuel, and because of its high flash point, JP-5 is the jet fuel carried aboard aircraft carriers.

Jet B is a blend of gasoline and kerosine fractions and is similar to military JP-4 fuel, which is the most widely used fuel for military jet aircraft.

Both types of jet fuel have a higher viscosity than gasoline, which allows them to readily hold contaminants. Water is the most prevalent contaminant, and it can remain entrained in the fuel until the temperature drops enough for it to condense out and form ice on the strainers. An additive, called PFA 55MB, or Prist, may be mixed with the fuel to lower the freezing point of any water that condenses out. In addition to the problem of shutting off

flash point. The temperature to which a material must be raised for it to ignite when a flame is passed above it, but it will not continue to burn.

the fuel by freezing on the strainers, the water that condenses from the fuel supports the growth of bacteria. These bacteria form a scum that holds the water against the aluminum alloy of which the fuel tanks are made. This water causes corrosion inside the tank. The additive that lowers the freezing point of the water also acts as a biocidal agent that destroys these bacteria.

Neither gasoline nor jet fuel burn in a liquid state, but vapors of both combine with oxygen in the air to form combustible mixtures. Gasoline evaporates at a relatively low temperature, but the mixture of vapor and air above gasoline in a storage tank is normally too rich to burn. Kerosine, on the other hand, requires a higher temperature to evaporate and the vapors above a storage tank of Jet A or Jet A-1 normally form a mixture that is too lean to burn. Jet B fuel has some of the characteristics of both gasoline and kerosine, and it evaporates over such a wide temperature range that its vapors mix with oxygen in the air to form a combustible mixture over a wide range of storage temperatures.

Kerosine has approximately 18,500 Btu of heat energy per pound and weighs 6.7 pounds per gallon. Aviation gasoline has 20,000 Btu per pound and weighs 6 pounds per gallon. Therefore kerosine, with 123,950 Btu per gallon, has a higher heat energy per unit volume than gasoline with 120,000 Btu per gallon.

Many aviation gas turbine engine manufacturers allow some aviation gasoline to be used in their engines when turbine fuel is not available. The amount of time aviation gasoline can be used is limited for two reasons: the tetraethyl lead in the aviation gasoline causes deposits to form on the turbine blades, and aviation gasoline does not have the lubricating properties that kerosine has. Using too much gasoline can cause excessive wear on the fuel control.

STUDY QUESTIONS: AVIATION FUELS

Answers are on Page 647. **Page numbers refer to chapter text.**

11. Two reasons the use of aviation gasoline should be limited in turbine engines are:
    a. _____
    b. _____
    Page 620

12. The reason jet fuel must not be used in reciprocating engines is that it causes
    _____ . *Page 618*

13. The viscosity of jet fuel is _____ (higher or lower) than that of aviation gasoline. *Page 619*

14. Give the color of each of these grades of aviation gasoline.
    a. Grade 80 _____
    b. Grade 100 _____
    c. Grade 100LL _____
       Page 617

15. Aviation gasoline whose antidetonation characteristics are better than those of the reference fuel (100-octane) are rated in _____ . *Page 617*

16. The antiknock characteristics of aviation gasoline is increased by using _____ as an additive. *Page 618*

17. Lead contaminants are purged from the combustion chamber of a reciprocating engine by adding _____ to the gasoline. *Page 618*

18. The heat energy content per gallon of jet fuel is _____ (greater or less) than that of aviation gasoline. *Page 620*

19. An uncontrolled burning, or explosion, of the fuel-air mixture within the cylinder of a reciprocating engine is called _____ . *Page 616*

20. If its vapor pressure is too high, a fuel will vaporize too _____ (readily or slowly). *Page 616*

21. Vapor lock can occur when the vapor pressure of the fuel is too _____ (high or low). *Page 616*

22. The designations of jet engine fuel _____ (do or do not) relate to the performance of the fuel in the engine. *Page 619*

23. In the dual-number rating system for aviation gasoline, 100/130 aviation gasoline has an octane rating of 100 with a _____ (lean or rich mixture). *Page 617*

24. Liquid gasoline _____ (will or will not) burn. *Page 616*

Aircraft Fueling

One of the most important operations performed by flight line personnel is that of fueling aircraft. An engine may be destroyed if the aircraft is serviced with the incorrect fuel, and numerous airplane crashes with their attendant loss of human lives have been attributed to improper fueling.

Precautions must be observed to prevent fire when the aircraft is being fueled and a CO_2 fire extinguisher must be available. In general aviation operations, the person fueling an aircraft is normally the point of contact between the aircraft owner and the operator selling the fuel. For this reason it is important that special care be taken to gain the confidence of the owner by maintaining a professional appearance and servicing the aircraft in a careful and professional way. Verifying the requested type of fuel and the quantity, whether in gallons, liters, or pounds, are always part of safe and professional line service.

When fueling an aircraft, one must be sure that the correct grade of fuel is used. All fuel tanks used on reciprocating-engine-powered aircraft are required to be marked near the filler opening with the word "avgas" and the minimum permissible grade of fuel.

Since it is so extremely important that no jet fuel be used in reciprocating-engine-powered aircraft, special adapters may be fitted into the filler neck of the tank that will not allow a jet fuel nozzle to enter.

Preparation for Fueling

An aircraft must be prepared for fueling by moving it to a well ventilated area and making certain that only electrical circuits necessary for the fueling process are energized. No one should be doing anything in nor on the aircraft that could create a fire hazard, and smoking in the vicinity of an aircraft being fueled is, of course, prohibited.

All solid contaminants and water must be removed from the fuel before it is put into the aircraft tanks. For this reason the fuel is passed through a water separator as the tank truck is being filled. Temperature changes will cause water to condense in partially filled tank trucks, so the fuel should be passed through water separators on the truck any time there is any indication of water being dispensed with the fuel.

If an aircraft is to be fueled from drums or cans, the fuel should be poured into the tank through a strainer-funnel that removes particles as small as five microns. (A human hair has a diameter of about 100 microns.) If no such filter is available, the fuel may be strained through a chamois skin.

Static electricity causes a special danger when fueling aircraft tanks. As fuel flows through the hose a charge of static electricity builds up, and if the hose and the aircraft are not connected together electrically, a spark is likely to jump between the fuel nozzle and the aircraft tank opening. This area is rich with gasoline fumes and the spark is likely to cause an explosion and a fire. If the aircraft is fueled through a chamois skin and funnel, special care must be exercised to ground the chamois through the metal screen in the funnel and keep it grounded until the fuel has stopped flowing. Plastic buckets and funnels must never be used as they do not allow the static charges to flow into the aircraft structure.

The fuel truck must be grounded with a static strap to dissipate any static charges that have built up, and it must be connected to the aircraft with a bonding cable. Before the fuel tank cap is removed, the nozzle should be bonded by plugging the ground wire into the receptacle located near the tank filler opening. See these grounding and bonding locations in Figure 10-7; the numbers represent the sequence of securing the connections.

Over-Wing Fueling

All small aircraft are fueled from the top of the fuel tank, and most large aircraft have provisions for this method of fueling if pressure fueling equipment is not available.

When fueling an aircraft by the over-wing method, the fuel truck is positioned ahead of the aircraft and the bonding wires are attached. The fuel hose is brought over the leading edge of the wing and the bonding wire connected, then the fuel tank cap is removed. Care should be taken to prevent the end of the nozzle damaging the bottom of the fuel tank, but the metal of the nozzle should rest solidly against the side of the tank opening to prevent a static electricity-induced spark jumping from the nozzle to the tank. When the proper amount of fuel has been pumped into the tank, the nozzle is removed and its protective cap replaced. The tank cap is replaced and properly secured, then the bonding wire is removed, and the hose is returned to the fuel truck.

Safety and attention to details cannot be stressed too highly. Even the relatively simple task of replacing the fuel cap can be accomplished improperly. Some tank caps have a vent line that is bent to point forward to pick up ram air pressure to slightly pressurize the tank and assist the fuel flow. If this type of cap is installed backwards the tank loses this assistance and the fuel flow will be decreased. Other types of fuel caps should seal tightly, and if they are improperly installed, the low pressure of the air above the wing will draw fuel from the tank and can force the aircraft to make an unscheduled landing for fuel.

It is important when fueling an aircraft by the over-wing method that fuel not spill on the rubber deicer boots, and that these boots not be damaged by the hose or by the bonding wire.

chamois skin. A soft pliable leather from the skin of a chamois, a goat-like antelope.

Chamois skin is used to filter gasoline. Gasoline will pass through it but water will not. Gasoline that has been filtered through a chamois skin may be considered to be free of water.

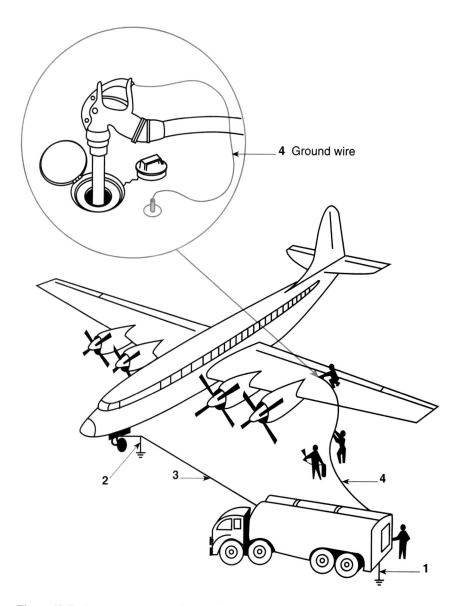

4 Ground wire

Figure 10-7. *The proper sequence for attaching the ground wires when preparing an aircraft for fueling*

Pressure Fueling

Most large aircraft are fueled by the single-point, or pressure, fueling method. A large hose carried on the fueling truck is connected to an underground fuel hydrant and to the fueling port under the aircraft wing, using a bayonet-type fueling nozzle such as the one in Figure 10-8.

At the fueling port there is a fueling control panel which contains fuel quantity gages for each tank, fueling valve switches that activate the fueling valves, lights to show the position of the fueling valves, a fueling power switch, and a fuel gage test switch. The maximum permissible fueling supply pressure and the maximum permissible defueling pressure are marked on a placard at the fueling control panel. *See* Figure 10-9.

If the selected tank is to be completely filled, the fueling valve will automatically close when the tank is full, but if the tank is to be partially filled, the valve can be closed by the fueling operator when the fuel quantity gage shows the appropriate amount of fuel is in the tank.

Figure 10-8. *International standard bayonet fueling nozzle for single-point fueling*

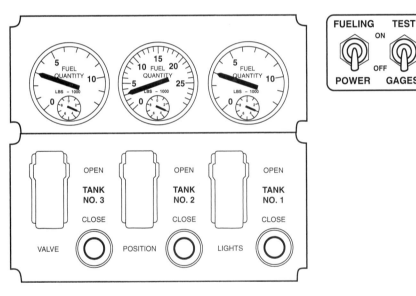

Figure 10-9. *Fueling control panel under the wing of a jet transport aircraft*

underground fuel hydrant. The terminal of an underground fuel system installed at many large airports. The fuel truck which has the required pumps, filters, and metering instruments but no storage tank is connected to the fuel hydrant, and its hoses are connected to the fueling panel of the aircraft.

bayonet-type fueling nozzle. A type of nozzle used to fuel aircraft with a pressure, or single-point, fueling system. The nozzle is connected to the fueling receptacle in the aircraft and the handles are turned a portion of a turn to lock it in place.

Defueling

When it is necessary to remove fuel from an aircraft tank, the same procedures should be followed as are used for fueling. The defueling process must never be conducted in a hangar, but should be done in an area where there is adequate ventilation. The aircraft should be properly grounded to protect against a static electricity buildup. The fuel removed from the aircraft should be protected against contamination and identified so it can be returned to the proper storage facility.

STUDY QUESTIONS: AIRCRAFT FUELING

Answers are on Page 647. Page numbers refer to chapter text.

25. Two bits of information must be marked on the fuel tank for a reciprocating-engine-powered aircraft are:
    a. _____
    b. _____
       Page 622

26. If the aircraft is equipped for pressure fueling and defueling, two bits of information are displayed at the fueling control panel. These are:
    a. _____
    b. _____
       Page 625

27. Water is removed from the fuel carried in a fuel tank truck by passing the fuel through a _____ before it is pumped into the aircraft. *Page 622*

28. Before fuel is pumped into an aircraft fuel tank, the fuel nozzle should be electrically connected to the aircraft structure, the fuel truck should be connected to the aircraft, and both the fuel truck and the aircraft should be electrically connected to the _____ . *Page 623*

29. A fire extinguisher must be readily available when fueling an aircraft. The recommended type of extinguisher uses _____ as the extinguishing agent. *Page 622*

30. What important precaution should be taken before pumping fuel into a fuel tank by the over-wing method? The fuel nozzle and the aircraft should be _____ . *Page 623*

31. It _____ (is or is not) normally safe to defuel an aircraft in an air-conditioned hangar. *Page 626*

Aircraft Movement

Because aircraft are designed to fly, their movement on the ground is often awkward and requires careful planning and skill to prevent damage to the aircraft being moved and to other aircraft.

Towing Aircraft

When towing an aircraft always use the correct tow bar and attach it the way the aircraft manufacturer recommends. Tail wheel aircraft may be towed by attaching a tow bar to eyes on the main landing gear or by using a smaller tow bar attached to the tail wheel. These methods are seen in Figure 10-10. As soon as the movement of the aircraft has stopped, chocks should be placed in front of and behind at least one of the wheels.

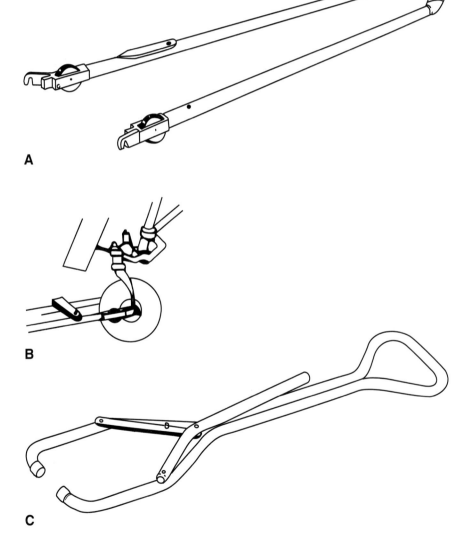

A

B

C

Figure 10-10

A. *Tow bar for moving a tail wheel aircraft from the main landing gear*

B. *Tow bar for moving a tail wheel aircraft from the tail wheel*

C. *Tow bar for moving a small tricycle gear aircraft by hand*

When towing a tricycle-gear airplane, the nosewheel scissors should be either disconnected or set so they will go into full swivel operation (whichever the aircraft manufacturer recommends). If this is not done, there is a good possibility that the tow bar can turn the nosewheel enough to break the steering stops.

Moving large aircraft normally requires a power tug or tractor, and extreme caution must be used when starting, stopping, and turning an aircraft with such a power device to assure that no damage is done to the aircraft.

Taxiing

When taxiing an aircraft in close quarters such as on a crowded ramp, always have a taxi signalman stationed in such a position that allows a clear view of the nose of the aircraft, the wing tip, and the person in the cockpit or the tug operator. This position is shown in Figure 10-11. Standard hand signals such as those seen in Figure 10-12 should be thoroughly familiar to all those involved in moving the aircraft and should be used to prevent any misunderstanding.

When moving an aircraft at night, the taxi signalman should use lighted wands. Since it is difficult, when using wands, to distinguish between the signal for "stop" and "come ahead," the signal for stop at night is the signal for "emergency stop" made by crossing the wands to form a lighted X above and in front of the head.

When it is necessary to taxi an aircraft into the flight area, radio contact must be established with the ground controller in the control tower, or at some airports, it is permissible to follow light signals from the tower. The light signals and their meaning are seen in Figure 10-13.

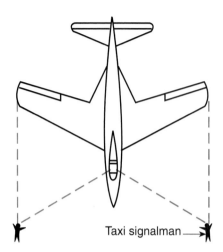

Figure 10-11. *When directing an aircraft moving into a parking area, the taxi signalman should be in a position that allows him to be seen by the pilot and allows him to see the wing tip.*

Taxi signalman

Light color	Meaning
Flashing green	Cleared to taxi
Steady red	Stop
Flashing red	Taxi clear of the runway in use
Flashing white	Return to starting point
Alternating red and green	Exercise extreme caution

Figure 10-13. *Light signals used to control taxiing aircraft*

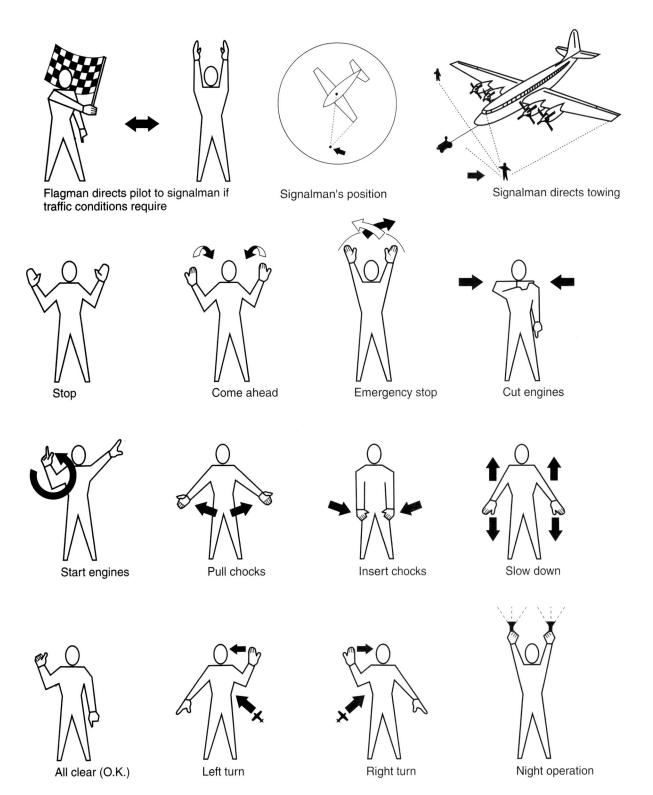

Flagman directs pilot to signalman if traffic conditions require

Signalman's position

Signalman directs towing

Stop

Come ahead

Emergency stop

Cut engines

Start engines

Pull chocks

Insert chocks

Slow down

All clear (O.K.)

Left turn

Right turn

Night operation

Figure 10-12. *Standard FAA hand signals used for directing an aircraft on the ground*

Figure 10-14. *Standard hand signals used for directing a helicopter*

AVIATION MAINTENANCE TECHNICIAN GENERAL

Helicopter Movement

When directing a helicopter into or out of a parking area, use the standard hand signals seen in Figure 10-14. Be sure to stand in a location that is clearly visible to the pilot and use exaggerated movements that are clear to the pilot.

STUDY QUESTIONS: AIRCRAFT MOVEMENT

Answers are on Page 647. **Page numbers refer to chapter text.**

32. Refer to the figure below. Identify the meaning of each of these signals.
    a. Signal A: _____
    b. Signal B: _____
    c. Signal C: _____
    d. Signal D: _____
    Page 629

A	**B**	**C**	**D**

33. Refer to the figure below. Identify the meaning of each of these signals.
    a. Signal A: _____
    b. Signal B: _____
    c. Signal C: _____
    d. Signal D: _____
    Page 630

A	**B**	**C**	**D**

Aircraft Tiedown

Many aircraft spend almost all of their ground life tied down outside of a hangar. This naturally shortens the life of the aircraft, but in many cases it must be done. It is important that the aviation maintenance technician understand the correct way to secure an aircraft.

Normal Tiedown

Most airport flight lines are equipped with either tiedown rings or cables, and the aircraft may be secured with either ropes or chains.

When using ropes, one made of a synthetic material such as nylon or polypropylene is preferred over manila because the synthetics do not shrink when they are wet, as manila does. Use a bowline knot such as the one illustrated in Figure 10-15 and do not tie the aircraft to the wing struts, but use the tiedown rings that are installed for that purpose. Allow about an inch or so of movement to avoid straining the aircraft while, at the same time, preventing the aircraft jerking against the ropes in the wind.

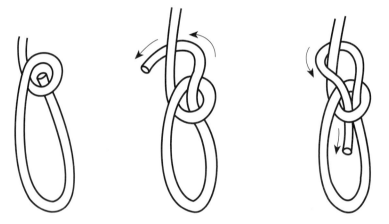

Figure 10-15. *Steps in tying a bowline knot*

When using chains and clips to secure the aircraft, do not depend upon the clip, but pass one link of the chain through another link and use the clip to prevent the link coming out. This procedure is shown in Figure 10-16.

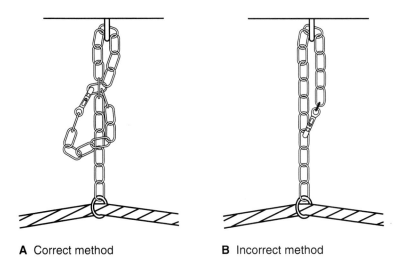

A Correct method   **B** Incorrect method

Figure 10-16. *When securing an aircraft with chains and clips, do not depend upon the clip to sustain a tensile load.*

Many airports have two parallel wire cables secured to the flight line ramp. Aircraft are secured to these cables with short lengths of chain that are free to move up and down the cable. This arrangement allows the tiedown chains to always be vertical when the aircraft are tied down.

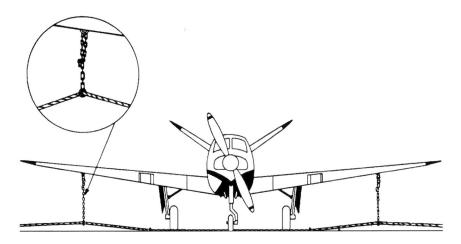

Figure 10-17. *Method of securing aircraft to a wire cable on the flight line ramp*

Preparation for Severe Weather

When high winds are forecast for the area in which the aircraft is tied down, special precautions should be taken. The aircraft control surfaces should be locked, either from the cockpit or with external locks, as in Figure 10-18. If a tail wheel aircraft is tied down facing the wind, the elevators should be secured in the full up position, and if it is facing away from the wind the elevators should be secured in the full down position. Tricycle gear airplanes should have their elevators secured in a neutral position.

Spoiler boards may be tied to the upper surface of the wing just above the front spar to prevent air flowing over the wing from producing enough lift to strain the tiedowns (*see* Figure 10-19). These boards can be made of 2-inch by 2-inch lumber with an inch of foam rubber attached to the bottom with waterproof cement. Holes in the boards allow nylon or polypropylene rope to pass through to tie the board to the wing.

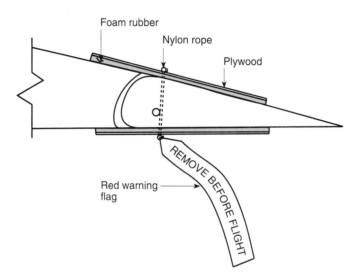

Figure 10-18. *Control surface locks should prevent the surface banging in the wind and should have a red streamer attached to help the pilot remember to remove them before flight.*

Securing Helicopters

If helicopters are to be tied down outside during severe weather, they should be headed into the direction of the strongest forecast wind and positioned at least a rotor-span away from any buildings or other aircraft. The brakes should be set and chocks installed in front of and behind the wheels. The rotor blades should be secured in the manner recommended by the helicopter manufacturer, and the fuselage should be secured with tiedown ropes or chains to secure ground anchors.

AVIATION MAINTENANCE TECHNICIAN   GENERAL

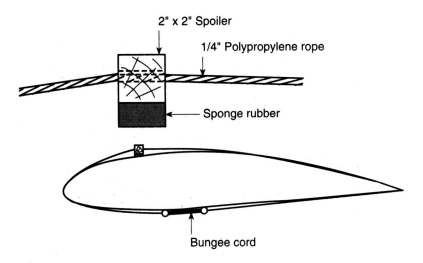

Figure 10-19. *A spoiler board tied to the upper surface of the wing above the front spar will prevent the wind producing enough lift to strain the tiedowns.*

STUDY QUESTIONS: AIRCRAFT TIEDOWN

Answers are on Page 647. **Page numbers refer to chapter text.**

34. The proper knot for securing an aircraft to its tiedown with a rope is a _____ knot.
    Page 632

35. When a tail wheel airplane is tied down facing the wind, the elevators should be secured in their full
    _____ (up or down) position. *Page 634*

36. When a tail wheel airplane is tied down facing away from the wind, the elevators should be secured in their
    full _____ (up or down) position. *Page 634*

37. One of the drawbacks for the use of manila rope for tying down an aircraft is the fact that manila rope
    _____ (shrinks or stretches) when it gets wet. *Page 632*

Figure 10-20. *Jack placement for raising one wheel for wheel or brake maintenance*

Aircraft Jacking and Hoisting
Aircraft Jacking

It is sometimes necessary to lift an aircraft on jacks, either a single wheel for brake or wheel maintenance, or the entire aircraft for landing gear maintenance or weighing. It is important that any jacking be done in a location where wind cannot rock the aircraft. No one should be allowed inside the aircraft while it is on jacks.

Each type of aircraft has specific requirements for jacking, and the manufacturer's instructions must be followed in detail to prevent damage to the aircraft or injury to personnel. Figure 10-21 shows a high-wing, single-engine airplane on jacks. The jack points (A) are aft of the center of gravity of the aircraft and when the aircraft is on the jacks, (B) it is nose heavy. To counter this nose-heavy condition, a weighted tail stand (C) must be attached to the tail tiedown ring.

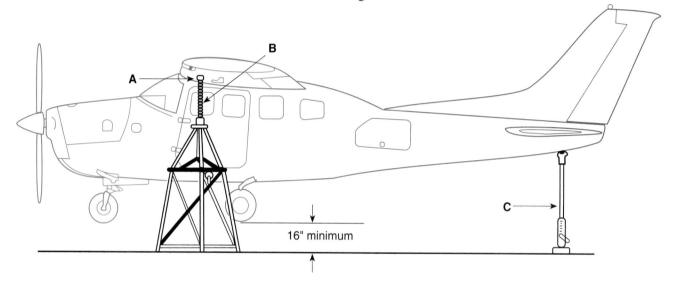

16" minimum

Figure 10-21. *Jacking airplanes with the jack points ahead of the aircraft CG requires a weighted tail stand to be attached to the tail tiedown ring.*

Some aircraft require that jack pads such as the one in Figure 10-22 be installed. In some installations, stress plates must be installed so that the stresses concentrated at the jack pad are distributed through the aircraft structure. Be sure to follow the aircraft manufacturer's recommendations in detail when jacking the aircraft.

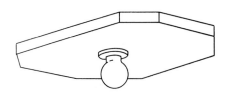

Figure 10-22. *Typical jack pad used under the main wing spar of an airplane*

All of the jacks used should have some method of locking the strut in its extended position if the hydraulic pressure should leak off. This is normally done with a large nut, or collar, screwed on the threaded jack strut. As the strut is extended, the collar is screwed down to prevent the strut from retracting. Some of the smaller jacks have their struts drilled and pins are stuck through the appropriate hole as the strut is extended.

Three jacks should be used to raise an aircraft and they should be raised together so it will remain in its level flight position at all times. If it is allowed to tilt, there is a possibility that it could slip off of the jacks.

Before lowering the aircraft be sure to remove all work stands and equipment that could be struck as the aircraft settles down, and be sure that the landing gear is locked in its down position. Lower all of the jacks together to keep the aircraft level as it comes down.

Aircraft Hoisting

It is sometimes necessary to hoist an aircraft rather than lift it with jacks. For example, if an aircraft has been involved in a gear-up landing or if the landing gear has collapsed, it is often impossible to get the jacks in the correct position and a crane must be used to raise the aircraft.

When hoisting the aircraft, attach the cables to the hoisting eyes, and if necessary place spreader bars between the cables to keep them directly in line with the hoisting eyes.

STUDY QUESTIONS: AIRCRAFT JACKING AND HOISTING

Answers are on Page 647. Page numbers refer to chapter text.

38. It is necessary when installing jack pads on some aircraft that the stress from the pad be evenly distributed through the structure by the installation of _____ . *Page 637*

39. A wing jack is prevented from collapsing because of a hydraulic leak by the use of a _____ screwed on the threaded jack strut. *Page 637*

Aircraft Icing Protection

Aircraft operating in winter months are often faced with the problem of taking off in conditions of snow and ice. Test data indicate that ice, snow, or frost formations having a thickness and surface roughness similar to medium or coarse sandpaper on the leading edge and upper surface of a wing can reduce wing lift by as much as 30 percent and increase drag by as much as 40 percent. For this reason all snow, ice, and frost must be removed.

Federal Aviation Regulations prohibit takeoff when snow, ice, or frost is adhering to the wings. It is the responsibility of the aviation maintenance technician to operate the equipment that deices and anti-ices the aircraft.

Small aircraft that have been sitting in the open and which are covered with snow may be prepared for flight by sweeping the snow off with a brush or broom, making very sure that there is no frost left on the surface. Frost, while adding very little weight, roughens the surface enough to destroy lift. An engine heater that blows warm air through a large hose may be used for deicing, but care must be taken to prevent water that is melted from running down inside the aircraft structure and refreezing.

deicing. Removal of ice from an aircraft structure.

anti-icing. Preventing the formation of ice on an aircraft structure.

There are two methods of ice control for large aircraft: deicing and anti-icing, and there are two types of freezing-point depressant (FPD) fluids used: Type I and Type II. Deicing and anti-icing may be accomplished by two procedures: the one-step procedure or two-step procedure.

Deicing is the removal of ice that has already formed on the surface, and anti-icing is the protection of the surface from the subsequent formation of ice. Just before takeoff large aircraft are both deiced and anti-iced.

The FPD fluids used for icing protection are made up of propylene/diethylene and ethylene glycols with certain additives. These fluids are mixed with water to give them the proper characteristics.

Type I FPD fluids contain a minimum of 80% glycols and are considered "unthickened" because of their relative low viscosity. Type I fluid is used for deicing or anti-icing, but provide very limited anti-icing protection.

Type II FPD fluids contain a minimum of 50% glycols and are considered "thickened" because of added thickening agents that enable the fluid to be deposited in a thicker film and to remain on the aircraft surfaces until time of takeoff. These fluids are used for deicing and anti-icing, and provide greater protection than Type I fluids against ice, frost, or snow formation in conditions conducive to aircraft icing on the ground.

The deicing and anti-icing may be done in either the one-step or the two-step procedure. In the one-step procedure, the FPD fluid is mixed with water that is heated to a nozzle temperature of 140°F (60°C) and sprayed on the surface. The heated fluid is very effective for deicing, but the residual FPD fluid film has very limited anti-icing protection. Anti-icing protection is enhanced by using cold fluids. In some instances, the final coat of fluid is applied in a fine mist, using a high trajectory to allow the fluid to cool before it touches the aircraft skin.

For the two-step procedure, the first step is deicing, and heated fluid is used. The second step is anti-icing, and cold fluid is used, so it will remain on the surface for a longer period of time.

STUDY QUESTIONS: ICING PROTECTION

Answers are on Page 647. **Page numbers refer to chapter text.**

40. Removal of ice after it has formed on an aircraft structure is called _____ .
    Page 638

41. Preventing the formation of ice on an aircraft structure is called _____ . *Page 638*

42. Deicing is normally accomplished by using _____ (heated or cold) FPD fluid. *Page 638*

43. The FPD fluid that is best suited for anti-icing is Type _____ (I or II). *Page 638*

Engine Operation

The Powerplant section of the *Aviation Maintenance Technician Series* covers the operation of both reciprocating and turbine engines, but in this General section we will cover the most important points of starting both types of engines and discuss some of the safety precautions that should be observed during the engine runup.

Reciprocating Engines

By far the greatest number of aircraft in the General Aviation fleet are powered by reciprocating engines. While their operation has been simplified over the years, there are still certain procedures and precautions that must be observed when operating them. In this section we will discuss the procedure for starting engines equipped with both float carburetors and fuel injection systems.

reciprocating engine. A form of heat engine in which the crankshaft is turned by the linear action of pistons reciprocating, or moving back and forth, inside the cylinders.

Almost all modern aircraft reciprocating engines are of the horizontally opposed type, and these are the ones we consider in the starting procedures. But there are still some radial and inverted inline or V-type engines flying, and these engines require a special procedure for starting.

Radial and inverted engines have some cylinders below the engine centerline, and when these engines are shut down oil may seep past the piston rings and into the combustion chambers of the lower cylinders. Before starting these engines that have been shut down for a period of time, the propeller should be rotated by hand for at least two revolutions to be sure that sufficient oil has not seeped into any combustion chamber to form a hydraulic lock.

Since oil is essentially noncompressible, if the engine fires when there is an appreciable quantity of oil in any of the combustion chambers, the engine will sustain major structural damage. If there is oil in any of the cylinders, remove one of the spark plugs from the affected cylinder and rotate the propeller in the direction of normal rotation to force out all of the oil.

hydraulic lock. A condition that can exist in an inverted reciprocating engine or in the lower cylinders of a radial engine, in which oil leaks past the piston rings in the lower cylinders and fills the combustion chambers. If the engine is forced to rotate, the oil-filled cylinders will be seriously damaged.

Starting Engines Equipped with Float Carburetors

When starting an aircraft engine, first check the fuel and oil supply, and then make sure that there are no obstructions in the inlet air ducts and that the cowling is securely in place. Chock the wheels and set the parking brake, then follow this starting procedure:

Place the fuel selector valve to the tank that you desire to use for the engine run.

Turn the master switch ON to supply power to the starter and the necessary instruments.

Check to be sure that the avionics master switch is turned OFF so none of the electronic equipment will be damaged by spikes of induced voltage when the starter is used.

Place the carburetor heat control in the COLD position so the air that enters the engine will be filtered. When it is in the HOT position, air bypasses the air filter and flows around part of the exhaust system to pick up heat.

Place the mixture control in the FULL RICH position since no fuel can flow from the carburetor until air is flowing through the venturi.

Prime the engine to introduce raw gasoline into the cylinders. This fuel allows the engine to start firing and draw enough air through the carburetor venturi to start the fuel flowing through the carburetor. Be careful not to over prime it because the excessive gasoline can cause an induction system fire and can wash oil from the cylinder walls and pistons.

Visually check the area around the propeller to be sure that there is no one in the way, and assure that the area remains clear by calling out the word "Clear."

When you are sure that there is no one in the way of the propeller, place the ignition switch in the BOTH position and engage the starter.

When the engine starts, check for an indication of oil pressure. If there is no pressure indicated on the oil pressure gage within 30 seconds, shut the engine down and determine the cause.

If the engine fails to start and you determine that it is flooded, clear it of excessive fuel by placing the mixture control in the CUTOFF position to shut off all flow of fuel to the cylinders. Turn the ignition OFF, open the throttle, and crank the engine with the starter or by hand until the fuel charge in the cylinders has been cleared.

If an induction system fire occurs, try to keep the engine running or keep it turning with the starter to pull the fire into the cylinders. If it cannot be kept running or turning, discharge a carbon dioxide (CO_2) fire extinguisher into the carburetor air inlet. CO_2 does not damage the engine, nor does it leave any residue to clean up.

flooded engine. A reciprocating engine that has too much fuel in its cylinders for it to start, or a turbine engine that has so much fuel in its combustors that it would create a fire hazard or a hot start if the fuel were ignited.

Starting Engines Equipped With a Fuel Injection System

Many modern horizontally opposed aircraft engines are equipped with constant-flow fuel injection systems. Starting these engines is somewhat different from starting one equipped with a float carburetor. The prestarting procedure of chocking the wheels, setting the parking brake, checking the fuel and oil, selecting the proper fuel tank, and turning on the master switch and checking that the avionics master switch is OFF, are the same as for an engine with a float carburetor. The differences are seen in these steps:

Place the mixture control in the FULL RICH position and turn the boost pump ON until there is an indication of flow on the fuel flow meter; then place the mixture control in the IDLE CUTOFF POSITION. This procedure puts gasoline into the cylinders for starting but prevents flooding the engine. The flowmeter indicates only when fuel is actually flowing through the injector nozzles.

Visually check the area around the propeller to be sure that there is no one in the way, and assure that the area remains clear by calling out the word "Clear."

When you are sure that there is no one in the way of the propeller, place the ignition switch in the BOTH position and engage the starter.

When the engine starts on the fuel in the cylinders, place the mixture control in the FULL RICH position and check for an indication of oil pressure. If there is no pressure indicated on the oil pressure gage within 30 seconds, shut the engine down and determine the cause.

If the engine fails to start and there is a steady flow of fuel from the internal supercharger drain valve, there is a probability that the mixture control was left in the FULL RICH position, rather than being returned to IDLE CUTOFF after the engine was primed. When the mixture control is in its FULL RICH position, fuel flows into the induction system and drains down into the supercharger section and out the drain valve.

internal supercharger drain valve. A pressure-operated valve in the bottom of the internal supercharger section of a reciprocating engine that is open when the pressures inside and outside the supercharger are the same. This allows excess fuel to drain out of the engine if the engine is flooded during the starting procedure.

Hand Cranking a Reciprocating Engine

All modern aircraft engines have starters, but sometimes the batteries may be dead and the engine must be cranked by hand. Small engines can be safely cranked by hand if certain precautions are observed, but large engines should be left to someone who is experienced in "propping" these engines. It is always far better to charge the battery than to hand crank large engines.

To safely prop a small engine, follow these steps:

1. Move the aircraft to an area where you can stand on level ground with no rocks or wet grass that could cause your foot to slip. Place chocks in front of and behind the wheels.

2. Place a responsible person in the cockpit to operate the ignition switch and throttle. This person should turn the fuel ON, the ignition switch OFF, prime the engine, set the parking brake, and crack the throttle slightly.

3. Stand close enough to the propeller that you are not leaning into it, and place the palms of your hands on the blade. Don't grip the blade or curl your fingers over it. This prevents the propeller pulling you into it if the engine should kick back or start to run in the opposite direction.

4. When you are ready, call "Contact."

   The person in the cockpit checks to be sure that everything is as it should be and replies "Contact" and *then* turns the ignition switch to the BOTH position.

5. Move the propeller blade down sharply, and with a smooth follow-through action, swing your body away from the propeller. If the engine does not start on the first try, do not touch the propeller until you have called "Switch off" and the person in the cockpit has turned the switch OFF and has replied "Switch is off."

Turbine Engines

Turbojet, turboshaft, and turboprop engines are far simpler in principle than reciprocating engines, but far more complex in their actual operation. For this reason, much of the starting procedure is programmed and is automatic in its operation. The steps listed here for starting turbine engines are purely generic. When actually starting these engines, be sure to follow the instructions of the aircraft manufacturer in detail.

Turbine Engine Starting

Before starting a turbine engine, be sure that all of the inlet duct and exhaust covers have been removed and that there are no foreign objects in the inlet ducts. Turn the compressor over by hand to ascertain that the engine rotates freely. Make sure that a power source of the proper capacity is connected and ready to supply compressed air or electricity as needed.

FOD (Foreign Object Damage). This is a common acronym for damage caused by debris such as nuts, bolts, safety wire, small parts, or tools being sucked into an operating aircraft turbine engine. Inflight damage caused by the ingestion of ice or birds is also considered to be FOD.

Be sure that there are no loose objects on the ground ahead of the engine and that the area behind the engine is clear of anything that could be damaged by the hot blast. Figure 10-23 shows the danger areas both ahead of and behind operating turbojet engines.

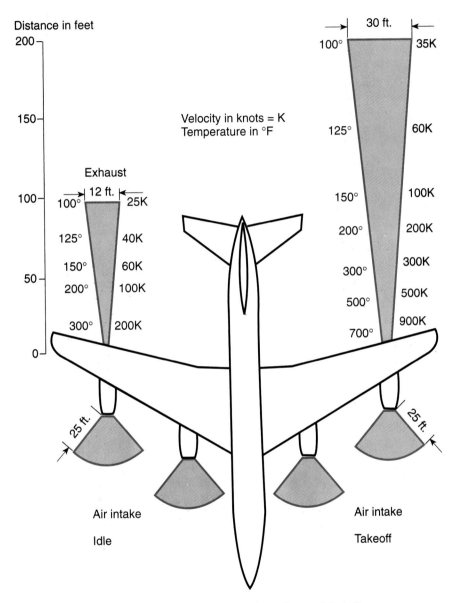

Figure 10-23. *Turbojet engine intake and exhaust hazard areas (shaded)*

When the start switch is placed in the START position, a series of events takes place that starts the compressor turning. When it reaches the proper speed, the ignition is energized, and then fuel is sprayed into the combustors. A proper start is indicated by an indication of oil pressure and an increase in exhaust gas temperature within a specified number of seconds after the start switch is closed. The engine should accelerate smoothly to the correct idling speed and stabilize at this RPM.

Improper Starts

The starting sequence for a turbine engine is automatic, but it is possible for faulty starts to occur, and when they do, immediate action should be taken to prevent damage to the engine.

No Oil Pressure

If there is no oil pressure indication after a turbine engine has reached a specified speed, turn the fuel and ignition off, discontinue the start, and make a thorough investigation to find the cause of the problem.

hot start. A start of a turbine engine in which the exhaust gas temperature exceeds the allowable limits.

Hot Start

If the exhaust gas temperature (EGT) or turbine inlet temperature (TIT) rises above its allowable limit, the engine is experiencing a hot start. Turn the fuel and ignition off and discontinue the start. An engine can be seriously damaged by a hot start, so make a careful investigation to find the cause and to determine if any damage has been done. Hot starts are usually caused by too rich a fuel-air mixture. This is the result of too much fuel for the amount of air being moved through the engine by the compressor.

hung start. The malfunctioning start of a turbine engine in which the engine starts, but fails to accelerate to a self-sustaining speed.

Hung Start

A hung, or false, start of a turbine engine is a start in which the engine lights off as it should, but does not accelerate to a speed that allows it to operate without help from the starter. If you encounter a hung start, shut the engine down and determine the reason it did not attain the required speed.

A hung start is often caused by insufficient power to the starter or the starter cutting off before the engine reaches its self-accelerating speed.

Answers are on Page 647. Page numbers refer to chapter text.

44. When starting an aircraft engine equipped with a float-type carburetor, the carburetor heat control should be in the _____ (hot or cold) position. *Page 640*

45. The most satisfactory fire-extinguishing agent for putting out an induction fire in an aircraft engine is _____ . *Page 641*

46. Oil collected in the lower cylinders of a radial engine can cause a problem known as _____ . *Page 640*

47. A horizontally opposed engine equipped with a fuel injection system is primed by placing the mixture control in the _____ position and turning on the boost pump. *Page 641*

48. A flooded reciprocating engine using either a float carburetor or a fuel injection system can be cleared of excessive fuel by placing the mixture control in the _____ position. Turn the ignition off, open the throttle, and crank the engine with the starter or by hand until the fuel charge in the cylinders has been cleared. *Page 641*

49. As soon as a reciprocating engine is started, you should check for an indication of _____ . *Page 641*

50. The mixture control of a float-type carburetor should be placed in the _____ position for starting the engine. *Page 640*

51. A turbine engine start in which the engine lights off but does not accelerate to a speed that allows it to operate without help from the starter is called a/an _____ start. *Page 644*

52. A turbine engine start in which the engine lights off but its temperature exceeds the allowable limits is called a/an _____ start. *Page 644*

53. The hazard area extends out ahead of an idling turbojet engine for about _____ feet. *Page 643*

54. The hazard area extends out behind an idling turbojet engine for about _____ feet. *Page 643*

55. A hot start of a turbojet engine is often caused by an excessively _____ (rich or lean) mixture. *Page 644*

Answers to Chapter 10 Study Questions

1. a. fuel
   b. oxygen
   c. heat
2. A
3. B
4. C
5. D
6. green triangle
7. red square
8. blue circle
9. yellow star
10. more
11. a. Lead deposits form on the turbine blades.
    b. Avgas does not have the lubricating properties of jet fuel.
12. detonation
13. higher
14. a. red
    b. green
    c. blue
15. performance number
16. tetraethyl lead
17. ethylene dibromide
18. greater
19. detonation
20. readily
21. high
22. do not
23. lean
24. will not
25. a. the word "Avgas"
    b. minimum permissible grade of fuel
26. a. maximum fueling pressure
    b. maximum defueling pressure
27. water separator
28. ground
29. CO_2
30. grounded
31. is not
32. a. stop
    b. come ahead
    c. emergency stop
    d. cut engines
33. a. go up
    b. start engine
    c. stop the rotor
    d. engage the rotor
34. bowline
35. up
36. down
37. shrinks
38. stress plates
39. collar
40. deicing
41. anti-icing
42. heated
43. II
44. cold
45. CO_2
46. hydraulic lock
47. FULL RICH
48. CUT OFF
49. oil pressure
50. FULL RICH
51. hung
52. hot
53. 25
54. 100
55. rich

REGULATIONS AND MAINTENANCE PUBLICATIONS

REGULATIONS AND MAINTENANCE PUBLICATIONS

11

Federal Control of Aviation

The Wright brothers' first successful flight of a heavier-than-air flying machine was made in 1903, and for the next few years, flying was limited mainly to short hops around fields. The airplanes of this era had no practical use, but in 1910 a law was passed to determine "whether aerial navigation may be utilized for the safe and rapid transmission of the mails." September of 1911 marked the first time mail was carried by airplane. The flights were of only about ten miles distance and were demonstrations at an air meet held on Long Island, New York. Throughout 1912, there were other successful attempts at carrying the mail by air, but it was not until 1916 that the U.S. government actually appropriated money for the carriage of mail by air. However, because of our involvement in World War I, airmail potential went untapped until the U.S. Post Office began carrying the mail in May of 1918.

After World War I ended in November of 1918, thousands of people trained in aviation returned to civilian life, and hundreds of airplanes and engines were made available to these veterans. This opened the age of barnstorming and flying circuses, and individual pilots toured the United States, introducing flying to the American public. Interest was created, but aviation still served little real public service.

The Airmail Act of 1925 started things moving when it awarded 12 contract airmail routes that covered most of the United States. The operators who held these contracts made the first serious use of the airplane.

The Air Commerce Act of 1926 was passed to "promote air commerce." This act charged the federal government with the operation and maintenance of the airway system as well as all aids to air navigation, and to ensure safety in air commerce through a system of regulation. Safety regulations were to be administered by the Department of Commerce through its Bureau of Air Commerce.

Safety regulations included the registration and licensing of aircraft, and the certification and medical examination of pilots. Enforcement of these regulations was assured by the authorization to impose civil penalties for their violation.

The Civil Aeronautics Act of 1938, and its later amendment in 1940, created the Civil Aeronautics Board (CAB) to investigate aircraft accidents and to exercise legislative and judicial authority over civil aviation. It also created the Civil Aeronautics Administration (CAA) which had responsibility for the execution of safety regulations. This included the enforcement and promotion of aviation safety and the operation of the airways system.

A series of serious accidents brought about the Federal Aviation Act of 1958, which included most of the old Civil Aeronautics Act, but changed the Civil Aeronautics Administration to the Federal Aviation Agency. This was removed from the Department of Commerce and placed on an independent level that answered only to the Congress and the President. The Department of Transportation was organized in 1966, and the Federal Aviation Agency was placed under its control and became the Federal Aviation Administration.

The next major change in governmental involvement came with the Airline Deregulation Act of 1978. This act relaxed the control of the CAB over the airlines. In 1985 the CAB was terminated. Deregulation opened the way for new airlines to operate and others to merge and has effected major changes in the airline portion of the aviation industry. When the CAB was terminated, the National Transportation Safety Board (NTSB) took over the responsibility for investigating aircraft accidents.

The Federal Aviation Administration (FAA)

The FAA consists of an administrator, a deputy administrator, and associate administrators. Aviation maintenance is regulated by the Associate Administrator for Aviation Standards who is charged with the responsibility for promoting safety of civil aircraft in air commerce by assuring, among other things, airworthiness of aircraft and competence of crewmembers.

Under the Associate Administrator for Aviation Standards is the Office of Airworthiness. This office has several divisions which include the Aircraft Engineering Division, Aircraft Manufacturing Division, and Aircraft Maintenance Division. The Aircraft Maintenance Division has two branches, the Air Carrier Branch and the General Aviation Branch.

There are nine FAA Regional Offices located in the continental United States and one in Europe. These offices are responsible for handling the various practical problems encountered in their geographical areas. The domestic regional offices and the areas they cover are shown in Figure 11-1.

FAA Regional Boundaries

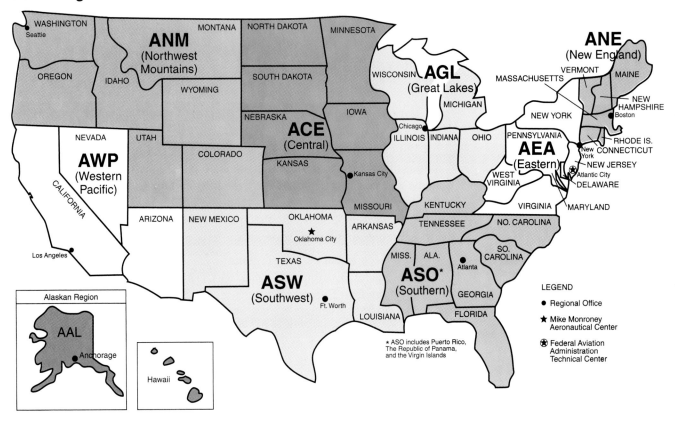

Figure 11-1. *Domestic regions of the Federal Aviation Administration*

Each of the FAA regions are divided into districts with a Flight Standards District Office (FSDO) which is a technician's main contact with the FAA, and is a source of information and assistance for maintenance personnel.

The FAA Mike Monroney Aeronautical Center, located in Oklahoma City, Oklahoma, houses many of the functions that involve aviation maintenance technicians. All of the maintenance technician tests are created here, and the Airmen Certification Branch has the records of all airmen certificates that have been issued. The FAA Academy, one of the largest aeronautical training facilities in the country, is located here.

Flight Standards District Office (FSDO). An FAA field office serving an assigned geographical area. It is staffed with Flight Standards Personnel who serve the aviation industry and the general public on matters relating to the certification and operation of both air carriers and general aviation aircraft.

Federal Aviation Regulations

Federal Aviation Regulations. Regulations relating to the certification of airmen and aircraft. These have been changed to Title 14 of the Code of Federal Regulations (14 CFR). Compliance with regulations is mandatory.

When the Civil Aeronautics Administration took on the responsibility of promoting the safety of aviation, it made a series of rules known as the Civil Air Regulations (CARs). When the Federal Aviation Administration came into being, these were changed to Federal Aviation Regulations. These have been changed again to Title 14 of the Code of Federal Regulations (14 CFR) which are the actual laws that govern operations today. These laws are issued by the Federal Aviation Administration and published by the U.S. Government Printing Office.

It is the responsibility of maintenance technicians to be aware of all regulations that affect us in those that are available. Some of them are sold on a single-sale basis while others are available only on a subscription basis.

An Advisory Circular AC 00-44, *Status of Federal Aviation Regulations,* listing all the regulations with their price, is available free of charge by writing and requesting it. The address is:

U.S. Department of Transportation
Subsequent Distribution Office, SVC-121.23
Ardmore East Business Center
3341 Q 75th Avenue
Landover, Maryland 20785

Advisory Circulars (ACs). Information published by the FAA that explains the Federal Aviation Regulations and describes methods of performing certain maintenance and inspection procedures. Compliance with ACs is not mandatory, and the information in the ACs is not necessarily FAA-approved data.

The cost of all of the applicable regulations is quite high, but for a person to become familiar with their contents, ASA, Inc. reprints and makes available in two volumes the federal regulations most widely used by maintenance technicians. These volumes are updated twice a year. Figure 11-2 lists the regulations most used by maintenance technicians.

Part 1:	Definitions and Abbreviations
Part 13:	Investigative and Enforcement Procedures
Part 21:	Certification Procedures for Products and Parts
Part 23:	Airworthiness Standards: Normal, Utility, Acrobatic, and Commuter Category Airplanes
Part 25:	Airworthiness Standards: Transport Category Airplanes
Part 33:	Airworthiness Standards: Aircraft Engines
Part 34:	Fuel Venting and Exhaust Emission Requirements for Turbine Engine Powered Aircraft
Part 35:	Airworthiness Standards: Propellers
Part 39:	Airworthiness Directives
Part 43:	Maintenance, Preventive Maintenance, Rebuilding, and Alteration
Part 45:	Identification and Registration Marking
Part 47:	Aircraft Registration
Part 65:	Certification: Airmen other than Flight Crewmembers
Part 91:	General Operating and Flight Rules
Part 121:	Operating Requirements: Domestic, Flag, and Supplemental Operations
Part 125:	Certification and Operations: Aircraft Having a Seating Capacity of 20 or More Passengers or a Maximum Payload Capacity of 6,000 Pounds or More
Part 135:	Operating Requirements: Commuter and On-Demand Operations
Part 145:	Repair Stations
Part 183:	Representatives of the Administrator

Figure 11-2. *Some of the regulations most often used by aviation maintenance technicians*

STUDY QUESTIONS: FEDERAL AVIATION REGULATIONS

*Answers are on Page 675. **Page numbers refer to chapter text.***

1. The issuance of an Airworthiness Certificate for a normal category airplane is governed by 14 CFR Part
_____ . *Page 655*

2. Information regarding instrument range marking for an airplane certificated in the normal category is furnished in 14 CFR Part _____ . *Page 655*

3. Information regarding certification of aircraft maintenance technicians is found in 14 CFR Part
_____ . *Page 655*

Advisory Circulars

approved data. Approved data is required for major repairs and major alterations and can be type design drawings, Airworthiness Directives, Designated Engineering Representative Data, Supplemental Type Certificate information, Parts Manufacturer Approval Drawings, Designated Alteration Station Data, and Appliance Manufacturer's Data.

Advisory Circulars, ACs, are nonregulatory information put out by the FAA to help maintenance personnel understand and comply with the regulations. Advisory Circulars show a way things can be done, and they are neither specific nor mandatory. Some information in ACs may be used as approved data for repairs and alterations, but not all of it can be used in this manner.

Some ACs are as simple as single sheets advising us of the availability of certain information, while others are bound books with several hundred pages.

Two of the most helpful ACs for aviation maintenance technicians are AC 43.13-1B, *Acceptable Methods, Techniques, and Practices—Aircraft Inspection and Repair*, and AC 43.13-2A, *Acceptable Methods, Techniques, and Practices—Aircraft Alterations*. AC 43.13-1B is a book of more than 700 pages which gives examples of methods of inspection and repair that are acceptable, but are not the only acceptable procedures, nor are they approved for all aircraft. This AC also contains many useful charts and tables listing suitable materials and illustrating the proper use of hardware.

AC 43.13-2A includes examples of acceptable radio installations, anti-collision light installations, ski installation, oxygen system installation, helicopter external-load device installation, tow-hitch installation, shoulder harness installation, and battery installation. All of the techniques and practices in this AC are acceptable, but because of the complexity of modern aircraft, this information is not considered to be approved data for an alteration.

ACs are available from the U.S. Government Printing Office (GPO), and you may get a list of all available ACs by writing to the same address as used for the *Status of Federal Aviation Regulations* and asking for AC 00-2 *Advisory Circular Checklist and Status of Other FAA Publications*.

Some ACs are free and others have a price. The Checklist includes order blanks and information on getting all the ACs.

STUDY QUESTIONS: ADVISORY CIRCULARS

Answers are on Page 675. Page numbers refer to chapter text.

4. Advisory Circular 43.13-2A *Acceptable Methods, Techniques, and Practices—Aircraft Alterations* _____ (is or is not) considered to be approved data for making an alteration to a certificated aircraft. *Page 656*

5. The Advisory Circular that gives such information as the standards regarding of bolts, studs, screws, and self-locking nuts is AC _____ . *Page 656*

Aircraft Certification

The design criteria for civilian aircraft are included in Federal Aviation Regulations for each category of aircraft. The regulations that include this information are listed in Figure 11-3.

Part	Category
23	Airworthiness Standards: Normal, Utility, Acrobatic, and Commuter Category Airplanes
25	Airworthiness Standards: Transport Category Airplanes
27	Airworthiness Standards: Normal Category Rotorcraft
29	Airworthiness Standards: Transport Category Rotorcraft
31	Airworthiness Standards: Manned Free Balloons
33	Airworthiness Standards: Aircraft Engines
35	Airworthiness Standards: Propellers

Figure 11-3. *Federal Aviation Regulations describing the design criteria for various categories of aircraft, engines, and propellers.*

Approved Type Certificates (ATC)

When an aircraft, engine, or propeller is designed, a prototype is built and tested. Any deficiencies are corrected, and it is retested until it is proven that it conforms to all of the requirements of the appropriate part of the regulations. It is then issued an Approved Type Certificate (ATC) in accordance with 14 CFR Part 21 *Certification Procedures for Products and Parts.* A Type Certificate Data Sheet (TCDS) accompanies the ATC that lists all of the pertinent specifications that must be adhered to for the ATC to continue to be effective.

Type Certificate Data Sheets, Aircraft Specifications, and Aircraft Listings

Any time an aircraft is given an annual or 100-hour inspection, the person approving it for return to service must inspect it for conformity to the TCDS. The aircraft is not legally airworthy if it does not conform.

Aircraft, engines, and propellers certificated before January 1, 1958 were certificated under the Civil Aeronautics Administration and did not have TCDS's issued, but this same information was furnished on Aircraft, Engine, or Propeller Specification Sheets.

Aircraft Listings is a document that contains the most pertinent specifications for certificated aircraft of which there are fewer than 50 still registered with the FAA.

TCDS, *Aircraft Specifications*, and *Aircraft Listings* are available from the FAA in the six volumes listed in Figure 11-4.

Type Certificate Data Sheet (TCDS). Documentation that includes the pertinent specifications for currently produced certificated airframes, engines, and propellers.

Aircraft Listings. Documentation that includes many of the pertinent specifications for certificated aircraft of which there are fewer than 50 still registered.

Aircraft Specifications. Documentation that includes the pertinent specifications for older aircraft that were certificated under the Civil Aviation Regulations. Specifications are also available for Engines and Propellers.

Volume I	Single-Engine Airplanes
Volume II	Small Multiengine Airplanes
Volume II	Large Multiengine Airplanes
Volume IV	Rotorcraft, Gliders, and Balloons
Volume V	Aircraft Engines and Propellers
Volume VI	Aircraft Listing and Aircraft Engine and Propeller Listing

Figure 11-4. *Volume number and contents of Type Certificate Data Sheets, Aircraft Specifications, and Aircraft Listings*

ATC number
Name and address of the ATC
  holder
Model number, seating arrange-
  ment, category, and date of
  certification
Approved engine models
Approved fuel
Engine limits
Approved propellers and propeller
  limits
Airspeed limits
CG range, EWCG range, and
  maximum allowable weights
Number and location of seats
Maximum baggage
Fuel capacity
Oil capacity
Maximum operating limits
Control surface movements
Serial numbers eligible
Location of the datum
Leveling means
Certification basis
Production basis
Required equipment
Notes regarding weight and balance
  information, required placards, and
  other information that is pertinent
  to the specific aircraft.

Figure 11-5. *Information included in an aircraft Type Certificate Data Sheet*

Volumes I through V are available only as subscriptions, and Volume VI is available as a single-copy sale. They may be ordered from the Government Printing Office, and information on their purchase is in the *Advisory Circular Checklist*. All of this information is available in either paper or Microfiche format. This information is also available in computer data banks, but, at this time, not from the FAA.

A typical TCDS for an airplane includes the information seen in Figure 11-5. A typical TCDS for an engine includes the information shown in Figure 11-6. A typical TCDS for a propeller includes the information shown in Figure 11-7.

ATC number
Name and address of the ATC holder
Model number
Type, includes number of cylinders, cylinder arrangement, method of cooling,
  and any applicable modification identifiers.
Power ratings
  Maximum continuous horsepower and RPM
  Takeoff horsepower and RPM with any time limits
Fuel, minimum grade
Lubricating oil, SAE viscosity (required for various ambient temperatures)
Bore and stroke
Piston displacement in cubic inches
Compression ratio
Weight, dry
Center of gravity location
Propeller shaft
Fuel metering
Ignition, type
Ignition timing
Spark plugs, type
Oil sump capacity
Notes regarding maximum permissible temperatures, fuel and oil pressure
  limits, information on the accessory drives, comparison between the models
  and other information that is pertinent to the specific engine.

Figure 11-6. *Information included in an engine Type Certificate Data Sheet*

Production Certificates

An ATC is approval for the design of an aircraft, engine, or propeller but it does not cover the production process. When each aircraft having an ATC is produced, it must be inspected to assure the FAA that it conforms in all ways to the provisions of the ATC.

When a large number of aircraft are produced under the same ATC, it is convenient and cost effective for the FAA to issue a Production Certificate under 14 CFR Part 21 to a manufacturing facility allowing them to produce the aircraft. This certification governs the location of the facility, the quality control system, and the various inspections of materials and finished products. The FAA can keep check on the production facility rather than having to inspect each aircraft produced. When an aircraft conforms to the ATC and is built under a production certificate, it may be given its Airworthiness Certificate without any further inspection.

Airworthiness Certificate

An Airworthiness Certificate is issued under 14 CFR Part 21 to an aircraft when it is first certificated, and it is transferred to the new owner when the aircraft is sold.

There are two classes of Airworthiness Certificates: Standard, and Special. Standard Airworthiness Certificates are issued to aircraft certificated in the normal, utility, acrobatic, commuter, and transport category, and to manned free balloons. Special Airworthiness Certificates are primary, restricted, limited, and provisional, and special flight permits and experimental certificates.

Standard Airworthiness Certificates and airworthiness certificates issued for primary, restricted, or limited category aircraft are effective as long as the maintenance, preventive maintenance, and alterations are performed in accordance with 14 CFR Parts 43 and 91. Special flight permits are effective for the period of time specified in the permit. An experimental certificate for research and development is valid for one year from the date of issue or renewal. Experimental certificates for amateur-built, exhibition, and racing aircraft are normally unlimited unless the Administrator finds for good cause that a specific period should be established.

Supplemental Type Certificates (STC)

An Approved Type Certificate does not afford a manufacturer the same type of protection as a patent, and an individual other than the manufacturer is free to make changes to the approved product and to make available information that allows others to make the same changes.

Authorization for these changes is made under a Supplemental Type Certificate (STC) issued under 14 CFR Part 21, and the applicant for an STC must allow the FAA to make any ground and flight tests they feel are necessary to show that the altered aircraft, engine, or propeller still conforms to the applicable regulations.

ATC number
Name and address of the ATC holder
Type
Engine shaft
Hub material
Blade material
Number of blades
Hub models eligible
Blades eligible
Certification basis
Production basis
Notes showing the hub model designation, blade model designation, pitch control, whether the propeller is feathering or reversing, and information about left-hand models. Notes also include information on interchangeability of blades and propellers and a table of approved propeller-engine combinations.

Figure 11-7. *Information included in a propeller Type Certificate Data Sheet*

Airworthiness Certificate. A document carried in an aircraft that identifies the aircraft as one certificated under the appropriate part of the Federal Aviation Regulations.

An STC allows the holder to obtain an airworthiness certificate for an altered aircraft; to obtain approval for installation of an altered engine or propeller on a certificated aircraft; and to obtain a production certificate for the altered product.

An STC does not give the holder exclusive rights for the alteration, and STCs covering the same alteration may be issued to more than one applicant so long as each applicant shows compliance with all the applicable airworthiness requirements.

The information included in an STC is approved data for the alteration. After an aircraft has been altered in accordance with an STC, it must be inspected for compliance with the provisions of the STC before it can be approved for return to service.

Supplemental Type Certificate (STC). A certificate of approval for an alteration to a certificated airframe, engine, or appliance.

A Summary of Supplemental Type Certificates containing a description of all effective STCs along with the name and address of the STC holders is available from the FAA. Information on obtaining a copy of this summary is included in the current volume of the *Advisory Circular Checklist*.

An example of an STC that is currently popular is the modification of an aircraft certificated to operate on aviation gasoline to fly on unleaded automobile gasoline.

STUDY QUESTIONS: AIRCRAFT CERTIFICATION

Answers are on Page 675. **Page numbers refer to chapter text.**

6. Information on aircraft certificated after January 1, 1958, is available from the FAA in the form of
_____ . *Page 657.*

7. Information on the number of degrees of control surface movement allowed for a particular aircraft is available from the FAA on the appropriate _____ .
Page 658

8. A listing of the engines approved for a particular airplane is included in the
_____ (aircraft, engine, or propeller) TCDS. *Page 658*

9. The location of the datum required for weight and balance computations for a particular aircraft is available from the FAA on the appropriate _____ . *Page 658*

10. Suitability for use of a specific propeller with a particular engine-airplane combination can be determined by reference to the appropriate _____ (airplane, engine, or propeller) Type Certificate Data Sheet. *Page 659*

11. Technical specifications for a certificated propeller is found in the appropriate
_____ Type Certificate Data Sheet. *Page 659*

12. Placards required to be in an aircraft are specified by the FAA in the appropriate
_____ or _____ .
Page 658

13. Information on aircraft certificated before January 1, 1958, is available from the FAA in the form
_____ . *Page 657*

14. Information on aircraft of which there fewer than 50 still in service is available from the FAA in the
publication entitled _____ . *Page 657*

15. An STC may be issued to more than one applicant for the same design change, providing each applicant
shows compliance with the applicable airworthiness requirements. This statement is
_____ (true or false). *Page 660*

16. The information included in an STC _____ (is or is not) considered to be approved data for
use by a person altering an aircraft in conformance with the STC. *Page 660*

17. Two classes of Airworthiness Certificates are:
a. _____
b. _____
Page 659

18. When an aircraft is sold, the Airworthiness Certificate is transferred to the _____ .
Page 659

Airworthiness Directives

If a condition is found that causes a particular design of aircraft, aircraft engine, propeller, or appliance to fail to meet its certification for airworthiness, the FAA can issue an Airworthiness Directive (AD). An AD describes the unsafe condition and the corrective action that must be taken to return the device to the conditions specified for its certification.

ADs are actually Federal Aviation Regulations and are published in the *Federal Register* as amendments to 14 CFR Part 39. They apply to aircraft, aircraft engines, propellers, or appliances, which are referred to as "products," and are issued when an unsafe condition is found to exist in a product when that condition is likely to exist or develop in another product of the same type design. Compliance with ADs is mandatory, and the compliance must be recorded in the aircraft maintenance records, showing the date and method of compliance and the name and certificate number of the person performing the work. If the AD is of a recurring type, the date or number of hours of operation for the next compliance must be included in the record.

There are four categories of ADs, each with their own effective date and method of notice to affected owners. These categories are shown in Figure 11-8.

Notice of Proposed Rulemaking (NPRM)—An NPRM is issued and published in the Federal Register when an unsafe condition is discovered in a product. Interested persons are invited to comment on the NPRM by submitting such written data, views, or arguments as they may desire. The comment period is usually 60 days, and proposals contained in the notice may be changed or withdrawn in light of the comments received.

When an NPRM is adopted as a final rule, it is published in the *Federal Register*, printed, and distributed by first-class mail to the registered owners of the product affected.

Immediately Adopted Rule—ADs of an urgent nature are adopted without the NPRM process, as immediately adopted rules. These ADs usually become effective less than 30 days after publication in the Federal Register and are distributed by first-class mail to the registered owners of the product affected.

Emergency ADs—Emergency ADs are issued when immediate corrective action is required. Emergency ADs are distributed to the registered owners of the product affected by telegram or priority mail and are effective upon receipt. Emergency ADs are published in the *Federal Register* as soon as possible after the initial distribution.

ADs Issued to Other than Aircraft—ADs may be issued which apply to engines, propellers, or appliances installed on multiple makes or models of aircraft. When the product can be identified as being installed on a specific make or model aircraft, AD distribution is made to the registered owners of those aircraft. However, there are times when a determination cannot be made, and direct distribution to the registered owner is impossible.

Figure 11-8. *Classification of Airworthiness Directives*

Publication of Airworthiness Directives

Individual ADs are distributed to the owners of the affected products and are also made available to maintenance personnel by subscription from the FAA, as described in AC 00-44, Status of the Federal Aviation Regulations. ADs are published in six books:

Small Aircraft and Rotorcraft—Book 1, Summary of Airworthiness Directives, dated January 1990. This book was not revised and it contains all ADs currently in effect but issued during the time period 1940 through 1979.

Small Aircraft and Rotorcraft—Book 2, Summary of Airworthiness Directives, dated January 1996. This book contains all ADs currently in effect but issued during the time period 1980 through 1989.

Small Aircraft and Rotorcraft—Book 3, Summary of Airworthiness Directives, dated January 1996. This book contains all ADs currently in effect but issued during the time period 1990 through 1995.

Biweekly Supplements, Small Aircraft and Rotorcraft, Summary of Airworthiness Directives. This package contains all biweekly supplements for small aircraft and rotorcraft from January 1996 through December 1997. An index is included which relates to books 1, 2, and 3 and reflects revised and superseded ADs. The index is updated twice during the subscription period.

There are also three books and biweekly summaries for large aircraft that include the same information as is furnished for small aircraft.

ADs are also available in microfiche form and the older ADs are available on a CD-ROM. Biweekly supplements are available free by downloading them from the FAA's website on the internet: http://afs600.faa.gov, then click on the AFS610 link.

AD subscriptions may be ordered from:

U.S. Department of Transportation
Federal Aviation Administration
P.O. Box 25461
Attn: AMZ-330
Oklahoma City, OK 73125
Phone: (405) 954-4103 • Fax: (405) 954-4104

Each AD contains four areas of information:

Applicability—This section specifies the product (aircraft, aircraft engine, propeller, or appliance) to which it applies. Unless specifically limited, ADs apply to the make and model set forth, regardless of the kind of Airworthiness Certificate issued for the aircraft. When there is no reference to serial numbers, all serial numbers are affected.

Compliance time—No person may operate the affected product after the expiration of the stated compliance time without an exemption or a special flight authorization when the AD specifically permits such operation.

The compliance time may be specified in several ways; typical are

- Before further flight
- Before further flight except with a ferry permit
- Within a specified number of hours time in service after the effective date of this AD
- Within the next specified number of landings after the effective date of this AD
- Within a specified number of operation cycles after the effective date of this AD
- Within a specified number of days after the effective date of this AD

Some AD compliances are repetitive, allowing recurring inspection at specified intervals in lieu of a final fix. This type of compliance is used because of costs, or until a fix is developed.

Required action—This is the most important part of the AD and it may require and describe an inspection or the replacement of a certain part. It may also specify that a certain inspection be performed by the effective date and again at certain intervals until the final fix of the replacement of the affected part is accomplished, at which time the recurring inspections are no longer required.

Effective date—The effective date of the AD and of any revisions is noted near the end of the AD.

To better understand the way a compliance statement works, consider the excerpt from the AD in Figure 11-9, and this information on the affected airplane:

Total time in service 468 hours
AD complied with at 454 hours

We can find the number of additional hours in service that can be accumulated before this AD must be complied with by analyzing each of the paragraphs.

The aircraft has less than 500 hours total time in service, so compliance falls within paragraph I.

The AD has been complied with, and the aircraft has operated for 14 hours since the compliance. Future compliance is required with each 200 hours of time in service, so the aircraft can operate for another 186 hours before the AD must be complied with again.

According to 14 CFR Part 91 *General Operating and Flight Rules*, it is the ultimate responsibility of the aircraft owner or operator to determine that all applicable AD notes are complied with and that their compliance is recorded in the aircraft maintenance records. But it is the responsibility of the technician performing annual and 100-hour inspections to comply with every AD applying to the airframe, engine, propeller, and all appliances.

When an aircraft is scheduled for an inspection, the technician must get the model and serial number of the airframe, engine, propeller, and all appliances that are covered by the AD system. Then he or she must check through the AD Summary indexes and all of the biweekly updates that have been issued since the date of the Summary.

Since it is so important that no AD be overlooked, and because of the large amount of time involved in conducting an exhaustive search, there are companies that offer computerized searches. If the technician supplies them with the required model and serial numbers, they can furnish the technician with an up-to-date list of all applicable ADs.

When an AD is complied with, the technician is required to enter in the aircraft maintenance records the AD number, the date of compliance, and the method of compliance. If it is a recurring AD, the date or time the next compliance is required must be indicated. This entry must be signed by the technician and must include his or her certificate number and class of certificate.

Compliance required as indicated, unless already accomplished:

I. Aircraft with less than 500-hours' total time in service: Inspect in accordance with instructions below at 500-hours' total time, or within the next 50-hours' time in service after the effective date of this AD, and repeat after each subsequent 200 hours in service.

II. Aircraft with 500-hours' through 1,000-hours' total time in service: Inspect in accordance with instructions below within the next 50-hours' time in service after the effective date of this AD, and repeat after each subsequent 200 hours in service.

III. Aircraft with more than 1,000-hours' time in service: Inspect in accordance with instructions below within the next 25-hours' time in service after the effective date of this AD, and repeat after each subsequent 200 hours in service.

Figure 11-9. *Example of a compliance statement in an Airworthiness Directive*

General Aviation Airworthiness Alerts

The Service Difficulty Program of the FAA functions as an information gathering and disseminating service in which information gathered from Malfunction and Defect Reports is fed into a computer data bank where it is analyzed and categorized. When a trend becomes evident it is written up in the *General Aviation Airworthiness Alerts* (AC 43-16A) which are distributed to interested maintenance personnel. Their contents include items that have been reported to be significant, but which have not been fully evaluated by the time the material went to press. When additional facts such as cause and corrective action are identified, the data is published in subsequent issues of the Alerts. The corrective action specified in an Airworthiness Alert is advisory in nature and does not become mandatory unless or until it is published as an Airworthiness Directive.

Airworthiness Alerts are sent automatically to technicians holding an Inspection Authorization, approved repair stations, air taxi operators, aviation maintenance technician schools, and Designated Mechanic Examiners, but anyone may purchase them from the FAA at the address below. See the latest copy of the *Advisory Circular Checklist* AC 00-2 for the current price.

U.S. Department of Transportation
Subsequent Distribution Office, SVC-121.23
Ardmore East Business Center
3341 Q 75th Avenue
Landover, MD 20785
Phone: (301) 322-4961 • Fax: (301) 386-5394

STUDY QUESTIONS: AIRWORTHINESS DIRECTIVES

Answers are on Page 675. **Page numbers refer to chapter text.**

19. The FAA notifies the registered owner of an aircraft of an unsafe condition by means of a/an
   _____ . *Page 663*

20. The FAA sends a copy of an Airworthiness Directive to the _____ of an
   affected aircraft. *Page 663*

21. An emergency AD is sent to the registered owner or operator of an aircraft by
   _____ or _____ . *Page 662*

22. Compliance with an Airworthiness Directive is _____ (mandatory or optional).
   Page 661

23. Compliance with an applicable Airworthiness Directive must be recorded in the aircraft _____ . *Page 665*

24. Four devices that are covered by the Airworthiness Directive system are:
    a. _____
    b. _____
    c. _____
    d. _____
    Page 661

25. Compliance with an Airworthiness Directive _____ (does or does not) require an entry in the maintenance record of the affected equipment. *Page 665*

26. The information in General Aviation Airworthiness Alerts is gathered through _____ reports sent into the FAA by mechanics and repair stations. *Page 666*

27. The corrective action listed in a General Aviation Airworthiness Alert is _____ (advisory or mandatory). *Page 666*

Technical Standard Orders (TSO) and Parts Manufacturer Approval (PMA)

A Technical Standard Order (TSO) authorization, issued under 14 CFR Part 21, is a minimum performance standard for a specified article (materials, parts, processes, or appliances). A part manufactured under the provision of a TSO is approved for installation on certificated aircraft. But just because a part has been built under a TSO does not mean that it is approved for installation on *all* certificated aircraft. Typical parts that are manufactured under TSOs are seat belts and harnesses, aircraft fabric, emergency locator transmitters (ELT), parachutes, radios and tires.

Technical Standard Order (TSO). An approval for the manufacture of a component for use on certificated aircraft.

A Parts Manufacturer Approval (PMA) is also authorized under 14 CFR Part 21, and it is an approval for the manufacture of a modification or replacement part that is to be installed on a certificated product. It is usually issued to someone other than the original equipment manufacturer (OEM) of the certificated product.

Parts Manufacturer Approval (PMA). An approval, granted under 14 CFR Part 21, that allows a person to produce a modification or replacement part for sale for installation on a type certificated product.

A PMA does not apply to the following:

- Parts produced under a Type or Production Certificate
- Parts produced by an owner or operator for maintaining or altering his own product
- Parts produced under an FAA TSO
- Standard parts such as bolts and nuts conforming to established industry or U.S. specifications

Typical examples of parts manufactured under FAA/PMA authorization are replacement engine parts such as bearings and valves and replacement magneto coils.

For an applicant to be granted a PMA, he or she must furnish the FAA with drawings and information on the part to be manufactured, along with test reports and computations proving that the part meets all of the specifications for the product on which it is to be installed. The FAA can monitor the applicants' facilities to ensure that the quality control is adequate to guarantee that the finished parts conform to the provisions of the PMA.

STUDY QUESTIONS: TECHNICAL STANDARD ORDERS AND PARTS MANUFACTURER APPROVAL

Answers are on Page 675. **Page numbers refer to chapter text.**

28. **An item manufactured under a Technical Standard Order is approved for installation on any certificated aircraft. This statement is _____ (true or false).** *Page 667*

29. **A replacement part manufactured under a PMA _____ (does or does not) have to be produced by a facility holding a Production Certificate.** *Page 668*

Manufacturer's Maintenance or Service Manuals

Manufacturer's maintenance or service manuals are FAA-acceptable data that provide information allowing a technician to maintain a specific aircraft in the manner specified by the manufacturer. Some manufacturers provide this service information in hard-copy form and others have it available for technicians only on microfiche.

The continuing increase in concern for proper documentation and the significant advances in computer technology will soon make it possible for a technician to have access to all of the latest service information immediately on his or her personal computer.

Regardless of the form in which the information is available, it is the responsibility of the technician to know that only the most current information is used when performing any maintenance.

manufacturer's maintenance or service manual. A document issued by the manufacturer of an aircraft or component and approved by the FAA. It details procedures to be followed for the maintenance of a specific aircraft, engine, propeller, or other major accessory or component.

acceptable data. Acceptable data may be used for all maintenance procedures other than major repairs and major alterations, and it includes manufacturer's service manuals and bulletins, Advisory Circular 43.13-1B, 2A, and 14 CFR Parts 121 and 135 Maintenance Manuals.

Figure 11-10 is a typical excerpt from an airplane service manual regarding lubrication of the nose gear assembly. Codes represented by symbols indicate the frequency of lubrication required and the method of lubrication. For example, the torque links should be lubricated with a grease gun every 50 hours, using MIL-G-81322A general purpose grease. *See* Figure 11-10.

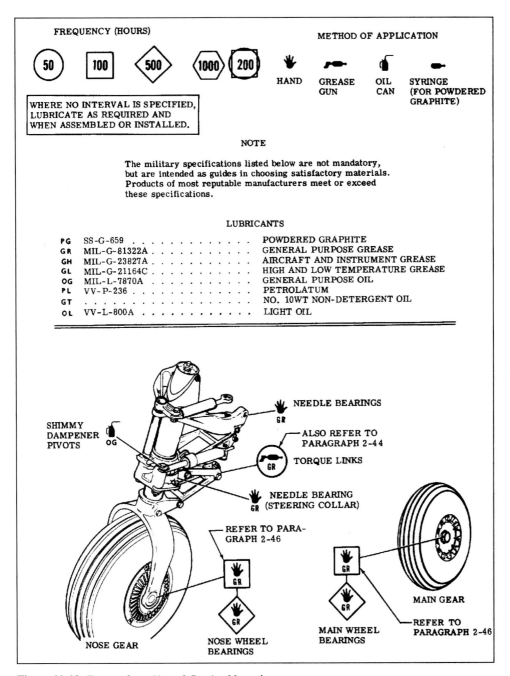

Figure 11-10. *Excerpt from Aircraft Service Manual*

Check thrust bearing nuts for tightness on new or newly over-hauled engines at the first 50-hour inspection following installation. Subsequent inspections on thrust bearing nuts will be made at each third 50-hour inspection.

Figure 11-11. *Time interval specified for checking thrust bearing nuts*

Maintenance Intervals

Most aircraft and engine service manuals contain inspection schedules that specify the maximum time interval recommended for certain operations. An example of such a time interval is shown in Figure 11-11.

Figure 11-11 gives the information that the thrust bearing nuts must be inspected at the first 50-hour inspection, but after this, inspection is required only at 150-hour intervals.

STUDY QUESTIONS: MANUFACTURER'S SERVICE MANUALS

*Answers are on Page 675. **Page numbers refer to chapter text.***

30. Refer to Figure 11-10 and supply this information:
    a. The shimmy damper pivots are lubricated with _____ .
    b. This lubricant is applied with a/an _____ .
    c. How often should the shimmy damper pivots be lubricated?

    _____

    Page 669

31. Refer to Figure 11-11. If the thrust bearing nuts were checked for tightness after 200 hours in service, they will next need to be checked at _____ hours time in service. *Page 670*

ATA 100 Specifications

Air Transport Association (ATA) Specification No. 100. A numerical classification of aircraft systems and components that allows standardization of maintenance information.

The Air Transport Association (ATA) is an organization of air carriers which has established standards and procedures to make airline operation more effective and efficient.

The ATA Specification 100 standardizes the maintenance information so that the maintenance manuals furnished by all manufacturers follow the same format. This indexing system makes it easy for a technician to find information on any subject for any aircraft by simply calling the information up on a microfiche or computer under its system and subsystem numbers. For example, if you want to find the correct oil to use in the airborne auxiliary power unit, look under 49.90.

Figure 11-12 is an example of the classification of maintenance items listed in ATA Specification 100.

System		
Subsystem		
Subject		

5	**Time Limits/Maintenance Checks**			10	HF		70	Water Lines
	00	General		20	VHF/UHF		80	Detection
	10	Time Limits		30	Passenger Addressing and	**31**	**Indicating/Recording Systems**	
	20	Scheduled Maintenance			Entertainment		00	General
		Checks		40	Interphone		10	Unassigned
	30	Reserved		50	Audio Integrating		20	Unassigned
	40	Reserved		60	Static Discharging		30	Recorders
	50	Unscheduled Maintenance		70	Audio & Video Monitoring		40	Central Computers
		Checks	**24**	**Electrical Power**			50	Central Warning System
6	**Dimensions and Areas**			00	General	**32**	**Landing Gear**	
	00	General		10	Generator Drive		00	General
7	**Lifting and Shoring**			20	AC Generation		10	Main Gear
	00	General		30	DC Generation		20	Nose Gear/Tail Gear
	10	Jacking		40	External Power		30	Extension & Retraction,
	20	Shoring		50	Elect. Load Distribution			Level Switch
8	**Leveling and Weighing**		**25**	**Equipment and Furnishing**			40	Wheels & Brakes
	00	General		00	General		50	Steering
	10	Weight and Balance Computer		10	Flight Compartment		60	Position, Warning & Ground
9	**Towing and Taxiing**			20	Passenger Compartment			Safety Switch
	00	General			System		70	Supplementary Gear Skis,
	10	Towing		30	Buffet/Galley			Floats
	20	Taxiing		40	Lavatories	**33**	**Lights**	
10	**Parking and Mooring**			50	Cargo Compartment		00	General
	00	General		60	Emergency		10	Flight Compartment &
	10	Parking/Storage		70	Accessory Compartments			Annunciator Panel
	20	Mooring	**26**	**Fire Protection**			20	Passenger Compartments
	30	Return to Service		00	General		30	Cargo & Service
11	**Required Placards**			10	Detection			Compartment
	00	General		20	Extinguishing		40	Exterior Lighting
	10	Exterior Color Schemes and		30	Explosion Suppression		50	Emergency Lighting
		Marking	**27**	**Flight Controls**		**34**	**Navigation**	
	20	Exterior Placards and		00	General		00	General
		Marking		10	Aileron & Tab		10	Flight Environment Data
	30	Interior Placards and		20	Rudder/Ruddervator & Tab		20	Attitude & Direction
		Marking		30	Elevator & Tab		30	Landing & Taxi Aids
12	**Servicing**			40	Horiz. Stabilizer/Stabilator		40	Independent Position
	00	General		50	Flaps			Determining
	10	Replenishing		60	Spoilers, Drag Devices &		50	Dependent Position
	20	Scheduled Servicing			Variable Aerodynamic Fairings			Determining
	30	Unscheduled Servicing		70	Gust Lock & Dampener		60	Position Computing
20	**Standard Practices Airframe**			80	Lift Augmenting	**35**	**Oxygen**	
	00	General	**28**	**Fuel**			00	General
21	**Air Conditioning**			00	General		10	Crew
	00	General		10	Storage		20	Passenger
	10	Compression		20	Distribution/drain Valves		30	Portable
	20	Distribution		30	Dump	**36**	**Pneumatic**	
	30	Pressurization Control		40	Indicating		00	General
	40	Heating	**29**	**Hydraulic Power**			10	Distribution
	50	Cooling		00	General		20	Indicating
	60	Temperature Control		10	Main	**37**	**Vacuum/Pressure**	
	70	Moisture/Air Contaminant		20	Auxiliary		00	General
		Control		30	Indicating		10	Distribution
22	**Auto Flight**		**30**	**Ice & Rain Protection**			20	Indicating
	00	General		00	General	**38**	**Water/Waste**	
	10	Auto Pilot		10	Airfoil		00	General
	20	Speed/Attitude Correction		20	Air Intakes		10	Portable
	30	Auto Throttle		30	Pitot & Static		20	Wash
	40	System Monitor		40	Windows & Windshields		30	Waste Disposal
23	**Communications**			50	Antennas & Radomes		40	Air Supply
	00	General		60	Propellers & Rotor			

Figure 11-12. *ATA 100 Specifications*

System		
Subsystem		
Subject		

39 Electrical/Electronic Panels and Multipurpose Components
- 00 General
- 10 Instrument & Control Panels
- 20 Electrical & Electronic Equipment Racks
- 30 Electrical & Electronic Junction Boxes
- 40 Multipurpose Electronic Components
- 50 Integrated Circuits
- 60 Printed Circuit Card Assemblies

49 Airborne Auxiliary Power
- 00 General
- 10 Power Plant
- 20 Engine
- 30 Engine Fuel & Control
- 40 Ignition/Starting
- 50 Air
- 60 Engine Controls
- 70 Indicating
- 80 Exhaust
- 90 Oil

51 Structures
- 00 General

52 Doors
- 00 General
- 10 Passenger/Crew
- 20 Emergency Exit
- 30 Cargo
- 40 Service
- 50 Fixed Interior
- 60 Entrance Stairs
- 70 Door Warning
- 80 Landing Gear

53 Fuselage
- 00 General
- 10 Main Frame
- 20 Auxiliary Structure
- 30 Platex/Skin
- 40 Attach Fittings
- 50 Aerodynamic Fairings

54 Nacelles/Pylons
- 00 General
- 10 Main Frame
- 20 Auxiliary Structure
- 30 Plates/Skin
- 40 Attach Fittings
- 50 Filets/Fairings

55 Stabilizers
- 00 General
- 10 Horizontal Stabilizer/Stabilator
- 20 Elevator/Elevon
- 30 Vertical Stabilizer
- 40 Rudder/Ruddervator
- 50 Attach Fittings

56 Windows
- 00 General
- 10 Flight Compartment
- 20 Cabin
- 30 Door
- 40 Inspection & Observation

57 Wings
- 00 General
- 10 Main Frame
- 20 Auxiliary Structure
- 30 Plates/Skin
- 40 Attach Fittings
- 50 Flight Surfaces

61 Propellers
- 00 General
- 10 Propeller Assembly
- 20 Controlling
- 30 Braking
- 40 Indicating

65 Rotors
- 00 General
- 10 Main Rotor
- 20 Anti–Torque Rotor Assembly
- 30 Accessory Driving
- 40 Controlling
- 50 Braking
- 60 Indicating

71 Power Plant
- 00 General
- 10 Cowling
- 20 Mounts
- 30 Fireseals & Shrouds
- 40 Attach Fittings
- 50 Electrical Harness
- 60 Engine Air Intakes
- 70 Engine Drains

72(T) Engine Turbine/Turboprop
- 00 General
- 10 Reduction Gear & Shaft Section
- 20 Air Inlet Section
- 30 Compressor Section
- 40 Combustion Section
- 50 Turbine Section
- 60 Accessory Drives
- 70 By-pass Section

72(R) Engine Reciprocating
- 00 General
- 10 Front Section
- 20 Power Section
- 30 Cylinder Section
- 40 Supercharger Section
- 50 Lubrication

73 Engine Fuel & Control
- 00 General
- 10 Distribution

- 20 Controlling/Governing
- 30 Indicating

74 Ignition
- 00 General
- 10 Electrical Power Supply
- 20 Distribution
- 30 Switching

75 Bleed Air
- 00 General
- 10 Engine Anti–Icing
- 20 Accessory Cooling
- 30 Compressor Control
- 40 Indicating

76 Engine Controls
- 00 General
- 10 Power Control System
- 20 Emergency Shutdown

77 Engine Indicating
- 00 General
- 10 Power
- 20 Temperature
- 30 Analyzers

78 Engine Exhaust
- 00 General
- 10 Collector/Nozzle
- 20 Noise Suppressor
- 30 Thrust Reverser
- 40 Supplementary Air

79 Engine Oil
- 00 General
- 10 Storage (Dry Sump)
- 20 Distribution
- 30 Indicating

80 Starting
- 00 General
- 10 Cranking

81 Turbines (Reciprocating Engines)
- 00 General
- 10 Power Recovery

82 Water Injection
- 00 General
- 10 Storage
- 20 Distribution
- 30 Dumping & Purging
- 40 Indicating

83 Remote Gear Boxes (Engine Driven)
- 00 General
- 10 Drive Shaft Section
- 20 Gearbox Section

84 Propulsion Augmentation
- 00 General
- 10 Jet Assisted Takeoff

Figure 11-12. *ATA 100 Specifications (cont.)*

*Answer to this question is on Page 675. **Page number refers to chapter text.***

32. Give the location according to the ATA 100 Specifications for maintenance information on each of these items:
    a. Automatic pilots _____
    b. Fuel dump systems _____
    c. Flight crew oxygen systems _____
    d. Thrust reversers _____
       Page 671

Component Maintenance Manuals (CMM)

Figure 11-13 is a cover of a typical CMM. Note that the part numbers of the OEM who manufactured the specific component, QCS Quality Control Systems (QCS), and of the prime manufacturer, Wildex Development Company (WDC), are shown. The ATA code is printed in the lower right corner. This number 78-30-06 indicates that this actuator is part of the engine exhaust system (78). The subsystem (30) indicates that it is for a thrust reverser. The specific number 30-06 is assigned by the prime manufacturer and the OEM of the component to distinguish it from others which apply to other thrust reversers.

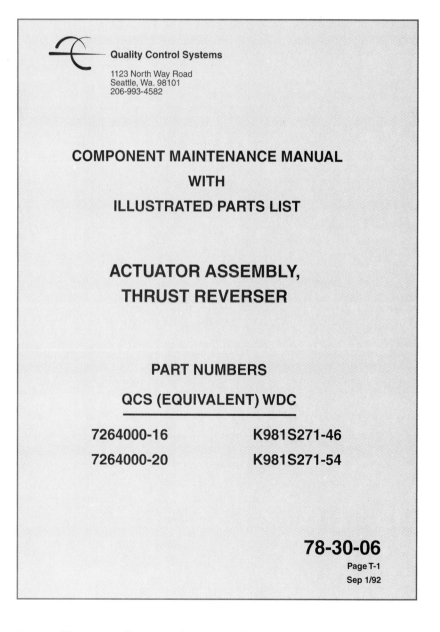

Figure 11-13. *The cover of a typical Component Maintenance Manual (CMM).*

Answers to Chapter 11 Study Questions

1. 23
2. 23
3. 65
4. is not
5. 43.13-1B
6. Type Certificate Data Sheet
7. Type Certificate Data Sheet
8. Airplane
9. Type Certificate Data Sheet
10. Propeller
11. Propeller
12. Aircraft Specifications, Type Certificate Data Sheet
13. Aircraft Specifications
14. Aircraft Listings

15. true
16. is
17. a. Standard
    b. Special
18. new owner
19. Airworthiness Directive
20. registered owner
21. priority mail, telegram
22. mandatory
23. maintenance records
24. a. aircraft
    b. aircraft engines
    c. propellers
    d. appliances
25. does

26. Malfunction and Defect
27. advisory
28. false
29. does not
30. a. MIL-L-7870A General Purpose Oil
    b. oil can
    c. as required and when assembled or installed
31. 350
32. a. 22-10
    b. 28-30
    c. 35-10
    d. 78-30

MECHANIC PRIVILEGES AND LIMITATIONS

12

MECHANIC PRIVILEGES AND LIMITATIONS

12

Introduction

In Chapter 11 we saw some of the basic Federal Aviation Regulations that pertain to aviation maintenance. In this chapter we will look at the specific regulations that affect us as technicians. When we are dealing with a specific regulation, it is quoted beside the text at the edge of the page.

Maintenance Classifications

Title 14 of the Code of Federal Regulations (14 CFR) Part 1, *Definitions and Abbreviations*, defines maintenance as inspections, overhaul, repair, preservation, and the replacement of parts but excludes preventive maintenance. This section will consider the different classifications of maintenance and the different types of maintenance personnel and match the personnel with the maintenance he or she is authorized to perform.

---

14 CFR Part 1: Definitions and Abbreviations

Airframe means the fuselage, booms, nacelles, cowlings, fairings, airfoil surfaces (including rotors but excluding propellers and rotating airfoils of engines), and landing gear of an aircraft and their accessories and controls.

Major alteration means an alteration not listed in the aircraft, aircraft engine, or propeller specifications—
(1) That might appreciably affect weight, balance, structural strength, performance, powerplant operation, flight characteristics, or other qualities affecting airworthiness; or
(2) That is not done according to accepted practices or cannot be done by elementary operations.

Major repair means a repair:
(1) That, if improperly done, might appreciable affect weight, balance, structural strength, performance, powerplant operation, flight characteristics, or other qualities affecting airworthiness; or
(2) That is not done according to accepted practices or cannot be done by elementary operations.

Aircraft engine means an engine that is used or intended to be used for propelling aircraft. It includes turbosuperchargers, appurtenances, and accessories necessary for its functioning, but does not include propellers.

Maintenance means inspection, overhaul, repair, preservation, and the replacement of parts, but excludes preventive maintenance.

Inspections

One of the most important operations of an aviation maintenance technician is that of inspection. The FAA requires several inspections to be conducted on certificated aircraft, each with a different purpose and frequency.

Preflight Inspection

The preflight inspection is not actually a maintenance inspection, but it is required by 14 CFR Part 91, *General Operating and Flight Rules*, that the pilot-in-command of the aircraft determine that it is safe for the planned flight.

Figure 12-1 shows a typical preflight inspection checklist for a commercial twin-engine airplane. Each model of aircraft has its own specific checklist, and only that list should be followed.

PREFLIGHT INSPECTION. This inspection is for the crew chief and/or mechanic and should become part of the airplane operator's operational routine and/or preflight inspection before each flight.

a. The propeller blades are free of nicks and the spinner and hub are free of cracks or damage.
b. There are no grease or oil leaks around the propellers.
c. The engine oil is at the proper level. (Dipsticks are marked for left and right engines. Use correct side of stick when checking oil level.)
d. There are no obvious oil leaks.
e. The cowling is clean. There are no loose or missing fasteners and all inspection covers are secured.
f. The tires are properly inflated and not excessively worn or cut.
g. The landing gear oleo struts have proper extension and fluid level.
h. The brakes are working and there are no leaks in the hydraulic lines.
i. The fuel cells are full or at a safe level of proper fuel.
j. There are no visible leaks in the fuel system.
k. The fuel cell caps are secure and the vents are open.
l. The fuel tanks and sediment bowls, strainers and lines are free of water and sediment by draining sumps and strainers.
m. There is no external damage, cracks or operational interference to the control surfaces, wings or fuselage.
n. The windshield and windows are free of defects and clean.
o. The emergency exit window latch is secure.
p. The baggage door latch and hinges and cabin entrance doors and window are free of damage and operate safely.
q. The seats and seat belts are securely fastened.
r. The landing, navigation, cabin and instrument lights are all operating.
s. The fuel selector and valves are operating properly.
t. The throttles, alternate air, mixture and propeller governor controls are all operating properly.
u. All systems are operating properly.

Figure 12-1. *A typical preflight inspection checklist for a commercial twin-engine airplane*

Annual and 100–Hour Inspections

14 CFR §91.409(a) requires that an aircraft must not be operated unless, within the preceding 12 calendar months it has had an annual inspection and been approved for return to service by a technician holding an Inspection Authorization, a certificated repair station, the manufacturer of the aircraft, or the holder of an air carrier certificate. There are some exceptions to this; these are:

- Aircraft carrying a special flight permit
- Aircraft carrying a current Experimental Certificate
- Aircraft carrying a provisional Airworthiness Certificate
- Aircraft inspected in accordance with an approved inspection program under Part 125, 127, or 135.
- Aircraft under a progressive inspection program
- Aircraft under the inspection program required for large airplanes to which Part 125 is not applicable.

14 CFR §91.109(b) requires that all aircraft carrying persons for hire or used for giving flight instruction for hire must have a complete inspection each 100 hours of operation. This 100-hour limit can be exceeded by up to 10 hours to get the aircraft to a place where the inspection can be performed. If this time is exceeded, the excess must be subtracted from the time the next inspection is due. For example, if the aircraft is operated for a total of 105 hours between 100-hour inspections, the next inspection will be due after 95 hours of operation.

---

14 CFR §91.409 (a), (b): Annual and 100-Hour Inspections

(a) Except as provided in paragraph (c) of this section, no person may operate an aircraft unless, within the preceding 12 calendar months, it has had—

(1) An annual inspection in accordance with part 43 of this chapter and has been approved for return to service by a person authorized by §43.7 of this chapter; or

(2) An inspection for the issuance of an airworthiness certificate in accordance with part 21 of this chapter.

No inspection performed under paragraph (b) of this section may be substituted for any inspection required by this paragraph unless it is performed by a person authorized to perform annual inspections and is entered as an "annual" inspection in the required maintenance records.

(b) Except as provided in paragraph (c) of this section, no person may operate an aircraft carrying any person (other than a crewmember) for hire, and no person may give flight instruction for hire in an aircraft which that person provides, unless within the preceding 100 hours of time in service the aircraft has received an annual or 100-hour inspection and has been approved for return to service in accordance with part 43 of this chapter or has received an inspection for the issuance of an airworthiness certificate in accordance with part 21 of this chapter. The 100-hour limitation may be exceeded by not more than 10 hours while enroute to reach a place where the inspection can be done. The excess time used to reach a place where the inspection can be done must be included in computing the next 100 hours of time in service.

Annual and 100-hour inspections are identical, except for the person authorized to perform them. A technician with both Airframe and Powerplant ratings can perform a 100-hour inspection, but only a technician with an Inspection Authorization can perform an annual inspection.

Each person performing an annual or 100-hour inspection must use a checklist. This checklist may be one recommended by the aircraft manufacturer or one of the inspector's own design, but it must include the scope and detail of the items listed in 14 CFR Part 43, Appendix D. This is reproduced in Figure 12-2.

APPENDIX D—SCOPE AND DETAIL OF ITEMS (AS APPLICABLE TO THE PARTICULAR AIRCRAFT) TO BE INCLUDED IN ANNUAL AND 100-HOUR INSPECTIONS

(a) Each person performing an annual or 100-hour inspection shall, before that inspection, remove or open all necessary inspection plates, access doors, fairing, and cowling. He shall thoroughly clean the aircraft and aircraft engine.

(b) Each person performing an annual or 100-hour inspection shall inspect (where applicable) the following components of the fuselage and hull group:

(1) Fabric and skin—for deterioration, distortion, other evidence of failure, and defective or insecure attachment of fittings.

(2) Systems and components—for improper installation, apparent defects, and unsatisfactory operation.

(3) Envelope, gas bags, ballast tanks, and related parts—for poor condition.

(c) Each person performing an annual inspection shall inspect (where applicable) the following components of the cabin and cockpit group:

(1) Generally—for uncleanliness and loose equipment that might foul the controls.

(2) Seats and safety belts—for poor condition and apparent defects.

(3) Windows and windshields—for deterioration and breakage.

(4) Instruments—for poor condition, mounting, marking, and (where practicable) improper operation.

(5) Flight and engine controls—for improper installation and improper operation.

(6) Batteries—for improper installation and improper charge.

(7) All systems—for improper installation, poor general condition, apparent and obvious defects, and insecurity of attachment.

(d) Each person performing an annual or 100-hour inspection shall inspect (where applicable) components of the engine and nacelle group as follows:

(1) Engine section—for visual evidence of excessive oil, fuel, or hydraulic leaks, and sources of such leaks.

(2) Studs and nuts—for improper torquing and obvious defects.

(3) Internal engine—for cylinder compression and for metal particles or foreign matter on screens and sump drain plugs. If there is weak cylinder compression, for improper internal condition and improper internal tolerances.

(4) Engine mount—for cracks, looseness of mounting, and looseness of engine to mount.

(5) Flexible vibration dampeners—for poor condition and deterioration.

(6) Engine controls—for defects, improper travel, and improper safetying.

(7) Lines, hoses, and clamps—for leaks, improper condition and looseness.

(8) Exhaust stacks—for cracks, defects, and improper attachment.

(9) Accessories—for apparent defects in security of mounting.

(10) All systems—for improper installation, poor general condition, defects, and insecure attachment.

Figure 12-2. *14 CFR Part 43, Appendix D, the scope and detail of the items that must be inspected on Annual and 100-hour inspections*

An actual checklist for a typical twin-engine airplane that includes items to be inspected on 50-hour, 100-hour, 500-hour, and 1,000-hour inspections is seen in Figure 12-3 on Pages 684-688.

(11) Cowling—for cracks, and defects.

(e) Each person performing an annual or 100-hour inspection shall inspect (where applicable) the following components of the landing gear group:

(1) All units—for poor condition and insecurity of attachment.

(2) Shock absorbing devices—for improper oleo fluid level.

(3) Linkages, trusses, and members—for undue or excessive wear fatigue, and distortion.

(4) Retracting and locking mechanism—for improper operation.

(5) Hydraulic lines—for leakage.

(6) Electrical system—for chafing and improper operation of switches.

(7) Wheels—for cracks, defects, and condition of bearings.

(8) Tires—for wear and cuts.

(9) Brakes—for improper adjustment.

(10) Floats and skis—for insecure attachment and obvious or apparent defects.

(f) Each person performing an annual or 100-hour inspection shall inspect (where applicable) all components of the wing and center section assembly for poor general condition, fabric or skin deterioration, distortion, evidence of failure, and insecurity of attachment.

(g) Each person performing an annual or 100-hour inspection shall inspect (where applicable) all components and systems that make up the complete empennage assembly for poor general condition, fabric or skin deterioration, distortion, evidence of failure, insecure attachment, im-

proper component installation, and improper component operation.

(h) Each person performing an annual or 100-hour inspection shall inspect (where applicable) the following components of the propeller group:

(1) Propeller assembly—for cracks, nicks, binds, and oil leakage.

(2) Bolts—for improper torquing and lack of safetying.

(3) Anti-icing devices—for improper operations and obvious defects.

(4) Control mechanisms—for improper operation, insecure mounting, and restricted travel.

(i) Each person performing an annual or 100-hour inspection shall inspect (where applicable) the following components of the radio group:

(1) Radio and electronic equipment—for improper installation and insecure mounting.

(2) Wiring and conduits—for improper routing, insecure mounting, and obvious defects.

(3) Bonding and shielding—for improper installation and poor condition.

(4) Antenna including trailing antenna—for poor condition, insecure mounting, and improper operation.

(j) Each person performing an annual or 100-hour inspection shall inspect (where applicable) each installed miscellaneous item that is not otherwise covered by this listing for improper installation and improper operation.

Figure 12-2. *Continued*

Nature of Inspection	Inspection Time (hours)			
	50	100	500	1000
A. Propeller Group				
1. Inspect spinner and back plate	●	●	●	●
2. Inspect blades for nicks and cracks	●	●	●	●
3. Check for grease and oil leaks	●	●	●	●
4. Lubricate per Lubrication Chart		●	●	●
5. Check spinner mounting brackets		●	●	●
6. Check propeller mounting blots and torque		●	●	●
7. Inspect hub parts for cracks and corrosion		●	●	●
8. Rotate blades and check for tightness		●	●	●
9. Check propeller air pressure (Check at least once a month)		●	●	●
10. Check condition of propeller De-Icer system		●	●	●
11. Remove propellers, remove sludge from propeller and crankshaft			●	●
12. Overhaul propeller				●
B. Engine Group				
CAUTION: Ground Magneto Primary Circuit before working on engine				
1. Remove engine cowl	●	●	●	●
2. Clean and check cowling for cracks, distortion, and loose or missing fasteners	●	●	●	●
3. Drain oil sump (See Note 2)	●	●	●	●
4. Clean suction oil strainer at oil change (Check strainer for foreign particles)	●	●	●	●
5. Change full flow (cartridge type) oil filter element (Check element for foreign particles)	●	●	●	●
6. Check oil temperature sender unit for leaks and security		●	●	●
7. Check oil lines and fittings for leaks, security, chafing, dents and cracks		●	●	●
8. Clean and check oil radiator cooling fins		●	●	●
9. Remove and flush oil radiator			●	●
10. Fill engine with oil as per Lubrication Chart	●	●	●	●
11. Clean engine		●	●	●
12. Check condition of spark plugs (Clean and adjust gap, .015 to .018, as required)		●	●	●
13. Check ignition harnesses and insulators		●	●	●
14. Check magneto main points for clearance – Set clearance at .016		●	●	●
15. Check magneto retard points for proper retard angle (30° 30')		●	●	●
16. Check magnetos for oil leakage		●	●	●
17. Check breaker felts for proper lubrication		●	●	●
18. Check distributor block for cracks, burned areas or corrosion		●	●	●
19. Check magnetos to engine timing (20° BTC)		●	●	●
20. Overhaul or replace magnetos (See Note 3)				●
21. Remove air cleaner screen and clean	●	●	●	●
22. Remove and clean fuel injector inlet line screen (Clean injector nozzles as required) (Clean with acetone only)	●	●	●	●
23. Check condition of alternate air door and box		●	●	●
24. Check intake seals for leaks and clamps for tightness		●	●	●
25. Inspect condition of flexible fuel lines		●	●	●
26. Replace flexible fuel lines (See Note 3)				●
27. Check fuel system for leaks		●	●	●
28. Check fuel pumps for operation (engine driven and electric)		●	●	●
29. Overhaul or replace fuel pumps (engine driven and electric) (See Note 3)				●
30. Replace hydraulic filter element and check for contamination		●	●	●
31. Check hydraulic pump and gasket for leaks		●	●	●
32. Overhaul or replace hydraulic pump (See Note 3)				●
33. Check pressure pumps and lines		●	●	●

Figure 12-3. *An inspection checklist for a typical twin-engine general aviation airplane*

Nature of Inspection	Inspection Time (hours)			
	50	100	500	1000
B. Engine Group *(Continued)*				
34. Overhaul or replace pressure pumps			●	●
35. Check throttle, alternate air, injector, mixture and propeller governor controls for travel and operating condition		●	●	●
36. Check exhaust stacks and gaskets (Replace gaskets as required)	●	●	●	●
37. Check breather tube for obstructions and security		●	●	●
38. Check crankcase for cracks, leaks, and security of seam bolts		●	●	●
39. Check engine mounts for cracks and loose mounting		●	●	●
40. Check all engine baffles		●	●	●
41. Check rubber engine mount bushings for deterioration		●	●	●
42. Check firewalls for cracks		●	●	●
43. Check firewall seals		●	●	●
44. Check condition of alternator and stater		●	●	●
45. Check condition and tension of alternator drive belt		●	●	●
46. Replace pressure inlet filter		●	●	●
47. Replace pressure line filter			●	●
48. Lubricate all controls (Do not lubricate Teflon liners of control cables)		●	●	
49. Overhaul or replace propeller governor (See Note 3)				●
50. Complete overhaul of engine or replace with factory rebuilt				●
C. Turbocharger Group				
1. Visually inspect system for oil leaks, exhaust system leaks, and general condition	●	●	●	●
2. Inspect the compressor wheel for nicks, cracks, or broken blades		●	●	●
3. Check for excess bearing drag or wheel rubbing against housing		●	●	●
4. Check turbine wheel for broken blades or signs of rubbing		●	●	●
5. Check rigging of alternate air control		●	●	●
6. Check oil inlet and outlet ports in center housing for leaks		●	●	●
7. Check turbine heat blanket for condition and security		●	●	●
8. Check linkage between bypass valve and actuator		●	●	●
9. Inspect induction and exhaust components for worn or damaged areas, loose clamps, cracks and leaks			●	●
10. Inspect fuel injection nozzle reference manifold for deteriorated hose, loose connections, leaks or obstructions		●	●	●
11. Check fluid power lines for leaks and security		●	●	●
12. Inspect for oil leakage from the controller		●	●	●
13. Check operation of compressor bypass door		●	●	●
D. Cabin Group				
1. Remove inspection panels		●	●	●
2. Inspect cabin entrance, door and windows for damage and operation		●	●	●
3. Check emergency exit latching mechanism		●	●	●
4. Check upholstery for tears		●	●	●
5. Check seats, seat belts, security brackets and bolts		●	●	●
6. Check trim operation		●	●	●
7. Check rudder pedals		●	●	●
8. Check parking brake		●	●	●
9. Check control wheels, column, pulleys and cable		●	●	●
10. Check landing, navigation, cabin and instrument lights		●	●	●
11. Check instruments, lines and attachments		●	●	●
12. Check gyro operated instruments and electric turn and bank (Overhaul or replace as required)		●	●	●

Figure 12-3. *Continued*

Nature of Inspection	Inspection Time (hours)			
	50	100	500	1000
D. Cabin Group *(Continued)*				
13. Check pitot tube(s), lines and static vents for condition, security and stoppage		●	●	●
14. Check altimeter (calibrate altimeter system in accordance with FAR 91.170, if appropriate)			●	●
15. Change manifold pressure gauge filters			●	●
16. Drain crossfeed line			●	●
17. Check operation – fuel selector valve		●	●	●
18. Check operation – crossfeed valve		●	●	●
19. Check operation – emergency shutoff valve		●	●	●
20. Check operation – heater fuel valve		●	●	●
21. Check switches to indicators registering fuel tank quantity		●	●	●
22. Check condition of heat ducts		●	●	●
23. Check oxygen outlets for defects and corrosion		●	●	●
24. Check oxygen system for operation and components		●	●	●
E. Fuselage and Empennage Group				
1. Remove inspection plates and panels		●	●	●
2. Check baggage door latch and hinges		●	●	●
3. Check fluid in brake reservoir (Fill as required)	●	●	●	●
4. Check battery, box and cables (Check at least every 30 days. Flush box as required and fill per instructions on box)	●	●	●	●
5. Check heater for fuel or fume leaks		●	●	●
6. Check recommended time for overhaul of heater per Piper Service Manual				●
7. Check electronic installations		●	●	●
8. Check bulkheads and stringers for damage		●	●	●
9. Check antenna mounts and electric wiring		●	●	●
10. Check hydraulic power pack fluid level (Fill as required)	●	●	●	●
11. Check power pack and lines for damage and leaks		●	●	●
12. Check fuel lines, valves and gauges for damage and operation		●	●	●
13. Check security of all lines		●	●	●
14. Check vertical fin and rudder surfaces for damage		●	●	●
15. Check rudder and tab hinges, horns and attachments for damage and operation		●	●	●
16. Check vertical fin attachments		●	●	●
17. Check rudder and tab hinge bolts for excess wear		●	●	●
18. Check rudder trim mechanism		●	●	●
19. Check horizontal stabilizer and elevator surfaces for damage		●	●	●
20. Check elevator and tab hinges, horns and attachments for damage and operation		●	●	●
21. Check horizontal stabilizer attachments		●	●	●
22. Check elevator and tab hinge bolts and bearings for excess wear		●	●	●
23. Check elevator trim mechanism		●	●	●
24. Check aileron, rudder, elevator cables, trim cables, turnbuckles, guides and pulleys for safeties, damage and operation		●	●	●
25. Clean and lubricate elevator and rudder trim drum screw		●	●	●
26. Check rotating beacon for security and operation		●	●	●
27. Lubricate per Lubrication Chart		●	●	●
28. Check condition of Pneumatic De-Icers		●	●	●
29. Check security of AutoPilot Servo bridle cable clamps		●	●	●

Figure 12-3. *Continued*

Nature of Inspection	Inspection Time (hours)			
	50	100	500	1000

F. Wing Group

	50	100	500	1000
1. Remove inspection plates and panels		●	●	●
2. Check surfaces, skins and tips for damage and loose rivets		●	●	●
3. Check ailerons and tab hinges and attachments		●	●	●
4. Check aileron and trim cables, pulleys and bellcranks for damage and operation		●	●	●
5. Check aileron balance weight for security		●	●	●
6. Check flaps and attachments for damage and operations		●	●	●
7. Inspect condition of bolts used with flap and aileron hinges (Replace as required)				●
8. Check all exterior bearings			●	●
9. Lubricate per Lubrication Chart		●	●	●
10. Check wing attachment bolts and brackets		●	●	●
11. Check engine mount attaching structure		●	●	●
12. Remove, drain and clean fuel filter bowl and screen (Drain and clean at least every 90 days)	●	●	●	●
13. Check fuel cells and lines for leaks and water		●	●	●
14. Fuel tanks marked for capacity		●	●	●
15. Fuel tanks marked for minimum octane rating		●	●	●
16. Check fuel cell vents		●	●	●
17. Check condition of Pneumatic De-Icers		●	●	●

G. Landing Gear Group

	50	100	500	1000
1. Check oleo struts for proper extension (Check for proper fluid level as required)		●	●	●
2. Check nose gear steering control and travel		●	●	●
3. Check wheels for alignment		●	●	●
4. Put airplane on jacks		●	●	●
5. Check tires for cuts, uneven or excessive wear and slippage		●	●	●
6. Remove wheels, clean, check and repack bearings		●	●	●
7. Check wheels for cracks, corrosion and broken bolts		●	●	●
8. Check tire pressure (N42 – M60)		●	●	●
9. Check brake lining and disc		●	●	●
10. Check brake backing plates		●	●	●
11. Check brake and hydraulic lines		●	●	●
12. Check shimmy dampener		●	●	●
13. Check gear forks for damage		●	●	●
14. Check oleo struts for fluid leaks and scoring		●	●	●
15. Check gear struts, attachments, torque links, retraction links and bolts for condition and security		●	●	●
16. Check downlock for operation and adjustment		●	●	●
17. Check torque link bolts and bushings (Rebush as required)			●	●
18. Check drag and side brace link bolts (Replace as required)				●
19. Check gear doors and attachments				●
20. Check warning horn and light for operation		●	●	●
21. Retract gear – check operation		●	●	●
22. Retract gear – check doors for clearance and operation		●	●	●
23. Check anti-retraction system		●	●	●
24. Check actuating cylinders for leaking and security		●	●	●
25. Check position indicating switches and electrical leads for security		●	●	●
26. Lubricate per lubrication chart		●	●	●
27. Remove airplane from jacks		●	●	●

Figure 12-3. *Continued*

Nature of Inspection	Inspection Time (hours)			
	50	100	500	1000
H. Operational Inspection				
1. Check fuel pump, fuel cell selector and crossfeed operation	●	●	●	●
2. Check fuel quantity and pressure or flow	●	●	●	●
3. Check oil pressure and temperature	●	●	●	●
4. Check alternator output	●	●	●	●
5. Check manifold pressure	●	●	●	●
6. Check alternate air	●	●	●	●
7. Check parking brake	●	●	●	●
8. Check gyro pressure gauge	●	●	●	●
9. Check gyros for noise and roughness	●	●	●	●
10. Check cabin heater operation	●	●	●	●
11. Check magneto switch operation	●	●	●	●
12. Check magneto RPM variation	●	●	●	●
13. Check throttle and mixture operation	●	●	●	●
14. Check propeller smoothness	●	●	●	●
15. Check propeller governor action	●	●	●	●
16. Check electronic equipment operation	●	●	●	●
I. General				
1. Aircraft conforms to FAA Specifications	●	●	●	●
2. All FAA Airworthiness Directives complied with	●	●	●	●
3. All Manufacturers Service Bulletins complied with	●	●	●	●
4. Check for proper flight manual	●	●	●	●
5. Aircraft papers in proper order	●	●	●	●

Note 1: Both the periodic and 100-hour inspections are complete inspections of the airplane – identical in scope. Inspections must be accomplished by persons authorized by the FAA.
Note 2: Intervals between oil changes can be increased as much as 100% on engines equipped with full flow (cartridge type) oil filters provided the element is replaced each 50 hours of operation.
Note 3: Replace or overhaul as required or at engine overhaul. Refer to Lycoming Service Instructions No. 1009

Figure 12-3. *Continued*

If the aircraft meets its requirements for certification, the person approving it for return to service must record the inspection in the aircraft maintenance records. But if it fails to pass the inspection, a list of the discrepancies or a notice of the defect that caused the aircraft to fail must be furnished to the owner. These discrepancies must be corrected before the aircraft can be approved for return to service. The aircraft does not have to be returned to the IA who failed it, nor does the technician who approves it for return to service have to hold an Inspection Authorization. Any certificated technician who holds the appropriate rating can approve the aircraft for return to service after the discrepancies have been corrected.

If an aircraft that failed to pass an annual inspection is considered by the technician conducting the inspection to be safe for flight, it may be issued a special flight authorization, or ferry permit, under the provision of 14 CFR § 21.197(a)(1), to allow the aircraft to be flown to another maintenance base where the required maintenance can be performed.

Progressive Inspection

Some aircraft are kept so busy that their operator does not want to take them out of service long enough to perform a complete inspection at one time. In these instances, the aircraft may be placed on a progressive inspection schedule that allows the maintenance required on the annual or 100-hour inspection checklist to be performed in smaller segments.

Before starting a progressive inspection, the inspection schedule must be prepared and approved by the local FAA FSDO, and the aircraft must be given a complete annual inspection. This program must include:

- The name of the certificated technician holding an Inspection Authorization, or the repair station or aircraft manufacturer who will supervise or conduct the progressive inspection.

- An Inspection Procedures Manual that details the progressive inspection, including the continuity of inspection responsibility, the making of reports, and keeping of records and technical reference material.

- Enough housing and equipment for necessary disassembly and proper inspection of the aircraft.

- Appropriate current technical information for the aircraft.

The frequency and detail of the inspection shall provide for a complete inspection of the aircraft within each 12 calendar months and be consistent with the manufacturer's recommendations and field service experience for the type of operation in which the aircraft is engaged.

If the progressive inspection is discontinued, the local FAA FSDO must be notified in writing. The next 100-hour inspection is due 100 hours after the last complete inspection, and the next annual inspection is due within 12 calendar months after the last complete inspection.

Continuous Airworthiness Inspection Program

Large airplanes to which Part 125 is not applicable, turbojet multiengine airplanes, turbopropeller-powered multiengine airplanes, and turbine-powered rotorcraft have special inspection considerations, and they are too complex to be satisfactorily inspected under either the annual and 100-hour system or the progressive inspection program. These aircraft may be placed under an inspection program that conforms to:

- An approved continuous airworthiness inspection program that is currently in use by a person holding an operating certificate issued under Part 121, 127, or 135 that is operating the same make and model of aircraft

- An aircraft inspection program approved under 14 CFR § 135.419

- A current inspection program recommended by the aircraft manufacturer

- Any other inspection program established by the registered owner or operator of the aircraft and approved by the FAA

Special Inspections

In addition to the complete inspection of aircraft just described, there are special inspections that are required.

Altimeter and Static System Inspection

An aircraft cannot be operated in controlled airspace under Instrument Flight Rules unless the altimeter and the aircraft instrument static air system has been inspected by a certificated repair station with the appropriate ratings within the preceding 24 calendar months. An exception to this is that a certificated technician with an Airframe rating can perform the static pressure system tests and inspections.

ATC Transponder Tests and Inspection

No person may use an ATC transponder unless within the preceding 24 calendar months it has been inspected by a certificated repair station with the appropriate ratings.

Other Special Inspections

An aircraft should be given a special inspection when it has encountered severe turbulence or a lightning strike or has experienced an overweight landing or sudden stoppage of the engine. The extent of these inspections is covered in the appropriate aircraft maintenance manuals.

Repairs

A repair is an operation that restores a device to a condition of safe operation after it has become deteriorated or has been damaged. The FAA subdivides repairs into two classifications: major and minor.

A major repair is an extensive repair to an aircraft structure, engine, or propeller that could affect its strength, performance, or flight characteristics. A minor repair is simply defined as a repair other than a major repair.

14 CFR Part 43, Appendix A, lists a number of items that are classified as major repairs. Figure 12-4 lists examples of airframe major repairs, Figure 12-5 lists examples of powerplant major repairs, Figure 12-6 shows examples of propeller major repairs, and Figure 12-7 lists examples of major repairs to appliances. *See* Page 692.

Airframe major repairs consist of repairs to the following parts of an airframe and repairs of the following types, involving the strengthening, reinforcing, splicing, and manufacturing of primary structural members or their replacement, when replacement is by fabrication such as riveting or welding.

Box beams

Monocoque or semimonocoque wings or control surfaces

Wing stringers or chord members

Spars

Spar flanges

Members of truss-type beams

Thin sheet webs of beams

Keel and chine members of boat hulls or floats

Corrugated sheet compression members which act as flange materials of wings or tail surfaces

Wing main ribs and compression members

Wing or tail surface brace struts

Engine mounts

Fuselage longerons

Members of the side truss, horizontal truss, or bulkheads

Main seat support braces and brackets

Landing gear brace struts

Axles

Wheels

Skis and ski pedestals

Parts of the control system such as control columns, pedals, shafts, brackets, or horns

Repairs involving the substitution of materials

The repair of damaged areas in metal or plywood stressed covering exceeding six inches in any direction

The repair of portions of skin sheets by making additional seams

The splicing of skin sheets

The repair of three or more adjacent wing or control surface ribs or the leading edge of wings and control surfaces, between such adjacent ribs

Repair of fabric covering involving an area greater than that required to repair two adjacent ribs

Replacement of fabric on fabric covered parts such as wings, fuselages, stabilizers, and control surfaces

Repairing, including rebottoming, of removable or integral fuel tanks and oil tanks

Figure 12-4. *Examples of airframe major repairs*

Powerplant major repairs consist of repairs of the following parts of an engine and repairs of the following types:

Separation or disassembly of a crankcase or crankshaft of a reciprocating engine equipped with an integral supercharger

Separation or disassembly of a crankcase or crankshaft of a reciprocating engine equipped with other than a spur-type propeller reduction gearing

Special repairs to structural engine parts by welding, plating, metalizing, or other methods

Figure 12-5. *Examples of powerplant major repairs*

Propeller major repairs consist of repairs of the following types:

Any repairs to, or straightening of steel blades
Repairing or machining of steel hubs
Shortening of blades
Retipping of wood blades
Replacement of outer laminations on fixed-pitch wood propellers
Repairing elongated bolt holes in the hub of fixed-pitch wood propellers
Inlay work on wood blades
Repairs to composition blades
Replacement of tip fabric
Replacement of plastic covering
Repair of propeller governors
Overhaul of controllable-pitch propellers
Repairs to deep dents, cuts, scars, nicks, etc., and straightening of aluminum blades
The repair or replacement of internal elements of blades

Figure 12-6. *Examples of propeller major repairs*

Appliance major repairs consist of repairs of the following types to appliances:

Calibration and repair of instruments
Calibration of radio equipment
Rewinding the field coil of an electrical accessory
Complete disassembly of complex hydraulic power valves
Overhaul of pressure-type carburetors and pressure type fuel, oil, and hydraulic pumps

Figure 12-7. *Examples of appliance major repairs*

Alterations

The FAA lists in the Type Certificate Data Sheets or Aircraft Specifications for an aircraft certain alterations that have been approved. For example, an airplane may be approved for operation with either wheels or skis, and the part number of the approved skis is included in the TCDS.

Alterations, like repairs, are classified by the FAA as either major or minor. A major alteration is a change to an aircraft, engine, or propeller that is not listed in the appropriate TCDS or Specifications and that affects the airworthiness of the aircraft. A minor alteration is considered to be any alteration that does not fit the definition of a major alteration and includes all alterations that are listed in the TCDS or Specifications. In the example of the wheels and skis, replacement of the wheels with the approved skis is a minor alteration.

14 CFR Part 43, Appendix A, lists a number of items that are classified as major alterations. Figure 12-8 shows examples of airframe major alterations, Figure 12-9 lists examples of powerplant major alterations, Figure 12-10 contains examples of propeller major alterations, and Figure 12-11 lists examples of major alterations to appliances.

Airframe major alterations are alterations of the following parts and alterations of the following types, when not listed in the aircraft specifications issued by the FAA:

Wings
Tail surfaces
Fuselage
Engine mounts
Control system
Landing gear
Hull or floats
Elements of an airframe including spars, ribs, fittings, shock absorbers, bracing, cowling, fairings, and balance weights
Hydraulic and electrical actuating systems or components
Rotor blades
Changes to the empty weight or empty balance which results in an increase in the maximum certificated weight or center of gravity limits of the aircraft
Changes to the basic design of the fuel, oil, cooling, heating, cabin pressurization, electrical, hydraulic, deicing or exhaust systems
Changes to the wing or to fixed or movable control surfaces which affect flutter and vibration characteristics

Figure 12-8. *Examples of airframe major alterations*

Powerplant major alterations are alterations of a powerplant when not listed in the powerplant specifications issued by the FAA:

Conversion of an aircraft engine from one approved model to another, involving any changes in compression ratio, propeller reduction gear, impeller gear ratios or the substitution of major engine parts which requires extensive rework and testing of the engine

Changes to the engine by replacing aircraft engine structural parts with parts not supplied by the original manufacturer or parts not specifically approved by the Administrator

Installation of an accessory which is not approved for the engine

Removal of accessories that are listed as required equipment on the aircraft or engine specification

Installation of structural parts other than the type of parts approved for the installation

Conversion of any sort for the purpose of using fuel of a rating or grade other than that listed in the engine specifications.

Figure 12-9. *Examples of powerplant major alterations*

Propeller major alterations are alterations of a propeller when not listed in the propeller specifications issued by the FAA:

Changes in blade design
Changes in hub design
Changes in the governor or control design
Installation of a propeller governor or feathering system
Installation of propeller deicing system
Installation of parts not approved for the propeller

Figure 12-10. *Examples of propeller major alterations*

Appliance major alterations are alterations of the basic design not made in accordance with recommendations of the appliance manufacturer or in accordance with an FAA Airworthiness Directive.

In addition, changes in the basic design of radio communication and navigation equipment approved under type certification or a Technical Standard Order that have an effect on frequency stability, noise level, sensitivity, selectivity, distortion, spurious radiation, AVC characteristics, or ability to meet environmental test conditions and other changes that have an effect on the performance of the equipment.

Figure 12-11. *Examples of appliance major alterations*

Preventive Maintenance

In order to make the maintenance aspects of private aircraft ownership less costly, the FAA has created a list of operations that are excluded from the classification of maintenance. These are called preventive maintenance. Preventive maintenance consists of simple or minor preservation operations and the replacement of small standard parts not involving complex assembly operations. Preventive maintenance may be performed by the holder of a pilot certificate on any aircraft owned or operated by that pilot which is not used under 14 CFR Part 121, 127, 129, or 135.

In late 1992, the FAA created a primary category of aircraft that are not permitted to be used for carrying persons or property for hire. The pilot of a primary category aircraft is allowed to perform more preventive maintenance functions than those listed in Figure 12-12, but he or she must first success-fully complete an FAA-approved preventive maintenance training program for the particular aircraft.

Preventive maintenance is limited to the following work, provided it does not involve complex assembly operations:

Removal, installation, and repair of landing gear tires

Replacing elastic shock absorber cords on landing gear

Servicing landing gear shock struts by adding oil, air, or both

Servicing landing gear wheel bearings such as cleaning and greasing

Replacing defective safety wiring or cotter keys

Lubrication not requiring disassembly other than removal of nonstructural items such as cover plates cowlings, and fairings

Making simple fabric patches not requiring rib stitching or the removal of structural parts or control surfaces.

In the case of balloons, the making of small fabric repairs to envelopes (as defined in, and in accordance with, the balloon manufacturer's instructions) not requiring load tape repair or replacement

Replenishing hydraulic fluid in the hydraulic reservoir

Refinishing decorative coating of fuselage, balloon baskets, wings, tail group surfaces (excluding balanced control surfaces), fairings, cowlings, landing gear, cabin, or cockpit interior when removal or disassembly of any primary structure or operating system is not required

Applying preservative or protective material to components where no disassembly of any primary structure or operating system is involved and where such coating is not prohibited or is not contrary to good practices

Repairing upholstery and decorative furnishings of the cabin, cockpit, or balloon basket interior when the repairing does not require disassembly of any primary structure or operating system or affect the primary structure of the aircraft

Making small simple repairs to fairings, nonstructural cover plates, cowlings, and small patches and reinforcements not changing the contour so as to interfere with proper air flow

Replacing side windows where that work does not interfere with the structure or any operating system such as controls, electrical equipment, etc.

Replacing safety belts

Replacing seats or seat parts with replacement parts approved for the aircraft, not involving disassembly of any primary structure or operating system.

Troubleshooting and repairing broken circuits in landing light wiring circuits

Replacing bulbs, reflectors, and lenses of position and landing lights.

Replacing wheels and skis where no weight and balance computation is involved

Replacing any cowling not requiring removal of the propeller or disconnection of flight controls

Replacing or cleaning spark plugs and setting of spark plug gap clearance

Replacing any hose connection except hydraulic connections

Replacing prefabricated fuel lines

Cleaning or replacing fuel and oil strainers or filter elements

Replacing and servicing batteries

Cleaning of balloon burner pilot and main nozzles in accordance with the balloon manufacturer's instructions.

Replacement or adjustment of nonstructural standard fasteners incidental to operations

The interchange of balloon baskets and burners on envelopes when the basket or burner is designated as inter changeable in the balloon type certificate data and the baskets and burners are specifically designed for quick removal and installation

The installation of anti-misfueling devices to reduce the diameter of fuel tank filler openings, provided the specific device has been made part of the aircraft type certificate data by the aircraft manufacturer, the aircraft manufacturer has provided FAA-approved instructions for installation of the specific device, and installation does not involve the disassembly of the existing tank filler opening

Removing, checking, and replacing magnetic chip detectors

Figure 12-12. *Examples of preventive maintenance*

Answers are on Page 706. **Page numbers refer to chapter text.**

1. Two conditions that require a special inspection of an airframe are:

   a. _____

   b. _____

   Page 690

2. A person authorized to conduct an annual inspection must hold a/an

   _____ . *Page 681*

3. The required scope and detail of items required for an annual and 100-hour inspection is found in Appendix D of 14 CFR Part _____ . *Page 682*

4. The use of a checklist _____ (is or is not) required when performing an annual or 100-hour inspection. *Page 682*

5. A private airplane that is not operated for hire _____ (is or is not) required to be given 100-hour inspections. *Page 681*

6. Before an aircraft can be started on a progressive inspection schedule, it must be given a complete _____ inspection. *Page 689*

7. An aircraft fails an annual inspection because of a discrepancy that requires a minor airframe repair. The certificated technician performing the repair and approving the aircraft for return to service _____ (does or does not) have to hold an Inspection Authorization. *Page 688*

8. The person responsible for making the entry in the maintenance records of an aircraft after an annual, 100-hour, or progressive inspection is the person who _____ . *Page 688*

9. If an annual or 100-hour inspection reveals a defect that causes an aircraft to be unairworthy, the person disapproving it must furnish the owner with a/an _____ . *Page 688*

10. An aircraft was not approved for return to service after an annual inspection. In order for the owner to fly the aircraft to another maintenance base, he or she must obtain a/an _____ . *Page 688*

11. Altimeters used in controlled airspace under IFR flight must be inspected every
_____ calendar months. *Page 690*

12. ATC transponders must be inspected every _____ calendar months. *Page 690*

13. Recovering a control surface with a different but approved fabric is considered to be a
_____ . *Page 693*

14. An operation to an aircraft structure that restores the structure to a condition for safe operation after it has
become deteriorated or has been damaged is called a/an _____. *Page 690*

15. Identify each of these operations as a major or minor repair:
    a. Replacing an aileron with an identical new aileron from the aircraft manufacturer _____
    b. Strengthening a wing spar by riveting on a reinforcement _____
    c. Major overhaul of a pressure carburetor _____
    d. Major overhaul of a direct-drive, normally aspirated engine _____
       Pages 691 – 692

16. The classifications of items that constitute major and minor repairs and major and minor alterations are
found in 14 CFR Part _____ , Appendix _____ . *Page 690*

17. Replacing a seat belt with an identical seat belt from the aircraft manufacturer is considered to be
_____ . *Page 695*

18. Replacing the fabric on a fabric-covered control surface is considered to be a
_____ (major or minor) repair. *Page 691*

19. Replacing a bolted-on engine mount with an identical new one from the aircraft manufacturer is considered
to be a _____ (major or minor) repair. *Page 691*

20. Installing a piece of equipment that is approved for installation on the aircraft is considered to be a
_____ (major or minor) alteration. *Page 693*

21. Replacement of an engine with a different type engine that increases the maximum certificated weight of
an aircraft is considered to be a _____ (major or minor) alteration. *Page 693*

22. Servicing a landing gear shock strut with air is considered to be _____ .
Page 695

Classification of Maintenance Airmen

Aviation maintenance personnel are certificated by the FAA under the provisions of 14 CFR Part 65, *Certification: Airmen Other Than Flight Crewmembers*. There are two types of certificates issued, mechanic and repairman. The mechanic certificate has two ratings, airframe and powerplant, and an experienced holder of a mechanic certificate with both of these ratings may apply for an inspection authorization. There are two types of repairman certificate, the regular repairman certificate and a special repairman certificate (experimental aircraft builder).

Mechanic

There has been a great deal of discussion over the past decade about changing the title of an aircraft mechanic to an aviation maintenance technician (AMT). The aviation maintenance industry has pretty well accepted the change of title from mechanic to technician or AMT, and in ASA's *Aviation Maintenance Technician Series* we often use "technician" or "AMT" as a synonym for "mechanic."

Requirements for Certification

The requirements for a Mechanic Certificate are listed in 14 CFR Part 65, *Certification: Airmen Other Than Flight Crewmembers*. Basically, these requirements are:

- Be at least 18 years of age.

- Be able to read, write, speak and understand the English language. In the case of an applicant who does not meet this requirement and who is employed outside of the United States by a U.S. air carrier, he or she may have the certificate endorsed "Valid only outside the United States."

- Have passed all of the prescribed tests within a period of 24 months.

- Pass a written test covering the construction and maintenance of aircraft appropriate to the rating for which he or she seeks, the regulations in 14 CFR Parts 65, 43, and 91, and the basic principles covering the installation and maintenance of propellers for the powerplant test.

- Demonstrate the practical skill requirements by passing appropriate oral and practical tests.

- Have at least 18 months of practical experience in the procedures, practices, materials, tools, machine tools, and equipment generally used in constructing, maintaining, or altering airframes or powerplants appropriate to the rating sought. Or have at least 30 months of practical experience concurrently performing the duties appropriate to both the Airframe and Powerplant ratings.

A Certificate of Completion from an Aviation Maintenance Technician School approved under 14 CFR Part 147 satisfies the practical experience requirements for technician certification.

A Mechanic Certificate is effective until it is surrendered, suspended, or revoked. However, a certificated mechanic may not exercise the privileges of the certificate and rating unless, within the preceding 24 months, he or she has for at least 6 months served as a mechanic under the certificate and rating, technically supervised other mechanics, or has supervised in an executive capacity the maintenance and alteration of aircraft.

Privileges and Limitations of a Mechanic

A certificated mechanic may perform or supervise maintenance, preventive maintenance, or alteration of an aircraft or appliance, or a part thereof for which he or she is rated. This excludes, however, major repairs to and major alterations to propellers and any repair to or alteration of instruments.

A mechanic may not supervise the maintenance, preventive maintenance, or alteration of, or approve for return to service, any aircraft or appliance or part for which he or she is rated unless the work concerned has been satisfactorily performed at an earlier date. A mechanic may show the ability to do the work by performing it to the satisfaction of an FAA inspector, or under the direct supervision of a certificated and appropriately rated mechanic or a certificated repairman who has had previous experience in this specific operation.

A mechanic may not exercise the privileges of the certificate and rating unless he or she understands the current instructions issued by the manufacturer in the maintenance manuals for the specific operation concerned. And, it is the responsibility of the mechanic performing the maintenance to be sure that the materials used in the repair conform to the appropriate standards.

A certificated mechanic holding both Airframe and Powerplant ratings can perform a 100-hour inspection and approve the aircraft for return to service. In order to exercise this privilege, the mechanic must be current, must have the necessary experience, and must have all of the required equipment and technical data needed for the inspection.

A certificated mechanic can also approve an aircraft for return to service after the completion of a minor repair or minor alteration for which he or she is appropriately rated.

An Airframe rating is required for a mechanic to work on the rotors of a certificated helicopter, and a Powerplant rating is required to perform inspections and minor repairs and minor alterations to propellers.

A certificated mechanic may perform inspections on the appropriate instruments, but a Mechanic Certificate does not authorize either minor or major repairs or alterations to aircraft instruments. All repairs and alterations to instruments must be performed by a certificated repair station approved for the particular operation.

Inspection Authorization

An Inspection Authorization (IA) is not a rating attached to the mechanic certificate, but is a special authorization that may be held by an experienced mechanic who meets all of the requirements for its issuance.

Requirements for IA Certification and Renewal

To be eligible for an Inspection Authorization a person must:

- Hold a currently effective Mechanic Certificate with Airframe and Powerplant ratings. Each rating must have been in effect for at least 3 years.

- Have been actively engaged for at least the past 2 years in maintaining certificated aircraft.

- Have a fixed base of operation at which he may be located in person during a normal working week.

- Have available to him the equipment, facilities, and inspection data necessary to properly inspect airframes, powerplants, propellers, or any related appliance.

- Pass a written test on his ability to inspect according to safety standards for returning aircraft to service after major repairs and major alterations and annual and progressive inspections.

An Inspection Authorization expires on March 31 of each year, and to be eligible for renewal, the applicant must have:

- Performed at least 1 annual inspection for each 90 days he or she has held the IA, or

- Performed at least 2 major repairs or major alterations, for each 90 days he or she has held the IA, or

- Performed or supervised and approved at least one progressive inspection, or

- Attended and successfully completed a refresher course acceptable to the Administrator of not less than 8 hours of instruction during the 12-month period preceding the application for renewal, or

- Passed an oral test by an FAA inspector to determine that the applicant's knowledge of applicable regulations and standards is current.

Privileges and Limitations of a Mechanic with an Inspection Authorization

A mechanic who holds an IA can exercise all of the privileges of a mechanic with both Airframe and Powerplant ratings. In addition he or she can inspect and approve for return to service an aircraft or related part after a major repair or major alteration if the work has been done in accordance with technical data approved by the Administrator. He or she can also perform an annual inspection and approve the aircraft for return to service and can supervise a progressive inspection.

The holder of an IA shall keep the authorization available for inspection by the aircraft owner, the mechanic who has submitted the repair or alteration for approval, and for any representative of the FAA, the NTSB, or any federal, state, or local law enforcement officer. When the holder of an IA changes his fixed base of operation, he must notify, in writing, the FSDO for the area in which the new base is operated.

Repairmen

Rather than having a proliferation of ratings for specialized areas of maintenance tied to the mechanic's certificate, the FAA has a Repairman Certificate that recognizes specialization. For example, a person who is highly skilled in overhauling turbine engine fuel controls does not need the diversity of knowledge and experience required for a Mechanic Certificate in order to be certificated by the FAA.

A Repairman Certificate can be issued to a person who meets these basic requirements:

- Be at least 18 years of age.

- Be specially qualified to perform the maintenance appropriate to the job for which he or she is employed.

- Be employed by a Certificated Repair Station, a Certificated Commercial Operator, or a Certificated Air Carrier to perform the job for which he or she is qualified.

- Be recommended for certification by his or her employer and approved by the FAA.

- Has had at least 18 months of practical experience in the procedure, practices, inspection methods, materials, tools, machine tools, and equipment generally used in the maintenance duties of the specific job for which the person is to be employed and certificated; or has completed formal training that is acceptable to the Administrator and is specifically designed to qualify the applicant for the job for which he or she is to be employed.

- Be able to read, write, speak, and understand the English language.

The basic limitations to the Repairman Certificate are that it is valid only for performing the operations specified in the certification and only for so long as the repairman is employed by the certificate holder that recommended him or her for certification.

There is another type of Repairman Certificate, this one for the builders of experimental aircraft. To qualify for this certificate, a person must:

- Be at least 18 years of age.
- Be the primary builder of the aircraft to which the privileges of the certificate are applicable.
- Show to the satisfaction of the Administrator that he or she has the requisite skill to determine whether the aircraft is in a condition for safe operation.
- Be a citizen of the United States or an individual citizen of a foreign country who has lawfully been admitted for permanent residence in the United States.

The Repairman Certificate (experimental aircraft builder) is valid only for condition inspections and work on the aircraft constructed by the holder of the certificate and in accordance with the operating limitations of that aircraft.

Answers are on Page 706. Page numbers refer to chapter text.

23. A certificated Airframe and Powerplant mechanic is authorized to approve an aircraft for return to service after a/an _____ (100-hour or annual) inspection. *Page 699*

24. A certified mechanic holding a Powerplant rating _____ (is or is not) authorized to perform a 100-hour inspection on a powerplant or propeller or any component thereof and approve the same for return to service. *Page 700*

25. In order for a certificated Airframe and Powerplant mechanic to be authorized to approve an aircraft for return to service after an annual inspection, he or she must hold a/an _____ . *Page 701*

26. A certificated mechanic operating under his or her general certificate privileges _____ (is or is not) authorized to perform minor repairs to an aircraft instrument. *Page 700*

27. A certificated mechanic with a Powerplant rating operating under his or her general certificate privileges _____ (is or is not) authorized to perform minor repairs to an aircraft propeller. *Page 700*

28. A certificated mechanic with a Powerplant rating _____ (is or is not) authorized to perform the work called for in an Airworthiness Directive on a propeller that requires a minor alteration to the propeller. *Page 700*

29. Major and minor repairs to an aircraft instrument must be performed by a certificated _____ . *Page 700*

30. In order for a certificated mechanic to work on a helicopter rotor, he or she must hold a/an _____ rating. *Page 700*

31. In order for a certificated mechanic to perform a minor repair to a propeller, he or she must hold a/an _____ rating. *Page 700*

32. In order for a certificated airframe and powerplant mechanic to be authorized to approve an aircraft for return to service after a major repair, he or she must hold a/an _____ . *Page 701*

Continued

33. The requirements for certification as a mechanic are covered in 14 CFR Part _____ .
    Page 698

34. A certificated mechanic shall not exercise the privileges of the certificate and rating unless, within the preceding 24 months, the Administrator has found that the certificate holder is able to do the work, or the certificate holder has served as a mechanic of the certificate and rating for at least _____ months. *Page 699*

35. The person performing a repair on a certificated aircraft and approving it for return to service is responsible for making sure that all of the material used conforms to the appropriate standards. This is a _____ (true or false) statement. *Page 699*

Answers to Chapter 12 Study Questions

1. a. overweight landing
   b. flight into severe turbulence
2. Inspection Authorization
3. 43
4. is
5. is not
6. annual
7. does not
8. approves the aircraft for return to service
9. list of discrepancies
10. ferry permit
11. 24
12. 24

13. major alteration
14. repair
15. minor
16. a. minor
    b. major
    c. major
    d. minor
17. preventive maintenance
18. major
19. minor
20. minor
21. major
22. preventive maintenance
23. 100-hour

24. is
25. Inspection Authorization
26. is not
27. is
28. is
29. repair station
30. Airframe
31. Powerplant
32. Inspection Authorization
33. 65
34. 6
35. true

Maintenance Forms and Records

13

Maintenance Forms and Records

13

Maintenance and Inspection Records

Proper maintenance depends upon a good recordkeeping system. The resale value of an aircraft may vary significantly, depending on the adequacy and organization of the maintenance records. Well-kept records which properly document all maintenance and inspections eliminate the need for reinspection and/or rework to establish airworthiness.

Only that information required to be a part of the maintenance record, however, should be included, as voluminous and irrelevant entries reduce the value of the records.

The FAA places the ultimate responsibility for proper maintenance records on the owner or operator of the aircraft, but it is the responsibility of the maintenance technician to make the proper entries in these maintenance records.

Today the record keeping aspect of aviation maintenance is more important than ever. When we conduct an inspection or make a repair or alteration, we are required to make an entry of the work done in the aircraft maintenance records. This is fine, because it helps the technician performing later work on the aircraft know exactly what was done and when. But there is another, even more important, reason for making accurate record entries and keeping our own copies of these records. We may have to defend a record entry in a court of law.

Required Maintenance Records

14 CFR § 91.417 requires each registered owner or operator of an aircraft to keep two types of records: temporary and permanent.

Temporary records as described in 14 CFR § 91.417(a)(1) must include these items:

- Records of maintenance performed
- Records of preventive maintenance performed
- Records of alterations made
- Records of 100-hour, annual, progressive and other required or approved inspections

14 CFR § 91.417: Maintenance records

(a) Except for work performed in accordance with §§91.411 and 91.413, each registered owner or operator shall keep the following records for the periods specified in paragraph (b) of this section:

(1) Records of the maintenance, preventive maintenance, and alteration and records of the 100-hour, annual, progressive, and other required or approved inspections, as appropriate, for each aircraft (including the airframe) and each engine, propeller, rotor, and appliance of an aircraft. The records must include—

(i) A description (or reference to data acceptable to the Administrator) of the work performed; and

(ii) The date of completion of the work performed; and

(iii) The signature, and certificate number of the person approving the aircraft for return to service.

(2) Records containing the following information:

(i) The total time in service of the airframe, each engine, each propeller, and each rotor.

(ii) The current status of life-limited parts of each airframe, engine, propeller, rotor, and appliance.

(iii) The time since last overhaul of all items installed on the aircraft which are required to be overhauled on a specified time basis.

(iv) The current inspection status of the aircraft, including the time since the last inspection required by the inspection program under which the aircraft and its appliances are maintained.

(v) The current status of applicable airworthiness directives (AD) including, for each, the method of compliance, the AD number, and revision date. If the AD involves recurring action, the time and date when the next action is required.

(vi) Copies of the forms prescribed by § 43.9(a) of this chapter for each major alteration to the airframe and currently installed engines, rotors, propellers, and appliances.

(b) The owner or operator shall retain the following records for the periods prescribed:

(1) The records specified in paragraph (a)(1) of this section shall be retained until the work is repeated or superseded by other work or for 1 year after the work is performed.

(2) The records specified in paragraph (a)(2) of this section shall be retained and transferred with the aircraft at the time the aircraft is sold.

(3) A list of defects furnished to a registered owner or operator under §43.11 of this chapter shall be retained until the defects are repaired and the aircraft is approved for return to service.

These records must include at least this information:

- A description of the work performed or reference to data that is acceptable to the Administrator
- The date of completion of the work
- The signature and certificate number of the person approving the aircraft for return to service

The records must be retained until the work is repeated or superseded by other work or for one year after the work is performed. An exception to this is that the records of the required inspections for altimeters and ATC transponders must be retained until the inspection is repeated or for two years.

When a list of defects is furnished to the registered owner of an aircraft listing unairworthy conditions that prevented the aircraft passing a required inspection, this list shall be retained until the defects are repaired and the aircraft is approve for return to service.

Permanent records, as described in 14 CFR § 91.417(a)(2), must contain the items listed here, and they must be retained and transferred with the aircraft when it is sold:

- The total time in service of the airframe, engines, propellers, and rotors.

- The current status of all life-limited parts.

- The time since last overhaul of all items installed on the aircraft which are required to be overhauled on a specified time basis.

- The current inspection status of the aircraft, including the time since the last required inspection.

- The current status of applicable Airworthiness Directives including the AD number and revision date and the method of compliance. If the AD involves recurring action, the time and date when the next action is required.

- Copies of the Form 337 for each major alteration to the airframe and currently installed engines, rotors, propellers, and appliances.

Figure 13-1 shows a typical AD compliance record sheet. It is a good idea to keep a separate record for each airframe, engine, propeller, rotor, and appliance, as it facilitates record searches and allows the record to be transferred with the item if it is removed from the aircraft.

Maintenance Record Entries

Maintenance technicians are required to make two kinds of record entries, those for maintenance and those for inspections. These record entries are described in 14 CFR §§ 43.9 and 43.11.

AIRWORTHINESS DIRECTIVE COMPLIANCE RECORD N _____												
AIRCRAFT, ENGINE, PROPELLER, ROTOR, OR APPLIANCE												
MAKE _____ MODEL _____ SERIAL NUMBER_____												
AD Number and Amendment Number	Date Received	Subject	Compliance Due Date Hours/ Other	Method of Compliance	Date of Compliance	Airframe Total Time In Service at Compliance	Component Total Time In Service at Compliance	One Time	Recur-ring	Next Compliance Due Date Hours/ Other	Authorized Signature, Certificate Type and Number	Remarks

Figure 13-1. *Typical Airworthiness Directive Compliance record. It is a good idea to have a page for each category.*

Maintenance Entries

14 CFR § 43.9(a) requires that each maintenance record entry contain the following information:

- A description (or reference to data acceptable to the Administrator) of the work performed.

- The date of completion of the work performed.

- The name of the person performing the work if other than the person approving the work.

- If the work has been performed satisfactorily, the signature, certificate number, and kind of certificate held by the person approving the work. The signature constitutes the approval for return to service only for the work described in this record entry.

The time in service is not required for this type of record entry as it is for an inspection record entry, but it is good practice to include the time in service on all entries.

14 CFR § 43.13 requires that each person performing maintenance, alteration, or preventive maintenance on an aircraft, engine, propeller, or appliance shall use the methods, techniques, and practices prescribed in the current manufacturer's maintenance manual or Instructions for Continued Airworthiness prepared by its manufacturer, or other methods, techniques, and practices acceptable to the Administrator. He shall use the tools, equipment, and test apparatus necessary to assure completion of the work in accordance with accepted industry practices. If special equipment or test apparatus is recommended by the manufacturer involved, he must use that equipment or apparatus or its equivalent acceptable to the administrator. The work shall be

---

14 CFR § 43.9 Content, form, and disposition of maintenance, preventive maintenance, rebuilding, and alteration records (except inspections performed in accordance with Part 91, Part 123, Part 125, §135.411(a)(1), and §135.419 of this chapter).

(a) *Maintenance record entries.* Except as provided in paragraphs (b) and (c) of this section, each person who maintains, performs preventive maintenance, rebuilds, or alters an aircraft, airframe, aircraft engine, propeller, appliance, or component part shall make an entry in the maintenance record of that equipment containing the following information:

(1) A description (or reference to data acceptable to the Administrator) of work performed.
(2) The date of completion of the work performed.
(3) The name of the person performing the work if other than the person specified in paragraph (a)(4) of this section.

(4) If the work performed on the aircraft, airframe, aircraft engine, propeller, appliance, or component part has been performed satisfactorily, the signature, certificate number, and kind of certificate held by the person approving the work. The signature constitutes the approval for return to service only for the work performed.
In addition to the entry required by this paragraph, major repairs and major alterations shall be entered on a form, and the form disposed of, in the manner prescribed in Appendix B, by the person performing the work.

done in such a manner and the materials used shall be of such a quality that the condition of the aircraft, airframe, aircraft engine, propeller, or appliance worked on will be at least equal to its original or properly altered condition (with regard to aerodynamic function, structural strength, resistance to vibration and deterioration, and other qualities affecting airworthiness).

If the maintenance performed could have appreciably changed the flight characteristics, or substantially affected the operation of the aircraft in flight, the aircraft must be flight tested by an appropriately rated pilot holding at least a private pilot certificate. This pilot must make an operational check of the maintenance performed or alteration made and the flight must be recorded in the aircraft records.

In the description of the work done, reference the data used for authorization. This data, for all maintenance other than major repairs and major alterations, must be acceptable data, which is that information included in manufacturer's maintenance manuals, service bulletins and letters, and AC 43.13-1B and -2A. For major repairs and major alterations, use approved data, and this is found in such documents as the appropriate Type Certificate Data Sheets, Specification Sheets, Supplemental Type Certificates, and Airworthiness Directives.

Technicians are required when performing an inspection to use a checklist. While not specifically required for other forms of maintenance, it is an excellent idea to follow a checklist and keep it with the maintenance records. This checklist documents exactly what was done.

When parts are replaced, it is the responsibility of the technician approving the aircraft for return to service to be sure that only approved parts are used. Any new parts should be purchased from the original equipment manufacturer (OEM) or manufactured under a parts manufacturer approval (PMA) and have the correct part number.

If an overhauled component is installed, it should have a properly completed copy of an FAA Form 337, *Major Repair and Alteration Airframe, Powerplant, Propeller, or Appliance.* If it was overhauled by an approved Repair Station, it should have a copy of a signed and dated work order and a maintenance release. The work order should give a description of the work done, the service bulletins and ADs complied with, and the approved data used. The maintenance release should have a statement similar to this:

The aircraft, airframe, aircraft engine, propeller, or appliance identified above was repaired and inspected in accordance with the current regulations of the Federal Aviation Administration and is approved for return to service. Pertinent details of the repair are on file at this repair station under: Order No. _____ Date _____.

Signed _____ (authorized representative for the repair station).

Repair station address and certificate number _____.

When a technician performs a maintenance operation, such as a repair or alteration, and makes the proper entry in the aircraft maintenance records, his or her signature is the authorization for return of the product to service. This record entry, in essence, states that the aircraft is airworthy as of this moment, and the technician is accepting the responsibility only for the airworthiness of the operation described. The technician is responsible for that maintenance until the part is again worked on, replaced, damaged, or has exceeded its life limit, or until the next required inspection in which an airworthiness determination is made.

Inspection Entries

Even though 14 CFR Part 1 includes inspection as a part of maintenance, it is handled differently as far as record keeping is involved. 14 CFR § 43.11(a) gives the requirements for the record entries to be made for inspections. These records require the following information:

- The type of inspection and a brief description of its extent

- The date of the inspection, and aircraft total time in service

- The signature, certificate number, and kind of certificate held by the person approving or disapproving the device for return to service

- Except for progressive inspections, if the aircraft is approved for return to service, a statement such as — "I certify that this aircraft has been inspected in accordance with a 100-hour inspection and was determined to be in airworthy condition."

- Except for progressive inspections, if the aircraft is not approved for return to service, a statement such as — "I certify that this aircraft has been inspected in accordance with a 100-hour inspection, and a list of discrepancies and unairworthy items dated June 7, 2000 has been provided for the aircraft owner or operator."

- For progressive inspections, a statement such as — "I certify that in accordance with a progressive inspection program, a routine inspection of the fuselage and a detailed inspection of the landing gear were performed and the aircraft is approved for return to service." If the aircraft was disapproved, the entry must also include a statement such as "and a list of discrepancies and unairworthy items dated June 7, 2000 has been provided to the aircraft owner or operator."

14 CFR § 43.11 Content, form, and disposition of records for inspections conducted under Parts 91 and 125 and §§135.411(a)(1) and 135.419 of this chapter.

(a) *Maintenance record entries.* The person approving or disapproving for return to service an aircraft, airframe, aircraft engine, propeller, appliance, or component part after any inspection performed in accordance with Part 91, 123, 125, §135.411(a)(1), or §135.419 shall make an entry in the maintenance record of that equipment containing the following information:

(1) The type of inspection and a brief description of the extent of the inspection.

(2) The date of the inspection and aircraft total time in service.

(3) The signature, the certificate number, and kind of certificate held by the person approving or disapproving for return to service the aircraft, airframe, aircraft engine, propeller, appliance, component part, or portions thereof.

(4) Except for progressive inspections, if the aircraft is found to be airworthy and approved for return to service, the following or a similarly worded statement—"I certify that this aircraft has been inspected in accordance with (insert type) inspection and was determined to be in airworthy condition."

(5) Except for progressive inspections, if the aircraft is not approved for return to service because of needed maintenance, noncompliance with applicable specifications, airworthiness directives, or other approved data, the following or a similarly worded statement—"I certify that this aircraft has been inspected in accordance with (insert type) inspection and a list of discrepancies and unairworthy items dated (date) has been provided for the aircraft owner or operator."

(6) For progressive inspections, the following or a similarly worded statement—"I certify that in accordance with a progressive inspection program, a routine inspection of (identify whether aircraft or components) and a detailed inspection of (identify components) were performed and the (aircraft or components) are (approved or disapproved) for return to service." If disapproved, the entry will further state "and a list of discrepancies and unairworthy items dated (date) has been provided to the aircraft owner or operator."

(7) If an inspection is conducted under an inspection program provided for in Part 91, 123, 125, or §135.411(a)(1), the entry must identify the inspection program, that part of the inspection program accomplished, and contain a statement that the inspection was performed in accordance with the inspections and procedures for that particular program.

An annual inspection approves the entire aircraft for return to service, and since there are no "Aircraft" maintenance records, the record of an annual inspection is only required to be entered in the airframe maintenance record or logbook, while other inspections should have separate entries made in the airframe, engine, propeller and appliance logbooks. For practical purposes, however, records of all inspections can be made in each of the individual logbooks to facilitate transfer of the record with each item when ownership changes.

A typical maintenance record entry specified in 14 CFR § 43.11(a)(4) for an annual inspection is shown in Figure 13-2.

```
Date: _____

Aircraft time in service _____ hours

I certify that this aircraft has been inspected in accordance with a/an
_____ (annual or 100-hour) inspection and
was determined to be in an airworthy condition.
     The records of this inspection are contained in Work Order No. 3428.


_____ (signature)
A&P 691916 IA
```

Figure 13-2. *Maintenance record for an aircraft that has passed an annual or 100-hour inspection*

If the aircraft did not pass the inspection, a record should be made in the maintenance record similar to that in Figure 13-3.

```
Date: _____

Aircraft time in service _____ hours

I certify that this aircraft has been inspected in accordance with a/an
_____ (annual or 100-hour) inspection and a list
of the discrepancies and unairworthy items dated _____
has been provided for the aircraft owner or operator.
     The records of this inspection are contained in Work Order No. 3428.

_____ (signature)
A&P 691916 IA
```

Figure 13-3. *Maintenance record for an aircraft that has not passed an annual or 100-hour inspection*

Answers are on Page 723. Page numbers refer to chapter text.

1. The record of a 100-hour inspection must be kept for _____ or until the next 100-hour inspection is performed. *Page 710*

2. The proper write-up to use in recording a 100-hour inspection in the aircraft records is found in 14 CFR Part _____ . *Page 710*

3. The person responsible for maintaining the required maintenance records for an aircraft is the _____ . *Page 709*

4. A pilot authorized to conduct a flight test after maintenance must hold at least a _____ pilot certificate. *Page 713*

Maintenance Forms

Major Repair and Alteration FAA Form 337

An FAA Form 337 must be completed for each major repair and major alteration performed on a certificated airframe, engine, or propeller.

At least two copies of the Form 337 must be made. The original goes to the aircraft owner to be kept with the aircraft maintenance records, and the duplicate is forwarded to the FAA FSDO within 48 hours after the aircraft is approved for return to service. It is a good policy for the technician who executed the Form 337 to keep a copy in his or her own records.

Refer to Figure 13-4. Examine each of the numbered items to see the correct information to be placed in these blocks:

Item 1—This is the make, model and serial number found on the aircraft manufacturer's identification plate. The Nationality and Registration mark is the same as shown on the Certificate of Aircraft Registration, Form 8050-3, that must be in the aircraft.

Item 2—This is the name and address of the aircraft owner, and it must be the same as that shown on Form 8050-3.

NOTE: When a major repair or major alteration is made to a spare part or appliance, items 1 and 2 are left blank, and the original and duplicate of the form remain with the part until such time as it is installed on an aircraft. The person installing the part will then enter the required information in blocks 1 and 2, give the original form to the aircraft owner or operator, and forward the duplicate copy to the local FAA district office within 48 hours after the work is inspected.

<table>
<tr><td colspan="3">

US. Department
of Transportation

Federal Aviation
Administration

</td><td colspan="2">

MAJOR REPAIR AND ALTERATION
(Airframe, Powerplant, Propeller, or Appliance)

</td><td colspan="2">

Form Approved
OMB No. 2120-0020

For FAA Use Only

Office Identification

</td></tr>
</table>

INSTRUCTIONS: Print or type all entries. See FAR 43.9, FAR 43 Appendix B, and AC 43.9-1 (or subsequent revision thereof) for instructions and disposition of this form. This report is required by law (49 U.S.C. 1421). Failure to report can result in a civil penalty not to exceed $1,000 for each such violation (Section 901 Federal Aviation Act of 1958).

1. Aircraft	Make	Cessna	Model	182
	Serial No. 15-10521		Nationality and Registration Mark	N-3763

2. Owner	Name *(As shown on registration certificate)* William Taylor	Address *(As shown on registration certificate)* 36 Main Street Cambria, Pennsylvania 15946

3. For FAA Use Only

The data identified herein complies with the applicable airworthiness requirements and is approved for the above described aircraft, subject to conformity inspection by a person authorized by FAR Part 43, Section 43 ~~Ralph Burlingame~~

AEA-GADO-19   April 5, 1986   Ralph Burlingame

District Office   Date   Signature of FAA Inspector

4. Unit Identification / **5. Type**

Unit	Make	Model	Serial No.	Repair	Alteration
AIRFRAME	～～～～～～ *(As described in Item 1 above)* ～～～～～～			X	
POWERPLANT					
PROPELLER					
APPLIANCE	Type Manufacturer				

6. Conformity Statement

A. Agency's Name and Address	B. Kind of Agency		C. Certificate No.
George Morris High Street Johnstown, Pennsylvania 15236	X	U.S. Certificated Mechanic	1305888
		Foreign Certificated Mechanic	
		Certificated Repair Station	
		Manufacturer	

D. I certify that the repair and/or alteration made to the unit(s) identified in item 4 above and described on the reverse or attachments hereto have been made in accordance with the requirements of Part 43 of the U.S. Federal Aviation Regulations and that the information furnished herein is true and correct to the best of my knowledge.

Date March 19, 1987	Signature of Authorized Individual George Morris

7. Approval for Return To Service

Pursuant to the authority given persons specified below, the unit identified in item 4 was inspected in the manner prescribed by the Administrator of the Federal Aviation Administration and is   ☒ APPROVED   ☐ REJECTED

BY	FAA Flt. Standards Inspector	Manufacturer	X	Inspection Authorization	Other *(Specify)*
	FAA Designee	Repair Station		Person Approved by Transport Canada Airworthiness Group	
Date of Approval or Rejection April 9, 1987	Certificate or Designation No. 237412		Signature of Authorized Individual Donald Pauley		

FAA Form 337 (4-87)

Figure 13-4 (a). An FAA Form 337 must be completed for each major repair or major alteration performed on a certificated airframe, engine, or propeller.

NOTICE

Weight and balance or operating limitation changes shall be entered in the appropriate aircraft record. An alteration must be compatible with all previous alterations to assure continued conformity with the applicable airworthiness requirements.

Description of Work Accomplished
(If more space is required, attach additional sheets. Identify with aircraft nationality and registration mark and date work completed.)

1. Removed right wing from aircraft and removed skin from outer 6 feet. Repaired buckled spar 49 inches from tip in accordance with attached photographs and figure 1 of drawing dated March 6, 1987.

   DATE: March 15, 1987, inspected splice in Item 1 and found it to be in accordance with data indicated. Splice is okay to cover. Inspected internal and external wing assembly for hidden damage and condition.

   Donald Pauley

   Donald Pauley, A&P 237412 IA

2. Primed interior wing structure and replaced skin P/Ns 63-0085, 63-0086, and 63-00878 with same material, 2024-T3, .025 inches thick. Rivet size and spacing all the same as original and using procedures in Chapter 2, Section 3, of AC 43.13-1A, dated 1972.

3. Replaced stringers as required and installed 6 splices as per attached drawing and photographs.

4. Installed wing, rigged aileron, and operationally checked in accordance with manufacturer's maintenance manual.

5. No change in weight or balance.

   END

☐ Additional Sheets Are Attached

Figure 13-4 (b)

Item 3 — In this block, the FAA states that the data submitted complies with the applicable airworthiness requirements and is acceptable for the repair or alteration for this aircraft. The work can be approved if it is done in conformity with this data.

NOTE: If the data used for the repair or alteration has not been previously approved by the FAA, it should be sent to the FAA FSDO along with both copies of the Form 337. If the FAA determines that the data complies with applicable regulations and is in conformity with accepted industry practices, the data is accepted, and block 3 of both copies are filled in and signed, and both copies and the supporting data are returned to the person performing the repair or alteration.

Item 4 — This block identifies the unit that is repaired or altered.

Item 5 — This block specifies whether the unit was repaired or altered.

Item 6 — This is the conformity statement in which the person performing the work certifies that it has been done in conformity to the approved data.

A — This is the name and address of the mechanic, repair station, or manufacturer that performed the repair or alteration.

B — This identifies the type of agency performing the work.

C — This is the certificate number of the mechanic or the air agency certificate number for the repair station.

D — This is the signature of the mechanic who did the work, and the date the work was completed.

Item 7 — This is the approval or rejection for return to service statement. It indicates whether the work was approved or rejected and includes the type of agency, the certificate number, and the authorized signature along with the date of approval or rejection.

Item 8 — This is the description of work accomplished and takes up the entire back side of the form. If more space is needed for the description, additional sheets may be used. Each additional sheet must be identified with the aircraft N number and the date the work was completed.

This should be a clear, concise, and legible statement of the work accomplished, and should describe the location of the repair or alteration on the aircraft or component.

Records of all major repairs and major alterations are entered in the aircraft maintenance records. These records must contain a description of the work done, the date the work was completed, and the name and certificate number of the person approving the aircraft for return to service. These repairs are referenced to the Form 337 that describes them.

Minor repairs performed on an aircraft must be recorded in the aircraft's permanent records, but no special form is required.

Malfunction or Defect Report

In order to keep track of weaknesses found in certificated airframes, powerplants, and propellers, the FAA requests that any maintenance personnel discovering a malfunction or defect to fill out a Malfunction or Defect Report, FAA Form 8010-4, Figure 13-5, and mail it in to the FAA FSDO office. The FAA enters this information into their computer and observes any trends or abnormal rates of similar occurrences. Airworthiness Alerts and Airworthiness Directives usually come from information sent to the FAA in the form of M or D reports.

Figure 13-5. *Malfunction or Defect Report card*

DEPARTMENT OF TRANSPORTATION
FEDERAL AVIATION ADMINISTRATION

INSPECTION REMINDER

The next inspection of this aircraft is required by Federal Aviation Regulation

Section:_____

Hours in Service: _____

OR

Date due: _____

FAA FORM 8600-1 (4-78)
FORMERLY FAA FORM 8320-2

Figure 13-6. *Inspection Reminder form*

Inspection Reminder

When an inspection is completed, the technician fills out the maintenance record in the airframe and powerplant logbooks and fills out an Inspection Reminder, Figure 13-6, attaching it in a conspicuous location to remind the pilots who fly the aircraft when the next inspection is due. These forms are available at your local FAA FSDO.

STUDY QUESTIONS: MAINTENANCE FORMS

*Answers are on Page 723. **Page numbers refer to chapter text.***

5. When a minor repair is made on a certificated aircraft, a record entry must be made in the aircraft _____ . *Page 720*

6. The record of a major airframe repair must be recorded on a FAA Form _____ .
   Page 720

7. When a major repair or a major alteration has been made to any equipment that requires an FAA Form 337, _____ copies of the form must be prepared. The original of this form goes to the _____ and the copy is sent to the _____ within _____ hours after the work is completed. *Page 720*

Answers to Chapter 13 Study Questions

1. 1 year
2. 43
3. owner
4. private
5. maintenance record
6. 337
7. aircraft owner, FAA, FSDO, 48

TOOLS FOR AIRCRAFT MAINTENANCE

14

TOOLS FOR AIRCRAFT MAINTENANCE

14

Measuring and Layout Tools

Aviation manufacture and maintenance became an exact science rather than an art with the advent of mass production and the requirement for interchangeability of parts. This step increased the importance of accurate measurement.

For many years all dimensions in the United States were noted in such units as inches and fractions, both common and decimal, and in feet, yards, and miles. This system was formerly called the English system, but today is more accurately referred to as the U.S. Customary system, or simply "U.S." The metric system, in which the basic unit of length is the meter, has been legal in the United States since 1866, but it has not been universally accepted except in scientific applications. The U.S. Congress enacted the Metric Conversion Act of 1975 and established the U.S. Metric Board to coordinate the voluntary conversion to the metric system. This transition is gradually taking place, and as we enter the twenty-first century, many technicians have two sets of wrenches and measuring tools—one set in U.S. sizes and one in metric (Figure 14-1).

Steel Rule

One of the most common measuring tools in a technician's toolbox is the six-inch steel rule, or scale. The better rules are made of flexible satin-finish stainless steel and are graduated in $\frac{1}{32}$- and $\frac{1}{64}$-inch increments on one side, and 0.1- and 0.01-inch increments on the other. Metric rules are also available graduated in centimeters and millimeters.

When making a measurement with a steel rule, do not use the end of the rule; rather, for greater accuracy, measure the distance between two marks away from the end (Figure 14-2).

Hook rules are a special type of steel rule that are usually stiff and have a hook on one end accurately aligned with the end of the rule. Hook rules are used to measure from the edge of an object when a radius is involved. (*See* Figure 14-3.)

Combination Set

In addition to the flexible six-inch steel rule, most technicians have a combination set (Figure 14-4) which consists of a 12-inch steel rule with three heads held onto the rule by clamps. One head is the stock head, which converts the rule into a square for measuring 90° and 45° angles. The stock head also has

Fraction		Decimal	MM
1/64		0.0156	0.397
1/32		0.0313	0.794
3/64		0.0469	1.191
	1/16	0.0625	1.588
5/64		0.0781	1.984
3/32		0.0938	2.381
7/64		0.1094	2.778
	1/8	0.125	3.175
9/64		0.1406	3.572
5/32		0.1563	3.969
11/64		0.1719	4.366
	3/16	0.1875	4.762
13/64		0.2031	5.159
7/32		0.2188	5.556
15/64		0.2344	5.953
	1/4	0.250	6.350
17/64		0.2656	6.747
9/32		0.2813	7.144
19/64		0.2969	7.541
	5/16	0.3125	7.937
21/64		0.3281	8.334
11/32		0.3438	8.731
23/64		0.3594	9.128
	3/8	0.3750	9.525
25/64		0.3906	9.922
13/32		0.4063	10.319
27/64		0.4219	10.716
	7/16	0.4375	11.112
29/64		0.4531	11.509
15/32		0.4688	11.906
31/64		0.4844	12.303
	1/2	0.500	12.700
33/64		0.5156	13.097
17/32		0.5313	13.494
35/64		0.5469	13.891
	9/16	0.5625	14.287
37/64		0.5781	14.684
19/32		0.5938	15.081
39/64		0.6094	15.478
	5/8	0.625	15.875
41/64		0.6406	16.272
21/32		0.6563	16.669
43/64		0.6719	17.066
	11/16	0.6875	17.463
45/64		0.7031	17.860
23/32		0.7188	18.256
47/64		0.7344	18.653
	3/4	0.750	19.049
49/64		0.7656	19.447
25/32		0.7813	19.844
51/64		0.7968	20.239
	13/16	0.8125	20.638
53/64		0.8281	21.034
27/32		0.8438	21.431
55/64		0.8594	21.828
	7/8	0.875	22.225
57/64		0.8906	22.622
29/32		0.9063	23.018
59/64		0.9219	23.416
	15/16	0.9375	23.812
61/64		0.9531	24.209
31/32		0.9688	24.606
63/64		0.9844	25.003
	1	1.000	25.400

Figure 14-1. *Fraction, decimal, and metric conversions*

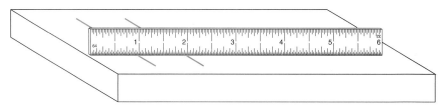

Figure 14-2. *For greater accuracy when using a steel rule, measure between two marks away from the end.*

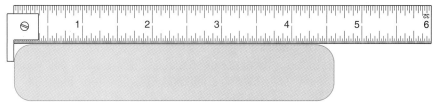

Figure 14-3. *Hook rules are used to measure distances from an edge when a radius is involved.*

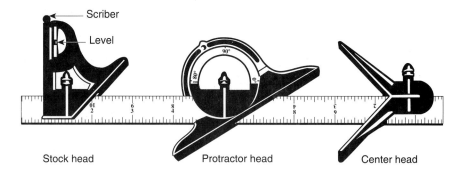

Figure 14-4. *A combination set consists of a 12-inch steel rule with three heads that may be placed anywhere along the rule.*

a bubble level and a scriber. A protractor head can be attached to the rule, and it can be set to measure any angle between the rule and the bottom of the head. The third head is the center head, in which one edge of the rule bisects the two arms of the head that are 90° apart. When the two arms are held against a circular object, the edge of the rule passes across the object's center.

Dividers

Dividers are used to transfer distances from a steel rule to a piece of sheet metal that is being laid out. They are also used for dividing a line into equal increments (*see* Figure 14-5).

Calipers

Calipers resemble dividers except the ends of the legs are rounded rather than pointed, and the ends are bent so they are at right angles to the axis of the legs.

On outside calipers, the ends of the legs are pointed inward so that the outside of an object can be measured. The legs are adjusted with the ends exactly the same distance apart as the outside of the object being measured. The distance between the ends is then measured with a steel rule.

The legs of inside calipers point outward, allowing the inside of an object to be measured. The legs are adjusted so the ends exactly fit into the object being measured, and then the distance between the ends is measured with a steel rule.

Hermaphrodite calipers are a combination of one leg like that of an outside caliper and one like that of dividers. They are used to scribe a line along a piece of material a specific distance from its edge (Figure 14-8).

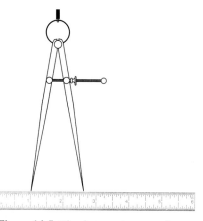

Figure 14-5. *The distance between the points of a divider is measured with a steel rule.*

Figure 14-6. *Outside calipers for measuring the outside of an object—the distance between the tips of the legs is measured with a steel rule.*

Figure 14-7. *Inside calipers for measuring the inside of an object—the distance between the tips of the legs is measured with a steel rule.*

Figure 14-8. *Hermaphrodite calipers are used to scribe a line along an object a specific distance from its edge.*

Scribers

A scriber is a tool with a needle-sharp point used to mark very fine lines on the surface of a piece of metal to be cut. The metal is usually sprayed with a thin coat of layout dye or zinc chromate primer so that the mark made by the scriber will show up clearly. Scribers that have points tipped with tungsten carbide are for use on very hard steel parts. The point of the pocket scriber in Figure 14-9 can be reversed and stored inside the handle to avoid damage in the toolbox.

Figure 14-9. *Use a scriber to mark very fine lines on a piece of metal to be cut.*

Scribers should not be used to mark the bend lines in a piece of aluminum alloy sheet, as this will weaken the metal. In the case of clad aluminum alloy, it will penetrate the protective coating of pure aluminum. A sharp-pointed soft lead pencil should be used in these instances.

Vernier Calipers

Vernier calipers (Figure 14-10) are used to make rapid and accurate inside and outside measurements over a greater range than that of a micrometer caliper. The accuracy of these calipers is based on the vernier principle. Each inch on the main scale is divided into 10 numbered increments that represent $\frac{1}{10}$ inch (0.1 inch). There are 4 spaces between each small number, each representing $\frac{1}{40}$ of an inch or 0.025 inch. One inch on the vernier scale is divided into 25 increments, with each increment representing $\frac{1}{25}$ inch or 0.040 inch. The difference in the space between the marks on the main scale and the marks on the vernier scale is $\frac{1}{25}$ of 0.025 inch, or $\frac{1}{1,000}$ inch (0.001 inch).

vernier principle. The principle by which two scales having different calibrations function together to allow very small measurements to be made.

For example, two calibrated scales are placed side by side. A space on one scale is divided into 10 increments and the same-sized space on the adjacent vernier scale is divided into 11 increments. Only one mark on the main scale lines up with a mark on the vernier scale. When the vernier scale is moved until the next two marks line up, the vernier scale has moved a distance that is equal to the difference between the marks on the two scales.

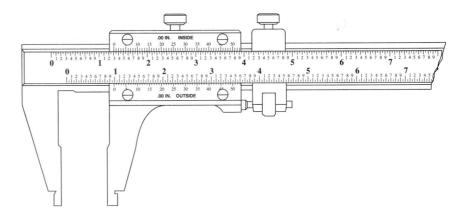

Figure 14-10. *This U.S. vernier caliper measures from 0 to 8 inches in increments of 0.001 inch.*

To read the vernier caliper in Figure 14-11, note that the 0 on the vernier scale has moved beyond the 3-inch mark on the main scale (3.000). It has also moved past the $\frac{4}{10}$-inch mark (0.400) and past one of the $\frac{1}{40}$-inch marks (0.025). There is only one mark on the vernier scale that aligns with a mark on the main scale; this is the 11 mark, as identified by the asterisks. Add 0.011 to the total just found: 3.000 + 0.400 + 0.025 + 0.011 = 3.436 inches.

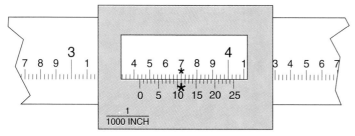

Figure 14-11. *Vernier scale on a U.S. vernier caliper*

Metric Vernier Caliper

With the metric system gaining prominence in the U.S., it is important that all aviation maintenance technicians are able to read metric calipers.

The main scale of the metric vernier caliper in Figure 14-12 is graduated directly in millimeters, with each space representing 0.5 mm. The vernier scale has 50 divisions, with each space representing 0.02 mm. Zero on the vernier scale has moved out beyond 41.5 mm on the main scale. The only line on the vernier scale that aligns with one of the marks on the main scale is the .18 mark, as is identified by the asterisks. Add 0.18 to 41.5 to get a total reading of 41.68 mm.

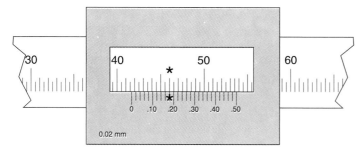

Figure 14-12. *Vernier scale on a metric vernier caliper*

Micrometer Calipers

Micrometer calipers are one of the technician's most widely-used precision measuring instruments (Figure 14-13). They are available as inside and outside calipers, with ranges from 0 to 1 inch, to special calipers that measure up to 60 inches.

When the thimble of the micrometer caliper is rotated, the spindle moves out to adjust the space between the two measuring faces. When the measuring faces touch, the zero on the thimble aligns with the reference line on the barrel, or sleeve. When the thimble is rotated one complete revolution, the zero is again lined up with the reference line. But the edge of the thimble has moved out to the first mark that crosses the reference line on the barrel. This line represents 25 thousandths (0.025) of an inch. Each mark on the beveled edge of the thimble represents one thousandth of an inch (0.001 inch). An ordinary micrometer caliper can be read directly to one thousandth of an inch.

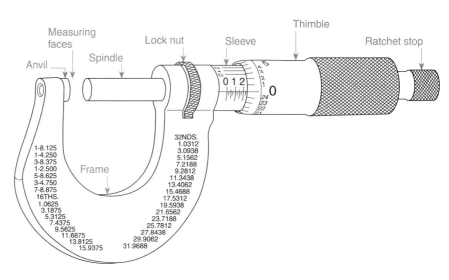

Figure 14-13. *Micrometer caliper*

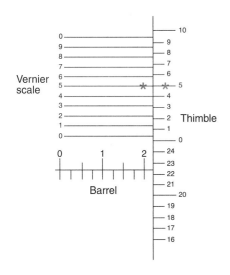

Figure 14-14. *U.S. vernier micrometer caliper scale*

A vernier micrometer caliper can be read directly to one ten-thousandth of an inch (0.0001 inch) by using the vernier scale, which is a series of parallel lines on the barrel that are parallel with the reference line. These lines are so placed that only one of them lines up with a mark on the thimble at any time. When the thimble has moved out enough for the next vernier line to align with one of the thimble marks, the spindle has moved out one ten-thousandth of an inch (0.0001 inch).

In the vernier micrometer caliper scale in Figure 14-14, the thimble has been screwed out more than eight complete turns, which has moved the spindle out two tenths of an inch (0.200). It has almost moved out another complete turn, but has stopped with the reference line on the barrel between the 22 and 23 thousandth-inch marks on the thimble. The measuring faces are between 0.222- and 0.223-inch apart. The 5 line on the vernier scale is lined up with one of the marks on the thimble. This means that the spindle has moved out 5 ten thousandths of an inch beyond 0.222. The total separation of the measuring faces is 0.2225 inch.

Metric Vernier Micrometer Caliper

As with other types of measuring devices, micrometer calipers are available in metric units as well as in U.S. units.

The reference line on the barrel, or sleeve, is graduated in millimeters and half millimeters, from 0 to 25, with every fifth millimeter mark being numbered. The beveled edge of the thimble is graduated in 50 divisions, each representing one hundredth of a millimeter (0.01 mm) with every fifth mark numbered. One revolution of the thimble moves the spindle in or out one-half (0.5) millimeter. Each graduation on the thimble therefore is equal to $\frac{1}{50}$ of 0.5 mm, or 1 one-hundredth (0.01) of a millimeter.

The vernier scale has five divisions, each of which equals one-fifth of a thimble division. This is $\frac{1}{5}$ of 0.01, or 0.002 mm.

The thimble in Figure 14-15 has moved out more than 8.5 mm, as shown by the marks on the barrel, and the thimble has moved more than 25 graduations, or 0.25 mm, beyond the reference mark. The vernier mark representing 6 divisions is aligned with one of the marks on the thimble, indicating that the spindle has moved 0.006 mm beyond 0.25. The total separation of the measuring faces is therefore $8.5 + 0.25 + 0.006 = 8.756$ millimeters.

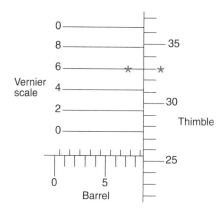

Figure 14-15. *Metric vernier micrometer caliper scale*

Dial Indicators

Dial indicators are versatile tools that are especially useful in aviation maintenance for such measurements as end-play in shaft installations, gear backlash, bevel gear preload, and shaft out-of-round or runout. The basic dial indicator, as shown in Figure 14-16, is available with a variety of dials, hardware for mounting, and types of contact points.

To measure the runout of a propeller shaft flange, or the amount it is bent, for example, mount the dial indicator with an adapter attached to the nose section of the engine. Adjust the adapter so it will press the contact point lightly against the shaft flange at the correct measuring position, and deflect the needle slightly to show a positive contact with the surface to be measured. Rotate the dial until the indicating needle points to zero. Very carefully rotate the propeller shaft and watch the indicator needle. As the contact point rides over the surface of the flange, the needle will indicate the amount the flange is run out.

Dial indicators are available with either metric or U.S. graduations.

Figure 14-16. *Dial indicator*

Feeler Gages

Feeler gages, also called thickness gages, are leaves of tempered steel ground to the correct thickness and marked with their thickness. These leaves, or blades, are usually assembled in sets in a protective steel case that allows easy access to the blades for use and replacement when necessary. (*See* Figure 14-17.)

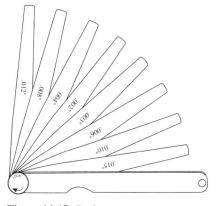

Figure 14-17. *Feeler gages*

A typical set of feeler gages has from 8 to 13 blades with thickness ranging from 0.0015 to 0.200 inch in the U.S. sizes, or from 0.04 to 3.0 mm in the metric sizes. Special-purpose blades are available that are bent so they fit into tight locations where straight blades cannot go.

Feeler gages are used for measuring clearances in valve trains and breaker points, gear backlash, piston ring end-gap and side clearance, and the flatness of objects when used with a precision surface plate.

Small-Hole Gages and Telescoping Gages

Small holes up to approximately ¹⁄₂ inch in diameter may be accurately measured with small-hole gages. Place a ball-type small-hole gage like the one in Figure 14-18 into the hole to be measured and twist the knurled end of the handle to expand the ball end until it exactly fits in the hole. Remove the gage and measure its diameter with a vernier micrometer caliper.

The diameter of larger holes, such as cylinder bores, may be accurately measured with telescoping gages like those in Figure 14-19. Select the gage with the proper range and place it in the bore. Loosen the knurled end of the handle, to release the hardened steel plungers in the telescoping head and allow an internal spring to force the plungers out against the walls of the cylinder bore. Hold the gage so the T-head is perpendicular to the inside wall of the bore and tighten the end of the handle. Remove the gage and measure the distance between the ends of the plungers with a vernier micrometer caliper.

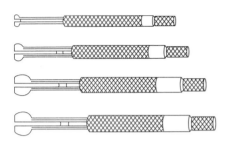

Figure 14-18. *Ball-type small-hole gages*

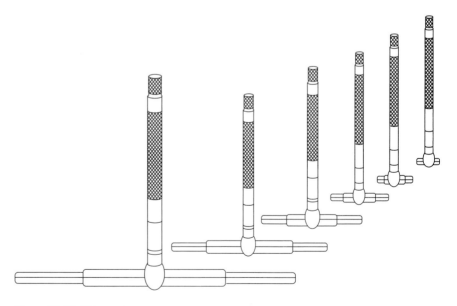

Figure 14-19. *Telescoping gages*

Holding Tools

Holding tools are some of the most widely varied tools in aircraft maintenance shops. They range from vises installed on work benches to the various
types of pliers in technicians' toolboxes.

Bench Vise

Bench vises are the standard vise found in most aviation maintenance shops.
Normally they have replaceable serrated jaws to hold the material without
slipping, and are mounted on a swiveling base. The size of a vise is indicated
by the width of the jaws, which normally range from 3½ to 6 inches. It is
important when using a vise to hold finished products or soft material, to install
soft metal jaws or cover the steel serrated jaws with a smooth protector made
of soft aluminum or brass. The vise in Figure 14-20 also has a set of jaws for
holding pipes and round stock.

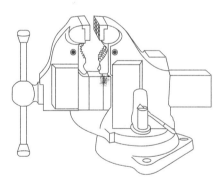

Figure 14-20. *Bench vise*

Drill-Press Vise

Drill-press vises have a flat bottom with slots that allow them to be bolted to the table of a drill press (Figure 14-21).

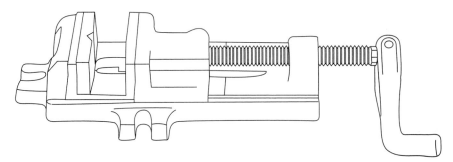

Figure 14-21. *Drill-press vise*

Pliers

Pliers are some of the handiest tools in a technician's toolbox—they are an extension of a technician's hand for gripping and holding. They are available in a variety of styles for specific purposes.

Combination/Slip-Joint Pliers

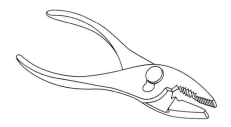

Figure 14-22. *Combination/slip-joint pliers*

These are the standard pliers with serrated jaws for gripping round objects and flat jaws for holding flat materials (Figure 14-22). When the jaws are open wide, the handle pivot may be slipped from one pivot hole to the other, allowing the jaws to open wider to hold larger objects. Most of these pliers have a short wire-cutting blade between the jaws near the pivot. Combination/slip-joint pliers are available in lengths from 4½ to more than 9 inches.

Water Pump Pliers

Figure 14-23. *Tongue-and-groove type water pump pliers*

These handy pliers are also called adjustable-joint pliers (Figure 14-23). They have long handles for applying force to the jaws and torque to the object being turned. They are available with a slip-joint adjustment, or with a tongue-and-groove type of adjustment that cannot slip. These pliers are available in lengths from 4½ inches (with parallel jaws that open to ½ inch), to 16 inches (with jaws that open to more than 4 inches).

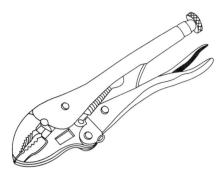

Figure 14-24. *Vise-Grip® pliers*

Figure 14-25. *Needle-nose pliers*

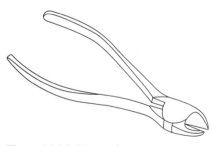

Figure 14-26. *Diagonal cutters*

Figure 14-27. *Duckbill pliers for twisting safety wire.*

Vise-Grip® Pliers

These patented locking pliers have a knurled knob in the handle that adjusts the opening of the jaws (*see* Figure 14-24). When the handles are squeezed together, a compound-lever action applies a tremendous force to the jaws, and an over-center feature holds them tightly locked on the object between the jaws. A trigger in the handle of the movable jaw may be squeezed to release the jaws from the object. These pliers are available in lengths from 4 to 10 inches with a wide variety of jaw configurations to hold objects of various shapes.

Needle-Nose Pliers

There are a number of types of needle-nose pliers used to hold wires or small objects and to make loops or bends in electrical wires. Some have straight jaws and others are bent to reach into obstructed areas. These pliers are available in lengths from 4½ to more than 10 inches, and many have wire cutters and insulated handles for use with electrical equipment.

Safety-Wiring Tools

Vibration is a characteristic of aircraft that requires all threaded fasteners to have some method of preventing them from becoming loose in operation. One of the most widely used methods is safety wire. Stainless steel, galvanized steel, or brass wire is attached to the fastener, twisted, and anchored to the structure or to another fastener. This wire pulls on the fastener in the direction of tightening so that vibration cannot loosen it.

Diagonal Cutters

Diagonal cutters, or "dikes," are used to cut safety wire and cotter pins. The name of these pliers is derived from the shape of the jaws that have an angled cutting edge.

The angled cutting edge makes diagonals unsuited for cutting rivets to length, but there are special rivet cutters which look much like diagonal cutters, except the jaws are ground flat on one side to cut the end of the rivet shank so it is smooth rather than angled.

Diagonals are not recommended for cutting the pigtails on electronic components such as transistors, because they cut with a pinching action that can damage the sensitive elements. Cutters for these components have overlapping jaws that cut with a shearing action.

Duckbill Pliers

These long-handled, flat-jaw pliers have been used since the beginning of aviation maintenance to twist safety wire. The wide serrated jaws hold the wire firmly as it is being twisted.

Safety Wire Twisting Tools

Duckbill pliers are capable of twisting safety wire for many applications, but modern turbine engine technology requires so much safety wiring that must be done efficiently and uniformly, special reversible safety wire twisting tools are necessary. The tool shown in Figure 14-28 grips the wire securely, and the jaws lock on the wire. When the knob in the handle is pulled out, the tool twists the safety wire with a uniform twist. This tool can be used to give the wire a right-hand or a left-hand twist.

Figure 14-28. *Milbar safety wire twister*

STUDY QUESTION: SAFETY-WIRING TOOLS

Answer is on Page 776. Page number refers to chapter text.

8. Diagonal cutters _____ (are or are not) suited for cutting rivets to length. *Page 739*

Bending and Forming Tools

Because most modern aircraft are made of thin sheet metal, it is important the AMT be familiar with the shop and hand tools for bending and forming this material in straight and compound curves.

Cornice Brake

The cornice, or leaf brake is found in most aviation maintenance shops that do extensive sheet metal repair (Figure 14-29). These heavy shop tools are used to make straight bends across a piece of sheet metal. The bend radius appropriate for the thickness and temper of the metal can be chosen by using the appropriate radius block on the upper jaw of the brake.

A box, or finger brake is similar to a cornice brake, except instead of the upper jaw being solid, it is made up of a number of heavy steel fingers so all four sides of a box can be folded up (*see* Figure 14-30). To form a sheet metal box:

1. Fold up two opposite sides in the way they would be folded on a cornice brake;

2. Adjust the fingers so the folded-up edges will pass between adjacent fingers;

3. Raise the leaf to fold the other sides.

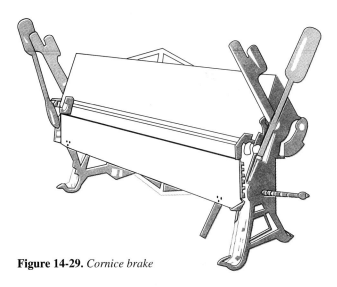

Figure 14-29. *Cornice brake*

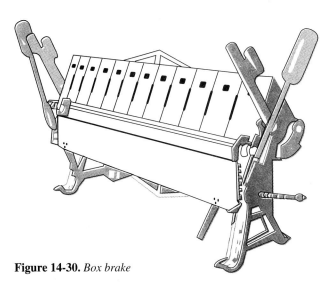

Figure 14-30. *Box brake*

Press Brake

When a large number of duplicate pieces of material having exactly the same amount of bend must be made, a press brake is used. This tool is normally found in aircraft factories. The metal is placed over the female die whose inside radius is the same as the outside radius of the finished bend. A matching male die, or punch, with the correct radius forces the material into the die with energy stored in a large flywheel, or with hydraulic pressure. Angles and channels are formed on press brakes (*see* Figure 14-31).

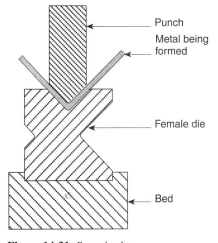

Figure 14-31. *Press brake*

Slip Roll Former

A slip roll former like the one in Figure 14-32 is used for making large radius bends across a piece of sheet metal. The metal is clamped between the drive roller and the gripping roller, as shown in Figure 14-33, and the handle is turned to pull the metal through the machine against the radius roller, which is adjusted to control the radius of the bend. For making a bend with a fairly small radius in a large sheet of metal, make a very small bend with the first pass, and then make a number of passes through the rollers with the radius roller readjusted between each pass. Continue this process until the final curvature is the one desired.

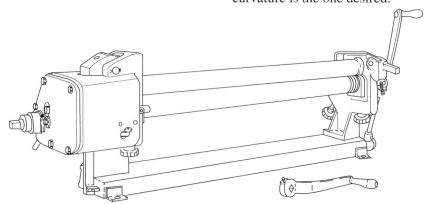

Figure 14-32. *Slip roll former*

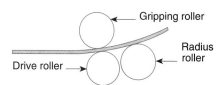

Figure 14-33. *Rollers in a slip roll former*

STUDY QUESTIONS: BENDING AND FORMING TOOLS

*Answers are on Page 776. **Page numbers refer to chapter text.***

9. The sides of a box or tray may be formed with a _____ or _____ brake.
   Page 740

10. Large radii bends may be formed in a piece of sheet metal with a/an _____
    _____ . *Page 742*

Tools for Forming Compound Curves

Brakes and slip roll formers make straight bends across a piece of metal. For making compound curves in large sheets of metal, such as fuselage and wing skins, aircraft factories use drop hammers or stretch presses. For small pieces, hydropresses are used.

Drop Hammers

Compound-curved wing and fuselage skins may be formed with a drop hammer. Large dies are made of a lead and zinc alloy called Kirksite, and a matching punch is made of lead. The skin blank is placed over the die and the heavy punch is raised high above it and dropped, forcing the metal to conform to the shape of the die. Parts that require deep drawing are formed with several dies and punches that progressively form the required shape.

Stretch Press

Stretch pressing skins is more economical than forming them with a drop hammer because the dies are less expensive.

The edges of the large sheets of aluminum alloy are held in special clamps. The large male die, which is in the exact shape desired for the skin, is pressed into the sheet, causing the metal to stretch over the form. After the metal is formed, the edges are trimmed.

Hydropress

Small compound-curved parts are usually formed on a hydropress. A steel male die is made of the exact shape of the inside of the part to be formed. One or two locating pins are normally used to hold the blank in place.

Blanks of the metal are cut, and holes are drilled or punched for the locating pins. The blank is placed over the die which is mounted on the bed of the hydropress. A rubber pad about four to six inches thick held in an open-face heavy steel frame is forced down over the die with a force of many tons. The rubber pad forces the metal blank down around the male die without wrinkling.

Sandbag

Maintenance and repair shops do not normally use the production methods of forming compound-curved parts. When large skins are damaged, they are usually replaced with new skins, available from the aircraft factory. These skins have pilot holes for the rivets.

Small compound-curved parts of which only one or a few are required are formed with a soft-face mallet and a sandbag. The best bags are made of leather, but many are made of heavy canvas and are usually filled with sand, but can be filled with lead shot. To form a part, lay the sandbag on a work bench and make a depression in the bag that is roughly the shape of the piece being formed. Use the mallet to work the metal down into the depression, beginning with the center and working out toward the edges in a spiral pattern. Periodically check the amount of bend by comparing the bend with a template of the desired shape.

English Wheel

The English wheel is a sheet-metal tool that gained popularity during the 1990s. Aluminum sheets are formed by stretching them, which is initially done with a sandbag, resulting in a rough surface that must be smoothed out. The smoothing is done by placing the stretched aluminum sheet over a smooth steel dolly and tapping it gently with a lightweight flat-face steel hammer. A much more satisfactory and quicker method of smoothing the metal is by using an English wheel (*see* Figure 14-34).

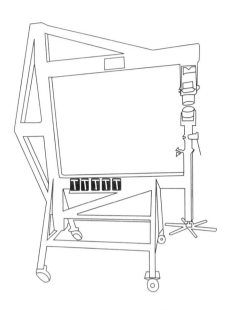

Figure 14-34. *An English wheel produces a smooth-surface compound curve in sheet aluminum.*

An English wheel actually has two wheels, one above the other. The upper wheel is a large cast-iron wheel with a highly polished and very slightly concave surface. A smaller, lower wheel is adjustable so it can be moved closer to or further from the upper wheel. The lower wheel has a convex surface, and there are a number of wheels available with differing radii in order to vary the radius of the metal being formed.

The metal being worked is moved back and forth between the two wheels to smooth and form it.

Shrinkers and Stretchers

Shrinkers and stretchers are a pair of shop tools that are extremely handy for curving angles to fit the contour of wings or fuselages. Each of these tools has two sets of jaws operated by a foot pedal.

When the pedal on the stretcher is released, the jaws open and the two sets of jaws move close together. The metal to be stretched is placed between the jaws, and the pedal is depressed. The jaws close to grip the metal tightly, and the two sets of jaws move apart, stretching the metal between them.

The shrinker works in the same way, except when the pedal is released, the jaws open and the two sets of jaws move apart. When the pedal is depressed, the jaws grip the metal and move close together, shrinking the metal between them.

STUDY QUESTION: TOOLS FOR FORMING COMPOUND CURVES

Answer is on Page 776. Page number refers to chapter text.

11. Compound curves may be formed in a small piece of aluminum alloy sheet by using a
_____ and a _____ . *Page 743*

Cutting Tools

It is extremely important to use the correct tool to cut metal—both sheet metal and bars or plate. There are three basic types of cutting tools used in aviation maintenance shops: shears, saws, and files.

Shears

As their name implies, shears cut metal by shearing it between two sharp blades in much the same way scissors cut across paper. Aviation maintenance shops normally have squaring shears to cut across large sheets of metal and several forms of smaller shears for cutting metal by hand.

Squaring Shears

Squaring shears are large enough to accept a 48-inch-wide sheet of metal. Foot-treadle-operated shears like the one in Figure 14-35 are able to make a straight cut across aluminum alloy sheets up to approximately 0.051-inch thickness and mild steel of 22-gage or thinner. Power-operated shears that use a small electric motor to store a large amount of energy in a heavy fly-wheel can cut much thicker sheets.

The metal to be cut is placed on the bed, or table, of the shears and is squared by holding it against the squaring fence. A hold-down clamp, locked in place with a toggle handle, holds the metal tight on the table and keeps the operator's fingers out of the way of the blade. The blade is angled so that it slices its way through the sheet when the foot-treadle is pressed, or when the energy stored in the flywheel forces the blade down.

Throatless Shears

Throatless shears (Figure 14-36) have two short cutting blades that cut much like a pair of scissors. The lower blade is fixed to the base and the upper blade is operated by a long handle. Throatless shears can cut completely across any size sheet of metal and can cut metal considerably thicker than squaring shears are able to cut.

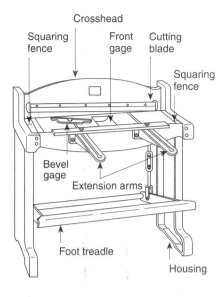

Figure 14-35. *Squaring shears*

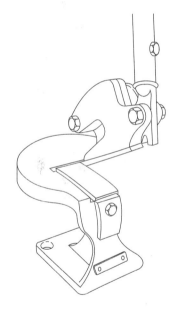

Figure 14-36. *Throatless shears*

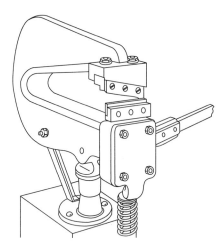

Figure 14-37. *Scroll shears*

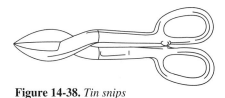

Figure 14-38. *Tin snips*

Cuts left—red handle

Cuts straight—yellow handle

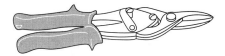

Cuts right—green handle

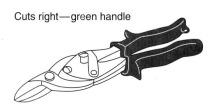

Figure 14-39. *Compound shears*

Scroll Shears

Scroll shears (Figure 14-37) are used to pierce a piece of sheet metal and cut irregular curves on the inside of the sheet without having to cut through to the edge. The upper blade, which has a sharp point for piercing the metal, is fixed to the frame of the shears, and the lower blade is raised against the upper by the compound action of a hand-operated handle.

Tin Snips

These hand shears are widely used in commercial sheet metal shops. They are used in aviation maintenance shops to cut sheets of aluminum alloy of up to about 0.032-inch thick, to roughly the size needed to fabricate a part. Final cutting and trimming is done with other tools. Tin snips have relatively short blades, similar to those of a pair of scissors, and long handles to provide the needed leverage. *See* Figure 14-38.

Compound Shears

Compound shears are the most useful sheet metal cutting hand tool available to the aviation maintenance technician. They are also known as aviation shears or Dutchman shears. These shears have short serrated blades, actuated by a compound action from the handles. There are three shapes of blades, one designed to cut to the left, one to cut to the right, and one to make straight cuts. The serrated blades leave a rough edge that must be filed off to prevent stress risers.

The handles of these shears are often color coded, as shown in Figure 14-39. Shears with red handles cut to the left, green handles cut to the right, and yellow handles cut straight.

Saws

Saws cut metal by the chisel action of a large number of teeth. Most well-equipped aviation maintenance shops have a band saw for cutting metal, wood, and plastic. Technicians have hacksaws in their toolboxes for a wide variety of cutting operations.

Band Saw

The most versatile band saw for aviation maintenance shops is the contour saw with a work table that can be adjusted for tilt, and a variable-speed drive that allows the cutting speed of the blade to be adjusted to meet the requirements for the material being cut.

The band saw pictured in Figure 14-40 has a cutter, welder, and grinder that allows the saw to be used for cutting inside a piece of sheet material without cutting through to the edge. A hole is first drilled or punched into the area to be sawed and the blade removed from the wheels of the saw. The blade is cut in two and the end placed through the hole in the material. The two ends of the blade are then clamped in the butt welder on the saw, and electric current flows through them, heating them enough to melt the ends so they flow together. The current is shut off and the joint allowed to cool, and it is then ground smooth. The blade is reinstalled over the wheels, and the inside of the material is cut.

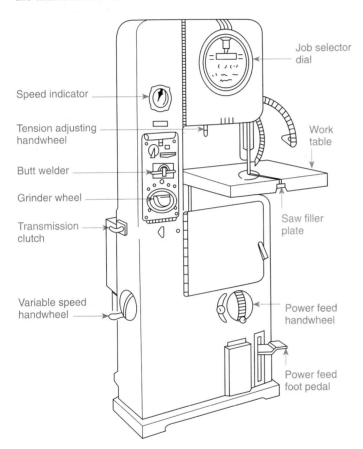

Figure 14-40. *Contour band saw*

Hacksaw

A hacksaw is a hand-operated metal cutting tool that uses a narrow replaceable blade held under tension in a steel frame. The blades are available in 10-inch and 12-inch lengths and from 14 to 32 teeth per inch. Some blades are very stiff for making straight cuts, and others are flexible for making slightly curved cuts without breaking.

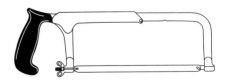

Figure 14-41. *Hacksaw frame*

A hacksaw blade should be chosen that will allow at least two teeth to be on the material at all times, and when cutting, pressure should be applied on the forward stroke and relaxed on the return stroke.

Wood Saws

There are a number of types of handsaws used for cutting wood. The most widely used are the crosscut and ripsaw for general cutting.

Crosscut Saw

A crosscut saw (Figure 14-42) is a handsaw used for cutting across the grain of wood. The teeth, or points, are filed so they have a knife-like cutting edge on the same side of each alternate tooth. The teeth are set by bending every other tooth to one side and the alternate teeth to the opposite side.

When the saw is pushed through the wood the teeth cut the fibers. The set of the teeth results in a cut that is wider than the saw blade. This widened cut, called the kerf, keeps the blade from binding in the cut.

kerf. The slit made by a saw blade as it cuts through wood. The set of the teeth determines the width of the kerf.

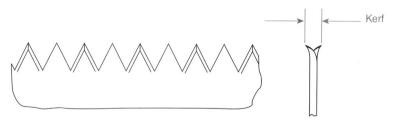

Figure 14-42. *Teeth of a crosscut saw*

Ripsaw

Ripsaws are similar to crosscut saws except for the shape and number of the teeth. They have fewer teeth per inch than a crosscut saw and the teeth are shaped to act as chisels and dig into the wood fibers. (*See* Figure 14-43.)

Figure 14-43. *Teeth of a ripsaw*

Compass, or Keyhole Saw

A compass saw, often called a keyhole saw (Figure 14-44), is a small saw with teeth similar to those of a crosscut saw. The blade is thin and tapered so it can enter a drilled hole and cut curves or circles.

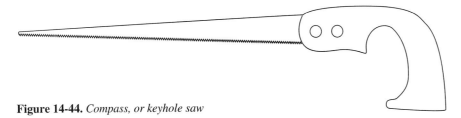

Figure 14-44. *Compass, or keyhole saw*

Backsaw

Backsaws have teeth similar to crosscut saws, but they are much smaller with more teeth per inch and less set. The blade has a stiffener across its back to keep it from bending (*see* Figure 14-45). Backsaws produce a smooth cut across the grain for wood stringers or capstrips; they are often used with a miter box.

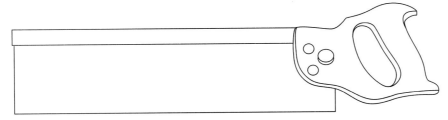

Figure 14-45. *Backsaw*

Chisels

Chisels are used to cut metal with a shearing action when the end of the chisel is hit with a hammer. Two types of chisels that are found in most aviation maintenance shops are the flat chisel and the cape chisel.

A flat chisel is made of a piece of hardened steel ground with a cutting angle of 70°, and the cutting edge is ground to a convex shape to concentrate the force of the hammer blows at the point the cut is being made.

Cape chisels (Figure 14-47) have a narrow cutting edge used to remove the head of a solid rivet after the head has been drilled through.

The shank of a chisel takes a tremendous amount of pounding and, over time, it becomes mushroomed from the hammer blows. It is extremely important that the mushroomed end be ground off to prevent chips being broken off and injuring anyone near, and to prevent its cutting your hand as you hold the chisel.

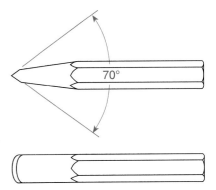

Figure 14-46. *The cutting edge of a flat chisel is ground to an angle of 70° and it is rounded to concentrate the blows.*

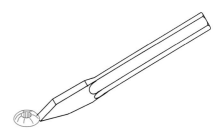

Figure 14-47. *A cape chisel is used to remove the head of a rivet after it has been drilled through.*

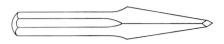

Figure 14-48. *A diamond-point chisel is used for cutting V-shaped grooves in metal.*

Figure 14-49. *A round-nose chisel is used for cutting radii in the bottom of grooves in metal.*

tang. The tapered shank sticking out from the body of a file. A handle for a file is slipped over the tang.

Diamond-point chisels are forged to a sharp-cornered square and the end is ground to an acute angle to form a sharp pointed cutting edge. Diamond-point chisels are used for cutting V-shaped grooves, and for cutting the sharp corners in square or rectangular grooves.

Round-nose chisels look much like the diamond-point chisel in Figure 14-48 except the cutting edge is ground to a circular point. They are used for cutting radii in the bottom of grooves (Figure 14-49).

Files

Files are used to remove small amounts of material to get the final dimensions of a part and to smooth a surface. Files are available in a number of lengths, shapes, and tooth cuts (*see* Figure 14-50). Standard lengths range from 6 to 12 inches (this does not include the tang), and the tooth cuts are made in single-cut, double-cut, rasp, and vixen, or curved-tooth.

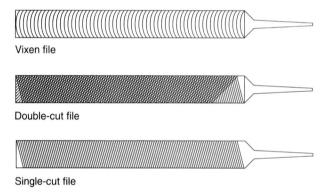

Vixen file

Double-cut file

Single-cut file

Figure 14-50. *Typical metalworking files*

There are a number of file shapes used in aviation maintenance:

- A flat file has a rectangular cross-section and is tapered toward the point in both width and thickness.

- A hand file has a rectangular cross-section, its sides are parallel, and it tapers in thickness. One of the edges is safe; that is, there are no teeth cut on it. Hand files are used for finishing flat surfaces.

- A half-round file has a flat side and a rounded side. It tapers in both width and thickness. Half-round files are used to file the inside of large radius curves.

- A triangular, or three-square file is a tapered, double-cut file with a triangular cross-section. Triangular files are used to file acute internal angles and to restore damaged threads.

- A round file, commonly called a rattail file, is circular in cross-section and is tapered in its length. It is used to file the inside of circular openings and curved surfaces.

- Knife files are tapered in both width and thickness and have a cross-sectional shape much like a knife blade. Knife files are used for filing work with acute angles.

- Vixen files have curved teeth cut across the file and are used for removing large amounts of soft metal.

- Wood rasps resemble files, except the teeth are formed in rows of individual round-point chisels. Wood rasps are used to remove large amounts of wood and they do not leave a smooth surface.

There are six degrees of coarseness in the teeth of a file. The coarsest is the rough cut, then the coarse cut, the bastard cut, second cut, smooth cut, and the smoothest is the dead smooth cut.

File should never be used without first placing a handle over the tang. These handles are available in wood and plastic and are installed by tapping them in place over the tang. When using a file, apply pressure only on the forward stroke and lift the file on the return stroke. The exception to this rule is when filing soft aluminum or lead: some pressure can be applied on the return stroke to clear the metal from the teeth.

File cards, or file brushes, are useful for keeping metal filings out of the spaces between the teeth. This imbedded metal can scratch the surface being filed. A file card is similar to a steel brush with a series of very short steel wire bristles mounted on a wood or plastic back. A sharp pick is included with the file card to remove stubborn filings from between the teeth.

Twist Drills

One tool widely used by AMTs is the twist drill. It is a simple tool, but its simplicity often causes it to be misused. It must be sharp and have the correct point angle for the material being drilled. It must be tightly chucked into the drill motor or drill press, and it must be turned at the correct speed for the material. The correct amount of pressure must be applied to ensure that the drill continues to cut.

Twist drills are available in two materials, carbon steel and high-speed steel. The carbon drills cost less but do not have nearly as long a life as high-speed drills and therefore have limited use.

High-speed drills are made of alloy steel and maintain their sharpness even when they are hot. These are the most widely used drills in aircraft maintenance shops. They are available in three groups of sizes: number, letter, and fraction—these are shown in the chart in Figure 14-52. Notice that in the number drills, the larger the number, the smaller the drill.

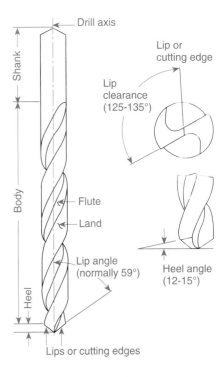

Figure 14-51. *Twist drill nomenclature*

Number or Letter	Fraction	Decimal Equivalent	Number or Letter	Fraction	Decimal Equivalent
80		0.0135	22		0.1570
79		0.0145	21		0.1590
78		0.0160	20		0.1610
	1/64	0.0156	19		0.1660
77		0.0180	18		0.1695
76		0.0200		11/64	0.1719
75		0.0210	17		0.1730
74		0.0225	16		0.1770
73		0.0240	15		0.1800
72		0.0250	14		0.1820
71		0.0260	13		0.1850
70		0.0280		3/16	0.1875
69		0.0290	12		0.1890
68		0.0310	11		0.1910
	1/32	0.0313	10		0.1935
67		0.0320	9		0.1960
66		0.0330	8		0.1990
65		0.0350	7		0.2010
64		0.0360		13/64	0.2031
63		0.0370	6		0.2040
62		0.0380	5		0.2055
61		0.0390	4		0.2090
60		0.0400	3		0.2130
59		0.0410		7/32	0.2187
58		0.0420	2		0.2210
57		0.0430	1		0.2280
56		0.0465	A		0.2340
	3/64	0.0469		15/64	0.2344
55		0.0520	B		0.2380
54		0.0550	C		0.2420
53		0.0595	D		0.2460
	1/16	0.0625	E	1/4	0.2500
52		0.0635	F		0.2570
51		0.0670	G		0.2610
50		0.0700		17/64	0.2656
49		0.0730	H		0.2660
48		0.0760	I		0.2720
	5/64	0.0781	J		0.2770
47		0.0785	K		0.2810
46		0.0810		9/32	0.2812
45		0.0820	L		0.2900
44		0.0860	M		0.2950
43		0.0890		19/64	0.2969
42		0.0935	N		0.3020
	3/32	0.0937		5/16	0.3125
41		0.0960	O		0.3160
40		0.0980	P		0.3230
39		0.0995		21/64	0.3281
38		0.1015	Q		0.3320
37		0.1040	R		0.3390
36		0.1065		11/32	0.3438
	7/64	0.1094	S		0.3480
35		0.1100	T		0.3580
34		0.1110		23/64	0.3594
33		0.1130	U		0.3680
32		0.1160		3/8	0.3750
31		0.1200	V		0.3770
	1/8	0.1250	W		0.3860
30		0.1285		25/64	0.3906
29		0.1360	X		0.3970
28		0.1405	Y		0.4040
	9/64	0.1406		13/32	0.4062
27		0.1440	Z		0.4130
26		0.1470		27/64	0.4219
25		0.1495		7/16	0.4375
24		0.1520		29/64	0.4331
23		0.1540		15/32	0.4688
	5/32	0.1562		31/64	0.4844
				1/2	0.5000

Figure 14-52. *Twist drill sizes*

Drill Gage

The number stamped on the shank of a drill is often difficult to read, and it is time consuming to use micrometer calipers to measure the drill diameter. To make this job quicker and easier, precision tool manufacturers provide drill gages with holes the size of the drill shank (Figure 14-53). To identify the size of the drill, find the hole that exactly fits the drill; the number beside the hole is the size of the drill. Most drill gages also have the decimal equivalent of the drill diameter stamped beside the number.

Twist Drill Sharpening

Twist drills are perhaps the simplest cutting tool used by an aviation maintenance technician, but it is important that they be properly sharpened for the material they are used to drill. Figure 14-54 shows the point angles for aluminum alloys and brass, hard and tough metals, and transparent plastics and wood.

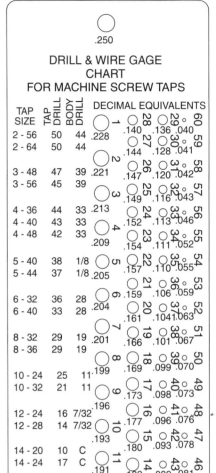

Figure 14-53. *Twist drill gage*

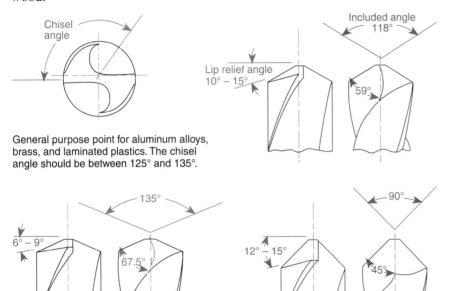

General purpose point for aluminum alloys, brass, and laminated plastics. The chisel angle should be between 125° and 135°.

Point ground for hard and tough metals. The chisel angle should be between 115° and 125°.

Point ground for transparent plastics and wood. The chisel angle should be between 125° and 135°.

Figure 14-54. *Twist drill points*

Material	Included angle	Lip relief angle
Aluminum, mild steel, brass	118°	10° – 15°
Hard and tough materials	135°	6° – 9°
Plastics, wood	90°	12° – 15°

Figure 14-55. *Recommended angles for twist drill points*

When sharpening a drill, be sure that the lengths of the lips, or cutting edges, are the same, and the included angle and lip relief angle are correct for the material that will be drilled (Figure 14-55).

Because the points of most drills used in routine aviation maintenance are ground to an included angle of 118°, or 59° either side of center, a handy drill point gage is available to determine that the angle is proper and the lips are of the same lengths. (*See* Figure 14-56.)

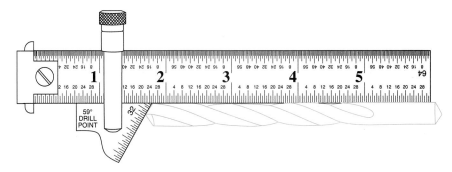

Figure 14-56. *Drill point gage*

Figure 14-57. *Auger bit for drilling wood*

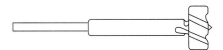

Figure 14-58. *Forstner bit for boring flat-bottomed holes in wood*

Figure 14-59. *Flat wood boring bits are mounted in an electric or pneumatic drill motor to bore holes in wood.*

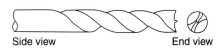

Side view   End view

Figure 14-60. *Brad-point drills are used to drill Kevlar without leaving fuzz inside the hole.*

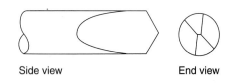

Side view   End view

Figure 14-61. *Spade drill for drilling graphite material.*

Drills for Wood and Composite Materials

Auger bits like the one in Figure 14-57 are turned with a bow-type brace. The feed screw in the end of the bit screws into the wood and pulls the bit in. Sharp cutting edges parallel with the axis of the bit cut a circle in the wood and the cutting edge perpendicular to the axis of the bit cuts the chips from within the circle. The chips travel up the spiral flutes and out of the hole.

Forstner bits are mounted in a drill press and are used for boring flat-bottomed holes in wood (Figure 14-58). The vertical cutting edge cuts a circle the size of the hole being bored and the horizontal edge cuts the chips from the area within the circle.

Flat wood-boring bits like the one in Figure 14-59 are available in sizes from $\frac{1}{4}$ inch to more than one inch. These bits are chucked into an electric or pneumatic drill motor. The pointed pilot keeps the bit centered in the hole as the cutting edge of the bit cuts the chips and moves them out of the hole.

Brad-point drills are used for cutting Kevlar reinforced material (Figure 14-60). The drill is chucked into a high-speed electric or pneumatic drill motor and pressed into the material with little pressure. The cutting edges cut the fibers and produce a fuzz-free hole.

Spade drills like the one in Figure 14-61 are used to drill graphite materials. This drill provides ample space for the graphite dust to leave so it will not enlarge the hole. These drills are turned at a high speed in an electric or pneumatic drill motor, using very little pressure.

Reamers

Reamers are special cutting tools with sharp knife-edge blades, or flutes, cut into their periphery. These blades are extremely hard and are easily chipped. When preparing a hole for close-tolerance bolt, drill the hole about one to three thousandths of an inch (0.001 to 0.003 inch) smaller than the outside diameter of the reamer. Be sure that the reamer is perfectly aligned with the hole and turn it steadily in its proper cutting direction to prevent it chattering. Never turn the reamer backward after it has begun to cut as this will dull the reamer.

Fixed-diameter reamers such as those in Figure 14-62 enlarge the hole to the most accurate dimensions, but an expansion reamer like that in Figure 14-63 may be used to ream a hole slightly larger than that cut with a fixed reamer. The adjustment on the end of the cutter is turned to increase the diameter of the cutters which can be measured with a vernier micrometer caliper.

Cutters for Large Holes

The twist drills used by aviation maintenance technicians are seldom larger than one-half inch diameter. When it is necessary to cut larger holes in thin sheet metal or wood, a hole saw or fly cutter may be used.

Hole Saw

Hole saws, such as the one in Figure 14-64, are used to cut large-diameter holes in thin sheet metal or wood. Different diameter saws can be installed on the arbor; these saws are available from $\frac{9}{19}$ inch up to more than 4 inches. The arbor has a shank that fits into a drill press or a hand drill motor, and the pilot drill has a short section of flutes with a longer smooth shank. This allows the drill to cut the pilot hole; then when the saw reaches the material, the shank of the pilot drill is in the hole and therefore does not enlarge the hole, yet holds the saw centered.

Fly Cutters

Fly cutters are also used to cut large holes in thin sheet metal, but they are not limited to specific-sized holes, as is a hole saw. A cutting tool is mounted in the arm of the fly cutter, and the arm is adjusted so the tip of the cutter is exactly the radius of the desired hole from the center of the pilot drill. The shank of the fly cutter is chucked in a drill press, and the pilot drill cuts the guide hole. As shown in Figure 14-65, the pilot drill has a long smooth shank so that it will not enlarge the guide hole when the metal is being cut.

The drill press is operated at a slow speed, and the cutter is fed into the work very slowly and carefully in order to cut rather than grab the material.

WARNING: It is important when cutting holes in thin sheet metal that the metal be supported on a piece of scrap plywood and the metal and plywood firmly clamped to the drill press table. This prevents the metal from becoming a lethal spinning knife if the cutter should dig into it.

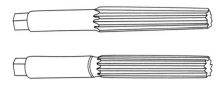

Figure 14-62. *Fixed diameter reamers. The top reamer is tapered and the bottom reamer has straight flutes.*

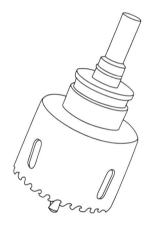

Figure 14-63. *Expansion reamer*

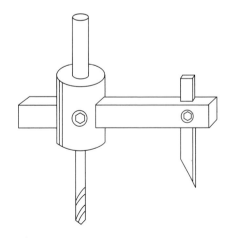

Figure 14-64. *Hole saws are used to cut large-diameter holes in thin sheet metal or wood.*

Figure 14-65. *A fly cutter is an adjustable hole cutter.*

The cutter can be reversed in the arm to cut holes with the edge of the hole either straight or beveled.

Countersinks

Flush rivets and structural screws are essential for a streamlined surface. Thick skins are countersunk to produce a flush surface, and thin skins are dimpled. Skins that are thicker than the head of the fastener are countersunk by beveling the edges of the holes so the fastener heads will be flush with the skin. The heads of most flush fasteners have an included angle of 100°. The stop countersink shown in Figure 14-66 has a countersink cutter that cuts a 100° bevel.

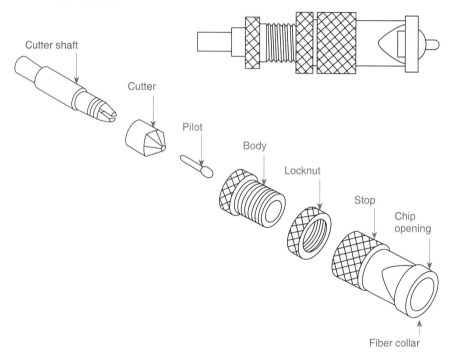

Figure 14-66. *A stop countersink allows you to countersink a series of holes exactly the correct depth for the fastener being installed.*

A stop countersink has an adjustable stop which ensures the material is countersunk to the correct depth. When the fiber collar contacts the skin being countersunk, the mounted cutter can go no deeper. The depth can be adjusted by changing the distance the cutter protrudes from the stop. The stop countersink has provisions for using different-sized pilots to match the diameter of rivet being installed.

To determine the correct adjustment of the stop, make some test countersinks in scrap material until the recess is just deep enough for the top of the fastener being installed to be flush with the surface of the metal.

Answers are on Page 776. **Page numbers refer to chapter text.**

12. At least _____ (how many) teeth of a hacksaw blade should be on the material while it is being cut.
    Page 748

13. Which type of wood saw has the fewer teeth, a ripsaw or a crosscut saw? A _____ .
    Page 748

14. A _____ (what type of saw) is used with a miter box to cut angles. *Page 749*

15. A _____ (what type of file) file has curved teeth and is used for removing large amounts of soft metal. *Page 751*

16. A number 20 high-speed twist drill has a _____ (larger or smaller) diameter than a number 30 drill. *Page 751*

17. A properly ground twist drill to be used for drilling aluminum alloy or soft steel should have an included angle of _____ degrees. *Page 754*

18. A/an _____ (what type) wood boring bit should be used to bore a flat-bottomed hole. *Page 754*

19. A _____ (fixed-diameter or expansion) reamer reams holes to the most accurate dimensions. *Page 755*

20. Large holes of nonstandard diameter can be cut in thin sheet metal with a/an _____ .
    Page 755

Screw size	Threads/inch	
	UNF	UNC
#0	80	
#2	64	56
#4	48	40
#6	40	32
#8	36	32
#10	32	24
#12	28	24
Bolt size		
3/16	32	24
1/4	28	20
5/16	24	18
3/8	24	16
7/16	20	14
1/2	20	13
9/16	18	12
5/8	18	11
3/4	16	10
7/8	14	9
1	14	8

Figure 14-67. *Threads per inch for various diameter screws and bolts using the Unified and American Standard threads.*

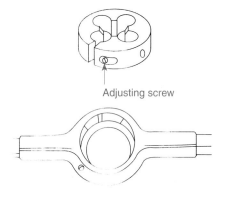

Adjusting screw

Figure 14-68. *Adjustable die and die stock*

Threads and Threading Tools

There are a number of forms of threads used on bolts and screws, but the Unified and American Standard Thread form has been accepted as the standard for most aircraft hardware. This thread form is available in both fine (UNF), and coarse (UNC) threads.

There are two basic ways of forming threads on a screw or bolt: rolling and cutting.

Rolled threads are formed by squeezing the shank between rotating dies that displace the metal and force it into the threads of the die. Rolled threads are superior to cut threads because the cold-working of the metal produces a better grain structure in the threads as well as a burnished thread surface.

Cut threads are formed with a die like the one in Figure 14-68. The adjusting screw is screwed in to spread the split in the die in order to shallow the threads that are being cut. The die is put in the die stock, and the four set screws are tightened to hold the die in place. The die is then placed over the end of the rod to be threaded, and turned to cut the threads. The depth of the threads can be increased by screwing out the adjusting screw.

Threads are cut inside a hole using a series of taps like those in Figure 14-69. There are three kinds of taps for each diameter and pitch. A taper tap is used to start the threads as the first several threads are ground back so the tap will enter the hole and easily begin to cut the threads. For thick material, a plug tap is used to follow the taper tap. Plug taps have only a short portion of the threads ground away so it can cut many more full-depth threads than a taper tap. If the threads are to extend all the way to the bottom of a blind hole, a bottoming tap is used to follow the plug tap. The threads on a bottoming tap are full depth all the way to the end. Taps are held in a tap wrench that is turned with both hands to ensure that the tap is perpendicular to the material as threads are cut.

Figures 14-70 and 14-71 list the body drill and tap drill sizes for screws and bolts having the Unified and American Standard Threads with a medium fit.

There is a special series of National Taper Pipe (NPT) threads used on fluid line fittings that screw into engine castings and instrument cases. The size of these fittings does not relate to their physical size, but is rather the size of the hole in a nominal iron pipe of the diameter given. For example, a 1/8-inch pipe thread actually has a root diameter of 0.3339, almost 3/8 inch. The threads taper 1/16-inch to the inch to ensure a leakproof seal.

An AMT will seldom find the need to cut tapered threads on the outside of a pipe or rod, but since a number of fittings for fluid lines have pipe threads on them, it may be necessary to cut internal threads for these fittings. Figure 14-72 lists the tap drill to be used for five of the most commonly used pipe threads.

Metric sizes are being increasingly used in aircraft manufacture and maintenance; Figure 14-73 lists the sizes of a metric tap drill to use with the various metric threads.

Taper tap

Plug tap

Bottoming tap

Figure 14-69. *Taps for cutting threads inside a hole*

Size and threads	Body diameter	Body drill	Preferred hole diameter	Tap drill
0-80	0.060	52	0.0472	3/64
1-72	0.073	47	0.0591	53
2-64	0.056	42	0.7000	50
3-56	0.099	37	0.0810	46
4-48	0.112	31	0.0911	42
5-44	0.125	29	0.1024	38
6-40	0.138	27	0.1130	33
8-36	0.164	18	0.1360	29
10-32	0.190	10	0.1590	21
12-28	0.216	2	0.1800	15
1/4-28	0.250	F	0.2130	3
5/16-24	0.3125	5/16	0.2703	I
3/8-24	0.375	3/8	0.3320	Q
7/16-20	0.4375	7/16	0.3860	W
1/2-20	0.500	1/2	0.4490	7/16
9/16-18	0.5625	9/16	0.5060	1/2
5/8-18	0.625	5/8	0.5680	9/16
3/4-16	0.750	3/4	0.6688	11/16
7/8-14	0.875	7/8	0.7822	51/64
1"-14	1.000	1"	0.9072	59/64

Figure 14-70. *Body and tap drill sizes for UNF threads*

Nominal pipe size (inch)	Threads per inch	Root diameter of pipe	Tap drill
1/8	27	0.3339	Q
1/4	18	0.4329	7/16
3/8	18	0.5676	9/16
1/2	14	0.7013	45/64
3/4	14	0.9105	29/32

Figure 14-72. *Tap drill for National Taper Pipe thread series*

Metric threads	Metric tap drill
M2.5 x 0.45	2.05
M3 x 0.5	2.5
M3.5 x 0.6	2.9
M4 x 0.7	3.3
M5 x 0.8	4.2
M6.3 x 1	5.3
M8 x 1.25	6.8
M10 x 1.5	8.5
M12 x 1.75	10.2
M14 x 2	12.0
M16 x 2	14.0
M20 x 2.5	17.5
M24 x 3	21.0

Figure 14-73. *Tap drill sizes for metric threads*

Size and threads	Body diameter	Body drill	Preferred hole diameter	Tap drill
1-64	0.073	47	0.0575	53
2-56	0.086	42	0.0682	51
3-48	0.099	37	0.078	5/64
4-40	0.122	31	0.0866	44
5-40	0.125	29	0.0995	39
6-32	0.138	27	0.1063	36
8-32	0.164	18	0.1324	29
10-24	0.190	10	0.1476	26
12-24	0.216	2	0.1732	17
1/4-20	0.250	1/4	0.1990	8
5/16-18	0.3125	5/16	0.2559	F
3/8-16	0.375	3/8	0.3110	5/16
7/16-14	0.4375	7/16	0.3642	U
1/2-13	0.500	1/2	0.4219	27/64
9/16-12	0.5625	9/16	0.4776	31/64
5/8-11	0.625	5/8	0.5315	17/32
3/4-10	0.750	3/4	0.6480	41/64
7/8-9	0.875	7/8	0.7307	49/64
1"-8	1.000	1"	0.8376	7/8

Figure 14-71. *Body and tap drill sizes for UNC threads*

Screw Pitch Gage

It is difficult and time-consuming to count the threads on a bolt or nut to identify the thread type and size. For this reason, precision tool manufacturers provide screw pitch gages that have a series of blades, or leaves, in a steel case. Each leaf has teeth corresponding to the threads with the number of threads per inch stamped on it. To find the number of threads per inch on a bolt or nut, select the leaf whose teeth fit exactly into the threads and note the number stamped on the leaf.

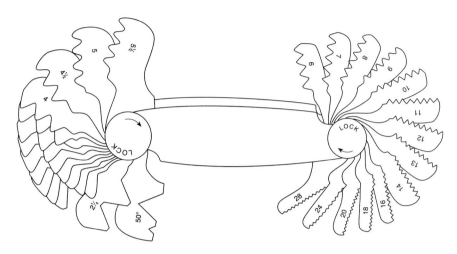

Figure 14-74. *A screw pitch gage saves time in determining thread pitch on a bolt or a nut.*

STUDY QUESTIONS: THREADS AND THREADING TOOLS

Answers are on Page 776. **Page numbers refer to chapter text.**

21. Two basic ways of forming threads on a screw or bolt are:
    a. _____
    b. _____
       Page 758

22. A _____ (what type) of tap is used for cutting threads to the bottom of a hole in a casting. *Page 758*

23. Pipe threads form a leakproof seal because they are _____ . *Page 758*

AVIATION MAINTENANCE TECHNICIAN   GENERAL

Torque and Torque Wrenches

Threaded fasteners are one of the most widely-used methods of joining aircraft components. The vibration encountered by the modern lightweight aircraft makes it imperative that the AMT understands the way to get the strongest joint when using bolts or cap screws. The strongest threaded joint is one in which the load applied to the fastener when it is installed is greater than the maximum load that will be applied to the joint in service.

Aircraft and engine manufacturers have determined the maximum load that will be applied to each joint and specify the proper torque for each fastener. This recommended torque is normally given for clean, dry threads, but if the threads are to be lubricated, the type and amount of lubricant will be specified.

When torquing a self-locking nut on a bolt, first determine the amount of torque needed to run the nut down on the bolt before it contacts the surface (this is called prevailing torque). The final torque on the nut must be the sum of the prevailing torque plus the desired torque.

If a threaded fastener does not fail when it is being properly torqued, it will not fail in service. When the fastener is being torqued, it is subjected to both torsional and tensile stresses. After the installation is complete, the fastener is subjected only to the tensile stress.

There are three ways the torque applied to a bolt may be measured, and the airframe or powerplant manufacturer will specify the correct method to use to determine the torque.

1. Using a torque wrench:

    Torque wrenches measure the amount of torque, or twisting force, applied to the tool used to install the fastener. This method is widely used on airframe and many engine applications.

2. Measuring the amount the bolt stretches:

    The torque applied to certain highly-stressed engine bolts is determined by measuring the length of the bolt with a vernier micrometer caliper before the torque is applied, then tightening the nut until the bolt has stretched a specified amount.

3. Turning the nut a specified amount after it reaches the bearing surface:

    This is a useful method in which the nut is turned until it contacts the bearing surface, then turned a specified number of degrees. This is usually specified by the flats of the nut. Turning a hex nut one flat is turning it 60°. The advantage of measuring torque by this method is that the final torque is not affected by the prevailing torque, nor by lubrication or lack of lubrication on the threads.

Figure 14-75. *A click-type torque wrench can be adjusted so it will click, or snap, when the desired torque is being applied.*

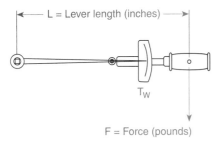

L = Lever length (inches)

T_W

F = Force (pounds)

Figure 14-76. *A typical deflecting-beam torque wrench*

The toggle, or micrometer click-type torque wrench such as the one in Figure 14-75 is popular because it is not necessary to look directly at the wrench when the torque is being applied. Twist the handle until a reference mark on the handle aligns with a graduation on the shaft of the wrench. This graduation indicates the foot-pounds of torque at which the wrench will click. Place the correct socket on the wrench and put it on the fastener to be torqued. Be sure that the wrench is perfectly square with the fastener, and apply a smooth pull on the wrench until it clicks.

Click-type torque wrenches do not limit the amount of torque that can be applied; rather, they indicate that the set amount of torque is being applied when they click. Stop the pull as soon as the wrench clicks.

Deflecting-beam torque wrenches such as the one in Figure 14-76 are widely used in aviation maintenance. It is important when using this type of wrench that the wrench be square on the fitting and the force applied to the wrench be concentrated at the pivot point on the handle. The torque read on the wrench (T_W) measured in inch-pounds, is the product of the lever length (L) in inches and the force (F) in pounds.

It is often necessary to use an adapter on a torque wrench. The arm of the adapter must be considered when determining the torque being applied to the fastener.

When the adapter adds to the lever length, as in Figure 14-77, you must use the formula to determine the torque reading on the wrench (T_W) to attain the required amount of torque applied to the fastener by the adapter (T_A). When the extension subtracts from the lever length of the wrench, use the formula in Figure 14-78.

The torsion-bar torque wrench is an accurate type of rigid-frame torque wrench. The critical component is the torsion bar which is a piece of hardened steel, circular in cross section with a square drive on one end. The other end is attached to the frame of the wrench in such a way that when torque is applied, the bar twists about its longitudinal axis. This bar is quite short, and its angular movement is limited. To be able to read the indication, a lever arm is attached to the torsion bar, and on the end of this arm is a rack gear which rotates a pinion on the shaft of a dial indicator. As torque is applied, the bar twists, the lever arm moves the rack and rotates the pinion which indicates on the dial indicator the amount of torque being applied.

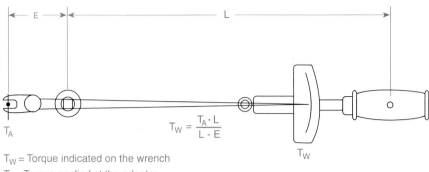

$$T_W = \frac{T_A \cdot L}{L - E}$$

T_W = Torque indicated on the wrench
T_A = Torque applied at the adapter
L = Lever length of torque wrench
E = Arm of the adapter

Figure 14-77. *Determine the proper torque indication when using an extension that adds to the lever length of the wrench.*

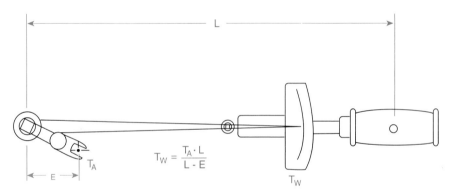

$$T_W = \frac{T_A \cdot L}{L - E}$$

T_W = Torque indicated on the wrench
T_A = Torque applied at the adapter
L = Lever length of torque wrench
E = Arm of the adapter

Figure 14-78. *Determine the proper torque indication when using an extension that subtracts from the lever length of the wrench.*

Torque Conversion

Figure 14-79 shows the most widely used units of torque and their conversion into other units.

Inch grams	Inch ounces	Inch pounds	Foot pounds	Centimeter kilograms	Meter kilograms
7.09	0.25				
14.17	0.5				
21.26	0.75				
28.35	1.0				
113.40	4.0	0.25			
226.80	8.0	0.50			
453.59	16.0	1.00	0.08	1.11	
	96.0	6.00	0.50	6.92	
	192.0	12.00	1.00	13.83	0.138
	384.0	24.00	2.00	27.66	0.277
	576.0	36.00	3.00	41.49	0.415
	768.0	48.00	4.00	55.32	0.553
	960.0	60.00	5.00	69.15	0.692
		72.00	6.00	82.98	0.830
		84.00	7.00	96.81	0.968
		96.00	8.00	110.64	1.106
		108.00	9.00	124.47	1.245
		120.00	10.00	138.31	1.383

Figure 14-79. *Torque conversion*

Recommended Torque Values for Nut and Bolt Combinations

It is extremely important to use the torque values listed in the manufacturer's service manuals for all threaded joints; but if no torque is specified, the values in Figures 14-80, 14-81, and 14-82 may generally be used for clean, dry threads.

Nut-Bolt size	Standard AN and MS steel bolts in tension				High strength MS and NAS steel bolts in tension			
	Nuts tension torque limits (in.-lbs.)		Nut shear torque limits (in.-lbs.)		Nuts tension torque limits (in.-lbs.)		Nut shear torque limits (in.-lbs.)	
	Min.	Max.	Min.	Max.	Min.	Max.	Min.	Max.
8-36	12	15	7	9				
10-32	20	25	12	15	25	30	15	20
1/4-28	50	70	30	40	80	100	50	60
5/16-24	100	140	60	85	120	145	70	90
3/8-24	160	190	95	110	200	250	120	150
7/16-20	450	500	270	300	520	630	300	400
1/2-20	480	690	290	410	770	950	450	550
9/16-18	800	1,000	480	600	1,100	1,300	650	800
5/8-18	1,100	1,300	660	780	1,250	1,550	750	950
3/4-16	2,300	2,500	1,300	1,500	2,650	3,200	1,600	1,900
7/8-14	2,500	3,000	1,500	1,800	3,550	4,350	2,100	2,600
1-14	3,700	4,500	2,200	3,300	4,500	5,500	2,700	3,300
1-1/8-12	5,000	7,000	3,000	4,200	6,000	7,300	3,600	4,400
1-1/4-12	9,000	11,000	5,400	6,600	11,000	13,400	6,600	8,000

Figure 14-80. *Recommended torque values for fine-thread-series steel fasteners*

Standard AN and MS steel bolts in tension				
Nut-Bolt size	**Nuts tension torque limits (in.-lbs.)**		**Nuts shear torque limits (in.-lbs.)**	
	Min.	**Max.**	**Min.**	**Max.**
8-32	12	15	7	9
10-24	20	25	12	15
1/4-20	40	50	25	30
5/16-18	80	90	48	55
3/8-16	160	185	95	110
7/16-14	235	255	140	155
1/2-13	400	480	240	290
9/16-12	500	700	300	420
5/8-11	700	900	420	540
3/4-10	1,150	1,600	700	950
7/8-9	2,200	3,000	1,300	1,800
1-8	3,700	5,000	2,200	3,000
1-1/8-8	5,500	6,500	3,300	4,000
1-1/4-8	6,500	8,000	4,000	5,000

Figure 14-81. *Recommended torque values for coarse-thread-series steel fasteners*

Aluminum bolts in tension				
Nut-Bolt size	**Nuts tension torque limits (in.-lbs.)**		**Nuts shear torque limits (in.-lbs.)**	
	Min.	**Max.**	**Min.**	**Max.**
8-36	5	10	3	6
10-32	10	15	5	10
1/4-28	30	45	15	30
5/16-24	40	65	25	40
3/8-24	75	110	45	70
7/16-20	180	280	110	170
1/2-20	280	410	160	260

Figure 14-82. *Recommended torque values for fine-thread-series aluminum alloy fasteners*

STUDY QUESTIONS: TORQUE AND TORQUE WRENCHES

Answers are on Page 776. **Page numbers refer to chapter text.**

24. Three ways of determining that the correct torque has been applied to a bolt and nut are:

a. _____

b. _____

c. _____

Page 761

25. Click-type torque wrenches _____ (do or do not) limit the amount of torque that can be applied to a fastener. *Page 762*

26. A deflecting beam torque wrench must indicate _____ inch-pounds, if 50 inch-pounds of torque is to be applied to a fastener by a wrench with a lever length of 12 inches and an extension that adds 2 inches to the length of the wrench. *Page 762*

Continued

Answers are on Page 776. **Page numbers refer to chapter text.**

27. A deflecting beam torque wrench must indicate _____ inch-pounds, if 50 inch-pounds of torque is to be applied to a fastener by a wrench with a lever length of 12 inches and an extension that subtracts 1 inch from the length of the wrench. *Page 762*

28. If no specific lubrication is specified for the threads of a fastener that is to be torqued, they should be _____ (coated with oil or clean and dry). *Page 764*

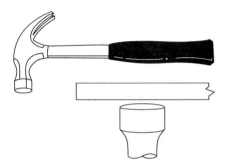

Figure 14-83. *The face of a carpenter's claw hammer is slightly crowned to concentrate the force for control when driving nails.*

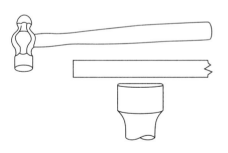

Figure 14-84. *The face of a ball peen hammer is flat.*

Pounding Tools

Hammers and mallets are some of the simplest tools, yet they do have specific purposes. Care must be taken that the wrong type of pounding tool is not used on a job.

Carpenter's Claw Hammer

This hammer used for driving and removing nails is seldom used when working on an aircraft. This type of hammer is not designed for use in metal working because its face is slightly crowned to concentrate the force when driving nails (*see* Figure 14-83).

Ball Peen Hammer

This is the most widely-used hammer for general aviation maintenance, and it is available with head weights from a few ounces to several pounds. The face of the hammer is flat with slightly rounded edges, and the opposite end of the head is rounded like a ball, as shown in Figure 14-84.

Metalworking Hammers

There are sheet metal applications that call for a hammer with a flat face like the ball peen hammer but with a wedge-shaped peen end. If the wedge is parallel to the handle, it is called a straight peen hammer, and if it is across the handle, it is a cross peen hammer.

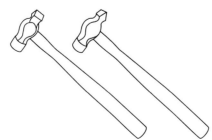

Figure 14-85. *Straight peen and cross peen hammers*

When forming compound curves in sheet aluminum, the metal may be stretched by hammering it into a sandbag. Then it is smoothed out by hammering it over a smooth, steel dolly block with a planishing, or body hammer. This is a lightweight hammer that has a large-area smooth face (Figure 14-86).

Mallets and Soft-Face Hammers

Sheet aluminum is formed by first stretching it and then smoothing it so the stretched metal forms the desired curves. The initial stretching is done by pounding the metal into a sandbag or around a form with a soft-face hammer, or mallet. These hammers may have replaceable faces of soft metal, resilient plastic, or coils of rawhide. Some of the faces are domed to better stretch the metal; some are flat to do some of the initial smoothing.

Sledgehammers

Sledgehammers are long-handled, heavy-head hammers that have two parallel flat faces. They are wielded with two hands and are used for heavy pounding work, and for driving stakes into the ground.

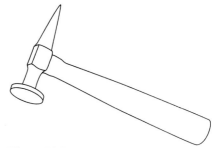

Figure 14-86. *A planishing, or body hammer is used to smooth an area in a piece of sheet metal that has been stretched.*

Figure 14-87. *Soft-faced mallets are used in sheet metal work to form the metal without damaging it with hammer blows.*

STUDY QUESTION: POUNDING TOOLS

Answer is on Page 776. Page number refers to chapter text.

29. A _____ (what type) hammer should be used when smoothing sheet aluminum by hammering it over a smooth steel dolly block. *Page 767*

Punches

There are a number of punches that are useful to the AMT. Figure 14-88 shows some of the most widely-used punches.

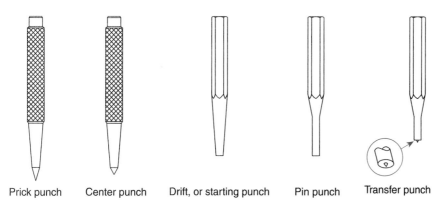

Prick punch   Center punch   Drift, or starting punch   Pin punch   Transfer punch

Figure 14-88. *Punches*

A prick punch has a sharp point and is used to mark the exact location for drilling a hole in a piece of sheet metal. The location for the hole is identified, the point of the prick punch is placed at this location, and the punch is tapped with a lightweight hammer. This leaves a small indentation at the location for the hole.

A center punch is similar to a prick punch, but its point is blunter and ground to an angle of approximately 60° (which is correct for starting a properly-ground twist drill to cut). The point of the center punch is placed in the indentation formed by the prick punch, and the punch is hit with a hammer to create a depression to hold the drill as it begins to cut.

A drift, or starting punch has a tapered shank, and is used to drive bolts from their holes and to align parts for assembly. Drift punches are especially useful when installing wings or other large components on an airplane. The wing is put in place, and a drift punch is used to align the holes in the wing spars and the fuselage before the bolts are put in place.

Pin punches are used to remove rivets after the manufactured head has been drilled through. A punch of the proper size is placed in the drilled hole, and the rivet head is broken off. The punch is then tapped with a lightweight hammer to punch the rivet shank from the hole. Pin punches are also used to align components being assembled.

Transfer punches are used to locate rivet holes when making a new aircraft skin using the old skin as a pattern. The skins are placed together, and a transfer punch whose outside diameter is the same as the diameter of the rivet hole is placed in the hole in the old skin. The punch is tapped with a lightweight hammer and the sharp point in the center of the flat end of the punch makes a small indentation in the new skin. This indentation is used as a location for a center punch.

Automatic center punches, such as the one in Figure 14-89, are especially handy when a large number of holes must be marked. The punch has a spring inside the handle whose compression is adjusted by twisting the handle. To use this punch, place the point in the indentation made by a prick punch and press the punch into the metal. As you press, the spring is compressed, and when the proper compression is reached, the spring automatically releases and drives the point into the metal.

Figure 14-89. *An automatic center punch saves time when a large number of hole locations must be marked.*

STUDY QUESTION: PUNCHES

Answer is on Page 776. Page number refers to chapter text.

30. The location of a hole that is to be drilled should be marked with a/an _____ (what kind) punch. *Page 768*

Wrenches

Various types of wrenches are used in aviation maintenance, and they are made in many sizes and shapes. Some of the most generally-used wrenches are described here.

Most wrenches are made of high-grade vanadium steel because of its toughness, and are heavily chrome-plated for appearance, protection against rust, and ease of cleaning.

Open End Wrenches

Open end wrenches have parallel jaws on each end (*see* Figure 14-90). These jaws are angled 15° to the axis of the wrench to allow the wrench to be flipped over to get a new grip on the fastener when turning it in a confined space.

Most open end wrenches have different-sized openings on the ends. Figure 14-91 lists the most commonly-used sizes in both U.S. and metric.

Figure 14-90. *Open end wrench*

U.S. wrench sizes (inches)	Metric wrench sizes (mm)
1/4 - 5-16	6 - 8
3/8 - 7/16	7 - 9
1/2 - 9/16	10 - 11
5/8 - 3/4	12 - 14
11/16 - 13/16	13 - 15
3/4 - 7/8	16 - 18
25/32 - 13/16	17 - 19
15/16 - 1	20 - 22
1-1/16 - 1-1/8	21 - 23
1-1/4 - 1-5/16	24 - 26

Figure 14-91. *The most popular sizes for open end and box end wrenches*

Adjustable Open End Wrench

Adjustable open end wrenches are often called "Crescent" wrenches. They are made by almost all of the quality hand-tool manufacturers and are available in standard lengths from 4 to 12 inches. (*See* Figure 14-92.)

Adjustable end wrenches have one fixed jaw, and one jaw that slides in a groove moved by a worm gear that is rotated by the user. It is important when using an adjustable open end wrench to place the wrench on the fastener so the pull is away from the fixed jaw. When the wrench is held in this way, the strain is placed on the base of the fixed jaw where it is the strongest.

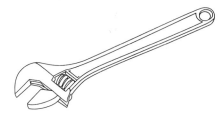

Figure 14-92. *Adjustable open end wrench*

Ratcheting Open End Wrench

A ratcheting open end wrench allows a fastener to be turned down or removed without having to remove the wrench each time it is necessary to get another grip. These wrenches look much like an ordinary open end wrench, except one of the jaws is much shorter than the other. When you pull the wrench toward you, the pressure is applied near the end of the long jaw and the root of the short jaw. When the direction of wrench movement is reversed, the short jaw moves around to the next flat.

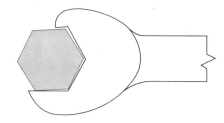

Figure 14-93. *Ratcheting open end wrench*

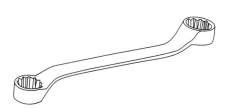

Figure 14-94. *Box end wrench*

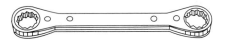

Figure 14-95. *Ratcheting box wrench*

pawl. A driving link in a ratchet wrench. It allows the handle to turn the socket in one direction but prevents its turning in the opposite direction.

Figure 14-96. *Combination wrench*

Figure 14-97. *Flare nut wrench*

Box End Wrenches

It is possible when a large amount of torque is applied to a fastener with an open end wrench, that the jaws will be sprung, and it is possible for the wrench to slip off the fastener. Much more torque can be applied with a box end wrench than with an open end, because they cannot be sprung open.

Box end wrenches are available with both 6-point and 12-point ends, with the gripping surfaces offset so the wrench can be flipped over to get a new grip on the fastener when working in close quarters. The handles of some box end wrenches are offset so the handle extends upward when the box of the wrench is flat. This gives clearance over adjacent fasteners. (*See* Figure 14-94.)

Box end wrenches have different-sized openings on the ends, and the typical sizes are listed in Figure 14-91.

Ratcheting Box Wrenches

Ratcheting box wrenches are extremely handy tools. Two thin 6- or 12-point open sockets are mounted in the ends of the wrench in the same way as the box ends of a standard box end wrench. The outside of the sockets have ratchet teeth cut in them, and the ratchet pawls are inside the wrench handle. (*See* Figure 14-95.)

To use a ratcheting box wrench, place it over the fastener and use it as a normal wrench. However, the wrench does not have to be removed to get a new grip on the fastener—just ratchet the handle for a new grip each time the pawl slips over a ratchet tooth. To reverse the wrench, remove it and flip it over. Ratcheting box wrenches are made with both straight and offset handles.

Combination Wrenches

A very popular wrench configuration is the combination wrench. This wrench has a box end and an open end of the same size. This is handy when removing tight fasteners. The box end is used to apply maximum torque for breaking the fastener loose, and then the open end is used because it is much quicker to get a new grip with an open end than it is with a box end.

Flare Nut Wrench

The many fluid lines in a modern airplane make a set of flare nut wrenches an important addition to a technician's toolbox. These wrenches resemble a straight box end wrench with a portion of the box removed so the wrench will slip over the fluid line to loosen or tighten the fitting (Figure 14-97).

Flare nut wrenches are weaker than box end wrenches and should not be used in place of a box end wrench for general nut tightening or loosening.

Socket Wrenches

Socket wrenches make it possible for a technician to have a wide range of wrench sizes and handles with a minimum number of expensive tools (*see* Figure 14-98). The handles are available with four basic sizes of square drives. The smallest ¼-inch square drive is widely used for aircraft maintenance, because many of the fasteners on an aircraft are small.

The next size, a ⅜-inch square drive, is the most popular. This is because most fasteners in an aircraft can be turned with wrenches using this size drive, and more torque can be applied with this drive than with a ¼-inch drive.

The ½-inch square drive is commonly used in automobile maintenance, but its use is limited in aircraft maintenance. The largest wrenches that are commonly available have a ¾-inch square drive and are used in aircraft maintenance only for very special applications.

square drive. The drive coupling between a socket wrench and the handle that turns it.

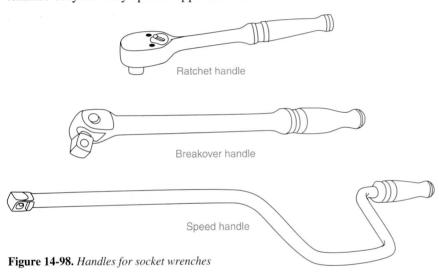

Ratchet handle

Breakover handle

Speed handle

Figure 14-98. *Handles for socket wrenches*

The most popular handles are the ratchet-type. This allows a socket to be placed on a fastener, and by moving the handle back and forth, it is possible to tighten or loosen the fastener without removing the socket.

A break-over handle, or breaker bar, is a long handle with the socket drive mounted on a pin that allows its angle relative to the handle to be varied. Break-over handles can apply the maximum torque to a fastener to tighten or loosen it.

Speed handles, or speeders, resemble a crank that allows a fastener to be rapidly spun into place. Very little torque can be applied with a speed handle.

Air-driven ratchets are available that allow nuts to be spun onto their bolts very quickly. Impact wrenches are used in automobile maintenance shops, but are not normally recommended for aviation maintenance. This is because the torque produced by these wrenches is in a series of impulses that do not produce the smooth torque needed for most of the highly stressed, lightweight structure found in an aircraft.

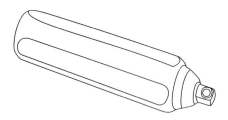

Figure 14-99. *Hand-impact driver for loosening stubborn screws and nuts*

There is, however, one handy hand-impact tool used in aviation maintenance to break loose nuts and screws that have been corroded or rusted to the extent that an ordinary socket or screwdriver cannot budge them. This is the hand impact driver in Figure 14-99. This is especially useful when fitted with a screwdriver bit to loosen structural screws in stressed inspection plates. The recess in the screw is cleaned out, and the screwdriver bit is installed on the driver and placed in the recess and the end of the driver is struck with a ball peen hammer. The blow rotates the screwdriver bit and at the same time prevents it from jumping out of the recess.

Sockets are available in both 6- and 12-point openings, in U.S. and metric sizes. They are available as shallow sockets, semi-deep sockets, and deep sockets. Sockets with universal joints are available, and universal joints that can be placed between a normal socket and a drive are also available.

Crowfoot wrenches that have an open end or a flare-nut end can be mounted on an extension to turn fasteners that cannot be reached by any other type of wrench.

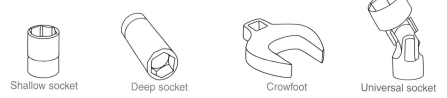

Shallow socket   Deep socket   Crowfoot   Universal socket

Figure 14-100. *Typical socket wrenches used in aviation maintenance*

Extensions are available that can place the socket away from the handle to allow the wrench to turn fasteners inaccessible to any other type of wrench (Figure 14-101). Straight extensions are available from less than two inches long to more than 36 inches. Some extensions are made of double-wrapped steel wire and are flexible so the socket can be oriented at any angle relative to the drive handle.

Universal joints are available that allow any socket to be used as a universal socket. Ratchet adapters can be installed between a handle and a socket, or between an extension and a socket; then the socket can be ratcheted.

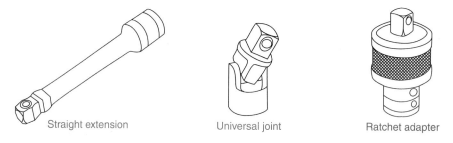

Straight extension   Universal joint   Ratchet adapter

Figure 14-101. *Extension and adapters used with socket wrenches*

Allen Wrenches

Some structural screws and bolts have internal wrenching heads. This type of head allows the fastener to be recessed in a close-fitting hole without needing to allow space for a normal socket wrench.

Allen wrenches are made of hardened tool steel with a hexagonal cross section. They are in the shape of the letter L with a long and a short leg (*see* Figure 14-102). They normally come in sets and have dimensions across their flats of from $\frac{1}{16}$ inch to $\frac{5}{8}$ inch.

Figure 14-102. *A typical set of Allen wrenches*

STUDY QUESTIONS: WRENCHES

Answers are on Page 776. **Page numbers refer to chapter text.**

31. When using an adjustable end wrench, it should be placed on the fastener so the pull on the handle is _____ (toward or away from) the fixed jaw. *Page 769*

32. A _____ (box end or open end) wrench should be used to apply maximum torque to a fastener. *Page 770*

33. A _____ (what kind) handle should be used with a socket wrench to apply the maximum amount of torque. *Page 771*

34. Impact wrenches _____ (are or are not) normally approved for use on an aircraft. *Page 771*

Screwdrivers

There are many applications in an aircraft where screws are used. Nonstructural screws are used for such applications as mounting instruments in panels, attaching fairings, and some inspection plates. Structural screws are used for attaching inspection plates in highly stressed areas where the surface must be flush.

Screwdrivers are available in many sizes and shapes and with wood or high-impact plastic handles. The blade lengths vary from about one inch for the short stubby screwdriver to some with shanks longer than 20 inches. The shanks of many are round, but some have square shanks. Some of the better round-shank screwdrivers have a short hexagonal section near the handle that can be turned with a wrench for greater torque.

Screwdrivers used for electrical applications have plastic handles that are electrical insulators. Screwdrivers used for miniature electronics applications have a rotatable knob on the end that allows better control when turning small screws.

One type of screwdriver that is becoming very popular is the magnetic screwdriver that has a ¼-inch hex socket at the end of its shank. This socket is magnetized so it will hold screwdriver bits and prevent their falling out. Some of the better screwdrivers have a ratcheting handle and come in sets with one handle and a number of various sizes and types of bits.

The very large quantity of screws in the stressed inspection plates on many modern airplanes require some type of power screwdriver. These are available as pneumatic or battery-operated electrical units that use ¼-inch hexagon bits, and the rotation of these power screwdrivers is reversible. Many power screwdrivers have a torque-limiting clutch that prevents over-torquing of the screws.

CAUTION: Some reversible, high-torque electric drill motors may be fitted with screwdriver bits and used to drive or remove screws. These are often universal motors that spark at the armature. They should *never* be used where there is any possibility of explosive fuel vapors. Any power tool used in a possibly explosive environment must be approved for that type of operation.

Slot Screwdrivers

Slot-head screws have a rather limited use in aircraft because they cannot be installed or removed with power screwdrivers — the blade slips out of the screw slot and can damage the component into which the screw is being driven. Slot-head screws have been replaced with recessed-head screws.

Slot screwdrivers are still ubiquitous tools in a technician's toolbox and can be the most universally misused of all tools. They should never be used as pry bars, chisels, or punches. The blade of a slot screwdriver must be properly sharpened to prevent damage to the screw or the component in which the screw is installed. The sides of the tip should be ground parallel with the shank, and the edges should be sharp to grip the screw at the bottom of the slot (Figure 14-103).

Screws are often installed in locations where a straight screwdriver cannot be used on them. For these applications, offset screwdrivers such as the one in Figure 14-104 is used. Some offset screwdrivers have bits for recessed-head screws.

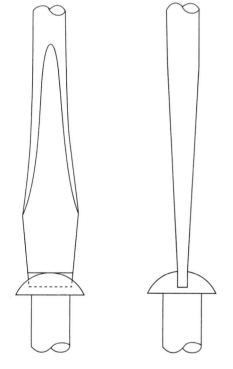

Figure 14-103. *The tip of a slot screwdriver should be ground so its sides are parallel, and it should fill approximately 75% of the width of the slot in the screw.*

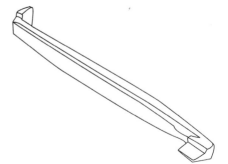

Figure 14-104. *Offset screwdriver*

Recessed-Head Screwdrivers

Power screwdrivers require a screw head that will not allow the bit to slip out. There have been two types of recessed-head, or cross-point screws used in aviation maintenance for decades. The recess in these screws looks similar, and the points of the screwdrivers look much alike, but they are different, and only the proper screwdrivers should be used for them. These are the Phillips and the Reed & Prince shown in Figure 14-105.

Notice that the point of the Phillips screwdriver is blunt, and the sides of the point have a double taper. The Reed & Prince, on the other hand, has a sharp point and a single taper.

The airlines and the military use screws with other types of recessed heads that hold the point of the screwdriver bit more tightly in order to prevent it from slipping out when used with a power screwdriver. Figure 14-106 shows some of the recessed heads.

The Pozidriv screwdriver tips are an improvement on the Phillips because the tip is not as tapered as on the Phillips, and it has wedges that ensure a tight fit in the screw head. Phillips screwdriver bits should not be used on Pozidriv screws because they will ride up out of the recess and round the corners of both the screw head and the screwdriver bit.

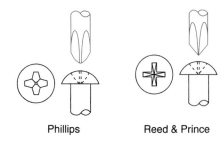

Phillips   Reed & Prince

Figure 14-105. *The Phillips and the Reed & Prince screws are the most widely used recessed head screws in general aviation.*

Hi-Torque®   Torq-Set®   Tri-Wing®   Pozidriv®   Torx®   Spline

Figure 14-106. *Screw heads for special structural screws. Screwdriver bits are made to fit all of these special screws.*

STUDY QUESTION: SCREWDRIVERS

Answer is on Page 776. **Page number refers to chapter text.**

35. A _____ (slot or recessed head) screwdriver bit is not normally used with a power screwdriver. *Page 774*

Answers to Chapter 14 Study Questions

1. soft lead pencil
2. 0.001
3. 0.02
4. 0.0001
5. 0.002
6. dial indicator
7. ball-type small hole gage
8. are not
9. box, finger
10. slip roll former
11. sand bag, soft-face
12. 2
13. ripsaw
14. backsaw
15. vixen

16. larger
17. 118
18. Forstner
19. fixed-diameter
20. fly cutter
21. a. rolling
    b. cutting
22. bottoming
23. tapered
24. a. use a torque wrench
    b. measure the amount the bolt has stretched
    c. turn the nut a specific amount after it reaches the bearing surface

25. do not
26. 42.8
27. 54.5
28. clean and dry
29. planishing, or body
30. prick
31. away from
32. box end
33. break-over
34. are not
35. slot

ENTERING THE FIELD OF AVIATION MAINTENANCE

15

ENTERING THE FIELD OF AVIATION MAINTENANCE

15

Once you have your treasured Aircraft Mechanic Certificate in hand, you are ready for the most important step of all, making it pay for all the work you have put into getting it. In this section we want to consider the different types of job opportunities available and look at some of the ways to get the job you want.

The Aviation Industry

World conditions change, our economy changes, and, most of all, aviation changes. In its short nine decades of existence, aviation has become a vital part of our economy, and every day new uses for aviation are found. All changes are not good, but without change, there is no progress. We need to examine both sides of the industry's progression.

The Down Side

In times of economic growth and industrial expansion, jobs are plentiful and easy to find. But in the 1990s this is not the case, and aviation has been hit particularly hard.

The military services are facing cutbacks, and as a result many highly experienced technicians will be facing the prospect of finding civilian jobs in their skill area. Military contracts in the aerospace industry are being scaled back, thus eliminating many job possibilities. Airlines are in financial difficulties, so some are merging while others are being forced into bankruptcy. The out-of-control rise in the cost of private aircraft ownership has wiped out a large segment of private flying and the services that support it. This has reduced job opportunities even more.

The Up Side

But, all is not bleak and discouraging. Aviation has replaced the railroads and steamship lines as people movers, and even though the number of airlines is decreasing, the number of passenger-miles and pound-miles flown is increasing. The night skies are full of airplanes moving express and mail so businesses will have on hand the things they need for each day. Many businesses have their own corporate aircraft to efficiently meet their transportation needs.

Aircraft do far more than just transport people and things. They are used to control forest fires, to plant, to fertilize, and to control pests in agricultural crops; and to survey traffic conditions and to save lives by rushing accident victims to hospitals. The uses of aircraft are increasing daily. The real up side for us is that as aircraft usage increases, the need for maintenance increases.

A recently released study indicates that the component repair and overhaul area of aviation maintenance is expected to double by the year 2010. This same study predicts that the airline fleet will increase by 50% to 16,000 aircraft by 2010. These figures emphasize that the need for aviation maintenance technicians will increase.

You have already identified the field in which you want to work and have taken the major step of obtaining your aircraft mechanic certificate. This narrows your job search and gives you a definite advantage over other applicants who do not have this certification.

Even though you may never use your mechanic certificate to certify an aircraft as being airworthy, having it is a definite asset, and for employment with some companies, it is a requirement. Having the certificate assures the potential employer that you have enough ambition and foresight to get the certificate, and that you have a recognized level of knowledge and skills.

What Do You Want?

There are basically two classifications of people ready to fill the slots open in aviation maintenance: recent graduates from the Aviation Maintenance Technician schools who have little or virtually no real world experience, and those who are leaving the military services and have specialized experience in aircraft maintenance.

Aviation maintenance is such a broad term and it encompasses so many different types of positions that there is a job to suit everyone. The problem is to define the one you most want, look at some of the steps to take in getting the job, and then being in the right place at the right time.

Life is too short to spend it doing something you do not enjoy or at a job that does not give you satisfaction. Some of us enjoy creating new things, others enjoy fixing things, while others enjoy working with people. Some of us are self starters and enjoy working with a minimum of supervision and restrictions, while others enjoy working in a more structured environment where we do things "by the book."

Naturally, when we limit ourselves to a certain geographic area, we are cutting down on our options, but aviation maintenance is so widely distributed that we can likely find a job that suits us in our local area.

How to Go About Getting the Job of Your Choice

Figure 15-1 contains excerpts from a recent survey published in the *Occupational Outlook Quarterly*. There are other methods of job hunting than those listed, but they were used by a smaller percentage of persons and proved to be less effective.

The tabulations in Figure 15-1 show that the most effective method of job hunting and the one used by the most people is that of applying directly. Here, we will look at this as being the primary method of job hunting, but, naturally it should be augmented with other methods as the opportunities arise.

Method	% of Total Jobseekers Using This Method*	Effectiveness rate **
Applied directly	66.0%	47.7%
Asked friends about jobs where they work	50.8%	22.1%
Answered local newspaper ads	45.9%	23.9%
Used private employment agencies	21.0%	24.2%
Used Federal/State employment agencies	33.5%	13.7%
Applied at union hiring halls	6.0%	22.2%

* Most jobseekers use more than one method.
** Effectiveness rate is found by dividing the number of jobseekers who found work by this method by the total number of jobseekers who used this method, whether they were successful or not.

Figure 15-1. *Use and Effectiveness of Job Search Methods*

Analyze Yourself

The person is fortunate, indeed, who enjoys the work with which he or she earns a living. When entering the job market or changing jobs is the time to locate the job that will give you the most long-term satisfaction. The way to do this is to match your talents and desires with the jobs in the aviation maintenance industry. It is always a good idea to be flexible, and to be alert to new opportunities as they develop. The aviation working environment provides a network of various jobs, the scope and nature of which are always changing.

Analyze yourself to find the type of job you want to do. Consider both the things you do best and the things you enjoy most. Some of the questions you should ask yourself are:

Exactly what type of work do I do best?

Which do I enjoy most, working with people, things, or information?

Do I work best by myself or with others?

Would I rather work in a small or a large company?

Do I enjoy variety in my work, or would I rather be specialized?

Do I enjoy working outdoors, or would I rather work indoors?

In what geographical area do I want to work?

Fit Your Expertise to the Right Type of Organization

When you have analyzed your personal likes and dislikes, consider the types of organizations that use aviation maintenance technicians. As we consider each of these basic types of operations, we will look at some of their basic characteristics. (There is such a wide range of salaries and security issues, and these are constantly in such a state of change, that we will not consider these issues in this overview.)

The Air Carriers

- Major, or trunk, carriers

- Commuters

- Contract carriers

- Freight and express carriers

Air carriers are perhaps one of the largest users of aviation maintenance technicians, and they offer the greatest diversity of locations in which a person may work. Therefore, advancing within the company often requires moving from one base to another.

Air carrier maintenance is done under the provisions of the individual airline's maintenance manual. This allows the airline to recommend to the FAA individuals who have had extensive specialized training and experience for certification as repairmen.

Air carriers normally have a relatively high pay schedule and offer such perquisites as discounted travel privileges. The large airlines have extensive training departments and all have good access to manufacturer's training, which allows you to keep current with the latest equipment. Because of the round-the-clock operation, work is done on a shift basis, and seniority is an important function in job security.

Aircraft, Equipment and Component Manufacturers and Rebuilders

The manufacturers of large civilian and military aircraft and engines employ an extensive workforce that covers a very wide range of skill and knowledge requirements. These operators offer a diversity of job opportunities in the actual manufacturing processes for specialists, such as machinists, tool and die makers, heat treat specialists, and painters.

Certified mechanics working in a factory will probably never have the need or opportunity to actually use their certificate to sign off an operation; but many factories place value on the fact that a job applicant has demonstrated the discipline and knowledge needed to certify as an aircraft mechanic.

Manufacturers offer many jobs other than those in the actual shops and assembly lines in which the knowledge requirement for certification is a great help. Technicians work in the experimental and prototype shops, test labs, scheduling, inspection departments, and training departments, and as liaison technicians between the engineering department and the actual assembly departments.

Almost all factories are unionized and much job security is based on seniority. This may subject a person to layoffs as the economy changes, but job security increases with seniority.

Fixed Base Operations (FBOs)

- Flight schools
- Aircraft sales and service
- Parts sales
- Line service
- Large aircraft overhaul facilities
- Charter flights
- Repair stations

The profitable small FBO has just about passed from the scene. Today the FBOs that are flourishing are those that are well financed and often have more than one operation.

Employment with an FBO normally provides a relatively stable work schedule, and it does not require much relocation. Since much of the work is done on aircraft other than those owned by the FBO, this work provides the opportunity to work directly with the customer. Some of the more successful FBOs recognize the importance of the maintenance technicians keeping current, and they make it possible for their technicians to attend manufacturer's training schools and seminars.

Flight training by the smaller FBOs has decreased in volume, but there are some large flight schools that maintain large fleets of aircraft and operate what is known as ab-inito training. This is flight training that takes the student from the very beginning up through commercial, multiengine, and instrument certification. Maintenance personnel in these schools work primarily on school aircraft and have little direct contact with private aircraft owners.

Specialty Operators

- Air ambulance operators
- Aerial photographers
- Aerial fire fighters
- Offshore helicopter operators
- Agricultural operators
- Aircraft caterers

Many of the specialty operators have relatively few employees and offer the individual an opportunity to be easily recognized for his or her abilities. Advancement on the basis of merit is usually easier than it is in a larger operation, but because of their small size, salaries, perks and job security may not equal those of the larger companies.

Because of the extremely wide diversity of operations, there are likely facilities in the geographic location of your choice.

Locating Your Potential Employer

After analyzing your strengths and desires and matching them with the particular branch of civilian aviation you want to pursue, your next step is to locate the actual companies you would like to work for.

If you are a recent graduate of an AMT school or have received your AMT training from a transition assistance program in the military, your instructor should be able to direct you to someone who has a current copy of the *World Aviation Directory*. This almost 2,000-page volume is periodically updated and gives information on just about every company involved in aviation activities throughout the world. Entries include the company name, address, and phone number and concise information on the activities of the company.

Once you have made a list of the companies that most interest you, your next step is to arrange for an interview with the person who can actually hire you. For an entry-level job in a large company, you will almost always have to go through the personnel department. You can usually learn the name of key persons by talking with someone who works in the company. If you do not know any one connected with the company, ask your friends and acquaintances who they know. One of the best places to meet people involved in aviation maintenance is at the Professional Aviation Maintenance Association (PAMA) meetings. You can get information on these meetings by calling PAMA headquarters at (202) 730-0260, or locate them on the worldwide web at www.pama.org.

Before you make your first contact, learn everything you can about the company, and have in your mind what you can contribute to the objectives of the company.

Your Résumé

A résumé is not the device that gets you the job, but it represents you. Your résumé and its cover letter must sell you to your prospective employer well enough to get an interview and to serve as an outline for this interview.

There are many books written on résumés, and there are services that will prepare a professional-looking résumé for you. One thing you should realize, though, is that there is no single résumé that will satisfy all employers.

There are essentially three types of résumés: functional, chronological, and technical. Functional résumés allow you to focus on the kinds of things you did as an employee, and chronological résumés emphasize the number of jobs you have held and the length of time you spent in each. Since we are considering only a specialized type of work, the technical résumé is the one we will discuss. The technical résumé focuses on the specific skills in your area of expertise.

Some of the basic points in technical résumé preparation are:

Write the résumé yourself. You know exactly what you want to convey to your prospective employer, and by being intimately familiar with its contents, you will be able to effectively use it in your interview. Leave out any reference to age, gender, height, weight, health, marital status, children, and hobbies.

- *Be specific.* State your job objective clearly and concisely. Be able to document your abilities.

- *Be relevant.* Do not put anything in your résumé that is not directly related to your job objective.

- *Be accurate.* You will really shoot yourself down if you make any claims that are not true.

- *Be positive.* Emphasize your accomplishments. Remember, your résumé must sell you.

- *Be brief.* Use short sentences and words that denote action. Do not make the résumé more than one page long.

- *Be civilian.* Unless the résumé is for military work or work for the government, avoid the use of military acronyms and MOS (Military Occupational Specialty) numbers. Civilians do not understand these terms.

Terry T. Worker

123 South Whichway Street   Home Phone (309) 597-8572
Anyold Place, Illinois 61004   Work Phone (309) 590-2500

Employment Goal
> Turbine engine mechanic

Experience
> Work experience
>> Hot section inspections PT6 engines
>> Turbine engine removal and replacement, including rigging and trimming
>> Flight line servicing and troubleshooting
>> Turbine engine test cell operation
>
> Safety management
>> Supervised flight line safety including fire fighting and enforcement of safe
>> work practices

Education and training
> PT6 Specialized training by Airwork, Inc.
> Newville Community College Aviation Technician Program
> U.S. Navy Aviation Turbine Engine Machinists Mate Course

Licenses Held
> FAA Mechanic Certificate with Airframe and Powerplant ratings

References
> Available on request

Figure 15-2. *A typical technical résumé*

Your résumé must be error free and professional looking. Have someone check your spelling and grammar. It is an excellent approach to use a word processor and a good quality printer to make the final copies. Also, having your résumé and cover letter on a word processor disk allows changes to be made so that each letter you send can be custom tailored to the company or individual to whom you are sending it.

The Cover Letter

Your résumé states the pertinent information about you. The cover letter that accompanies it is a short, personal, friendly letter that introduces you to the person with whom you want to interview. It emphasizes your high points and makes the person want to meet you. The cover letter must be friendly, enthusiastic, and professional. *See* Figure 15-3 on Page 788.

The Job Application

After you have made the first meaningful contact with the company, you will be required to fill out an employment, or job, application. This form gives a lot of information about you, but it does not give you the control to emphasize those high points you feel are important. Do not consider the job application to take place of your résumé. They serve two entirely different purposes.

When filling out a job application, be extremely neat, write legibly, and give only the information asked for. Be sure not to say anything that is untrue; untruths will return to haunt you.

The Interview

Your cover letter and résumé are written to get you the all-important interview. By this time, you should have done your homework and become familiar enough with the company to know exactly how you can be most profitable for both yourself and the company. Remember, in this interview, you are not begging for a job, but you have something to sell that your prospective employer needs; that is you. The goal of any successful job interview is a win-win situation. You have something the employer needs, and he has something you need. The object is to get these needs together.

The first impression you make on the interviewer is the most important one. Some basic pointers on the interview are:

- Be neat and clean and wear conservative clothes.

- Arrive a few minutes early, but never more than 10 minutes.

- Bring along two extra copies of your résumé. You will need one for yourself, and the extra one is in case the one you sent the company has been lost, or if two people conduct the interview.

- Have a pleasant and positive attitude toward everyone you meet. You will be hired for your attitude almost as much as for your knowledge and skill.

123 South Whichway Street
Anyold Place, Illinois 61004
April 31, 2000

Mr. John Jones, Maintenance Supervisor
Ontime Airlines, Inc.
P.O. Box 1662
Newville, Illinois 61317

Dear Mr. Jones:

Your engine shop foreman, Mr. Paul Somebody, recently spoke at a PAMA meeting in Anyold Place and told of the expansion Ontime Airlines is planning.

I have four years of experience in maintaining and servicing PT6 engines and recently completed the PT6 course held by Airwork. Most of my work has involved line maintenance and troubleshooting and one year was spent in the shop performing hot-section inspections.

I would appreciate the opportunity to meet with you and discuss the possibilities of joining the Ontime Airline maintenance crew. I will call you next week to arrange a meeting at your convenience.

Sincerely,

Terry T. Worker

Terry T. Worker

Figure 15-3. *A typical cover letter to accompany your résumé*

- Don't smoke during the interview, or even in the reception area. No one is hired because they smoke, but sometimes people may not be hired because they *do*.

- Keep eye contact with the interviewer, and be positive. You are doing the company as much a favor as they are doing you.

- Be prepared to discuss in detail anything that you have on your résumé.

- Answer all of the questions in good plain English. Be careful to not use the acronyms that are so common in military talk, and do not try to snow the interviewer.

- If you do not know the answer to any question, be honest and admit it. Bluffing is a red flag that will shoot you down.

- Do not criticize your former employer or any one with whom you have worked. Remember, an interview must be positive all the way through.

Most employment interviews should not last more than 20 minutes. The hiring decision is normally made during the first 10 minutes, and the last 10 minutes confirms the decision.

Never ask questions about job benefits. This will come with the negotiations after you have been given a positive offer. Impress on the interviewer the fact that you want to learn, to work hard, and to advance in the company. Since each company and sometimes departments within the company have their own "character," an additional benefit of the interview is for you to learn more about the company, and its expectations of the employees. Consider the interview as a two-way street; i.e., you are also seeking information about the company.

The Follow-Up

After the interview, send a follow-up letter to the interviewer, thanking him or her for the opportunity to be considered for employment. This letter gives you an opportunity to ask questions or supply additional information, and it keeps your name before the interviewer and marks you as a considerate person.

If you have not heard from the company after about two weeks, call or write to determine whether or not the job has been filled. If you receive a positive response, you are ready for the final negotiations; but if you receive a negative response, take a deep breath, review your job-hunting skills, and go for another company. Don't be discouraged, there is a right job for you!

GLOSSARY

abrasive. A material containing minute particles of some hard substance which when rubbed on a surface will wear away that surface.

absolute humidity. The actual amount of water in a given volume of air.

absolute pressure. Pressure that is measured from zero pressure, or from a vacuum. Absolute pressure is measured with a barometer.

absolute temperature. Temperature measured from absolute zero. Absolute temperature is measured in degrees Kelvin or degrees Rankine.

absolute zero. The temperature at which all molecular movement inside a material stops. It is zero degrees on both the Kelvin and Rankine scales and -273°C and -460°F.

acceleration due to gravity. 32.2 feet per second, per second.

accelerate. To increase speed or to make an object move faster.

acceleration caused by gravity. The change in speed of an object falling in a vacuum caused by the pull of gravity. The object will increase its speed 32.2 feet per second each second it falls.

acceptable data. Acceptable data may be used for all maintenance procedures other than major repairs and major alterations. It includes manufacturer's service manuals and bulletins, Advisory Circular 43.13-1B, 2A, and 14 CFR Parts 121 and 135 Maintenance Manuals. *See* approved data.

acid. A chemical substance that contains hydrogen, has a characteristically sour taste, and reacts with a base, or alkali, to form a salt.

addition. The process of finding the combined value of two or more numbers.

Advisory Circulars (ACs). Information published by the FAA that explains the Federal Aviation Regulations and describes methods of performing certain maintenance and inspection procedures. Compliance with ACs is not mandatory, and the information in the ACs is not necessarily FAA-approved data.

aging. A change in characteristics of a material that takes place over a period of time under specified environmental conditions.

Air Transport Association (ATA) Specification No. 100. A numerical classification of aircraft systems and components that allows standardization of maintenance information.

aircraft. A device that is used or intended to be used for flight in the air. For maintenance purposes, an aircraft consists of both the airframe and its powerplant.

Aircraft Listings. A document that contains many of the pertinent specifications for certificated aircraft of which there are fewer than 50 still registered.

Aircraft Specifications. Documents that includes the pertinent specifications for older aircraft that were certificated under the Civil Air Regulations. Specifications are also available for Engines and Propellers.

airfoil. Any surface designed to obtain a useful reaction, or lift, from air passing over it.

airframe. The basic structure of an aircraft that includes the fuselage, wings, landing gear, and rotors of a helicopter. Propellers and engine components are not a part of the airframe.

Airworthiness Certificate. A document carried in an aircraft that identifies the aircraft as one certificated under the appropriate part of the Federal Aviation Regulations.

Airworthiness Directives (ADs). Notices sent by the FAA to the registered owners or operators of aircraft identifying an unsafe condition in the affected aircraft and specifying a method for its correction. Compliance with ADs is mandatory.

airworthy. A condition in which the aircraft or component meets the requirements of its type design and is capable of safe operation.

Alclad. The registered trade name for high-strength sheet aluminum alloy that is protected from corrosion by a thin coating of pure aluminum rolled onto its surfaces.

alkali. A chemical substance, usually a hydroxide of a metal. An alkali has a characteristically bitter taste and it reacts with an acid to form a salt.

allowance. The difference between the nominal dimension of a part and its upper or lower limit.

alloying agent. A metal, other than the base metal in an alloy.

alodizing. A method of corrosion protection by the formation of a hard, airtight oxide coating on the surface of aluminum alloy parts by chemical means. The name is taken from the registered trade name of the chemical Alodine.

alpha iron. The arrangement of the molecules in iron when its temperature is below 911°C.

alteration. A change to a certificated aircraft, aircraft engine, propeller, or appliance.

alternating current (AC). Electricity that continually changes its voltage and periodically reverses its direction of flow.

ammeter. A measuring instrument installed in series with an electrical load to measure the amount of current flowing through the load.

ampere. A flow of current equal to one coulomb per second.

angstrom. A convenient unit used to measure the wavelength of light. One angstrom, or A, is equal to 1/10,000,000 meter. The wavelengths of visible light are between about 3,800 and 7,800 angstroms.

annealing. A form of heat treatment in which a metal is made soft.

annual inspection. A complete inspection required for all U.S. certificated aircraft that are not operated under some other inspection program. An annual inspection must be performed by an A&P technician who holds an Inspection Authorization, and it must be performed at least once every 12 calendar months.

anode. The end of a semiconductor diode that is made of P-type material and is represented in the schematic symbol by the arrowhead.

anodic area. An area inside a piece of metal that has lost some of its electrons. This leaves a net positive charge which attracts negative ions from the electrolyte. Positive metallic ions and negative ions from the electrolyte unite to form the salts of corrosion.

anodizing. A method of preventing corrosion of aluminum alloy parts. A hard oxide film is formed on the surface of the metal by an electrolytic process. This film prevents oxygen reaching the surface of the metal.

anti-icing. Preventing the formation of ice on an aircraft structure.

apparent power. Power in an AC circuit that is the product of the circuit voltage and all of the current. It is measured in volt-amps.

approved data. Approved data is required for major repairs and major alterations and can be type design drawings, Airworthiness Directives, Designated Engineering Representative Data, Supplemental Type Certificate information, Parts Manufacturer Approval Drawings, Designated Alteration Station Data, and Appliance Manufacturer's Data.

Arabic. Numerals. The symbols 0, 1, 2, 3, 4, 5, 6, 7, 8, and 9 used to represent values in the decimal number system.

aramid. An aromatic polymide fiber sold under such registered trade names as Dupont's Kevlar. Aramid fiber has a much higher tensile strength than aluminum, and it stretches appreciably before it breaks.

arbor. A precision ground shaft that fits in the bearings of a connecting rod. The arbor is used with parallel bars and feeler gages to measure connecting rod twist.

Archimedes' principle. The principle that states that a body immersed in a fluid undergoes an apparent loss of weight equal to the weight of the fluid it displaces.

arm. The distance, in inches, between the center of gravity of an object and the reference datum. An arm ahead of the datum is negative, and an arm behind the datum is positive.

armature. The rotating element of an electric motor or generator.

aromatic naphtha. A coal tar derivative that is used as an additive in certain reciprocating engine fuels, but is not used for cleaning aircraft parts.

artificial aging. A method of aluminum alloy heat treatment in which the part is heated and quenched (solution heat-treated) and then held at a slightly elevated temperature for a period of time. The metal gains additional strength by this process. Artificial aging is also called "precipitation heat treatment."

aspect ratio. The ratio of a wing span to its chord.

assembly drawing. A drawing that shows the way components are assembled to form a complete unit.

atom. The smallest particle of a chemical element that can exist, either alone or in combination with other atoms. An atom is made up of a nucleus, which contains protons and neutrons, and electrons, which spin around the nucleus. In a balanced atom, there are as many electrons spinning around the nucleus as there are protons in the nucleus.

austenite steel. Gamma iron into which carbon can dissolve. Below its critical temperature, iron carbides are scattered throughout the iron matrix in a physical mixture. At its critical temperature, the carbon dissolves into the matrix and becomes a solid solution rather than a physical mixture.

auxiliary view. A view used on some aircraft drawings made at an angle to one of the three views of the main drawing.

bacteria. Microscopic plant life that lives in the water that is entrapped in fuel tanks. The growth of bacteria in jet fuel tanks forms a film of scum which holds water against the aluminum alloy surfaces and causes corrosion to form. *See also* microbes.

base. The number in an exponential expression that is multiplied by itself the number of times shown by the exponent.

basic operating weight (BOW). The weight of the aircraft, including the crew, ready for flight, but without payload and fuel. This term applies only to transport category aircraft.

bayonet-type fueling nozzle. A type of nozzle used to fuel aircraft with a pressure, or single-point, fueling system. The nozzle is connected to the fueling receptacle in the aircraft and the handles are turned a portion of a turn to lock it in place.

bend allowance. The amount of material used in the bend of a piece of metal.

Bernoulli's principle. The principle that states that if energy is neither added to nor taken away from a fluid in motion, any increase in its velocity will cause a corresponding decrease in its pressure. The velocity of the moving fluid relates to its kinetic energy, and its pressure relates to its potential energy.

bilge. The lowest part of an aircraft structure where water, dirt, and other debris collect. Corrosion is likely to form in the bilge areas.

biocidal action. The function of certain fuel additives which kill microbes and bacteria living in the water that accumulates inside aircraft fuel tanks. Biocidal action prevents the formation of scum, thus preventing corrosion in these tanks.

block diagram. A drawing using blocks to show operational parts of a system. The block shows what enters and what leaves, but it has no indication of what is in it.

Boyle's law. The law that states that the product found by multiplying the pressure of a gas by its volume will always be constant. If the volume of a container of gas is decreased without changing temperature, the pressure of the gas will increase.

break line. A line showing that a part has been broken off and only a portion of the object is shown.

brine. A solution of salt and water.

brinelling. Damage to a metal surface by some force pressing hard enough to make an impression in the surface.

British thermal unit (Btu). The amount of heat energy needed to raise the temperature of 1 pound of pure water from 60° to 61°F.

buoyancy. The uplifting force that acts on an object when it is placed in a fluid.

burnishing. A method of smoothing the surface of metal that has been damaged by a deep scratch or gouge. The metal piled up at the edge of the damage is pushed back into the damage with a smooth, hard steel burnishing tool.

calendar month. A period of time used by the FAA for inspection and certification purposes. One calendar month from a given day extends from that day until midnight of the last day of that month. A calendar month beginning on June 6 ends at midnight of June 30.

call-out. Numbers and names used to identify components or parts in an aircraft drawing.

calorie. A small calorie is the amount of heat energy needed to raise the temperature of 1 gram of water 1°C. A large calorie is the amount of heat energy needed to raise the temperature of 1 kilogram of water 1°C.

capacitance (C). The amount of electrical energy that can be stored in an electrostatic field in a capacitor. Capacitance is measured in farads, microfarads, or picofarads.

capacitive reactance (X_C). The opposition to the flow of AC caused by capacitance. It drops voltage, but does not cause heat or use power.

capacitor. An electrical component used to store electricity in the form of electrostatic fields.

carbon tetrachloride. A halogenated hydrocarbon-type fire extinguishing agent. Carbon tetrachloride is no longer used because of the poison gas it generates when it is exposed to open flame.

caret. A small inverted "V" used to show the new location of the decimal in multiplication and division problems using decimal fractions.

case hardening. A type of metal heat treatment in which the surface of the metal is hardened and made brittle while the core of the material remains relatively soft and tough.

cathode. The end of a semiconductor diode that is made of N-type material and is represented in the schematic symbol by the bar.

cathodic area. An area within a piece of metal to which electrons from the anodic area have migrated.

cathodic protection. Another name for sacrificial corrosion. A material that is more anodic than the material being protected is attached to or plated on the material. This becomes the anode and is corroded, while the part that is being protected is the cathode and it is not damaged.

center of gravity (CG). The point in an aircraft at which all of the weight is considered to be concentrated. The algebraic sum of the moments about the center of gravity is zero. The center of gravity may be expressed in inches from the datum or in percent of the mean aerodynamic chord. The symbol for the location of the CG on an aircraft is ◕ .

center of gravity limits. The specified forward and aft points beyond which the CG must not be located during flight. These limits are indicated in the Type Certificate Data Sheets (TCDS) for the aircraft.

center of gravity range. The distance between the forward and aft CG limits shown in the pertinent Type Certificate Data Sheets.

chamfer. The tapered, or beveled, end of a cylindrical object.

chamfered edge. A beveled edge.

chamois skin. A soft pliable leather from the skin of a chamois, a goat-like antelope. Chamois skin is used to filter gasoline. Gasoline will pass through it but water will not. Gasoline that has been filtered through a chamois skin may be considered to be free of water.

Charles's law. The law which states that if the pressure of gas in a container is held constant and its absolute temperature is increased, its volume will also increase.

chemical salt. The result of the combination of an alkali with an acid. Salts are generally porous and powdery in appearance, and they are the visible evidence of corrosion in a metal.

chord. An imaginary line drawn through an airfoil from its leading edge to its trailing edge.

circular magnetization. Magnetization of a part in which the magnetic field extends across the material. Circular magnetism is used to detect faults along the length of the part.

circumference of a circle. The distance around the outside of a circle.

clad aluminum. An aluminum alloy sheet that has a coating of pure aluminum rolled onto its surfaces. Aluminum alloys are corrosive, but pure aluminum is not. The pure aluminum cladding protects the core alloy sheet from corrosion.

cladding. A method of protecting aluminum alloys from corrosion by rolling a coating of pure aluminum onto the surface of the alloy. Cladding is done in the rolling mill, and because the pure aluminum coating is weaker than the alloy sheet, cladding reduces the strength of the material somewhat.

clearance. The distance or space that allows free movement between parts.

cold flow. A deep, permanent impression left in a flexible hose by the pressure of a hose clamp.

color. The characteristic of light that is caused by the different wavelengths of electromagnetic energy that make up light. Violet light has the shortest wave lengths, and red has the longest.

common fraction. A fraction written in the form of one number above another. The number on the bottom is the denominator, indicating the number of parts into which the whole is divided, and the top number is the numerator indicating the number of parts being considered.

compound curve. A curve formed in more than one plane. The surface of a sphere is a compound curve.

compression ratio. The ratio of the volume of an engine cylinder with the piston at the bottom of its stroke to the volume of the cylinder with the piston at the top of its stroke.

concentration cell corrosion. A type of corrosion in which the electrode potential difference is caused by a difference in ion concentration of the electrolyte instead of a difference in galvanic composition within the metal.

concentric. Having the same center. The shafts that hold the hour hand and minute hand of a clock are concentric.

conduction. The method of heat transfer by direct contact.

conductor. Any device or material that allows the flow of electrons under a reasonable amount of electrical pressure, or voltage.

continuous magnetic particle inspection. Magnetic particle inspection in which the part is inspected while the magnetizing current flows either through the material or through a coil, or solenoid, wrapped around the part.

convection. The method of heat transfer by vertical currents within a fluid.

conversion coating. A chemical solution that is used to form a dense, nonporous oxide film on the surface of magnesium or aluminum.

corrosion. An electrochemical attack on metal that changes some of the metal into its salts. Corrosion destroys the strength of the metal.

cosecant. The trigonometric function of a right triangle which is the ratio of the length of the hypotenuse to the length of the side opposite an acute angle.

cosine. The trigonometric function of a right triangle which is the ratio of the length of the side adjacent to an acute angle to the length of the hypotenuse.

cotangent. The trigonometric function of a right triangle which is the ratio of the length of the side adjacent to an acute angle to the length of the side opposite the angle.

coulomb. A measure of electrical quantity. One coulomb is 6.28 billion, billion (6,280,000,000,000,000,000 or $6.28 \cdot 10^{18}$) electrons.

critical temperature of a metal. The temperature at which the internal structure of a metal takes on a crystalline form.

current (I). The flow of electricity. Current is measured in amperes.

cutaway drawing. A drawing which shows the inside construction or contents of an object as well as its outside.

Dalton's law. The gas law which states that there will always be the same number of molecules of gas in a container when the gas is held at a uniform pressure and temperature. Dalton's law explains the partial pressure of the gases which make up the air in our atmosphere.

data plate. A small tag, usually made of metal that is attached to a component which provides the name of the manufacturer, model number, part number, serial number, and other important information.

datum. A reference plane from which measurements are made. Datum lines are chosen by the engineers at the aircraft factory to define longitudinal, lateral, and vertical locations. Fuselage stations are measured in inches aft of the longitudinal datum. Waterlines are measured in inches above or below the vertical datum and butt lines are measured in inches to the right or left of the lateral datum.

DC electrical power. The product of current and voltage. Power is measured in watts.

decibel (acoustic). The basic unit for measuring sound intensity. One decibel (dB) is the smallest change in sound intensity the normal human ear can detect.

decimal fraction. A fraction which has a multiple of ten as its denominator.

deicing. Removal of ice from an aircraft structure.

delaminated. A condition caused by exfoliation corrosion in which the layers of grain structure in a metal extrusion separate from one another.

delta CG (Δ CG). A change in the center of gravity of an aircraft.

delta iron. The molecular arrangement in iron at temperatures between 1,392°C and 1,538°C. Pure iron melts at 1,538°C.

denominator. The quantity below the line in a common fraction, indicating the number of parts into which the numerator is divided.

density. The amount of mass in a unit volume. The density of air is measured in slug per cubic foot with the standard sea-level density being 0.002378 slug per cubic foot.

detail drawing. A drawing that contains enough information to allow a component to be built.

detonation. An explosion-like uncontrolled burning of the fuel-air mixture inside the cylinder of a reciprocating engine when the fuel-air mixture reaches its critical pressure and temperature. Detonation causes a rapid rise in cylinder pressure, excessive cylinder head temperature, and a decrease in engine power.

dew point. The temperature to which a body of air must be lowered before the water vapor it contains condenses out and becomes visible, liquid water.

diameter of a circle. The distance from one side of a circle to the other, passing through the center.

dichromate solution. A solution of potassium or sodium dichromate used to form a hard, airtight film on the surface of magnesium parts to prevent corrosion.

difference. The amount by which one quantity is greater or less than another. The difference is the answer in a subtraction problem.

dimpled. Recessed to allow something to fit flush with the surface. Rivet holes in thin sheet metal are dimpled by forcing the edges of the hole into a recessed die to form a tapered depression that allows the head of a countersunk rivet to be flush with the surface of the metal.

⁄ode. A semiconductor check valve that allows electrons to flow in one direction, but blocks their flow in the opposite direction.

direct current (DC). Electricity that flows in the same direction all of the time.

discontinuity. In nondestructive inspection, any interruption in the normal physical structure or configuration of a part. A discontinuity may or may not affect the usefulness of a part.

dissimilar-metal corrosion. Corrosion that forms where two different metals are in contact with each other. The severity of the corrosion is determined by the relative location of the metals in the electrochemical series.

dividend. The quantity in a division problem that is divided.

divisor. The quantity in a division problem by which the dividend is divided.

domains. Clumps of molecules in a piece of ferromagnetic material that change their magnetic alignment as a group rather than as individual molecules.

dope. A finishing material used to shrink cotton or linen material, making it airtight and weatherproof. Dope is made of a cellulose film base mixed with suitable solvents, thinners, and plasticizers.

doping. The process of adding small amounts of certain chemical elements as impurities to a semiconductor element to alter its electrical characteristics.

double flare. A flare made on a piece of rigid tubing in which the tubing wall is folded back on itself, giving two thicknesses of material in the flare.

ductility. The property of a material that allows it to be drawn, or stretched, into a thin section without breaking.

dye-penetrant inspection. Inspection of a material by soaking it in a penetrating liquid. After the liquid has soaked into any surface faults, it is washed off, and the surface covered with a developer powder which pulls the penetrant from the fault. The fault shows up as a vivid line or mark.

eddy current inspection. Inspection of a material by inducing eddy currents into it. The amount of eddy current induced in the material varies as the physical condition of the material changes, and it is affected by the presence of faults.

edge distance. The distance between the edge of a part and the center of a hole.

effective voltage. A measure of AC voltage that is 0.707 times the maximum instantaneous voltage. Effective voltage is also called rms (root mean square) voltage.

elastic limit. The maximum amount of stress a solid material can withstand before it is permanently deformed.

electrical. Relating to the application of the flow of electrons through conductors.

electrode potential. A voltage that exists between different metals and alloys because of their chemical composition. An electrode potential causes electrons to flow between these materials when a conductive path is provided.

electrolyte. A chemical, either a liquid or a gas, which conducts electrical current by releasing ions that unite with ions on the electrodes.

electromotive force. A force that causes electrons to move from one atom to another in an electrical circuit. It is the difference in electrical pressure or potential that exists between two points.

electronic. Relating to the application of the flow of electrons through semiconductor devices and across a vacuum.

electroplating. An electrochemical method of depositing a film of metal on some object. The object to be plated is the cathode, and the metal which is to be deposited on the cathode is the anode. Both the cathode and the anode are covered with an electrolyte which forms ions of the plating metal.

electrostatic field. An electrical force caused by an excess (negative field) or deficiency (positive field) of electrons.

EMF (electromotive force). The force that causes electrons to move in an electrical circuit.

empennage. The tail section of an airplane.

empty weight. The weight of the airframe, engines, and all items of operating equipment that have fixed locations and are permanently installed in the aircraft. It includes optional and special equipment, fixed ballast, full reservoirs of hydraulic fluid, and engine lubricating oil. It includes only unusable, or residual, fuel.

empty-weight center of gravity. The center of gravity of the aircraft as it is weighed. It includes all of the items required in aircraft empty weight.

empty-weight center of gravity range. The distance between the allowable forward and aft empty-weight CG limits. When EWCG limits are given for an aircraft, and the empty-weight CG falls within these limits, you cannot legally load the aircraft in such a way that its operational CG will fall outside its operational CG limits.

emulsion-type cleaner. A chemical cleaner which mixes with water or petroleum solvent to form an emulsion (a mixture which will separate if it is allowed to stand). Emulsion-type cleaners are used to loosen dirt, soot, or oxide films from the surface of an aircraft.

energy. Something that changes, or tries to change, matter. There are two basic types of energy: potential and kinetic. Common forms of energy are: chemical, electrical, light, and heat.

equivalent resistance. The resistance of a single resistor that is the same as that of several resistors connected in a circuit.

ethylene dibromide. A compound added to leaded aviation gasoline that converts some of the lead oxides into more volatile lead bromides so that they will pass out of the cylinder with the exhaust gases. This reduces lead fouling of the spark plugs.

exfoliation corrosion. An extreme case of intergranular corrosion in an extruded metal part. The corrosion causes the metal to separate in layers.

exploded-view drawing. A drawing showing all of the parts spread out to show their relative location in the component.

exponent. A small number written above and to the right of a base number to show the number of times the base is multiplied by itself.

extension line. A line on a drawing used to mark the location from which a dimension is taken.

FAA Form 337. The form that must be completed when a major repair or major alteration is accomplished.

fatigue crack. A crack caused by a metal being hardened by vibration or continual bending back and forth.

fayed surface (faying surface). The metal that is covered in a lap joint.

Federal Aviation Regulations (14 CFR). Regulations relating to the certification of airmen and aircraft. These have been changed to Title 14 of the Code of Federal Regulations (14 CFR). Compliance with the regulations is mandatory.

ferrite steel. Alpha iron into which some carbon has been dissolved. It exists at temperatures below its critical temperature.

ferrous metal. Iron or any alloy that contains iron.

ferrule. A metal ring or cap used to reinforce the end of a tube, to form an electrical contact at the end of an insulating tube, or to act as a sealing surface for a fluid line fitting.

fiber optics. An optical inspection procedure using a tool composed of tiny glass rods which conduct light and vision. The flexibility of a bundle of fiber rods makes inspection around corners practicable.

filiform corrosion. A thread- or filament-like corrosion which forms on aluminum skins beneath a dense paint film.

fire sleeve. A protective covering installed around flexible hoses installed in the engine areas of an aircraft. A fire sleeve does not increase the service temperature of the hose, but it protects the hose from direct fire long enough to allow appropriate action to be taken.

flammable. Easily ignited. Flammable replaces the older term "inflammable" which can be misinterpreted to mean "not flammable."

flash point. The temperature to which a material must be raised for it to ignite when a flame is passed above it, but it will not continue to burn.

Flight Standards District Office (FSDO). An FAA field office serving an assigned geographical area. It is staffed with Flight Standards personnel who serve the aviation industry and the general public on matters relating to the certification and operation of both air carriers and general aviation aircraft.

flooded engine. A reciprocating engine that has too much fuel in its cylinders for it to start, or a turbine engine that has so much fuel in its combustors that it would create a fire hazard or a hot start if the fuel were ignited.

fluorescent penetrant inspection. A type of penetrant inspection in which the penetrating liquid pulled from a surface fault glows, or fluoresces, when it is inspected under an ultraviolet light.

FOD (foreign object damage). This is a common acronym for damage caused by debris such as nuts, bolts, safety wire, small parts, or tools being sucked into an operating aircraft turbine engine. Inflight damage caused by the ingestion of ice or birds is also considered to be FOD.

force. Energy brought to bear on an object that causes or tries to cause change in its direction or speed of motion.

frequency. The number of complete cycles of a recurring event that takes place in one unit of time.

fretting corrosion. Corrosion that forms between metal parts that allow some slight relative movement. The movement continually wipes away the protective oxides that form on the surface. These oxides act as an abrasive to further damage the metal.

friction. Opposition to the relative movement between two objects.

fuel grade. A system of rating aviation gasoline according to its antidentonation characteristics. This is based on the older system of octane rating or performance number in which the higher the number, the more resistant the fuel is to detonation.

fuel load. The expendable part of the load of the aircraft. It includes only the fuel that is usable in flight.

fuse. A circuit protection device made of a strip of metal that melts when excessive current flows through it. When it melts, it opens the circuit.

fuselage center line. A line parallel to the longitudinal axis of an airplane that divides the fuselage into symmetrical halves.

fuselage station. A location along the longitudinal axis of an airplane measured in inches from the datum.

gage block. A precision ground block of hardened and polished steel used to check the accuracy of micrometer calipers. Their dimensional accuracy is normally measured in millionths of an inch.

galvanic action. Electrical pressure within a substance which causes electron flow because of the difference of electrode potential within a material.

galvanic corrosion. Corrosion that is caused by the presence of dissimilar metals.

galvanic grouping. An arrangement of metals in a series according to their electrode potential difference.

galvanizing. The application of a coating of zinc on steel by dipping the steel in a vat of molten zinc.

gamma iron. The molecular arrangement of iron at temperatures between 911°C and 1,392°C.

gas. The physical condition of matter in which a material takes the shape of its container and expands to fill the entire container.

gear backlash. The amount of clearance between the teeth of two meshing gears. Backlash is measured by holding one gear rigid and measuring the amount the other gear can move.

General Aviation Airworthiness Alerts. Documents furnished by the FAA to mechanics alerting them of problems that have been found in specific models of aircraft and suggesting corrective action. Compliance with the suggestions in an Airworthiness Alert is not mandatory.

halogenated hydrocarbon. A chemical compound containing hydrogen and carbon and one of the halogen-family elements such as fluorine, chlorine, or bromine. The vapors of halogenated hydrocarbons are particularly effective as fire extinguishing agents as they chemically prevent the combination of oxygen with the fuel.

heat. A form of energy that determines the speed of movement of molecules in a material.

heel of a bend. The outside of a bend. The metal in the heel of a bend in rigid tubing has been stretched and is thinner than in other parts of the tubing.

henry. The basic unit of inductance. One henry of inductance will induce one volt of pressure in a circuit when the current is changing at the rate of one ampere per second.

hidden line. A line that shows a surface of a part that is not visible in the view shown.

high metal ion concentration cell corrosion. Corrosion that results from a concentration of metallic ions in the electrolyte. The area of high concentration of metallic ions is the cathode of the cell.

Hooke's law. The law which states that the strain within an object is directly proportional to the stress that causes it until the elastic limit of the material is reached.

horsepower. A measure of mechanical power equal to 33,000 foot-pounds of work done in 1 minute, or 550 foot-pounds of work done in 1 second. One horsepower is equal to 746 watts of electrical power.

hot start. A start of a turbine engine in which the exhaust gas temperature exceeds the allowable limits.

hung start. The malfunctioning start of a turbine engine in which the engine starts, but fails to accelerate to a self-sustaining speed.

hydraulic lock. A condition that can exist in an inverted reciprocating engine or in the lower cylinders of a radial engine, in which oil leaks past the piston rings in the lower cylinders and fills the combustion chambers. If the engine is forced to rotate, the oil-filled cylinders will be seriously damaged.

hydrometer. A device used to measure the specific gravity of the electrolyte in a lead-acid battery.

hypotenuse. The side of a right triangle that is opposite the right angle.

impedance (Z). The total opposition to the flow of AC. Impedance is the vector sum of resistance and reactance.

improper fraction. A common fraction in which the numerator is greater than the denominator.

inclusion. A fault caused by an impurity introduced into the metal when it was rolled in the mill or when it was cast.

inductive reactance. The opposition to the flow of AC caused by inductance. It drops voltage, but does not cause heat or use power.

inductor. A coil of wire, normally wound around a soft iron core. Inductors oppose the flow of AC by producing inductive reactance.

inertia. The characteristic of all matter that causes an object to remain in its present condition.

inhibitive film. A film of material on the surface of a metal which inhibits the formation of corrosion. It does this by providing an ionized surface which will not allow the formation of corrosive salts on the metal.

installation drawing. A drawing that contains all the information needed to install a component in an aircraft.

insulator. A material whose valence electrons are so tightly bound to the atom that they resist any force that tries to move them from one atom to another.

integer. A whole number, or counting number. Integers include negative numbers, positive numbers, and zero.

intergranular corrosion. Corrosion that forms along the grain boundaries in a piece of metal.

internal supercharger drain valve. A pressure-operated valve in the bottom of the internal supercharger section of a reciprocating engine that is open when the pressures inside and outside the supercharger are the same. This allows excess fuel to drain out of the engine if the engine is flooded during the starting procedure.

inverse ratio. A ratio of the reciprocals of two quantities.

inverse square law. The intensity of a physical quantity varies inversely with the square of the distance between the source and the point at which it acts.

ion. An atom of a chemical element that does not have the same number of electrons spinning around it as there are protons in its nucleus. A positive ion has fewer electrons than protons, and a negative ion has more electrons than protons.

iron carbide. The form in which carbon exists in steel. The amount of iron carbide and its distribution in the metal determine the hardness of the steel.

iso-octane. The hydrocarbon fuel used as the high reference when rating the antidetonation characteristics of aviation gasoline.

isometric drawing. A drawing made in such a way that three faces of an object are visible and are drawn in such a way that they are equally inclined to the surface of the drawing. Vertical lines are drawn vertical to their true length, while horizontal lines are drawn at an angle of 30° to the horizontal and are also drawn to their true length.

jack pad. A fixture that attaches to the structure of an aircraft to fit the jack used to raise the aircraft for weighing or for service.

kerf. The slit made by a saw blade as it cuts through wood. The set of the teeth determines the width of the kerf.

kilo (k). The metric prefix meaning 1,000.

kindling point. The temperature to which a material must be heated for it to combine with oxygen from the air and burn.

kinetic energy. Energy in an object caused by its motion.

Kirchhoff's voltage law. The sum of the voltage drops in a series circuit is equal to the sum of the source.

latent heat. Heat that changes the state of a substance without raising its temperature.

lay line. A colored line that runs the length of a piece of flexible hose. It is used to indicate whether or not the hose was twisted during installation. If the lay line spirals around the hose, the hose is twisted.

layup. A method of fabricating aircraft structure with composite materials. Several layers of reinforcing materials such as glass, graphite, or aramid are impregnated with resin and pressed together to exclude all air and hold pressure on the layers until the resin cures.

least significant digit. The digit on the extreme right in a decimal number.

LEMAC. Leading edge of the mean aerodynamic chord. When the CG of an airplane is given in % MAC, LEMAC is specified in inches from the datum to allow weight and balance computations to relate % MAC to the datum.

leveling means. The method specified by the aircraft manufacturer to determine the level-flight attitude of an aircraft. The leveling means are specified in the TCDS for the aircraft, and leveling may require the use of a spirit level or a plumb bob.

lever. A rigid bar, free to pivot, or rotate about a point called the fulcrum. An input force is applied at one point, and an output force is taken from the lever at another point.

litmus paper. An indicator paper used to determine whether a solution is acidic or basic (alkaline). Litmus paper turns red when wet with an acidic solution and blue when wet with a basic solution.

load cell. A weighing device placed between a jack and jack pad when weighing an aircraft. Load cells contain strain gages that change their resistance proportional to the amount of weight the load cell supports.

longitudinal magnetization. Magnetization of a part in which the magnetic field extends lengthwise in the material. Longitudinal magnetization is used to detect faults across the part.

low oxygen concentration cell corrosion. Corrosion that forms between the lap joints in aircraft skins and under labeling tape. The lack of oxygen in these areas prevents the formation of hydroxide ions. When electrons leave this area, it becomes anodic and corrosion forms.

magnetic particle inspection. Inspection of ferrous metal parts by magnetizing the part and flowing a liquid containing iron oxide over the surface. Any faults form magnetic poles which attract the oxide and show up the fault.

magnitude. A measure of quantity, or amount.

maintenance. Inspection, overhaul, repair, preservation, and replacement of parts, but excluding preventive maintenance.

maintenance release. A statement made by an Approved Repair Station in lieu of a Form 337 that approves a product for return to service after a major repair.

major alteration. A change to an aircraft, engine, or propeller that affects its strength, flight characteristics, or weight and balance. For example, putting a larger engine in an airplane is a major alteration.

major repair. An extensive repair to an aircraft structure, engine, or propeller that could affect its strength, performance, or flight characteristics. Repairs that involve welding, replacement of a sheet metal skin, and the complete overhaul of an engine with an internal supercharger are examples of major repairs.

Malfunction and Defect Report (M&D Report). A small postcard-like form used by repair stations, maintenance shops, and technicians to report an unacceptable condition to the FAA. Information from these forms provides the basis for the General Aviation Airworthiness Alerts and subsequent Airworthiness Directives.

malleability. The characteristic of a material that allows it to be stretched or shaped by rolling or hammering it.

mandrel. A long steel rod with a rounded end that is inserted into a piece of thin-wall metal tubing when it is being bent in a tube bending machine. The rounded end is held at the point the bend is started to prevent the tubing flattening as it is bent.

manifold pressure. The absolute pressure inside the induction system of a reciprocating engine.

manufacturer's maintenance or service manual. A document issued by the manufacturer of an aircraft or component and approved by the FAA. It details procedures to be followed for the maintenance of a specific aircraft, engine, propeller, or other major accessory or component.

mass. The amount of matter in an object.

matrix. The bonding material that encapsulates the fibers in a composite structure to transfer the stresses into the fibers. Epoxy and polyester resins are common matrix materials.

matter. Anything that takes up space and has weight.

maximum landing weight. The maximum weight at which an aircraft may normally be landed. The maximum landing weight may be reduced to a lesser weight when runway length or atmospheric conditions are adverse.

maximum takeoff weight. The maximum allowable weight at the start of the takeoff run. The aircraft may be initially loaded to a greater weight to allow for fuel burnoff during ground operation. The takeoff weight for a particular flight may be reduced to a lesser weight when runway length, atmospheric conditions, or other variables are adverse.

maximum weight. The maximum authorized weight of the aircraft and all of its equipment as specified in the TCDS for the aircraft.

mean aerodynamic chord. The chord of an imaginary airfoil that has the same aerodynamic characteristics as the actual airfoil. The length of the MAC is given for many aircraft, and the CG is expressed in percent of the mean aerodynamic chord (% MAC).

mechanical advantage. The increase in force or speed produced by mechanical devices such as levers, pulleys, gears, or hydraulic cylinders.

mega (M). The metric prefix meaning 1,000,000.

METO. The acronym that means Maximum Except Take Off. METO horsepower is also called the maximum continuous horsepower.

micro (μ). The metric prefix meaning 1/1,000,000, or 0.000 001.

microbes. Extremely small living plant and animal organisms, including bacteria, mold, and algae. The term "microbes" is more generally replaced with the term micro-organisms.

milli (m). The metric prefix meaning 1/1,000, or 0.001.

minimum fuel for balance purposes. Minimum fuel for balance purposes is $\frac{1}{12}$ gallon per maximum-except-takeoff (METO) horsepower, and is the maximum amount of fuel which could be used in weight and balance computations when low fuel might adversely affect the most critical balance conditions. To determine the weight of fuel in pounds, divide the METO horsepower by 2.

minor repair. A repair other than a major repair.

minuend. The quantity in a subtraction problem from which another quantity is to be subtracted.

mixed number. A number that contains both an integer and a fraction.

molecule. The smallest particle of a substance that retains the characteristics of the substance.

moment. A force that tries to cause rotation. In weight and balance, a moment is found by multiplying a weight by its arm. Moments are expressed in pound-inches. A moment that causes a nose-down condition is a negative moment, and one that causes a nose-up condition is a positive moment.

moment index. The moment divided by a constant such as 100, 1,000, or 10,000. Moment indexes are used to simplify weight and balance computations for large aircraft where heavy items and long arms result in large, unmanageable numbers.

moment index envelope. A graphical representation of the forward and aft CG limits of an airplane using weight moment indexes. If a horizontal line representing the weight of the aircraft and a vertical line representing its total moment index (the moment divided by a reduction factor) intersect within the envelope, the aircraft weight and balance conditions are within allowable limits.

momentum. A force caused by the inertia of a moving body trying to keep the object moving in the same direction, at the same speed. It is the product of the mass times the velocity of an object.

monocoque. A type of aircraft structure that carries all of its stresses in its outside skin.

most significant digit. The digit on the extreme left in a decimal number.

MS flareless fittings. Fluid-line fittings that form their seal with a ferrule around the tubing rather than with a flare.

multiplicand. The number in a multiplication problem that is multiplied by another number.

multiplier. The number in a multiplication problem that is used to multiply another number (the multiplicand).

Mylar. The registered trade name for a strong, flexible polyester film that is widely used as an electrical insulator and as film on which high quality drawings can be made.

nacelle. An enclosed compartment in an aircraft in which an engine is mounted.

negative number. A number less than zero. It is a number that is preceded by a minus sign.

nitride. A compound of nitrogen and a metal. Aluminum nitride is formed inside a reciprocating engine cylinder to provide a hard, wear-resistant surface.

nitriding. A method of case hardening steel by heating it in an atmosphere of ammonia. The nitrogen in the ammonia reacts with alloying elements in the steel to form extremely hard nitrides on the surface.

noble. Inactive or inert. In the electrochemical series of metals, the metal in a combination that does not corrode is the more noble.

normalizing. A form of heat treatment in which stresses are removed from a metal that has been welded, rolled, or otherwise unevenly hardened.

numerator. The number in a common fraction written above the line.

OEM. Original Equipment Manufacturer.

ohm ( ). The basic unit of electrical resistance, or opposition, to current flow.

ohmmeter. An instrument used to measure resistance in an electrical circuit or component. A known voltage is applied across the unknown resistance, and the resulting current is measured.

one-hundred-hour inspection. A complete inspection of an aircraft that is operated for hire that must be conducted every 100 hours. A 100-hour inspection is identical to an annual inspection except for the requirement that an annual inspection be conducted by an A&P mechanic holding an Inspection Authorization.

operational CG. The center of gravity of an aircraft when it is loaded for flight.

orthographic projection. A method of showing all the sides of an object. There are six possible views of an object.

overhaul. The maintenance procedure in which a device is disassembled to the extent needed to determine the condition of all of its parts. Each part is inspected and, if damaged or excessively worn, is repaired or replaced. The device is then reassembled and tested to approved service limit requirements. A unit which successfully passes this testing is approved for return to service.

oxidation. The chemical action in which a metallic element is united with oxygen. Electrons are removed from the metal in this process.

parallel circuit. An electrical circuit in which the components are arranged in such a way that there is more than one path for electrons to follow from one terminal of the power source to the other terminal.

part number. A number assigned by the engineering department to a detail drawing. This number identifies the part made from that drawing. Some part numbers are followed by a -1 or a -2 to indicate mirror image parts. A left-hand part is identified as a -1 part and the right-hand part is a -2 part.

partial pressure. The pressure caused by each of the gases in a mixture.

Parts Manufacturer Approval (PMA). An approval, granted under 14 CFR Part 21, that allows a person to produce a modification or replacement part for sale for installation on a type certificated product.

parts list. A list of all items and their part numbers that are included on an assembly drawing. A parts list is also called a Bill of Materials.

Pascal's law. The law that states that when pressure is applied to a fluid in an enclosed container, the pressure is transmitted equally throughout all of the fluid, and it acts at right angles to the walls that enclose the fluid.

pawl. A driving link in a ratchet wrench. It allows the handle to turn the socket in one direction but prevents its turning in the opposite direction.

pentavalent element. A chemical element that has five electrons in its valence shell. Nitrogen, arsenic, antimony, and bismuth are pentavalent elements.

performance numbers. An antidetonation rating system for aviation gasoline whose performance characteristics are better than those of iso-octane, which is used as the top value in the octane rating system. Aviation gasoline ratings above 100 are called performance numbers.

permeability. The ease with which a material conducts magnetic lines of force.

perspective view. A view of an object in which parallel lines do not appear parallel, but converge at a vanishing point off of the drawing.

phantom line. A line used to show the location of a part that is not visible in the view shown, but is used as a reference.

pickling. A method of treating magnesium with chromic acid to form a hard, protective oxide film to prevent water reaching the metal and causing corrosion.

pickling. The treatment of a metal surface with an acid to remove surface contamination.

pictorial diagram. A drawing using illustrations of the components rather than accepted symbols.

piezoelectric. The characteristic of certain materials that causes them to produce an electrical pressure when they are bent or twisted or when pressure is applied to them.

pip. The display of a received pulse on the screen of a cathode-ray tube. This is also called a blip.

pitot tube. An open-end tube that points directly into the air flowing over an aircraft structure. The pitot tube samples the pressure of the ram air.

plan area. The area of a surface as viewed from the top.

plumb bob. A pointed weight with a string attached to a hole in line with its point. When the string is fastened to an object, the point of the plumb bob is directly below the point of attachment. A freely hanging plumb bob always points directly toward the center of the earth.

position line. A line used to show the extreme position to which a part can be moved.

positive number. A number greater than zero.

pot life. The length of time a resin will remain workable after the catalyst has been added.

potable water. Water carried in an aircraft for the purpose of drinking.

potential difference. The force that causes electrical current to flow. Potential difference is measured in volts.

potential energy. Energy in an object caused by its position, configuration, or chemical composition.

potentiometer. A variable resistor with three connections.

poundal. The unit of force in the foot-pound-second system of measurement that is required to accelerate a mass of 1 pound, 1 foot per second, per second.

power (electrical). The ability of an electrical device to produce work. The basic unit of electrical power is the watt, which is the product of current times the voltage that causes the current to flow.

power factor. The percentage of current in an AC circuit that is in phase with the voltage. Power factor is found by dividing the circuit resistance by the circuit impedance. It is also the cosine of the phase angle.

power of a number. The number of times a number is multiplied by itself.

power (mechanical). The time rate of doing work. It is found by dividing the amount of work done, measured in foot-pounds, by the time in seconds or minutes used to do the work. Power can be expressed in terms of foot-pounds of work per minute or in horsepower. One horsepower is 33,000 foot-pounds of work per minute or 550 foot-pounds per second. In the metric system, power is measured in watts. One watt is equal to 1/746 horsepower.

powerplant. The powerplant of an airplane includes the same items specified in the FAA definition of an aircraft engine. A Powerplant Rating is required for a technician to work an aircraft engine or propeller.

powers of ten. Another name for scientific notation. A handy mathematical tool in which very large and very small numbers are changed to numbers between 1 and 9 with a superscript to show the number of places to move the decimal point. Numbers greater than 0 have a positive exponent, and numbers smaller than 0 have a negative exponent.

pressure. Force per unit area. Pressure is normally expressed in such a term as pounds per square inch.

preventive maintenance. Simple or minor preservation operations and the replacement of small standard parts not involving complex assembly operations.

product. The answer in a multiplication problem.

Production Certificate. A certificate issued under 14 CFR Part 21 that allows a certain certificated aircraft, aircraft engine, or appliance to be manufactured by the specified facility.

progressive inspection. An inspection of an aircraft that is scheduled to be conducted over a period of time, rather than all at one time.

proper fraction. A common fraction in which the numerator is smaller than the denominator.

pumice. A very fine abrasive powder used to polish metal surfaces.

Pureclad. A registered trade name for clad aluminum alloy sheets.

Pythagorean formula. The length of the hypotenuse of a right triangle is equal to the square root of the sum of the squares of the lengths of the other two sides.

$$H = \sqrt{A^2 + B^2}$$

quenching. Rapid cooling of a metal as part of the heat treating process. The metal is removed from the furnace and it is submerged in a liquid such as water, oil, or brine.

quotient. The answer in a division problem.

radiation. The method of heat transfer by electromagnetic wave action.

radical sign. A sign used to indicate the root of a number.

$$\sqrt{}$$

radiographic inspection. Inspection of the interior of a structure by passing radiographic energy through the structure and either exposing a photographic film or exciting a fluorescent screen. Faults appear because their density is different from that of sound material. X-rays and gamma rays are used in radiographic inspection.

ram air pressure. Pressure produced when moving air is stopped.

ramp weight. The maximum takeoff gross weight plus the weight of the fuel burned during taxi and runup. Ramp weight is also called taxi weight.

rarefying. Decreasing the pressure of air.

reactance (X). The opposition to the flow of AC caused by both inductive and capacitive reactances.

rebuild. The maintenance procedure in which a device is disassembled to the extent needed to determine the condition of all of its parts. Each part is inspected and, if damaged or excessively worn, is repaired or replaced. The device is then reassembled and tested to the same limits as a new item. A unit which successfully passes this testing is approved for return to service.

reciprocating engine. A form of heat engine in which the crankshaft is turned by the linear action of pistons reciprocating, or moving back and forth, inside the cylinders.

reciprocal. The reciprocal of a number is 1 divided by the number. For example, the reciprocal of 4 is 1/4.

rectifier. A device or circuit that changes alternating current into direct current.

reduction factor. A constant which, when divided into a moment, results in an index. Reduction factors of 100, 1,000, and 10,000 are used to simplify weight and balance calculations.

relative humidity. The relationship between the amount of water in the air to the amount of water the air can hold at its existing temperature.

relief tube. A urinal installed in some special-purpose aircraft.

remainder. The number left in a division problem when the divisor does not go into the dividend an even number of times.

Repair Station. A certificated maintenance facility approved by the FAA to perform certain specific maintenance functions. These facilities are certificated under 14 CFR Part 145.

repair. The restoration of a device to a condition for safe operation after damage or deterioration.

residual magnetic particle inspection. Magnetic particle inspection in which the part is magnetized and removed from the magnetizing field. The inspection is made with the magnetism that is retained in the material.

resilient sealant. A sealing compound that hardens to the consistency of rubber. It does not get brittle.

resistance (R). Opposition to the flow of electricity. Resistance is measured in ohms. It drops voltage, causes heat, and uses power.

resonance. The condition of a vibrating object that causes it to have the greatest amplitude of vibration for the amount of energy put into it.

resonant frequency. The frequency of AC at which inductive and capacitive reactances are the same.

resultant vector. A single vector which is the sum of two or more vectors.

retentivity. The ability of a material to retain magnetism.

retort. A sealed container in which a ferrous metal may be heated in a controlled atmosphere. Nitriding is done by heating a metal part in a retort that contains an atmosphere rich in nitrogen.

revision letter. A sequentially assigned letter appended to a drawing number to document a change made to the drawing. Revision letters help maintain control of the changes and assure that only the drawing containing the latest changes is used.

rheostat. A variable resistor with two connections.

rigging load. The tension on aircraft control cables.

right triangle. A triangle that contains one right (90°) angle.

root. A number which, when multiplied by itself a specified number of times, will give a specific number.

sacrificial corrosion. A method of corrosion protection in which a surface is plated with a metal that is less noble than the metal itself. Any corrosion that occurs will attack the plating rather than the base metal.

SAE. Society of Automotive Engineers. An organization that has established standards for materials and processes that are widely used in the aviation industry.

safety. A method of securing a threaded device so it cannot accidentally turn. Bolts, screws, and turnbuckles are often safetied by passing soft steel or brass wire through holes in them, twisting the wire, and attaching it to the structure in such a way that it pulls in the direction to tighten it.

scaling. The measuring of a distance on a blueprint by using a ruler or scale. This is not an acceptable practice, as the paper shrinks or stretches. All dimensions and tolerances must be clearly indicated on the drawing so that there is no need for scaling.

schematic diagram. A diagram of an electrical circuit in which the components are represented by symbols rather than drawings or pictures of the actual devices. A schematic diagram shows the location of individual components with respect to each other in the operation of the system.

scientific notation. A mathematical procedure in which very large or very small numbers are made more manageable by changing them to numbers between 1 and 9, raised to a power showing the number of places the decimal point was moved.

sea level pressure. 29.92 inches of mercury, or 1013.2 millibars.

secant. The trigonometric function of a right triangle which is the ratio of the length of the hypotenuse to the length of the side adjacent to an acute angle.

sectional drawing. An aircraft drawing that shows the inside of a part.

semiconductor. A material whose electrical characteristics may be changed from that of a conductor to that of an insulator by changing its circuit conditions.

sensible heat. Heat that raises the temperature of a substance without changing its state.

serial number. An identification number assigned sequentially to items which have the same part number.

series circuit. An electrical circuit in which the components are arranged in such a way that there is only one path for electrons to flow from one terminal of the power source to the other terminal.

shelf life. The normal length of time a resin may be expected to keep its usable characteristics if it is stored and not used.

short circuit. A malfunction in an electrical circuit that allows electrons to flow with no opposition.

sine. The trigonometric function of a right triangle which is the ratio of the length of the side opposite to an acute angle to the length of the hypotenuse.

sine wave. The waveform of AC voltage and current produced by a rotary generator. The value of the voltage or current varies as the sine of the angle through which the armature has rotated.

single flare. A flare made on a piece of rigid tubing in which there is only one thickness of the tubing material in the flare.

sintered plate. A plate of a nickel-cadmium battery made of powdered metal that has been heated and molded to form a strong, cohesive material. Sintered material is used because its granular structure gives it a large surface area.

sketch. A simple, rough drawing of an object that contains only enough detail to serve the purpose of the sketch. Sketches are normally made without the use of drawing instruments.

solid solution. A state in which a base metal and alloying agents are united to form a single solid metal.

solid-state electronics. Electronic circuits which use semiconductor devices such as diodes and transistors rather than vacuum tubes.

specific heat. The ratio of the amount of heat energy needed to raise the temperature of a certain mass of a material 1°C to the amount of heat energy needed to raise the temperature of the same mass of pure water 1°C.

specific gravity. The ratio of the density of a material to the density of pure water.

specific weight of air. 0.07651 pounds per cubic foot.

speed of sound. Sound travels at 661.7 knots, or 761.6 miles per hour at sea level under standard conditions of pressure and temperature.

spirit level. An instrument used to determine when an object is level, or perpendicular to a line pointing directly toward the center of the earth. A curved glass tube partially filled with a liquid is mounted in a long, straight metal or wood bar. When the bar is perfectly level, the bubble in the liquid is in the center of the curve in the tube.

spontaneous combustion. Ignition of a material without an external source of heat. The heat that causes the ignition is provided by oxidation, and if it is not allowed to escape, the temperature will rise to the combustion temperature of the material.

square drive. The drive coupling between a socket wrench and the handle that turns it.

square of a number. The product of a number multiplied by itself.

square root. A number which, when multiplied by itself, will give a particular number.

squat switch. A landing gear safety switch mounted on the main landing gear strut in such a way that it is actuated when weight is on the landing gear and the oleo strut is compressed. A squat switch in the landing gear retraction circuit prevents the landing gear being inadvertently retracted when weight is on the wheels.

standard day conditions. Conditions of the atmosphere that have been agreed upon by scientists and engineers who work with the atmosphere to allow them to correct all measurements to the same conditions.

Temperature .... 15° Celsius
Pressure at sea level .... 29.29 inches of mercury
1013.2 millibars
14.69 pounds per square inch
Acceleration due to gravity .... 32.174 feet per second
9.809 meters per second, per second
Specific weight of air ..... 0.07651 pounds per cubic foot
1.225 kilograms per cubic meter
Density 0.0023769 lb/sec2/ft4
0.12492 kg/sec2/m4
Speed of sound .... 761.6 miles per hour
1,225.35 kilometers per hour
661.7 knots
34,046.16 centimeters per second

standard weights. Values used when specific weights are not available:

gasoline .... 6.0 pounds/U.S. gallon
turbine engine fuel .... 6.7 pounds/U.S. gallon
lubricating oil .... 7.5 pounds/U.S. gallon
water .... 8.35 pounds/U.S. gallon
General Aviation
crew & passengers .... 170 pounds
Air Carrier
passenger (summer) .... 160 pounds
passenger (winter) .... 165 pounds
male cabin attendant .... 150 pounds
female cabin attendant .... 130 pounds
other crewmembers .... 170 pounds
checked baggage .... 23.5 pounds
carry-on baggage .... 5 pounds

station. A location on an aircraft identified by a number designating its distance in inches from the datum.

steel. An alloy of iron that usually contains between 0.1 and 1.5% carbon with other elements used to give it desirable characteristics.

stiffener. A piece of formed sheet metal or extrusion that is riveted to a large piece of thin sheet metal to give it rigidity and stiffness.

strain. A deformation, or physical change caused by stress in a material.

stress. A force set up within an object that tries to prevent an outside force changing its shape.

subtrahend. The number in a subtraction problem that is to be subtracted.

sum. The answer in an addition problem.

Supplemental Type Certificate (STC). A certificate of approval for an alteration to a certificated airframe, engine, or appliance.

surface corrosion. Corrosion that forms on the surface of a metal that is covered with some form of electrolyte. Surface corrosion shows up as pits filled with a powder.

swaged. A process of attaching a terminal to a steel control cable. The cable is inserted into the tubular end of the steel terminal, and the terminal is compressed in such a way that the metal is pressed into the cable. A swaged connection is as strong as the cable.

swaged fitting. A fitting on a flexible hose that is installed by forcing the material of the fitting into the hose. Swaged end fittings are not reusable. Swaged fittings are also used on rigid lines used in high-pressure hydraulic and pneumatic systems.

tang. The tapered shank sticking out from the body of a file. A handle for a file is slipped over the tang.

tangent. The trigonometric function of a right triangle which is the ratio of the length of the side opposite an acute angle to the length of the side adjacent to the angle.

tare weight. The weight of the chocks or other devices used to hold an aircraft on the scales for weighing. Tare weight is subtracted from the scale reading to find the weight of the aircraft.

Technical Standard Order (TSO). An approval for the manufacture of a component for use on certificated aircraft.

Technician Certificate. A certificate issued under 14 CFR Part 65 (*Certification: Airmen Other Than Flight Crewmembers*) to a person who demonstrates the required experience, knowledge, and skills. This certificate must be accompanied by either an Airframe or Powerplant rating or both.

TEMAC. Trailing edge of the mean aerodynamic chord.

temperature. A measure of the intensity of heat.

tempering. A form of heat treatment in which some of the hardness and brittleness is removed from a metal that has been hardened by heat treatment.

terminal strip. A component in an aircraft electrical system to which wires are attached for the purpose of connecting sections of the wire. Terminal strips are normally installed in junction boxes.

tetraethyl lead (TEL). A poisonous compound added to aviation gasoline to increase its critical pressure and temperature. TEL inhibits detonation and improves the performance of the fuel in the engine. Fuels containing TEL are being phased out.

thermal expansion. The increase in size of a material caused by the absorption of heat energy.

theta (Θ). The Greek letter normally used to represent an unknown angle.

thrust. A forward aerodynamic force produced by a propeller or a turbojet engine as it accelerates a mass of air to the rear.

time in service. Time in service with respect to maintenance records is that time from the moment an aircraft leaves the surface of the earth until it touches it at the next point of landing.

tines. The prongs which extend from a fork-like object.

tolerance. The difference between the extreme possible dimensions of a part.

torque. A turning or twisting force.

traceability. The assignment of serial numbers to individual parts to aid in controlling or tracing them in the event of an investigation or recall.

transducer. An electrical device that either changes electrical energy into mechanical movement or changes mechanical movement into electrical energy.

transformer. An electrical component consisting of two or more coils of wire wound around a laminated soft iron core. AC flowing in one winding induces a voltage in the other windings.

trapezoid. A closed, four-sided plane figure with only two of its opposite sides parallel.

triangle. A closed, three-sided plane figure. The sum of the angles in a triangle is always equal to 180°.

trichresyl phosphate (TCP). An additive to aviation gasoline that helps scavenge lead deposits from the cylinders by converting lead bromides to the more volatile lead phosphates.

trivalent element. A chemical element that has three electrons in its valence shell. Boron, aluminum, gallium and indium are trivalent elements.

true power. Power in an AC circuit that is the product of the circuit voltage and only that part of the current that is in phase with the voltage. It is measured in watts.

truss. A type of aircraft structure made up of longerons and cross braces. Compressive loads are carried by cross members at right angles to the longerons, and tensile loads are carried by diagonal members.

Type Certificate Data Sheets (TCDS). The official specifications of an aircraft, engine, or propeller issued by the Federal Aviation Administration. TCDS for an engine lists the minimum grade of fuel approved for its use.

U.S. gallon. A measure of quantity equal to 231 cubic inches, or 0.1333 cubic foot.

ultrasonic inspection. Inspection by vibrating the part with ultrasonic energy. The physical condition of the material and the presence of faults affect the passage of the energy through the part.

ultrasonic vibrations. Vibrations at a frequency higher than the human ear can normally hear. Ultrasonic vibrations are higher than 20,000 hertz (cycles per second).

underground fuel hydrant. The terminal of an underground fuel system installed at many large airports. The fuel truck which has the required pumps, filters, and metering instruments but no storage tank is connected to the fuel hydrant, and its hoses are connected to the fueling panel of the aircraft.

useful load. The difference between the empty weight of an aircraft and its maximum allowable gross weight. Useful load is the weight of the pilot, copilot, passengers, baggage, fuel, and oil.

vapor lock. A condition in a fuel system in which the fuel has vaporized and formed pockets of gas in the fuel line. Vapor lock prevents liquid fuel flowing to the engine.

vapor pressure. The pressure of the vapor above a liquid required to prevent the liquid releasing additional vapors.

vector. A quantity which has both direction and magnitude.

veneer. Thin sheets of wood cut from a log with a knife held against the log as it is rotated in the cutter. Veneer is used for making plywood.

vernier principle. The principle by which two scales having different calibrations function together to allow very small measurements to be made.

For example, two calibrated scales are placed side by side. A space on one scale is divided into 10 increments and the same-sized space on the adjacent vernier scale is divided into 11 increments. Only one mark on the main scale lines up with a mark on the vernier scale. When the vernier scale is moved until the next two marks line up, the vernier scale has moved a distance that is equal to the difference between the marks on the two scales.

viscosity. The resistance of a fluid to flow. The higher the viscosity, the "thicker" the fluid.

volatility. The characteristic of a liquid that relates to its ability to vaporize, or change into a gas.

volt-amp. The basic unit of apparent power in an AC circuit.

volt. The basic unit of electrical pressure. One volt is the amount of pressure required to force 1 ampere of current to flow through 1 ohm of resistance.

voltmeter. An electrical instrument used to measure voltage. Most analog voltmeters determine the voltage by measuring the current forced through a series of precision resistors.

warp and fill. Threads in a piece of woven fabric. Warp threads run the length of the material and fill threads run across the material.

wash primer. A self-etching primer that is used on aluminum or magnesium. It is often used to prepare the surface for an acrylic lacquer topcoat.

watt (W). The basic unit of electrical power.

weighing points. Locations on an aircraft, designated by the manufacturer, for the placement of the scales or load capsules when the aircraft is being weighed.

weight. A measure of the force of gravity acting on a body.

work. The product of a force and the distance an object moves under the influence of the force. Work is measured in foot-pounds.

working drawings. The classification of drawings that includes detail drawings, assembly drawings, and installation drawings.

zero fuel weight. The weight of an aircraft without fuel. It is the basic operating weight of the aircraft plus the payload.

zinc chromate primer. A primer that releases chromate ions and inhibits the formation of corrosion on the surface of aluminum alloys.

zones. Numbers along the bottom and letters along the right side of a large drawing, used to aid in locating a part by defining a grid pattern on the drawing.

INDEX

AVIATION MAINTENANCE TECHNICIAN SERIES
GENERAL

Copy Editing	Sally Clark, Kitty Crane
Design & Production	Dora McClurkin Muir
Editing & Production	Jennifer Trerise
Production	Cynthia Wyckoff, Jennifer Shontz, David Gagley
Additional Illustration	Virginia Wright

Produced at
ASA's Graphic Design & Publications Department
in Times and Helvetica Black using Microsoft Word, Macromedia
FreeHand, Adobe Illustrator and PageMaker,
Hewlett Packard DeskScan II, and Zedcor DeskPaint

Product names are trademarks or registered trademarks of their respective holders.

READER RESPONSE

Dear Aviation Maintenance Technician:

You have made an investment in your future by purchasing this textbook from ASA's *Aviation Maintenance Technician Series*. We hope you were pleased with your selection. Your input is invaluable to us. Please take a moment to provide us with your comments and suggestions. Include your name and address so we can thank you.

— *Aviation Supplies & Academics, Inc.*

Please print clearly.

NAME _____ DATE _____

TITLE *(Student, Instructor, other)* _____

BUSINESS/SCHOOL _____

ADDRESS _____

CITY _____ STATE _____ ZIP CODE/POSTAL CODE _____

COUNTRY _____ TELEPHONE *(optional)* _____

WHERE DID YOU PURCHASE THIS **GENERAL** AVIATION MAINTENANCE TEXT? _____

WAS THE TEXT RECOMMENDED TO YOU? _____ BY WHOM? _____

DO YOU INTEND TO PURCHASE ASA'S TWO ADDITIONAL TEXTS IN THE SERIES? AIRFRAME _____ POWERPLANT _____

COMMENTS AND SUGGESTIONS
Please tell us what you liked or disliked about the text: content, subject matter, ease-of-use, illustrations and figures, etc.

_____

_____

_____

_____

_____

_____

MAIL OR FAX THIS FORM TO:

Aviation Supplies & Academics, Inc.
7005 132nd Place SE
Newcastle, Washington 98059-3153
Fax: 425.235.0128

Please photocopy or remove this page.